TRIAL ADVOCACY

SECOND EDITION

By

JAMES W. JEANS, Sr.

Professor of Law,
University of Missouri-Kansas City

ST. PAUL, MINN.

WEST PUBLISHING CO.

1993

COPYRIGHT © 1975 WEST PUBLISHING CO.
COPYRIGHT © 1993 By WEST PUBLISHING CO.
                    610 Opperman Drive
                    P.O. Box 64526
                    St. Paul, MN 55164-0526
                    1-800-328-9352

Library of Congress Cataloging-in-Publication Data
Jeans, James W., 1928-
    Trial advocacy / by James W. Jeans. — 2nd ed.
        p.   cm.
    Includes index.
    ISBN 0-314-01904-9
    1. Trial practice—United States. 2. Practice of law—United
States.
    KF8915.J4   1993
    347.73'7—dc20
    [347.3077]   93-14110
                                            CIP

ISBN 0-314-01904-9

    Jeans—Trial Advoc.2d

Preface

When the first edition of this book was published in 1975 the preface read as follows:

It has been my observation throughout two decades of intensive involvement in the practice and teaching of advocacy that we have never created a systemized approach to the subject. Our present state of development might be likened to that of the musicians as it existed hundreds of years ago. Someone diddling upon his lute or lyre would happen upon a happy combination of sounds that were pleasing to the ear. Other diddlers, seeking to emulate the pleasant sounds, would muddle their way by trial and error through a series of experiments until a reasonably similar series of sounds were accomplished. Now we advocates, like the musicians of old, will listen to our colleagues perform, recognize a "pleasing" examination, voir dire or summation and then attempt to emulate the same by trial and error when our turn comes to perform.

The musicians were able to evolve beyond this haphazard stage with the development of a discipline—the invention of scales, notes, bars, rests and the like. The copying was no longer left to chance. A tune could be analyzed and expressed in terms of rhythm, pitch, tone and intensity. Only with such capacities could music develop to the state of sophistication which it enjoys today.

Advocates similarly must develop a discipline of their own. We must demonstrate that ours is not simply an unstructured art form depending upon hokum, gimmickry and trial ploys. To do so we must create standards by which we can analyze the component parts of an examination, a voir dire, a summation and express those standards by professional terminology. This book represents a beginning of this awesome task.

Furthermore, it is my hope that we writers of advocacy develop a particular form as well as a definitive content. We must deal with the problems of advocacy in a straight forward, realistic fashion. We must not evade the questions of tactics and ethics which pervade every facet of our art. It has been my endeavor to deal with these problems in such a fashion—as if the reader were a fellow professional in the same law office. The importance of improving

PREFACE

our skills and sensitivities demands an approach no less frank and open.

Since then, a host of trial advocates and professors of trial advocacy have risen to the challenge and the student of advocacy (which should include all of us since all of us have much to learn) has a wide selection of worthy books to feed upon. Why then a second edition? Most of the recent offerings in the areas of advocacy have explored the more sophisticated aspects of our art. They have evolved, as one might suspect, to a more elevated and more complicated state. Good for the seasoned practitioner, not so good for the neophyte law student. So it is that this edition seeks to explore advocacy from the ground up. Nothing is taken for granted, no assumptions made that the reader is already familiar with what goes on in a courtroom or, indeed, what the courtroom looks like, who is in it and what they do. If some of such information is too basic for you, skip on to more pertinent stuff; but sometimes it is profitable to go back to the basics, even when you know them.

When I was in college, I had the pleasure of playing for and later coaching with a great gentleman and an extraordinary football mentor, Weeb Ewbank. Whenever we lost a game you could be sure what happened on Monday—intensified drills on blocking and tackling. "That's what the game is all about" he would say. "Perfect the basics and we'll win." And so it is with advocacy.

JAMES W. JEANS, SR.

SUMMARY OF CONTENTS

*

TABLE OF CONTENTS

TABLE OF CONTENTS

TABLE OF CONTENTS

TABLE OF CONTENTS

CHAPTER 5.   TAILORING THE SUIT

A.   IN GENERAL

B.   CHOICE OF FORUM

TABLE OF CONTENTS

C. PARTIES

D. THEORIES OF RECOVERY AND DEFENSE

CHAPTER 6. PLEADING PRACTICES

A. PLAINTIFF'S PETITION OR COMPLAINT

B. DEFENDANT'S MOTION PRACTICE

CHAPTER 7. TRIAL PREPARATION

TABLE OF CONTENTS

CHAPTER 8.   THE COURTROOM

B.   GEOGRAPHY

C.   PERSONNEL

D.   PROTOCOL

E.   DYNAMICS

CHAPTER 9.   VOIR DIRE

A.   PROCEDURE

TABLE OF CONTENTS

TABLE OF CONTENTS

TABLE OF CONTENTS

TABLE OF CONTENTS

TABLE OF CONTENTS

CHAPTER 15. CROSS–EXAMINATION

A. IN GENERAL

B. TECHNIQUES OF INTERROGATION

C. FORMS OF QUESTIONING

D. STRUCTURING THE INTERROGATION

TABLE OF CONTENTS

TABLE OF CONTENTS

TABLE OF CONTENTS

TABLE OF CONTENTS

TABLE OF CONTENTS

C. METHODS OF PRESENTATION

D. SELLING THE CLIENT

TRIAL ADVOCACY

SECOND EDITION

*

CHAPTER 1

ADVOCATES AND ADVOCACY

"You've got to have a dream.
If you don't have a dream, how you
going to have a dream come true?"
South Pacific—Oscar Hammerstein II

Analysis

§ 1.1   Genesis of the Advocate

Time was when there were no trial lawyers. Other means were utilized to resolve disputes without the use of interlopers. The problem of course was not an easy one—trying to ascertain the nugget of truth amidst the dross of stories. It was a job more suited for the Almighty and so it was that the burden was thrust on Him. Was a person thought guilty of stealing? Have him put his hand in a pot of boiling oil. If he was burned the guilt was his. If he was innocent a Kindly Providence would intervene, and, mirabile dictu, the hand would be withdrawn unharmed. The scheme was speedy and simple (two attributes which has always been considered of significance in the judicial process) and afforded the prosecutor a damn fine win-loss record. In fact, too good a record. The innocents with blistered paws finally rose up and

1

trial by ordeal was abandoned to give way to a fairer and more logical way of dispensing justice—trial by battle. Two disputants were pitted against one another with the certain knowledge that "right meant might" and that the purveyor of truth would surely prevail. Again the formula had the benefit of simplicity, the legal accouterments consisting of two cudgels and a pit, and the participants the litigants themselves. No judge, no jury, no appeal. But again the results didn't prove too satisfactory. The "right" was found to reside in a disproportionate degree with the "big guys." A good right was equated with *the* right and the little guys were losing lawsuits and winning bumps with unremitting regularity. Then on one unremembered day in history a "little guy" litigant had an idea. Not relishing the threat of having his cranium caressed by his opponent's cudgel, he accosted a puissant passerby and suggested *he* might want to enter the fray as a substitute swinger. The passerby, intrigued by the promise of a full blown elbow and belly-button donnybrook nodded assent—and thus was born the first trial lawyer.

Several hundred years have passed and, though time has brought some modest modifications, the trial lawyer remains essentially the same. He is a substitute samurai, a free swinging surrogate, an alter-ego for a pusillanimous patron. He is called upon to fight for his client, to use his skills in his service, to advance those arguments which his client, if given the training and talents, would make on his own behalf. He is, in essence, a hired gun.

§ 1.2 Legal Advocacy

If that's what an advocate is, what is advocacy? Let us start with Webster but let us not end there. He says advocacy is "the act of advancing or supporting a cause." That tells what it is but we're trying to find out how to do it. For that purpose we have to flesh out the definition.

First of all it's not a science—a body of knowledge with definitive rules and objective standards. One doesn't learn how to advocate by means such as memorizing multiplication tables or reciting rules. Advocacy is an art. Now that doesn't mean there aren't any rules. Even art has rules. If you're painting you have to stay on the canvas and if you're sculptoring your end product will be dictated by the medium with which you work. Certain well defined skills must be mastered and these will involve the knowledge and application of specific information. The painter must know the chemistry of color and the sculptor the science of stone.   Similarly they should be acquainted with the technique and works of the masters that went before.   But being an artist can not be assured by acquiring the color creativity of Titian or mimicking Michelangelo.   The artist brings *himself* to his work. The skills are the departure point of his endeavors, not the terminus.   His effectiveness will depend upon his own unique make-up, that peculiar blend of soul, mind and spirit that identifies the individual.   As Claude Bernard stated, "Art is I; science is we."

So it is with the trial lawyer.   His art is that of advocacy—of advancing a cause in his own particular way.   Not *any* cause, a *legal* cause in a legal setting, restrained by rules of procedure, confined to theories of recovery and defense and gentled by the awareness of a conscience.   It is this art of which we will speak, but not this alone.   Art presupposes knowledge, in this case knowledge of the law, and so we must deal, at least to some extent, with matters of procedural and substantive law.   Such reference will be peripheral only to our main thrust.   Remember, the emphasis will not be on science, the body of the law, but on art, your own personal skills and talents that will adorn that body.

§ 1.3   Traits of an Advocate—Generally

How then do we come by these "hired guns" who have mastered the art of advocacy?   Are they born or are they made? The products of training and experience or some fated happenstance?   Are the occupational prerequisites those of intellect or chromosomal pattern?   Is the practice of trial law cerebral or visceral?   These are fundamental questions that must be answered.   If it is your attempt to learn how to be an advocate it seems reasonable that you determine if it can be learned at all and, if so, what you must bring to the learner's seat.

Let us attempt a response to the aforementioned conundrums by considering first the attributes of a good trial lawyer.   If we know what these are we should have our answer.

§ 1.4   Traits of an Advocate—Intellectual Breadth

It is obvious that there are some initial demands for mental acumen if one is to be an advocate.   Of course the same is true of any branch of law.   Each facet of the law demands its own area of competence which requires a certain degree of intellectual capacity and scholarship to attain.   But trial law demands something

3

more than a grasp of Procedure, Torts and Evidence. Lawsuits don't exist in a vacuum. The dispute in any given case will involve facts that will carry the advocate far beyond the field of legal studies. Perhaps you're representing a client who has been injured by a faultily designed lawnmower. If such is the case you must be savvy in the fields of engineering, metallurgy and medicine. Does your client seek a dissolution of his partnership in an automobile agency? The need for knowing accounting as well as the customs and practices of the automobile business will be thrust upon you. Are you turning to trial work because you have gagged in the sawdust of trusts and future interests? Forget it, for you are fated to handle a will contest case that will necessitate a knowledge of those very areas of the law.

If the trial lawyer must be equipped with special intellectual traits it will be the need for breadth not depth. The Roman philosopher Terrence stated in a euphoric moment of transcendent brotherhood, "Nothing that is human is alien to me." The same might be said of trial law, with a bit of paraphrasing. "Anything that is human is likely to be litigated" and when that happens it will be two trial lawyers who will have to know about that "anything." So we have our first essential characteristic of a trial lawyer—an intellect and an interest capable of learning something about anything. Now that is something that can be taught— right?

§ 1.5　Traits of an Advocate—Desire

Assuming that you have the intellectual capacity to become an advocate and assuring you can learn the law you will have one leg up. But the beast is far from being straddled. You're going to have to *want* to become a trial lawyer.

During World War II the story was told of a visit made by General "Hap" Arnold to the paratrooper training camp at Fort Benning, Georgia. As he passed down the line of paratroopers he frequently stopped to ask a trooper a question. He paused before one and making "small talk" said, "Do you like to jump son?" The soldier, holding himself at attention, replied, "No sir." "Well why are you in the paratroopers then?", queried the general. "Because I like to be with the men who like to jump," the soldier explained. Not a bad answer. It is always nice to be associated with exciting people even if you don't like excitement. The paratrooper might have justified his involvement quite adequately but that response won't work for a trial lawyer. If you become a

4

trial lawyer it must be because you like to try cases—not because you like to be with people who try cases. Well why shouldn't you like to try cases, don't all lawyers? No! The number of lawyers who appear regularly in court in adversary proceedings numbers less than ten per cent of the bar. Why? Because for the most part they don't like to jump. That prompts a second question. Why don't they like to jump? As in most such cases, it is a fear of failure, a feeling of inadequacy that restrains them. The law they have learned will not suffice. Some unlearned talents are required.

§ 1.6   Traits of an Advocate—Active Mental Metabolism

Aside from an intellect capable of learning substantive and procedural law and the myriad facts that constitute legal proceedings, there is yet another kind of mental acuity required, and that is the ability to "think on your feet." This attribute is quite unrelated to "knowing the law." Such so called "book lawyers" can draft a brief or analyze a tough tax problem in scholarly fashion—given the time. Their minds function best in an environment suited to reflection and concentration. Thrown into the bear pit of a trial court they are out of their element and cannot cope. They may be likened to the intense craftsman who in solitude fastidiously labors in the quiet sanctity of his garage to perfect the innards of a racing car—and then is thrust into the noisome, smoky, whirling milieu of the Indianapolis 500. The automotive skills demanded of the mechanic and the driver are poles apart and, in fact, at times incompatible. The former must be cautious and deliberate as he plans to meet the predictable problems of design and maintenance. The latter must be daring and impulsive if there is to be success in overcoming the unpredictable contingencies that arise with explosive suddenness during the race.

Has the analogy been overdrawn? Only slightly. The implication is that you are one or the other, mechanic or driver, book man or trial man. Of course that isn't true. The driver must have a knowledge of automotives. He must know the difference between a "hawk and a hand saw" or a partridge and a piston. Being merely a gutsy daredevil won't suffice. Similarly it isn't enough that a trial lawyer possess a salesman's bravado and a hair trigger tongue. He too must know the law, but having the kind of intellect by which the law can be known won't get the job done in the court room. Here is where the extras are needed: the quick draw objection to an opponent's improper questioning; the speedy analysis of the tack being taken by an adversary; the knee jerk ameliorative response to an unexpected statement from a witness. The lack of these "moves" keeps many a lawyer off the trial gridiron. Query: can this be learned?

Even though adequately "equipped" with the "smarts" and the "moves" a lawyer might still disdain a courtroom duel. The head is willing but the flesh is weak. Other anatomical equipment is demanded and it is a sine qua non that the trial lawyer be equipped with all three.

§ 1.7 Traits of an Advocate—Combativeness

The trial lawyer must possess a combativeness, a bellicosity which responds to the challenge of impending conflict. By some unconscious remembrance there is a link to that first stand-in trial combatant and as an heir it is he who now grasps the cudgel to swing on behalf of your client. There must be no agonizing uncertainty, no hesitation of the thrill to the exhilaration of the coming conflict. It is not enough to merely tolerate the tooth and nail—you must yearn for it. You must relish the thwack of a well landed left hook, tingle with the thump of a crushing block. The physical crudities will not be there but the verbal jousting, the tactical thrusts, the legal clouts will be. It's heady stuff this advocacy and you'll have to have a spirit of combativeness to play the game. Query: Can learning supply this ingredient?

§ 1.8 Traits of an Advocate—Stomach

There is a second anatomical requirement. A trial lawyer is required to undertake a number of chores for which the average lawyer will not have the stomach. Making the contact with the client, briefing him on the essentials of his claim or defense, "coaching" a witness—all have elements of unpleasantness about them from which the squeamish will withdraw. The specifics will be developed in the chapter on ethics. Suffice to say at this point that absent the stomach for this aspect of advocacy the candidate for the courtroom is missing a significant organ of the trial anatomy. Query: Can stomachs be doled out in the classroom?

§ 1.9 Traits of an Advocate—Sensitivity

There is yet a third requirement. The true trial lawyer must have a heart. Being equipped with the other attributes will provide the intellectual and competitive necessities but the advocate must be something more than a technician. Hopefully you will master your craft but that cannot be the end all to your calling. You must be about the task of improving the structure of the law. Building on, revising, perhaps tearing down but in any case working on the edifice we call "Justice." To do that you must be sensitive to the social problems of the day, discerning of those segments of our culture which need buttressing and those which call for change. Absent this awareness the advocate becomes an argumentative automaton for sale to the highest bidder. But blessed with this last and greatest gift the advocate reaches the fullness of his potential and realizes his true identity. Quintilian, the master of the art of rhetoric was once asked his definition of an orator. The expectation was that he would list the various skills needed for a man to fulfill that role; a broad vocabulary, expressive gestures, good diction, et cetera. His reply instead was, "An orator is a good man who speaks well." Quintilian realized that the most meaningful attribute, far greater than the technical skills, was that of moral integrity and social commitment. The same needs are no less for an advocate. If such is your calling let it be said of you "He was a good man who tried a lawsuit well." Query: Can morals be taught?

How does the final tally shape up? The trial lawyer must have a whole carload of characteristics. Some are skills, some are talents. Some can be taught, some must be experienced and others must spring from the genes of your forebears. If you have stayed with us so far, I sense that whatever it is, you have what it takes.

§ 1.10 Analytical Methodology

Some ancient moralist suggested a sure-fire test to determine if a rumor should be repeated. Ask yourself three questions: first, is it true? second, is it needful? third, is it kind? Unless you can respond affirmatively to all three, best not repeat it.

Without getting sidetracked as to the merits of the moralist's approach, it does provide a methodology readily adaptable to learning those elements of advocacy capable of being taught. Each step in the trial of a lawsuit from pleading to closing argument should be subjected to a similar three tiered test, the three questions being: first, *can* I do it?, second, *how* do I do it?, and third, *should* I do it?

The initial query that must be asked before undertaking any tact is whether or not the law permits you to do it. Let us take an example. You are defending an intersection accident case and your opponent asks the plaintiff, "You have never been cited for careless driving have you?" Is relief available? Can I object to that form of suggestive interrogation which is not relevant to the issues? The answer may be found in the law of evidence and that answer will resolve our first problem. Yes, you *can*.

We now pass to the second—*how* do I do it? Continuing with the illustration, the trial lawyer would have to know the proper verbiage necessary to impose an objection and the most effective posturing to be adopted in making that objection. The answer will be—stand and state in the hearing of the jury, "I object your honor, the question is leading and suggestive and is not relevant to the issues."

On to the third—*should* I do it? The answer to the first query is a matter of law; the second, a matter of mechanics; the third, a matter of judgment. Back to our illustration. Your opponent has asked an improper question about traffic citations. You know that you can object and you know how to do it. But your file reveals that the plaintiff has been arrested twice for drunken driving and once for running a red light. If you object and are sustained the matter is closed and the jury will probably infer that plaintiff had a clear record (or else why would you have objected?) If you don't object the relevancy of plaintiff's past driving record will be established and the plaintiff will be fair game on cross-examination. *Should* you object? No.

As we progress through the trial process there will be the three questions to which we shall continually address ourselves. Each problem as it were, will be looked at through tri-focal glasses. If you are able to see what you can do, how to do it and what factors to consider to determine if you should do it—you will be well on your way.

§ 1.11 Establishing Priorities

The trial of a lawsuit is a succession of choices, choices that encompass an infinite range of subject matter. Success or failure will depend on your recognition of the choices that are available and the wisdom of the choices made.

Some of the areas in which options are to be excused are more obvious than others.

The first, should the case be taken?

8

The second, what fee should be charged?

Assuming a lawyer-client relationship is established and a claim is to be made, we must choose the time and manner of presenting that claim, and if we opt for litigation, choices must be made regarding the identity of the parties, the venue, the theories of recovery, the sequence and tools of discovery, the type of evidence to be presented, the sequence of proof and other matters to be dealt with in subsequent chapters.

Other choices that transcend matters of procedure and tactics must be considered by the thinking advocate, matters of goals, attitude and style. To these too often neglected areas let us direct our attention.

§ 1.12 Establishing Priorities—Goals

Ask a lawyer the goal he pursues in the trial of a lawsuit and the knee jerk response will be, "To win."

Sounds obvious doesn't it? But a deeper delve into the advocate's psyche will often reveal a more basic goal—to survive.

The appearance in a public forum in full view of your client, an adversarial fellow professional, the judge, court personnel and a random sampling of the community sitting in the jury box can create an elevated state of anxiety that diverts one's mind from the appointed task. Fear generates a relentless centripetal energy that sucks the life's forces into the comforting confines of your inner self. Concerns are directed within and not without. Questions of "How do *I* look?" "How do *I* sound?" "How will *I* make it through this valley of the shadow of death?" predominate over regard for the processes of communication and persuasion.

The physical manifestations of the advocate's angst can be awesome and express themselves in such polar phenomena as dry mouth or wet palms, quaking knees or stiffened neck, quickened pulse or slackened speech.

The question is not how do I rid myself of these disquieting displays but rather how can I curb them so that they are merely discomforting and not disabling. As one speech instructor observed,[1] "One never gets rid of the butterflies in the stomach. All you can hope for is to get them to fly in formation." Failing to discipline those butterflies and create a formulated flight pattern will result in the advocate utilizing the traditional twin techniques

1. Joseph Guastaferro.

of survival—passivity ("playing possum") and predictability ("don't rock the boat"). The measure of success will not be in winning, but in surviving. The plaudits will not come from an appreciative client for a fight well fought but from a patronizing judge for a restrained and deferential performance. The reward sought is not the laurel crown of a winner to bedeck your brow but a passel of billable hours to cram your time sheet.

Such can never be the goal of the advocate. As Emerson reminds us, "Let us not flag in paltry works which serve our pot and bag alone." The alternative—"Hitch your wagon to a star" and seek the goal of excellence in your chosen profession.

§ 1.13 Establishing Priorities—Attitudes

The poet reminds us that "it isn't the gale but the set of the sail that makes the ship to go." Granting the truth of that aphorism we must ask ourself "How does the advocate set his sail in order to drive the trial ship in a favorable direction?" We begin with the Golden Rule—"Do unto others as you would have them do unto you."

Once we have freed ourselves from the fear which drives us to introspection and self centeredness we can focus on the needs of the multiple identities with which we must deal during the investigation, initiation and trial of a case.

Once we subdue the predator of fear we encounter another adversary of a more subtle sort—that bundle of elements intrinsic within our profession (power, attention, adulation) which pull us from the heights of service to others to the depths of consuming conceit. The greater our success, the greater the pull. "Fame is the public destruction of a person in the process of becoming" and many are the advocates who have been destroyed by their successes.

The remedy is the continuing application of chilling, humbling homilies to the swelling sense of self importance—ameliorative mantras that remind us that "Pride goeth before a fall" and "Before honor is humility."

CHAPTER 2

ETHICS OF ADVOCACY

"Every move you make,
every step you take,
every smile you fake,
I'll be watching you."
I'll be watching you—The Police

Analysis

---

§ 2.1 Introduction

Mark Twain complained that everyone talked about the weather but no one did anything about it. In the case of legal ethics we seldom do either. Not that lawyers aren't concerned,

11

it's just that everyone has his own idea on the subject. True, the American Bar Association has promulgated rules of ethics that have been adopted by a goodly number of states and which do a credible job in attempting to aid in the search for standards but, unfortunately, many lawyers resist such guidance. Since such rules fall short of the tablets from Sinai they seek help from other sources. Some provide a very simplistic solution, "All you have to know concerning the propriety of your conduct as a lawyer is to apply those principles you learned at your mother's knee." The test seems a bit haphazard. As some cynic remarked, "The only thing most kids learn at their mother's knee is how to dodge cigarette ashes."

Whether or not the suggested test is adequate, it does provide a necessary element—an individual sensitivity to what is "right" and what is "wrong." The problem with this is apparent. It is wholly subjective and the moral sensitivity of those who practice trial law constitutes a pretty broad spectrum. The "good guy's" sensitivity to right will restrain him at every turn while the "bad guy's" indifference to this same consideration will provide him an unfettered romp. The problem is aggravated by the fact that these two will be pitted against each other in an adversary proceeding. Granted the moral advocate will have some things going for him (Gallahad reputedly had the strength of ten "because his heart was pure"), it is a bit naive to think that a breastplate of righteousness will do much good against a well-aimed kick to the crotch.

In the absence of the adequacy of an individual's sense of fairness with its sliding scale, we attempt to employ some group standard. Ethics Committees at both the local and state bar levels are created which judge specific complaints (most often on an ad hoc basis) and if the sensibility of the group is offended by an individual's errant behavior, sanctions are imposed. The guidelines for what is right or wrong, as provided by the directives of the American Bar Association may serve as the Rosetta Stone to conventional conduct but just as often they do not. But even if they did, other difficulties arise.

First, someone has "to blow the whistle," make a formal complaint and initiate the action. Sometimes it will be a dissatisfied client, but too often these are merely malcontents with a streak of paranoid and little merit to their gripes. It is the fellow practitioner who must yell "cop" and for most, that is hard to do. Consequently the lawyer who operates on the border of propriety with occasional sorties beyond will never know the lash of retribution. You see we lawyers too have our "conspiracy of silence" and that silence shelters all save the knave who is guilty of aggravated offenses of a continuing nature. Most of us would agree to that homily which holds, "Shame on the bird that fouls its own nest." But some would elaborate, "Double shame on the bird who evicts the bird that fouls its own nest." Why should this be so? It's not simply because of some peer group passion within the legal fraternity. Other reasons exist. The plaintiff lawyers file no complaints against their unethical adversaries claiming that they will go unheeded because the "silk stocking" boys of the defense bar control the disciplinary machinery. The defense lawyers stand mute because, as some state, disbarment of the ambulance chasers will eliminate the incompetents against whom they have much better success than the ethical lawyers into whose hands these cases otherwise would come. Add to this the truism that "no one likes a snitch" and its corollary "everyone likes to be liked" and we have a silence inducing combination of pussilanimity and ego preening that gives the illusion that all is well with legal ethics.

Second, the ethical guidelines are not always adequate. With any codification of rules regarding human conduct the exceptions soon outnumber the examples. The lawyer, particularly the trial lawyer, confronted with an ethical situation will find himself adrift with a particular problem between two shores of generalities. The rules function well in defining the proprieties of legal listings and announcing office openings but where is the definitiveness in dealing with the complexities of coaching a witness, negotiating a settlement or wooing a would be client? It is tough to envision rules that could adequately deal with such problems. Where then do we go for help? Back to momma's knee—with a few suggestions.

Since little headway can be made in listing criteria for "right" and "wrong" and attempting to impose one person's sense of morality on another, let us not make the effort. Let us instead consider the points of views to be taken rather than the conclusions to be reached. We will leave those to you.

Every decision which demands ethical consideration should be viewed from three different points of view: what effect will your decision have upon your client, upon the law, upon yourself (not necessarily listed in the order of importance). If any of the three suffer by reason of your resolution of the problem it is a good bet you have failed to abide by good ethical standards. Let us put it

13

another way. When confronted by a problem of professional ethics put yourself in the position of your client and ask what would he have me do? Then slip into the role of watch dog of our profession. What should be done to maintain the integrity of the law, the righteousness of the administration of justice? Lastly, ask yourself what will this decision do to me, as a practitioner, as an officer of the Court, as a person? I guess a fourth effort at role playing should be made. I advance no claim of authorship, the idea having been conceived almost 2,000 years ago, "Do unto others as you would have them do unto you." If your proposed action meets all four, go ahead. It is bound to be alright.

There are a number of recurring ethical problems that confront the trial lawyer. Let us meet them head on, and restricted by neither pussy footing nor moralistic mouthings, let us see if some sensible, ethical (they go together) resolution can be made.

§ 2.2   Making the Attorney–Client Connection

Wouldn't it be nice if the relationship of attorney and client were initiated in the same fashion as that of physician and patient? The client waiting his turn in the ante-room eager to seek the solace of the healing hand. Or the anxious telephone message plaintively inquiring about the possibility of a house call. Not so with the lawyer. Oh, there might be a few exceptions when a friend calls from the local jail at 1:00 A.M. protesting that he had only two beers and demanding that you effect his release. But aside from events such as this, the conception of the lawyer-client relationship is hesitant and obtuse.

First of all the client isn't at all sure that he needs you. He has been involved in some incident that has left him injured in body and damaged in pocketbook but he feels that he might be able to "work it out himself" and avoid the expense of legal fees. The astute businessperson, who dares not entertain the thought of diagnosing the sharp pain in his right side as an appendicitis and who would think it madness to try a self executed excision, seriously thinks that he is sufficiently perspicacious about the law to "know his rights" and then match wits with the claims adjuster regarding the evaluation and settlement of his claim. And even if they do recognize the need for legal assistance, they more or less back into a commitment.

They will not call and say, "Hurry over I need your help." The message is more apt to be, "I've been involved in an accident, what do you think I should do?" You know very well what he should do—hire you! But will you tell him that? Probably not. The response will probably be a long list of advice: don't talk to an adjuster, try to find out if there are any witnesses, etc. All the while you're hoping that the magic invitation "Will you handle the case?" will be forthcoming. It usually isn't. Why? Not because the caller doesn't need you (he wouldn't have called if he didn't recognize some need), but because he is ignorant of the lawyer's sense of protocol in initiating the relationship. He is unaware of the lawyer's sensitivity to "chasing." After all, when he calls the doctor, he simply says, "My child is sick." There is no superfluous query, "Will you handle the case?" The nurse, responds with "Bring him in." The lawyer should be similarly conditioned. When the caller says, "I've got a problem" the response should be, "Come to the office." If the problem is big enough, a superior retort would be, "I'll be right out!" The recitation of a legal problem initiated by a prospective client is tantamount to a request for representation. Once they have dropped the hanky, the courtship begins and should culminate in a lawyer-client relationship.

Complications arise, however, when the hanky is dropped by a third party. An accident victim lies in a hospital bed suffering from a serious injury. An ex-client calls and says, "There's an injured friend of mine who wants to talk to you." Now what do you do? A number of responses might be given:

1. "Good, what's his room number, I'll be right out."

2. "When will you be available to go to the hospital with me to see him?"

3. "If he wants to talk to me why don't you suggest that he give me a ring."

4. "Sorry, unless he calls me seeking my representation, I'm afraid I can't be of any help."

How would you characterize the number one respondent?

Perhaps a multiple choice should be offered. Check the appropriate space.

Unethical ____ "Pushy" ____ Smart ____ Hungry ____
                                    (temporarily)

And number four?

Ethical _____ Self righteousness _____ Stupid _____ Hungry _____
                                                   (perpetually)

Change that conversation a bit and new problems arise. "My friend is injured and he wants to talk to a lawyer." Or, "My friend is injured and unconscious. I think you ought to talk to his wife." Now which of the responses should be made?

The ethical problems don't cease with the initial confrontation between you and the perspective client. How is the relationship to be consummated? Will I have to "sell" myself and, if so, how self laudatory may I be? Should there be a formal contract and, if so, what should be the terms? These are not idle inquiries. Remember you might be at the hospital bed simply because the injured party wants "to talk to a lawyer." Suppose you have made sufficient inquiry to know it is a good case with serious injury. You feel that the injured party needs a lawyer and you know you're competent to do the job. How nice it would be if someone else could extol your virtues and give the prospective client the assurance he seeks. But no one is there—but you. Is there any ethical problem in telling of your experience, similar type cases you have handled, successful jury verdicts you have won? That fellow lying there is in big trouble. The resolution of his claim might hold the key to his economic future. He wants and needs a good lawyer as much as he wanted and needed a good medic to treat his injuries. Ever hear a doctor assure a patient by reciting his experiences and skills? Undoubtedly you have and if you have been the patient you appreciated the assurance that your surgeon had not confined his practice to lancing boils. If he needs this assurance from you—give it to him.

Unfortunately, he might seek other assurances—such as the promise of financial help. Picture a seriously injured victim of a well insured tort-feasor. He has incurred substantial medical bills, he has been off work six months and his injuries are such that he will be off work for a long time to come. There has been a substantial settlement offer but no where near the potential value of the case. He would like to hire you as his attorney but the wife and the kids must be fed and he needs at least $600.00 a month just to get by. What do you do now Counselor?

The ethical demands in such a situation are clear. Any offer of financial help as a quid pro quo for creating the lawyer-client relationship is blatantly improper. A more difficult question may

16

arise later when the suit is in litigation, approaching trial and the economic situation of your client threatens to necessitate a premature and inadequate settlement. What then can the lawyer do? Advance support money? Co-sign a note? Arrange for temporary financial help through a third person? The answers do not come as readily.

§ 2.3   Initiating the Suit or Invoking the Defense

Some office wag has authored what has become a well known truism: "No person is a hero to his or her secretary". How true. Continuing exposure to a person lessens our opinion for that person, and familiarity—whether with persons or things—breeds contempt. Lawyers are familiar with pleadings. Allegations of negligence will roll of a lawyer's tongue as easily as litanies off the lips of a mother superior. Accusations of riotous misconduct, mayhem and fraud can be crammed into a one page petition and nothing more will be thought of it than a perfunctory pleading. Wholesale claims of injuries are recited within the complaint that no more resemble those of the plaintiff than Hamlet resembled Hercules. And how does the defendant respond to this purple prose? With prose of his own of even deeper hue. He solemnly denies that he was guilty of negligence; that the accident occurred, or, indeed, that the street on which it happened was "open and public." And besides, if the street was open and public and the accident occurred and he was negligent, the plaintiff caused it all himself by reason of his own riotous misconduct, mayhem and fraud.

The wisdom of such pleadings shall be dealt with elsewhere, but what of the ethics? How does the defendant react when he is served with the summons and reads such Hammurabian hyperbole? What will be his impression of the truthfulness much less the majesty of the law? The American Bar Association Discipline Rule 7–102(A) provides: "In his representation of a client, a lawyer shall not file a suit, assert a position, conduct a defense . . . or take other action on behalf of his client when he knows or when it is obvious that such action would serve merely to harass or maliciously injure another."

But despite the above American Bar Association admonition, unthinking lawyers, contemptuous through their familiarity with pleading ploys, continue to profane the practice.

Even before the pleading is filed, an ethical decision should be made to ascertain the verity of the claim or the defense. This is particularly true in alleging legal theories which carry an imputation of moral wrongdoing or professional incompetence. Take the medical malpractice case. A client comes to the office claiming that the family doctor has malfunctioned. He hasn't run a red light, he left a sponge in the belly. Should you precipitously file suit and thus advertise the medic's oversight? Or should you call on the doctor, arrange for a settlement conference with his carrier and make a good faith endeavor to dispose of the case before suit? Ethics might not mandate such pre-suit efforts but courtesy to a fellow professional might.

§ 2.4   Educating the Client

Every time a screeching line drive curves foul the likelihood is that among the spectators there will be some to mouth the familiar clichés appropriate to the occasion—"A miss is as good as a mile" says one fan of the fielding team. "Close only counts in horseshoes" reminds another. Their counterpart cracks a resigning smile and observes, "Baseball is a game of inches."

And so it is with the law. The validity of a legal theory will often be a "matter of inches." If the facts fall inside the playing field it is a home rule. If not, it is just another strike. A few questions will illustrate the difference:

Query: Is your client a licensee or a trespasser?

Key: Was she using the store as a short cut (foul) or was she intending to make a purchase? (fair).

Query: Was the victim of a negligent driver a "guest" or a "passenger?"

Key: Was he riding for free (foul) or was he going to chip in for the gas? (fair).

Query: Is the company owned yacht a business expense which is tax deductible?

Key: Is the "business" transacted monkey (foul) or otherwise? (fair).

Obviously if the appropriate theory of defense or recovery is going to be available (if the ball is going to land fair) the evidence to support those theories will have to be forthcoming and the source of that evidence must usually be your client. Which brings us to the question with the ethical crunch—how are the facts of a given incident to be adduced from the client?

The choices are essentially two and it is simply a matter of chronology. You either advise the client *first* of the essential ingredients of his legal position then inquire into his knowledge of those ingredients or you elicit from the client "all he knows" about the state of facts and *then* advise him whether or not he has a valid claim or defense. It boils down to a matter of timing—but therein lies all the difference.

Let us take the three fact situations mentioned earlier. (Areas, incidentally, in which current case law is changing rapidly). First, the status question of licensee or trespasser. The two options of client interview might be as follows:

First

Lawyer: "Ms. Jones I understand you slipped and fell while walking through the street level, main aisle of Macy's. In presenting this claim it will be important to determine your purpose in being in the store. If you were there as a customer rather than someone just using the store as a short-cut, the chances of your recovery will be substantially greater."

Ms. Jones: "You mean that whether or not I recover from my fractured hip that resulted in a two inch shortening in my leg and ruined my career as lead ballerina for the Bolshoi will depend on whether I was a shopper or short-cutter?"

Lawyer: "Yes, that's true."

Ms. Jones: "I unquestionably was shopping."

Second

Lawyer: "Now tell me Ms. Jones all about the accident."

Ms. Jones: "Well I had just come from the bank and I was walking through Macy's main aisle when I fell."

Lawyer: "Had you purchased anything at Macy's?"

Ms. Jones: "No."

Lawyer (Agonizing): "Were you *intending* to purchase anything at Macy's?"

Ms. Jones: "I don't know."

Lawyer: (Poor but proud) "I'm sorry Ms. Jones under those circumstances, I'm afraid I can't help you."

How true! Such a lawyer can't "help" his client—one who obviously needs help. Let us take the second situation, the rider who is injured by reason of the driver's negligence.

First

Lawyer: "Fred, it's apparent that your driver was negligent in causing your injuries but he wasn't guilty of willful and wanton negligence in my opinion. Now we have a guest statute in this State that will prevent you from recovery unless we can prove that you were a passenger in the car and not a guest?"

Fred: "What's the difference?"

Lawyer: "Well, if you were paying for the ride or if you intended to share expenses then you would be considered a passenger and entitled to recover."

Fred: "You mean whether or not I recover for $5,000 medical expenses and $10,000 in loss of wages will depend on whether I intended to pay for half a fill up at the gas station?"

Lawyer: "Exactly."

Fred: " 'Course I wasn't going to sponge a ride. We had planned to split the gas and any other expenses that would have been incurred."

Second

Lawyer: "Now tell me Fred all about the accident." (You know about the rest).

Don't think that the ethics of client interviewing is confined to the personal injury case. It is just as substantial a problem, and perhaps more so, for the corporate, criminal or tax lawyer. In each instance the client wants to know the pertinent elements of the applicable law and what information is necessary to present his case effectively. In fact, it is not unusual for the lawyer to be confronted with a blunt, "What do you want me to say?" The invitation to suborn perjury must of course, be rejected. But there are those who say that telling a client the facts necessary to support his case is just that—perhaps a bit more subtle and subliminal—but still subornation. Where do good ethics lie? Who is the candidate for disbarment—the lawyer who advises his client accused of a crime to "just tell the policeman all you know" or the one who says, "If you want to get out of this alive take my advice and say you shot in self defense." In both instances the role of the lawyer has been profaned and each of the erring advocates should have his ticket torn from the wall. The true advocate will seek the golden mean. He can neither passively sit by while his charge "spills his guts" nor can he write the script for his pliant client. He must acquaint his client with the legal facets of the case, tell him of the significance of his testimony and then let the truth come forth. Ah, but can it be the truth when tempered so? Indeed it can. Experience has shown that the "fudging" that goes on by litigants is more likely to occur with the unadvised client. Let us take a simple example. Hubert has struck down a young pedestrian while traveling 25 miles per hour in a school zone. The child has negligently attempted to cross the street in the middle of the block and if there is to be recovery it must be through invocation of the "last clear chance" doctrine. The "truth" of the matter is that Hubert didn't have a prayer as far as avoiding the accident. But, unadvised as to the legal implications of his testimony, he states on deposition that he was traveling 15 miles per hour and "could have stopped on a dime." Hubert has "fudged" in the wrong direction and has rationalized himself into a lawsuit. Adequate, ethical counselling would have spared him that unfortunate result.

Even in matters that do not directly affect the factual issues of the case, the lawyer must recognize the need to give direction not to suggest erroneous responses, but to prevent the unguided client from rationalizing into a lie. Take the instance where the witness' cross examination has been interrupted by a recess. The first question upon resumption is, "Did you talk to your lawyer during the recess?" The witness reacts like a parson caught reading Playboy. "Why no!" he says, and the jury, probably having seen an innocuous conference taking place, knows that he is capable of lying and discredits his entire testimony. Shame on the lawyer who has not anticipated such a question and advised his client of the most effective response—the truth.

§ 2.5 Investigation

Perhaps it is incongruous to talk of "ethics" and "investigation." There is something about the quest for information which seems to override a consideration of propriety. The reporter on a hot assignment feels little restraint in the use of a repertory of ruses to get the story. Even Sergeant Friday, while circumventing constitutional guarantees by banging down doors and making warrantless searches seemed to be functioning properly since his goal was simply "to get the facts, Ma'am." What then of the lawyer? May he employ ruses, misrepresentations, and little white subterfuges in his search for information about his case?

It is easier to pose the problem than to supply the answers. Here are a few of the problem areas that confront the investigating lawyer. The first set will concern dealings with the opposing litigant, the second, with potential witnesses.

The police report indicates the name of the potential defendant. You have been hired by the injured party and consequently are anxious to ascertain the facts of the incident, the names of witnesses, commit the defendant to an unfavorable story and determine the extent of financial responsibility.

Query number one: May I ethically contact the potential defendant for the purpose of securing such information?

Query number two: What if you have been notified by the local claims person for Shifting Sands Mutual that they represent the potential defendant and are willing to discuss settlement? May you then contact the insured?

Query number three: The incident will probably involve the liability of a corporation which you know has a staff of attorneys which tends to their corporate legal affairs. Do you interview the potential defendant under those circumstances?

Perhaps the written guidelines will provide some comfort and direction but the main burden of ascertaining right from wrong, aggressive representation from overreaching, will fall upon your conscience.

Seeking help from witnesses is another problem. You are trying to track down an illusive witness who holds the key to your case. Apparently he is avoiding bill collectors or a summons server because every inquiry directed to neighbors or friends about his whereabouts is countered with feigned ignorance. Can a "smart" investigator legitimately offer a reward for information about the witness' whereabouts? Can he misrepresent himself as a legal investigator seeking the witness as the legatee of a will? How far can imaginative investigation go before becoming fraudulent misrepresentation?

§ 2.6 Pleading Practices

Unfortunately the subject of legal ethics is seldom related to pleading practices. As mentioned before (§ 2.3) the plaintiff's petition and the defendant's response are frequently as fanciful as a realtor's blurb for a retirement village in the Sunshine State. Overdrawn accusations and demonic denials do much to stultify the law. But shoddy ethics in the pleading stage do not end there. The proliferation of discovery practice has placed in the hands of the parties a variety of tools each of which is capable of use and abuse. Depositions of the litigants are full blown revelations of the pedigree, life style and thought processes of the deponent. Restricted only to the extent that the inquiries must be peripherally "relevant" and "not privileged," the inquisitor will range hither and yon gathering minutiae with feckless, fumbling interrogation. Despite the magnitude of the litigation you can be assured that some young lawyer armed with a checklist and an abiding mistrust of plaintiffs will thoroughly inquire into past residences ("And where did you live before *that*?"), past employment ("And did you have any summer jobs in high school?"), past medical history (were you a full term baby?) and past everything.

It is not unusual for the deposition of a litigant in a simple case to consume three or four hours of such reprehensible rambling. What is the explanation? Perhaps there are a number (taking them in descending order of propriety).

1. The interrogator doesn't know any better and hopes that his "thoroughness" will smokescreen his ignorance. The better you are at any given endeavor the less effort is necessary to accomplish your goal. And so it is with interrogation.

2. The interrogator has been victimized by the current trend to overtry a case. Law, like medicine, has fallen into the practice of doing everything possible in the representation of the client. Does Johnny have a sprained ankle? Take three x-rays of the site, run some blood tests, and hospitalize him overnight for observation. Does Mary have a few thousand dollars? Write a will, create a trust, prepare a power of attorney. Do whatever can be done and charge what the traffic will bear.

3. The investigator has his "meter running" and thus, being paid by the hour, will be able to justify a substantial bill for his thorough questioning.

4. The interrogator is involved in a war of attrition. His client has more resources than yours and ultimately he will wear you down. When this deposition is completed he will serve notice that others will be taken all over the country.

Unfortunately this type of advocacy is being practiced more and more. There no longer is a small case that can be investigated in a few weeks and tried in a few days. And the reason, in too many instances, is the unethical conduct of some who pose as advocates.

§ 2.7 Trial—Generally

"All things are fair in love and war." So say the lovers and the warriors—and there are some lawyers who would include a lawsuit as a third activity in which fairness is a missing factor. After all, there are some similarities in the three endeavors—only one can win, a lot rides on the outcome, and there is no red ribbon for second place. Besides, your opponent is a mature person, parading as a competent advocate learned in the law—why should any favors be expected from you? Perhaps that query begs the question. Maybe the real question is better expressed "Is fairness a favor—or an expectation?" Or putting it in Pilatean terms, "What is fair?"

Let us ponder a few problems that are illustrative of the trial lawyer's dilemma that puts him between "the rock and the hard place."

You represent a defendant who is seventeen years of age at trial time. Local procedure dictates that litigants under eighteen be represented by a guardian ad litem. A judgment rendered against a minor without benefit of a guardian is void. Your opponent has neglected to fulfill this procedural requirement and absent a last minute recognition of this oversight your client is guaranteed a "free ride"—a defendant's verdict will bind the plaintiff, but a plaintiff's verdict will be worthless.

What do you do—advise your opponent of the deficiency, or play things cozy and see how the trial comes out? Arguments exist for either decision. Those adhering to the former would say that the problem is simply another application of the query that was mouthed by Cain at the dawn of history and, although never affirmatively answered, there exists a strong implication of such a response by the celestial Chief Justice himself. Those who would adhere to the latter would point out that an answer was never given to that question. Further, if an advocate's role is the keeping of his brother or sister lawyer, he can do so only at the expense of his client. For them a more legitimate question is, "Am I my client's keeper?" and to that there can be only one answer.

This illustration demonstrates the dilemma—duty to client equalling one horn, courtesy to colleague the other. The form in which the dilemma materializes will vary. In the above, the attorney faced with the decision had not precipitated the problem. He merely had to react to a bad situation created by his opponent.

The law never has invoked a duty to rescue—so it might be argued that passivity can be justified. "If I'm not compelled to extend a hand to a drowning child why should I save a struggling adversary?" Maybe you're not, if he is the one who jumped in the water. Most of the ethical problems during trial however can not be analogized to a rescue duty. In most instances the question is, "When can I push him in?"

The pushing can occur in countless ways. A few of the more common ones as excerpted from appellate decisions are set forth in the sections which follow.

§ 2.8   Voir Dire

Facts: The following inquiry was made of the jury panel:

"Now, some three or four months ago there were—two or three articles in the newspaper, an item or two on television and two or three news items on the radio about the fact that (plaintiff) was flying in his private plane down to one of the South Sea Islands and he dropped his airplane in the Atlantic Ocean—Is there anyone on the panel who has any recollection of that matter such that it would cause you to have any feeling in leaning one way or another in this case?"

Held: "It seems perfectly obvious that the most probable effect of this incident would be to create in the mind of the jurors the impression that the plaintiff was a person of considerable means, if he could fly overseas in his own private plane. The idea that the incident would create sympathy for him seems most illusory. We are impelled to find that counsel knowingly used this incident to create prejudice against the plaintiff."

This is one reason that more and more jurisdictions are confining jury interrogation to the judge. If you are fortunate enough to practice in a jurisdiction which does afford the right to question the prospective jurors, don't abuse the process with tricks such as that.

§ 2.9   Direct Examination—Generally

Facts: On direct examination plaintiff testified that she was employed at the County Courthouse and started to work the first part of June, 1974. She was then asked the following additional questions:

Q. "How come you went to work the first part of June, 1974?"

    A. "I lost my husband in May, 1974."
    Q. "Your husband passed away?"
    A. "Yes, sir."
    Q. "Did you have to go to work?"
    A. "Yes, sir."

Held: Evidence of plaintiff's family status or the persons in plaintiff's family is improper; the theory being that such an inquiry is ordinarily made only for the purpose of appealing to the sympathy of the jury.

The ethical dilemmas confronting the lawyer at trial are not unlike those encountered during the investigative process. How carefully can you guide your interrogation so as to emphasize those elements favorable to your case and de-emphasize or ignore those elements which do violence to your cause?

§ 2.10 Direct Examination—Selective Interrogation

A classic example of such "guidance" is demonstrated in the Sacco–Vanzetti case, the cause celebre in which two Italians of left wing political persuasion were tried on a charge of the murder of a factory guard. The following excerpts are taken from the opinion, Commonwealth v. Sacco, 255 Mass. 369, 151 N.E. 839.

At the time of his arrest, there were found in the possession of Sacco "a .32 Colt automatic pistol" and "twenty-three .32 calibre automatic cartridges" of various makes. "The pistol was fully loaded; eight cartridges in the clip and one in the barrel." A bullet of .32–calibre, introduced in evidence and marked Exhibit 18, was taken from Berardelli's body which, in the opinion of the Commonwealth's medical expert, had caused his death. The Commonwealth called William H. Proctor and Charles J. Van Amberg, who qualified as experts on the construction as well as the practical use of firearms, bullets, and different styles of cartridges. l. c. 452.

After the trial the witness Proctor filed an affidavit in which he outlined the manner in which his expertise was solicited and developed at trial.

"During the preparation for the trial, my attention was repeatedly called by the district attorney and his assistants to the question: whether I could find any evidence which would justify the opinion that the particular bullet taken from the body of Berardelli, which came from a Colt automatic pistol, came from the particular Colt automatic pistol taken from

Sacco. I used every means available to me for forming an opinion on this subject. I conducted, with Captain Van Amberg, certain tests at Lowell, about which I testified, consisting in firing certain cartridges through Sacco's pistol. At no time was I able to find any evidence whatever which tended to convince me that the particular model bullet found in Berardelli's body, which came from a Colt automatic pistol, which I think was numbered 3 and had some other exhibit number, came from Sacco's pistol and I so informed the district attorney and his assistant before the trial. This bullet was what is commonly called a full metalpatch bullet and although I repeatedly talked over with Captain Van Amberg the scratch or scratches which he claimed tended to identify this bullet as one that must have gone through Sacco's pistol, his statements concerning the identifying marks seemed to me entirely unconvincing. At the trial, the district attorney did not ask me whether I had found any evidence that the so called mortal bullet which I have referred to as number 3 passed through Sacco's pistol, nor was I asked that question on cross-examination. The district attorney desired to ask me that question, but I had repeatedly told him that if he did I should be obliged to answer in the negative; consequently, he put to me this question: 'Q. Have you an opinion as to whether bullet number 3 was fired from the Colt automatic which is in evidence?' To which I answered, 'I have.' He then proceeded, 'Q. And what is your opinion?' 'A. My opinion is that it is consistent with being fired by that pistol.' After stating that he is still of the same opinion he goes on: '... but I do not intend by that answer to imply that I had found any evidence that the so called mortal bullet had passed through this particular Colt automatic pistol and the district attorney well knew that I did not so intend and framed his question accordingly. Had I been asked the direct question: whether I had found any affirmative evidence whatever that this so called mortal bullet had passed through this particular Sacco's pistol, I should have answered then, as I do now without hesitation, in the negative.'" l. c. 453–454.

The court on appeal held that no error had been committed by the trial judge who considered the post trial affidavit and found that "neither the district attorney nor his assistant intentionally solicited an ambiguous answer to the questions under consideration for the purpose of obtaining a conviction." l. c. 457.

No need to argue the merits of the court's decision. The test, if not the application of that test, appears well stated. The intentional solicitation of a misleading response through ambiguous questioning is unethical.

§ 2.11 Direct Examination—Illustrations of Selective Interrogation

Let us now try the above test on a few run-of-the-mill trial occurrences. You represent a plaintiff who has been struck by a fire truck which has run a red light. The defense is that the siren was sounding and red light flashing and that the emergency vehicle had properly usurped the right of way. You find a witness who was in an automobile one half block from the crash who is willing to testify that he did not hear the siren. He further explains that his windows were rolled up, that his radio was on full blast playing "Thunder and Lightning" by the Stentorians and that he receives a government pension by reason of a 30% hearing loss suffered during military service. What questions do you ask on direct examination?

You represent a defendant who has been charged with defective design of a Widget which malfunctioned and seriously injured plaintiff. You are anxious to prove that such a mishap has never happened before. There have been no previous complaints from customers but in a number of tests undertaken after the plaintiff's casualty it was discovered that the Widget frequently failed under duplicated conditions. What questions do you direct to your design engineer—if any?

You represent a plaintiff in a personal injury suit claiming injuries to his back. Although he has never suffered any previous injury to his neck or back in the sense of an accident he has had "trouble" with his back in that on several occasions he has been awakened with a sharp pain in his back with shooting pains down his leg and after a hard day's work frequently has to have several hours of bed rest to relieve a "strained feeling." How do you interrogate about his pre-accident condition?

§ 2.12 Cross Examination—Generally

Facts. On cross examination of the witness ..., appellant's attorney attempted to ask the following question: "You are a practicing homosexual ...?" The prosecutor made timely objection to the question, which was sustained by the trial court. Appellant claims the question was proper as an attempt to impeach the credibility of the witness.

Held: "It is difficult to see what the practice of homosexuality has to do with credibility of a witness in a case of this kind."

This particular incident illustrates the viciousness of cross-examining in an area in which there may be a factual basis for the questions asked but no legitimate relevance. When such a transgression occurs by the plaintiff in a civil case or a prosecutor in a criminal matter, the opponent may seek appropriate relief from the trial court. But if the defense attorney has injected the poison there is little, if any, antidote available. Mistrials are, from a practical point of view, undesirable (who wants to abort a year of docket waiting, and the expense of an unfinished trial?) and that admonition to "disregard the testimony" is meaningless. Only two factors can prevent such unethical cross examining:

one, the advocates own sensitivity to the civilities of trials, and;

two, the threat of a well directed crotch kick in retaliation.

§ 2.13   Cross Examination—Suggestive Interrogation

A more aggravated ethical aberration occurs when interrogation suggests information of a relevant nature but for which there is no factual support. Perhaps some would quarrel about the designation of such tactics as ethical matters rather than simply "trial ploys and gambits." True, everytime an advocate gets a hand slapped by an adverse ruling doesn't mean that the bounds of propriety have been overstepped. The trial of a lawsuit might be likened to "courting." There are a number of liberties you can take with your passive colleague or date (as the case might be), which properly fall within the rules of the game. But there are some things which "nice" people just don't do—and suggestive interrogation without evidence to support it is one such thing.

§ 2.14   Cross Examination—Illustrations of Suggestive Interrogation

Let us take a criminal matter as our first example. The accused is charged with murder. The trial ploy is to raise the implication of self defense—although there will be no evidence forthcoming to support such a theory. The police officer called to the scene of the street shooting is being cross examined.

Q. Now officer where was it that you found the decedent's 38
    caliber revolver that he was brandishing at the time he was
    shot?
A. We didn't find any gun belonging to the decedent.
Q. You didn't find it? Well, how long was it after the shooting
    that you arrived at the scene?
A. About 10 minutes.
Q. And were there a lot of people gathered around?
A. Oh yes.
Q. And did you ask any of those people what had happened to
    the gun?
A. Why no, there was no—
Q. No further questions.

Undoubtedly in defending a man on a murder charge the lawyer is
entitled, and indeed obligated, to pursue the development of facts
which might provide a defense. Is this type of pursuit ethical?

Let us try a few similar situations on the civil side. Defendant on deposition has testified that shortly before the accident he
had dropped by a local tavern to pay off a debt he owed to the
bartender and had left immediately without having anything to
drink. In your pre-trial investigation you find that the bartender
confirms this story, and you believe him, but you ascertain he will
be out of town at trial time. What do you do at trial?

1. Ask no questions as to where defendant has been.
2. Ask simply, "Did you have anything to drink immediately
    before the accident?"
3. Inquire as follows:
    Q. How much intoxicating beverage had you consumed imme-
        diately before this accident?
    A. Why none.
    Q. Well you had just come from a tavern hadn't you?
    A. Yes, but I didn't have anything to drink. I paid off a loan
        I had made with the bartender.
    Q. What is the name of the bartender?
    A. Fred Jones.
    Q. And is he a friend of yours?
    A. Enough to lend me ten bucks.
    Q. Does he know how much you had to drink that day?
    A. Yes. He knows I didn't drink anything.

Now the scene is set for a closing argument that since the
defendant's friend was not produced to confirm his story, it is
unrealistic to believe that defendant had just come from a tavern
and hadn't had anything to drink.

You are defending a wrongful death case. The widow of the deceased has since remarried. This evidence is inadmissible but the jury's knowledge of the remarriage, you believe, will mitigate the damages considerably.

Consider the following interrogation:

Q. How long were you married to Mr. Jones?
A. Eighteen years.
Q. And are you still living at the family residence?
A. Yes.
Q. And who is the man living with you now?

What does the plaintiff's lawyer do? Object and have it appear that his client is "living in sin?" Ask for a mistrial and incur the delay and expense always felt more keenly by the plaintiff than the defendant? Or does the client respond that it is her present husband who is living with her? How would you characterize the ethics of such interrogation?

It is not enough simply to say that such is the rough and tumble of litigation. Football is also a rugged competitive struggle. Among the participants are numbered "rough" players and "dirty" players. The distinction is sometimes difficult to make— to both the officials and the spectators. But the players know. The same is true in the game of advocacy. You'll soon distinguish the "rough" opponents from the "dirty" ones.

§ 2.15   Closing Argument—Generally

Facts: In the closing argument defense counsel noted that there was no evidence that there was blood on the bed where state's witnesses testified the stabbing occurred. In his closing argument, the prosecutor stated: "(The defense) has made quite a point of the absence of blood on the bed. Maybe I should have brought in the bloody bed sheets."
Defense Counsel: "I'm going to object to the Prosecutor testifying as to facts that are not in evidence, and certainly we have no right to cross examine, and no one has any idea whether they exist or not."
The Court: "Objection sustained and the jury is directed to disregard the mention of the bed sheets or bloody sheets, to strike from their mind and not to consider it in any way in arriving at their verdict."
Defense Counsel: "And I move for a mistrial."
The Court: "Denied."

31

Held: The trial court promptly and unequivocally instructed the jury to disregard the argument directed to the bloody sheets. Whether the statement of the prosecutor was so prejudicial as to require a mistrial was a matter within the trial judge's discretion.

Facts: Counsel stated, "The plaintiff in this case is a 'Dutchman,' and the defendant is the son of an 'Irishman,' and it is nothing but an attempt on the part of an 'Irishman' to beat a 'Dutchman' out of an honest debt."

Held: It is with great reluctance that we reverse the judgment. Nor do we do it, did we not have reason to believe, that the amount of the verdict might have been the result of the statements made by plaintiff's counsel to the jury."

§ 2.16 Closing Argument—Retribution

"Self help" is, and always has been, a significant feature of the law—and it applies to lawyers as well as litigants. The most frequent application of this venerable doctrine as applied to advocacy occurs during closing argument. The evidence is concluded, the instructions are prepared and just when the judicial process is about to grind out a result, some impropriety occurs in the closing argument which threatens to abort the entire effort of judge and jury and further delay a resolution for the litigants. When confronted with such a problem what options, within the realm of proper ethics, are available?

Comment has already been made of the frequent inadequacy of a motion for new trial. If your opponent is a defendant seeking to perpetuate the status quo he would relish such "relief" being granted.

An objection could be made but again a sterile pronouncement by the court that your position is "sustained" will seldom suffice to offset the damage sustained. Even an admonition to counsel or a request that the jury perform the impossible and "disregard that statement" still leaves the offender advantaged.

In the absence of judicial ability to treat the poison can you ethically apply your own antidote? Frequently, the answer is "yes."

§ 2.17 Closing Argument—Retribution—Illustration

The defendant in a civil case argues.

"Here is a claim that has "fraud" written all over it. This plaintiff, from another state, comes into our back yard and brings a suit against one of our good neighbors, Lion Trucking Company. He wants to put his hand into our company's pocket and get a ton of money for a phony injury."

Such an argument is, of course, chuck full of errors and cries out for a reply.

A retaliatory argument might go something like this:

"Counsel for defense characterizes the Lion Trucking Company as a "good neighbor" and plaintiff as a stranger in your midst. Why didn't he tell you that his client is a Delaware corporation and that the principal owner is John Aster from New York who has probably never set foot in this community? They are no "neighbor" much less a "good neighbor." Every six months they have a labor dispute with the men from this community that work there. And this comment about "putting hands in the company's pockets." He knows that his company is insured with Shifting Sands Mutual and that not one cent of any judgment which you render for my client will come out of this company's pocket."

Strong argument? You bet—but so was the argument that precipitated it. Unethical? Not so in my book. The opponent asked for it and he got it. Reversible error? Hard to tell—but look up the law in your jurisdiction and you'll be surprised how much "self help" is available as retaliatory argument.

§ 2.18 Post–Trial Motions

There has been little consideration given to the ethics of filing those forms of post-trial motions which contain wholesale allegations of error citing the court's incompetence in every facet of the case from initial pleading through the reception of the verdict. There are a number of reasons advanced for such a practice but the one usually relied on is that, "We can't take a chance. We'll include everything lest we overlook something." Of course what this does is to make opposing counsel and the court slog through a morass of minutiae to find an issue worthy of contention.

This prolixity of pleading can threaten the case at any stage of its development. The indiscriminate charges of misconduct in the pleading or answer, the mimeographed interrogatories which include questions unrelated to the particular case and unduly repetitive of information secured by deposition, the submission of countless requests for instructions, etc. In each case such practice is unprofessional and inept—and in some instances it can reach such a level of abuse that it best be labelled "unethical."

33

§ 2.19 Informal Negotiations—Generally

During the course of a dispute, particularly during the settlement negotiation stage, the lawyers will exchange information and attitudes regarding the case, their clients and themselves. Sometimes these exchanges are representations of fact and culminate in a formal commitment. "Fred, I have given you a complete copy of the hospital record. I'd like to avoid the expense and trouble of having to subpoena the medical librarian. Is it ok that we just admit the copy?" If Fred says "yes" it means two things; one, the factual representation that it is a complete copy must be true; and two, Fred can't object at trial time that the records have not been properly identified. If either the statement of fact is knowingly false, or Fred reneges on his promise, there has been a serious breach of ethics.

But other exchanges are less formal and more nearly resemble the puff and banter of used car dealers than commitments of professional men. "This is the best case in my office and worth a bundle" will be countered with, "You're lucky if we agree to pay the court costs to get rid of it." Both statements are just comic interludes in the otherwise serious game of doing justice. But what about the countless negotiating ploys that lie somewhere in between? How do they square with good ethics? There follows a few of the more common gambits.

§ 2.20 Informal Negotiations—"The Phantom S.O.B."

You have reached a stage of negotiation where the opponent has made a proposition that is satisfactory to your client but falls a trifle short of your own expectations. Squeezing that last drop out of a long time professional associate can be a nasty affair that might mark you as an unreasonable bully. The script reads like this: "Paul, I've passed your offer on to the client and recommended that we dispose of the matter on that basis. But you know what that rascal did? He told me he just wouldn't settle and he didn't care if we had to go to trial or not. Personally I wish we could get rid of this case but we've got a real son of a bitch on our hands."

Sometimes the script varies. Occasionally the settlement offer is acceptable to both client and counsel but the lawyer is fearful that a willing acceptance on his part might be an indication of weakness. In that case, it goes like this: "Paul, I told him his claim was worth more and it shouldn't be settled. But he's strapped for money right now and told me to go ahead and take the offer. If my client had a little more guts we'd clean your plow for twice as much." In each instance the "image" of the lawyer is protected, and the blame is shunted to a phantom.

§ 2.21 Informal Negotiations—Bogus Bellicosities

A million and one things can impair a party's preparedness for trial. Perhaps the client is ill, a witness can't be found, or the lawyer has another commitment that he wants to keep. Such problems are best kept from your adversary for if your plight were known, the opposition would stiffen and any compromise would be less than that which was "dealt from strength." When these problems occur, how ethical is it to deceive your opponent?

"Will you be ready for trial Monday John?"

"You bet—we're ready to go!" (The client is on a week-end drunk. Your doctor has been jailed for income tax evasion and your key witness has left for the Peace Corps).

"But I'll tell you what. I'll give you one more chance to work this out before we go to bat. If you come up with $3,000 I'll recommend it to my client and I'll do all I can to make him take it." (The old sot has already said he'd be satisfied with $1,500.)

§ 2.22 Informal Negotiations—Factual Footsies

Withholding certain information from your opponent regarding your condition for trial is one thing. Withholding certain facts to which he is entitled is another.

Defendant exercises his right for a medical examination of the plaintiff who is claiming that defendant's negligence caused a whip lash injury which resulted in $5,000 in damages. The defendant's doctor calls counsel and advises him that his examination has disclosed a compression fracture of C6 which undoubtedly came from the accident. The following ensues: "Tom, thought I'd give you a call about the Jones case. Maybe your demand of $5,000 isn't too far off. I've got a couple of other important things on for next week. If I can get you $4,500 will you take it?"

"Well I'd rather see your doctor's report first before I'd do any compromising."

"I haven't received a written report yet Tom but you know ole Doc Phelps. He'd certify that Helen Keller had 'only subjective complaints.' I'll send releases in the next mail."

How say you, Zarathustra?

§ 2.23   Vis-a-Vis Judge

What are the ethical considerations in dealing with a judge? What is the proper attitude to be assumed that will guide you ethically and identify you neither as a sycophant nor an obstructionist?

The problem as to the latter has been given considerable attention. The travails endured by Judges Medina and Hoffman have been well documented and the Smith Act trial and the Chicago Seven trial have become classics in their illustration of what ethical lawyers should not do in their relationships with a trial judge. But what of the former? Is there a similar breach of ethics when the trial lawyer obsequiously defers to the judgment of the trial court and raises no opposition to actions of the judge when such actions stultify the judicial process and demean the stature of the lawyer?

The obstreperous lawyer is "a sometime thing"—a similarly characterized judge is not as rare. Any trial lawyer can recite instances when a judge has acted capriciously or even tyrannically and thus has abused his position. But seldom does the lawyer tell of how such a judge has been reminded of his derelictions. What chuckles we get with the telling of the story about the autocratic judge who bellowed to the lawyer, "Are you trying to show this court contempt?" "No," replied the lawyer, "I'm trying to conceal it." It is considered "gutsy" to make even an ambiguous suggestion that yes, a trial judge too, can overstep his proper role in the administration of justice.

The syndrome of the tyrannical judge occurs with sufficient frequency that trial lawyers have identified it by name—"federalitis." What is its cause and why does it proliferate among those who wear the woolsack of the trial judge? It would be fruitless to attempt an analysis of all those who ascend to the bench. Suffice to say there are some strong characters who feel omnicompetent in the role of judge. They consider themselves the professional heirs of Roy Bean and the younger Holmes. They speak of "my" courtroom and "my" docket and of even "trying" the lawsuit in which they serve as judge. They appear as speakers and panelists at judicial conferences to bolster the ego of their less "progressive" judicial brethren (who still harbor such concepts as the judge being a passive arbiter and the lawyers trying "their" lawsuits).

36

It is not an easy job to confront raw power under any circumstance but is is doubly difficult when the lawyer realizes that his confrontation might penalize his client. And so it is that the martinet who wears his judicial robes as if they were canonical garment and acts as if he had been anointed and ordained as the sole agent to see that justice be done continues in his role unchallenged. Sometimes a Don Quixote will arrive on the scene to plant a barb. One such was a St. Louis lawyer whose presentation was constantly being interrupted by the trial judge asking questions and volunteering advice. Finally after a particularly inappropriate intrusion the lawyer approached the bench and said, "Judge, I don't mind your trying my case, but, for God's sake, don't lose it!"

CHAPTER 3

ADVOCACY FROM THE STUDENT'S PERSPECTIVE

"I am still learning"
Michelangelo

Analysis

A. GENERALLY

A. GENERALLY

§ 3.1 Introduction

From the standpoint of the law student or seminar attendee the role of advocate does not begin with a client interview from which the factual basis for a claim or defense will be generated. Pedagogical considerations dictate that the fact situation from which discrete exercises will be assigned be presented as a fait accompli complete with pleadings, reports, exhibits and witness statements. Of course as a practitioner the role of advocate will begin much earlier, and indeed, much of your success in the courtroom will depend on your skill in the foundational arts of framing the proper pleadings, selecting appropriate exhibits and generating the operational facts.

These matters will be left to future chapters. For now let us concentrate on the problems which beset the student of advocacy and defer those which confront the practitioner.

§ 3.2 Case Analysis

There is a tremendous temptation to break down a trial into its component parts and deal in insolation with the problems of voir dire, opening statement, direct examination, etc. A trial doesn't work that way. The mathematical maxim that the whole is simply the sum of its parts doesn't apply to a trial. Each part must be seen as interacting with the other with the synergistic effect transcending the sum of those parts. This gestalt approach dictates that we take an overview and that takes the form of case analysis.

A method developed by the National Institute for Trial Advocacy is to begin case analysis with a complete awareness of all the facts of the case and an evaluation of those facts as "good" or "bad".

Let's take a fact situation with which all of us are apt to have some familiarity—the assassination of President John F. Kennedy. Assume that you would be assigned the defense of Lee Harvey Oswald. Begin with a review of the facts as they present themselves to your memory and categorize them as "good" or "bad" for the defendant.

Your analytical sheet could look something like this:

Good	Bad
No eye witnesses	Worked near site from which shots were fired.
Was seen on 2nd floor a few minutes after shooting and conveyed neither apprehension nor excitement	Gun found near site was traced to him.
Witnesses identify source of shots as "grassy knoll"	Identified as man who shot Officer Tippet.
Type of gun found incapable of rapid, accurate fire	Had history of political activism.
Oswald's denial of guilt	Married to Russian woman.

Let's stop here. The list could go on and on but you get the point. It is only after you have identified the strengths and weaknesses of a case that you can then understand the issues that must be exploited and those which must be countered. Of course this step is not always obvious. Most fact elements will logically fall into a category of "good" or "bad" but it takes an understanding of human nature to classify the importance of these elements.

Let's consider a few examples. When prepared cake mixes first appeared on the market the presumption was made that their greatest appeal was that they were cheaper and simplified the cake making procedure. There was substantial market resistance. A psychologist consultant suggested that making a cake was not just another kitchen chore. It symbolically simulated gestation (no doubt drawing on the colloquial expression of pregnancy— "she's got a cake in the oven"). Appealing to thrift and ease in this substantially symbolic endeavor was offensive to some homemakers—so the thrust of the advertising theme was changed. Cake mixes were treated as being tastier and more nutritious. Homemakers who used cake mixes, consequently, were not identified as selfishly attempting to save time by using a cheap product. They could proudly proclaim that they were altruistically advancing the health and enjoyment of the family.

This same psychology has been applied in the marketing of certain luxury items. The sales of a haute couture perfume rose briskly when the price was increased. Prospective buyers rejected the product when its "cheap" price was incompatible with the claims of elite quality. They were satisfied that they were getting a better product when they paid more.

§ **3.3** Selection of Theme

Those illustrations become relevant as we select our theme, for now we are faced with ranking the importance of our "good" and "bad" factors to present a salable product to the jury. Sticking with our analogy, which of the "good" facts are most persuasive in the defense of Oswald? The object in ranking the importance of the available evidence is not to find a single fact and translate it to a theme. Rather the task is to find specific facts which are compatible with a general premise. Certain specific facts (absence of gun powder stains, incapability of the gun to fire rapidly, a malfunctioning scope sight) translate to a general theme that there is no scientific objective proof of Oswald's connection with the crime. The specific facts of the involvement of others (shots from the grassy knoll, Oswald's own statement that he was "a patsy") could translate to a conspiracy theme in which Oswald was an innocent dupe.

Perhaps the theme will be more general, encompass a host of constituent minor themes and translate to the standard position that the state hasn't met the burden of proof. As a rule, the appeal of the theme is directly related to its specificity. Rifles are better than shotguns in bringing down a courtroom opponent. If you were defending a person accused of a crime, how would you categorize a series of previous convictions for the same offense? Most of us would immediately say "bad". But in some cases a record can be used to advantage. "Why did they arrest my client? It was the same mentality you see in the movies 'Round up the usual suspects.' Every time something is missing in the neighborhood they sing the same song. Without my proof, without any witnesses they simply say, 'Arrest Jones, he must have stolen it.' And that's what they did in this case."

§ **3.4** Evidentiary Analysis

This same method of case analysis applies to each bit of evidence that you adduce. Don't think of an exhibit as an appropriate something that you're throwing in the pot in the hope that it savors the stew. Know the identity of the stew you wish to serve, determine the recipe that will produce the desired dish—then follow that recipe.

So too with witnesses. Ask yourself:

1. What contribution can this witness make? (or if you like an athletic metaphor, "How will this witness advance the ball?")

2. How does this contribution relate to the elements of proof?

3. How does this contribution relate to the theme of the case?

B. CASE PROBLEM

§ 3.5 Introduction

The trial of a law suit is not simply the sum of its parts. One must know the skills identified with each aspect of the trial from pleading to post-trial motions but of even greater importance is putting it all together. That is the challenge with which you will now be faced. The fact pattern was one used in a national student competition sponsored by the American Bar Association.

§ 3.6 Statement of Facts

On Saturday May 26, 1992, at 7:00 p.m., an automobile collision occurred at the intersection of State Road 7 and Atlantic Drive in Palm Bay, Calvert County, State of Nova. At this location, State Road 7 is a four-lane thoroughfare running north and south, divided by a median strip, with left-turn lanes for both northbound and southbound traffic. Atlantic Drive is a two-lane thoroughfare running east and west. The intersection of these thoroughfares is controlled by a traffic light. At the time of the accident, the weather was clear, the roads were dry and level, and the traffic was light.

The drivers involved in this collision, Herb Millman and Sarah Cassidy, are in dispute as to who had the right of way at the intersection. The investigating police officer suggests that Sarah Cassidy ran the red light while traveling in an easterly direction on Atlantic Drive. Her vehicle collided with the left front side of Herb Millman's automobile, which was traveling north in the inside land of State Road 7. The collision occurred in the middle of the intersection. The impact catapulted Mr. Millman's vehicle approximately forty feet, through the intersection, into a cement pole. Mr. Millman sustained various injuries that required immediate medical attention. He was taken to Palm Bay General

Hospital by Go Gettum Ambulance Company. Mr. Millman's 1990 Buick Riviera automobile was damaged in excess of $7,500.

The investigating officer, State Trooper Jane Wright, arrived at the scene of the accident moments after it had occurred. Trooper Wright approached the intersection from the southbound lane of State Road 7 and parked her vehicle in the middle of the crossroad to act as a warning for oncoming traffic. Officer Wright proceeded to Sarah Cassidy's vehicle, a 1986 Pontiac LeMans, located in the intersection; Sarah Cassidy was still in her vehicle.

As Trooper Wright reached the driver's open window, she detected a faint smell of beer. Upon helping Ms. Cassidy out of her vehicle, the trooper noticed six cans of beer—two were open and empty—on the seat next to her. The officer then went to the Millman vehicle and stayed with Mr. Millman until the paramedics arrived.

After charging Ms. Cassidy with careless driving with open alcohol in the car, the officer allowed her to call a friend to drive her home. The officer did not charge her with drunken driving, nor did she administer a breathalyzer test.

Both vehicles involved in the accident had to be towed from the scene. There were no eyewitnesses to the accident.

Herb Millman is a 65–year–old retired mailman, residing with his wife, Inez, at 2107 Elm Street, Palm Bay, Nova. At the time of the accident, Mr. Millman owned a 1991 Buick Riviera, BJE 074, which was insured through Protective Insurance Company.

As a result of the collision, Mr. Millman sustained lower back damage, compounded by an injury to his right knee. He has had a lower back problem for over twenty years, which made him miss an occasional day of work. He was driving without his shoes, because his feet were tender after many years as a letter carrier.

Sarah Cassidy is a single, 22–year old dental student, residing at 704 N.W. 12th Street, Apt. 19, Palm Bay, Nova. Ms. Cassidy owns a 1986 Pontiac LeMans, NVM 442, insured through Cheetum Company. Ms. Cassidy did not sustain any significant injuries as a result of the accident. Ms. Cassidy maintains that she had entered the intersection under a green traffic light and that the collision occurred while she could see the amber warning signal. She asserts that Mr. Millman was negligent in overanticipating his traffic signal.

Ms. Cassidy was coming from an all-day picnic. She states that she had taken six cans of beer to the picnic, had drunk only two, and then put the two empty cans in the car. She claims that the smell of beer came either from the empty cans or the fact that some beer was left in one and spilled during the accident.

Herb Millman, through his attorney, filed suit against Sarah Cassidy in civil court asserting that she was negligent and demanding damages in excess of $5,000 and trial by jury. Discovery procedures have been accomplished to the satisfaction of both parties, and the issues ready to be litigated include both causation and damages.

Medical testimony has already been heard concerning the plaintiff's injury and diagnosis. Millman sustained a tibial plateau fracture of the right knee, which required surgery to correct, and a cervical strain requiring analgesic medication and fifteen weeks of hot pack and ultrasound treatment. Millman's surgeon has testified that he has suffered permanent physical impairment and the loss of physical function in 10% of the body as a whole.

Sarah Cassidy has already appeared in county court concerning her careless driving citation. Ms. Cassidy pled nolo contendere and was fined $50.

§ 3.7 Complaint

IN THE CIRCUIT COURT FOR THE FIFTH JUDICIAL CIRCUIT OF NOVA, IN AND FOR CALVARY COUNTY. CIVIL DIVISION CASE NO 84–5475 CV (J)

HERB MILLMAN, and INEZ MILLMAN,

Plaintiffs

v.

SARAH CASSIDY,

Defendant.

COMPLAINT

Plaintiffs, HERB MILLMAN and INEZ MILLMAN, sue the Defendant, SARAH CASSIDY, and allege:

GENERAL ALLEGATIONS

1. This is an action for damages that are in excess of the sum of FIVE THOUSAND DOLLARS ($5,000.00), exclusive of costs, interest, and attorneys' fees.

2. At all times material hereto, the Defendant, SARAH CASSIDY, was a resident of the City of Palm Bay, County of Calvert, State of Nova.

COUNT I

3. On or about May 26, 1992, the Defendant, SARAH CASSIDY, negligently operated a motor vehicle owned by the Defendant, on a road in Calvert County designated as Atlantic Drive such that the vehicle was caused to collide with the vehicle that was owned by the Plaintiff, HERB MILLMAN.

4. That as a direct and proximate result of the carelessness and negligence of the Defendant, SARAH CASSIDY, the Plaintiff, HERB MILLMAN, was caused to suffer bodily injury and resulting pain and suffering, disability, disfigurement, mental anguish, loss of capacity for the enjoyment of life, expense of hospitalization, medical and nursing care, treatment, and aggravation of any previously existing condition. The losses are either permanent or continuing and Plaintiff will suffer the losses in the future.

WHEREFORE, the Plaintiff, HERB MILLMAN, demands judgment for punitive damages against the Defendant, SARAH CASSIDY, in an amount in excess of FIVE THOUSAND DOLLARS ($5,000.00) exclusive of costs, interest, and attorney's fees, and further demands trial by jury.

COUNT II

5. Plaintiff, HERB MILLMAN, realleges and adopts all allegation of Count I as though the same were fully set forth herein.

6. At all times material hereto, the Defendant, SARAH CASSIDY, had a duty to the Plaintiffs, and to the public at large, to use due care in the operation of a motor vehicle, including the duty not to operate a motor vehicle while under the influence of alcohol.

7. That the Defendant, SARAH CASSIDY, breached her duty of care and furthermore demonstrated a willful and wanton disregard for the safety of others, including the

Plaintiffs, in that she deliberately operated a motor vehicle while under the influence of alcohol, such that her motor vehicle collided with the motor vehicle owned by the Plaintiff, HERB MILLMAN.

8. As a direct and proximate result of the aforementioned deliberate act of the Defendant, SARAH CASSIDY, the Plaintiff, HERB MILLMAN, was caused to suffer bodily injury and resulting pain and suffering, disability, disfigurement, mental anguish, loss of capacity for the enjoyment of life, expense of hospitalization, medical and nursing care and treatment, and aggravation of a previously existing condition. The losses are either permanent or continuing, and the Plaintiff will suffer the losses in the future.

WHEREFORE, the Plaintiff, HERB MILLMAN, demands judgment for punitive damages against the Defendant, SARAH CASSIDY, in an amount in excess of FIVE THOUSAND DOLLARS ($5,000.00), exclusive of costs, interest, and attorneys' fees, and further demands trial by jury.

COUNT III

9. Plaintiffs reallege and adopt all allegations of Counts I and II as though the same were fully set forth herein.

10. The Plaintiff, INEZ MILLMAN, has been and will continue to be substantially deprived of the love, companionship, affection, society, comfort, solace, sexual relations, and the services of her husband, the Plaintiff, HERB MILLMAN. In addition, she has incurred great medical, hospital, and nursing expenses for the care and treatment of the injuries sustained by her husband, and these losses were proximately and directly caused by the Defendant, SARAH CASSIDY.

WHEREFORE, Plaintiff, INEZ MILLMAN, demands judgment for damages against Defendant, SARAH CASSIDY, in an amount in excess of FIVE THOUSAND DOLLARS ($5,000.00), exclusively of costs, interest, and attorneys' fees, and further demands trial by jury.

Respectfully submitted,

_____

BENJAMIN FRANKLYN
Attorney for Plaintiffs

§ 3.8 Defendant's Answer

IN THE CIRCUIT COURT FOR THE FIFTH JUDICIAL CIRCUIT
OF NOVA, IN AND FOR CALVERT COUNTY.

CIVIL DIVISION CASE NO. 84–5475 CV (J)

HERB MILLMAN, and INEZ MILLMAN,

Plaintiffs

v.

SARAH CASSIDY,

Defendant

DEFENDANT'S ANSWER AND AFFIRMATIVE DEFENSES
TO PLAINTIFFS' COMPLAINT FOR DAMAGES

The Defendant, SARAH CASSIDY, by and through her under-
signed attorney, files this Answer to the Complaint and states as
follows:

1. Paragraph 1 of Complaint is a jurisdictional statement
   and requires no response.

2. Paragraph 2 of Complaint is admitted.

3. Paragraph 3 of Complaint is admitted.

4. Paragraph 4 of Complaint is denied in that defendant did
   not operate the vehicle negligently.

5. Paragraph 5 of Complaint is denied.

6. Paragraph 6 of Complaint is denied.

7. Paragraph 7 of Complaint is denied.

8. Paragraph 8 of Complaint is denied in that the Defendant was not operating her motor vehicle under the
   influence of alcohol.

9. Paragraph 9 of Complaint is denied.

10. Paragraph 10 of Complaint is denied.

11. Paragraph 11 of Complaint is denied.

AFFIRMATIVE DEFENSES

1. The Complaint fails to state a cause of action for which relief can be granted.

2. The Plaintiff was himself negligent and careless and was the sole contributing cause of the injuries and damages, if any, and, therefore, is barred from recovery in whole or in part.

3. Any injury or damage sustained by the Plaintiff, if any, was proximately caused by the misuse or abuse of the Plaintiff's motor vehicle, in that he failed to use the seat belt restraint available to him in his vehicle.

4. The Complaint fails to state a claim for punitive damages under Nova law, for which such relief can be granted.

WHEREFORE, Defendant, SARAH CASSIDY, respectfully moves that the Honorable Court enter a judgment of no cause of action in favor of the Defendant and against Plaintiffs and further provide such other relief as this Court deems proper.

IT IS HEREBY CERTIFIED that a true copy of the foregoing has been furnished, by mail the 21st day of July, 1984, to Benjamin Franklyn, Esquire.

Respectfully,

_____

BRET MARSHALL
Attorney for the Defendant

§ 3.9 Plaintiff's Deposition

Deposition of Herb Millman

Q. Mr. Millman, can you please tell us, in your own words, how the accident on May 26, 1992, occurred?

A. Certainly. I had been running errands, and was driving north on Route 7 heading home for supper. I passed through a green light at the intersection of 7 and Atlantic, but this girl ran the red light and hit me broadside.

Q. Did you see Ms. Cassidy's car approaching?

A. Only at the last second—the intersection was clear as I drove into it. I honked my horn when I saw her, but it didn't seem to slow her down any.

Q. What injuries did you receive as a result of the accident?

A. My back hasn't been the same since—I was thrown about the car, both from her hitting me, and from hitting the pole. The doctors said its severely strained, and anyway it has hurt me from that day. My knee was also broken, and I had an operation to fix that.

Q. Were you wearing your seat belt?

A. No, I was only a short distance from home.

Q. Have you ever had problems with back pain prior to the accident?

A. Occasionally, yes. I was a mailman for over thirty years, and the lifting and walking of that job naturally caused me some backaches over the years.

Q. Had doctors prescribed any medication or treatment for that back pain?

A. They had suggested exercise—as if a mailman needed any!— and sometimes heat or muscle relaxants. I was hospitalized once for it, but that was ten or twelve years ago when I slipped on some ice while working.

Q. Were there any significant changes in the degree of back pain following the accident?

A. Hell, yes. My back hurts all the time now, and worse than it ever did before—even that time I fell.

Q. Does this pain affect your everyday life in any way?

A. Well, it is not debilitating, if that's what you mean. I can still get around, but it hurts like hell every time I bend, or lift, or stand for a long time, or walk too far. I just can't do as much as I used to—and that's a major effect, if you ask me. And my knee bothers me if it's going to rain, or if I'm tired.

Q. Have your ever been involved in a traffic accident before?

A. No, sir. I've been driving over fifty years and have never caused any accident, ever. I'm real proud of that.

§ 3.10 Defendant's Deposition

Deposition of Sarah Cassidy

Q. Ms. Cassidy, would you please tell us exactly how the accident occurred on May 26, 1992?

A. Well, I was driving home from the picnic—it was about 7 o'clock—and had reached the intersection of Atlantic Drive and Route 7. The light was green as I approached the intersection, and it turned yellow just as I got there. So, I drove through the intersection, but Millman ran his red light and I couldn't avoid hitting him.

Q. Exactly how far were you from the intersection when the light turned yellow?

A. I'm not very good at estimating distances, but I would say that I was about twenty feet or so.

Q. And did you look into the intersection before proceeding?
A. Yes, it appeared clear—he seemed to come from nowhere.
Q. Were you injured in the accident?
A. No, I was really lucky—I was just a little shaken up and bruised. Plus I was wearing my seat belt.
Q. Have you ever been involved in an automobile accident before this?
A. Well, I rear-ended someone when I was sixteen, but that was a long time ago, when I first learned to drive.
Q. Had you drunk any alcohol on the day of May 26, 1992, prior to the car crash?
A. Yes. I had a single light beer. I remember it very clearly since I had been carrying around this single empty beer can most of the day and people had been teasing me about it.
Q. Did you use marijuana or any other intoxicating drugs on that day?
A. No. I've never used illegal drugs in my life.

§ 3.11 Deposition of Plaintiff's Witness

Deposition of Nova state trooper Jane Wright

Direct examination

Q. Would you please state your full name?
A. Jane Wright.
Q. Your age?
A. Thirty-nine years old.
Q. By whom are you employed?
A. State of Nova Highway Patrol
Q. For how long have you been a trooper, Ms. Wright?
A. For fifteen years.
Q. Trooper Wright, do you remember what transpired on the evening of May 26, 1992, at approximately 7:00 p.m.
A. At approximately 7:00 p.m., I was travelling south on State Road 7. As I approached the intersection of Atlantic Drive, I saw that a car had smashed into a cement light pole.
Q. What did you do next?
A. I pulled my squad car into the middle of the intersection, to act as a warning. There was a vehicle stopped in the intersection and one that had hit the pole. I got out of my car and walked to the Pontiac, where I noticed Sarah Cassidy.
Q. Go on, please, Office Wright.
A. I approached the open driver's window, when I detected a faint smell of beer. The driver, Ms. Cassidy, was apparently in a mild state of shock, so I opened her door to assist her out of the car. As I helped her out, I saw beer cans on the floor of

51

the passenger's side of the vehicle. I brought her to the side of the road and she sat down.

Q. Did you issue a citation to Sarah Cassidy?

A. I gave her a citation for careless driving with open alcohol in the car.

Q. Officer Wright, were the traffic lights in working order when you arrived on the scene of the accident?

A. Yes, they appeared in working order.

Q. Can you please tell us, based on your knowledge of the evidence, who was at fault in this accident?

A. Based on an examination of the vehicles, the skid marks, and the scene itself, it is my opinion that the driver of the Pontiac, Sarah Cassidy, ran a red light, and so struck the Buick as it crossed the intersection on a green light.

Cross-examination

Q. Officer Wright, why did you approach Ms. Cassidy's vehicle as you pulled into the intersection of State Road 7 and Atlantic Drive on the evening of May 26, 1992?

A. I felt that she was unsafe remaining in her car in the middle of the intersection.

Q. Is that why you wanted to help her out of her car—for her safety?

A. Yes, that is correct.

Q. Officer Wright, when did you first smell what you thought was beer?

A. When I came up to the driver's window.

Q. Trooper Wright, how was it your occasion to recognize the smell of beer?

A. Through my years of experience, I have gained the olfactory knowledge to recognize the smell of beer.

Q. Was your head, or any other part of your body, inside Ms. Cassidy's window, when you smelled the odor?

A. No.

Q. Officer Wright, you said you helped Ms. Cassidy out of her car.

A. That is correct.

Q. Did you open the door of her vehicle?

A. Yes, I believe I did.

Q. Officer Wright, why did you feel that Ms. Cassidy needed to be helped out of her car?

A. She seemed disoriented.

Q. Did she have any problem regaining her feet?

A. No, she did not.

Q. Was she able to walk without assistance?

A. Yes, she seemed stable.

Q. Officer Wright, did Ms. Cassidy at any time display any action that would indicate to an officer of your experience that she was in any way intoxicated or under the influence of a drug?
A. No. She seemed very normal.
Q. Did you administer a breathalyzer?
A. No, I didn't think it was necessary.
Q. Officer, why was the Defendant allowed to go home following the accident?
A. I felt it was within my discretion to allow Ms. Cassidy to call a friend to drive her home.

§ 3.12 Deposition of Defendant's Expert Witness

Deposition of Major Frank Neil, Ph.D.

Expert witness for Defendant

Direct examination

Q. Sir, please state your name and address.
A. Frank Neil, 1275 Oak Street, Palm Bay, Nova.
Q. Mr. Neil, would you describe briefly your education following high school?
A. I earned a B.S. degree in mechanical engineering at Harvard University and then received a Ph.D. in biomechanical engineering from Stanford University.
Q. What was your first job following this training?
A. I was a member of the U.S. Air Force, and I was put in charge of studying the crash resistance of cockpit canopies in our high speed aircraft.
Q. For how many years were you with the Air Force?
A. Twenty-five years.
Q. Are you still a member of the Air Force?
A. No. I retired some years ago.
Q. What was your rank when you retired?
A. Major.
Q. Are you familiar with automobile collision reconstruction?
A. Yes, that has been my specialty since I left the Air Force.
Q. Are you considered an expert in the field of automobile collision reconstruction?
A. Yes.
Q. Mr. Neil, have you examined all of the reports concerning the accident of May 26, 1992, and upon which you are required to base your conclusion for this deposition today?
A. Yes, I have.
Q. Mr. Neil, based on the reports, would you please describe the direction and velocity of the respective vehicles prior to the collision?

A. Vehicle one, Mr. Millman's car, was traveling in a northern direction at approximately forty miles per hour on State Road 7. Vehicle two, Ms. Cassidy's automobile, was traveling east, on Atlantic Drive, at approximately thirty-five miles per hour.

Q. How were these velocities of each respective automobile calculated?

A. Information based on the skid marks, the type of vehicles involved, the amount of damage to each vehicle, and the vectors the vehicles took following impact is all entered into a complicated formula that determines the estimated speed of the vehicles.

Q. Please describe the exact location of impact between the two vehicles.

A. The line of impact indicates that Mr. Millman's left front quarter panel struck the leading edge of the defendant's vehicle, which was the front of her car.

Q. Did the plaintiff's vehicle have operational seat belts at the time of the accident?

A. Yes, it did.

Q. What type of operational seat belts did the vehicle contain?

A. Mr. Millman's automobile had both lap seat belts and shoulder harness restraints present and operational at the time of the accident.

Q. Mr. Neil, based on your investigation, was Mr. Millman wearing his safety belt restraints at the time of the accident?

A. No, he was not wearing any type of seat belt.

Q. Did the plaintiff have knowledge of the safety advantages of seat belts?

A. Yes, Mr. Millman stated that he knew they were a measure of safety, but he added that he was only going to the grocery store and didn't think that they were necessary.

Q. Mr. Neil, please describe the direction in which Mr. Millman's vehicle went following the impact with the defendant's vehicle.

A. The impact caused Mr. Millman's automobile to veer off at a forty-five degree angle. He continued in this direction for approximately forty feet.

Q. Would you please explain the trajectory of the plaintiff's body within his automobile after the first impact with the defendant's car?

A. The crash caused Mr. Millman first to be jolted to his immediate left. His body struck the inside of the car, causing a slight dent in the left door. After striking the driver's door, the impact deflected Mr. Millman across the front seat to his right.

Q. Did these series of secondary collisions within his vehicle render the plaintiff unable to control his vehicle?

A. Yes, the series of impacts caused him to be unable to control his vehicle.

Q. Would the plaintiff have remained in front of the steering wheel and in a position to control his vehicle if he had been wearing his safety belt?

A. Yes.

Q. It appears from the police diagram that the plaintiff struck a cement light pole, located on the northeast corner of the intersection in question.

A. That is correct. It was about forty feet from the point of impact.

Q. Would you consider the police investigation diagram a true and accurate representation of the facts surrounding the accident on May 26, 1992, at the intersection of State Road 7 and Atlantic Drive?

A. Yes, I would.

Q. At what speed did the plaintiff strike the cement light pole?

A. Reviewing the relative damage done to the pole and to the plaintiff's vehicle, I would estimate that he was traveling at least twenty-five miles an hour when he struck the pole.

Q. Do you consider that an unusually fast speed to strike the pole, considering the forty feet between the site of the collision and the pole?

A. Yes, that is a substantially high rate of speed, considering the distance, but that can be explained. When Mr. Millman received the initial impact from the defendant's car, he was thrown to his left, then to his right, as was previously explained. This abnormal positioning of the driver rendered him unable to control his vehicle or remain behind the brake pedal to allow him to bring it to a stop.

Q. Mr. Neil, in your opinion, would the plaintiff have been able to avoid the pole had he remained behind the steering wheel?

A. Yes, in my opinion, he could have directed his vehicle away from the pole had he remained behind his steering wheel.

Q. Mr. Neil, in your opinion, considering the forces acting on Mr. Millman, would a seat belt have allowed him to remain behind the wheel, thus allowing him to negotiate his vehicle clear of any obstruction?

A. Yes, a seat belt would have allowed Mr. Millman to safely bring his vehicle to a stop without striking any object in the intersection.

Q. Mr. Neil, would you please describe the trajectory of the plaintiff's body after hitting the stationary cement light pole at the above-mentioned speed?

A. Mr. Millman's vehicle struck the cement light pole with the left front bumper. This collision caused Mr. Millman to be thrown in a forward motion, with sufficient force to put a two-

and-a-half-inch dent into the steel dash. This forward trajectory caused the plaintiff's right knee to strike the front dash,
creating the dent.

Q. Mr. Neil, please describe the relationship, if any, between the
events in Mr. Millman's vehicle crash and his injuries.

A. The initial impact between the two vehicles, which caused the
plaintiff's left-to-right motions, is almost certainly related to
his lower back problems, due to the impact with which he
struck the driver's door. The second collision—that is, the
collision between his vehicle and the light pole—caused the
plaintiff's right knee to be thrust into the front dash, thereby
absorbing all of the force.

Q. Was it this substantial change in velocity that caused the
severe damage to the plaintiff's knee?

A. Yes, it was.

Q. In your opinion, Mr. Neil, would these injuries have occurred
but for the fact that the plaintiff was not wearing his available seat belt?

A. No, the injuries would not have occurred if he had been
wearing his seat belt.

Q. Mr. Neil, in your opinion, do you feel that the plaintiff would
have sustained any substantial injury if he had been wearing
his seat belt?

A. No, I believe the plaintiff would not have been injured as he
was because he would have been able to control and/or stop
his vehicle if he had remained behind the steering wheel.

Q. Mr. Neil, was there any intrusion into the driver's compart-
ment of the plaintiff's vehicle as a result of this accident?

A. No, there was not.

Q. Was the defendant, Sarah Cassidy, wearing her seat belt at
the time of the accident?

A. Yes, she was.

Q. Was Ms. Cassidy injured in this accident?

A. No, she was not.

§ 3.13 Relevant Statutes and Law

The applicable law in this case is that of the State of Nova,
which in pertinent part reads as follows:

   a. The defense counsel may choose whether or not to give
       his/her opening statement immediately following Plain-
       tiff's, or to defer it until the presentation of his/her case.

   b. The *ad damnum* can, if counsel so wishes, be mentioned in
       the opening statement.

   c. The rule of comparative negligence in this jurisdiction is
       as follows: comparative negligence will apply unless the

negligence of the Plaintiff is found to be 50% or greater, in which case the Plaintiff will not recover. N.S. 375.2(a).

d. Negligence is defined as "the doing of something that a reasonable person would not, or should not, have done, or the failure to do something that a reasonable person would have, or should have, done." N.S. 379.1(b).

e. A party's failure to use an available, functional seat belt is hereby adopted by the State of Nova as an affirmative defense, but only as to mitigation of damages. N.S. 795.1.

All other aspects of law in this case are to be determined by the Federal Rules of Evidence and Civil Procedure.

§ **3.14** Ambulance Bill

GO GETTUM AMBULANCE COMPANY
INVOICE

Emergency services—Saturday, May 26, 1992

Called by Police

Delivered Herbert Millman to Palm Bay General Hospital

Charges —	Ambulance	$150.00
	Emergency Technicians Services	150.00
	Equipment	22.50
		$322.50

§ **3.15** Doctor's Bill

DR. JAMES DOWNEY, M.D.
Practice Limited to Orthopedics
INVOICE

Services included 15 office visits in May and June, 1992

$11,363.26

§ **3.16** Transcription of Radio Dispatch Reports
PALM BAY, NOVA

TRANSCRIBED COPY OF RADIO REPORTS TO POLICE DISPATCHER FROM 26 MAY, 1992

7:15 p.m.   Radio transmission received:
"This is Trooper Jane Wright. I'm calling from the

scene of an accident at the intersection of Atlantic Drive and State Road 7."

"Send an ambulance and wrecker ASAP."

"My investigation reveals one person needing to go to the hospital emergency room."

"I will mark accident to warn on-coming drivers, care for injured person, and conduct arrest of intoxicated driver who appears to have caused the accident."

§ 3.17 Excerpt From Police Manual

CALVERT COUNTY, STATE OF NOVA
Manual for Police Practice

ALCOHOL AND DRUGS IN MOTOR VEHICLES

Whenever an officer encounters a driver of a motor vehicle in a situation that suggests ingestion of alcohol or other intoxicants, very careful attention must be paid to the possibility of intoxication. This care is necessary both for purposes of documentation of the intoxication for evidentiary purposes in cases of prosecution and also because of the potential threat to safety created by the driver of the motor vehicle while in an intoxicated state.

If imbibing of alcohol is suspected, a breathalyzer should be administered to document the intoxication and/or to prove sobriety, so that the officer can ensure that the release of the person to continue driving will not create a threat to safety.

§ 3.18 Résumé of Plaintiff's Witness

JANE R. WRIGHT
100 Elm Avenue
Palm Bay, Nova 12345

EDUCATION	Nova University
	B.S. in Criminology, 1976
	Police Academy, 1977
	1st Place Medal—Marksmanship
EXPERIENCE	Palm Bay Police Department, 1977–present
	Patrol Officer
	Medal of Valor, 1990
PROFESSIONAL MEMBERSHIPS	American Society of Professional Enforcement
	Nova Police Officer's Society
	Fraternal Order of Police
	National Rifle Association

§ **3.19** Curriculum Vitae of Defendant's Expert Witness

CURRICULUM VITAE

Name:		Major Frank Neil, Ph.D.
Date and Place of Birth:		August 8, 1930
		Cape May, New Jersey
Marital Status:		Single
Education:	1947–1953	B.S., Harvard College, 1948
		Medical Engineering
	1954–1958	Ph.D., Stanford University
		Biomedical Engineering
Certification:		Biomedical Engineer
Military Service:		
	1959–1984	U.S. Air Force (Major)
		Tripler Army Medical Center, Hawaii
		Specialized in analyzing the crash resistance of cockpit canopies in high speed aircraft.
Employment	1985–Pres.	Accident Reconstructionist

C. ANALYSIS OF CASE FILE

§ **3.20** Plaintiff's Point of View

The originating petition or complaint is the opening shot in the battle that is to follow. Too often it is dismissed as being of little importance. T'ain't so. Consider what impact it will have.

First, if there are multiple defendants, the order in which they are named will determine the sequence of presentation at voir dire, opening statement, cross-examination of the plaintiff's witnesses, the defendants order of proof and closing argument.

Second, this initial pleading will usually be the defendant's first notice that a claim is being made against him. That alone will be upsetting. Will you further aggravate the situation by making hyperbolic claims of misconduct on his part, injuries on your part and conclude with an outrageous claim for damages? No need to unnecessarily infuriate an opponent. It reduces the likelihood of a peaceful settlement.

Third, the liberalization of our pleading practices has not eliminated the need to make specific allegations in certain circumstances. Special damages, such as medical bills, lost wages, permanent injuries, are often overlooked and when they are, the errant pleader will be denied proof of such damages at trial.

§ 3.21 Pleadings

The notice pleadings identify no specific allegation of negligence, but the testimony of the witnesses indicate that the only submissible charge of negligence against the defendant, Sarah Cassidy, would be violating the stop signal. Care should be given to determine the authority by which the stop signals have been erected. The fact that the accident occurred on a state road and was investigated by a state trooper suggests that the signal was erected and maintained by the state, and the sanctions are imposed by statute. If such is the case, the state court can take judicial notice[1] of the statutes that authorize this stop sign and create traffic regulations. If, however, the accident occurred in an incorporated area and the signal was authorized by sanctions described by local ordinance, then other rules apply.

If the plaintiff wishes to rely on a negligence per se submission for violation of the ordinance, many jurisdictions require specific pleadings alleging that the signal had been erected under duly enacted ordinances then and there in full force and effect (identifying the ordinances) and describing (in haec verba) the duty of motorists to stop in compliance with a red light.[2]

Allegations seeking punitive damages are properly alleged in a separate count, as is the derivative claim for loss of consortium. Although some jurisdictions may permit a separate suit to be filed for loss of consortium, the nature and extent of these injuries suggests that the two claims be joined.

The defendant has pleaded contributory negligence in the same generic fashion. If there is any question that the claim will involve anything other than running a red light (she admits that she didn't see him until the last second), a motion for a more definite statement should be filed. The plaintiff is further advised that his failure to wear a seat belt will be introduced to mitigate damages. It should be anticipated that the issue will arise at two levels:

1. WEST DIGEST, Evidence, Key Numbers 27–30.

2. WEST DIGEST, Evidence, Key Number 32.

1. Was the plaintiff's loss of control of his car after the initial collision affected by his failure to use a seat belt?

2. Was the force of the impact of his knee against the dashboard affected by his failure to use a seat belt?

§ 3.22 Proof

The proof that the defendant negligently ran the red light comes from two sources: the testimony of the plaintiff, and the opinion of the state trooper. The trooper's conclusion is "iffy" at best, both as to admissibility and weight. Basically the case will be a swearing match between the parties.

The evidence of the defendant's intoxication will not support a claim for punitive damages. The only witnesses to this issue are the defendant (who admits to only one beer all afternoon and denies any adverse effects) and the officer. But what does the officer have to say? She confirms that there were two empty beer cans in the car and that she detected a faint odor of alcohol. But she doesn't identify the source of that odor, and so we are left to speculate whether it came from the beer cans or the breath of the defendant. The transcribed copy of the radio reports quotes the trooper as having said, "I will ... conduct arrest of intoxicated driver who appears to have caused accident". But how can this be introduced? If you call the trooper you are faced with these problems:

• she describes defendant's condition after the accident as a state of shock;

• she denies at her deposition that defendant was intoxicated;

• she didn't administer a breathalyzer test (although the manual for police practice mandates its use when alcohol is suspected); and

• she didn't issue a citation for driving under the influence.

The radio report indicating intoxication can be admitted only as an impeachment of your own witness after she admits the defendant was not intoxicated—hardly a persuasive element of proof.[3]

---

3. Rule 607 of the Federal Rules of Evidence provides "The credibility of a witness may be attacked by any party, including the party calling him."

§ 3.23 Defenses

The seat belt defense shouldn't be taken lightly. The plaintiff is claiming that the defendant should have been more careful to protect the plaintiff—but how careful was the plaintiff in protecting himself? The big problem in the seat belt defense is establishing causation, being able to adduce expert testimony that the failure to wear the seat belt aggravated the injuries. Pre-trial discovery reveals the presence of the defendant's expert, who is willing to supply the causative link.

§ 3.24 Tactical Considerations

The introduction of evidence concerning drinking is basically a tactical problem for the plaintiff. Will the jury hold it against the defendant for having drunk a beer or two at a picnic, or will they hold it against the plaintiff for attempting to accuse the defendant of drunken driving with inadequate proof?

§ 3.25 Defendant's Point of View

The same admonitions given the plaintiff are relevant to the defendant in drafting a responsive pleading. Most states identify by statute or court rule those affirmative defenses that must be pleaded if they are to be relied upon. The list is impressive: from accord and satisfaction to waiver.

As each party analyses the pleadings, his job will be to carefully examine his own efforts to see that he has met all the procedural demands imposed upon him and to make the same careful analysis of his opponent's efforts.

§ 3.26 Pleadings

Notice pleading provides little help in determining the specific acts of negligence that may ultimately be submitted. Thorough pre-trial discovery must determine the facts upon which the plaintiff will rely to make a submissible case. We know that the plaintiff will claim that your client ran the red light. That will suffice to make a submissible charge of violating a traffic signal. But what other admissible evidence is available to the plaintiff?

§ 3.27 Proof

A substantial part of the defense will be conducted before trial in an effort to preclude evidence favorable to the plaintiff. The issue of the defendant's drinking should not be presented to the

jury, in voir dire or opening statement, unless the plaintiff can
assure the court that sufficient evidence can be adduced to support
a finding that defendant's senses were impaired and that such
impairment contributed to the accident.   No such proof has been
developed in pre-trial discovery.   Absent such proof, evidence of a
beer at a picnic becomes irrelevant.   An order should be sought to
foreclose the plaintiff from mentioning, during voir dire and
opening statement, the defendant's drinking, with the court reserving his ruling on the evidence on this subject as it is adduced.[4]

A second potential dangerous item of evidence is the defendant's plea of nolo contendere to the charge of careless driving.
The general rule is that the issuing of a citation for a traffic
charge, as well as a finding of guilt on such a charge, is inadmissible.[5]   If a party pleads guilty, however, to the charge, it becomes
admissible as a statement against interest.[6]   Where does that
leave a nolo contendere plea?   Is it to be considered as an
admissible statement?   Research of the local law is required,[7] and
if it's determined to be inadmissible, the court should be requested
to instruct the plaintiff to make no inquiries in this subject area.
With proper pre-trial protective orders the issue of defendant's
negligence should be confined to a "yes, you did"—"no, I didn't"
confrontation between the parties.

§ 3.28   Tactical Considerations

The drinking issue presents itself as a tactical problem for the
defendant as well as the plaintiff.   If the plaintiff elects to present
evidence of Ms. Cassidy's alleged intoxication, the defendant can
either:

   • attempt to suppress the issue through pre-trial procedures
   referred to before; or

   • permit the plaintiff to attack with his unconvincing, inferential evidence and then counterattack with much stronger
   evidence supporting her contention of sobriety.

A loss on this issue could taint the plaintiff's entire case.

A second tactical decision must be made with respect to the
issue of damages.   As in most civil cases the defendant is faced
with the question, "Will a spirited defense regarding the issue of

---

4.   See Motions in Limine, *infra.*

5.   31 A.C.J.S. § 300, p. 771.

6.   WEST DIGEST, Evidence, 207(4).

7.   Neibling v. Terry, 352 Mo. 396,
177 S.W.2d 502, 152 A.L.R. 249 (1944).

damages be regarded as a concession of liability?" In this instance the plaintiff's claim for damages is vulnerable to attack.

1.   His low back problem is a chronic condition dating back
     twenty years.

2.   He suffered a traumatic injury to his back ten or twelve
     years ago, which required hospitalization.

3.   His knee problems are minor, being confined to com-
     plaints of their being bothersome when "it's going to rain
     or I'm tired."

In addition, there is strong evidence that Millman's own
failure to wear a seat belt was the most substantial reason for the
second impact with the pole and the resultant injury to his knee.
In addition, there is the fact that Millman was driving without his
shoes. Although this does not rise to the dignity of a legal claim
of contributory negligence, it does suggest that his capacity to
respond to an emergency situation requiring braking was somewhat impaired.

Good tactics will demand that the defendant attack on all
fronts—liability, affirmative defense, and damages.

D.   PRESENTATION OF THE PLAINTIFF'S EVIDENCE

§ 3.29   Direct Examination of the Plaintiff

Some thought must be given to the order of presentation of
the evidence. The proof in this case, both as to the issue of
liability and damages, is limited. Not too many options present
themselves. Who goes first, the plaintiff or his expert? Logic
dictates that the juror must first hear the facts from the former
upon which the opinion of the latter rests. Call your client first.

§ 3.30   Personal Information

Q.   Mr. Millman, please state your full name for the record.
A.   Herbert A. Millman.

Why is information adduced on direct examination: to
convince a jury, or to make a record? It is frequently stated

that a trial lawyer is obliged to "preserve the record for appeal," but the chief concern must always be the effect that the interrogation will have on the jury. Our initial task in direct examination is to introduce the witness to the jury—not to provide information for the record.

The hackneyed beginning above is even more inappropriate in those jurisdictions where the judge instructs the witness to identify himself and provide the proper spelling of his name to the court reporter. Having witnessed this recording process, the jury realizes that the lawyer's request to repeat the name is not a needed recitation for the record, but rather is a mindless cliché. Why not try, "Would you introduce yourself to the jury, please," or "Let me ask you some questions so that the jury can become acquainted with you."

Q. Mr. Millman, where do you live?
A. I live at 2107 Elm Street, here in Palm Bay.
Q. How long have you lived at that address?
A. Thirty years.
Q. How old are you?
A. Sixty-five.
Q. Are you married?
A. Yes. To Inez.
Q. How long have you been married?
A. Forty-three wonderful years.
Q. Do you have children?
A. Yes. We have two daughters. They are both married and living out of state.
Q. Are you employed?
A. No, sir. I am retired.
Q. What did you do before you retired?
A. I was a mail carrier for the U.S. Postal Service for thirty-five years.
Q. When did you retire?
A. In April of 1989.
Q. Does Inez work?
A. Yes. She is a bookkeeper.

First, a few general comments. This series of questions elicits the necessary statistical information and does so in a crisp, staccato style. But is this desirable for this stage of the interrogation? In this introduction phase of direct examination, there are three goals:

• to provide the jury with biographical information;

• to afford the jury an opportunity to gain a "feeling" for the witness; and

• to put the witness at ease so that his effectiveness in reciting his testimony will be enhanced.

The first two goals are directed to the issue of credibility. The jury has been or will be instructed that they have the sole task of assessing credibility, and they will be invited to consider the appearance, attitude, and behavior of the witness; the interest of the witness in the outcome of the suit; the relation of the witness to any party to the suit; the inclination of the witness to speak truthfully or untruthfully; the probability or improbability of the witness's statements; and all other facts and circumstances in evidence.

This <u>Dragnet</u>-style questioning ("just the facts, ma'am") accomplishes the first goal of providing biographical information, but the short questions calling for short answers furnish little opportunity for the witness to warm up for the task ahead, nor does it allow the jury to glimpse the "real" Herbert A. Millman. Those goals would be better achieved by asking questions that will prompt responses that are more conversational and more revealing of the witness's personality. Scratch the statistical check list approach ("Are you married?"; "How long have you been married?"; "Do you have any children?") and substitute a more inviting, "Tell us about your family life." Now we'll hear about Inez and the children in a more natural fashion.

Now for a few comments regarding specific questions. Be aware of how far you can go in eliciting family situations. Some judges will consider marital status, number of children, and length of marriage as merely an attempt to generate sympathy and irrelevant. The response to that position is that such information is relevant to the issue of credibility (although one might question the relationship of fecundity to credibility).

Even if there is no challenge to this line of questioning, be sensitive to the manner in which it is adduced. The witness's answer of "forty-three wonderful years" in response to the question "how long have you been married?" is in jarring contrast to his other laconic answers and sounds a bit phony. It would fit more comfortably in a narrative response to a general question about family life.

One could question the advisability of eliciting information of his wife's occupation. Will her role as wage earner undercut his request for money? Remember: If there is no reason to ask a question, there is a reason not to.

§ 3.31   Accident Information

Q.   I want you to direct your attention to the early evening of May 26. As you recall, what were you doing that evening?

Transitions from one topic to another are important, and one should never be content with such a tired triteness as "Directing your attention to. . . ." In this case, as in most cases, there is no dispute that the litigation-inducing event occurred. No doubt both parties alluded to the May 26th automobile accident in voir dire and their opening statements. Why be so tentative about how we introduce the details of that event to the jury? When the conversation is over, let everyone know the next topic of discussion with something as simple as: "I'm going to ask you some questions about this automobile collision that occurred on May 26th. What were you doing earlier that evening?"

One more comment. Eliminate the needless phrase "as you recall." All of the testimony will recite recollections; indeed, personal knowledge is a requisite to establish witness competence. Throwing in such extraneous phrases as "if you remember" and "are you aware" suggests that the witness's memory might be impaired. In addition, the witness tends to mimic this tentative style and is apt to preface his response with some mushy phrase such as "Well, I remember" (as did this witness); "To my best recollection"; "If I can recall"; or some other conditional modifier that weakens the persuasiveness of the testimony.

A.   Well, I remember my wife sent me to the grocery store about 6:15 or 6:30 p.m. She was making lasagna for supper that evening, and she discovered she was short of cheese about half-way through the recipe. So I went to buy some more cheese.

Q.   Where is the grocery store?

A.   I drove to the A & P on State Road 7, just about half a mile south of Atlantic Drive.

Q.   After you left the A & P with your cheese for dinner, where did you go?

Here we see an illustration of an interrogation anomaly for which the advocate must develop "rabbit ears." In this case, the effect is inconsequential and would not justify an objection, but opposing counsel should be aware of what happened. The interrogator, by his question, filled in a void for which there was no proof. "After you left the A & P with your cheese for dinner"—there is no testimony that he left the store (although his presence in court suggests that he did at some time), nor is there testimony that he left "with ... cheese." Harmless minutiae in this instance, but it illustrates a common inclination for interrogators to abhor a vacuum as much as nature. Interrogators will supply the missing ingredient by "assuming facts not in evidence"—an objection that must sit lightly on the tongue of every advocate.

A. I intended to drive straight back home, but I never made it.
Q. What time did you start home from the grocery store?
A. About 7:00 p.m.
Q. What was the weather like that evening?
A. The sky was clear. It was a warm spring evening.
Q. Was it light outside?
A. Oh, yes. It doesn't get dark that time of year until 8:00 or 8:30.

Usually it is advisable to set the stage before we proceed with the dynamics of an event. The jury will be asked to recreate in their minds what happened on the evening of May 26th. They can do that better if you supply the details of time and circumstances.

Q. As you were driving back home that evening, did anything unusual happen?
A. It certainly did. I was involved in a car wreck.

Another uninspired transition that does nothing to introduce a recitation of the dynamic event. Not only is the phrase "did anything unusual happen" trite and predictable, it can sometimes confuse the witness. A New York prosecutor reports that a witness to a subway mugging (a routine event, unfortunately, in New York City) responded in the negative when asked, "Did you witness anything unusual on the night of April 10th?" If an introductory statement is needed, why not, "Now let's talk about the details of the collision"?

Q. Where did this car wreck happen?
A. At the intersection of Atlantic Drive and State Road 7.
Q. I'm showing you what's been marked as Plaintiff's Exhibit Number One. Is that a fair and accurate representation of the intersection as it existed back on May 26?
A. Yes, it is.
Q. Would it help you describe the car wreck to the jury if you could use this diagram?
A. Yes, it would.
Q. Your Honor, with your permission, I'd like to have the witness step down and use this diagram to answer some questions.
Court: Go ahead.

The transcript does not reveal the nature of the exhibit. It could be an eight by eleven drawing or transparency, or it could be a large chart to be displayed on an easel. If it is of such a size that the jury can distinguish details, you might draw an objection if it is displayed to them before it is authenticated. To avoid this possibility, either authenticate the exhibit in a pre-trial procedure or position the exhibit so it can be seen by the witness and not the jury.

Note that the magic words are used and that the form is a bit leading, but it is proper, inasmuch as leading is permitted in laying foundations for exhibits.[8] Furthermore, it might appear to be inconsistent to rail against legal clichés and then endorse the use of "fair and accurate representation" as the

8. C.J.S. Witness § 329 et seq.; WEST   seq.
DIGEST, Witnesses, Key Number 239 et

foundational standard. In most instances you should avoid such clichés, because you will be framing your interrogation so that it will be appealing to the jury. In this instance, however, the language is for the judge. He's used to "fair and reasonable representation." It has a soothing sense of familiarity about it—so use it. The other foundation ingredient is also present, supplied by the simple phrase "as it existed back on May 26th." The appearance of the site of the accident at any other time would be irrelevant.

The witness's acknowledging that the exhibit would be helpful to him in describing the "car wreck" is not a foundational requisite, but it does have a tactical advantage. Any objection to its admission would appear to be an attempt by the opponent to handicap the witness in presenting the facts.

Note that this is the third time that the interrogator has referred to the incident as a "car wreck." Some studies conducted by Dr. Elizabeth Loftus [9] have indicated that a juror's perception of the violence of an event such as this is affected by the words or phrases chosen to describe the event. Think of the descriptive range available:

Mr. Witness, please describe:
"how the cars came together," or
"how the cars came into contact with
each other," or
"the collision," or
"the crash," or
"the wreck."

Each option connotes its own sense of violence, and "car wreck" implies a contact of some significance.

Q. Mr. Millman, using this diagram, please show the jury the position of your car as you drove toward the intersection.
A. (Pointing to diagram) I was traveling north on State Road 7, in the left lane here.

Whenever your witness refers to a diagram and says "here" or "there," you must either:
1.   verbally describe the position he has indicated ("you have indicated you were traveling in the westernmost of the northbound lanes"); or

9. Goodman & Loftus, *Social Science*   52, 54 (Apr. 1984).
Looks at Witness Examination, TRIAL

2. physically indicate on the diagram, by a self-identifying mark, the position indicated ("please mark a rectangle on the diagram to indicate in which lane you were traveling and place your initials in the rectangle"). If the diagram is to scale, it is best if your rectangles of the vehicles also be to scale.

Q. How fast were you traveling?
A. About forty miles per hour.
Q. What were the traffic conditions like at the intersection of Atlantic Drive and State Road 7?
A. Pretty light; not much traffic at all.
Q. What did you do when you got to the intersection?
A. Well, I just covered the brake pedal and proceeded on through.
Q. Why didn't you stop?
A. I had the green light—plain as day. No reason to even slow down.

When describing a dynamic event such as the collision of two moving vehicles, you will find it necessary to indicate differing speeds and positions as the action unfolds. Here we have a single statement as to the speed of the Millman automobile with no reference to its position at that time. The question should be (after he indicates his position on the diagram), "How fast were you traveling *at that time?*" Now it might be that his speed remained the same up until the time of impact, but that significant fact should not be left to conjecture. The witness states that he "covered the brake pedal." Did he do that with the right foot, necessarily removing that foot from the accelerator and causing the car to slow down? More explanation is needed.

It's always refreshing to hear a real, honest-to-goodness question on direct examination. Here the interrogator has utilized such a device—and it is effective. Further, it's a question the jury wants to know, and that's the best description of any interrogation, direct or cross—"Ask a question the jurors would ask if they had the chance." What better way to coax an exculpatory explanation than to ask, "Why didn't you stop?"

71

Q. What happened, if anything, as you drove through that intersection?

Isn't it interesting how a defensive mind-set can precipitate meaningless circumlocution? Fearful of being accused of leading his witness (apparently that's the reason), the interrogator throws in "if anything" after inquiring "what happened." Wouldn't it sound more logical to ask "Tell us what happened as you drove through the intersection"?

A. Well, about half way through the intersection, the other car smashed into the left side of my car.
Q. Where did this other car smash in your car?

Here is an example of loop-back questioning. Having heard the witness describe the event in plain-talk and violent terms ("smashed into"), the interrogator incorporates that phrase in the next question. Many lawyers would have been content with "What part of your car was hit?" or "Where was your car impacted?" (Save *that* pretentious verb as an adjective to describe teeth.) Reinforce what the witness said through simple repetition.

A. On the left-front fender area.
Q. What happened immediately after the collision?
A. Well, the impact knocked my car across the intersection and into a cement pole.
Q. Where did your car finally stop?
A. Up against this cement pole here.
Q. Please return to the witness stand.

After demonstrating his ability to employ the loop-back technique, the interrogator abandons it by switching to the more general, less violent, and non-accusatory word "collision." Let us instead inquire, "What happened immediately after the defendant's car smashed into you?" But doesn't this question assume a fact not in evidence, that the other car was the defendant's car? Technically yes, but is there to be a dispute as to identity of the car? Of course not—and it's time the jury sees this incident for what it is. The case is not about one car hitting another car; it's about a car driven by the defendant hitting "you."

How often the repetitive phrase is used is a matter of judgment. Note the ease with which it could follow the last question, if you so desired: "Where did your car finally come to a stop after the defendant had smashed into you?"

Once more we see the failure of the interrogator to dress up the record when the witness points to the diagram and says "here." How simple it would be to add, "Would you please mark that cement pole where your car came to a stop with a red X."

The stage direction, however, is right on the button. Once the use of the diagram is completed, get the witness back on the stand. There are a number of reasons that this should be done:

1. The testimony of a witness is more effective when presented from the witness stand. It is a valuable prop that enhances the credibility of your witness's testimony, the pulpit from which sworn testimony is delivered.

2. People standing near exhibits tend to look at the exhibit as they talk, even when the content of the testimony is unrelated to the exhibit. The projection, of course, should be to the jury.

3. When lawyer and witness are positioned together near the exhibit, there is an almost irresistible temptation to have the public interrogation deteriorate into a private tête-à-tête. Reduce that temptation by truncating the time away from the stand.

Q. As you were sitting there in your car, seconds after the collision, what do you remember?

A. Well, at first I really wasn't sure what had happened. I was kind of shaken up. But I remember my back was killing me. These sharp, stabbing pains running from my lower back to

my shoulders. I'd had headaches before, but never anything
like this. Also, my right knee felt like someone had taken a
hammer and busted my knee. I also had various cuts and
bruises.

Q. What happened next?

A. Well, just a few minutes later the police arrived. And then
the ambulance arrived.

The interrogation subject matter is good (allow the witness to describe the immediate effects of the accident), but the
questioning is awkward. The question "what do you remember?" is vague and open ended and will probably draw an
objection on the ground that it calls for a narrative and is
irrelevant. Better to ask, "What were the immediate effects
of the crash?"

"What happened next?" is a complete abdication of the
advocate's responsibility to direct the examination. You are
dumping the entire responsibility of the narration into the lap
of the witness. This style of interrogation (or should we call
it non-directed questioning) is employed so frequently by
neophyte prosecutors that the consensus of the criminal defense bar is that one can prepare to be a prosecutor by
following a simple two-step procedure: develop the accepted
interrogation technique (learn to say, "What happened
next?"); and develop the proper mind set (that of someone
about to stomp on baby chicks.)

Is there any excuse for this prolific use of non-directive
questioning? This type of question probably arises as an
alternative to other more direct forms of interrogation that
have been thwarted by objections made by nitpicking lawyers
and sustained by even pickier judges. Consider this scenario:

Q. Did the police arrive at the scene?

Opponent: Objection—leading.

Court: Sustained

Q. Who arrived at the scene?

Opponent: Objection—assumes that someone arrived at
the scene.

Q. What happened next?

Don't be intimidated by such antics. Anticipate that
such foolishness may occur and ask, "Did anyone arrive at the
scene?" and "Who was it?"

----

§ 3.32   Injuries

Q. Did you go to the hospital?
A. Yes, the ambulance took me to Palm Bay General.
Q. Who called the ambulance?
A. I don't know. It wasn't me. I didn't request it.

You will be fighting the abbreviated attention span of jurors; consequently, you should make every question count. What difference does it make who called the ambulance? And you see the kind of answer it provokes—a gratuitous "I didn't request it," which sounds like a denial of an injury.

Q. Did you receive medical treatment at the hospital?
A. Yes. I spent two nights there. My back injuries were treated, and so was my knee.
Q. After your two nights in the hospital, were you okay after that?
A. Far from it. I went back for knee surgery about ten days later to repair damage done in the car wreck. I had to have a pin put in my knee. I also had fifteen weeks of ultrasound treatment on my back.

The above is not a bad technique: assume that the plaintiff was okay after two days in the hospital and have the denial and amplifications come from the witness. Too often the lawyer and the plaintiff join hands and skip together through an overly solicitous recitation of all the injuries and ensuing complaints. The result is often a prolonged, whiny recitation of medical procedures, aches, and pains that fails to persuade. The records themselves and the hospital personnel are the best sources for describing in detail the treatment and travails that were experienced in the hospital. Save the plaintiff for those complaints that are undocumented, which he alone can describe.

Q. Did you have any health problems before the collision with Ms. Cassidy?

A. Nothing serious. My back did bother me from time to time because I carried mail for thirty-five years—nothing some aspirin wouldn't cure. I did slip and fall at work on some ice about ten years ago and hurt my back, but that got a lot better with time. Also, my feet are a little tender from delivering mail al¹ those years.

The plaintiff's pre-accident condition is an important issue in this case. The plaintiff, fortunately, has the initial opportunity of dealing with it, and full advantage should be taken of an opportunity to "de-fang the tiger." Note again the possibility of making this "pre-emptive strike" with a quasi-adversarial question: "You did have some physical disabilities before this accident, Mr. Millman, didn't you?" Would this enhance the credibility of your presentation? Perhaps.

Q. How did this car wreck affect Mrs. Millman?
A. She had to miss about two weeks of work to stay home with me cause I couldn't get around too well for a while?
Q. Did you lose any household income as a result of your wife missing work?
A. Yes, we did.
Q. How much?
A. Fifteen hundred dollars.

Now we know why the plaintiff mentioned his wife's work status at the beginning of the interrogation, but we still might question the tactical wisdom of introducing such testimony. Sure, there were losses of $1,500, but what is the legal basis for their recovery, and how will the jury respond to the request? Too many questions might be provoked:

1. Wasn't she merely performing those chores that should be performed by someone aiding an injured spouse?
2. Did she have to lay off two weeks because her husband "couldn't get around too well for a while?"
3. What if she had been a $3,000 a week executive? Would she be demanding $6,000 for helping her husband get around?

76

4. Isn't the real measure of damages the value of her services, and, if so, where is the testimony that helping someone "get around" for two weeks is worth $1,500?

Q. I'm handing you Plaintiff's Exhibit Number Two. Can you identify that?
A. Yes. It's a copy of the ambulance bill in the amount of $322.50.
Q. Your Honor, I offer Plaintiff's Exhibit Number Two into evidence.
Judge: Any objection, counsel?
A. No, your Honor.
Judge: It will be admitted.
Q. How much was the charge for the surgery that was performed upon you after the accident?
A. The bill was $11,363.26.
Q. Handing you Plaintiff's Exhibit Number Three, do you recognize that?
A. Yes, it's the surgeon's bill.
Q. I offer Plaintiff's Exhibit Number Three into evidence.
Judge: Any objection, counsel?
A. No, sir.
Judge: It will be admitted.
Q. What were the damages to your automobile from the collision?
A. Three thousand five hundred dollars.

Visual aids are particularly valuable in presenting statistical information, and in this case it is advisable to get those expense figures before the jury in written as well as oral form. But don't forget the foundation for their introduction. For the medical expenses it must be shown that: they were reasonably necessary for the treatment of the injuries suffered; and the charges were reasonable.[10] For the automobile damages, the measure is usually expressed as the difference in market value before and after the collision.[11]

The law affords some assistance in meeting these demands for proof. Payment of the bill rendered will suffice to

---

10. Spica v. McDonald, 334 S.W.2d 365 (Mo.1960).

11. WEST DIGEST, Damages, Key Number 103; Hughey v. Graham, 604 S.W.2d 626 (Mo.App.1980).

prove reasonableness of a medical bill,[12] and the owner of property is qualified to express the value of that property.[13] Of course, the easiest way to meet the demands of the law is to get a pre-trial stipulation as to the admissibility of these expenses. If a recalcitrant opponent resists a stipulation, file a motion to admit the validity of the charges; if they respond with a denial you'll be in a position to seek reimbursement for the cost of proving these items.[14] Remember: The proof of auto damage is not the cost of repair—it's the difference in value before and after the accident. The questioning should be:

Q. How much was your car worth before the collision?
A. Ten thousand dollars.
Q. And how much after the collision?
A. Six thousand five hundred dollars.

Q. Has your lifestyle changed at all since the collision with Ms. Cassidy?
A. It certainly has. I used to play golf on a regular basis, I swam at the YMCA three times a week, and Inez and I always had a garden. I had looked forward to retirement so I could truly enjoy all of these activities. But I can't since the car wreck.
Q. What else, if anything, has changed?
A. Well, Inez and I had planned to drive across the U.S. after I retired—you know, take about a month to really see this great country—but since my car wreck I just can't sit in a car for much more than an hour before my knee really starts throbbing.
Q. Is anything else different as a result of the collision with Sarah Cassidy?
A. Well, before the car wreck, my wife and I enjoyed a very satisfying sex life. But now my back just hurts too badly to make love.
Q. Mr. Millman, since this collision, are you ever without pain?
A. No, never.

The plaintiff's lawyer had good instincts. He wants to relate the change in lifestyle to the collision, which in turn is

12. Gooch v. Avsco, Inc., 340 S.W.2d 665 (Mo.1960).

13. WEST DIGEST, Evidence, Key Number 474(16); Tull v. Housing Authority of City of Columbia, 691 S.W.2d 940 (Mo.App.1985).

14. Fed.R.Civ.P. 2, 36 and 37.

related to the errant behavior of Ms. Cassidy. But how effectively does he translate this instinctive desire into his interrogation? He speaks of pain "since the collision with Ms. Cassidy." Consider these alternatives: "Has your life-style changed at all ...

1. "since the defendant broke the law by violating the red light and negligently crashed into the left side of the car?"

2. "since the defendant ran the red light and crashed into the side of your car?"

3. "since the defendant smashed into the left side of your car?"

The first is obviously argumentative and would, or at least should, draw an objection. The second is less argumentative, but since there is no direct evidence that the defendant ran the red light (only inferential, since the plaintiff testified that he had the green light), an objection might be made and sustained. But what is the objection to the third? First, isn't it better to refer to the other party as "the defendant," rather than personalize her with a "Ms. Cassidy" in one case and "Sarah Cassidy" in another? And if the phrase "smashed into the left side of the car" was so desirable before, why change it to "collision"?

Loss of consortium is a possible element of damages in this case, but, as is characteristic of the claim, it's a sensitive topic to be approached with caution. Is it worth pursuing when the injured party is sixty-five and his mate approximately the same age? (There is no evidence of Inez's age, but we know they've been married forty-three years, so she's probably in the same age range). Herbert thinks so, and that's all you need to know as his advocate (get ready with those arguments that "a dollar is most important to the man who has only one left"). The question here is whether Herbert has presented his claim in the best way possible. Talking about his ability to "make love," in response to a general question whether "anything else is different," can sound a bit clinical and self-centered.

Perhaps this is the proper time to recognize the delicate nature of the subject matter and acknowledge to the jury the need to explore this awkward area.

Q. Mr. Millman, this jury is going to be asked to determine if the injuries you suffered when the defendant's car smashed into you had any effect beyond what you have told us. I know that you are hesitant to talk about it, but I must ask—did those injuries affect your relationship with your wife?"

Don't turn your witness loose with any old answer. Remember the spouse has a separate claim of her own. It's not simply that *he* can't make love. *They* can't enjoy the companionship, comfort, and nurturing that they had previously known. Find out how he expresses that loss—then dress it up.

The interrogator obviously has given attention to the organization of his direct. He ends with the plaintiff's present complaints and a nice, pithy declaration of a gloomy prognosis for the future. The only suggestion: Reaffirm that this never ending pain has existed not "since the collision" but "since the defendant smashed into the side of my car."

---

§ 3.33 Cross–Examination of Plaintiff

The manner in which the jury perceives the plaintiff as an individual will be critical to your defense. Will they see him as a sympathetic victim, a whining complainer, a belligerent antagonist? It will depend on how you analyze him yourself and how you will treat him on cross-examination.

§ 3.34 Information Available

- Statement of facts
- Deposition
- Police diagrams of scene
- Deposition of reconstruction expert

§ 3.35 Analysis of Information

The statement of facts reveals a single bit of information—that the plaintiff was driving in his stocking feet.

The deposition reveals

1. he didn't see the other vehicle until "the last second"; yet,
2. the intersection was clear when he entered it;
3. he "honked my horn when I saw her";
4. he wasn't wearing a seat belt.

The police diagram indicates that the overall width of Atlantic Drive is forty feet and the overall width of State road is eighty feet.

The accident reconstruction expert estimates the relative speeds of Millman and Cassidy to be forty miles per hour and thirty-five miles per hour, respectively.

§ 3.36 Coordinating the Information

Millman's recitation of the incident is intrinsically inconsistent and subject to attack on several grounds:

1. He says that the intersection was clear when he entered it—yet Cassidy, traveling at a slower speed, passed through the two southbound lanes, the median strip, and the left-turn lane for northbound traffic (approximately fifty feet into the intersection) while Millman was traveling the width of the eastbound lane of Atlantic Drive (approximately twenty feet). Obviously it was Cassidy who entered the intersection first.

2. He states he sounded his horn before the collision. Traveling at forty miles per hour, he was moving sixty feet per second. Even if the honk was simultaneous with the impact, he was forty-five feet south of the impact (or twenty-five feet south of the intersection) when he reacted to Cassidy's presence. Could he have taken another kind of evasive action, such as swerving or slowing? Was his failure to apply the brakes related to his driving without shoes?

3. He wasn't wearing a seat belt. One capacity that an advocate must develop is that of creating scenarios—being able to envision an event as it probably occurred. Picture Herb Millman getting into his car. He is sixty-five years old, retired, living alone with his wife of many years, a government employee for over thirty years—a definite anal-retentive type. He slowly and deliberately gets open the car door (he, of course, had locked it), places the parcels on the right front seat, positions himself behind the wheel, takes off his shoes (because he has bad feet, they are high top with multiple laces), places them on the seat next to his parcels and drives off. Why didn't this ritual include the one thing of importance, putting on his seat belt?

81

§ 3.37 Executing the Cross–Examination

The first task is to exploit the physical impossibility of the plaintiff's version of the accident.

Q. Mr. Millman, you state that as you approached the intersection you were traveling about forty miles an hour?
A. Yes.
Q. And you know that at forty miles an hour you are traveling about sixty feet a second.
A. I don't know that.
Q. Well, if an accident reconstruction expert with a doctorate degree in physics were to say that, you wouldn't disagree, would you?
A. No.

One sure-fire way to get information before a jury on cross-examination is to ask the witness if they know something. Whether they know it or not is unimportant. You have given the information to the jury so they can appreciate the context of your questioning.

Q. You don't know the rate of travel of Ms. Cassidy's car, do you?
A. No, I don't.
Q. Let's assume that she will testify that she was traveling thirty-five miles per hour. (Aside) There will be such evidence, your Honor. (To the witness) Now your speed remained the same from the time you approached the intersection until the impact occurred, didn't it?

Note the contrast between the defendant's "rate of travel" and the plaintiff's "speed."

A. Sure, I had the green light.
Q. That's for the jury to decide, Mr. Millman.

—————

One of the most common hazards in cross-examination is the gratuitous exculpatory phrase injected by the witness. Some reply must be made, lest silence be interpreted as acquiescence, but you don't want a fight with the witness. The best retort?   "The jury will decide that, Mr. Witness."

—————

Q. Will you look at the diagram of this intersection, your Exhibit Number One, the diagram that's part of the official report, and tell us what distance you traveled in the intersection at forty miles per hour before the impact occurred?

—————

Note how we endorse the diagram.   It is their exhibit, which is "part of the official report."   How can the witness dispute its accuracy?

—————

A. My front bumper was right in the center line of Atlantic Drive. I went about twenty feet.
Q. And can you tell the jury how far Ms. Cassidy had traveled in the intersection at thirty-five miles an hour before the impact occurred?

—————

This form of questioning invites a response and gives more control to the witness.   Whether you elect to risk this invitation depends on your evaluation of your psychological control.   A safer way would be as follows:

—————

Q. Let's figure out how far Ms. Cassidy traveled at thirty-five miles an hour. She passed the curb lane of southbound traffic on State Road, correct?
A. Yes.
Q. And the inside lane of southbound traffic?
A. Yes.
Q. The width of the median strip?

83

A. Yes.

Q. The width of the left-turn lane for northbound traffic on State Road?

A. Yes.

Q. And partially into the inside lane for northbound traffic on State Road?

A. That's what it looks like.

Q. Well, that's what the diagram from the official report that you introduced to this jury, isn't it?

Several things to note:

1. Witnesses equivocate and seek to evade your control. They frequently do this by a response such as "you can say that," "I guess so," or in this instance, "That's what it looks like." Don't permit this attempt to jump the traces. Reassert your domination, as was done in this instance. One warning: Don't be argumentative, just firm.

2. Note the contrast in describing the distances traveled by the respective vehicles. With Millman the phrase is neutral, the "distance traveled"; with Cassidy we mention how "far" she traveled. The use of "far" will help convey the concept of a greater distance.

3. Some themes should be developed slowly in order to let the point sink in. The interrogator could well have lumped all this in one question, but by stringing it out and pointing to each lane of traffic Cassidy passed (in contrast to Millman's single lane), the difference in the distance traveled in the intersection is much more apparent.

Q. Would it be fair to say, Mr. Millman, that Ms. Cassidy traveled approximately twice the distance through the intersection before the collision than you did?

If he's "fair" he must acknowledge that fact. As an additional proof of your thesis the diagram itself shows that Millman was one car length in the intersection at time of impact and Cassidy was two car lengths inside the intersection. When you know what the answer must be, give the

witness an opportunity to respond. This is much more effective than stating, "She traveled over twice the distance in the
intersection than you did, didn't she?"

———————

A. I guess she did.
Q. Then since you were traveling about the same speed, she must
have entered the intersection first, correct?

———————

One goal of cross-examination is to provide material for
your closing argument. With the response to the previous
question, you have the information from which you can argue
that Ms. Cassidy had, indeed, entered the intersection first.
Whether you want to adduce more direct evidence by a
concession from the witness is one of those tactical decisions
that makes our craft so challenging. The danger is that you
may provoke an explanation you hadn't anticipated. One
witness in a similar situation was asked to explain how a car
traveling sixty miles an hour and a train traveling thirty
miles an hour had both moved the same distance in the same
amount of time. The witness thought a moment, then responded, "Well, the train had these real big wheels, and the
car had these little wheels."

———————

A. Yes.

———————

Now we have to decide if we want to take this any
further. It depends upon the mood of the witness. Is he
vulnerable to another humbling experience? If so, go on.

———————

Q. Well, when you testified that the intersection was clear when
you entered it, you were mistaken, weren't you?
A. I guess so.
Q. And you could be mistaken about other recollections you have
about the accident, isn't that true?

85

Here is a question to which you don't know the answer and don't care. You make your point just by asking the question. Note the other options available to you. The interrogator chooses to refer to the previous testimony as a "mistake." Why not another option, "When you testified under oath that the intersection was clear, that was a lie, wasn't it?" This sounds a bit rough, and the jury might penalize you for it. Cicero once remarked, "It's better to have someone ask you, 'Why isn't your statue in the square?' than to have him ask, 'Why is your statue in the square?' " Translated to advocacy the rule becomes: It is better to have the jury wonder, "Why isn't he more indignant towards the witness?" than to have them wonder, "Why is he so indignant toward that witness?"

Our second task is to exploit the witness's statement that he honked his horn before impact.

Q. You say that you had time to honk your horn before the collision?

A. I sure did.

Q. When you first saw Ms. Cassidy's car, you had time to realize that a collision was about to happen and to react to that situation by moving your hand to the horn?

A. Yes, sir.

Q. There were no cars in that left-turn lane for northbound traffic, were there?

A. No.

There is a temptation to make the next question, "Well, why didn't you swerve to the right or to the left to avoid the collision?" This is one of those "why" questions best left unanswered. You have the facts to argue the point. Save it for argument.

Q. When you saw Ms. Cassidy's car, you didn't apply the brakes, did you?

A. I didn't have time.

You see the position the interrogator is in. He wants to confirm that Millman didn't apply the brakes, and then ask about his lack of shoes, to imply that perhaps that was why he didn't apply the brakes. When the question is asked directly, the witness will become defensive and give an exculpatory explanation. You could follow with:

1. "Well, you did have time to sound the horn, didn't you?"; or
2. "That's for the jury to decide, Mr. Millman." But if you want to avoid this exchange, you could make the question less direct.

Q. You have told us all that you did to avoid the accident after seeing Ms. Cassidy, is that true?
A. Yes.
Q. You weren't wearing your shoes, were you, Mr. Millman, when you saw the Cassidy car?
A: No.

We all like to think that we're good at figuring things out, that we have the gift of insight that provides us with the wherewithal to solve mysteries. Some jurors will get the point you're making and will be pleased with their perspicacity. For the others you'll argue: "Mr. Millman had time to honk the horn. Why didn't he apply the brakes? Was it because he was in his stocking feet and didn't have the capacity to apply forceful pressure on the brake pedal?"

Our third task is to develop the importance of the plaintiff's failure to wear a seat belt.

Q. Let's review for the jury just what you did when you approached and entered your car before your trip home. Did you unlock your car?
A. Yes.
Q. What did you do with the parcels you had purchased?
A. I placed them on the passenger seat.
Q. Did you then position yourself in the driver's seat?
A. Yes.

Q. You know that seat belts are required by law, don't you, Mr. Millman?

A. Yes.

Q. And you knew that on the day of this accident, didn't you?

By now you should see the pattern developing, a step-by-step recitation of what Mr. Millman did and what he knew. The effect is to emphasize that his decision not to wear a seat belt (let's call it a "safety restraint" from now on) was a deliberate and dumb decision.

Q. The seat belt or safety restraint was in position and ready to be used, wasn't it?

A. Yes.

Q. But you didn't buckle up when you first positioned yourself behind the wheel.

A. No.

Q. What you did instead was to untie one of your shoes.

A. Yes, my feet are tender from walking so much as a mailman, so I usually drive in my stocking feet.

Q. So you took off one shoe?

A. Yes.

Q. Where did you put it?

Who cares where he put it? No one—but by prolonging the recitation of the act you demonstrate how deliberate his actions were in taking off his shoes and leaving off the seat belt.

A. On the passenger seat next to the parcels.

Q. Then you untied and took off your other shoe, I suppose.

A. Yes.

Q. And you placed that alongside the other shoe?

A. Yes.

Q. Now, after taking off your shoes, did you buckle up?

A. No.

Q. Then, as I understand it, as you pulled away from the parking lot you had taken off your shoes, but you hadn't applied the safety restraints?

A. Yes.
Q. That decision, not to wear your safety restraint, which was there in the car and which the law required you to wear, was a deliberate decision on your part. Correct?
A. Yes. It was only a short distance to my house.
Q. Yes, but a long enough distance for you to be involved in an accident, wasn't it?

———————

Here again we have an attempt at an exculpatory explanation that shouldn't go unanswered. The trouble is you can't always anticipate what kind of excuse the witness will advance. You just have to stay alert and hope that an appropriate (and not a smart-alecky) response will jump from your lips.

———————

§ 3.38   Direct Examination of Officer Wright

Here is your most persuasive witness. She is professional and neutral. You must enhance those characteristics through your direct examination.

§ 3.39   Personal Information

Q. Please give your full name.
A. Jane R. Wright.
Q. Where do you live?
A. 100 Elm Avenue in Palm Bay.
Q. For how long?
A. About ten years.
Q. What formal education do you have?
A. I have a Bachelor of Science degree in criminology from Nova University.
Q. Where are you employed?
A. Palm Bay Police Department.
Q. For how long?
A. Since 1977.
Q. Have you received any honors?
A. Yes. I won a first-place medal in marksmanship, and I was awarded the Medal of Valor in 1990.

This pithy, perfunctory line of questioning provides the jury with statistical information about the witness, but it does little to accomplish the other two goals of this phase of the interrogation: to "warm-up" the witness, and to "personalize" the witness. Let's explore some modifications that will serve to achieve all three goals. First, let's call this witness by her title and afford her a little more respect. It won't cost any more to refer to her as "Officer Wright."

Second, let's elaborate on the formal education. How many law enforcement officers do you know that have a college degree in criminology? This one has, and the jury should be given a few more details, i.e., length of study, types of courses, number of courses, etc. Don't be so stingy with your inquiry into her present employment status. Which elevates her more in the eyes of the jury: "Where are you employed?", or "After completing your four-year college preparation, what type of professional activity did you undertake?"

And why don't we hear more details about this Medal of Valor? Forget that you're in a courtroom. You are introducing Officer Wright to a friend. If you said, "And oh yes, she once won a medal of honor!", the friend would ask, "What did you do to win that award?" The jury will be just as curious, so let them know.

Q. How many automobile accidents have you investigated?
A. Several hundred.
Q. Do you have any formal training in accident investigation?
A. Yes, I received two weeks of special training in accident investigation at Northwestern University about ten years ago, and we have periodic refresher courses at our local police academy.
Q. Any other experience in investigation and reconstruction?
A. Well, each one of the hundreds of accidents I have investigated provides experience in both getting the information and reaching conclusions from the information I get.
Q. Have you testified in other automobile accident cases?
A. Yes, many times.

One of the critical evidentiary rulings will be in regard to this witness's conclusion that the accident was the fault of the defendant Sarah Cassidy. Now is the time to elaborate on the credentials so that the judge will permit such testimony and the jury will be apt to believe it. In this case, the second inquiry should be, "In addition to your four-year courses in criminology, do you have any formal training in accident investigation?" The next question should be, "Any other experience in the investigation and reconstruction of automobile accidents such as this?"

If her previous experience in testifying is important, make it clear that she testified as an expert. Continue with two more questions: "Did you testify in those other cases as an expert in accident reconstruction?" and "Did the judges in those other cases accept your qualifications as an expert?"

This last question may draw an objection, but the ruling will have little consequence on the point you have to make.

---

§ 3.40 Accident Information

Q. Were you on duty on May 26, 1992, at 7:00 p.m.?
A. Yes.
Q. Did you investigate this collision?
A. Yes.
Q. How did you come upon the scene?
A. I was conducting my regular patrol, approaching the intersection of State Road 7 and Atlantic Drive, when I saw this automobile smashed up against a cement light pole.
Q. Would a diagram aid you in explaining to the jury what you saw?
A. Yes, it would.
Q. Do you recognize this diagram, previously marked as Plaintiff's Exhibit Number One?
A. Yes, it's the intersection of Atlantic and Route 7.
Q. Is Plaintiff's Exhibit Number One a fair and accurate representation of the scene as it appeared on May 26, 1992?
A. It is.

This exhibit has already been authenticated and received in evidence, so although no further authentication is required, it is best to have this professionally trained and experienced expert confirm the accuracy of the exhibit. Remember, the name of the game is not "admissibility," but "persuasion."

Q. With the use of this diagram, please generally describe the intersection of Highway 7 and Atlantic.
A. State Road 7 is a north-south four-lane road separated by a median strip. Atlantic Drive is a two-lane road running east and west, intersecting 7 at a right angle.
Q. Where was Mr. Millman's vehicle?
A. It was here against the light pole.
Q. Where was the defendant's auto?

Again, as noted above, whenever a witness uses the words "here" or "there" in describing a location on a plat, the interrogator must respond in one of two ways:
1. Verbally describe the act of the witness ("You have indicated a circle on the northeast corner of the intersection, which has been designated as a 'cement pole' "); or
2. Direct the witness to mark on the exhibit the location she has described ("Will you please indicate where it was located when you arrived on the scene by drawing a rectangle representing Mr. Millman's car").

Obviously, the diagram can be used to best advantage if the jury is afforded a visual depiction of the car's location. The only difficulty might be in the shape and size that the "artist" gives to the car. To avoid this problem, you should create another exhibit (a rectangular shape, drawn to scale, representing the car) and have the witness position this and secure it to the diagram.

A. It was still in the intersection, right in the middle, facing east in the eastbound lane.

The defendant's car should be given the same treatment as that of the plaintiff (incidentally, note the studied use of the impersonal, legal description of "defendant," as opposed to the personal reference to "Mr. Millman"). The verbal description is not too exact. If this officer is as well-trained as her résumé indicates, she would have referenced the location of the car to well-defined east-west and north-south land-marks: "The front bumper of the car was thirty feet west of the east curb line of State Road Seven, and the left side of the car was two feet south of the center line of Atlantic Drive."

Q. How did these vehicles appear?

A. The car against the light pole had damage to the left front and the left side. The other one was damaged all across the front end.

Q. In performing your duties, what was the first thing you did when you approached the intersection?

A. I pulled my squad car into the middle of the intersection and turned on my flasher to warn other drivers.

Q. What did you do after you parked your car in the intersection with the lights on?

A. I went to the car that was in the intersection, the Pontiac driven by Sarah Cassidy.

Q. What was the first thing you noticed as you approached the defendant's car?

A. I noticed the smell of alcohol.

Q. What kind of alcohol did you smell?

A. Beer.

Q. How did you know it was beer?

A. Well, I'm familiar with the smell of beer from many investigations I've conducted involving drunken driving.

Q. How strong was the odor?

A. It was faint.

One must question why this question was asked. The witness has committed herself in her deposition with the response of "faint." It would be better to leave it alone. If the defendant wants to bring it up, let him. No need for you to emphasize it.

Q. How far away were you when you noticed it?

A. Several feet from the car.

Use pronouns sparingly. Avoid "when you noticed it."
Instead, repeat the inflammatory phrase, "when you noticed
the smell of alcohol from the defendant's car."

Q. What did you do as you got to the defendant's vehicle?
A. I helped her out of the car.
Q. Why did you help Ms. Cassidy out of her car?
A. She appeared to need help.
Q. Did you find anything in the car about the source of the odor
   of beer?
A. Yes.
Q. Turn to this jury and tell them what you found in Ms.
   Cassidy's car.

One must always be conscious of the need to emphasize
the importance of certain evidence. The six beer cans in the
front seat is important. Counsel emphasizes its importance
by prefacing his question with the direction, "Turn to this
jury and tell them."

Q. Did you find any physical evidence at the scene of the colli-
   sion?
A. Yes, I did.
Q. What was that physical evidence?
A. There was debris on the street and some scuff marks.
Q. Whose fault was this collision?
A. Sarah Cassidy.

The brevity of the question and its chronological position
in the interrogation gives the appearance that the plaintiff's
counsel is attempting to "slip in" significant testimony that is
marginally admissible. Whose fault it was is obviously an
ultimate conclusion that normally falls within the jury's
province. Whether it is a proper opinion of an expert as
contemplated by Rule 704 will be a matter for judicial inter-

pretation, and the call could go either way. The defendant, through pre-trial discovery, is well aware of what the officer's response will be. He cannot afford to wait until the trial begins to raise this evidentiary point. The mere asking of the question, even if objected to (and the objection sustained), raises the inference that the response would be favorable to the lawyer asking the question, another reason this matter must be taken up in a pre-trial conference.

Q. Where did you find skid marks?
A. Running from the point of impact here, for a few feet towards the position where the Millman car came to rest.

Let's make full use of the diagram. Pointing out the location of the scuff marks is not enough. Ask the witness to draw them on the diagram. If this information is important enough to hear, it's important enough to remember. The diagram, fully marked, can be used in closing argument, and perhaps even admitted into evidence and given to the jury during their deliberations.

Q. What is debris?
A. Debris is the glass, metal, and dirt that usually results when two cars collide.
Q. Why is debris important?
A. Its location usually indicates the point of impact.
Q. Where did you find debris?
A. In the eastbound lane of Atlantic Drive about two feet from the center line of Atlantic and about thirty feet west of the east curb line of State Road Seven.
Q. Did you take any measurements?
A. Yes.
Q. What were they?
A. I measured the distance between the point of impact and the cement light pole where the Millman car came to rest, and I found that it was forty feet.
Q. Describe the damage to the defendant's car.
A. It was damaged across the entire front end.
Q. What damage did Mr. Millman's car suffer?

A. It had damage to the left front quarter panel where it was
struck and to the left front bumper where it struck the light
pole. There was also some damage to the inside of the car: a
slight dent in the left door and a two-and-one-half-inch inden-
tation in the dashboard.
Q. Based on the above, did you reach a conclusion as to the cause
of this collision?
A. Yes, I did.

Assuming that the officer's testimony regarding the collision is admissible, you should ask yourself, "How can I make
this officer's opinion about this pivotal issue sound more
impressive?"

Don't use the shorthand phrase, "based on the above."
Tell us what the "above" is, and make the recitation of all
those elements sound important. Now is the time to make all
those credentials relevant: "Officer, based upon your formal
education, resulting in a college degree in criminology; your
experience in investigating hundreds of accidents; and the
information you received in your official investigation of this
incident; [now ask the question] did you reach a conclusion as
to the cause of this collision?"

Q. What is that conclusion?
A. The collision was caused by Sarah Cassidy's failure to stop for
the red light.

§ 3.41 Cross–Examination of Officer Wright

There is a special challenge in cross-examination of a witness
who, because of age, station in life, appearance or demeanor,
engenders sympathy and believability. A woman police officer
presents such a challenge. How do you do it? The technique is
similar to that of porcupines making love—proceed very carefully.

§ 3.42 Information Available

• Statement of facts

• Police report and diagram

• Deposition

§ 3.43 Analysis of Information

The statement of facts reveals that the officer did not charge Cassidy with drunken driving, nor did she administer a breathalyzer test, as required by the police manual when "imbibing of alcohol is suspected."

The deposition confirms that the officer did not feel that the defendant was intoxicated.

§ 3.44 Executing the Cross–Examination

Obviously, there are two elements of the direct examination that must be met head-on. The first is the implication that the defendant's driving ability was impaired by her having consumed a beer or two. The second is the conclusion that the accident was the defendant's fault.

———————

Q. Officer, my opponent asked you some questions regarding the smell of beer in my client's car. I want to ask some questions about that, too. Ms. Cassidy seemed normal, didn't she?
A. Yes, only a little disoriented.
Q. But she had not trouble standing?
A. No.
Q. She was stable and able to walk without assistance?
A. Yes.
Q. Your police manual instructs you to administer a breathalyzer test if a driver is suspected of having imbibed alcohol, isn't that true?
A. Yes.
Q. And as an officer with fifteen years of experience you were familiar with that regulation when you investigated the accident, weren't you?
A. Yes, sir.
Q. And you conducted a proper and professional investigation?
A. Yes, sir.
Q. And you didn't give Ms. Cassidy a breathalyzer test, did you?
A. No.
Q. Tell the jury why.
A. I didn't think that she had imbibed any alcohol.

———————

How simple it is when your only task in cross-examination is to get the witness to acknowledge that she is a competent, conscientious person. In this instance we know that the rules obligated the officer to administer a breathalyzer test if she thought Cassidy had been drinking. We know that a breathalyzer test was not given. The only facts missing are the officer's knowledge of the regulation and her compliance with it. Note how unlikely it is that the officer would deny either one of these elements of proof.

There really is no need for the last question. The fact that a breathalyzer test wasn't given would seem to be proof enough that the officer didn't think Cassidy was drunk. The last invitation to "tell the jury why" is simply a demonstration that sometimes even a "why" question can be asked when you know what the answer must be.

Our second task is to undercut the officer's conclusion that the accident was our client's fault (assuming that you have lost your motion in limine seeking to foreclose such a conclusion as an ultimate issue that invades the jury's province).

Q. Officer Wright, now let's talk about what you didn't see. You didn't see the accident occur, did you?

A. No, I didn't.

Q. You didn't see the color of the lights as Ms. Cassidy and Mr. Millman drove into that intersection, did you?

A. No, sir.

Q. Let's talk about what you saw when you arrived at the scene of the accident. You saw the position of the vehicles?

A. Yes, sir. Mr. Millman's car was up against a pole on the northeast corner of the intersection facing north, and the Cassidy car was in the middle of the intersection facing east.

You might want to end your interrogation at this point. Remember the overall goal of cross-examination is to get the raw material for your closing argument. You have that and are free to argue: "How can someone know the color of a light at the time of the accident when she wasn't there to see it? The same damage to the vehicle, the same position of the vehicles, the same skid marks would be there as seen by the officer if these same two cars collided and there had been no lights at the intersection." If you elect to proceed, do so with caution.

Q. Officer, you have investigated automobile accidents that have
    occurred in intersections where there have been no traffic
    control signals, haven't you?
A. Certainly.
Q. And in those situations you observe the damage to the vehic-
    les, the position of the vehicles, and you might find skid
    marks, correct?
A. Correct.
Q. And those observations would be made by you and would be
    the same if there were no traffic lights at the intersection.
A. Yes.
Q. Or if there were traffic lights that were not working.
A. Yes.
Q. Or if the lights were one color or another.
A. Yes.

E. PRESENTATION OF THE DEFENDANT'S EVIDENCE

§ 3.45 Direct Examination of the Defendant

The manner in which you address your witness will be a
subtle but significant manner in which the jury will accept her
testimony. She is a twenty-two year old single student who is
accused of drinking and driving. Your demeanor and choice of
address will set the stage for the story your witness will relate.
Forget a cheery "Sarah, tell the jury your full name". Our goal is
to dignify her as much as possible and acknowledge the gravity of
the charge against her.

§ 3.46 Personal Information

Q. Ms. Cassidy, please tell the jury a little about yourself. What
    is your full name?
A. Sarah F. Cassidy.
Q. Where do you live?
A. 704 N.W. 12th Street, Apt. 19, Palm Bay, Nova.
Q. How old are you?
A. Twenty-two.
Q. Are you married?
A. No.
Q. Are you employed?
A. No, I'm a second-year dental student at Nova U.
Q. How are you paying for school?
A. Student loans, summer jobs.

The opening questions avoid the predictable "state your name for the record" approach, but a little grooming of the questions is in order. Why ask if she's employed? A question like that could end up like the old vaudeville routine: "Does your father work?"—"No, he's a policeman." It is better to ask, "What are you doing now?" and let her respond, "Preparing to be a dentist. I'm a second-year dental student at Nova University." How she's paying for school is irrelevant, but if it is asked, a better response would be, "I'm working my way through as best I can, but I usually end up having to go into debt with a student loan." There are some phrases that sound responsive chords. "Working my way through college" has a nice connotation. "Going into debt" evokes sympathy. It's up to you to have your witness express herself in as effective a way as possible.

Q. Now, Ms. Cassidy, the plaintiff seems to want to direct this jury's attention away from the accident to your activities earlier on the day of May 26, 1992, so let's talk about that.

You should use topic sentences to introduce a new topic of interrogation, but this is much too argumentative. It would, and should, draw an objection. It's not a bad idea to meet the issue head on, but let's do it with a bit more finesse:

Q. There's been some mention of your activities before the accident, so let's talk about that.

Q. Where were you on the afternoon of May 26?
A. At a family reunion in Lake Park.
Q. What did you do at this reunion?
A. Played softball, volleyball, Frisbee—just got out and enjoyed the weather.
Q. What kind of day was May 26, 1992?
A. Gorgeous—just about a perfect May day—warm and sunny.
Q. What did you have to eat at this reunion?

100

A. Hamburgers, hot dogs, chips, potato salad, barbecue beans—all kinds of stuff.
Q. Along with all this food, did you have anything to drink?
A. Yes, I had one can of light beer—it was a pretty warm day.

Driving after drinking is always a potentially dangerous element. Defendant must present this issue in its most favorable light by explaining:
- the amount imbibed;
- the prevailing conditions; and
- the effect of the intoxicant at the time of the accident.

The defendant does a credible job, but a sober second thought suggests some minor revisions.

The phrase "along with all this food" is well chosen. Most of us realize that the effect of alcohol is diminished when accompanied by food ingestion. Let's make the drinking sound inevitable, however, by completing the phrase with "you, of course, had something to drink?"

Q. What time did you have that one beer?
A. Around noon.
Q. How is it that you recall having only one beer?
A. Well, most of the day I was carrying around this one empty beer can, and some of my relatives teased me about it.

The reasons for remembering are always important. Remembering what you did three months ago on a particular day is a most challenging task—unless that particular day was your birthday. Remembering how many beers you had at a picnic is not the sort of minutiae with which we crowd our memory—unless someone made a point of it.

Q. Now, Ms. Cassidy, I want you to turn to this jury and tell them, did that one beer you had at noon affect your ability to drive at 7:00 p.m. that evening?
A. No, not at all.

Here comes the important point, and we know it's important because of the introduction—an invitation for the defendant to look the jurors in the eye and deny the inference that she was under the influence of intoxicants at the time of the accident. The interrogator has framed a good question, but let's emphasize the time interim more emphatically. "Did that one beer you drank at noon, along with the hamburgers, hot dogs, and all the other food you had, affect your ability to drive *seven hours later* at 7:00 that evening?"

§ 3.47 Accident Information

Q. Ms. Cassidy, I'd like to talk about the time immediately after the accident. How did you feel after the accident?

A. I was in a state of shock; it happened so quickly. I just couldn't believe he ran the red light.

Q. After the accident did Officer Wright give you a breathalyzer test? Make you touch your nose? Make you say the alphabet backwards?

A. No.

Q. What sort of sobriety test did Officer Wright give you?

A. None—she just sent me home with a friend.

An experienced officer investigating a serious accident would certainly do something to determine the driving capabilities of a driver who exhibited some indications of being intoxicated. That is the point you want to make. The only suggestion is—ask your questions with more deliberation. Give the jury time to make the inference you want them to make. Structure a whole series of questions that will evoke a simple "no":

- Did she make you blow into a balloon?
- Did she draw a blood sample?
- Did she use *any* kind of scientific test to discover if you were under the influence of alcohol?
- Did she make you walk a straight line?
- Did she ask you to recite the alphabet backward?
- Or have you touch your nose with your eyes closed?

- Ms. Cassidy, did this officer investigating the accident give you any test at all to determine if your driving capacity was affected?

If a point is worth making, it's worth making well.

Q. I'd like for you to tell this jury how the accident happened. What time did you leave the reunion?
A. 6:30 p.m.
Q. Where were you going?
A. Heading home for supper.
Q. What direction was home?
A. My apartment is east of Lake Park. I went eastbound on Atlantic Drive.
Q. What did you see as you approached the intersection of Highway 7 from the west?
A. My light was green.
Q. Did you see the plaintiff's car?
A. Yes; as I approached the intersection, he was several hundred yards back from the intersection.
Q. Did your light stay green as you entered the intersection?
A. No, just as I entered the intersection, it changed to yellow.
Q. How fast were you going at that time?
A. Thirty to thirty-five miles per hour.
Q. Did you stop when your light changed to yellow?
A. No, I was practically in the intersection.
Q. Where were you when you next saw the plaintiff's car?
A. About halfway across the southbound lanes.
Q. Where in the intersection did the accident occur?
A. When he shot out in front of me; we collided just north of the northbound lanes.
Q. How far were you through the intersection when you collided?
A. More than halfway.

A good rule for direct examination is to use journalistic language. Begin your questions with who, what, where, when, and how (and sometimes why), and you'll keep the interrogation crisp and understandable.

One addendum could be made. After the defendant acknowledges that she was traveling thirty to thirty-five miles per hour, ask about the speed limit to assure the jury that the speed was lawful.

§ 3.48 Injuries

Q. Were you injured in this accident?
A. No.
Q. Why weren't you injured?
A. Because I was wearing my seat belt.
Q. Was the plaintiff wearing his seat belt?
A. No, he was not.

Neat ending. One of the defenses, or at least a fact from which the jury could find fault on the part of the plaintiff and reduce the verdict, is that the plaintiff wasn't wearing a seat belt, and therefore his injuries were caused not by the collision but by the impact with the light pole after he lost control of his car. The question "why weren't you injured?" could draw an objection as calling for a conclusion, but so what? If an objection is made and sustained go right on to the next question: "Were you wearing a seat belt?" Follow this with the other side of the coin, "Was the plaintiff wearing a seat belt?" The contrasting answers and the contrasting effects will make your point.

§ 3.49 Cross–Examination of Defendant

An intelligent, articulate graduate student will be a difficult target for cross examination. She has no apparent vulnerability as a personality. The attack must be directed against her story.

§ 3.50 Information Available

We have a number of sources of information about Sarah Cassidy that might provide material for cross-examination:

• Statement of facts

• Deposition

• Police report diagram

• Transcribed copy of radio transmission

§ 3.51 Analysis of Information

The statement of facts reveals that Sarah Cassidy had drunk two beers at the picnic and that she put the two empty cans in the car. Her plea to the careless driving charge was nolo contendere.

The deposition reveals two facts:

1. The plaintiff, Millman "seemed to come from nowhere."

2. She had a "single light beer" (contradicting the statement of facts, which indicates she had two beers).

The diagram confirms that the front of her car struck the side of the plaintiff's car.

The transcribed copy of the radio dispatch indicates that the investigating officer intended to "conduct arrest of intoxicated driver that appears to have caused accident."

§ 3.52 Executing the Cross–Examination

Our first task is to exploit the defendant's admission that the plaintiff seemed to "come from nowhere." More thorough interrogation at the deposition would have pinned her down by an inquiry, "Where was the front of the plaintiff's automobile in respect to the south curb line of Atlantic Drive when you first saw it?" We'll do the best with what we got.

Q. Ms. Cassidy, on the day of the accident you were twenty-two years of age and in good health. Is that correct.
A. Yes.
Q. You had excellent eyesight?
A. Yes.
Q. The day was clear and sunny?
A. Yes.
Q. Your windshield was clear?
A. Yes.
Q. And there weren't any buildings or trees or anything else to obscure your vision as you approached the intersection of Atlantic Drive and State road?
A. That's right.

You have laid the foundation for the argument, "Why didn't she see him?" Of course, your client is blackened by the same brush. He admits that he didn't see her "until the last second." The prevailing law precludes recovery by the plaintiff unless the defendant's negligence is greater than that of the plaintiff. Maybe this line of questioning will convince the jury that they're both guilty of the same offense (failing to keep a lookout), and that plaintiff shouldn't recover. The same danger is inherent in proving that the defendant took no evasive action, but if you wish to exploit that possibility, proceed as follows.

Q. Your car was in good mechanical condition?
A. Yes.
Q. The steering worked?
A. Yes.
Q. The brakes were working?
A. Yes.
Q. There were no other automobiles either to the right or left of you as you entered the intersection?
A. No.
Q. Your horn was in working order?
A. Yes.
Q. Now tell the jury, when you finally saw this other automobile, did you apply those brakes in good working order?
A. No.
Q. Did you swerve to the left or right?
A. No.
Q. You didn't do anything to avoid this collision after you saw the plaintiff, Mr. Millman, did you?

You can anticipate that somewhere in that line of questioning Sarah will protest, "I didn't have time to." When she does, respond with "That's for the jury to determine," or "If you had seen him sooner you would have had time, wouldn't you?"

The second task will be to utilize the different stories concerning the number of beers consumed. We've already discussed the possible impediments to the reception of this evidence, but since the witness testified on direct examination that she had one beer, the subject is now relevant to test credibility. Although the statement of facts does not disclose the source of the information that she had two beers, and that two empty cans were in her car at the time of the accident, let us assume that she disclosed such information to the investigating officer.

Q. Ms. Cassidy, you just told the jury that you had drunk only one beer at the picnic, is that right?

A. Yes.

Q. You remember being asked that same question by Officer Wright immediately after this accident, don't you?

A. Yes, I guess she asked me.

Q. And you told her the truth then, didn't you?

A. Yes.

Q. And you told her that you had drunk two beers, didn't you?

A. Yes.

Q. So when you told the jury that you had only one beer at that picnic, you weren't telling them the truth, were you?

This scenario seems too neat and unrealistic. Undoubtedly there will be some explanation for the different stories. The important thing to remember is that you want to use these differing versions to undercut credibility, rather than to prove that Cassidy was intoxicated. You want to prove that the witness attempted to fool the jury, and therein lies the harm. Note that the reference is not simply to her "prior testimony," but rather to "what you told the jury." When it comes to characterizing the two versions consider the options you have. "So when you told the jury that you had only one beer at the picnic ...

    1.   "you were confused, weren't you?"
    2.   "you were mistaken, weren't you?"
    3.   "you weren't telling the truth, were you?"
    4.   "you were lying, weren't you?"

The choice depends on the identity of the witness and how tough you want to be.

The third task is to exploit the observation by the police officer that Cassidy was intoxicated and arrested for careless driving. Such information cannot be easily incorporated into a cross-examination. The officer's behavior and her testimony discounts the fact that Cassidy was drunk, and in all likelihood the nolo contendere plea is inadmissible. This presents one of those instances in which the information is more apt to come before the jury in statement form from the attorney.

Q. You were intoxicated at the scene of the accident, weren't you?
A. No, I wasn't.
Q. Well, Officer Wright informed the dispatcher that you were intoxicated, didn't she?

Is this "dirty pool"? The statement will probably draw an objection—it is hearsay and there's no readily apparent exception—and it will probably be sustained. Is that an ethical concern?

The issue of the nolo contendere plea raises a similar issue. How legitimate is the question: "When you were charged with reckless driving, you didn't deny it, did you?" Add another issue to the ethical problem: Do you risk a motion for mistrial? All things considered, it is probably for the best that these two matters be left unexplored.

---

§ 3.53 Direct Examination of Major Frank Neil

An expert witness presents a peculiar challenge for the direct examiner. Frequently they will have a mind of their own as to how their testimony should be presented. Remember, you are the captain of the ship and bear the ultimate responsibility for your client's cause. Consequently you are the one to structure the sequence, the content, and the style of the testimony.

§ 3.54 Personal Information

Q. Please state your full name for the record.
A. Major Frank Neil.
Q. Major Neil, what do you do for a living?

108

It is exceedingly important that you develop a mindset towards a witness that will help you integrate your presentation. You are presenting him as an expert, one whose credentials you want to develop so that the jury will respect him as a man of learning and experience. He identifies himself with a title. The interrogator repeats the title. Okay so far. But what is the question posed? "What do you do for a living?" Is that the impression you want to create in the minds of the jury: that this witness is simply engaged in making a living? He's an "expert," by Jupiter! A man who pursues his profession for the pure intellectual stimulus it provides. He is a dedicated professional man of science, a seeker of truth unconcerned with such mundane matters as "making a living." You would not ask Pope John Paul II or Billy Graham "what do you do for a living?", would you? A more appropriate question for Major Neil would be, "What is your profession?"

A. I am an accident reconstructionist.

Q. What does an "accident reconstructionist" do?

A. Well, we investigate various types of accidents and collisions. By applying the principles of physics and various sciences, we determine the causes and effects of these collisions.

Perhaps the most significant rule of the interrogator of an expert is to serve as an interpreter of esoteric words and phrases. We begin in this instance, as in many cases involving expert testimony, with a need to explain the area of expertise. Mankind's tendency toward obfuscation and braggadocio seems to manifest itself most frequently in the area of job description. Garbage collectors identify themselves as "sanitary engineers"; janitors magically metamorphose into "maintenance engineers"; the unmistakable moniker "beekeeper" transmogrifies to the bewildering appellation "apiarist." Don't leave the jury perplexed and frustrated by such conceits.

Q. Do you have a specialty in the area of accident reconstruction?

A. Yes. Since 1985 I have studied automobile collisions almost exclusively.

109

Q. For whom do you do this type of study?
A. Various corporations contract out different types of research projects. Most of my work has involved automobile crash testing for the major auto makers in America and in Japan.
Q. Do you ever testify in trials such as this one?
A. Sometimes.
Q. Are you being paid for your time today?
A. Of course; I'm missing work to be here.

Why do lawyers always approach the subject of expert witness fees with such fear and trembling? Is there a realistic possibility that jurors will consider a lawyer's agreement to pay an expert as some perfidious pact to corrupt the fact-finding process?

Consider these factors:
1. Jurors are accustomed to having professionals charge for their services.
2. If you have a paid expert, chances are your opponent has a paid expert.
3. Unless your expert habitually testifies on your behalf, there is little likelihood that fee payment will be the subject of cross-examination.

Now, what decision do you make regarding the subject matter of expert witness fees? You have two choices:
1. Leave it alone.
2. Ask a question that attempts to legitimatize the payment.

The interrogator opted for number two. Let's analyze his effort. He asks if the witness is being paid "for your time today." The word choice has become a cliché. Somehow being paid for "time" is better than acknowledging that one is being paid for "testimony." But this studied effort to elevate your witness's motivation is not without danger. An aggressive opponent could well object to this editorializing conclusion: "I object your honor; it's up to the jury to decide why this witness is being paid."

The response, too, carries potential for harm. The witness responds, "Of course; I'm missing work to be here." If that's the true basis for his payment, then the amount of payment should jibe with the amount of money lost from his work. What is his "work"? In this instance he's a retired military officer. Will his retirement pay be reduced by the amount of the fee received? Of course not. In all likelihood his only work is testing and testifying. Now we're caught in a dog-chasing-his-own-tail puzzler. We can't discover how much he is getting paid to test and testify in this case until we find out how much he's losing because of his inability to test and testify in another case. (Couldn't a cross examiner have fun with this?) In this case it probably would have been better if option one had been followed.

Q. What has been the primary focus of your research since 1985?
A. Automobile seat belts. I have been hired by various corporations to help in the research and development of more effective seat belts.
Q. What is the nature of research?
A. Well, we study both real automobile collisions and simulated collisions to determine how effective seat belts are in preventing injuries to real people and dummies in such collisions. We monitor injuries to real people and dummies in various types of collisions at different speeds.
Q. What types of collisions have you studied?
A. Everything you can imagine—head-ons, broadsides, brick walls, even collisions with cattle and deer. We don't use real deer or cattle, of course.
Q. What is the extent of your formal education?
A. Well, I have a B.S. in mechanical engineering from Harvard, 1953, and a Ph.D. from Stanford, 1958, in biomechanical engineering.
Q. What is "biomechanical engineering"?
A. Very simply, it is the study of human movement and the effect of different types of physical force on the human body.

The sequence of the interrogation is a bit confusing. Chronologically it would have made more sense to get the formal education up front before a recitation of the expert's post-graduation experience. Once the expert has identified his specialty, why not ask, "Have you had any formal education that prepared you to develop this specialty in accident reconstruction?"

The recitation itself is not too convincing. Of what significance is it to a typical juror with a high school education that the expert has a "B.S." and a "Ph.D." in biomechanical engineering? If Ph.D. is frequently interpreted as "piled higher and deeper," you can imagine how jurors might interpret B.S.

Having an undergraduate degree translates to four years of college studies, which can include as many as thirty-six

111

semester hours (or approximately six hundred classroom hours) in the area of major study. A doctorate degree is a "terminal degree": the highest that can be attained in an academic field. It is awarded only after the presentation of a doctoral dissertation. Although unstated, it was necessarily preceded by a master's degree, which meant an additional two years of study and the writing of a master's thesis. Doesn't this sound more important than the perfunctory and succinct muttering of some meaningless initials?

Q. Do you have any professional certifications?
A. Yes, I am a certified biomechanical engineer.

Again, we presume too much from the jury. What does certification mean? Does it require some formal education, some experience in the field, some testing? The jury is entitled to know.

Q. What did you do after leaving Stanford in 1958?
A. I entered the U.S. Air Force.
Q. What military rank did you achieve in the Air Force?
A. Major.
Q. How long were you in the Air Force?
A. Twenty-five years.
Q. What did you do in the service?

Remember, your witness is under oath. Do you really want to make the general inquiry, "What did you do in the service?" Imagine the possible answers.

Seriously, it would be better to ask, "Did your official duties as an officer in the United States Air Force involve your area of expertise in biomechanical engineering?"

A. I put my education to work studying the crash resistance of airplane cockpit canopies. I worked with a team of research scientists and engineers to develop safer cockpits in military aircraft in crash or ditching situations.

Q. In the course of this research for the Air Force, did you do any research on the effectiveness of safety belts in plane crashes?

A. Yes, I did.

Q. About what percentage of the twenty-five years of research for the military involved the study of safety belts in plane crashes?

A. I'd say, roughly, about fifty percent.

Q. When did you leave the Air Force?

A. 1984.

Q. What was the nature of your leaving?

A. I retired.

Some questions trigger curiosity. When a person hears a witness being asked, "Why did you leave your job?", some other questions immediately spring to mind: "Was he fired?"; "Why?"; "Did he quit?"; "Did he have to?" Why face this possibility? Tell your witness, "When I ask you 'when did you leave the Air Force?', respond with, 'I retired in 1984.'"

Q. Your Honor, I tender this witness as an expert.
Court: His expert testimony will be received.

How this practice of tendering a witness as an expert ever began is a mystery. Why it is proliferating is more easily understood. It is a fact that one of the oldest and most respected institutes for training advocates had its genesis in Colorado, a state that follows the practice. Colorado jurists, sitting as presiding judges in the mock trials conducted by the National Institute for Trial Advocacy, insisted that the student advocates tender their witnesses to the judge as an expert.

The naive students, thinking that they were being instructed in prevailing trial protocol, took the practice back home to their native jurisdictions, and what was once a local anomaly is now posturing as a national norm. Thus, Colorado must bear the blame as the source of a second scourge (along with Rocky Mountain spotted fever)—the practice of tendering a witness to the court as an expert.

The better practice, of course, is simply to establish the credentials of your expert and then solicit his opinions. If your opponent questions those credentials, let him object and then let the court rule. The court's pronouncement that the witness is an expert unnecessarily creates confusion and intrudes upon the jury's function as sole evaluator of a witness's credibility.

---

§ 3.55   Accident Information

Q. Major Neil, have you investigated a collision involving the plaintiff in this case, Herb Millman, and Sarah Cassidy, which occurred on May 26, 1992?
A. Yes, I have.
Q. How did you come to investigate this particular collision?
A. At your request.
Q. When did I contact you?
A. Several months ago.
Q. Did I pay for your time?
A. Of course; I have bills to pay.

Again attention is directed to a payment made to the expert, a subject best left unemphasized. Remember the old maxim, "The more you stir it, the more it stinks." If you must ask the question, certainly the witness should be groomed to respond less defensively than, "Of course; I have bills to pay."

Q. How did you go about your investigation?
A. I studied police reports and photographs of the damaged automobiles.
Q. What did you do next?
A. I calculated the "speed estimate."
Q. What do you mean?
A. I figured out about how fast each car was traveling.
Q. How did you do that?

A. Based upon the weight of each vehicle, the damage to each vehicle, and the distance that the plaintiff's car travelled after impact, I calculated the relative speeds of each car at the time of impact.

Q. What were those speeds?

A. The plaintiff's car was traveling forty miles per hour; and the defendant's car was traveling thirty-five miles per hour at the time of impact.

Q. Describe the damage to each vehicle, as you observed them in the photographs.

A. The Buick, the plaintiff's car, sustained severe damage to the front fender area of the driver's side, consistent with a broad-side-type collision. The defendant's Pontiac was damaged severely in the front grill and hood area.

The basic formula for arranging the testimony of the expert is as follows:

- Who is he?
- What does he know about the subject matter of his testimony, generally?
- What does he know about the specific elements in the instant case?
- How did he get that information?
- What did he do with that information?
- What conclusion did he reach?

The interrogator follows that general approach by asking short, direct "journalistic" questions that permit the witness to give detailed explanations. There is no magic to the sequence, but it does bear the stamp of being chronological. Note that the Federal Rules permit the opinion to come before the bases of the opinion are elicited, an option that may in some instances be desirable.

---

§ 3.56 Injuries

Q. Do you have an opinion as to the effectiveness of automobile seat belts in the collision involving Mr. Millman and Sarah Cassidy?

A. Yes, I do.

Q. How certain are you of your opinion?

A. I am extremely confident in the accuracy of my opinion.

Every witness must express a requisite degree of certainty before his testimony has probative value. A lay witness testifying as to facts who states "the light may have been green," "the light could have been green," or "I think that the light was probably green" should have such speculations stricken.

The expert witness is no different. His opinion testimony must be stated with the requisite degree of certainty in order to overcome a challenge that it is speculation. The magic words that are most often used are "do you have an opinion based on reasonable scientific certainty...." The phrase is familiar and soothing to the trial judge, so it is the shibboleth of choice for most trial lawyers. But must this phrase, which expresses the minimal threshold expression of certainty, always be used? What if your witness is certain of his opinion? Must you water down his expression by having him say his opinion is based on a reasonable certainty? Ask yourself this question: If you were prosecuting a criminal case, would you rather have an eyewitness testify that he is "certain" of the defendant's identity or "reasonably certain" of his identity?

Q. What is your opinion?
A. Seat belts would have been very effective in reducing injuries in this particular collision.
Q. Why is that?
A. Well, in a collision of this type the driver of the car that was struck broadside would be thrown around—jolted pretty hard—without a seat belt. But, if worn, the seat belt would keep the driver behind the wheel and substantially reduce the violent jolt of the body. As for the other driver, a seat belt would possibly prevent that person from going through the windshield.

Now we come to that point where "the rubber meets the road," and just when the interrogator must tighten up the questioning and sharpen his inquiries, he begins to falter. First of all, the opinion solicited (and as a result, the response given) is much too general. We're not really interested if "seat belts would have been effective in reducing injuries." The question posed in the deposition is much more to the

116

point: "In your opinion, ... would these injuries have occurred but for the fact that the plaintiff was wearing his
available seat belt?" (Note the difference between "would
they have occurred" and "effective in reducing injuries.")
The response is correspondingly more assertive and more
convincing: "No, the injuries would not have occurred if he
had been wearing his seat belt." The interrogator would
have been well-advised to have reprised the deposition exchange.

Q. Major Neil, please assume that in the collision between Mr.
Millman's car and Sarah Cassidy's car that Mr. Millman was
not wearing his seat belt. Also assume that, as a result of the
collision, he sustained back injuries and a fractured tibial
plateau on his right knee. Assuming those facts as true, do
you have any opinion as to how effective a seat belt would
have been in preventing those injuries?

The facts upon which this expert is basing his opinion are
not in dispute. The speeds of the vehicles, the type of impact,
the weather conditions, the use or nonuse of seat belts—every
facet of the case is agreed upon by the parties. Why, then,
should we ask the witness to assume anything? It is much
more effective if he gives his opinion and then, when asked to
explain the basis for that opinion, states (as facts, not assumptions) that Millman was not wearing a seat belt and that he
sustained back injuries and a fractured tibial plateau.

A. Yes, I do.
Q. What is your opinion?
A. A seat belt would greatly lessen the "sideways jolt," which
can cause back injuries. Therefore, a seat belt would greatly
lessen, maybe even prevent, back injuries in a broadside-type
collision. As for the knee injury, a seat belt would probably
prevent that type of injury, since the knee would be prevented
from smashing into the dashboard of the car if a seat belt is
worn.
Q. How confident are you in this opinion?
A. I am very confident that seat belts would lessen or prevent
those types of injuries.

An expert can never be turned loose to express his opinion as the muse directs. This is the guts of the defense. The jury is being asked to disregard the relative skills of the drivers and the actual mechanics of the collision, and direct their attention to the plaintiff's failure to wear a seat belt and the significant consequences of that failure. Such a challenge demands assertive and convincing pronouncements.

The witness says, "A seat belt *would greatly lessen* the sudden 'sideways jolt.'" Bad. Change to "greatly lessens." Better. Additional editing is needed.

1. "Which can cause back injuries." Bad. "Causes back injuries." Better.

2. "A seat belt would greatly lessen, maybe even prevent, back injuries in a broadside-type collision." Bad. "A seat belt lessens back injuries and in my opinion would have prevented Mr. Millman's back injury in this broadside-type collision." Better.

3. "A seat belt would probably prevent that type of injury [to the knee] since the knee would be prevented from smashing into the dashboard." Bad. "In my opinion, if Mr. Millman had worn a seat belt, it would have prevented his knee from smashing into the dashboard and he would have suffered no knee injury." Better.

Don't think that we are simply dealing with the niceties of persuasive language. As the testimony now stands, especially with the use of "probably," there is a good likelihood that the expert's opinion would be stricken as being speculative.

§ 3.57 Cross–Examination of Major Frank Neil

The cross-examination of an expert witness is especially daunting for a neophyte advocate. Chances are he will be a more seasoned courtroom performer than you—and you'll be encountering him in his familiar area of expertise. The temptation is to simply say, "No questions, your Honor." Resist that urge. "Stiffen your sinews, summon the air of a tiger and charge into the breach. The first step for such an heroic undertaking is to refocus your perception of the expert who you are going to confront.

One technique used by a successful advocate is to picture the expert as a baby sitting in a bathtub and playing with a rubber ducky. Got that image in your mind? Now, go after him!

§ 3.58 Information Available

• Curriculum vitae

• Deposition

§ 3.59 Analysis of Information

We have the benefit of Major Neil's curriculum vitae and deposition. His education is impressive: an undergraduate degree from Harvard and a doctorate from Stanford. His experience is credible, but it is only obliquely related to the area in which he will be testifying. He considers himself an expert in "accident reconstruction," but where is his expertise in the use of seat belts and the effects arising from their use or non-use? The extent of his experience in this area should have been explored at the deposition, but since it wasn't, we must consider it to be a proper subject for cross-examination.

The deposition reveals that Major Neil will testify that, in his opinion:

1.   the original impact caused the plaintiff to be thrown to his left, denting the driver's door, and then be thrown to his right;

2.   the plaintiff was unable to control his vehicle;

3.   if the plaintiff had been wearing his seat belt he would have been "in a position to control his vehicle" (note the phrasing);

4.   the plaintiff struck the pole at a speed of twenty-five miles per hour;

5.   the plaintiff could have avoided the pole had he remained behind the steering wheel;

6.   the collision with the pole caused the plaintiff to be thrown forward with sufficient force to put a two-and-one-half-inch dent in the steel dash;

7.   the first impact is "almost certainly related to [the plaintiff's] lower back problems"; and

8.   the injuries to the plaintiff's back and knee would not have occurred had he been wearing his seat belt.

Some of his opinions are of little consequence because they are conceded facts—the speeds of the vehicles, the directions they were traveling, the point of impact, and the areas of damage on the cars. The other opinions listed are more significant, but they are subject to attack.

As you read the deposition, you come away with two impressions. First, the witness is an advocate, rather than a disinterested person of science seeking the truth. Notice how he describes this accident: "Mr. Millman's left front quarter panel struck the leading edge of the defendant's vehicle." A strange way to describe an indisputable broadside of the plaintiff's vehicle, as depicted in the police report.

Second, he is willing to express an opinion about anything that will help the cause. He states in his deposition that the initial impact "is almost certainly related to [the plaintiff's] lower back problems" and that the injury to the plaintiff's knee "would not have occurred if he had been wearing his seat belt."

These opinions were reached without any expertise in the field of medicine and without any scientific experiments or knowledge of important facts (Mr. Millman's size, the dimensions of the front seat, the amount of play in the seat belt had it been worn, etc.) Many experts are vulnerable because of the inadequacies of the information or experiments on which their opinions are based. Major Neil is such an expert.

Another area of cross-examination is revealed by a critical review of his opinion that the use of a seat belt would have afforded Millman an opportunity to avoid the light pole. Consider some undisputed scientific facts:

1. An object's speed expressed in feet per second is approximately one and one-half times its speed expressed in miles per hour. The expert stated Millman's speed at initial impact was forty miles per hour and that he struck the light pole at twenty-five miles per hour. If the deceleration was uniform, the average speed as it traveled those 40 feet (distance between point of impact and pole) was 32 miles per hour or 48 feet per second. This means that Millman had less than a second to avoid contact with the pole.

2. The average reaction time is three-fourths of a second. Certainly, when one is unexpectedly hit and jostled about (as Millman would have been even with the seat belt in

place) the time of reaction would be even longer. But even using average reaction time, the Millman car would have traveled 36 feet (¾ of 48) before he could have reacted by attempting to swerve or stop.

The cross-examination of Major Neil should include:

1. a challenge to his expertise in the limited area of safety restraints particularly relating to automobile accidents;

2. an attack on his lack of pertinent information and experimentation;

3. a review of the basic laws of physics, which refute his opinion that Millman could have avoided contact with the pole had he been wearing a seat belt; and

4. an acknowledgement that he is not a medical expert and is therefore incompetent to render an opinion on injury causation.

§ 3.60   Executing the Cross–Examination

The magic formula is "plan your work and work your plan." Having planned our cross-examination topics, we're ready for the second phase. Translating those ideas into questions can be an intimidating chore, but there are some techniques that can be employed that make the undertaking less threatening. Consider cross-examination as an opportunity to present information to the jury. For instance, you might want the jury to know that the witness is related to the party for whom he has testified. Procedure prevents us from turning to the jury and announcing, "This witness is the plaintiff's brother." But what we can do is direct that statement (note "statement," not "question") to the witness and request his confirmation. Thus, "You are the brother of the plaintiff, isn't that so?" This style of interrogation will afford us a significant measure of control, and if all goes well (but it never does), the cross-examination will consist of probing observations that the witness must confirm.

Although this method of basic, low-risk cross-examination has the obvious advantage of control, it can be deadly dull in the execution if the same confirmatory phrase is used without variation:

You're John Stevens, isn't that correct?

And you live at 1313 Stewart, isn't that correct?

121

You were a party to a contract with my client, Ben Healy, isn't that correct?

Even if the subject matter has some inherent interest, this repetitive "isn't that correct?" will bring on glazed eyes among the jurors. There are other phrases available, e.g., "correct?", "isn't that true?", "that's true, isn't it?", etc. In fact, rhythm and inflection alone can make it clear that a series of questioning statements are being made, and for much of your interrogation there will be no need to use any direct expression of confirmation.

Using this basic approach, let's see how we can frame some verbal thrusts on cross-examination. Our first task is to exploit the expert's limited experience.

Q. Major Neil, the title you bear is a military title, isn't it?
A. Yes.
Q. You were in the Air Force for a quarter of a century?
A. Yes, I was.
Q. Of course, you did no studies regarding automobiles and seat belts while you were in the service, did you?
A. No, I was in charge of studying crash resistance of cockpit canopies.
Q. And that was your primary line of work during a substantial part of your career, wasn't it?
A. Yes.

This line of cross-examination is neither high-risk nor high-yield; however, it is usually necessary to provide information to remind the jury that the elderly sage who sits before them had other interests in his life besides studying the effects of the non-use of seat belts.

Our second task is to demonstrate the expert's lack of pertinent information and experimentation.

Q. During the years you were an officer in the United States Air Force in charge of studying crash resistance of cockpit canopies, I am sure that you conducted many tests and experiments.
A. We certainly did.

Again, it's easy to get agreement when you seek confirmation of complimentary information.   Note how solicitous we are of the witness as we begin to coax him down the garden path.   He wasn't "in the service"; he was "an officer in the United States Air Force."   He wasn't "working on a project"; he was "in charge."   Our goal, of course, is to draw a contrast between his work in the Air Force, conducted in proper scientific fashion, and his off-the-cuff observations in the instant case.

Q.   In conducting those tests and experiments, you worked with other men who were well trained and educated, I assume.
A.   Yes, I was proud of our group.
Q.   Major Neil, I have seen tests on television where mannequins are used in moving automobiles and slow-motion movies are taken to demonstrate the effects of a crash.   Did you use similar tests in the service?
A.   Yes, we did.

You could follow this with an inquiry if such a test was conducted in this case, but it's questionable whether the jury would hold it against him for failing to undertake an expensive test in a case such as this.   But perhaps another tack can be followed.

Q.   There are certain testing devices, I assume, that can measure the effects of movement and force on human bodies without crashing a car into a wall, aren't there?
A.   Yes.
Q.   These devices and these tests can be conducted to determine the effect of wearing or not wearing a seat belt, can't they?
A.   Yes, hundreds of such tests have been conducted over the years.
Q.   Before coming to testify in this case, you, of course, conducted such tests and experiments using the particular facts of this accident.

Utilize a number of styles in your cross-examination interrogation. Here we have the anticipatory question. You are not asking ("Did you conduct a test?"), nor are you accusing ("You didn't conduct a test, did you?"). You are anticipating that any competent expert would have conducted a test.

A. No, I didn't. I didn't think it was necessary.
Q. Well, that's for the jury to determine, Mr. Neil. You didn't conduct any tests or experiments, did you?

This is much too critical a question to ask without knowing the answer. You should have requested information regarding tests on pre-trial discovery and determined that he didn't conduct any.

A. No, I didn't.
Q. Did the lawyer who hired you tell you to conduct any experiments or tests?
A. No.
Q. Did he tell you *not* to conduct any experiments or tests?

In contrast, you don't know the answers to these questions, but who cares whether the response is affirmative or negative. The answers will probably be "no," in which case the inference is that the lawyer doesn't care much about the case. If the answer is "yes," the disinterest lies with the witness.

Q. Mr. Neil, on direct examination you indicated that you reviewed the reports that were filed in this case.
A. Yes.
Q. And those reports afforded you all the information you had in reaching the conclusions you gave to this jury?

A. Yes.

The previous question demonstrates the technique of closing the door before you start chasing the cat. The witness has committed himself to the fact that *all* of his information was secondhand. You are now free to ask the following questions, knowing that the answers will be in the negative. Without this prefatory commitment, the witness might well respond in the affirmative. Does this suggest that expert witnesses might lie? Sad to say, yes.

Q. You didn't go to the scene?
A. No.
Q. You didn't examine the vehicles involved?
A. No.
Q. You didn't observe the appearance of the skid marks or the damage to the cement pole?
A. No.
Q. You didn't talk to either Mr. Millman or Ms. Cassidy?

Think of all the things he could have done and didn't. If you feel feisty enough, you might want to conclude by reprising your two-pronged inquiry as to whether the lawyer asked him to do these things or if he asked him not to.

The third task is to refute the conclusion that Mr. Millman could have avoided contact with the pole if he had been wearing his seat belt.

Q. You, then, Mr. Neil, have given your opinion to this jury based solely on information from reports, and I assume, the application of the laws of physics?
A. That's correct.
Q. First, let's review some of the information on those reports and the conclusions you drew from those reports. Mr. Millman was traveling forty miles per hour and Ms. Cassidy was traveling thirty-five miles per hour, correct?
A. Correct.

125

Q.   Incidentally, Mr. Neil, I believe you said on direct examination that the side of Mr. Millman's vehicle struck the front of Ms. Cassidy's vehicle. You misspoke when you said that, didn't you?

Some issues are best approached "incidentally." This is one of them. The diagram and the facts all indicate that Cassidy hit Millman. Why let this expert's cutesy remark that Millman's car "struck the leading edge of the defendant's vehicle" go unchallenged. Give him the benefit of having misspoke and let him recant with a "yes." If he says "no, he did strike the front of her vehicle with the side of his," just roll your eyes and proceed.

Q.   And you say that he struck the pole traveling twenty-five miles per hour.
A.   That's my opinion.
Q.   Well, that's what you're getting paid for, isn't it—your opinions?

Don't let him equivocate now. Hold his feet to the fire. This exchange could evolve into another "incidental" inquiry such as, "Incidentally, Mr. Neil, how much are you getting paid?"

Q.   Now let's see if we can agree on some points.

This preface is beguilingly disarming. People like people who are agreeable. This shows your own willingness to be non-confrontational and may help to move the proceedings along.

Q.   First of all, would you agree that when a car is struck broadside, as indicated in the diagram, by a car travelling thirty-five miles an hour that the driver will be jostled, regardless of whether he's wearing a seat belt or not?

———————

The ideal question to ask on cross-examination is one to which the jury responds before the witness. The juries will whisper "yes" to themselves. Who cares what the witness says?

———————

Q.   And that jostling, which will occur when hit by a three-thousand-pound vehicle traveling thirty-five miles an hour, can affect the ability of a driver to control the vehicle, whether he's wearing a seat belt or not, isn't that correct?

———————

Again, we don't care what the response will be. Either he buys into your proposition, or he runs the risk of losing his credibility.

How did we arrive at this figure of three thousand pounds? Ms. Cassidy was driving a 1986 Pontiac LeMans, which probably weights about a ton and a half. This illustrates a point that should be apparent to all advocates. It is possible to out-expert the expert—not in the extent of your knowledge, but in the extent of your preparation. It shouldn't take much research to determine the weight of a 1986 LeMans and the amount of force exerted when an object of that weight, moving thirty-five miles an hour, strikes something. From the deposition it is apparent that brother Neil didn't make those computations. Proceed as follows, asking questions that will have one of two results: They will confirm your point that the initial impact was severe enough to cause Millman to lose control regardless of his use of a seat belt; or, that this "expert" is either not so smart or not well-prepared.

———————

Q.   How do you scientific people figure out the amount of force exerted by a moving body?

Sometimes you can give a witness on cross-examination a free rein and know that you'll not be hurt. This is one such occasion.

Q. Using that method, will you compute how much force this 1986 LeMans traveling thirty-five miles an hour would have exerted?
A. I don't know how much a 1986 LeMans weighs.
Q. You didn't bother to find that out?
A. No.
Q. If I told you that I found out by calling a local Pontiac dealer that it weighs 2,940 pounds, would that sound correct?

See how much fun you can have? Don't be intimidated by experts. Get prepared and take them on.

Now test another area of his expertise. Let him tell the jury how speed in miles per hour translates to speed in feet per second.

Q. You told us Mr. Millman was traveling forty miles an hour when he was struck. How fast was he traveling in feet per second?
A. At forty miles per hour his vehicle was moving about sixty feet a second.
Q. How did you make that computation?
A. You take the number of feet in a mile, 5280, and divide by the number of seconds in an hour, 3600. That ratio is about one and one-half. So to get speed in feet per second from speed in miles per hour, you simply multiply by one and a half and you have the approximate figure.

You could stop here with your inquiry about Millman's speed, but fairness dictates further refinements.

Q. You also say he was traveling twenty-five miles per hour when he hit the pole.

A. Correct.

Q. His speed had diminished fifteen miles an hour in the forty feet he traveled between collision and impact?

A. Right.

Q. If that deceleration was gradual, would it be fair to say that having started at forty miles an hour and ended at twenty-five miles per hour, that the average speed of his automobile as it moved those forty feet was thirty-seven and one-half miles per hour?

A. Yes.

Q. And using your formula, tell us how much time passed between getting hit broadside by this LeMans traveling thirty-five miles per hour and hitting the pole.

A. Well, at thirty-seven and one-half miles per hour, he was traveling fifty-five feet per second. That would mean he traveled those forty feet in less than eight-tenths of a second.

See, you don't have to always lead in cross. Let the witness talk sometimes—when you know that you can't get hurt.

Q. Mr. Neil, tell this jury what reaction time is.

A. It's the time it takes for the body to receive a stimulus and respond to that stimulus in some fashion.

Q. Accident reconstructionists use this factor in reaching their expert opinions, don't they?

A. Yes, we do.

Q. Mr. Neil, I'll ask you a question that can be answered "yes" or "no." The figure accepted by experts who deal in automobile safety and accident reconstruction is that the average reaction time is three-fourths of a second. Correct?

A. Yes.

Q. And after the reaction time lapses, there is additional time that must pass before the vehicle can respond. That is, if the driver responds to an emergency by applying his brake, three-fourths of a second passes before his foot hits the brake, then additional time passes as the vehicle comes to a stop. Correct?

A. Correct.

You have laid the foundation for your argument. Millman had less than eight-tenths of a second to:

1. recover from the jostling,
2. react, and
3. have the vehicle respond.

You should be able to refute the expert's opinion that Millman could have avoided the cement pole if he had been wearing a seat belt.

Our fourth and final task is to exclude the witness's opinions regarding medical causation.

When an expert begins to expand his field of expertise into areas beyond his learning and experience, his excursion into omnicompetence should be aborted immediately, instead of waiting for cross-examination. On deposition the witness was permitted to respond to two questions involving medical causation: "Mr. Neil, please describe the relationship, if any, between Mr. Millman's vehicle crash events and his injuries"; and "In your opinion, Mr. Neil, would these injuries have occurred but for the fact that the plaintiff was not wearing his available seat belt?" If the direct examination at trial is a replay of the deposition, the opposing lawyer should have responded by objecting to both questions on the grounds that they called for a medical opinion. The objections could have been preceded by a request to "voir dire the witness" or "examine the witness in aid of an objection." This permits the interjection of a few questions directed to the information needed to make an objection. Leading questions can be used. In this instance the voir dire would proceed with the same type of questioning illustrated below. Your interrogation would be followed by an objection: "I object, your Honor. The witness is not qualified to testify to medical matters that call for medical expertise." Waiting to cross-examine is a poor second option.

Q. You told this jury on direct examination about what you thought had caused Mr. Millman's injuries.
A. Yes, I did—his failure to use a seat belt.
Q. It is *Mister* Neil, and not *Doctor* Neil?
A. Yes.
Q. You never received a degree in medicine?

A. No.
Q. You don't advertise yourself as a medical expert do you?
A. No.
Q. You do know that there are medical experts in this community qualified to give opinions as to the cause of injuries, don't you?
A. I guess there are.
Q. You aren't parading before this jury as such an expert, are you?
A. No.

F. CONCLUSION

§ 3.61 Lessons to Be Learned

The profession of advocacy is a demanding and exacting calling that requires the exercise of numerous skills. The foregoing exercise is designed to remind us that trial work is a two-step process, a process best expressed by the motto, "Plan your work, then work your plan."

A second lesson is that preparation and execution are inexorably linked together and that a trial is truly a gestalt experience. We often study the various features of a trial as if each were a discrete exercise, related to others only by the sequence in which they occur. Such is not the case. Our formal theories of recovery and defense, and our informal theories of persuasion, must permeate every facet of the case, from pleading to closing argument.

A third lesson that this exercise is meant to demonstrate that the persuasion process is seldom an explosive, love-at-first-sight experience. It is more properly likened to a gradually evolving relationship in which many seemingly insignificant events and experiences lead to ultimate conviction. As expressed by the lyricist, "Little things mean a lot." Those "little things" are the techniques that have been addressed in this case analysis.

CHAPTER 4

INITIATING THE ATTORNEY–
CLIENT RELATIONSHIP

*"You make a first impression only
once"*
Kenneth Albers

Analysis

§ 4.1 Expectation of the Client—Generally

The client who seeks the professional services of an advocate has a need. What that need and concomitant expectation is will vary with the client. Too often the advocate is willing to identify that need as simply winning a lawsuit. The plaintiff wants money—the defendant wants to keep from paying money. The plaintiff wants equitable relief—the defendant resists the relief sought. In a word, the plaintiff desires to upset the status quo and seize a prize. The defendant desires to be left undisturbed because he "lies possessed."

Certainly that simplistic approach will suffice in many cases. But the psychological factors involved in human disputes are varied indeed. Consider the following.

§ 4.2 Expectation of the Client—Exoneration

Mrs. Jones is involved in an intersection collision. Her seven year old daughter sitting in the front seat crashes into the windshield and suffers permanently disfiguring facial scars. Mr. Jones was aware that the seat belts were broken but had not had them repaired. The Joneses seek legal help. What are their needs? Just winning the lawsuit is not enough. Mr. and Mrs. Jones must be exonerated from the guilt they feel regarding their child's injury. A quick pre-trial settlement might not be enough to meet that need. Even if the attorneys agree as to amount, it might be best to let Mrs. Jones tell her story of her own careful driving and the fault of the other before terminating the case. Then capitulation by the opposition would more likely be interpreted as an acknowledgment of guilt and exoneration of the Joneses. Not just an informal settlement but a quasi-judicial resolution of innocence is the need.

§ 4.3 Expectation of the Client—Revenge

Thelma Meyer is a beautician who needs the help of an assistant. She hires Betty Conyer, a young girl living alone who has no schooling. Thelma patiently trains Betty in the skills of a beautician and shares with her the secrets of certain applications which she has developed through years in her profession. After three years Betty suddenly quits and within two weeks opens a competing beauty shop down the street and sends notices of the opening to all of Thelma's customers whose names she had secured from Thelma's personal file. Thelma hires a lawyer. What are her needs?

133

Basically, she wants revenge. A damage award is incidental. She couldn't bear to be within a stone's throw of that "thieving ingrate." Injunctive relief is needed—and quick!

§ 4.4 Expectations of the Client—Justification

Fred Brown, a bachelor engineer, started his business endeavors in a back alley shop manufacturing a mechanical device which he invented. Over a period of twenty years of hard work he has developed a large company hiring over two hundred employees and selling its product throughout the world. A commercial air plane equipped with Fred's product fails in flight and eighty-five passengers are killed. Lawsuits are filed naming Fred's company as one of the defendants, claiming that his product was defective and seeking millions in damages. Fred has $500,000–$1,000,000 coverage. He seeks legal help. What are his needs?

The pending lawsuits are a threat to his very existence. Not only does he face financial disaster but, even worse, a repudiation of the value of his life's work. An offer of settlement, even if paid for by insurance, would be considered as a confession that his inventiveness and engineering savvy were unworthy. The only thing that will satisfy him will be if the whole batch of claims are "thrown out of court." It will take a lot of patient counseling to meet Fred's needs and still avoid the risk of severe financial loss.

§ 4.5 Expectations of the Client—Third Party Resolution

Tom and Bill have been long time associates in business. Bill intends to retire. The two had made an agreement that the continuing partner would pay the retiring partner a certain percentage of the preceding year's profit in purchase of his interest. Tom thought the figure was 30%. Bill contends it was 35%. Both acknowledge the dispute to be an honest difference of opinion. They ask legal help. What are their needs?

No ill feelings with Tom and Bill. They both feel that they are honorable gentlemen with long years of pleasant association between them. Unfortunately, there's a pretty good sum of money involved but they disdain the thought of formal litigation to resolve a dispute between old friends. A voluntary "split the difference" approach might indicate that either one (particularly the one who might suggest it) was not so honest in his position. What they need is a third party to arbitrate the matter, hear both sides and announce the "fair figure."

Whatever the problem or the psychological factors involved, the prime expectation of the client is that the lawyer will be sensitive to his needs—and then fulfill them.

§ 4.6 Expectations From the Lawyer—Generally

Several years ago the Missouri Bar Association conducted a survey which attempted to ascertain the attitudes that the public had toward the legal profession in regard to our role and reputation, availability and adequacy of legal service and competence of the lawyer and satisfaction of the client. The raw responses were analyzed, conclusions were reached and recommendations made. The more pertinent information follows:

THE ROLE AND REPUTATION OF THE LAWYER

Objective

To determine public impressions regarding services performed by lawyers, the public reputation of lawyers in general and the effect the use of a lawyer's service has on this reputation.

Findings

Non-user—lawyers in general		*User—lawyers in general*	
Very Good	21.3%	Very Good	25.4%
Good	50.7%	Good	40.2%
Average	8.0%	Average	14.9%
Poor	10.7%	Poor	6.5%
Don't Know	9.3%	Don't Know	13.0%

The above figures take on new significance when compared with the ratings which the users give their own lawyers. See list below:

Users—personal attorney	
Very Good	48.9%
Good	36.0%
Average	2.2%
Poor	4.4%
Don't Know	8.5%

Note how the very good and good ratings climb ... and the average and poor ratings drop.

In rating the reputation of *lawyers in general* these same respondents considered the following influences (in order of importance): honesty, shady or crooked dealings, high fees and an attitude of getting as much as possible, political activity (bad), participation in civic and community affairs, participation in church affairs, drinking and marital discord, and wealth.

In rating their *own lawyer "average"* respondents mentioned the following factors, given in order of their importance: professional ability, honesty, politics (bad).

Respondents rating their individual lawyer's reputation "poor" considered the following influences, given in order of importance: drinking and marital discord, poor professional ability, shady and crooked dealings. These same respondents in rating lawyers generally mentioned only shady and crooked dealings.

Conclusion

Perhaps the most important findings in this area are those showing the factors which influence the public in judging the reputation of a lawyer. The most frequently mentioned was professional ability. Next in importance were honesty and participation in civic, church and governmental affairs. Lawyers do not seem to realize the importance placed on professional competency by the layman. Lawyers do realize, however, the importance placed by the layman on participation of the lawyer in civic and church affairs, and on his honesty and integrity.

Other factors which the layman use to a lesser degree in assessing a lawyer's reputation as favorable are family background, education and impressive clients such as banks and corporations.

Dishonesty, solicitation and other unethical practices are the most important factors which detract from the reputation of the profession in the opinion of both lawyers and laymen.

The private life of the lawyer does not escape the eyes of the public either. The most important factor affecting the individual's rating of his own lawyer's reputation as poor was drinking and marital discord.

The educational level of the layman does have an effect on his attitude toward the profession; the more highly educated groups rate the general reputation and professional ability of the lawyer higher than the less educated groups. Economic position does not affect attitude as much as does occupation or education, although persons in the upper income groups tend to have a better opinion of the professional ability of lawyers than do those in the lowest income groups. The reputation of lawyers in non-urban areas is better than in cities and the lawyers themselves realize this.

It is interesting to note that the representation of criminals does not appear to have much affect on the opinion of the public as to the reputation of the lawyer.

SATISFACTION OF CLIENT

Objective

To determine how well the public is satisfied with legal services; which facets of the attorney-client relationship produce positive and negative impressions on the client; and whether the lawyer recognizes which aspects of the relationship most affect his public image.

Findings

The responses to both the depth interviews and the questionnaire show that the overwhelming majority of clients are satisfied with the legal services they have received and would use the same lawyer again. The depth interviews indicated a 91 per cent incidence of satisfaction; the questionnaire 95 per cent. The depth interview question concerning the use of the same lawyer showed that 85 per cent of clients would use the same lawyer again.

Dissatisfaction was expressed by only 7 per cent of the depth interview respondents and 5 per cent of the questionnaire respondents. Lack of promptness and failure of the attorney to keep the client informed were two of the main reasons listed for dissatisfaction. It is interesting to note that less than 2 per cent of the 2500 questionnaire respondents listed results as the cause for dissatisfaction. The percentage of depth interviewees listing results as the cause for dissatisfaction was even smaller.

A comparison, in order of importance, placed on the various factors affecting the attorney-client relationship by the lawyer and the laymen points out the marked difference in emphasis.

Positive Factors

Laymen	Lawyer
1. Friendliness	1. Results
2. Promptness, businesslike manner	2. Honesty
3. Courtesy	3. Efficiency
4. Not condescending	4. Personality
5. Keeping client informed	5. Education

Negative Factors

Laymen		*Lawyer*	
1.	Superior attitude	1.	Procrastination
2.	Bored or indifferent attitude	2.	Failure to inform
3.	Impatient, impersonal, failure to inform	3.	Lack of frankness
4.	Rude, brusque	4.	Lack of courtesy

It is interesting to note that lawyers listed "results" as number one among factors having a positive effect on the attorney-client relationship, while among clients this rated as an insignificant factor in both the depth interviews and questionnaire responses. (less than 2 per cent of all respondents.)

It is obvious that the lawyers, while seemingly fulfilling the desires of the clients, fail to realize the importance clients place on the human aspect of the relationship.

Conclusion

The results of this series of questions show that the great majority of people are well satisfied with the services they obtain from their attorneys and will use the same attorneys again if legal services are needed. Most attorneys keep their clients well informed, turn over to them all papers upon completion of the work and treat the client exactly as he wants to be treated.

Of the very small percentage (7%) who indicated dissatisfaction with the service received from their lawyer, most indicated it was because of delay and failure of the attorney to keep them informed. "Results" are indicated as being a very minor cause of dissatisfaction since they were listed by less than 2 per cent of respondents.

Probably the most important factor brought out by this portion of the survey is the importance placed by the client on such attorney attitudes as friendliness, equality, helpfulness, courtesy, consideration, etc. While most attorneys seem to be meeting these desires of the clients, it is obvious from a comparison of the responses that they are doing it unconsciously and do not realize the great importance placed by the client on these personal considerations.

While the human aspects of the relationship are deemed of most importance by the client in the above comparison, we should be able to assume that factors listed by the lawyers as being most helpful or harmful to the attorney-client relationship are of at least equal importance even though the client does not realize the fact. Those areas deemed of most importance by the lawyers are:

(1) Prompt and full communication, to keep the client fully informed.

(2) Prompt handling of the client's work. In the lawyer responses the word "procrastination" is used more frequently than any other in describing conduct harmful to the attorney-client relationship.

(3) Honest and straightforward dealing with the client, including a careful evaluation of the case, a full explanation of the particular problems and procedures involved, and a frank and early discussion of fees.

(4) A courteous and sympathetic attitude of the attorney toward the client evidencing his personal and sincere interest in the client's problems.

(5) Competence and diligence in the handling of the client's affairs. Lawyers' responses indicate a great number of them believe that the lack of this factor often results from the lawyer's failure to obtain a proper basic education, inattentiveness to continuing legal education, and a failure to exert the required effort for a thorough and lawyerlike job.

IMPROVING LAWYER–CLIENT RELATIONSHIP

Objective

To determine how lawyers may better satisfy their clients and thereby improve lawyer-client relations.

Findings

Of the 282 laymen interviewed, 25 made suggestions relating to attorneys' fees generally giving the impression that the fee was too high or significantly that the fee was more than the client had expected although if the fee had been discussed at the beginning of the relationship or fully explained, it probably would have been acceptable by the client.

The remaining suggestions indicated constructive criticism of the profession as a whole and not dissatisfaction with their particular lawyer. These suggestions varied widely but dealt mainly with the lawyer's attitude toward and relationship with the client and the lawyer's public image. The general feeling was a need for more time, sincerity, warmth and friendliness from the lawyer toward his client and a need for the profession to encourage honesty, courtesy, sobriety and fairness on the part of lawyers as a whole to counteract the unfavorable image such as TV and movies depicting the lawyer as a "shyster," "ambulance chaser," or "crooked politician" and "fixer."

Conclusions

About 45 per cent of the people who have used lawyers had suggestions as to how lawyers could improve their services although only about 20 per cent of these indicated any dissatisfaction in their own experiences with lawyers.

Substantially all of the suggestions indicated the lawyer had not taken enough time with his client to discuss with the client fully, the fee and its basis, the problems and the plans for their solution and the progress of the matter.

A significant segment of laymen feel that the bar should create a better public image of the lawyer.

RECOMMENDATIONS

More time must be given to clients so that a frank and full appraisal of their problem may be given. The lawyer's fee and the basis for it should be thoroughly discussed with the client at the earliest opportunity.

Since clients expect leadership and positive action in the handling of their legal affairs, where definite positive advice cannot be given, the client should receive a complete briefing of the pros and cons concerning his matter.

The public should be informed concerning the qualifications and the ethical requirements of the legal profession.

The client should be informed by his attorney that in order to secure benefits for him, a lawyer must negotiate with opposing counsel and that such negotiations frequently are time consuming causing delay in the progress of the client's case.

Further study should be devoted to the present standards of legal training with an examination being made of the advisability of the establishment of apprenticeships. The possibility of a more extensive use of practicing lawyers as instructors in law schools should be studied with a view to increasing the practical aspects of a law student's training.

The bar should receive some sort of guidance, perhaps in the form of loose leaf services such as Prentice Hall, as to new developments respecting law offices layout, equipment, staffs and personnel with a view to promoting promptness and efficiency in handling client's affairs and avoiding unnecessary delays.

§ 4.7 Expectations From the Lawyer—Community of Approach

From that survey and general observation one may conclude that the client has some basic expectations. These expectations are discussed below.

The lawyer is his client's alter ego. Those personality traits which the client possesses, or which he wishes he possessed, he wants to see reflected in his attorney. Some litigants think of themselves as shrewd and clever. They will want a lawyer of the same stripe. Others are forthright and honest. They will choose a lawyer with those same attributes. Opposites may attract as mates—but you don't want a lawyer for a lover.

§ 4.8 Expectations From the Lawyer—Concern

Regardless of the personality traits, every client will demand that his lawyer will be concerned. For the litigant his legal problem is the most important matter in the world (all lawyers should have at least one legal dispute of their own in order to appreciate the truth of that homily). They want their lawyer to realize this and show a commensurate degree of concern. How will that concern be demonstrated? In a host of ways.

First, in the dispatch with which the matter is attended to. Most matters in litigation take time—and most litigants don't realize how much. They should be told of the pace of litigation and given explanation for the time lapses which will be involved. Otherwise they will interpret the delay as a lack of concern.

Second, in the intensity with which the matter is handled. When the client comes in for a conference he is entitled to your undivided attention. No one interrupts surgery with a telephone message that "Mrs. Jones wants to know if her prescription should be refilled". A legal conference holds the same significance for your client as does an appointment in an operating room. Block out a piece of your day—and hold the telephone calls. They realize that they are not your only client but you are their only lawyer and they deserve all of you when you're working on their case.

Third, in the sharing of information. Every lawyer knows what they want in a doctor—someone who will take them into their confidence, explain what the problem is, tell what course of treatment will be inaugurated and prognosticate the final outcome. Well, a legal client expects the same of you. Unlike a patient, most of the professional activity undertaken on his behalf won't even involve the client. Six months might pass between the client interview and the taking of a deposition. In the meantime a petition will be filed, witnesses interviewed, reports procured, etc. Let the client know what's going on. A carbon of your correspondence is little enough. Better yet a monthly report to the client. Aside from evidencing your concern, it will keep you on the ball. No one likes to admit, "Nothing was done on your case this month."

§ 4.9   Expectations From the Lawyer—Trust

The professional relationship will demand a third set of attributes that are best described as loyalty and discretion. The client will be taking you into his confidence concerning the most intimate details of his life. The lawyer's conference room must have the same sanctity as the confessional box—and the client should be given specific assurance of this. Some do not know of the lawyer's obligation to protect the secrets of their clients. Even if they do they will want to be reassured of the lawyer's sensitivity to this obligation.

§ 4.10   Expectations From the Lawyer—Professionalism

Underlying all the other expectations is the client's hope of hopes that his lawyer is a competent professional. How does the client get this message? In innumerable ways—dress, manner, office furnishings, personnel, etc. Professional image is a lot like obscenity—hard to describe but you know it when you see it.

§ 4.11   Lawyer's Motivations

Just as the client may have one of a multitude of needs in seeking legal advice so it is that the lawyer may have one of a number of motivations in providing the service that is sought. A lawyer's frank recognition of these varying motivations, some desirable and some not, may hasten his evolution into a true professional.

A story that well illustrates the point is that of the young man who encountered three workers all engaged in the same task, and to whom he addressed the same question, "What are you doing?" The first replied, "Making a buck;" the second, "Laying brick;" and the third, "Building a cathedral."

The three descriptions were not mutually exclusive. Each of course was making a buck, laying brick and building a cathedral. So it is with the lawyer. In his role as an advocate the lawyer will be earning a living, developing his craft and contributing to the edifice of justice. What he envisions as the main thrust of his endeavors is of greatest importance. Some advocates, young ones in particular, think the three evolve in the order stated. Initially you must develop economic security, then hone your competence and finally concern yourself with the more ethereal themes of "justice" and "the law." Oddly enough the opposite is true. The advocate who strives to fulfill his role in the judicial system must develop a competence for that role and the economic rewards will surely follow. A similar inverse transgression was enunciated some two-thousand years ago when an earlier counselor observed that if the kingdom of God was sought initially all other needs "will be added unto you."

§ 4.12   Client Interview—Generally

With the proper motivation established, the advocate will attempt to ascertain the client's needs and expectations. Sometimes the situation itself will suggest the answer but other times there might be some confusion as to what the lawyer must do to satisfy the client. In such instances it might be well to take a page from the book of Officer Pulver, the libido oriented lieutenant depicted in the play *Mr. Roberts*. When asked how he had seduced a 40 year old virgin he replied that he was the first who had ever asked. On occasion the client must be asked.

§ 4.13   Client Interview—Relationship of Law and Facts

With the needs of the client in mind it is now simply a matter of where we'll go and how we will get there. These decisions will be based upon the facts of the case and the applicable law. These elements are stated conjunctively as if they were two separate entities and some lawyers understand them as such. For them the development of a case is considered as a two part exercise: first, the indiscriminate marshalling of all the facts and then, a legal determination of the significance of those facts.

Other lawyers approach the problem from a different angle. The facts are gathered selectively with a view in mind of what legal theories might be available and what facts will be needed to support such theories. Each procedure evolves simultaneously, feeding off each other and deriving a thrust that is compatible to both.

Perhaps an illustration will serve to mark the distinction. Picture the lawyer as a chef who is seeking to prepare a six course Cantonese dinner (the analogy between a submissible case and a Cantonese dinner meal is rather valid. The ingredients of a law suit are as identifiable and necessary as the courses in a well ordered meal—and as esoteric to the litigant as Chinese cuisine). Somehow the food must be secured. The chef could tell the head of the household to go out to the store and bring back anything which he considers to be of importance in the preparation of the meal. Chances are the buyer wouldn't know the difference between bean curd and barley and, consequently, would overlook some of the essential components of the recipe.

Most chefs would make a list and state, in effect, "Here's what we need," listing everything from water chestnuts to soy sauce.

Of course the lawyer doesn't have that much control over the facts which make up the lawsuit. The recipe of a particular theory of recovery or defense will not be able to dictate the ingredients of the evidence. Quite the contrary. The available evidence will dictate what recipe must be followed. But the chef and the purchaser cannot operate independently of each other.

§ 4.14 Client Interview—Preparatory Set

The lawyer can inaugurate the first fact finding session with his client by asking a simple question. Why do you think you are entitled to relief? This question will serve two purposes—it will afford the client to tell the "why" of his claim or defense and will permit the lawyer to explain the "how."

Let us take a simple fact situation involving a personal injury to a customer who slips and falls in the local supermarket. An exchange may take place like this:

Lawyer: "Why do you think you're entitled to get some money for your injuries?"
Client: "Because I broke my leg."
Lawyer: "But many people break their legs without getting paid for it."
Client: "Yes, but I broke my leg in their store."
Lawyer: "That's not enough. What did they do that caused you to break your leg?"

Client: "I slipped on something. They should have swept their floor."

Lawyer: "True enough. But in order for you to recover we must prove something about what caused you to slip and perhaps how long the slippery condition existed before you fell. We must show specifically how someone's fault caused your injury."

Now at this point the lawyer must recognize the various potentials that exist for a "recipe of recovery"—and explore which, if any, combinations of ingredients are available.

§ 4.15 Client Interview—Initial Development of the Facts

First, the lawyer must discover what caused the floor to be slippery; a fact to be disclosed through direct or circumstantial proof from the client himself or others.

Acquaint the client of the importance of this ingredient before starting your interrogation. Let him know that you are seeking to discover if the storeowner was negligent in either causing or permitting a dangerous condition to exist in the store. "Did you see anything on the floor where you slipped? Did you feel or smell anything? Were there any stains on your clothing, any residue on your shoe, any statements by another customer or a store employee as to what might have caused you to slip?"

This type of questioning would reveal if you had the ingredients for an actual or constructive notice of a transient condition.

If you discover that the client slipped on a piece of lettuce but there is no evidence available, either direct or circumstantial as to how long the lettuce was there, then you will shift your inquiry to another line seeking to show some negligent type of display or other merchandising practice that might have created the danger. "Where was the lettuce in respect to the vegetable display counter? How was the lettuce displayed? Where was the lettuce trimmed before being displayed? Where was the lettuce kept in storage and how was it carried to the display case? etc."

If no luck, another tack could be employed to discover if a case could be made for a defective static condition: "What kind of floor was it? Did it appear to be waxed? Do you know how often it is waxed or what they use? etc."

If there are still insufficient facts for a case there might be another explanation for the fall; product liability for a defectively slippery shoe. Again, acquaint the client with the significance of the questions that you ask and the theory of recovery that you are exploring and then inquire as to the type of shoe being worn, the composition of the sole and heel, place of purchase, date of purchase, etc.

This interplay between the lawyer and the client in developing the facts involving a legal matter is a matter of great importance and creates some substantial problems. The lawyer must provide guidance as to type of information which he seeks and the legal significance of that information. Many lawyers (as demonstrated in Chapter 2, supra) feel that such advice, given before the facts are adduced, is in reality a subliminal form of suborning perjury and consequently grossly unethical. Others would take the position that a failure to so advise the client is non-professional and indeed unethical.

§ 4.16 Lawyer–Client Relationship—Generally

Perhaps this topic is misplaced and should appear at an earlier stage. But good sense frequently dictates that a professional relationship not be created until the lawyer has received sufficient facts to ascertain two things: whether he can be of any help to the prospective client, and whether he wants to be of any help to that particular client. One of the sweetest prerogatives of the professional is that we retain the capacity to say when the occasion demands, "Get out of my office." We won't feel the need often but when antipathy develops with the prospective client it is best to back away.

Other reasons other than personal feelings may occasion a refusal to enter into a client-lawyer relationship.

You might find that the client has a worthy case but that his expectations are too high. Remember, your professional capacity will be judged on the basis of whether or not you have satisfied your client. If that satisfaction depends upon a result which you know can't be attained then you have one of two courses to follow: bring those expectations down to reality, or don't get involved. Sometimes these unrealistic expectations are the product of the lawyer's own doing. "Sure we'll win this case Mrs. Jones and you'll end up with a bundle." Sounds good—but what happens when the case is lost or the "bundle" is more accurately characterized as a "pocket sized package"? A case should never be described as "cut and dried," "open and shut" or any other such conclusive conjunctive. First of all, in the law there isn't such a thing as a sure winner. Secondly, how are you going to justify a fat fee if it was all that easy? Lawyers should take a page from the doctor's book. "You have a serious problem Mrs. Jones. We will do all we can and I have reasonable expectations that everything will turn out all right."

§ 4.17 Lawyer–Client Relationship—Conflict of Interest

A potential "conflict of interest," or perhaps more generally expressed "an identity crisis" might prevent you from assuming the role of attorney in a given case. Sometimes the conflict is apparent. A driver and passenger request your representation for injuries received in an accident. The passenger will probably be better served if the driver is joined as a defendant. If *any* fault could be attributed to the driver, it's best that you not represent both. There may be some rare exceptions (if the driver is completely judgment proof or the passenger is convinced that it is the other fellow's fault and will not sue the host driver), that would allow representation of both but even in those cases the options should be fully explained to both clients and the potential conflicts pointed out and the assent to proceed secured in writing.

If both cannot be represented can a choice be made, who should it be and when should it occur? The potential conflict should be apparent from the very outset and intimate disclosures from each potential client regarding the facts of the accident should not be made. If such facts are disclosed and a conflict definitely established, the lawyer would probably have to refuse representation from both sides lest a confidential relationship be violated. If, for instance, the driver confessed that he really didn't see the stop light because he was under the influence of alcohol at the time, as lawyer for the passenger you would realize that the driver should be sued. But having received that information in a confidential relationship, you could not utilize it.

The best procedure to follow upon recognition of a problem, is first, find out from the individuals the nature of their injuries and the potential of the claims; second, determine from independent sources (such as a police report) the facts of the accident; third, explain the problem involved and, if both cannot be represented, choose which of the two you wish to represent and advise the other to seek counsel.

From a liability standpoint it will always be better to represent the passenger, but what if the driver's claim has ten times the potential as far as damages is concerned? You might want to represent the driver instead. Keep the option open by recognizing

147

the conflict immediately, secure the facts upon which a choice can be made and don't violate a confidentiality while doing so.

The "identity crisis" presents a different form of conflict. You are hired to defend a company in a product liability case. There are allegations that the product was designed defectively and packaged without adequate warning of its potential danger. The claim is substantial and if the plaintiff is successful, corporate heads will roll. It's not unusual in a case like this that each of the various departments involved in the research, production and marketing of the product be anxious to absolve themselves if it means hanging the blame on someone else in the company. You are defending a suit that exposes an insurance company to loss of funds, the company to a loss of prestige and future loss of sales and a host of individuals to a loss of employment. Where does your prime responsibility lie? The problem is more easily stated than solved. At least recognize that with one named defendant with multiple interests the same type of conflict can arise.

§ 4.18 Lawyer–Client Relationship—Fee Arrangement

If you elect to represent the client, then it is incumbent that several steps be taken. First, make certain the fee basis on which the case will be handled and reduce it to writing. Remember, however, that you are not two antagonists dealing at arm's length but a team who will be working together for a common end. Consequently the contract of employment should be as simple and non-technical as possible. Typical of such an agreement is that form frequently employed by lawyers representing plaintiffs in personal injury litigation.

"I employ Fred Brown to represent me in my claim for injuries arising out of an accident on June 1, 1992. His fee for professional services rendered shall be one-third of any amount recovered by settlement or trial. If nothing is received, Fred Brown is to receive nothing for professional services rendered."

If the case will involve the advance of costs on the part of the lawyer the agreement should spell out that any fee is in addition to litigation and investigation expenses whether paid initially by the client or advanced by the lawyer.

There is a great deal of truth in the homily that the cobbler's children go unshod. Frequently it is the lawyer that is left unprotected when the arrangements for the fee is made. A firm understanding at the outset will avoid one of the most unpleasant events that can befall a lawyer—a dispute over a fee.

§ 4.19   Marshalling of Client Information—Mechanics

Assuming you have elected to take the case, further information from your client will be necessary. It is advisable to develop a check list as a reminder of those many facets of a client's history which may be important. How this information is developed is of some concern to the lawyer simply because of the time commitment which it entails.

One of the following methods may be employed:

1. A casual conversation with the client with the pertinent items dictated as they are developed.

2. The use of a para-professional to record the pertinent information much as a nurse takes the patient's history for the doctor.

3. A check list given to the client to record on his own and return to the office.

§ 4.20   Marshalling of Client Information—Checklist

Regardless of the mechanics, a typical client's check-list for a run-of-the-mill vehicular accident would cover these areas:

Name

Birth Date

Weight

Height

Address _____ How long resided there

Previous address _____ How long resided there

Place of birth

Family history

    Name of parents

    Parent's occupation

    Number of siblings

Education

    Grade School

    High School

    College

Employment

> Present employer
>
> Earnings
>
> Length of service
>
> Immediate superior
>
> Previous employment

Medical History

> Congenital defects
>
> Childhood diseases
>
> Previous injuries
>
> Date
>
> Nature of injury
>
> Nature of treatment
>
> Hospitals
>
> Doctors
>
> Permanent results
>
> Claim filed
>
> Results

Previous Litigation

> Venue
>
> Lawyer
>
> Results

Previous Illnesses

> Date
>
> Nature of Treatment
>
> Hospitals
>
> Doctors
>
> Last treatment for illness or injury
>
> Date
>
> Nature of treatment
>
> Last Examination

Employment

Insurance Application

INJURIES

Have you told all injuries sustained?

Have any marks on body at time of accident?   Any now?

And are you alright now?

If there are complaints, describe:

> When do they occur
>
> What movements or activities precipitate complaint
>
> Type of pain (sharp, dull, aching, etc.)
>
> Frequency (continually, episodic, occasionally)
>
> Response to treatment

Previous condition

> Ever have such complaints before?
>
> Any part of body injured before?
>
> How did previous injuries occur?
>
> When?
>
> Type of complaints
>
> (a) Parts of body injured
>
> (b) Length of complaints
>
> Medical treatment received
>
> Claim made?   If so:
>
> (a) Against whom?
>
> (b) When?
>
> (c) Represented by counsel?
>
> (d) Suit filed?   Tried?
>
> (e) Disposition of claim

Any claims or litigation?

Health or accident insurance at time of accident

DAMAGES

Property damage

Date purchased, how much?

Value before accident

Photographs of damage

Where repaired, how much?

Loss of time from work

Were you docked time?

Any union or insurance benefits?

Unemployment compensation from state?

Medical expenses

Doctor bills

Hospital bills

X-rays

Ambulance

Medicine

Nurses

Treatment devices

CONCLUSION

Have you ever been convicted of a crime?

Have you fully understood the questions that I've asked you and have you answered them truthfully?

§ 4.21 Litigation Forms—General

The practitioner who engages in litigation must be efficient both as regard to his own time and that of his staff. Much of the work that must be done will be repetitive in nature and, consequently, such tasks are well suited to the development of a standard practice and the utilization of forms.

To what extent such forms are used is a matter of personal taste and professional judgment. Certainly there is something to be said for the personal touch that emanates from individually structured correspondence but this advantage must be weighed against the cost of time and effort. There are at least three areas in which forms can be used and those examples follow.

§ 4.22 Litigation Forms—Medical Authorization

Kindly permit my attorneys _____ or their representative, to examine, copy or photostat any and all records of your hospital concerning any treatment of myself, or _____, of any character at your institution at any time, including all correspondence, x-rays and reports, and particularly such records while a patient there on or about _____.

All previous authorizations are hereby revoked and I request that under no circumstances should any information be given to anyone other than my designated representative, the above.

_____

Subscribed and sworn to before me this _____ day of _____, 19__.

_____

Notary Public

My commission expires: _____

§ 4.23 Litigation Forms—Medical Report

In some instances it might be advisable to include a medical report form with the authorization.

MEDICAL REPORT

Dr._____

_____

Please furnish Mr. _____ the following report regarding my condition

Signed _____

---------(To be detached and retained by reporting physician if desired)---------

MEDICAL REPORT

PATIENT	Name _____ Age _____ Address _____
	Occupation _____ Employed by _____
HISTORY OF CONDITION	Date of Accident _____ 19__ History as described by patient _____
	_____
	_____

153

X–RAY	Date of first treatment _____ 19__ Date of last treatment _____ 19__ Date taken _____ 19__ Where taken _____ Findings _____
DIAGNOSIS (Describe and locate character and extent of injury)	_____ _____ _____ _____ _____
CONTRIBUTING FACTORS	In your opinion, is disability a result of above described accident solely? _____ _____ _____
PROGNOSIS (include estimate of Total and Partial Disability and of probable permanent results)	_____ _____ _____ Total disability estimate _____ weeks _____ days. Ended _____ 19__ Partial disability estimate _____ weeks _____ days. Ended _____ 19__ Cost of medical treatment to date _____

Signed _____
Date _____ 19__ Address _____

§ 4.24 Litigation Forms—Employment Information

NAME OF EMPLOYEE:

SOCIAL SECURITY NUMBER:

JOB CLASSIFICATION:

DUTIES:

WAGES:

DATE OF EMPLOYMENT:

ABSENCE FROM WORK FOLLOWING: _____

TOTAL WAGE LOSS:

DID EMPLOYEE RECEIVE ANY COMPENSATION DURING ABSENCE FROM WORK?

IF SO, FROM WHAT SOURCE AND IN WHAT AMOUNT?

DID EMPLOYEE PROVIDE EXPLANATION FOR ABSENCE?

IF SO, PLEASE RELATE:

HAS EMPLOYEE SUFFERED PREVIOUS INJURIES OR MADE PREVIOUS COMPLAINTS OF ILL HEALTH OR DISABILITY?   COMMENTS:

§ 4.25   Client's Diary

In almost every case there will be information developed subsequent to the initial interview. The lawyer must advise his client of the importance of making a record of such information. In the case of a plaintiff in an injury case the lawyer might prepare a form directive outlining the role of the client in this fashion.

CONTENTS OF DIARY

In order for the diary to fill the void and provide accurate answers to questions such as these, it will be necessary for the diary to include:

1. An accurate record of visits to the doctor.

2. An accurate record of significant episodes of pain and physical malfunctioning. This is particularly so if the injury suffered is of such a nature that there are periodic attacks such as blackouts, nausea, dizziness, cramping, etc.

3. An accurate record of the frequency with which medication is taken.

4. An accurate record of occasions when outside help is needed in order to accomplish tasks formerly performed by the injured party but are now impossible to perform by reason of disability.

5. A record of social events foreclosed to the injured party by reason of disability or ill health.

6. An accurate record of all medical, doctor and drug bills, along with related expenses such as rental of orthopedic devices, wheel chairs, etc.

§ **4.26** General Information to Client

The client interview should not be a one way street. It is important that you as the lawyer receive vital information from your client, but it is just important that the client receive information from you. How can the lawyer answer the questions that most clients will have about the legal process in general and their case in particular?

One such device is to prepare a video taped message for your new client. Put on the tape all the preliminary information that you think it is necessary that a new client knows then turn him loose in the library with the recording machine.

Another method is to prepare a pamphlet to be taken home by the client and perused at his leisure. Such a suggested pamphlet is set forth in the following section.

§ **4.27** Client's Handbook—Model

The following is an illustrative client's handbook as prepared by an attorney for plaintiff—civil litigation. Appropriate changes could be made to suit the particularities of any practice.

Introduction

You have suffered a loss, you have placed your claim in the hands of an attorney and we now begin our joint endeavor to bring about a just and successful disposition of that claim. This is probably the first such experience that you have had. There are no doubt a lot of questions in your mind about the procedures that will be followed, the nature of the law that is involved, the likelihood of recovery, the time that will elapse before a final disposition, and many others. We hope to answer these questions and to acquaint you with our system of jurisprudence and the role that you are to play in it.

What is an Attorney?

The history of the word itself pretty well tells the story. It is derived from an old French word meaning "to recognize one as the person in whose behalf one holds something". You have turned your case over to us. We will prosecute that case on your behalf. We are your proxy, your alter-ego in the presentation of your claim. This relationship which has been created is a most intimate one and it demands the strictest loyalty from both attorney and client. As your advocate we will advance your case as vigorously as our talent permits.

A greater duty lies only to the fulfillment of our professional ethics and our obligations as officers of the Court. In turn, you as a client owe us your trust and confidence. In order that we might represent you most effectively we must know not only the facts surrounding the particular incident giving rise to this litigation, but also many personal facts about you which might have a bearing on the case. These facts must be freely given with the complete assurance that they will be held by us in the strictest confidence and with the realization that such communication is held to be privileged in the same sense as that given to a clergyman or to a doctor.

Why Make a Claim?

Although you have engaged an attorney there might still be some reservations in your mind as to whether or not this step should have been taken. You might feel that your act will be misinterpreted by your friends or acquaintances and you will be considered as being "claim-minded," "greedy" or "wanting to get something for nothing." You need have no feeling of guilt in the presentation of a legitimate claim. We are seeking a just settlement of a dispute. Our Court houses were built and our laws were written for this very reason. No one need to be apologetic about that. In all probability this dispute will be settled by mutual agreement. However, if your case is one of the few that has to be presented before a jury, you must remember that there is nothing dishonorable about telling your story to twelve citizens who have been chosen at random from the community and allowing them under the law to reach a verdict. The United States is one of the few countries in the world that has such a system of settling disputes between her citizens. It is a cherished right that each of us possess and we should not deprive ourselves of this right merely because of the possibility of criticism from some shallow thinking persons.

Why File a Lawsuit?

Statistics show that about 90% of all claims that are made are settled without going to a trial. The question that might be asked is "Why is there a necessity of filing a lawsuit?" The way in which most voluntary agreements are made is that the parties involved recognize that if they do not mutually work out their problems that a solution will be thrust upon them by some other party. There is only one way in which a dispute can be settled in the event that the parties cannot voluntarily work it out, that is through the verdict of a Court. Before there can be a Court verdict the suit must be filed and the case processed. This procedure usually takes from six months to a year. Frequently it takes that same length of time before the full extent of your injuries can be determined. If several months elapse before the extent of the claim can be determined and then negotiations are entered into which do not result in a satisfactory settlement, an additional six months or a year will pass before the case can be filed and brought before a Court. Rather than face a possibility of this delay, it is best that a lawsuit be filed as soon as practical. The claim matures as the case is being processed through the Court. If for some reason a mutually satisfactory disposition of the claim is not reached, then the parties will be able to present the claim to the Court without additional delay.

There are other reasons for the necessity of filing suit. Under the law when a suit is filed there are a number of discovery procedures that are available to both parties. We, as plaintiff, are entitled to take the deposition or sworn statement of the opposite party and find out from them under oath their version of the incident. Similarly we may take depositions of witnesses who might otherwise not be willing to disclose the information that they have. A filing of this suit is the only way in which both parties are given the complete opportunity of finding out full information and thus enables both of them to appraise the claim more accurately.

What are the Legal Procedures in the Filing of a Lawsuit?

The filing of a lawsuit is merely a notice to the Court and to the persons against whom the claim is made. Generally speaking the place where the lawsuit is filed is determined by the place of the occurrence or the residency of the defendant. However, if more convenient, the claim can be filed in the county where you live if the defendant can be served by the sheriff in that county. A Petition is drafted by the attorney. This is merely a formal statement alleging briefly the facts of the accident, the complaints of negligence against the defendant and the injury or damage which has resulted. This Petition and copies are presented to the Court and the sheriff then serves a copy of the Petition to each of the defendants. Upon receipt of the Petition the defendant then has 30 days in which to file an Answer. Usually this is in the form of a denial of the allegations of negligence and in some instance a claim is made that the damages suffered were contributed to by your own fault. Frequently, however, there are Mo-

tions which are filed attacking the propriety of the Petition.
When this occurs, it necessitates a presentation of these Motions
before the Court and invariably means a delay. When an Answer
to the Petition is filed, the case then becomes "at issue" and can
then be set upon a trial docket. The time that elapses between
the filing of the Petition and the setting on the trial docket varies
according to many factors, but usually this interim is from nine
months to a year. The trial courts are closed during the summer
months, but from the middle of September through the middle of
June, with the exception of a few weeks for holidays, the Courts
are open for the trial of civil cases. On the Monday of each of
these weeks a trial docket of about 150 cases is prepared. The
order of which these cases appear on the docket is usually determined by the time that they were filed,—that is, the cases that
have been pending the longest appear at the top of the docket
while those that have been more recently filed appear farther
down. Each morning of the week the docket is called and the
attorneys respond as to whether or not they are in a position to
try the case. The manner in which the cases are disposed of at
the docket occur at a variable and unpredictable rate. Thus, if
your case is set No. 50 on the docket, it could not be ascertained
until the calling of the docket on the day on which it was set as to
what disposition was to be made of the 49 cases that proceeded
your case. Many of these cases will have been settled, some of
them will be continued, while others will answer that they are
ready to try the case. Those cases ready for trial are assigned out
to trial Courts and usually there are about six such courts available. As these cases are disposed of in the trial division new cases
are assigned to trial in the order that they appear on the docket.

What is Expected of Me?

Much of the preparation of the lawsuit will depend on you.
Of course a full and complete statement has to be given to the
attorney and all the facts and circumstances surrounding the
incident told in detail. From this initial interview, we then will
be able to follow through with interviews of the witnesses, pro-
curement of the police report and the medical information. Undoubtedly within several weeks the attorney representing the
defendant will request that your deposition be taken. Under the
law they have the right to take your deposition, that is, a sworn
statement as to the facts of the accident and the surrounding
circumstances. Although sometimes a witness or a party is subpoenaed in order to appear for the deposition, in most instances

the attorneys make arrangements for the voluntary appearance of their clients. Before you are interrogated, it is necessary that adequate time be spent with the attorney in order to acquaint you with the nature of the questions that will be asked. The depositions are usually held in the office of the attorney under informal circumstances. The interrogation is conducted by the attorney representing the opposite party. A court reporter records the interrogation and the transcription of the proceeding is made a part of the court record. Despite the informal setting and the courteousness and friendliness of the opposing party, the deposition is of prime importance and very frequently is a determining factor in the success or failure of your case. It is for that reason that you should have a full understanding of the nature of the proceeding and what will be expected of you.

First, it should be recognized that this is a compulsory proceeding. We are not voluntarily appearing in order to tell "all that we know about the accident." Instead you will be here to answer questions that will be put to you. In this sense you should think of yourself as a reluctant witness answering only those questions which are asked and not volunteering any information. Frequently a client will ask "shall I tell the lawyer such and such." There need be no worry on your part as to what information you should relay. If a question is asked and it is a proper question you will be obligated to answer. If no inquiry is made then you should not volunteer any information.

Second, listen to each question and answer it in as brief a fashion as possible. It is surprising how many questions can be answered with a simple "yes" or "no." There will be many questions that will be asked of which you will have no knowledge. In that case, the answer is "I don't know." Remember, regardless of the informality of the proceeding, this is not a conversational exchange. This is part of the legal process and the answers that you give and the manner in which you answer are of extreme importance.

Third, there undoubtedly will be questions concerning estimates of time, speeds and distances. The answers to such questions should be in terms of approximation. One cannot truthfully say, "I was traveling at 30 miles per hour." It would be much nearer the truth to say that "I was traveling *about* 30 miles per hour," or "*between* 25 and 30 miles per hour." Similarly, in the case of giving the estimation of a distance, it would be much more truthful to say that the street was *about* 40 feet wide rather than to make a flat statement as to its exact width.

Fourth, there will be questions directed not only to the facts of the accident, but to your own personal background. You might think it unnecessary that the opposing party ask you questions about your age, your address, your type of employment and whether or not you have been married before, etc., however, all of this information is considered relevant and must be answered. Remember, your attorney will be present during the taking of this deposition and if there is any improper matter which is sought to be adduced, an objection will be made.

Fifth, one of the important facets of the interrogation will concern the result or the nature of the injuries or damages which you have suffered. Facts of an injury cannot be relayed truthfully with merely "yes" or "no" answers. In order that a fair, full and complete picture of your injuries and damages can be appreciated by the opposing attorney it will be necessary to explain not only the nature of the injury but how it has affected you in your daily living. You will be asked not only the complaints that you have at the present time, but those that you suffered shortly after the accident. You will also be asked questions as to the amount of visits that you have made to the doctor, the type of treatment that he afforded you, the time that you have lost from work, the expenses that have been incurred, etc. For that reason, it is important that you come to the deposition prepared with information. From the very inception of your case a record should be kept regarding such information as the time lost from work and financial loss that has resulted, dates of visits to the doctor, expenditures made for drugs, nurses, braces, etc. This information is of primary importance in determining the true value of your loss. Very frequently the information can be known only by yourself.

After the deposition has been taken, and if you have suffered a personal injury, the defendant may request that you be examined by a doctor of his own choosing. The law affords this right and we must comply with this request. If you are asked to submit to such an examination you should remember the following points:

1. The doctor examining you will have but this one opportunity to talk to you and observe you and appraise your injury. Many of the initial effects of the injury such as bruises, and swellings will have disappeared and perhaps many of the complaints that you had at one time will have cleared up. For that reason, the doctor will rely most heavily upon your

own recitation as to how the injuries were sustained and what their past effects have been.

2.   Many of the complaints that persons have following injury are of a subjective nature, those that cannot be found by examination or clinical tests.   For instance, a headache is a subjective complaint.   No amount of x-rays or observation can indicate to an examining physician that a person is suffering from a headache.   Therefore, it is your obligation to recite to the doctor all of the complaints that you have had and are presently suffering from.

3.   The examination of the doctor is not meant to be an interrogation as to the details of the accident.   It will be important to him to determine how the injuries were suffered, that is, whether or not you were a pedestrian that was struck by a car or whether you slipped on a defective floor.   However, facts concerning the speeds of the automobiles or the nature of the defect of the floor is no concern to the doctor and should not be the subject of his examination.

4.   Do not be hostile to the doctor.   It is true that he is examining you on behalf of the opposing party, but generally speaking he has been chosen because he is a competent doctor whose opinion will be held in high regard by the judge or the jury.   Be cooperative in giving as much information as you can concerning your injuries.   Remember the difficulty under which he operates.   He has not seen you before, did not treat you and in this one short examination must form an opinion as to the nature and extent of your injuries.

During the pendency of your claim, you will no doubt be asked by many persons how your suit is progressing.   It is well not to talk about the nature of your claim, the facts of the accident nor the injuries that you have suffered.   It is possible that some of the statements that you make could be misinterpreted by friends or others and such statements would prove detrimental to your claim.   It is also true that many persons feel that they have a certain competency in the law and can give you advice concerning your claim.   Such advice from "curbstone lawyers" can only lead to uneasiness and worry.   You must have confidence in your attorney and that he, through his experience and special training, will be able to adequately protect your interests.

Settlement Negotiation

After depositions have been taken and you have been examined by a doctor of the defendant's choosing and the trial date approaches, settlement negotiations will be initiated. These negotiations will be relayed to you, and usually at that time a conference is arranged so that you may become fully aware of the features of the case, the likelihood of recovery, and the factors taken into consideration in evaluating your claim. Usually during the preparation of the case certain expenses will have been incurred. It is desirable that any consideration of settlement be made on the basis of the net settlement after attorney's fees and legal expenses. All of this information will be made known to you so that an intelligent decision can be made as to whether the offer should be accepted or rejected. In evaluating a claim about the only guide that can be used is the anticipation of what a jury is apt to do in the event that the case is tried. Of course, as you must realize, this is at best a guess. Regardless of the facts and the injuries involved, it is impossible to foresee what a jury of twelve persons might do in a particular case. Experience and knowledge of past cases which have been similar in circumstances provide some guidance but no two cases are alike and no two injuries are alike. All of the factors concerning the case will be presented to you along with our recommendations, but the final decision will rest with you.

Preparation for Trial

If it appears that the settlement negotiations are not satisfactory, preparations for trial will begin usually a week or two before the case is set. At that time, you will be called in for a pre-trial conference. The facts of the accident as well as the extent and nature of your injuries will be reviewed with you. Notices will be sent to the doctors and the witnesses alerting them to the possibility of having to testify in the event that the case is tried. Usually it is impossible to determine beforehand when your case might be called for trial. For that reason it is usually acceptable if you go about your regular routine, but that you hold yourself available for appearing in Court in the event that the case is called. There is usually about an hour or two available for such notice and plenty of time for another brief pre-trial conference before the case begins. Before testimony is adduced, a jury must be chosen and preliminary statements made by the attorneys. This usually takes about an hour or two and allows you to become acclimated to the courtroom.

Your Role During Trial

As a party to a lawsuit you have an important job to do. It is important not only because of the immediate result it will have on you, but also important to our system of justice. For a jury to make a correct and wise decision it must have all the evidence put before it in a truthful manner. Attention should be given not only to what you say, but the manner in which it is said. Testimony given in a stumbling, hesitant manner leaves the jury with a doubt as to whether or not all the facts are being told in a truthful fashion. If, however, the same facts are told in a confident, straightforward manner the jury has more faith in what you are saying. Here are a few suggestions which must be kept in mind in helping you to become a good witness.

1. Your physical appearance is important. Your clothing should be clean and conservative. Some persons are offended by others who wear too stylish clothes, excessive jewelry, severe hairdos, etc. This should be kept in mind.

2. Your whole demeanor should reflect to the jury that you are an intelligent, serious person that has a great deal of concern over the outcome of your case. When the oath is administered to you, you should stand erect, listen to the clerk carefully and respond in a clear, certain fashion.

3. You should recall that the answers which are given are not for the benefit of the attorney asking them nor for the judge, but primarily they are directed for the jury. For that reason, it is well to keep in mind that you are communicating with twelve persons taken from various walks of life and who are under oath to perform their job as jurors. They are conscientiously trying to find out what the truth is and you might turn to them during the course of the interrogation and make your answers directly to them in a clear, straightforward, friendly fashion. The acoustics in most of our courtrooms are not too good by reason of the high ceilings. Therefore, it is important not to cover your mouth, but to speak clearly and loudly so that the farthest juror can hear you easily.

4. Don't memorize your responses. You will be acquainted with the nature of the questions that will be asked you under direct examination, but there should be a certain amount of spontaneity to the way in which they are answered. Listen carefully to the questions asked you. Understand the ques-

tion before you respond. If you do not understand it, have it repeated. Do not give a snap answer without thinking. Sometimes an answer cannot be responded to in a simple "yes" or "no" fashion. You have a right to explain the answer and in most cases this will be necessary. You must recall that testifying for a jury is quite different than testimony that is given in a deposition. The purpose of the deposition is for the defendant to ascertain facts that will help him in the investigation of the case. As far as the jury trial is concerned it is your role as a plaintiff to place all of these facts before the jury and therefore you must be more communicative and detailed in explanation of the facts of the accident and the results therefrom.

5. Don't be a "smart alec" or cocky witness. You are not engaged in some type of a verbal duel with the opposing counsel. Your primary job is to convey truthful, meaningful information to the jury as best you can. It serves no purpose to be argumentative with the opposing counsel. Most persons do not like persons of this nature and if you respond to an argumentative question in a kind and courteous fashion it will inure to your benefit.

6. Sometimes during the course of the testimony there are objections. When an objection occurs, stop instantly when you are interrupted until the Court can rule on the propriety of the objection. Do not try to "sneak in" an answer.

7. Don't look to your attorney or the judge for help in answering a question. You are on your own and frequently if you look to your attorney the jury might get the idea that you are seeking some kind of a clue as to the proper answer. Remember, you are under oath, you are expected to tell the truth, and you know the answers to the questions that will be asked of you better than anyone else.

8. Do not respond to the testimony of others. You will be present during the entire case and it is quite foreseeable that other witnesses will testify to a version of the facts diametrically opposed to your testimony. When this occurs do not do anything by way of exclamation or gesture which suggests your opposition to such testimony.

What Happens After the Verdict?

With the return of the jury verdict, it does not necessarily mean that the case is ended. If any of the parties is disappointed with the result, he has the opportunity of filing a Motion for a New Trial within 15 days after the verdict. This motion is directed to the Trial Court and in effect asks the Court to correct mistakes in rulings of law that had been made during the trial. The Court must rule upon this within 90 days after its filing, and he will either sustain the Motion for a New Trial or overrule it. This action of the Court may be appealed by any of the parties. When an appeal is taken a transcript of the record must be prepared and the party seeking the transcript is given 90 days or in some cases a total of 180 days for the transcript to be prepared. After being prepared the case can then be set for a hearing before the appropriate appellate court. Briefs must be prepared by both parties and usually there will be an additional three or four months that will pass before the oral argument can be heard. After oral argument, it is usually several months before the written opinion is handed down. This initial opinion by the Court can in turn be questioned by either of the parties and Motions for a Re-hearing filed. However, in most cases, the initial opinion of the appellate court is final. The time usually elapsing between the verdict and the final disposition on appeal is approximately a year or fourteen months. If the verdict was initially in your favor and is sustained on appeal, then you are allowed 6% interest on the amount of the verdict during the pendency of the appeal.

Conclusion

We will be working closely together until your case is completed. We hope that you now have a better understanding of the events that will be occurring during these coming months. There might be other questions that you have. Remember, we are your attorneys and you can feel free to call upon us at any time to impart information or seek answers to your questions. However, please consider that our obligations to our clients and frequent commitments before the Courts make us unavailable much of the time and may delay our response to you. We are here to serve you and to use all of the proper means available to secure a fair, just and proper disposition of your claim.

§ 4.28 Client's Handbook—Deposition Instructions

The Lawyers and Judges Publishing Co., Inc. has published an excellent copyrighted booklet available to attorneys which acquaints the client (or indeed, any witness) with the ramifications of a deposition. The contents of this pamphlet follow:

Table of Contents

Your deposition has been scheduled for _____

Please be in our offices at _____

*If the above dates or times conflict with your
schedule, telephone at once.*

INTRODUCTION

Arrangements have been made for the taking of your deposition. You may be puzzled about this legal procedure and no doubt have questions concerning it. The purpose of the 95 questions and answers in this booklet is to explain what a deposition is, what will be required of you and what advance preparations you should make for it.

Please understand that these instructions are only guidelines. Every case, person, lawyer and situation is different. Always be guided by the advice, counsel and instructions of *your* lawyer. He will clarify any questions which you may have about your deposition after you have read this booklet.

Section I: GENERAL INFORMATION

Question: What is a deposition?

Answer: A deposition is sometimes referred to as a discovery procedure. It is a lawful method whereby what you know about your own case is *discovered* by the opposing lawyer through a series of questions he will ask you and your answers to those questions.

The significant difference between just talking about your case and a deposition is that you will be given an oath and sworn to tell the truth.

A deposition is most often taken after your case has been filed in court and before the actual trial.

Question: Why is my deposition being taken?

Answer: Your deposition is being taken so that the opposing lawyer can determine what *you* know about the facts and details of your case.

A deposition enables the lawyers to form an impression and to make an appraisal of *you, what* you have to say about your case, and *how* you say it.

Question: Who will be present when my deposition is taken?

Answer: Your lawyer will be there with you. The lawyer or lawyers representing the party or parties you are suing will be there. An official court stenographer will also be present. Very often the court stenographer is called a "court reporter." This does *not* mean the court reporter is a *newspaper* reporter. The word "reporter" means the same as "stenographer."

Question: Will there be any publicity in connection with my deposition?

Answer: In the vast majority of cases there is no newspaper or television publicity. If your case is one of public interest your lawyer will protect you from unnecessary publicity.

Question: Does the taking of my deposition at this time mean my case is going to trial soon?

Answer: Not necessarily. Your lawyer will estimate the expected trial date.

Question: Is the deposition conducted like a trial?

Answer: Not exactly. There will be no judge or jury present, but you will be testifying in somewhat the same manner as you would during a trial.

Question: Will the deposition take place in a courtroom?

Answer: No. It usually takes place in a lawyer's office. If it takes place in a courtroom it just happens to be the most convenient place for everyone to meet.

Question: How does the deposition start?

Answer: The official court stenographer will ask you to raise your right hand and take an oath to tell the truth. The general language of the oath is: "Do you swear to tell the truth, the whole truth and nothing but the truth as you shall answer to God." You

168

will, of course, answer "yes." If, for reasons of religious belief, you cannot take an oath, you will not be required to do so. Your lawyer will explain this to you and will answer any questions you might have on this subject. After the oath has been administered you will then be asked questions by the other lawyer.

Question: If a deposition is not the actual trial of my case, why will an official court stenographer be there?

Answer: Everything you are asked and the answers you give will be taken down in shorthand or by machine. Only an official court stenographer is permitted to do this by law. The deposition may later be transcribed (typed up into a book) by the stenographer. It is important that you answer truthfully and to the best of your knowledge. Understandably it will be difficult for you to make any major changes in your testimony once you have testified and the court reporter has recorded it.

Question: Will any other person connected with my case be present during the taking of my deposition?

Answer: Not ordinarily.

Question: Will I be told about the lawyer who will ask me the questions?

Answer: Yes. Your lawyer will discuss with you the type of questioning usually conducted by the opposing lawyer. He may even tell you about his personality, attitudes, tone of voice, speed of questioning, etc. If the opposing lawyer asks questions in rapid fire order, this should not cause you to give rapid fire answers. You should answer questions at your own pace.

Question: Will more than one lawyer be asking me questions?

Answer: This will depend on how many parties have been sued by you. If each of the parties you sued is represented by a different lawyer, each one of them may be permitted to ask you questions.

Question: Will a deposition be taken from anyone else connected with my case?

Answer: Probably. Your lawyer will take depositions if and when he feels it is necessary to do so.

Question: How long does a deposition take?

Answer: This depends on the particular case and the lawyer asking the questions. Ask your lawyer to estimate the time for your particular deposition. Your schedule should be arranged so that you will not be hurried or rushed for time when you testify.

Question: Is there some special way I should come dressed to the deposition?

Answer: Yes. Wear plain, neat, and comfortable clothing—the same as you would wear if you were going to church.

Women should avoid using heavy facial make-up and costume jewelry.

If you have suffered scar formations from your injury do not cover them with cosmetics.

Question: Will I be permitted to smoke during the deposition?

Answer: Yes, if you so desire.

Question: If the deposition is unusually long will I be permitted to go to the washroom or just take a break?

Answer: Yes. You should be as comfortable as possible at all times. Tell your lawyer about any personal problems or physical conditions which require special attention *in advance* of the deposition. He will arrange for the necessary recess.

Question: Can I bring anyone with me to the deposition?

Answer: Ask your lawyer in advance and he will tell you who may or may not sit in with you during the deposition.

Question: Is there some special way I should conduct myself at the deposition?

Answer: Yes. Be courteous. Never become angry, antagonistic or hostile. *Avoid asking questions in answer to questions.*

Do not become overly friendly with or tell jokes to the opposing lawyer or the court stenographer. A deposition is an important and a serious proceeding.

Even if the lawyers sometimes engage in informal talk among themselves or with the court stenographer, you should avoid taking part in these conversations.

Question: Will there be some special order to the questions I will be asked?

Answer: The deposition will cover about eight to ten general areas of information but not necessarily in the order here given.

(a) Your personal history and background;

(b) The facts of the accident;

(c) The injuries you claim to have suffered as the result of the accident;

170

(d) The medical treatment and care you have received;

(e) The complaints you now have resulting from the injuries you received in the accident;

(f) Your ability or lack of ability to partake in your usual daily activities;

(g) What effect your injuries have had upon your ability to work and to enjoy your off-work activities such as hobbies and sports (bowling, tennis, swimming, hunting, etc.);

(h) The damages (money) you lost, paid, or owe as the result of the injuries you claim to have suffered;

(i) A complete history of all illnesses or injuries that you have suffered before and after the date of the present accident.

Question: At the deposition can I relate any conversation I heard about the character of the party I am suing, or anything anyone has told me about the accident?

Answer: No. You should relate these details to your lawyer privately. What other people told you or what you overheard is generally not admissible evidence. Your lawyer may find admissible evidence and perhaps witnesses from an investigation of what you heard or what was told to you.

Question: What if the opposing lawyer interrupts the completion of my answer to a question by asking me another question?

Answer: Your lawyer will keep the record straight. He will recognize that you have not been permitted to complete your answer and will make the necessary comments for the record. It is possible that your lawyer may not be interested in having you complete your answer. Your lawyer may ask you if you care to complete your answer or he may decide that your interrupted answer is all opposing counsel is entitled to receive under the circumstances. If your completed answer is vital to your case your lawyer will make it possible for you to complete your answer. Listen carefully to what your lawyer says during the deposition and be guided by his instructions to you and his remarks to the stenographer or the opposing lawyer.

Question: If my deposition is *not* transcribed how will the insurance company know about me, my case or my testimony?

Answer: The opposing lawyer will furnish the insurance company with a review of your testimony and his personal appraisal of you,

171

your injury, how you testified, and his opinion of the value of your case.

The opposing lawyer and the insurance company will make a determination whether to settle your case or wait for a trial and a jury verdict.

Question: What if the court stenographer makes a mistake in recording my testimony?

Answer: If your deposition is transcribed you and your lawyer will be able to read it and check it for errors. Your lawyer will know what to do if the deposition is inaccurate. Stenographic errors can be avoided if you are careful not to talk at the same time someone else is talking. It is almost impossible for the court stenographer to record overlapping conversations. Speak loudly enough to be heard and clearly enough to be understood. There may be occasions when the court stenographer may ask you to spell a work or a name in order to prevent errors.

Question: Will the lawyer try to trick or confuse me with his questions?

Answer: This is a general misconception brought about by what you may have seen on television or at the movies. If the opposing lawyer's questions should be of this nature, your lawyer will be quick to recognize it. He will take the proper measures to prevent the continuation of this method of questioning.

Question: Would it be a good idea to memorize my testimony so I won't forget what to say?

Answer: Do not memorize your testimony. A deposition is not a memory contest. Do not bring papers or lists of items you want to remember. If your lawyer wants you to bring anything to the deposition he will tell you.

Question: Is there some special way in which I should answer questions?

Answer: Yes. You should be truthful. If you adhere to the truth you will be better able to remember the details. *Think* before you answer.

Consider that there are three parts to every question. First, you hear it. Second, you consider the answer in your own mind. Third, you will give the answer audibly. Answers should be brief and in direct answer to the question. Do not ramble on giving answers to questions which have not been asked. Many questions can be answered with a simple "yes" or "no." Take your time.

Listen and understand the question. Consider the answer. Then state the answer. Speak clearly and loudly enough for those in the room to hear you. *Do not nod your head in answer to a question.* The court stenographer may not know what you mean.

Question: Must I answer every question the opposing lawyer asks?

Answer: Yes, unless your lawyer enters an objection, or if you do not know or remember the details involved in the question. *Do not make up answers.*

Question: If I do not remember certain facts or figures and I am asked about them, what should I say?

Answer: Say that you do not remember, or words to that effect. If you can give a reasonable approximation then you may do so. For example: "about 20 feet," "about 35 miles per hour," "about 2 P.M." If your answer is based on an estimate, then say that it is an estimate. If you cannot make a reasonably accurate estimate or you do not recall the particular fact or facts, then simply say so.

Question: What is an objection?

Answer: If a question is put to you which your lawyer considers improper he will say "I object." The word "object" when spoken by either lawyer is your signal to stop talking. *You must never volunteer to give an answer when your lawyer makes an objection.* The lawyers may be interested in clearing up a point or making certain the question or answer is proper. This is not a signal for you to attempt to explain something. You should remain silent until you are instructed by your lawyer to continue with your testimony.

Question: What If I think the question should not be answered by me, but my lawyer does not make an objection?

Answer: Answer the question. Your lawyer is present in order to protect your interests and he knows when to enter objections. You should never say "I object" or "off the record" in order to explain answers.

Question: What if the opposing lawyer fails to ask me certain questions which I think are important?

Answer: The opposing lawyer will ask you those questions he feels are important. *Do not volunteer facts or answers to questions you have not been asked.* For example:

Q: What is your present residence address?

A: My present residence address is 5 West Elm. I have lived there for 10 years. I work at 5674 West Broadway and my employer is Henry Hopkins. My husband works for the Federal Government and we have three children.

You were only asked to give your *present residence address.* The answer should be given simply: "5 West Elm." Stop talking. Wait for another question. If you continue giving details you have not been asked about the deposition will be unduly long and disorganized.

Question: Will I be permitted to talk to my lawyer during the deposition, and before I answer certain questions?

Answer: Avoid doing this. Everything said at the deposition will be recorded by the court stenographer. If you do ask your lawyer questions he will undoubtedly say "off the record" to the court stenographer, and will talk to you. You may create doubt and suspicion where none should exist. Your lawyer will tell you to answer the question to the best of your ability. If you do not know the answer, then say so.

Question: What should I do if I did not hear the question or did not understand what the opposing lawyer meant?

Answer: Simply say that you didn't hear or that you didn't understand the question asked. The opposing lawyer will then either ask the court stenographer to reread the question to you or he will rephrase it until you do understand it.

Question: What if during the deposition I realize that I have given an incorrect or inaccurate answer to a previous question?

Answer: You may ask that the particular question you are concerned about be reread to you. You may also ask that the answer you gave be reread. Then think carefully about any change you wish to make in your testimony. The opposing lawyer may ask questions about the change in your testimony in an attempt to discredit your corrected answer.

Question: If I am asked: "Did you talk to your lawyer before coming to this deposition?" what should I say?

Answer: The truth. "Yes" if you did, and "no" if you did not. It is most probable that you went over the details of your case with your lawyer. There is absolutely no reason for you to hide the fact that you did talk to your lawyer before coming to the deposition.

Question: What if the lawyer says: "Did your lawyer tell you what to say at this deposition?"

Answer: Your lawyer will not tell you *what* to say. He will tell you to testify truthfully and to the best of your ability and knowledge. Your lawyer will prepare you for your deposition by referring to reports, notes and other documents in your file and will review the facts in order to refresh your recollection.

Question: Is it permissible for me to talk to my lawyer outside of the deposition room during a break or when there is a lull in questioning?

Answer: It is best not to talk about your case at any time except in answer to questions during the deposition. Do not talk about your case in lobbies, waiting rooms, washrooms and so forth. Some things you say may be misinterpreted by others. When the deposition is concluded, stop talking.

Section II: PERSONAL HISTORY AND BACKGROUND

Question: What has my personal background to do with this case?

Answer: A great deal. A deposition is a search for truth. You may be asked questions concerning your marital and divorce history, how many children you have, their names and ages, your age, where you were born, where you have resided in the past, your schooling and educational background, your employment history, if you have ever been in jail—and many similar questions. Your lawyer will object to any questions he considers improper.

Question: If there is something in my personal history which happened a long time ago, how can I keep the incident from coming out?

Answer: The only *positive* protection you can rely on is to confide in your lawyer. Unburden yourself of the worry you may have regarding incidents which occurred in your life. It is quite possible the incidents have nothing to do with the issues in your case and can be kept out as a matter of law. If you disclose your concern to your lawyer he will evaluate the problem, review its importance and advise you how the matter can best be handled. Obviously *if you fail to tell your lawyer* the matter may come out during the deposition and he will be unable to come to your assistance.

Question: This accident was not my fault. Why are these questions concerning my personal life so important?

175

Answer: A lawsuit makes some areas of your life an open book. The questions about your personal life may have nothing to do directly with the accident—indirectly, they may have significance. These questions have to do with who you are, how your accident has presently affected your life and how your life may be affected in the future.

Question: What is so important about my past divorce or remarriage history?

Answer: You must accept the fact that certain information you consider "your business" is no longer completely private and may be significant and proper areas for questioning. You should keep in mind that your lawyer must know these details before your deposition is taken.

All information given to your lawyer is confidential. If you fail to disclose the required information, your lawyer may not be able to enter an objection to information which would ordinarily be inadmissible. He will be unable to fully protect your rights at the deposition *if he is not fully informed.*

Question: What significance is attached to the places I have lived in the past?

Answer: The purpose of learning your past residences (in some cases all the way back to your date of birth) has to do, among other things, with any possible claim or accident you may have had in the past. *Any previous injuries may affect this case.* You must reveal these previous injuries to your lawyer so he will know how to deal properly with these facts.

Insurance companies maintain a thoroughly documented index of all claims and lawsuits. This information is indexed under your name, place of residence and other similar categories.

Question: Will I be asked if anyone ever sued me or if I was ever a party in a lawsuit?

Answer: Yes. If you are asked such questions, be prepared to answer truthfully. Be sure you tell your own lawyer about any lawsuits in which you were either the suing party, or the person against whom the lawsuit was filed.

Do not surprise your own lawyer at your deposition with the fact that you were sued or sued someone else. *Discuss any of these facts in advance of the deposition.*

SECTION III: FACTS OF THE ACCIDENT

Question: What will the lawyer ask me regarding the facts of the accident?

Answer: The questioning regarding the accident will probably start with the day, date, time and place it occurred. Thereafter, the questions will relate to *how* it occurred, and *what* happened to you personally. Be prepared to answer questions about everything you personally know about the accident. *You should not attempt to fill in details you do not know.*

Question: Will the opposing lawyer skip from one subject matter to another?

Answer: Every lawyer develops his own particular style of asking questions. Some skip from one subject to another and others follow a definite pattern. You can avoid confusion by paying close attention to the questions asked. Always remember you have the right to have a question repeated or clarified if you did not understand it or did not hear it. If you stick with the facts as you know them, no amount of skipping around should confuse you.

Question: How specific will the questions be that are asked of me?

Answer: This, of course, will depend upon the lawyer taking the deposition. You should answer specific questions with specific answers whenever it is possible.

Some lawyers may be purposely vague, others may be very specific. Some lawyers will dwell at great length upon what appear to be minor details. Your lawyer will know when to enter an objection to questions which are vague. If the opposing lawyer asks detailed questions, your own lawyer may determine it best not to enter objections. He may be learning much about your case that otherwise might not be known to him.

Question: Is it proper for me to visit the place where the accident happened before my deposition is taken?

Answer: Yes, if it is conveniently located. Do not travel out of town to visit the place of your accident without first checking with your lawyer. If you do visit the scene of the accident, estimate the distances involved, (how far you were from certain points to other points).

Observe the location of highway and road markings, signs, places of business, street lights, traffic lights and all other such objects.

Question: The accident happened so quickly I can't remember all the details. What should I do about that?

Answer: Take the time to think about how the accident happened. Go over the details in your own way. Retrace your activities. Take yourself back as far as necessary to piece together the events before, at the time of and after the accident.

Question: The accident happened so long ago I can't remember all the details. What should I do?

Answer: Your lawyer has many details in his file that you are probably unaware of. With your permission he has obtained police, hospital, medical, employment and other records. When he reviews your case with you, he will go over these items and will assist you in recalling the details you may have forgotten. Do not panic. Be calm. Refresh your memory.

Question: How should I review what happened in my accident?

Answer: Go over such things as where you had been before the accident happened. What was the weather like? What were you doing? Where were you going? Why were you going wherever you were going? What route did you take or how did you get to the place of the accident? How long did it take you to get there? How far did you travel? How were traffic conditions? As you think about these general questions, the details will probably come back to you.

Question: Will I be asked questions about the car I was operating or was riding in?

Answer: Yes. Be prepared to answer such questions if you know the answers. If not, your lawyer will probably have this information in your file.

It is likely that you will be asked if your car had an automatic transmission, seatbelts, a stick shift, power steering, power brakes; if the lights were on or off; if it was a four door or convertible, and other similar questions relating to the type of car and its condition. You may be asked about the tires on your automobile, and if the windshield wipers were working. Was the radio on? Was the heater or air conditioner working? Which windows were up or down? When and where did you purchase the car? Was it in good working condition before the accident?

Question: What measurements should I be prepared to talk about?

Answer: Generally—the length and width of your car, the width of the streets involved, the distance you were from certain objects

178

such as intersecting streets, traffic lights, other vehicles, cross-walks, street markings, traffic signs, curbs, edges of the road, etc. You should be aware of the posted speed limits at the time of the accident, how fast or slow you were traveling; if you were stopped and for what length of time.

Question: I didn't measure these things when the accident happened. How can I know them at the time of the deposition?

Answer: Answers to questions relating to distances and other measurements need not be exact. Your best judgment will be sufficient if you can give a reasonably accurate estimate. Your lawyer may have exact measurements, but he will not expect you to memorize and know them to the inch. When he prepares you for your deposition he will review these details with you.

Question: If the center of the roadway was not marked, how can I tell where I was in the roadway at the time of the accident?

Answer: Think about how close or how far your vehicle was from the curb or edge of the roadway on your right. Consider the width of your own car as compared to the width of the roadway. Recall (if you can) about cars that approached, passed, or were behind you before, at the time of, or after the accident.

Question: Is it important to recall about sounds, (like horns or the squealing of tires) or such other matters?

Answer: Yes. Tell your lawyer what you saw, heard and even smelled. He will determine the importance of every detail and he will relate these details to your whole case.

Question: If things were said to me by the other party, should I tell the other lawyer about them?

Answer: Only if you are asked to answer questions concerned with such conversations. By all means be sure to discuss with your lawyer *before* the deposition any conversations which took place at the scene of the accident. It is important to tell your lawyer where and when these conversations took place and who, if anyone, was present at the time.

Question: What should I be prepared to say about the police officer or officers who came to the scene of the accident?

Answer: What the police officers said to you and to the other parties will be important. Did the officers take photographs or make measurements of skid marks? Did they obtain the names and addresses of witnesses? *Before* your deposition tell your lawyer about the investigations made by the police officers.

Be sure to tell your lawyer when and if you signed anything for the police or any other person at the scene, in the hospital or at your home. If you did write or sign a statement for the police or any other investigator, you should try to remember what was written in the statement—and tell your lawyer all about it. If you have a copy of the statement you signed be sure to give it to your lawyer.

Question: Must I know the exact compass directions like East, West, North and South?

Answer: If you do not recall the directions your lawyer will be able to assist you. Were you headed uptown, downtown or cross-town? Were you going in the direction of a certain community or away from it? If you can read a map you should use one when going over the details of the accident at home or with your lawyer. By doing so you will be able to pinpoint your location and the direction involved as well as the other streets or roadways in the area where the accident occurred.

Question: I realize you cannot cover every single question I might be asked, but are there other areas of questioning that I should know about?

Answer: Yes: These are other general areas you should think about when you review your case in your own mind:

(a) Where in the roadway or in the intersection did the impact occur?

(b) Where did the vehicles come to rest after the impact?

(c) Did you see any dirt or debris in the roadway from the vehicles after the collision?

(d) Where was the debris located?

(e) Where was the damage to your vehicle?

(f) Where was the damage to the other vehicle or vehicles?

(g) Were the vehicles moved from the place of collision before the police arrived?

(h) Did you notice any skid marks from the vehicle or vehicles involved (including your own)?

(i) Where were these skid marks? What was the length of the skid marks?

(j) What were you doing and where were you looking just before the collision occurred?

(k) Was there any change in the speed or movement of your vehicle before the collision?

(*l*) Was your vehicle moved in any direction because of the impact? Which way? How far?

(m) Were there other vehicles at or near the scene of the collision (where were they and what were these vehicles doing)?

(n) If you were stopped before the collision, how long were you stopped? Pretend you are stopped, look at your wristwatch or clock second sweephand and try to judge the time lapse.

(o) Do you remember the type of road surface?

(p) What parts of the vehicles contacted each other?

(q) Did you apply your brakes? Did you blow your horn? Did you swerve? Did you go straight ahead?

(r) Was the contour of the roadway hilly, level, curving or straight?

Question: Will I be asked at the deposition to make a drawing of the scene of the accident?

Answer: Probably—so be prepared to do so. Try to make a rough sketch at home. Make streets wide enough to allow room to put cars and other objects in proper location and perspective. You are not expected to prepare an artist's drawing. Talk it over with your lawyer. He may not want you to make a sketch if you are asked to do so at the deposition. *Be guided by what your lawyer advises you to do.*

SECTION IV: INJURIES AND MEDICAL TREATMENT

Question: Will the other lawyer know what injuries I received in the accident?

Answer: In some cases, yes. In others no. Assume that he does not know about your injuries. You will then be better prepared to discuss them in detail.

Question: How will I recognize the questions that have to do with my injuries?

Answer: There are several key questions, one or two of which will probably be asked: "What happened to you?" or "Were you injured?" or "What injuries do you claim you received as the result of this accident?"

Question: What questions will I be asked concerning my injuries?

Answer: There are approximately four general categories of information relating to your injuries which you will be questioned about:

(a) The specific areas of your body which you claim to have injured;

(b) The hospital, medical and other care you received;

(c) Your complaints of pain and disability;

(d) Your present condition.

Question: Is there some special order I should follow in discussing my injuries?

Answer: Yes. If you sustained injuries to several areas of your body, then discuss them in their anatomical order—from your head on down to your toes. You will be better able to recall the injuries you suffered if you follow this anatomical order.

Question: What if the particular injury or injuries no longer give me any difficulty. What do I say about that?

Answer: The truth. For example:

Q: How long did you have these pounding headaches?

A: They lasted for about three months following the accident.

Q: And I take it you have had no trouble with headaches since that time, is that correct?

A: That is correct.

Question: Will the lawyer go through each of my injuries?

Answer: Yes. The lawyer will probably take each area of injury and go through the same process of questioning you about it. Answer truthfully to each series of questions regarding each injury. Do not exaggerate or minimize your injuries or complaints.

Question: If an injury still bothers me and I am not asked fully about it, what do I say or do?

Answer: Follow the questions carefully. If you have described each injury and the lawyer fails to ask you about any particular one of them, do not be disturbed. For example:

Q: Does your fractured knee still bother you?

Q: Yes.

If the lawyer asks no further questions regarding your knee do not offer to give any further answers. Your lawyer will cover your complaints thoroughly at the time of trial if the case is not settled.

Assume you will be asked to fully describe your complaints. Be prepared to do so.

Question: How thorough should my answers be if the particular injury does bother me and I am asked about it?

Answer: As thorough as the question requires you to be. For example:

Q: How does your knee bother you now?

A: It is painful to bend it. The pain shoots up my thigh and down my leg. I am unable to kneel on my knee—like at work or at church. It swells up at the end of the day. I can't climb ladders like I did before. At times it gets so painful I limp.

Q: Does your knee ache every day?

A: No.

Q: When does the knee not ache you?

A: When I am off my feet. Usually on my days away from work.

If the particular injury no longer bothers you, say so. For example:

Q: How does your right shoulder bother you now?

A: It no longer bothers me.

Q: When did it stop giving you difficulty?

A: It cleared up about two weeks after the accident.

Q: What difficulty did you have with the right shoulder during the two week period following the accident?

A: It ached and I had pain when I lifted it or moved it.

Question: Will I be required to show scars or injuries if exposing that part of my body may be embarrassing to me?

Answer: No. If the opposing side desires to know about such scars or injuries they will request a medical examination. But as embarrassing as it might be, you should answer questions truthfully and honestly regarding these areas of your body. Every effort will be made to avoid sensitive situations. You must bear in mind however that injuries which you refuse to discuss cannot be evaluated by the opposing lawyer or the insurance company.

Question: If I have an injury which is best demonstrated by walking or going through some particular motion, should I do so?

Answer: Only if you are asked to by your lawyer or by the lawyer asking you the questions.

Question: If my injury is visible and can be shown without disrobing or creating an embarrassing situation should I offer to exhibit it?

Answer: You should *not offer* to do so.

If asked to see it, then you may do so without hesitation. Anything that will help the lawyers understand your problem will assist them in assessing the injury and the relationship it may have with respect to the value of your case.

Question: If the lawyer wants to feel the lump, scar or deformity, should I comply?

Answer: It depends on its location and your willingness to permit it. There is a sincere desire to know the extent of your injuries and if feeling the injured area will add to the lawyer's knowledge of the problem, it should be permitted. Your lawyer will object if he feels the opposing lawyer's actions are inappropriate.

Question: If I have pain as the result of any of my injuries at the time my deposition is being taken should I say so?

Answer: Yes, if that is the truth.

Question: Will I be asked about the medical or hospital treatment I received?

Answer: Yes. Questions relating to this subject usually follow a discussion of your injuries.

You will probably be asked when you received medical or hospital treatment, who or what institution gave it, and the type of treatment given.

Question: Must I know the names of the doctors and hospitals and exact dates of confinements, visits and treatments?

Answer: Yes, if the information is requested. If you cannot recall exact dates of treatment, give an estimate of the date of the initial examination and the number of subsequent visits, and the general period of time covered. Your lawyer will verify the dates for you from the information he has in your file before you go to the deposition.

Question: If my lawyer referred me to a doctor or doctors for examination, should I tell about that if I am asked to do so?

Answer: Yes. Your lawyer has a right to send you to doctors to help him evaluate your injuries. If it was a friend, relative or your family doctor who recommended another doctor, say so. If it was your lawyer, say so.

Question: If I am asked what the doctor or doctors did for me am I permitted to answer?

Answer: Yes. You may tell what they did for you and the treatment recommended, as well as all medicine prescribed or given to you.

Question: Should I see my doctor or doctors and talk over any injuries or have another examination before I go to the deposition?

Answer: Only if your lawyer recommends that you do so. Ask him.

Question: Will I be asked about medical examinations by doctors who are not involved in the treatment and care of my injuries?

Answer: Yes. Answer truthfully about such examinations. Be sure you tell your own lawyer about any examinations which were done at work, for life insurance, health and accident insurance or other reasons.

Question: Will I be asked how I got to the hospital or the doctor's office?

Answer: Yes. If someone took you or you were taken by ambulance you should say so. If you drove yourself to the doctor do not hesitate to admit it. If you went by taxi or car driven by another person or in a public conveyance, say so.

Question: Will I be asked about illnesses or operations which had nothing to do with any accidents?

Answer: Yes. You should not *volunteer* information about operations or illnesses. Discuss them only if you are asked questions about them.

Question: What questions will I be asked about injuries I suffered before or after the date of the present accident?

Answer: You may be asked to describe the injuries you received and what complaints of pain you had and how long the pain persisted.

Question: If I was injured before or after the present accident *but I did not file a lawsuit,* and was paid by the insurance company, how do I answer if I am asked?

Answer: The manner in which you answer the question will depend on *exactly* what you are asked. For example, opposing lawyer asks:

Q: Have you ever *filed* a lawsuit in which you claimed damages for personal injuries?

A: No.

Q: Have you ever suffered any injury before or after the date of this accident?

A: Yes.

Q: Have you ever made a claim for injury before or after the date of this accident?

A: Yes.

If you *deny* having filed a lawsuit or *made a claim* when in fact you did, you may needlessly impair or completely destroy your right to recover damages in your present case. Search your memory carefully and thoroughly for any lawsuits, claims or injuries you suffered (regardless if you were or were not paid) and report them to your lawyer.

Section V: THE DAMAGES CLAIMED

Question: What does the word "damages" mean?

Answer: Damages are the dollars you lost, paid or owe as the result of injuries received in your accident. Be prepared to talk about the cost of first aid, ambulances, medical and hospital care and treatment, drugs and appliances (crutches, braces, etc.), nurses, loss of income or wages, property damage (your automobile, personal effects, clothing, luggage, etc.), therapy treatments, transportation expense to and from the doctors and special help at home during the period you were confined or unable to care for yourself or family.

Question: If I have not paid the bills, do these items count in adding up the damages I incurred?

Answer: Yes.

Question: At the time of the accident I carried insurance that paid for my hospital and doctor bills. Can I still claim these bills as damages in my case?

Answer: Yes. Any exceptions will be explained by your lawyer.

Question: If I lost time from work, but my employer paid me, what should I say?

Answer: If you are asked this specific question "were you paid for the time you claim you lost from work?", then your answer should be "yes." (If you used up vacation or accumulated sick leave time, be sure to tell your lawyer before going to the deposition).

Question: Will I be asked how my pay is figured (by the hour, salary, etc.)?

Answer: Yes. Be prepared to answer detailed information regarding your loss of income, the days, weeks or months you lost from work; overtime pay or bonus arrangements.

In answering questions regarding your rate of pay, your answers should be based on your *gross* pay check (the amount of your check before deductions for income tax, social security, union dues, etc.). For example if your pay check before deductions is $750.00 per week you should say "my weekly pay is $750.00 per week." *Your take home pay may be $500.00 or less,* but in discussing your wage loss at the deposition you should always refer to your weekly or semi-monthly or monthly pay as being $750, $900 or $1200—whatever your *gross* pay check is.

Question: The time I lost was not all at once. I lost some time right after the accident and then I lost a day every now and then. Will I be required to give exact dates?

Answer: Yes. The more accurate you are the more reliable will be the damages you claim. Your employer keeps an attendance record in order to make up the payroll. Ask your employer to give you a letter setting forth the exact days or part days you were off, the reason for the particular absence, and your rate of pay at the time of the absence.

Question: Will I be paid for the time I lost from work to come to the deposition?

Answer: If you are the party who brought the lawsuit, you will not be paid.

Question: My accident occurred while I was on the job and I received Workmen's Compensation for the time I was off. Also my doctor bills were paid by the Industrial Commission or Compensation Insurer. Will I be asked about Workmen's Compensation payments?

Answer: You should not volunteer information concerning a Workmen's Compensation claim. Your lawyer will object if he deems it necessary to do so. He will explain the law to you and how these questions should be answered if you are asked.

Question: Will I have to bring my tax returns to prove my loss of income?

Answer: Only if your lawyer says you should.

Question: Should I bring all of my bills to the deposition?

Answer: No. You should give all bills connected with your accident, whether they are paid or unpaid, to your lawyer.

Section VI: PERSONAL MEMORANDUM

Use this section to list any additional questions you wish to ask your lawyer.

_____

_____

_____

_____

CHAPTER 5

TAILORING THE SUIT

"Well begun is half done"
Horace

Analysis

A. IN GENERAL

A. IN GENERAL

§ 5.1 Creative Decisions

The trouble with the case book method of studying law is that the focus of attention is on the appellate decisions which dispose of legal issues which arose after litigation was initiated. The law student is apt to believe that lawsuits are auto genetic—that Lumley versus Guy was a fated feud and Winterbottom versus Wright an alliterative inevitability. Little or no attention is given to the creativity that was exercised by the lawyers in bringing the suit into being. It is important to read, with the hope of understanding, the views of Judges Cardozo and Andrews on proximate cause as stated in the *Palsgraf* case. But it is of equal importance to know why Mrs. Palsgraf's lawyer sued the Long Island Railroad for failing to assist a passenger and didn't sue the owner of the unstable scales for negligent maintenance.

A lawsuit is similar to a battle in many respects. The casual historian thrills to the charge at Balaclava and the retreat from Moscow. These matters are objective, easily understood and described. The military student ponders the problems of logistics, the choice of supply routes, the disposition of forces. He knows that these are the factors which will determine the success of the charge and the consequence of the retreat.

Similarly the third party observer to litigation is apt to concentrate on the issues of law raised on appeal. They are spelled out in the opinion and can be easily analyzed and discussed. The student of advocacy will study the choice of theories, choice of forums and choice of parties knowing that these are the factors which will set the stage for the litigation and determine the legal issues about which the judges will write.

B. CHOICE OF FORUM

§ 5.2 Significance of Choice of Forum—Generally

There are a number of decisions that must be made at the outset. One doesn't necessarily precede the other but each depends upon the other. One of these initial decisions is where the lawsuit should be filed. While this decision is controlled to a great extent by jurisdiction, venue, service of process, and other restrictions, the plaintiff will often have a choice of which court to bring the action in.

Recognition should be made of the fact that the value of any commodity is effected by the site of the market place. Refrigerators in Reykjavik are not as saleable as they are in Rio de Janeiro. Oddly enough this same rule of the market place applies with as much force with fractures as it does with Frigidaires. Where have most of the astronomically large personal injury verdicts been recorded? Note the statistics of the casualty insurance companies and they will reflect the "high verdict" and "low verdict" areas of the country and of each state. There may be a few exceptions but generally in the former category would be the urban, middle and lower economic class, "Democratic type" areas while in the latter would be the rural and suburban, middle and upper economic class, "Republican type" areas. No need to make your own sociological studies as to which is which. Just ask a veteran local trial lawyer—he will know.

§ 5.3 Procedural Factors—Generally

The choice of forum (assuming the jurisdiction, venue, etc., restrictions permit a choice) might be between courts within the same jurisdiction, courts of different states or courts of a state or those within the federal system.

In each instance there will be differences that exist.

As to the first, there might be a choice between a court of limited jurisdiction and general jurisdiction. As to the former, as they exist in some jurisdictions, there may be limited pretrial discovery, smaller sized juries, de novo trials on appeal and other significant procedural differences.

As to the second, there may exist local customs and court rules that create differences as well as the well known phenomenon of "high verdict—low verdict" counties.

As to the third, the procedural differences may be legion. We will consider the more important.

§ 5.4 Procedural Factors—Pretrial Conference

The differences that exist between pretrial discovery as it exists within state courts as compared to federal courts are becoming less and less as more of the states model their procedural rules on the Federal Rules of Civil Procedure. But even though the verbiage of the rules may be the same there are few state judges which have applied those rules with the same spiritual fervor as do their federal counterparts.

Take the matter of pretrial conference. Although provided for in most jurisdictions it is uniformly ignored in some and uniformly employed in others. For those courts which do utilize this procedural tool it may be a perfunctory get-together, more social than anything else, in which the judge informally explores the possibility of settlement and, if unsuccessful, ascertains the length of trial, marks the exhibits and asks for preliminary drafts of jury instructions. Or, for the more devoted jurist, the pretrial conference may be more accurately described as a mini-trial in which the parties exchange their list of witnesses, exhibits, jury instructions, expert's reports and witness statements and identify the issues that are conceded and those disputed. It is often literally an exchange of files. No wonder one lawyer was prompted to inquire at the conclusion of his first such procedure, "If I lose before the judge, do I have a trial de novo before the jury?"

To grasp the enthusiasm with which some courts employ pretrial procedures, the rules adopted by the United States District Court, Western District of Missouri follow in §§ 5.5 and 5.6.

§ 5.5 Procedural Factors—Pretrial Conference—Illustrative Orders (Federal–Civil)

[**Note:** *The following Orders are from the United States District Court, Western District of Missouri.*]

PRETRIAL INSTRUCTIONS

The success of a pretrial conference depends in great measure upon the thoroughness and care with which counsel are prepared and cooperate with the Court.

At the time a pretrial conference is held in this Court, the attorneys will be required to cover such of the following items as are appropriate to the instant action:

1. A brief statement of facts that the plaintiff expects to prove in support of his claim.

2. A brief statement of facts that the defendant expects to prove as a defense thereto.

3. Similar statements as to any counterclaim or crossclaim.

4. Any amendments required of the pleadings.

5. Any tender of issue in the pleadings that is to be abandoned.

6. Any stipulation of facts that the attorney is willing to make, or on which he requests an admission.

7. The details of the damages claimed, or any other relief sought, as of the date of the pretrial conference.

8. All documents and records to be offered in evidence at the trial must be produced at the conference.

9. The names and specialties of experts to be called as witnesses.

10. Any other pretrial relief which the attorney will request.

In some cases the Court will notify counsel to submit typewritten memorandums concerning such items. When so notified, each counsel will prepare and file in Court, and serve on opposing counsel, such a typewritten memorandum two (2) days before the pretrial conference is held.

In preparation for the pretrial conference, the attorneys are requested to discuss with each other the matters listed above.

The attorneys appearing at the pretrial conference must be prepared to discuss the action and be authorized to act for their clients. If an attorney for a party fails to appear at a pretrial conference, the Judge may act as in the case of a non-appearance for trial.

STANDARD PRETRIAL ORDER NO. 1

1. On or before the _____ day of _____, 19__, each party shall complete all discovery authorized by Rules 26 to 37, inclusive, of the Federal Rules of Civil Procedure and by Sections 1781 and 1783 of Title 28, U.S.C., including, but not limited to, depositions on oral interrogatories, deposi-

tions on written interrogatories, production of documents for inspection and copying, written interrogatories to parties, requests for admissions, examination for mental or physical condition, depositions on letters rogatory or by subpoena under Section 1783 of Title 28, U.S.C. No further or additional discovery shall be permitted thereafter except by leave of the Court for good cause shown, provided that supplementation of responses to a request for discovery under subparagraph (e) of Rule 26, F.R.Civ. P., shall not require leave of Court.

2. After the completion of discovery generally under this Rule or any special order of Court, any party may, without leave of Court, submit written interrogatories to determine whether there has been a change of relevant circumstances or relevant occurrences since the close of discovery; and before trial, and with leave of Court, may undertake additional discovery concerning changes of relevant circumstances and relevant occurrences since the close of discovery.

3. In any action in which the present, past, or future physical or mental condition of a person is in issue, neither the party or person whose condition is in issue nor any other party shall be entitled to prevent discovery by asserting any physician-patient privilege provided by state law against discovery of information concerning such physical or mental condition or prior history directly related thereto. Any abuse of discovery under this Rule may be made the basis of a motion for a protective order under Rule 26(c), F.R.Civ.P.

4. Interrogatories to parties, in forms approved by rule or order of the Court en banc, may be propounded in appropriate cases. No objection to the form or substance thereof should be made when so used.

Filing of Lists of Potential Witnesses.

1. Within 10 days after the time fixed for the completion of discovery by the provisions of this Rule, unless otherwise ordered by the Court, counsel for each party shall prepare, serve, and file (on a separate sheet or separate sheets of legal-size paper) a list of the names and addresses of all witnesses who may be called on behalf of his client at the

        trial, excepting witnesses who may be called for impeachment purposes only.

2. Except for good cause shown, and with leave of Court, and except solely for the purpose of impeachment, counsel shall not be permitted to call at the trial any witness who is not so listed by the counsel calling the witness.

3. After expiration of the time for filing lists of witnesses, no supplemental or amended list of witnesses shall be filed without leave of Court.

Numbering and Filing of Lists of Exhibits.

1. Within 10 days after the time fixed for the completion of discovery by the provisions of this Rule, unless otherwise ordered by the Court, counsel for each party shall prepare, serve, and file (on a separate sheet or separate sheets of legal-size paper) a list of all exhibits which may be offered in evidence at the trial on behalf of his client. Each plaintiff's exhibit shall be given an Arabic numeral such as "P. Ex. 1" and shall be described following the enumeration. Each defendant's exhibit shall be given an Arabic numeral such as "D. Ex. 1" and shall be described following the enumeration. If an exhibit consists of more than one page or parts, the number of pages or parts shall be included in the description. The enumeration of the exhibit shall be endorsed on each exhibit at the time of listing except as hereinafter provided. It shall not be necessary to list exhibits to be used for impeachment purposes only. X-rays to be offered in evidence which are in the possession of a radiologist, physician, hospital, or other professional practitioner, shall be enumerated separately. The description of an x-ray may be limited to the name of the person at whose direction the x-ray was taken or to the name of the custodian thereof, and to a description of the type thereof. Endorsement of identifying exhibit numbers on x-rays, original hospital records, and other original exhibits, copies of which are not available to the counsel listing the exhibit, may be reserved until trial.

2. Except for good cause shown, and with leave of Court, and except solely for the purpose of impeachment, no exhibit shall be received in evidence which is not so listed by the counsel offering the exhibit.

3. After expiration of the time for filing lists of exhibits, no supplemental or amended list of exhibits shall be filed without leave of Court.

Filing of Stipulation of Uncontroverted Facts and Standard Pretrial Order No. 2.

1. Within 20 days after the time fixed for the completion of discovery by the provisions of this Rule (or if the United States is a party, within 40 days thereafter), unless otherwise ordered by the Court, counsel for each party shall meet and enter into a stipulation of uncontroverted facts, waive objections to admissibility of exhibits on the ground of lack of identification when the identification thereof is not to be contested, and, at the option of counsel, agree upon the submission in writing, prior to trial, of any legal question or questions involved. At this conference counsel shall produce each exhibit (excepting x-ray, original hospital records, and other original exhibits, copies of which are not available) listed on behalf of his client for inspection by counsel for other parties and for waiver of objection to admissibility on the ground of lack of identification. The stipulation so agreed upon under this paragraph may be filed in a separate document or included in an agreed Standard Pretrial Order No. 2.

2. Unless otherwise ordered or agreed, counsel for plaintiff or plaintiffs shall initiate arrangements for this conference and cause to be prepared and filed within 40 days after the time fixed for the completion of discovery (or if the United States is a party, within 60 days thereafter) a separate document on legal-size paper which is in compliance with paragraph G.1. of this Rule.

3. Before the conclusion of the conference of counsel under this paragraph G., counsel shall undertake to agree upon a pretrial conference order in the form set forth in Standard Pretrial Order No. 2 attached hereto, the form of which agreed order shall be subject to amendment by order of the Court. The agreed order, if any, shall then be prepared and filed by counsel for the plaintiff or plaintiffs as soon as is reasonably possible and in no event later than 50 days after the time fixed for completion of discovery (or if the United States is a party, within 70 days thereafter), unless otherwise ordered by the Court.

4. Unless otherwise ordered by the Court, if counsel are unable to agree upon a Standard Pretrial Order No. 2 before the conclusion of the conference of counsel under this paragraph G., counsel for each party shall within 40 days after the time fixed for completion of discovery (or if the United States is a party, within 60 days thereafter) prepare, serve, and file a complete proposed form of Standard Pretrial Order No. 2 for consideration by the Court.

Filing of Lists of Voir Dire Questions and Requests for Instructions in Jury Cases.

1. In actions to be tried by a jury, on or before the third day prior to the date on which the cause is set for trial, counsel for each party
   a. Is requested to prepare, serve, and file (on a separate sheet or separate sheets of legal-size paper) a list of questions or topics for voir dire examination desired to be propounded by the Court;
   b. Is requested to submit in writing requests for instructions to the jury which can be anticipated. Each instruction shall be appropriately numbered and on a separate sheet of legal-size paper, shall cover no more than one subject, and shall have the source and authority upon which it is based and the name of the party submitting it noted at the bottom of the page. In any event, such written requests for instructions shall be served and filed after the case is called for trial and before the beginning of the opening statements; and
   c. May file a trial brief on any questions of fact or law which are expected to arise.

Filing of Trial Briefs and Suggested Findings of Facts in Non-jury Cases.

1. In actions to be tried without a jury, on or before the third day prior to the date on which the cause is set for trial, counsel for each party
   a. May serve and file a trial brief stating separately the factual and legal contentions for the party for whom the trial brief is filed, with citation of authorities relied upon in respect to each legal contention;
   b. Shall serve and file suggested findings of fact and suggested conclusions of law separately stated in separately numbered paragraphs.

Filing Hypothetical Questions in Jury or Nonjury Cases.

1. In actions to be tried by a jury or by the Court without a jury, on or before the third day prior to the date on which the action is set for trial, counsel for each party shall prepare, place in a labeled, sealed envelope, and file the hypothesis of any hypothetical question or questions that may be asked of any listed witness at the trial. The Clerk shall make such filing *in camera.* No hypothesis so filed will be revealed to opposing counsel before its use without order of the Court, but such an order may be requested by any party.

STANDARD PRETRIAL ORDER NO. 2

(including Stipulation of Uncontroverted Facts)

Following pretrial proceedings pursuant to Rule 16 of the Federal Rules of Civil Procedure (and Supplemental Admiralty Rules, if applicable) and Rule 20 of this Court,

IT IS ORDERED

I. This is an action for:
(Here state the nature of action, designate the parties and list the pleadings which raise the issues.)

II. Federal jurisdiction is invoked upon the ground:
(Here list the legal authority for jurisdiction and a concise statement of the facts requisite to confer Federal jurisdiction.)

III. The following facts are admitted, and require no proof:
(Here list each admitted fact, including jurisdictional facts.)

IV. The reservations as to the facts recited in Paragraph III above are as follows:
(Here set forth any objection reserved by any party as to the admissibility in evidence of any admitted fact and, if desired by any party, limiting the effect of any admission of fact as provided by Rule 36(b) of the Federal Rules of Civil Procedure, or Supplemental Admiralty Rules, as the case may be).

V. The following facts, though not admitted, are not to be contested at the trial by evidence to the contrary:
(Here list each).

VI. The following issues of fact, and no others, remain to be litigated upon the trial:
(Here specify each; a mere general statement will not suffice).

VII. The exhibits to be offered at the trial, together with a statement of all admissions by and all issues between the parties with respect thereto, are as follows:

(Here list all documents and things intended to be offered at the trial by each party, other than those to be used for impeachment, in the sequence proposed to be offered, with a description of each sufficient for identification, and a statement of all admissions by and all issues between any of the parties as to the genuineness thereof, the due execution thereof, and the truth of relevant matters of fact set forth therein or in any legend affixed thereto, together with a statement of any objections reserved as to the admissibility in evidence thereof).

VIII. The following issues of law, and no others, remain to be litigated upon the trial:

(Here set forth a concise statement of each).

  IX. The foregoing admissions having been made by the parties, and the parties having specified the foregoing issues of fact and law remaining to be litigated, this order shall supplement the pleadings and govern the course of the trial of this cause, unless modified to prevent manifest injustice, or to implement Rule 26(e), F.R.Civ.P.

————, 19—

_____
United States District Judge

Approved as to form and
content: _____
Attorney for Plaintiff

_____
Attorney for Defendant

STANDARD PRETRIAL ORDER NO. 3

Pretrial Order Providing for Filing of Questions for Voir Dire Examination, Submission of Requests for Instructions to Jury Prior to Trial, Trial Briefs at Option of Counsel, Filing of Suggested Findings of Fact and Suggested Conclusions of Law in Nonjury Cases, and Filing in Camera Hypothetical Questions

For good cause shown, it is hereby

ORDERED as follows:

1. In actions to be tried by a jury, on or before the third day prior to the date on which the cause is set for trial, counsel for each party

    a.   Is requested to prepare, serve, and file (on a separate sheet or separate sheets of legal-size paper) a list of questions or topics for voir dire examination desired to be propounded by the Court;

    b.   Is requested to submit in writing requests for instructions to the jury which can be anticipated. Each instruction shall be appropriately numbered and on a separate sheet of legal-size paper, shall cover no more than one subject, and shall have the source and authority upon which it is based and name of the party submitting it noted at the bottom of the page. In any event, such written requests for instructions shall be served and filed after the case is called for trial and before the beginning of the opening statements; and

    c.   May file a trial brief on any questions of fact or law which are expected to arise.

2.   In actions to be tried by the Court without a jury, on or before the third day prior to the date on which the cause is set for trial, counsel for each party

    a.   May serve and file a trial brief stating separately the factual and legal contentions of the party for whom the trial brief is filed, with citation of authorities relied upon in respect to each legal contention; and

    b.   Shall serve and file suggested findings of fact and suggested conclusions of law separately stated in separately numbered paragraphs.

3.   In actions to be tried by a jury or by the Court without a jury, on or before the third day prior to the date on which the action is set for trial, counsel for each party shall prepare, place in a labeled, sealed envelope, and file the hypothesis of any hypothetical question or questions that may be asked of any listed witness at the trial. The Clerk shall make such filing *in camera*. No hypothesis so filed will be revealed to opposing counsel before its use without order of the Court, but such an order may be requested by any party.

§ 5.6   Procedural Factors—Pretrial Discovery—Illustration (Federal–Criminal)

[**Note:** *The following "Omnibus Hearing Report" is from the United States District Court, Western District of Missouri.*]

OMNIBUS HEARING REPORT

A. **Presentment to Grand Jury**
    1.   Indictment No. _____; Returned _____.
    2.   The defendant has been advised and understands that the Government cannot file a felony charge against him un-

less the matter is presented to a Federal Grand Jury, who may or may not initiate the charge by indictment. With an understanding of his right to have the charges proposed by the Government presented to a Federal Grand Jury, and having been furnished with a copy of the proposed information, defendant states that it is his intention to (not) waive his right to have his case presented to a Federal Grand Jury.

3. Defendant(s) No.(s) _____ was a juvenile at the time of the commission of the offense and will be proceeded against as a juvenile delinquent and defendant will agree to be proceeded against as such.

4. The United States will file an information or complaint charging a minor or petty offense.

B. **Discovery by Defendant**

1. The defense states it has inspected the Government file (except) (If Government has refused discovery of certain materials, other than Grand Jury transcripts, defense counsel shall state nature of material _____)

2. The Government states it has disclosed all evidence in its possession, favorable to the issue of guilt.

3. Defendant, having had discovery of item Nos. B. 1 and B. 2, requests and moves for discovery and inspection of all further and additional information coming into the Government's possession as to item
Nos. B. 1 and B. 2.   (Granted)   (Denied)

4. Defendant requests and moves for the following information:

     4(a) Discovery of all oral, written, or recorded statements or testimony made by defendant to investigating officers, third parties or before a grand jury. (Rule 16(a)(1), (13))

                       (Granted)   (Denied)

     4(b) Reports or tests of physical or mental examinations of the defendant in the control of the prosecution. (Rule 16(a)(2))

                       (Granted)   (Denied)

     4(c) Reports of scientific tests, experiments or comparisons and other reports of experts in the control of the prosecution, pertaining to this case. (Rule 16(a)(2))

     4(d) Inspection and/or copying of any books, papers, documents, photographs, or tangible objects which the prosecution—

         (1) Obtained from or belonging to the defendant, and/or,

         (2) Which will be used at the hearing or trial. (Rule 16(b))

                       (Granted)   (Denied)

4(e) Discovery of the names and addresses of plaintiff's witnesses and their statements at least *10 days* prior to trial.

(Granted)   (Denied)

5. The defense requests the following information and the Government states:

5(a) The Government will (not) rely on prior acts or convictions of a similar nature for proof of knowledge or intent.

5(b) Information concerning all prior felony convictions of persons whom the prosecution intends to call as witnesses at the hearing or trial will be supplied to counsel for the defendant in writing *5 days* prior to trial.

5(c) Expert witnesses will (not) be called:
    (1) Names of witnesses, qualifications and subjects of testimony will be supplied to the defense in writing _____ days prior to trial.

5(d) Any information the Government has suggesting entrapment of the defendant will be supplied to the defense at least *20 days* prior to trial.

5(e) Prior convictions:
    (1) The Government knows of no prior felony convictions of the defendant.
    (2) The Government believes the defendant does have prior felony convictions but does not know the date or nature of the convictions at this time.
    (3) If the Government intends to use prior felony convictions of any defendant herein for impeachment of that defendant if he testifies, the Government will furnish to counsel for defendant a list of such prior felony convictions in writing _____ days prior to trial.

C. **Motions Requiring Separate Hearing**

6. The defense *moves*—

6(a) To suppress physical evidence in plaintiff's possession on the grounds of
    (1) illegal search
    (2) illegal arrest
    (3) other _____.

6(b) To suppress admissions or confessions made by defendant on the grounds of
    (1) delay in presentment to U.S. Magistrate
    (2) coercion or unlawful inducement
    (3) violation of the *Miranda* rule
    (4) unlawful arrest

(5) improper use of line-up

(6) improper use of photographs

6(c) To suppress prior to trial identification of the defendant by witness on the grounds of

(1) improper use of line-up

(2) improper use of photographs

6(d) Grand Jury proceedings:

The Government states:

(1) There were (no) proceedings before a grand jury relating to this case.

(a) Federal agent's testimony only was heard.

(2) Proceedings before the grand jury were (partially) (not) recorded.

(3) The defense moves for production of transcriptions of the grand jury testimony, or summaries of testimony not recorded, of the accused, and all persons whom the prosecution intends to call as witnesses at a hearing or trial.

6(e) The Government states:

(1) There was (not) an informer (or lookout) involved.

(2) The informer will (not) be called on as a witness at the trial.

(3) It has supplied the identity of the informer. (or)

(4) It will claim privilege of nondisclosure.

6(f) The Government states:

There has (not) been

(1) Electronic surveillance of the defendant or his premises.

(2) Evidence or leads to evidence obtained by electronic surveillance of persons or places other than of the defendant.

(3) The defense moves for inspection of all transcripts, logs, notes, reports, and other material concerning such electronic surveillance.

D. **Miscellaneous Motions**

7. The defense will move—

7(a) To dismiss the information or indictment for failure to state an offense.

7(b) To dismiss counts _____ of the indictment or information on the ground of duplicity or multiplicity.

7(c) To dismiss the indictment or information on constitutional grounds.

7(d) To sever the case of defendant _____ and for a separate trial.

7(e) To sever Count(s) _____ of the indictment or information and for a separate trial thereon.

7(f) For a Bill of Particulars. (Rule 7(f)).

(Granted)   (Denied)

7(g) To take a deposition of witness for testimonial pur-
poses and not for discovery. (Rule 15).
Name of witness _____
(Granted)   (Denied)

7(h) To require Government to secure the appearance of
witness _____, who is subject to Government direction and not subject to the usual power of subpoena, at the trial or hearing.
(Granted)   (Denied)

7(i) Other _____

_____
(Granted)   (Denied)

7(j) To Inquire into the Reasonableness of Bail.
Amount fixed. 1. $_____ Unsecured Secured
2. $_____ Unsecured Secured
3. $_____ Unsecured Secured
4. $_____ Unsecured Secured

(1) Request for review by Magistrate under Title 18,
Sec. 3146(d)
(Yes)   (No)
Date of hearing _____.
(Affirmed)
(Modified to) 1. $_____ Unsecured Secured
(Affirmed)
(Modified to) 2. $_____ Unsecured Secured
(Affirmed)
(Modified to) 3. $_____ Unsecured Secured
(Affirmed)
(Modified to) 4. $_____ Unsecured Secured

(2) Request for amendment of Order by the District
Court under Title 18, Sec. 3147
(Yes)   (No)
(Affirmed)
(Modified to) 1. $_____ Unsecured Secured
(Affirmed)
(Modified to) 2. $_____ Unsecured Secured
(Affirmed)
(Modified to) 3. $_____ Unsecured Secured
(Affirmed)
(Modified to) 4. $_____ Unsecured Secured

E. **Discovery by the Government**
(1) Statements by the defense in response to Government request:

8.   Competency and Insanity.

8(a) There is (not) (may be) a claim of incompetency of
defendant to stand trial.

8(b) Counsel for defendant (No. _____) will (not) file a motion for examination under Sec. 4244, Title 18, U.S.C.

8(c) Defendant will (not) (may) rely on a defense of insanity or other defense of lack of, or diminished, mental responsibility at the time of offense.

8(d) Defendant will (not) supply the name of his witnesses, both lay and professional, on the above issue.

8(e) Defendant will (not) permit the prosecution to inspect any copy of all medical reports under his control or the control of his attorney. (Rule 16(c)).

(Granted) (Denied)

8(f) Defendant will (not) submit to a psychiatric examination by a court-appointed doctor on the issue of his sanity or mental responsibility at the time of the alleged offense.

9. Nature of the Defense:

9(a) Defense counsel states that the general nature of the defense is—

(1) lack of knowledge of contraband.
(2) lack of specific intent.
(3) insanity or lack of or diminished mental responsibility.
(4) entrapment.
(5) alibi.
(6) illegal coercion.
(7) general denial—put Government to proof.

9(b) Defense counsel states there (is) (is not) (may be) a probability of a disposition without trial.

9(c) Defendant will (not) waive a jury and ask for a court trial.

9(d) Defendant will (not) (may) testify.

9(e) Defendant will (not) (may) call additional witnesses.

9(f) Character witnesses will (not) (may) be called.

9(g) Defense counsel will (not) supply to Government the names of witnesses for defendant *five days* before trial.

10. The Government moves for the defendant (No. _____) to:

10(a) Appear in a line-up.

10(b) Speak for voice identification by witnesses.

10(c) Be finger printed.

10(d) Pose for photographs (not involving a reenactment of the crime).

10(e) Try on articles of clothing.

10(f) Permit taking of specimens of material under the fingernails.

10(g) Permit taking samples of blood, hair, and other materials of his body which involve no unreasonable intrusion.

10(h) Provide samples of his handwriting.

10(i) Submit to a physical external inspection of his body.

10(j) Defendant No. _____ and counsel (do not) agree to and will (not) comply with Nos. _____.

11.   Scientific Testing:

Defendant will (not) furnish results of scientific tests, experiments or comparisons, books, papers, documents, tangible objects or copies or portions thereof, which the defendant intends to produce at the trial and which are within his possession, custody or control. (Rule 16(c).)

(Granted)   (Denied)

F. **Stipulations**

12.   It is stipulated between the parties:

12(a) That the venue of this case is properly laid in the Western District of Missouri.

12(b) That the United States District Court for the Western District of Missouri has jurisdiction to try defendant for the offense charged.

12(c) That if _____ was called as a witness and sworn he would testify he was the owner of the motor vehicle on the date referred to in the indictment (or information) and that on or about that date the motor vehicle disappeared or was stolen; that he never gave the defendant or any other person permission to take the motor vehicle.

12(d) That the official report of the chemist may be received in evidence as proof of the weight and nature of the substance referred to in the indictment (or information).

12(e) That if _____, the official Government chemist were called, qualified as an expert, and sworn as a witness, he would testify that the substance referred to in the indictment (or information) has been chemically tested and is _____, contains _____.

12(f) That there has been continuous chain of custody in Government agents from the time of the seizure of the contraband, or other evidential material, to the time of the trial.

12(g) That the bank (or savings and loan institution) was at all times, as mentioned in the indictment (or information), insured by the Federal Deposit Insurance Corporation (or Federal Savings and Loan Insurance Corporation).

12(h) Other _____

_____

_____

Conclusion—Defense Counsel States:

That defense counsel knows of no problems involving delay in presentment of the defendant before a United States Magistrate, the *Miranda* Rule or illegal seizures or arrest, or any other constitutional problems except as set forth above. That defense counsel has inspected the check list on this Omnibus Hearing Report form, and knows of no other motion, proceeding, or request which he desires to press, other than those checked thereon.

§ 5.7 Procedural Factors—Voir Dire

The manner in which the jury selection is made can vary appreciably from jurisdiction to jurisdiction and sometimes from judge to judge. The trend is in the direction of truncating the selection process and shifting the interrogation from counsel to court. Most trial lawyers, particularly those representing plaintiff, decry what they consider a usurpation of their right to visit with the prospective jurors and unfold their prejudices in their own peculiar way. Take for example, the typical plaintiff lawyer's questioning in a case involving a teenage motorcyclist. He will consider as pertinent questions regarding a juror's parental status, ownership of motorcycles, use of motorcycles by teenage children, accidents with motorcyclists, etc., and cap this line of general questioning with a specific inquiry to each venireman as to whether he can give this young motorcyclist a fair trial.

The judge might well be satisfied with a terse question directed to the panel as a whole as to whether they can treat both parties alike.

There are more "modern" judges to be found on the United States District Courts so that is where you are more likely to encounter this "modern trend." But keep in mind that there are few codes which spell out the respective roles of judge and counsel in voir dire and the form that is adopted is most often a matter of the judge's particular taste.

§ 5.8 Procedural Factors—Jury Instructions

The same extent of control vis-a-vis court and counsel exists at the conclusion of the case as well as in the beginning. The form and chronology in which the instructions of the law are given to the jury may be very critical.

As to the form, there are many state jurisdictions which have adopted pattern instructions which seek to enunciate the applicable law in an easily understood manner. Typical of a state court rule defining the form of such pattern instructions is that of Missouri which states "All instructions shall be simple, brief, impartial, free from argument, and shall not submit to the jury or require findings of detailed evidentiary fact."

Most instructions are read to the jury and then given to them in written form for further guidance in the jury room.

In federal courts and some state jurisdictions, the instructions are delivered orally without written submission and few can be characterized as simple, brief and free from argument. The judge may be free to comment on the evidence (as he is in federal court) and to express his statement of the applicable law in his own fashion frequently in a repetitive, rambling style. It is not unusual to have the judge's charge exceed the counsel's argument in length, if not in clarity. These differences in procedural practices may be critical in your choice of forum.

As to the chronology, the instructions from the court may come before or after closing argument. Most advocates like to get the "last word" and so it is not unusual that counsel would prefer that system which provides them that advantage. Again, the federal courts give that lever to the judge while in some state courts it is given to the lawyer.

§ 5.9 Procedural Factors—Closing Arguments to Jury

One feature of procedural differences that may exist regarding final argument is its chronology as related to instructions. Two other differences should be mentioned, time and order.

Most state and federal courts will impose a time limit on counsel's closing argument—and in some courts the limitations are severe. It has always appeared incongruous for the judicial procedure to limp along throughout the pleading, discovery, and evidentiary stages and then hurried along when it came time for closing argument. And yet that is what most courts do, frequently imposing an arbitrary limit of thirty minutes to each side. Granted that such time is usually adequate (recognition being given to the parson's observation that, "you don't save any souls after twenty minutes") it might be that an unrestricted time limitation would be, in a particular case, a procedural advantage. This is particularly true when there are multiple defendants to share a limited period of argument time.

The order of argument is also a matter of procedural difference. In every jurisdiction that party with the risk of nonpersuasion is given the benefit of the last argument. In some jurisdictions such litigant has the additional advantage of opening argument. Thus, if each side has thirty minutes of argument the plaintiff or prosecutor might argue twenty minutes, the defendant argue thirty and the plaintiff or prosecutor close with ten. When such a division of time is permitted there are usually three other features imposed: the initial portion must equal or exceed the time reserved for the closing portion; the content of the closing portion must be confined to rebuttal of those points raised by opponent's argument; if your opponent waives argument, then there is nothing to rebut and no closing portion may be given.

§ 5.10　Procedural Factors—Number for Verdict

This last factor may be the most important. In many state systems a verdict may be retained by a less than unanimous number. Not so in federal court. All the jurors must agree. The burden of unanimity is somewhat lessened with the use of a six person jury (a practice now utilized in most civil cases in federal court) but even so, it is an awesome impediment to persuasion. The plaintiff bearing the burden of the risk of nonpersuasion finds the pickins' more profitable when the conviction of two-thirds or three-fourths of the jurors can carry the day. Even if the plaintiff ultimately prevails in securing unanimity it is usually of the expense of a compromised amount. If a verdict can be returned by less than all, then those favoring the plaintiff are free to evaluate damages without accommodating those who question the liability issue. Nine jurors who believe plaintiff should win and should receive $10,000 in damages may return a verdict in that amount. If the unpersuaded three must be excluded, the "trade-off" is usually a reduced verdict. Three zeros averaged in brings that verdict down to $7,500. If such a procedural difference exists in your choices of forum, it will probably be the decisive factor of where the suit will be filed (if plaintiff) or if the suit will be removed (if defendant).

§ 5.11　Substantive Factors—Generally

One of the old maxims of the law, that the substantive law is determined by the lex loci, has become so shot through with exceptions that it is practically valueless. The liberalization of our concepts of the law of conflicts has increased the importance of the lex forum at the expense of the lex loci and the substantive law that will be applied will be more influenced by the plaintiff's choice of forum than the fortuity of the place where the litigation producing incident occurred.

Along with these liberalizing developments in the case law of conflicts, we have similar liberalizations in the statutory laws concerning service. Long arm statutes have proliferated to such an extent that almost any corporate defendant can be found to be "doing business" in a given jurisdiction so as to support venue for a "single tort."

The lawyer need not be confined to suits in the local courthouse. The choice of "where" has been substantially broadened— and the significance of that choice will be substantial.

§ 5.12 Substantive Factors—Evidence

Rules of evidence have in the past been fairly uniform but with the trend toward codification of evidentiary rules, particularly the introduction of Federal Rules of Evidence, the choice of forum and the consequent applicable rules of evidence might be the determining factor in whether you have a submissible theory of recovery or defense. Variances may exist in the admissibility of hearsay evidence, expert opinion, "Dead Man's Statutes," documentary evidence, etc. The thinking advocate will consider the matter of evidentiary rules when the choice of venue is made—and will be aware of the variances.

§ 5.13 Substantive Factors—Evidence—Illustration

To illustrate the differences that may exist between federal and state jurisdictions in the reception of evidence we need only review a selected number of changes incorporated in the Federal Rules of Evidence which substantially differ from most state jurisdictions.

As to content:

Rule 704: Permitting lay or expert opinion as to an ultimate fact.

Rule 803(18): Permitting content of learned treatise as substantive evidence.

Rule 804(b)(3): Dying declaration admissible in civil litigation and in prosecution for homicide.

Rule 804(b)(4): Statement against interest broadened to include "proprietary" interest.

As to form:

Rule 612: Permitting counsel to inspect writing used by opponent to refresh memory of witness.

Rule 705: Permitting statement of opinion without prior disclosure of underlying facts or data.

These examples serve to demonstrate that in a given case the submissibility of a claim or defense might well turn on the rules of evidence to be applied.

§ 5.14   Substantive Factors—Quantum of Proof

The amount of proof that is adequate to raise a jury issue differs from jurisdiction to jurisdiction. The language that is employed to describe the threshold of submissibility is fairly universal (must transcend evidence and inferences that are "mere speculation and guesswork") but the interpretation of that phrase can vary considerably.

The evolution of cases under the Federal Employee's Liability Act beautifully illustrates the difference between the submissibility of cases initiated in the federal courts and those initiated in the state courts. Scores of plaintiff jury verdicts were reversed by state courts because on appeal it was held that the evidence had not been substantial enough to raise a jury issue. On appeal to the United States Supreme Court the jury verdicts were reinstated with admonitions that the state courts should be more sensitive to the injured workmen's right to a trial by jury.

The same phenomenon is being evidenced to some degree in the area of product liability. Unlike F.E.L.A. litigation there is no statutorily imposed concurrent jurisdiction so the opportunity for comparison does not exist to the same extent. But it has already become apparent that the federal courts have expressed a solicitude for the consumer that has outstripped the concern of most state jurisdictions.

§ 5.15   Substantive Factors—Finality of Verdict

A final substantive difference might be the posture of the court regarding appellate manipulation of jury awards. In most federal circuits the decisions have unequivocally expressed a distaste for the practices of either remittitur or additur. Not so in some state tribunals. There are still some jurists extant who think that there is merit in the concept of uniformity of verdicts and consequently are inclined to reduce jury awards which exceed in amount previous verdicts for similar injuries. Most plaintiff's lawyers eschew such a philosophy and seek to avoid jurisdictions which second guess the twelvers and undercut the finality of the jury award.

§ 5.16 Pragmatic Factors—Generally

A final factor must be considered which transcends the issues of procedural, evidentiary or substantive law—the practicalities of your choice of forum. Some of these factors relate to personal convenience of counsel, client or witnesses. Is the courtroom nearby? What will be costs of travel and time if the case is brought in a remote jurisdiction? Will there be the need to associate local counsel thus adding to litigation expense? Will the critical witnesses be subject to subpoena and thus afford the enhanced effect of live testimony as compared to expensive deposition testimony? Will the opposing lawyer be determined by the location of the litigation and, if so, where will I be apt to encounter the least formidable adversary?

These are but a few of the practicalities which may affect your decision—along with two others which merit special discussion.

§ 5.17 Pragmatic Factors—Docket

A favorable venue is of little value unless the case can be reached for trial. Even though a substantial portion of litigation is settled, it is usually disposed of by compromise because a trial is imminent and the counsel are forced "to fish or cut bait." In any negotiation the parties must tender a solution or an "or else." In litigation the "or else" is "I'll see you in court." Such a threat carries no weight if that court room appearance is far off in the indefinite future. Consequently it is imperative that the plaintiff in particular (trying to upset the status quo) select a court in which the docket is current. Ascertain the hiatus between suit filing and trial setting. If that delay exceeds a year you're in trouble.

Witnesses disappear and forget, clients are pressed with financial obligations, wounds heal, bereaved widows remarry—all manner of events occur which lessen the value of a claim. Only with a current docket can you minimize such possibilities.

§ 5.18 Pragmatic Factors—Judge

Who will judge? The variables that one encounters among the judiciary are awesome indeed. They run the full spectrum from uniquely brilliant to outrageously incompetent. And the ranges are not confined to intellect. Some are "tough" (note the sobriquet of Judge Sirica, "Maximum John") and some are "soft." Some hard workers and others drones. Some who rule quickly on matters submitted to them and others who agonize over decisions and hold rulings "in pectore" for unconscionable periods of time. And some who express a judicial philosophy that marks them as "plaintiff minded," "defense oriented," "law and order," etc. Not to mention those judges, fortunately few, who might succumb to political considerations of a case or who have favorites or enemies at the bar.

It is a naive counsel indeed who would choose a forum without considering the factor of who will judge.

C. PARTIES

§ 5.19 Generally

The interplay between these various topics of choice becomes apparent from the outset. Your choice of parties might be subordinated to your choice of forum. Assume that for one or more reasons considered above you elect to be in federal court. Your only entry to that forum is through a diversity action. Your forum choice will dictate that no local defendant be joined. But assume for our discussion that the choice of the forum is of little importance. Assume further that there are no problems concerning a statute of limitations. The press of time and the threat of losing a potentially viable defendant will not precipitate a hasty decision to join a marginally liable party. We will analyze the problem of choice of parties without such confining considerations.

§ 5.20 Plaintiffs

Perhaps it is considered axiomatic that if you represent a party you must institute a claim on that person's behalf. Such might be the case in a large percentage of instances but there are some which force another decision. Assume you represent a surviving husband and three young children in a civil action arising out the wrongful death of the wife and mother. The fatal accident occurred with the mother a passenger in an automobile driven by the father under circumstances highly suggestive of contributory negligence on his part. Within six months of the death the father remarried.

What options does the lawyer have in this case? If the father and children are joined as party plaintiffs what will be the chances of success? Or put another way, will the children's cause of action be jeopardized if daddy's claim is joined with theirs?

Let us assume the same facts only this time momma survives but with serious injuries and monstrous medical expenses. Should the husband join in a loss of consortium claim? Can the wife sue for the medical expenses without the necessity of a separate count on behalf of the husband? How will the alignment of parties affect the ultimate outcome?

In the aforementioned cases certain rules of procedure and substantive law might restrict the options that are available. Perhaps the wife is foreclosed from bringing a claim for medical expenses incurred. Perhaps the spouse is mandated to join a loss of consortium claim with the injured spouse's suit. The choice involved might very well waive the right of one client in order to enhance the likelihood of recovery for another. Maybe the counsel will sense an irreconcilable conflict of interest that would dictate withdrawal. But the options should be explored and, the consequences of the decisions made, fully explained. Sometimes those consequences aren't as dire as waiving a claim for possible recovery. Let us go back to the possibly negligent father operating the automobile into collision with a third party and causing serious injury to himself and his passenger child. Must the two suits be joined? Of course not. Many lawyers, fearful that the negligence of the father might "slop over" onto the child, would elect to bring one case first then, after disposition, file the second. The choice of the initial suit would depend probably on the relative injuries (the most serious first) or the press of the statute of limitations (children's actions usually are tolled until they reach majority). Merely filing separate suits won't suffice. In most jurisdictions there would be a hasty consolidation. If suits could be entertained in different jurisdictions perhaps a simultaneous filing could be accomplished under those circumstances without fear of consolidation.

The point is that counsel frequently has tactical decisions that must be made at the very outset—who do I join as party plaintiffs?

§ 5.21   Defendants—Generally

There is a lengthy check list of factors to be considered in determining whether a potential defendant should be joined or omitted as a party. It is difficult to reach any definitive conclusions as to how to weigh these factors and ultimately what decision to reach. Trial lawyers, as one might suspect, are not in agreement as to what general philosophy to follow much less what factors to consider. Some express the opinion "sue everyone in sight" and they advance as their rationale the following:

1. The more contributors you have kicking into the kitty, the bigger your settlement will be.

2. If you fail to join a possible defendant the party defendants will accuse the missing culprit who won't be be able to defend himself. What is worse, the jury might speculate that he has settled and either reduce the size of the verdict or grant no verdict whatever.

3. The more adversaries on the other side the greater the illusion that it is the plaintiff against the world, David fighting Goliath, Robin Hood versus the Sheriff of Nottingham—all those good little guys against the big baddies.

4. The more defendants you name the greater the likelihood that you will create a cross-fire among them and nothing is more beneficial to a plaintiff than to have a falling out among thieves.

Others would be more selective in choosing party defendants and the arguments they would advance are as follows:

1. You just might ring in an opposing counsel who, through his persuasiveness, might tip the scales against you. With each added defendant you increase the odds of such an occurrence.

2. The joinder of a financially insecure or a jury appealable defendant tends to reduce the size of a verdict.

3. Sometimes cooperation is needed from a potential defendant. If he is joined as a party that cooperation vanishes and he is driven into the enemies' camp.

In each case these conflicting factors must be weighed and the choice made.

§ 5.22 Defendants—Procedural Factors

The rules of procedure will dictate a number of happenings during trial which may be determinative of your joining a party as a defendant. The defendants will proceed with voir dire examination, opening statement, cross examination of witnesses, presentation of evidence and summation in the order in which they are named as defendants.

On occasion good trial tactics may suggest that a party be joined in order to utilize this chronology of procedure to plaintiff's advantage. Let us assume that you represent plaintiff in a civil claim against one obvious tort feasor and two nominal defendants. If all three are joined with the target defendant named first, such defendant will find himself sandwiched between a hostile plaintiff and hostile co-defendants. Each time counsel for "Lucky Pierre" addresses the jury, each time he interrogates a witness (with the exception of his own) he will be preceded and followed by adverse counsel. And when time comes for summation the situation will be further aggravated. Not only will his argument be shot at from all sides, the time of argument will be diluted among the three defendants. Sometimes this truncation of summation alone is a worthy reason for joining peripheral defendants.

§ 5.23 Defendants—Substantive Factors

Frequently the admissibility of testimony will depend on the status of the declarant as a party or non-party. Consider the difference between a declaration against interest and the admission of a party. McCormick on Evidence characterizes these differences as follows. As to the former "first, the declaration must state facts which are against the pecuniary or proprietary interest of the declarant—second, the declarant must be unavailable at the time of trial." As to the latter, "the admissions need not have been against interest when made. The admitting party need not be, and seldom is unavailable. Nor does the party need to have personal knowledge of the fact admitted." Perhaps that declaration is a critical bit of evidence and perhaps its admissibility will depend on whether the declarant is a party or not.

The coin has a second side as well. The status of a would be witness might determine what evidence may be foreclosed from admission. Suppose the plaintiff has died before trial and a could be defendant is poised to testify adversely to plaintiff's position. Most "Dead Man's Statutes" will seal the lips of the surviving party to a transaction. But the survivor must be a party. Again trial tactics might suggest that this rule of law be invoked—and the only way to do that is to join the potential witness as a party.

§ 5.24 Defendants—Pragmatic Factors

There are some instances that occur with regularity in civil litigation that illustrate the pragmatic factors to be considered in selecting or rejecting defendants. The first is the typical master-servant situation, the railroad engineer who fails to sound a warning and kills or maims a plaintiff at a public crossing. Should the engineer be joined in such an instance? There might be good reason to do so.

Do you wish to avoid a removal to federal court by the foreign corporation's railroad by naming a local defendant? Then join him. Do you wish to invoke the "Dead Man's Statute" (if applicable)? Then join him. Do you wish to utilize a statement of the engineer as an admission of a party? If you are not operating under Federal Rules of Evidence, then join him.

But absent good reasons such as these, why humanize a corporate defendant by having good ol' Tom Brown sitting at the counsel table as the target of your accusations? Why have the jury wonder if he will have to pay the judgment or suffer some type of reprimand? If there is no reason to join him, there is reason not to.

The second situation is the product liability case where everyone in the chain of distribution could be named as defendants in a law suit. General Pharmaceutical, giant of the industry, manufactured the defective drug, kindly Dr. Welby (who delivered half of the babies in town) prescribed it. Charlie Smith, local owner of Smith's Drug Store (the ol' high school hang out) sold it. Are you going to join all three? Perhaps there will be reasons as recited above, but the advantages of not joining them are overwhelming. Besides, how are you going to generate any proof when you choose to make everyone your enemy? Most lawyers would want Dr. Welby and Charlie Smith on their side unloading on the drug company—and you don't make many friends by using a summons as your calling card.

D. THEORIES OF RECOVERY AND DEFENSE

§ 5.25   Generally

The concept of notice pleading has tended to minimize the advocate's awareness of theories of recovery but, aware or not, they still exist. Maitland's observation is as valid today as when it was first uttered. The common law actions have indeed, been pronounced dead but they rule us from their graves. This posthumous potentate dictates that careful attention be given by the advocate in choosing a theory of recovery.

§ 5.26   Procedural Factors—Statute of Limitations

The choice of theory will be determinative of a number of procedural matters that are of transcendent importance. First, the statute of limitations to be applied will be ascertained by the cause of action stated in the petition. Does your product liability case sound in tort, contract, or fraud? It is quite likely that each will have a different period of limitation and that each cause of action will accrue at a different point of time. Under a contract theory the statute might be triggered at the time of the sale, under a tort theory when the damage occurs, under a fraud theory when the misrepresentation was made.

Ascertain your time restrictions and or your pleadings to adopt that theory which is still "alive."

§ 5.27   Procedural Factors—Service of Process

Perhaps a service of process problem can be resolved by a judicious choice of theory. Is the prospective defendant an out-of-state corporation which has as its only nexus to your jurisdiction the sale of its product within the state? If so perhaps your only chance of securing service is through the invocation of a "single tort long arm statute." If such a statutory device is to be utilized then you must be careful to characterize the defendant's wrongdoing as a "tort" or the appropriate language of the statute.

§ 5.28   Procedural Factors—Fact Finder

Choice of theory might be determinative of who will serve as the finder of fact, the court or the jury. Keep in mind those actions, statutory in nature, which provide that the judge shall sit as a fact finder: Federal Tort Claims Act, Equal Employment Act, etc.

In addition if you seek equitable relief you might find yourself before a judge. Sometimes you have no choice but other times you do—and when the option is there, consider the difference.

§ 5.29　Substantive Factors—Elements of Proof

The significance of the choice of theory becomes quite apparent when we enumerate these elements of the case which will hinge on the theory adopted.

The necessary ingredients in the recipe for submissibility will be determined by the theory of the case. It is surprising how often lawyers are indifferent to this elementary truth and plead a theory which imposes upon their client some elements of proof that are not easily come by. As an example consider the situation when a person delivers furniture to a warehouseman for storage which is subsequently destroyed by fire. What theory of recovery should be advanced? If negligence is alleged the plaintiff must prove some wrongful act which caused the fire. If a bailment is alleged the plaintiff makes a submissible case by simply proving delivery to the defendant and a failure to redeliver. If there is a legitimate legal excuse for the nondelivery, such as an Act of God, destruction through an enemy force, etc., it is up to the defendant to adduce such proof. The respective burdens are considerably different and a judicious choice might well mark the difference between success and failure.

§ 5.30　Substantive Factors—Quantum of Proof

How much proof, as distinguished from what proof, may also be determined by choice of theory. A bottle of soft drink explodes and injures a customer in a supermarket. The theories of recovery available would include a breach of warranty or negligence. The first choice would entail proof of the element of a sale (since most jurisdictions consider a breach of warranty theory to be derived from a contractual relationship). If the bottle had exploded on the shelf injuring a passerby there could be no evidence to supply the proof of sale. If the explosion had occurred after the victim had placed the bottle in her shopping basket but before the actual purchase there might be a question as to whether a sale had been consummated. Thus (illustrative of the point made before), this problem could be finessed by choosing a theory of negligence rather than one of breach of warranty. But how should the negligence be pleaded? If a specific allegation is made, such as a failure to inspect the bottles, failure to properly carbonate the beverage, failure to properly handle, proof to support those allegations must be forthcoming. The quantum of proof will be reduced if an allegation of general negligence is made ("the bottle was negligently caused to explode"). Reliance in such instance will be placed on inferential evidence (or "res ipsa loquitur" if you will) and the plaintiff will not be burdened with the specifics of defendant's negligent acts or omissions. The important thing to remember is that the choice that will dictate the quantum of proof should be made at the initial stage of the pleading. Once you have pleaded specific negligence, many jurisdictions demand that you must prove those specifics and cannot retrench and rely upon a general allegation of negligence.

§ 5.31 Substantive Factors—Quality of Proof

Perhaps we are dealing in errant pedantry by differentiating between the quantum of proof and the quality of proof but there appears to be sufficient legal language incorporated in case law to justify the distinction. Legion are the references to those theories of recovery, such as fraud, inter vivos gift from a deceased donor, etc., which necessitate "clear, cogent and convincing proof." The degree of conviction is spoken of as a different quality than the usual "preponderance of the evidence." The importance of this peculiar language of the three c's will depend upon how it is employed. Most often it is used to describe the manner in which an appellate court will review the evidence on appeal. Of more significance is when such language is incorporated into the instructions to the jury. In either case this peculiarity of the law cannot be ignored in choosing your theory of recovery.

One other point should be made. There has been language employed in product liability decisions that suggest that a different quality of proof might apply in cases invoking strict liability under the Restatement, Second, Torts, § 402A from those relying upon common negligence. This possibility must be pursued and recognized as a potentially important factor in the framing of your petition.

§ 5.32 Substantive Factors—Statutory Requisites

A final word of caution. In choosing your theory you should be aware of the source from which it sprung and the essential elements by which it is characterized. Consider the statutes which create an action for wrongful death. Frequently the language will limit recovery to deaths arising from "tortious conduct" or "wrongful acts." Will such language accommodate a theory bottomed on breach of warranty?

And what of the Federal Tort Claims Act which prohibits recovery for willful and wanton acts? Will a casual allegation of "gross negligence" plead you right out of court?

The advocate must know the source from which his cause of action derives its viability and choose that theory which tracks that life-giving language.

CHAPTER 6

PLEADING PRACTICES

"The common law actions are dead but they rule us from their graves"
Frederick William Maitland

Analysis

A. PLAINTIFF'S PETITION OR COMPLAINT

A. PLAINTIFF'S PETITION OR COMPLAINT

§ 6.1 Generally

The lawsuit will be initiated by the plaintiff with the filing of a petition or a complaint. The all too usual route that the advocate follows is to seek out a handy form book and draft the pleading as if he were selecting stock paragraphs for a will. We consider pleadings to be a matter for the courts and our brother

222

lawyer and so our primary, and too often only, concern is that the petition (or complaint) meet the minimal test as a legal document. In reality it is more than that. It is the opening gambit in the game of advocacy. It is our first attempt in our endeavor to persuade. As such it assumes tremendous significance and is not a matter to be entered into lightly or ill-advised.

§ 6.2   Effects of Filing

Perhaps the best way to determine the adequacy of any given effort is to weigh its effects. We should know what consequences will follow the filing of the petition. After all, the initiation of formal litigation is not obligatory. Countless claims are settled without suit being filed and the matter which is now under consideration might be such a case. So before we leap on the legendary horse and "gallop off in all directions," let us consider what effects this filing will have.

§ 6.3   Effects of Filing—Statutory Limitations

Every claim will have a time period defined by statute in which the claim will have to be initiated. Sometimes these demands of the law are complicated and confusing. True, there are many instances in which this will provide no problem—if the theory of recovery to be invoked is easily defined, and if the parties reside in the same state, and if the activity which gave rise to the litigation arose in that state, and if both parties are still living, etc. But what if there is a question as to the theory? Or the theory chosen is statutorily defined with special restrictions for a timely filing? Or the defendant has died and notice of a claim must be filed against the estate? Or the event occurred in a foreign jurisdiction? Every day that your case reposes in the file drawer unfiled, the clock ticks off another unit of that continually shrinking statutory period.

Effect number one of the filing of the plaintiff's petition is that it satisfies the law's demands for a timely initiation of your suit.

§ 6.4   Effects of Filing—Trial Setting

As soon as the petition is filed one clock (that which measures the statute of limitations) stops running and another clock (that which measures the hiatus between filing and trial) begins.

The sequence of litigation is not unlike that of a checkers game. Each player's turn occurs alternately. As the opponent moves the onus for action is shifted to you and with your move the onus shifts to your opponent. Your first move is the filing of the petition. The game has begun which will, you hope, ultimately conclude with a settlement or trial. Now it is up to the defendant to respond and with each series of moves the time to trial shortens.

§ **6.5** Effects of Filing—Discovery

Many times the settlement of a claim is frustrated because of the disputants' inaccessibility to the facts. The plaintiff wants to know what witnesses the defendant has. The defendant wants a physical examination of the plaintiff. Each wants the report from the others' expert. True, this exchange of information could occur informally without the threat of sanctions from the court for non-compliance. But seldom does such occur and when it does there is always the fear that the information given may be incomplete or distorted. The only sure way is to have statements taken under oath, answers to interrogatories sworn to, etc.—which add up to formal pretrial discovery and that means filing a suit.

§ **6.6** Effects of Filing—Adverse

While each of the foregoing effects are desirable and, indeed, in most cases necessary, the practitioner must recognize that the filing of a petition has some negative effects, most of which have to do with relations with the newly created defendant. First, it will severely limit and in some instances foreclose any extra-legal pretrial discovery. Once suit is filed there is little likelihood that any informal search for information from the named defendant will succeed. Up until such time there is simply a "misunderstanding" which your "client" is seeking to "adjust"—and the opponent might just share some information with you. But once the suit is filed a "misunderstanding" is metamorphosized to a "cause of action," the "client" becomes a "party plaintiff" and the adjustment a "claim for damages." You can forget any cooperation from the informal investigative process. Consider it as a birth pang of the pleading's parturition.

Second, it will create hostility with the newly named defendant. Now there is nothing intrinsically harmful in creating ill will with a competitor but in the case of litigation this alienation may manifest itself in a number of ways. If a defendant feels a sense of indignation by reason of a claim he will be transformed from a passive insured ingenuously supplying information to help resolve a dispute to an active partisan generating facts in order to defeat a claim.

The latter is a far more dangerous opponent and this adverse effect of the pleading should be recognized and dealt with.

§ 6.7   Purposes—Generally

It should be apparent that the general purpose of the petition should be to achieve the three-fold beneficial effects of initiating suit while at the same time to minimize the twin threats generated by the hostility of the defendant.

To appreciate our task let us pause for a minute and consider the genesis of an average lawsuit from the defendant's point of view.

He is sitting at home one evening, relaxed in front of the "telly" when the doorbell rings. A strange fellow inquires in the impersonal and usually gruff fashion that is the inevitable result of routine, "Are you Sam Harding?" An affirmative response results in a perfunctory announcement, "I'm a deputy sheriff," the thrust of a paper into his hand and a friendless, silent withdrawal from this enigmatic intruder.

We are told that fear generates from the unknown and poor Sam has never known the experience of being served with court papers. Trembling hands unfold the document as he wonders which one of his past sins (flashing before him in serial form) has been uncovered.

He reads the summons and his apprehension heightens:

To the above-named defendant:

> You are hereby summoned and required to serve upon Philip Anderson, plaintiff's attorney, whose address is 700 Main Street, an answer to the complaint which is herewith served upon you, within 20 days after service of this summons upon you, exclusive of the day of service. If you fail to do so, judgment by default will be taken against you for the relief demanded in the complaint.

Thomas Benton

_____

Clerk of Court

When he gets to the petition other emotions surface. The "plaintiff" is recognized as the fellow he rear-ended about a month ago. Sure enough, there in the first paragraph it recites the time and place of the accident. Now things don't seem too bad. After all it was an innocent enough incident, a momentary lapse while he tuned his car radio, and the damages were less than two hundred dollars.

On to the second paragraph and the allegations of negligence. Sam reads them in disbelief. He is confronted with a full blown recitation of errant behavior which links him to the likes of Adolph Eichman and Genghis Khan. He is accused of "dangerous and excessive speed" "failure to swerve, dip or dart," and of "negligently colliding with great force and violence into the rear of plaintiff's vehicle."

The third paragraph is even worse. This fellow who denied being hurt at the scene, is now reciting a litany of complaints that sounds as if he were flattened by a steam roller rather than having been rear-ended by a Renault. The plaintiff's "head, neck, back, chest, arms, hands, legs" and all the "bones, muscles, tissues, tendons, joints, discs, organs, vessels and skin thereof" were severely "fractured, twisted, torn, dislocated, ruptured, strained, sprained, abraded, lacerated—and missing." The effects thereof, logically enough, being that "he has suffered great pain of body and anguish of mind in the past and will so suffer in the future," that he has "lost earnings and will in the future lose earnings," that he has "incurred substantial medical expense in the past and will incur substantial medical expense in the future" and that his "hopes have been shattered, his dreams denied and his life of golden promise turned to dross."

The final clincher is the prayer—$125,000. A cool $75,000 over his insurance coverage and enough to wipe out the equity in his house, the cash surrender value of his policies and the balance of his worldly possessions. He envisions complete ruin—his home auctioned on the courthouse steps, his favorite golf clubs sold at a garage sale, his children being shipped off as indentured servants.

But soon fear and despair is displaced with indignation and anger. He'll fight back. No fraudulent shyster is going to do this to him! He'll report to his insurance company and will make it perfectly clear that he is willing to do anything to win this lawsuit.

This scenario is repeated tens of times each day. Unthinking plaintiffs' lawyers dictate petitions from forms, make wholesale charges of negligent conduct, bizarre allegations of horrendous injuries and unrealistic prayers for damages. The only result is to alienate the defendant, create hostility and stiffen resistance to ascertaining the truth and making a favorable disposition of the case. Here are a few rules that might help in lessening the adverse effects of that initial petition.

§ 6.8   Purposes—Minimize Claim

In most jurisdictions the plaintiff's lawyer must specify the amount of damages sought. (An isolated few require only that the claim be identified as above or below $50,000 in order to determine the possibility of federal jurisdiction based on diversity of citizenship). Some amount will have to be stated, the question is how much? Some neophyte lawyers accept this unfettered freedom to choose the amount of the prayer as an invitation to publicity. They evidently derive satisfaction in seeing a blurb in the local paper that announces "$500,000 sought for injuries inflicted by drunken driver." Chances are that the name of the plaintiff's lawyer might be included—so where is the harm?

Ethics aside for the moment, there is a great deal of harm—as indicated before. The amount of the prayer should not be dictated by publicity value. As for the *initial* petition (or complaint) (it can always be amended later) choose as your prayer an amount that meets two tests.

1. Does it provide the proper jurisdictional limits?

2. Does it represent a satisfactory settlement figure?

Remember the defendant can always confess judgment, pay the amount of the prayer into the registry of the court and conclude your lawsuit. In your anxiety to lessen your opponent's opposition don't select a sum that jeopardizes your jurisdiction or is less than an adequate settlement.

The rule of minimization is not confined to the prayer but includes the elements of the charge and the specifics of the damages. Think back on the "bad example" stated before and recognize the value of:

1. A bare bones recitation of the claim, avoiding color words suggesting gross misconduct;

2. A modest allegation of damages confining the complaints to those easily verified.

This second suggestion is of particular importance in personal injury cases.

Any formal pleading which overstates the nature or extent of a disability can have devastating effects later on. Assume that you perfunctorily plead that plaintiff's back has been injured and that "all such injuries are painful, permanent and disabling." In reality plaintiff had a stiffness in the back which abated within a few days. Several years later, plaintiff is again involved in an incident from which a ruptured intervertebral lumbar disc is suffered. That prior allegation will come back to haunt you. Think of the cross-examination to which your client will be subjected—and the possible charge of malpractice that could be directed against you.

§ 6.9   Purposes—Obscure Theory

The petition may be viewed as a declaration of war. It is a formal pronouncement that plaintiff has a complaint against defendant and seeks relief. It goes further than that. The plaintiff is obligated to state with some particularity the nature of the complaint and the relief sought. The question is how detailed will this initial call to arms be?

Picture an invading army confronting an opposing force ensconced within the protection of its castle wall. The protocol of medieval combat dictates that the challenger announce his presence and his intention to assault the castle keep. But once that custom has been fulfilled the challenger is free to embellish his pronouncements as he wishes. Some, overcome with bravado, might disclose the entire battle plans by thundering from the far side of the moat, "Tonight at ten we're coming through the north gate to sack the town and rape the women!" But there are other tactics that could be employed. Alternative one, a deliberate obfuscation. "Someday we will get in somehow and perhaps seek some booty." Alternative two, a diversionary attempt. "Tomorrow at noon we're coming over the west wall to kidnap the queen."

These three choices are available to the plaintiff as the initial petition is framed. Assume a simple fact situation of a product failure. The blade of a lawn mower has disengaged, shattered the housing and seriously injured your client. Your initial investigation suggests that the best theory of recovery is that an improper aluminum alloy with minimal impact resistance has been selected for use as the housing.

Option one (bravado), plead with particularity the negligent choice of materials.

Option two (obfuscation), plead a general allegation that the lawnmower was "negligently caused to malfunction."

Option three (diversion), plead that the defendant negligently failed to assemble the device.

In each instance the original complaint should withstand a motion to dismiss. The opportunity for pretrial discovery will be triggered and depositions of the design engineers will be taken. Now, in which instance will your discovery be more fruitful?

Or asked another way, "Do you think that advising a hostile witness of your intentions increases your changes to uncover beneficial information or decreases those chances?"

For those who believe that such disclosure would decrease the opportunity for fruitful discovery, option two or three would be chosen.

Remember these suggested rules of pleading apply only to the initial pleading. After your pretrial discovery has been completed, amend your pleading accordingly identifying particular charges of misconduct, specific allegations of damages and a judicious prayer for damages.

B. DEFENDANT'S MOTION PRACTICE

§ 6.10 Generally

The Rules of Civil Procedure provide the defendant with a wide assortment of motions designed to either refine or eliminate issues. Any elementary course in civil procedure adequately explains the case law interpretations of the relatively unambiguous code or rule provisions and a host of pleading manuals and form books will provide the magic incantations which invoke the application of a given rule. The problem for the advocate is not the "what" or the "how" but the "why?" We shall confine ourselves to the last query.

§ 6.11 Purposes

Let us list the more common pretrial motions and attempt to list the purposes for which they are employed.

Motion to Quash Service—to abort the complaint in its present form either by reason of the impropriety of service or venue. (In essence, "you failed to follow proper procedure in securing service or you have served the party in the wrong place.")

Motion to Make More Definite and Certain —to refine the complaint in its present form by reason of the specificity of the allegations. (In essence, "you said enough to stay in court but not enough to get to trial.")

Motion to Strike —to abort a portion of the complaint in its present form either by reason of the inadequacy of the allegations to support an issue or the relevancy of certain allegations to support an issue or claim. (In essence, "you said enough to stay in court but not enough for some issues or too much for others.")

Motion for Judgment on the Pleadings —to abort the entire complaint in its present form by reason of the inadequacy of the allegations to support the complaint. (In essence, "you didn't say enough to stay in court.")

Summary Judgment —to secure a partial judicial disposition of an issue or a complete judicial disposition of a claim on the basis of the pleadings and supplementary probative materials.

§ 6.12 Improper or Ineffective Use

These listings of "purposes" are perhaps misleading. The various pleadings were designed to effect their respective legal purposes. In the everyday world of litigation they might be utilized for other reasons, some valid and some not. The mere filing of any motion regardless of its merit triggers two events—a bill to the client, a delay in the case. Unfortunately the filing of too many motions is prompted by the desire to either inflate a legal charge or effect a senseless delay. Neither are compatible with good ethics. (Note, however that the complaint is with "senseless delay." Frequently dilatory tactics are both effective and legitimate.)

But the abuse of motion practice is not confined to those instances. On many occasions a good faith utilization of a motion proves to be either valueless or even detrimental.

§ 6.13 Motion for More Definite Statement of Claim—Illustration

The plaintiff has filed a complaint wherein he claims that "the head, face, body and limbs of the plaintiff have been severely and permanently injured all to his damage in the sum of Fifty Thousand Dollars for which sum he pays damage together with his costs." The allegations of damages are obviously inadequate and could be subject to a motion to make more definite and certain. But what would the filing of the motion accomplish? The plaintiff would make specific allegations of broken limbs, lacerated face and recurring headaches. But defendant could have received all this necessary medical information from an examination of his own and an exchange of medical reports. In addition, the plaintiff will "beef up" the charge with allegations of medical bills, lost wages and other special damages the proof of which would have been foreclosed had the case gone to trial with the original petition.

The effect of the motion under these circumstances was nothing more than a reminder to the plaintiff to dress up his complaint—hardly the concern of the defendant.

§ 6.14 Motion for Judgment on the Pleadings—Illustration

A Wrongful Death Statute has a one year statute of limitations and requires that suit be brought by the personal representative of the deceased. The original petition filed eleven months after the fatal incident names as plaintiff the widow of deceased in her individual capacity rather than as administratrix of the estate. The defendant files a Motion for Judgment on the Pleadings pointing out the inadequacies of the petition. The plaintiff seeks leave to amend and properly modifies the complaint within a week of the statutory limitation. Need we review the sagacity of defendant's motion practice in this case?

§ 6.15 Motion for Summary Judgment—Illustration

The plaintiff's complaint adequately states that he was stopped in a line of traffic when he was rear-ended by a vehicle driven by the defendant. The defendant has a statement taken from the plaintiff in which he admits that he has no memory of the incident. The defendant files a Motion for Summary Judgment accompanied by affidavits of defendant and two witnesses, which have been uncovered through intense investigation, stating that plaintiff had made a sudden, unsignaled stop which precipitated the accident. The plaintiff files a counter affidavit stating he was stopped five to ten seconds before the impact. The motion of course would be denied by reason of the factual dispute. The defendant's filing had merely resulted in a complete revelation of his file and provided plaintiff with a cheap, effortless pretrial discovery.

The lesson to be learned from the foregoing illustrations is that defendant's motion practice should not be a perfunctory implementation of available pleading devices. Remember that many motions are simply a reminder to your opponent to "do it right." Others may effect a dismissal but most frequently this is only a temporary victory which does not dispose of the litigation. Only a Motion for Judgment on the Pleadings or a Motion for Summary Judgment are motions for a final disposition of a course of action, and as to the latter the courts are increasingly hesitant to provide such relief.

§ 6.16 Proper and Effective Use

Motion practice can be effective if it can truncate litigation and dispose of improper issues or claims without the need of full blown litigation. Take the case of a complaint seeking money damages from a governmental unit in a jurisdiction which heretofore has honored the concept of governmental immunity. A motion for judgment on the pleadings permits the parties to litigate the issue without the expense and delay of a trial.

Similarly if a given issue, such as grief and loss of society as a claimed item of damages in a wrongful death case, is subject to question then a Motion to Strike is an effective tool to test its propriety. Summary Judgment has a more restrictive use primarily because there has been an increasing reluctance on the part of appellate courts to sustain such motions. Reverse a trial judge a time or two for granting a Motion for Summary Judgment and he is apt to develop the attitude that all such motions should be denied (he avoids the threat of reversal with such a practice inasmuch as a denial of the motion is not a final judgment and consequently is not appealable).

The other motions provide few advantages to the defendant other than to put the case into momentary suspension and thrust the burden of proceeding back to the plaintiff. For that reason alone, busy defense attorneys will continue to file their boiler plate motions and, in doing so will buy some time at the price of dressing up their opponent's slipshod pleadings.

CHAPTER 7

TRIAL PREPARATION

"Plan your work and work your plan"
Anonymous

Analysis

§ 7.1 Philosophy of Persuasion

The initial stage in trial preparation is the preparation of the lawyer himself. The advocate should develop a philosophy of persuasion—a conceptual approach to the phenomenon of influencing another to accept the ideas advanced by you and your client. Some would say that it is simply adducing facts in a clear, cogent and convincing matter—that the cumulative effect of discrete bits of persuasive evidence inevitably leads to an ultimate conclusion which is compatible with those bits. A rather mechanistic, mathematical approach as expressed in the axiom "The whole is equal to the sum of its parts." If this is accepted as a valid concept then the advocate will concentrate on the parts (the evidentiary detail) and let the whole (the favorable result) take care of itself.

But others would say that human reasoning does not lend itself to such analysis—that a decision is not the end result of a chronologically ordered linear continuum of cumulative facts. They would advance the thought that decision making is more of a gestalt phenomenon—a three dimensional agitated blob of factual, impressionistic, inferential, prejudicial miscellany from which a decision spins forth trailing behind it sufficient selective supporting material to assuage the conscience and justify its genesis as a product of the rational mind. Such an approach rejects the application of an algebraic axiom and minimizes the importance of the evidentiary proof in the decision making process. "Trying to persuade a jury with factual evidence alone is like pushing a string", they will argue. "You must provide a *reason* for their decision, a *motivation* for reaching the result you desire. Pull the string from the emotional end and the factual end will follow."

If there is validity in this methodology, then the advocate must approach the trial of a case accordingly. He will not confine his efforts to the sterile adduction of facts. Every action, every word, every gesture of the attorney, his client, his witnesses will filter through the mind of each juror, assume the flavor of his experience and background, blend with the distillates from his fellow "fact finders" and generate a feeling for the case. This then will be the concern of the advocate—to create the proper "feeling", cultivate the responsive mood, generate a *desire* to reach the "right" conclusion. In doing so, you will incidentally, but only incidentally, produce the facts that will support that desire.

Of course such a superficial analysis of the philosophy of persuasion is totally inadequate for the serious advocate. There are countless theories and studies which must be explored if one has chosen advocacy as his profession. Sad to say the writings that do exist in our field are puny indeed and the advocate who wishes to learn the secrets of persuasion must seek out the literature of advertising and marketing. Any good library is glutted with works on "consumer behavior," "motivating the market," "product acceptance", etc., complete with surveys, statistics and empirical studies. Seems as if we find it more important to learn the techniques of selling soap than in doing justice.

§ 7.2 Subjects of Persuasion—Generally

Persuasion does not exist in a vacuum. There is always a "persuader" and "persuadee." Too often the trial lawyer consid-

234

ers himself as the only instrument of persuasion and ignores the other principals identified with his cause. All are important—client, client's family, witnesses—and each must be thought of as part of the persuasion process.

Nor can these persuaders be considered in isolation. The physical environment is an additional element in the process. Unfortunately most courtrooms were conceived with absolutely no thought given to the purpose for which they were to serve. Dimensions and design are hostile to good hearing and good viewing. The advocate must be sensitive to these shortcomings and attempt to ameliorate their ill effects. Some physical attributes of the courtroom must be lived with but you still are presented with some options. Recognize that there are such things as optimum distances with which to communicate. Interrogation of a witness is best carried out at eight to ten feet. Closer than that and you present a physical threat, more distant and you have lost the connection. Too often the interrogation takes place from a counsel table or a lectern which has been positioned at random by some bailiff. Don't let happenstance dictate where you stand to interrogate—make your position reflect instead psychological considerations.

The same is true in addressing a jury. Don't be influenced by all those movie and television presentations which portray the impassioned lawyer leaning over the jury rail while delivering his closing argument. Effective camera angles for dramatic viewing might dictate a particular position; effective advocacy quite another. Don't intimidate the jury with your threatening presence. Humans have territorial imperatives too. Back off until you hit that comfort zone and do your persuading from there.

Now let us turn from the persuader to the persuadee. No, the jury alone will not be the only subject of your persuasion. Others will be included.

§ 7.3   Subjects of Persuasion—Judge

Regardless of the type of trial judge you draw, whether an active participant or a passive presence, the role he will play during the course of the trial will have a significant impact on the outcome. You will feel the effects of his rulings, not only as to the legal issue that is decided but the manner in which it is pronounced. The mere "Sustained" to an objection to a repetitive question is one thing—"That objection is sustained. Let's stop this senseless repetition and get on with the trial," is quite another.

Such gratuities can be devastating. The jury member is usually conditioned to have great respect for the judge. They will be aware of his appraisal of each phase of the trial—not only the rulings but his general demeanor. Even the least sensitive to body language will be able to ascertain through his posture and countenance his approval or disapproval, interest or apathy, belief or incredulity.

It would be fruitless to explore all the possible reasons why judges act as they do but some good should come from an attempt to analyze why they rule as they do. Let us hazard a listing of a few potential factors which may influence their decisions along with suggestions as to how to satisfy those factors.

Factors of Persuasion

1. *A desire to follow existing law.* An obvious factor. The judge is under an oath to do just that and consequently he will be influenced (and perhaps compelled) by applicable case law.

Suggestion—prepare trial briefs which formally, decisively express prevailing law.

2. *A desire to reach a just result.* The subjective appraisal of the case will no doubt enter into the judge's decision making process. Most often this feeling for the case is developed early in the proceeding and is a result of the attitudes expressed by the lawyers rather than the evidence adduced at trial. How often will a trial judge call the advocates together before the trial begins and say, "Well gentlemen, what kind of a case do we have?" Here is the open invitation to exert your persuasiveness on the judge and create a climate in which his desire for a just decision will be reflected in judicial rulings favoring your client.

Suggestion—don't apologize about your case.

"Well judge it is a little claim involving a petty quarrel about a lease arrangement."

"It's one of those civil rights matters, judge, where my client claims he was fired because he's black."

"We probably owe some money on this one judge but the plaintiff is asking too much."

Now how can you expect the judge to be sympathetic with your case if you have introduced it in such a fashion?

Be convinced of the significance of the litigation and the righteousness of your cause and exude the attitude that reflects those convictions.

3. *A desire not to be reversed.* Peer approval, we are told by psychologists, is a powerful force in influencing the activities of us humans. Judges, being human, are subjected to this same phenomenon. They pride themselves on their judicial record and express with ill concealed contentment such conceits as "I've never been reversed on an instruction" or "I've had fewer reversals than any other trial judge in this circuit."

How can the advocate take advantage of this factor?

Suggestion—let the trial judge know that you are possessed of certain characteristics:

> knowledge of the law;
>
> confidence in your case;
>
> persistence to pursue litigation to an ultimate resolution;
>
> courage to make a record.

Let us assume an informal in chambers discussion regarding a point of evidence which you believe to be important and which you desire to mention in your opening statement. The judge's response is, "Not in my court you don't." Some lawyers would quit right there. If so, the judge has nothing to fear by way of appellate review. You have backed off your position, there has been no record made and the judge knows he is dealing with a "patsy" who is likely to be similarly intimidated when other matters of legal controversy arise.

How much more effective if, with this first test of strength, the advocate would respond, "Judge it is my firm conviction that the law which I have cited in my trial brief establishes my right to adduce such evidence. This is a critical matter in this case. I would like to call the court reporter in to make a record and preserve my position on appeal."

Now the judge knows that you mean business and in such cases it is not unusual that a sober second thought might result in a reversal of the court's initial position.

Laboratory scientists have accumulated hundreds of experiments dealing with the relative strengths of motivations which affect behavior. The methodology employed is to free a white rat in a maze and determine which of a number of circumstances will motivate the rat to learn the maze in the shortest period of time. In one instance the subject is starved and then rewarded with food at the successful completion of the run. In the second, the subject is deprived of his mate and is rewarded accordingly when he completes the run to find his pink eyed, snuggly white beauty. In the third, a well fed, sexually satisfied subject is given an electric shock each time he makes a wrong term.

A sense of romance suggests that the fulfillment of a physical need or the yearning for a lover would prove to be the greatest motivating forces. Not so. Fear of punishment is what gets the job done. Apply the lesson from the rats as you see fit.

§ 7.4 Subjects of Persuasion—Opposing Lawyer

In every case you should be attempting to persuade your opposing advocate. A number of reasons dictate that he is worthy of your persuasive attention.

1. Ninety per cent of litigation is settled. That statistic alone should be enough to make the point. Most of those settlements occur before trial but many are consummated during trial, some even as late as during jury deliberation. Convincing your opponent of the legitimacy of your appraisal will be a continuing effort.

2. You will have an on-going relationship with your opponent. The instant case will not be your last confrontation. Unlike the jury, who you will never meet again, here is a subject that will be encountered again and again. Your efforts with him will have a cumulative effect—both as to other litigation with this particular opponent and litigation before other members of the bar with whom this opponent will share his appraisal of your worth.

§ 7.5 Subjects of Persuasion—Opposing Lawyer—Techniques

Generally

There are a multitude of ways in which an opposing advocate can be persuaded. If we were to list the elements of such persuasion we would have to begin with the basic ingredient of any lawsuit—the facts. Time was, before the advent of the new civil procedure codes, that opposing lawyers held their cards close to their vests and revealed little or nothing of the nature of their claim or defense. It is surprising under those circumstances that any cases were settled—but a surprising number of pigs in pokes were sold. The climate is substantially different now. If you want to persuade your opponent you must disclose the nature of your lawsuit.

A second axiom is that you must not only have the facts and reveal them, you must demonstrate a willingness to use those facts by going to trial. Lawyers possess that same characteristic possessed by judges—they don't like to lose. But lawyers don't lose unless they have an opponent that is capable of winning—and they can't win without playing. The advocate who has not established a reputation for playing—actually trying lawsuits—will never be able to persuade an opponent.

But let us assume that we satisfy these two basics: we have the factual necessities and the willingness to try the case, what follows in our attempts to persuade our opponent? We shall review some of the standard gambits that are employed in order to "psyche" an opponent and accomplish the necessary persuasion.

False Assurance of Compromise

("Don't worry, we will work this one out")

If a case comes into the office that appears to be a good one to try, from either a plaintiff or defendant standpoint, it will serve no purpose to persuade your opponent that he has a fight on his hands and he had better get ready. All that will do is to intensify his preparation and help gird him psychologically for the imminent battle. Best if he would think just the opposite—that the matter will be "worked out" so that there really is no need to go through all the expenses and commotion of pre-trial preparation.

And so it is that frequently the defense lawyer will open communications in the following fashion.

"Say Frank, that Williams file has just been sent over to our office. Looks like you have a good one. I'm afraid our assured was the culprit. Tell you what you could do. Get all your medical reports, accumulate your specials and then let's sit down and see if we can't get rid of this one."

To the plaintiff's lawyer who is gun shy about going to court an invitation like this is seized upon as tantamount to a concession of liability accompanied by a tender of a blank check. Thoughts of filing suit and initiating discovery proceedings are abandoned and "visions of sugar plums" dance in the head of the bemused barrister. Even if the routine of filing suit and invoking pre-trial discovery is not affected, the attitudes of the lawyer and client will be. The opponent has identified himself as a fair-minded, non-contentious, peace loving individual. Hardly the kind with whom you will relish a good fight. You have been softened psychologically. Remember, a trial is combat and to be a good combatant you must "summon up the blood, stiffen the sinew and assume the air of a tiger." Settlement talk accomplishes just the opposite— the blood pressure recedes, the sinews soften and the air is that of a pussy cat.

Plaintiffs can play the same game by bad mouthing their client, depreciating liability and giving assurance that "this is one I'd be willing to close out cheap." The farce continues until trial time when it is suddenly discovered that "the damn claims committee won't pay over a $1,000" or that "stupid client wants his case tried."

Keep your guard up for that kind of gimmick. Neither Greeks nor opposing advocates can be trusted when they are bearing gifts.

Similar Case, Similar Result

("I had a case just like this last year and I won it")

One of the most glaring deficiencies in the law is the lack of empirical data concerning the disposition of claims. Our records are confined to those cases tried and appealed but what about the 90% that never get beyond the trial stage? Although a few records may now be accumulating in the computer banks of the insurance companies, for the most part the results of most trials remain in the ruminations and reminiscences of the ole trial dogs. "Now Henry, out of the last ten whiplashes I tried I didn't get less than $4,500." "This kind of a product case is a sure winner. Our office hasn't lost one in all the years I've been here." Now how do you counter an argument like that? Protocol forecloses a direct challenge to such "facts."

Even a Missourian wouldn't dare respond with a "Show me." That kind of persuading fire is fought with the same kind of fire. "This case will be tried before Judge Holmes and I've got a string of six wins in his court." "I'm not worried, I had a case just like this last year and the jury wasn't out fifteen minutes."

How does the advocate develop such persuasive patter? Well, get some experiences behind you to form some background material for your reminiscences—then spend a lot of time around fishermen and politicians.

Economic Appeal

("You can't afford to be out of your office for three days on a case
like this" or "You can't try a leg-off case for $5,000")

The purpose of this persuasive ploy is to undercut the fighting spirit of the opponent by appealing either to his pride or his pocketbook. The former works for all advocates, the latter is confined to the plaintiff's lawyer. It is rather flattering and disarming to be told that your professional skills should be directed to more important matters and when an opponent incredulously states, "Fred, I'm surprised to see you handling a case like this," it's not unlikely for Fred to respond, "Well if I didn't think we'd settle it I wouldn't be here." Fred has been finessed into making the first overture for settlement and has been forced into a non-litigating posture by an appeal to his pride. The corollary to the "This case is too little" ploy is understandably enough, it's the "This case is too big" gambit. Negotiations have petered out with the parties standing with a $100,000 demand and a $95,000 offer. Time has come for the defense lawyer to say, "You can't try this case for $5,000." It is a blatant appeal to the pocketbook and in most cases it is effective. Again the psychological edge has been taken off. No longer are you trying a $100,000 case, you are now trying a $5,000 case and the come down will no doubt blunt your enthusiasm.

This pocketbook approach manifests itself in other forms. The young lawyer particularly is apt to be challenged with, "We can give you $1500 right now" (enticing pause) "That's $500 for you." Another procedure being employed by an increasing number of insurance companies is to send an unsolicited settlement draft to the plaintiff's lawyer in an amount representing the "final offer." Your client-lawyer relationship dictates that the client be advised of the offer and chances are (as shown by the insurance company records) the lure of the "ready money" will precipitate a settlement.

§ 7.6 Subjects of Persuasion—Jury

Of course the jury is the main target of the advocate's persuasive powers. They will provide the ultimate test of your ability to convince. Before examining the techniques to be utilized let us recognize the scope of your efforts. Persuading the jury is not confined to the closing argument. Every facet of the case must be an integrated effort to sell your case. And the persuasion effort must not be limited to the actual trial. The convincing process pervades the entire case from the time the jury panel is brought to the courtroom until they reach a verdict. There are no "time-outs." You and your client will be on display that entire time and the jury's impression of you will include those respites during recess and the comings and goings from the courthouse. Those manifestations of your personality revealed in the corridor will be just as telling, perhaps more so, than those displayed in the courtroom. It will do little good to be on your good behavior during trial then impolitely shove your way into a crowded court-house elevator at the close of day.

And don't be guilty of behavior that confuses the jury. If you have engaged in spirited controversy during trial, don't exchange jokes with your opponent during recess. If you have told the jury at closing argument, "We'll be waiting for your verdict" don't skip off to the office and leave an empty counsel table for the jury to see when they recess during deliberations.

§ 7.7   Subjects of Persuasion—Jury—Techniques

Generally

The elements of jury persuasion are most often related to the subject matter of the litigation and the identity of the jurors. Consequently it is difficult to single out techniques that have universal application. To further the difficulty it is well nigh impossible to ascertain which techniques are indeed successful. Most lawyers are content to conclude that if a particular ploy was utilized in a winning effort that success was the result of that favored gambit. They are victimized by that old devil "Post hoc ergo propter hoc." Unfortunately there are no valid studies to establish why juries do as they do. The most ambitious was undertaken by Harry Kalven, Jr. and Hans Zeisel and appeared in a book entitled The American Jury. But even this "scientific" approach by professors of law and sociology was tainted with inadequate sampling, questionable methodology and biased ap-praisal. The job of establishing universal rules that apply to juries in general is an impossible task. The best we can do is to list two characteristics of persuasive counsel that merit special recognition.

Confidence

The jury expects a winning lawyer to be confident (aren't all winners?) and this confidence must include an extensive realm: confidence in self; in your cause; in your client; and in the system. But confidence in itself must stop short of cockiness. Confidence in cause must avoid the pitfall of disdain for the opposition. Confidence in your client must not result in blind faith that ignores potential weaknesses. Confidence in the system should not be displayed by obsequious subservience to the court. On the other hand a self-effacing lawyer who distrusts his client, bickers with the judge and treats the system with contempt will have little chance for success. As in most instances the manifestation of your confidence must be expressed with Aristotelian restraint by seeking the Golden Mean.

Courtesy

"Faith without works is dead" and confidence without courtesy is a sham. Courtesy is but a revelation of your confidence and if your faith in your self, your cause, your client, the system is there, the works of courtesy will follow.

At the risk of sounding like a Boy Scouts Manual, we could state that a courteous counsel—

> Doesn't elbow his way up to a side bar conference;
>
> Doesn't hassle a witness;
>
> Doesn't bicker with the judge;
>
> Doesn't grab exhibits from an opponent's hand; etc.

Attributes of gentleness are still appreciated and a courteous counselor is the most persuasive counsel.

§ 7.8   Pretrial Review

As the time for trial nears it is necessary to recheck that you have successfully completed your investigation and are prepared to litigate. The procedure to effect this important stage of preparation is to begin with a listing of the essential elements of your case and then check against that list the sources of proof to establish those elements.

Suppose you represent a client who has fallen in a store and suffered an injury. You will first ascertain what you must do to establish a submissible case. The best source of this information will be your own pleadings which, hopefully have been framed after considering the instructions of law which identify the cause of action of an invitee. List these elements on the left side of a sheet of paper and to the right list the manner in which you will adduce proof of that element. In the proposed problem it might appear as follows:

Elements of Case	Sources of Proof
Control of premises	Defendant's Answer Paragraph One admitting ownership
Status of plaintiff	Plaintiff's testimony that she was shopping
Existence of defect	Witness Martha Cohen that lettuce was in aisle
Knowledge of defect	Witness Jack Petty that manager said, "I meant to clean that up an hour ago."
Cause of injury	Plaintiff's testimony that she slipped and saw lettuce leaf under her
Nature of injury	Hospital Record Dr. Zieman
Future Pain	Dr. Zieman
Permanency	Dr. Zieman
Consequence of injury	
Loss of wages	Employment records—request for admission
Medical expenses	List of paid bills—Plaintiff
Future loss of wages	Personnel manager Ralph Furman.

§ 7.9   Order of Proof—Generally

Now that the necessary ingredients have been identified and their sources established, thought must be given to the most effective way in which the proof will unfold.

§ 7.10   Order of Proof—Psychological Considerations

There are three psychological phenomena which are of significance in determining the structuring of your case.

Primacy—the concept that first-heard is best retained.

Recency—the concept that last-heard is last retained.

Attention span—the realization that there are limits to our ability to sustain mental concentration for an unlimited period of time.

These principles must be employed in the structuring of every facet of the case; the individual's testimony, each segment of trial and the case as a whole. Utilize the first moments to grab attention, save the most important feature to last and do it all within a limited time framework.

There should be nothing to impair your utilization of this structuring for the individual witness but recognition should be made that practical problems frequently discombobulate the appearance of witnesses and the ideal order of proof. But at least this is the ideal for which we should strive.

§ 7.11   Order of Proof—Appraisal of Evidence

The recitation of these rules is just the first step. The advocate will have to utilize his own judgment in determining which evidence is the attention grabber, which is the most important and how long can attention be maintained. In order to make the choice more deliberate it is well to refer to your list of the sources of proof and then attempt to appraise their relative merits. Usually in civil litigation there will be two distinct areas of proof: liability and damages. The initial decision should be which of these two do you wish to begin and end your presentation? Once that decision is made, list the evidence to support each facet of the case. It will fall into several categories:

live witnesses;

depositions;

exhibits.

The subject matter and form of these types of evidence must also be taken into account. Is the live witness testifying as a fact witness, expert witness or character witness? Is the deposition televised or written? Is the exhibit a list of medical bills or a motion picture?

Now we are ready to proceed.

1. Determine the order of the issues to be proved.

2. Determine the chronology with which each issue should be developed.

3. Determine the relative importance of the evidence which supports each sub-issue.

    4. Determine the anticipated length of each item of evidence and develop a working schedule for each block of trial time.

§ 7.12   Order of Proof—Appraisal of Evidence—Illustration

Let us translate these suggestions to a given case. You represent a client who has suffered central nervous system disorders from anoxic encephalopathy during an operation. A malpractice action has been instituted against the anesthesiologist. Your proof as to liability involves:

> testimony of the operating surgeon;
>
> testimony of a nurse attendant;
>
> written deposition of a nurse anesthetist;
>
> video tape deposition of an expert witness;
>
> a hospital record;
>
> excerpts from the defendant's deposition.

Your proof as to damages involves:

> testimony of the treating doctor;
>
> testimony of a physical therapist;
>
> employment records;
>
> neighbor of client;
>
> wife of client;
>
> fellow employee who is a traveling salesman.

§ 7.13   Order of Proof—Availability of Witnesses

Now another fact, yet unmentioned, comes into play. Some of the evidence, concerning both liability and damages, is readily available at anytime and other evidence is not. In the liability phase we can produce at a moment's notice the written deposition of the nurse anesthetist, the video tape of the expert and the excerpts from defendant's deposition. Less available are the hospital records to be authenticated by the record librarian, the attending nurse and, least available, the operating surgeon. On the damages side the client and his wife will be immediately on tap, the employment records and neighbor reasonably available and the traveling salesman and professional witnesses less so.

246

Absent any problems of production we might want to arrange our schedule as follows:

First morning	Operating surgeon
First afternoon	Attending nurse, nurse anesthetist, excerpts from defendant's deposition
Second morning	Hospital records, video tape of expert
Second afternoon	Client, neighbor, fellow employee
Third morning	Treating doctor, employment records
Third afternoon	Physical therapist, wife of client

Practicalities might force a change. The doctors might have surgery scheduled, the traveling salesman might be out of town. If such is the case the chronology will have to be rearranged by scheduling those witnesses when their appearance is assured and using the readily available evidence as "fill in."

Note one aspect of the proposed scheduling. The professional witnesses, with the exception of the nurse anesthetist, are planned for the beginning of a morning or afternoon session. The purpose is three fold:

the testimony is important and utilizes the principles of primacy;

the time for court appearance is more easily controlled;

you will be provided an opportunity for an immediate pre-testifying review with the witness.

The first two items are self evident. The third merits elaboration. Suppose you have scheduled the neighbor as first witness at 9:30 A.M. and, anticipating approximately a thirty minute appearance, ask the physician to arrive at 10:00 A.M. The direct examination goes as expected but the cross examination drones on for an hour. Meanwhile the busy professional is fuming in the witness room, increasing his displeasure with the inconsiderate lawyer who has unduly inconvenienced him and decreasing his enthusiasm for his client's cause. It is true that on such occasions the court may withdraw the lay witness and put the professional on out of turn. But what if you have professionals back to back? Good practice dictates that you anticipate the vagaries of trial and minimize their effect by scheduling your busiest witnesses for the most predictable times.

§ **7.14** Logistics of Marshalling the Evidence—Generally

To many advocates this is the most distasteful and aggravating aspect of trying a lawsuit. We know what evidence we wish to adduce, we have decided on our order of proof—now what do we do to translate those statements and exhibits in our file to admissible evidence in court?

§ 7.15   Logistics of Marshalling the Evidence—Preparation of Witnesses

In the case of witnesses an irreducible ritual must be followed.

1. *The witness must be subpoenaed.* Although the power of the law need not be invoked to assure the appearance of every witness in court, it is good practice to subpoena them all.

   A. If for some reason the intended witness does not show up at trial the court will be unsympathetic to your problem (and can afford little relief) if that witness is not under the compulsion of law to appear.

   B. The subpoena will afford a ready explanation for an absence from work or some other competing commitment. It is easier to explain to a boss that "I have to go to court" than to say "I'm missing work to testify for a friend."

   C. The jury might regard a subpoenaed witness as less partial than one who appears voluntarily. The validity of this assumption is not universally accepted but there exists a goodly number of attorneys who inquire of all witnesses as to whether they have appeared under subpoena, with the thought that an affirmative response from their own witness will suggest impartiality and a negative response from an opponent's witness will establish an unnatural willingness to cooperate.

2. The witness must be contacted for the purpose of:

   A. *Reviewing testimony.* This is particularly important if a deposition has been taken or a statement given to the opposing side.

   B. *Giving assurances.* The typical witness will want to be reinforced as to the importance of the case, the significance of his testimony, the painless procedure of trial, the reimbursement for financial losses incurred through court appearance, etc.

   C. *Creating good will.* A concern for the convenience of the witness by inquiring as to his work schedule or other obligations will help immeasurably in keeping the witness "in your corner." Nothing alienates a witness more than having to spend dead time waiting to testify. To reduce the likelihood of such an event occurring, advise the witness that although the subpoena calls for his appearance at 9:30 A.M. on Monday, that the uncertain pace at which the trial moves makes it impossible to know when he will have to testify. Secure his telephone number at home and at work, find out how much notice he must have to appear in court and advise him that he need not appear unless contacted. Add, as an extra assurance of your concern, that if the case is settled and his appearance is not needed that he will be so notified.

§ 7.16   Logistics of Marshalling the Evidence—Preparation of Client

The client must be thoroughly prepared for court appearance. Each advocate develops his own style for preparing witnesses and although individual preferences may vary the routine somewhat, the basic needs are universally recognized.

Initial Preparation

A month before trial confer with the client for the purpose of:

1. *Advising the client of the status of the case.* The average client, be he plaintiff or defendant, will want to know what the prospects for trial will be.

    First, will the case actually be reached and, second, what is the likelihood of settlement? The lawyer should anticipate these concerns and advise his client accordingly.

2. *Securing current information on the client's condition.* If you represent a plaintiff in an injury case you will be anxious to ascertain the present physical condition. Perhaps new complaints have arisen which will necessitate additional medical attention, an amendment to the petition and even an increase in the prayer. (This possibility is what determines the timing of this initial pre-trial conference. The lawyer must have sufficient time to make a proper amendment without sacrificing the trial setting.)

3. *Preparing for a final dress rehearsal.* Undoubtedly your client's deposition has been taken and, in all likelihood, it has not as yet been reviewed. Give the deposition to your client, ask that he read it thoroughly and to mark the deposition for any errors of transcription or any incorrect responses.

4. *Scheduling a final pre-trial conference.*

Final Preparation

The week preceding trial the second conference will be held at which time the lawyer will:

1. review the current stage of negotiations.

2. advise the client of the likelihood of trial and the need for arranging a schedule for court appearance.

3. review the deposition, the theory of the claim or defense and the evidence to be adduced by the client.

4. arrange for an immediate pre-trial rendezvous in lawyer's office. The lawyer must be continually reminded of the apprehension that most clients go through on the eve of trial. That fear can be reduced if the client is told to come to the familiar setting of the lawyer's office so that the two of them can go to court together. (Remember how the terror of the dentist's office was somewhat lessened when you walked in holding mommy's hand?) Your client will find this arrangement much more comfortable than proceeding alone into the strange and foreboding environs of a courthouse.

Other necessary logistical problems will arise depending on the complexity of the case. Some are worse than others, most demand the help of competent aides, all present problems. But this much is sure—if you can't get the troops on the field there won't be any battle.

CHAPTER 8

THE COURTROOM

"You gotta know the territory"
Music Man—Meredith Willson

Analysis

A. IN GENERAL

A. IN GENERAL

§ 8.1 Composition and Dynamics

The courtroom is the site in which you will function, the arena in which the combat will take place, the stage on which the drama will unfold. Whichever of these metaphors you choose, it should be apparent that you must develop a sense of comfort in that environment, be it the coliseum or the theatre, in which the action will take place. That comfort can come only with knowledge: an awareness of the geography of the place, a sense of what will happen and where; a feeling of familiarity with the form of the structural components and the function they will serve. So let's begin the exploration.

The components of the courtroom, not listed in order of importance, are:

> the bench,
>
> counsel table,
>
> jury box,
>
> witness chair,
>
> court reporter's place,
>
> bailiff's place,
>
> clerk's place,
>
> visitor's gallery.

The three last named serve no function in the dynamics of the trial. The location of the two court officers, indeed, even their presence during trial is of no concern to those involved in the proceedings. As far as visitors it is important only that they be far enough removed from the jury that their comments cannot be easily heard and that they can come and go without interfering with the trial.

Other and more valid reasons dictate the location of the actual participants in the trial.

B. GEOGRAPHY

§ 8.2 The Judge's Bench

The judge's bench dominates the courtroom scene. It is usually located at the end of the room most distant from the public entrance. Located so, it affords the judge ready access from his chambers (usually to the rear or side of the bench) isolates him or her from the "great unwashed" in the visitor's gallery (who are further isolated by a rail) and permits the judge a full view of the scene before him and below him, (inasmuch as the bench is always elevated above floor level.)

§ 8.3   The Witness Chair

The witness chair is usually located along side the bench, with the witness facing in the same direction as the judge, but of course on a lower level. This proximity to the witness allows the judge easy communication and permits the judge the opportunity to present such shots as:

a cajoling "Please speak up, the jury can't hear you";

a cautioning "Answer only the questions you're asked"; or

a caustic "Remember you're under oath and the laws regarding perjury are severe."

This location also permits the possibility of the witness being privy to conversations to which he is not a party, the conferences which take place between judge and counsel at the bench. Many a witness has been educated, deliberately or by chance, concerning the nature and importance of pending questions as the result of the information exchanged at sidebar conferences. Example:

Q.	"Describe the location of the vehicles when you arrived at the scene officer."
Lawyer 1.	"I object your honor. May we approach the bench?"
Court.	"Yes." (Judge, counsel and court reporter huddle at center of bench within four feet of witness)
Lawyer 1.	"There's been no proof when the officer arrived at the scene and if he had personal knowledge of that information.
Lawyer 2.	(Stage whisper) He arrived at the scene within a matter of minutes and knew that the cars hadn't been moved because they were positioned in front of their skid marks.
Court.	"That hasn't been developed yet. If it is, I'll overrule the objection."

(The witness now knows the significance of his arrival time and the inferences that can be drawn from the location of the skid marks)

If the witness chair is located in such close proximity to the judges' bench, caution should be exercised to conduct bench conferences "sidebar," that is, at the extreme opposite end of the bench out of earshot of the witness.

§ 8.4   The Jury Box

The jury box is usually located against the side wall on the same side of the bench as the witness chair. Four factors should dictate the location of the jury box.

1. It must be located lateral to the witness chair and sufficiently near that all the jurors can easily understand the unamplified conversational tone of the witness.

2. It should be sufficiently forward of the witness chair so that the witness can readily turn to the jurors and speak directly to them without having to swing his head in an awkward ninety degree turn. Furthermore, the jurors who are the "sole judges of the credibility of the witnesses" should not be confined to only a profile view.

3. It should be sufficiently far from the counsel table and the visitors' gallery that sotto voce conversations at either site cannot be heard.

4. It should be convenient to an exit so that jurors can pass easily from jury box to jury room without being exposed to extraneous sights and sounds.

These "musts" are admittedly of little interest to the advocate who encounters a jury box in a less desirable location. However, identifying these significant factors of location of the jury box does serve to remind you of these maxims:

1. Each juror must be able to hear the witness without an undue strain on the witness to speak or the juror to hear.

2. Each juror must be able to observe the witness adequately to form an opinion of that witness's credibility.

3. Each juror should be shielded from any diversion during trial or while processing or recessing from the jury box.

If the existing geography of the courtroom does not assure that these conditions be met, then you must conduct yourself in such a way to minimize the difficulties.

One additional note. Most jury boxes are built to accommodate the traditional twelve jurors with two tiers of six chairs each. But in certain jurisdictions (civil trials in Federal Court) the number of jurors have been reduced and now that twelve occupant box is twice the size that is needed. How will the jurors be seated? It will make a difference in your communicative style if the six

254

jurors are strung out in a single line or bunched in two rows of three. Suggestion: request the configuration of your choice.

§ 8.5   The Counsel Table

The counsel tables' location should be determined primarily by the function they serve. In no case should counsel table or tables by located so near to the jury box that conversations between counsel can be heard by the jury. Ideally the table should be large enough to accommodate comfortably the trial notebooks and exhibits so that their contents cannot be seen by opposing counsel.

If the counsel table is to serve as the site from which interrogation takes place, the location and position relative to the witness assumes tremendous significance.

In almost every instance the location of the jury box will be such that one counsel will be positioned nearer to the jury than the other.

Thus, if the counsel table runs parallel to the jury box the, closer counsel will have the advantage of proximity but his opponent has the advantage of note taking (assuming he's right handed) without turning his back to the jury and his ability to observe the jury during the interrogation of witnesses is facilitated.

The only position which affords counsel the same proximity to the jury and the same facility for taking notes and observing the jury is to position the counsel table perpendicular to the jury box and across the room.

But such configuration affects the dynamics of communication and impedes your ability in direct examination to nurture your witness and in cross examination, to control the witness.

No longer can the counsel table be across the room. If so positioned, the witnesses will be pitching their responses to the interrogator while turning their back to the jury.

The situation will be aggravated if the local rule mandates that counsel remain seated at the counsel table during interrogation. Now the element of control during cross examination is rendered even more difficult and creates an unsolvable problem. If the seated interrogator is placed close enough to the witness to exert an intimidating presence (ten to twelve feet) counsel will have his back to some if not most of the jurors.

Again, the question arises as to whether these observations can be of any significance other than constituting a litany of complaints. One would hope not. One would hope that the counsel table could be positioned in the courtroom so that no advantage is gained be either counsel. If such is not possible, then local rules should dictate either the position of counsel for plaintiff or prosecutor and the defense or which counsel should be provided the choice.

It seems a tad unseemly to have opposing counsel engage in a foot race to ascertain their respective positions at counsel table. But if that's the game that is played, speed on!

§ 8.6 The Court Reporter

Ideally the court reporter will be so positioned that he can perform his function in a non obtrusive fashion without interfering with your task as communicator. His function of course, is to record all those proceedings which might be the subject of review be an appellate court. That will include:

1. the opening statements of counsel

2. the testimony of witnesses

3. the motions of counsel

4. the objections of counsel

5. the rulings of the court

6. argument of counsel

The jury selection or voir dire is not listed but only because in some jurisdictions a tradition has developed wherein these proceedings are not recorded. Seems like a foolish tradition. Reversible error can occur during this stage of the proceeding, but how can this error be preserved if no record is made?

In addition, the court reporter will record the identity of exhibits which are offered.

A review of the proceedings listed will reveal that there are several sites from which the court reporter must function in order to record the evidence from the witness stand, statements from counsel, the conferences of the bench and the conferences in the judge's chambers. Let us consider the geography of the courtroom as it concerns the role of the court reporter in recording evidence of witnesses and statements of counsel.

From an architectural view the court reporter is often the forgotten child. Either no permanent position is assigned to them, and they are left to set up their chair and portable stenotype machine where they can, or they are provided a single site from which they are expected to fulfill their various functions. This "one size fits all" philosophy usually results in the court reporter being position in front of, below, and on that side of the bench more proximal to the witness chair.

From this point the court reporter is in a good location to hear the questions from counsel and the responses from the witnesses. And, in most instances this configuration serves as a good site to record the opening statements and closing arguments—but is not always the case. Good communication at times dictates that you approach within a few feet of the jury rail and speak in low, intimate tones to the jurors. As you do so you will be facing the jury box with your back to the court reporter and pitching your voice to reach the jurors who are much closer to you than is the court reporter. The result? Your intimate, purring peroration will be interrupted with a jarring "Speak up counsel, I can't hear you."

[As a small boy visiting relatives on a farm, I directed a similar phrase to Uncle Marlowe who was quietly offering grace before dinner. His appropriate reply was, "I wasn't talking to you"]

The same problem can arise during jury selection. The panel cannot all be accommodated in the jury box and must be seated elsewhere in the courtroom. The reporter sits at his post as you gravitate to that position where you can most effectively communicate with the potential jurors. In most instances you can expect no help from the judge. The reporter will remain rooted and it is you who will be made to forfeit your advantageous position of optimum communication. Mohammed will not come to the mountain, the mountain must come to Mohammed.

It isn't that the reporter *cannot* move. When bench conferences occur the reporter must stand and join counsel as they huddle before the judge. And on occasion when a more extensive record must be made outside the hearing of the jury, the court reporter will demonstrate his ability to ambulate by standing *and* walking into the judge's chambers. But these movements are made to accommodate the judge. The advocate can expect no such considerations.

These are the constants that exist in every courtroom and these are the geographical elements that will be of the most significance in influencing your role as communicator in the classroom in the court house. But there are other elements of which you must be aware. Are there facilities for exhibiting visual aids? Is there a blackboard, an easel, a screen, a shadow box? Are they stationery or mobile? Where are the electric outlets? How can the courtroom be darkened? Are there acoustic "dead spots" or "echo chambers". The advocate who is sensitive to the elements of communication will find the answers.

C.   PERSONNEL

§ 8.7   Generally

Perhaps identifying the courtroom personnel appears to be more appropriate for a member of an eighth grade civics class than for a student of trial advocacy. But let us not confine ourselves to a simple "player roster". Let us explore the roles of each of the players and seek to understand the relationship which they have to each other. There is no need to list them in order of importance, indeed, there is no ranking to take place. The advocate must never think of himself as being positioned somewhere in a pecking order or hierarchy. Each participant, lawyer, judge, jury, witness, bailiff, clerk and reporter, is an essential player in the game and each must fulfill the task assigned. The endeavor of assigning rank is as fruitless and impossible as that of evaluating the relative importance of the senses.[1] Each must function within his own area of responsibility. All must cooperate in order that justice be done but that cooperation does not take the form of holding hands and skipping into the sunny uplands together. Rather, the relationship of the court officers (particularly that of judge and advocate) can be likened to that of the negative and positive charges within an atom. It is the tension between those two differing, and in some respect antagonistic, components that maintains the integrity of the atom and permits it to preserve its distinctive characteristic.

Indeed, such is the rule of the universe which applies to the celestial bodies that constitute the cosmos, the electrical charges which compose the minutest form of matter—and all the inani-

---

1. 1 Corinthians 12:14.

mate things which are found in between. This basic rule of structure applies to animate organisms as well, from the basic unit of the family to society as a whole—and all the social structures in between.

Here then is an attempt to identify the courtroom personnel as seen through the eyes of an advocate. They are not listed in order of importance.

§ 8.8 Judge

The judge is the referee or umpire who is present to see that the game is played by the rules. The advocate envisions him as a passive participant who rules only when rulings are sought. His role is likened to that of an umpire in a baseball game who observes that a runner has missed a base. He does not intrude by calling him out. It is only when someone on the fielding team calls for the ball and touches the base that the umpire is obliged to rule. Absent the appeal for a ruling, the umpire remains mute. Such is the analogy that the advocate hopes to have confirmed at trial—a hope that is not always fulfilled.

Passivity does not always characterize the role of the umpire. Egregious behavior on the part of a player, manager or coach can evoke sanctions, usually in the form of being thrown out of the game. The ejection is never preceded by a request from the opposing team. The umpire does it on his own. And so it is with the judge. Outrageous behavior by counsel, witness or juror can precipitate sanctions, sua sponte, ranging from reprimand to incarceration for contempt.

Another valid comparison can be made between judge and umpire. The umpire determines when the game should be called because of adverse conditions. The man in blue is the one who yells "play ball" and he's the one who determines when the game is called.

And so it is with the judge. It is he who starts the contest and it is he who, sensing adverse conditions which make fair play impossible, can yell "mistrial."

Now differences arise and the analogy breaks down. Unlike an umpire, a trial judge's call is never final. It is always (at least almost always) subject to an appeal to a higher court. For that reason a trial judge, unlike an umpire, can, and will on occasion change his mind.

And one further difference. The umpire is bound by specific rules of the game that are seldom subject to interpretation. The rules themselves are objective (three strikes are out, four balls are a walk, etc.) and the role of the umpire is confined to judgment alternatives (fair or foul, ball or strike, safe or out). Not so with the judge. Despite our quest for certainty, the "rules" (all of them; substantive "rules", procedural "rules", evidentiary "rules") are mushy at best and require a literal convention of casuists to plumb their meaning. The role of the judge is therefore not confined to a knee jerk thumbs up you're out or a palms down you're safe. He must take a myriad of fact situations and,

first, identify the applicable rule;

second, interpret the rule;

third, apply the rule to the instant facts;

fourth, exercise discretion as to its effect; and

fifth, make a ruling consistent with the rule and fair play.

Having said all that, what is the relationship that an advocate should have with the judge? Consider him a fellow officer of the court with tremendous responsibilities who needs the help of a well disciplined professional conversant with the law and the facts who can provide guidance through the thicket of an adversarial proceeding.

§ 8.9   Jury

The identity of the jury depends on the stage of the proceeding. Initially there is no jury, only potential jurors, individuals torn from familiar places and faces, called to perform an awesome task with an alien environment aided only by sinister outsiders. To them the judicial process is vague and complex; the courtroom, terra incognito; the lawyers, a suspicious breed of garrulous manipulators unworthy of trust or reliance. Each juror is a stranger, even to those who wear the same identifying badge. Each is afflicted with the same apprehensions so they withdraw into the safety of introversion and render themselves incapable of companionship.

That's how you'll find them in the courtroom when the trial begins and you confront them during voir dire.

What should your relationship be to them? You must be friend, counselor and guide. You must be sensitive to their needs. You must provide necessary information to them in order that they may understand the context of the questions that you will address to them. The information which you solicit from them must not appear to be either intrusive nor frivolous. You must demonstrate your concern for their privacy, an understanding and acceptance of their station in life and respect for the views they express. Above all you must not embarrass them.

You must neither be paternalistic nor pedagogic, judgmental nor juristic. Your initial interchange will be a friendly encounter between individuals (never think of them as a group) who have a common goal—to do their best to fulfill the role to which fate has assigned them.

As the trial progresses, the identity of the jury will too. The strangers become friends and the individuals merge to form a group. The veniremen who considered themselves as trespassers now are jurors with designated seats in the jury box and exclusive access to "their" jury room. They no longer function with the tentativeness of a tyro. They have been initiated into the club, sworn to their new task, instructed by the court, and now enjoy the ease that comes from acceptance and identifiable expectations. They no longer feel the need for solicitous handling. They now want the facts, delivered in a straight forward manner as one court officer to another so they can be about their job of doing justice.

§ 8.10 Opposing Counsel

Your adversary will be a continuing presence in the courtroom, somewhat of a mirror image of yourself. Your identities and your relationships are manifold. You are competitors seeking the same prize and knowing that only one can prevail.

You are representatives of your respective clients each of whom expect and deserve unflagging allegiance to their cause. You are fellow officers of the court engaged in a common enterprise—the awesome process of doing justice. You are members of the same profession bonded by common roots of training and tradition.

The range of duties, concerns and courtesies which spring from these diverse relationships are not easily sorted out. As difficult as that task might be, the advocate must, at least, recognize that contact with your opposing counsel will occur while differing roles are being played and you must suit your work and action to the appropriate role. True professionals can, as competing combatants, engage in heated controversy in the courtroom then, as officers of the court, exchange thoughtful legal theories in chambers, and then as brother and sister advocates raise a glass together in post-trial revelry.

§ 8.11 Your Client

Your client is your reason for being, the sine qua non for your presence in the courtroom. That word of reminder for the wise is sufficient—but too many advocates lack the wisdom to recognize this basic fact. The lawyer himself becomes the chief protagonist in the courtroom drama while the client is relegated to supernumerary status. True, much of the action during the trial proceedings will focus on the attorney and the client will be merely a presence at counsel table or in the front row. But it is the client for whom these clashes in the courtroom are performed and the client who must be incorporated into the action.

In a boxing match, the sound of the gong finds the boxer in his corner and at the end of each round it is this same corner to which he returns. So it should be with the advocate. The start of each session should find him with his client and at each recess or adjournment he should retire to his client's side. There will be tasks to be performed during these lapses in the trial but a reassuring base-touch with your client can prove as important as the phone calls, legal research and last minute reviews with witnesses which usually usurp recess time.

There are some specific times before, during and after trial when client nurturing is of particular importance. That initial trip to the courthouse before the trial begins can be a lonesome and loathsome experience for the first time litigator. The gospel singer tells us that on our way to the promised land we'll "have to cross Jordan alone" but no one dictates that the clients' trip to the courthouse be undertaken unaccompanied. Have him meet you at your office and steady his steps as you go to confront the foe together.

The conclusion of the jury selection process provides a special time during trial when you should be at your client's side. The decision as to who should be stricken from the jury panel should take into account the feelings of the client. Several factors lead to this conclusion:

First, the evaluation of prospective jurors, despite continuing efforts to reduce it to intellectual analysis, remains a gut decision.

Second, the client has had an opportunity to view the jury panel and to see various reactions unseen by the interrogating attorney.

Third, the chemistry between the client and the individual jurors will be an important factor in the outcome of the case.

Fourth, the client's ability to sense that chemistry is more valid than that of a third party.

Put them all together and they spell "consultation with client before your strikes are made." Go over the jury list with the client; share your appraisal of the individual jurors; remind him that there is no hard and fast rules that dictate your choice of strikes, ask him his feelings about the individual jurors, whether he likes their looks or not (a more specific test, "Who wouldn't buy a used car from you?")

This kind of consultation serves a number of purposes.

It will help you choose a better jury.

It will improve the client-lawyer relationship.

It eliminates post trial complaints such as "Why did he leave the accountant on the jury? I knew he'd be bad for us."

There are certain pronouncements which, though simple in form, initiate momentous events which in turn provoke an appropriate and complementary emotional response.

The car racer hears, "Gentlemen, start your engines" and his pulse quickens, his muscles tighten and he's ready to race. When the boxer hears, "Shake hands and come out fighting" he experiences a rush of adrenaline, primeval instincts resurface and he's combat ready. The magic phrase for the lawyer is "You may now retire and consider your verdict." When that pronouncement is made our stomach goes queasy, our forehead aches and we settle in for an interminable wait. Misery likes company. Your client probably feels the same way. Spend this time explaining the options that the jury has. Explain that if you win, the check wouldn't be in the mail tomorrow, that there will be post-trial motions and possible appeals that will assuredly take time and might even reverse the jury finding.

263

Conversely, if the verdict is unfavorable, we can file post trial motions and appeals which could reverse the results.

Explain about hung juries and mistrials and retrials. The client deserves to be advised and just talking will provide a therapeutic effect for both of you.

D. PROTOCOL

§ 8.12 Generally

It is interesting how often we use locale to describe various types of human behavior. We speak of "barnyard" humor, "gutter" language "mountaintop" experiences. Certain kinds of speech and conduct are associated with certain behavior and the individual sensitive to civility will make sure that the matching is compatible. Shakespeare observed that we should "suit the word to the action and the action to the word." He might well have added that the word and the action should also be suited to the place.

For advocates the "place" is the courtroom. What are the words and actions suited for the peculiarities of this place? The courtroom is an environment which encompasses several components. It is first of all, the site of the transaction of government business. It contains certain symbols, such as flags and seals, indicative of that governmental nexus. But the "business" that is transacted therein is of a special kind, the business of doing justice—a refinement which necessitates other trappings to the environment: paneled walls, elevated ceilings, richly appointed furniture and fixtures.

Another component must be added. The organism of justice is not an anaerobe, it can flourish only in an open air area exposed to the light of public scrutiny. Hence, the courtroom must serve as an auditorium, an open space adequate to accommodate the curious who can see and hear and, in so doing, confirm that justice is taking place.

And what is the focus of this search for justice, the alter to which the supplicants come? It is *The Bench*," sheathed in richly grained wood, rising in isolated elegance above the unpretentious plane on which mere mortals dwell, flanked by flags and backgrounded by the great seal of a sovereign state or an even more sovereign nation. Heady stuff.

To the physical environment add the accouterments of personnel:

the judge, robed in ecclesiastical garb and ensconced upon an elevated throne behind the alter;

the bailiff, uniformed and sometimes armed, conditioned to bracket the courtroom activities (and his own state of semi-somnolence) with variations of a "hear ye, hear ye" invocation and a "The court is adjourned" benediction;

the court reporter, poised and alert, positioned near the witness box and "at the ready" to metamorphose the spoken word to the enigmatic ideograms of the stenotype machine.

Now, how should one act in a place of such material grandeur, the awesomeness of which is intensified with occasional flourishes of spiritual pageantry marked by the uttering of incantations and the swearing of oaths? Obviously with a great deal of decorum. Court rules mandate, juror's expect and tradition compels the advocate to perform with dignity and civility in such an environment. Translated to the more common situations that means you stand when:

the jury enters or leaves the courtroom,

the court is being called to order,

you are addressing the judge,

you are addressing the jury.

Further, you address the Court by "Your Honor,", witnesses by mister, misses, or miss (unless a child), and your opponent in a similarly civil fashion. (Some jurisdictions maintain the practice of referring to opposing counsel as "my brother" an appellation utilized universally despite gender. Scratch "My learned colleague." No matter how uttered it drips with derision.)

Some judges, to satisfy the requirements of court rules or their own need for obeisance, require that counsel seek the court's permission before straying from a designated spot at lectern or counsel table in order to approach a witness or the bench. If such a practice doesn't exist, don't initiate it. If it does, no harm in complying unless it conditions you to play the role of obsequious wimp. One may grant a courtly bow but one does not grovel. It's not so much what you do as what it does to you what you do. If good advocacy dictates that you approach a witness or mandates that you approach the bench, a courteous request to do so should have no ego stripping effect—as long as you maintain the mindset that if the request is denied the result will be confrontation and not obsequious compliance. It's all a matter of attitude. Remember the general maxim, "You can't try a case on your knees."

E.   DYNAMICS

§ 8.13   Generally

Shakespeare would have us believe that all the world is a stage. We'll have to excuse Will for the hyperbole which universalizes his trade but at the same time acknowledge that as far as a trial is concerned he was right on the button.

The trial is drama, those who participate are the actors, the jury is the audience and the courtroom is the stage. The metaphor should be of help in considering positioning and movement—the dynamics involved in your presentation. We could go to the drama experts to learn the tricks of their trade and apply them as they relate to our role as director and actor. But few of us have played this role before. Our experience in the theatre has most likely been confined to that of play goer, so let's review the applicable rules from the vantage point of the audience—then translate them as they apply to your audience—the jury.

§ 8.14   Auditory Requisites

What is said must be heard.

The prime requisite for a theatre is good acoustics. Nothing is more frustrating and tiring than straining to hear the lines spoken by the actors.

Translation: position yourself so that the lines spoken in the courtroom, both from you and your witness, can be heard—by the jury and by the court reporter. (I'm not forgetting the opposing counsel and the judge. They may not want to hear).

Keep in mind certain principles:

1.   A person will usually choose the pitch and volume necessary to be heard by the person to whom they are talking. If you are standing ten feet from a witness he will speak loudly enough for you to hear him. But what if the farthermost juror is twenty feet away? A possible solution is to ask the witness to "speak up". But regardless of

how gently that suggestion is given it is a rebuff to the witness and could be upsetting. Best for you to remedy the situation with action of your own. Simply back up. The witness will respond by pitching his voice to reach you and the same result will be accomplished.

2.   A person will direct an answer to that person from whom the question has come. There is an almost irresistible inclination for the *public* interrogation of a witness for the benefit of the jury to disintegrate into a *private* tete a tete between witness and counselor. Consider two remedies:

one, position yourself near the end of the jury box farthest from the witness,

two, occasionally direct the witness to "turn to the jury and tell them '——' "

3.   An exhibit or an easel presents a seductive target for eye contact.

There's good news and bad news in the message. The good news is that a visual aid displayed on an easel can dramatically enhance a verbal presentation. The bad news is that if the exhibit remains in view of the jury beyond its relevant use it distracts all those exposed to its view—the jury, the witness, the lawyer. Watch a lawyer deliver an opening statement or closing argument with the aid of a visual. After appropriate reference he will continue to make frequent turns of the head directed to the visual aid as if it is part of the audience. The solution is to use the aid then either remove it or position yourself so that you'll not be tempted to sneak a meaningless peek.

§ 8.15 Visual Requisites

What is shown must be seen.

The lawyer using visual aids is confronted with two problems:

creating an exhibit on which the material presented is of such size, color and arrangement that the content can be readily understood;

positioning the exhibit in such a way that each juror can easily see it; and

presenting it in such a way that the visual information is coordinated with the complementary verbal component.

In respect to the initial problem of creating the exhibit certain maxims must be followed:

1.   Spontaneously created exhibits (a freehand drawing of an intersection, a list of figures or other written material) are more apt to create problems than exhibits containing the information which are prepared beforehand. Sometimes that problem is in establishing its admissibility. An opponent and a judge is more apt to interrupt your spontaneous scribbling on a blackboard than your presentation of a properly prepared and authenticated exhibit. But even if admissibility isn't the problem, the handwritten message will carry with it the intrinsic limitations of the medium used (chalk, pencil, etc.) aggravated by your own inadequacies in penmanship and sometimes your limitations of spelling. (The author well remembers the embarrassment suffered by a physician who boldly wrote on the blackboard that the injury had been caused by "trama.")

2.   Printed letters in bold color are more easily seen than cursive writing in white on black.

     The intrinsic limitations mentioned above can be lessened with a deliberate choice of a bold medium (such as a magic marker or felt tipped pen) and printed letters.

     We are all familiar with the instruction found on so many forms, "Please print." If jurors could express their choice they would echo that request.

3.   A professionally prepared exhibit bespeaks forethought, concern and competence and, thus, becomes a more effective tool of persuasion. Just as a properly prepared exhibit impels admission by the judge, it too will impel acceptance by the jury.

Confining ourselves to matters of size, color and legibility does not address the more provocative problem of having the message understood.

Again, some general principles will help with the problem.

Don't be guilty of a proliferation of evidence presented in visual form. Unrestricted use of exhibits can result in two adverse effects expressed in these truisms:

the worth of anything is related to its scarcity, consequently, too much of anything can cheapen it (that's why they have diamond cartels), to limit the number of "precious" gems on the market;

overloads cause circuit breaks which result in complete interruption of service.

Applying these truisms the advocate will not cheapen his visual aids with indiscriminate use and will endeavor to make the message conveyed meet the three c test of clear, cogent and concise.

Don't ignore the options available both as to content and to media. The choice should depend on such factors as:

cost;

ease of preparation;

ease of presentment;

persuasiveness;

ease of preserving in the trial record.

CHAPTER 9

VOIR DIRE

"Getting to know you, getting to know
all about you"
The King and I—Oscar Hammerstein II

Analysis

A. PROCEDURE

B. PURPOSES

A. PROCEDURE

§ 9.1 Generally

There are as many procedural ways to pick a jury as there are ways to pronounce "voir dire." Each jurisdiction seems to have adopted a unique methodology of its own. Some of these procedures deal with the respective role of the judge and the lawyer, some with the order of interrogation, others with the mechanics of the strike. An examination will be made of each with the understanding that the purpose is to provide a cursory overview of some representative species not a definitive recitation of all the mutants that may exist.

§ 9.2 Role of the Judge and Lawyer

Who is to assume the laboring oar of interrogating the jury? In most federal courts this responsibility has been assumed by the judge and the lawyer's role is confined to submitting written suggestions as to lines of inquiry or specific questions to be directed to the panel. Sometimes the lawyer is allowed to ask a few "mop-up" questions of his own but it is quite apparent that is strictly an ancillary function.

The pendulum swings as far the other way in most state courts. The lawyer is front and center asking all the questions and the judge is a passive umpire making an infrequent ruling but only when the other side yells "Foul."

No need commenting on the relative merits of these procedures as they exist in various parts of the country. Suffice to say that the advice of Harold Hill applies to lawyers as well as salesmen—"You gotta know the territory!"

§ 9.3 Order of Interrogation

The panel members may be interrogated as a whole, in groups of four, individually or alternately as a group and as individuals. Oddly enough these differences are seldom dictated by court rules but merely custom. (Perhaps an incongruous combination of adjective and noun. For a lawyer "custom" is never "mere.") Allowing for a personal observation, it appears a profligate waste of time to inquire of each juror if he knows the litigants or has heard of the incident or a score of other such questions. These can be asked once of the group and if affirmative responses are forthcoming additional questions confined to the ones involved. The absence of definitive court rules should allow for experimentation and the acceptance of a plan that will truncate the process but preserve the purposes.

§ 9.4 Method of Invoking Strikes

Here the differences proliferate and demonstrate the wide range of procedures under which lawyers have been content to function. We have eighteen candidates (veniremen) for twelve jobs (jurors). We, of course, wish to choose the best twelve. Now if the positions were those of typists in a secretarial pool, we know how an experienced office manager would undertake the task— interview all eighteen, compare their skills, temperament and all those undefinables which make for good employees, then render a decision. Of course the law is not selecting typists. These "employees" will listen to evidence, exercise their judgment, execute the conscience of the community and render a decision dealing with life, liberty and property. Their employment interview should be just as thorough and designed to pick the best of the lot (or eliminate the worst). Right? Sad to say in many jurisdictions. "Wrong." The candidates are examined one at a time. The lawyer must judge whether he wishes to exercise a peremptory challenge or not on the basis of which panel members are least desirable but rather on the basis of whether the panel member under consideration meets the minimal requirements of jury service. The use of the peremptory challenges must be made without knowledge of the qualifications of the jurors yet to be examined. Exhaust your challenges on so-so jurors and you might be saddled with some real clinkers later on. Those jurisdictions which examine in groups of four ameliorate the problem somewhat. Instead of measuring each juror against a hypothetical juror of minimum competence the jurors are measured against others in the group. But the basic problem still remains. It the challenges are used on jurors in this group what will I be faced with in the subsequent groups?

Good sense dictates that the lawyers be given the opportunity to see and interrogate the entire panel and then, with all the cards on the table face up, to screen the lot. Customs die hard but the piecemeal selection of jurors is one that should be dispatched.

But even in those jurisdictions in which the entire panel is interrogated then challenged some differences exist. Plan one— the plaintiff in a civil suit or the state in a criminal act exercises the total number of strikes designated by law then the opponent completes the process by doing the same. Plan two—the plaintiff or state makes the initial strike, the defendant follows with a strike and the parties alternate until the requisite number of jurors remain.

You can appreciate the difference. Suppose A and B are considered undesirable by both parties. In plan two, plaintiff (or the state) can hold back on the initial strike and perhaps finesse the defendant into striking A or B thus giving plaintiff an extra choice for elimination. In plan one no such maneuvering can take place. Plaintiff must eliminate the two least attractive with his one and only opportunity. The advantages have shifted to the defendant. Maybe one of his undesirables has already been stricken by the plaintiff. The "extra" strike now goes to the defendant.

§ 9.5 Announcing Strikes

The choices that the lawyer makes must be communicated to the court and the opponent. The particular court procedure may permit the peremptory challenges to be made without notice to the venireman as to which party dropped the ax. This can frequently be advantageous. Suppose in a highly technical product liability case the examination develops that one member of the panel is an engineer highly knowledgeable in that particular field about which the case is concerned. The lawyer who strikes such a potential juror might have the reasons for his strike interpreted as a fear that his case would suffer from the judgment of a fellow who "really knows." Best that the striking lawyer remain unknown.

But if peremptory challenges can, on occasion, be made clandestinely, challenges for cause cannot. Most often the lawyer must request the juror to be stricken in the hearing of the panel and the juror himself. That poses a potential problem. Let's say that the juror acknowledges that he has a business relationship with a corporate litigant. The lawyer states, "Well your honor, under that circumstance I don't see how Mr. Juror can be fair and I ask that he be stricken." Now that might not be too bad—if the judge rules in your favor. But what if your opponent intervenes "Pardon me your honor, may I voir dire Mr. Juror? Sir, would you be able to follow the instructions of this court and return a verdict based on the law and the evidence?" "Certainly" comes the righteous response. "Then I see no reason to strike Mr. Juror. I think he's aptly qualified." Now you are in an argument about the juror's fairness—right in front of him and his peers (many of whom have probably played bridge with him in the jury waiting room and have concluded that he is obviously an upright citizen). If you don't win that argument you are going to have to strike him—and maybe there are some who are worse.

Recognizing a danger such as this it is best to make the challenge less challenging. Don't use color words that accuse a venireman of unfairness and then ask that he be "stricken" (it sounds so violent). Better to say, "Mr. Juror, I'm sure you can appreciate my concern about your business relationship with Mr. Brown and how that might affect your ability to serve on this jury. Would you feel more comfortable if you were excused from this panel?" If he says "no" or if your opponent objects that "feeling comfortable" is not the test for jury service, then you might have to push further but at least you have provided him an "out" and a chance to be removed without having challenged him about his fairness.

Incidentally, it's not unusual to get involved in a tug of war concerning the merits of a challenge for cause. If it's a juror that looks good to you, don't let that challenge go unchallenged. Get your oar in there and ask if he can't "follow the law and the evidence" and insist that such is the proper test of a juror's qualifications. Failure to do so just provides your opponent with additional eliminations which further refine the jury according to his desires.

B. PURPOSES

§ 9.6 Generally

What is the purpose of voir dire? The answer depends on the identity of the person to whom the question is put. A venireman might understand it to be an exercise in curiosity which results in either the selection of the most "fair minded" or the "least intelligent" (depending on whether the venireman was selected or not). To a judge the purpose might appear to be the selection of an unbiased panel in the shortest time possible. To the advocate it's quite a different thing. His response will be in the content that voir dire is perhaps the most significant procedure in the whole trial process and that consequently, it is to be afforded such time and attention that such significance deserves. He will recognize that it is not a selection process at all (that was done when the names came out of the jury drum) but rather an elimination process. Contrary to common belief you are not "picking a jury" more accurately you are culling the undesirables or, if you insist, "picking non-jurors." He should realize that it is an introduction between the lawyer and the future fact finders and as such is a time for some "social preening." It is also an introduction, abbreviated as it may be, to the case at hand and the legal and social issues that it involves. Recognizing these factors, the advocate will identify the purposes of voir dire to be: elimination, ingratiation, indoctrination.

§ 9.7   Jury Selection Philosophy

Before submitting a less traditional approach to the voir dire process perhaps it would be well to review the philosophy of "jury selection" that has prevailed among trial lawyers for many years. What better representative to express that view than Clarence Darrow?

SELECTING A JURY BY CLARENCE DARROW [1]

Selecting a jury is of the utmost importance. So far as possible, the lawyer should know both sides of the case. If the client is a landlord, a banker, or a manufacturer, or one of that type, then jurors sympathetic to that class will be wanted in the box; a man who looks neat and trim and smug. He will be sure to guard your interests as he would his own. His entire environment has taught him that all real values are measured in cash, and he knows no other worth. Every knowing lawyer seeks for a jury of the same sort of men as his client; men who will be able to imagine themselves in the same situation and realize what verdict the client wants.

Lawyers are just as carefully concerned about the likes and dislikes, the opinions and fads of judges as of jurors. All property rights are much safer in the hands of the courts than of jurors. Every lawyer who represents the poor avoids a trial by the court.

Choosing jurors is always a delicate task. The more a lawyer knows of life, human nature, psychology, and the reactions of the human emotions, the better he is equipped for the subtle selection of his so-called "twelve men, good and true." In this undertaking, everything pertaining to the prospective juror needs be questioned and weighed; his nationality, his business, religion, politics, social standing, family ties, friends, habits of life and though; the books

---

1. Reprinted by permission of Esquire Magazine © 1936 by Esquire, Inc.

and newspapers he likes and reads, and many more matters that combine to make a man; all of these qualities and experiences have left their effect on ideas, beliefs and fancies that inhabit his mind. Understanding of all this cannot be obtained too bluntly. It usually requires finesse, subtlety and guess-work. Involved in it all is the juror's method of speech, the kind of clothes he wears, the style of haircut, and, above all, his business associates, residence and origin.

To the ordinary observer, a man is just a man. To the student of life and human beings, every pose and movement is a part of the personality and the man. There is no sure rule by which one can gauge any person. A man may seem to be of a certain mold, but a wife, a friend, or an enemy, entering into his life, may change his most vital views, desires and attitudes, so that he will hardly recognize himself as the man he once seemed to be.

It is obvious that if a litigant discovered one of his dearest friends in the jury panel he could make a close guess as to how certain facts, surrounding circumstances, and suppositions would affect his mind and action; but as he has no such acquaintance with the stranger before him, he must weigh the prospective juror's words, manner of speech and, in fact, hastily and cautiously "size him up" as best he can. The litigants and their lawyers are supposed to want justice, but, in reality, there is no such thing as justice, either in or out of court. In fact, the word cannot be defined. So, for lack of proof, let us assume that the word "justice" has a meaning, and that the common idea of the definition is correct, without even seeking to find out what is the common meaning. Then, how do we reach justice through the courts? The lawyer's idea of justice is a verdict for his client, and really this is the sole end for which he aims.

In spite of the power that the courts exercise over the verdict of a jury, still the finding of the twelve men is very important, sometimes conclusive. It goes without saying that lawyers always do their utmost to get men on the jury who are apt to decide in favor of their clients. It is not the experience of jurors, neither is it their brainpower, that is the potent influence in their decisions. A skillful lawyer does not tire himself hunting for learning or intelligence in the box; if he knows much about man and his making, he knows that all beings act from emotions and instincts, and that reason is not a motive factor. If deliberation counts for anything, it is to retard decision. The nature of the man himself is the element that determines the juror's bias for or against his fellow man. Assuming that a juror is not a half-wit, his intellect can always furnish fairly good reasons for following his instincts and emotions. Many irrelevant issues in choosing jurors are not so silly as they seem. Matters that apparently have nothing to do with the discussion of a case often are of the greatest significance.

In the last analysis, most jury trials are contests between the rich and poor. If the case concerns money, it is apt to be a case of damages for injuries of some sort claimed to have been inflicted by someone. These cases are usually defended by insurance companies, railroads, or factories. If a criminal case, it is practically always the poor who are on trial.

The most important point to learn is whether the prospective juror is humane. This must be discovered in more or less devious ways. As soon as "the court" sees what you want, he almost always blocks the game. Next to this, in having more or less bearing on the question, is the nationality, politics, and religion of the person examined for the jury. If you do not discover this, all your plans may go awry. Whether you are handling a damage suit, or your client is charged with the violation of law, his attorney will try to get the same sort of juror.

Let us assume that we represent one of "the underdogs" because of injuries received, or because of an indictment brought by what the prosecutors name themselves—"the state." Then what sort of men will we seek? An Irishman is called into the box for examination. There is no reason for asking about his religion; he is Irish; that is enough. We may not agree with his religion, but it matters not; his feelings go deeper than any religion. You should be aware that he is emotional, kindly and sympathetic. If he is chosen as a juror, his imagination will place him in the dock; really, he is trying himself. You would be guilty of malpractice if you got rid of him, except for the strongest reasons.

An Englishman is not so good as an Irishman, but still, he has come through a long tradition of individual rights, and is not afraid to stand alone; in fact, he is never sure that he is right unless the great majority is against him. The German is not so keen about individual rights except where they concern his own way of life; liberty is not a theory, it is a way of living. Still, he wants to do what is right, and he is not afraid. He has not been among us long, his ways are fixed by his race, his habits are still in the making. We need inquire no further. If he is a Catholic, then he loves music and art; he must be emotional, and will want to help you; give him a chance.

277

If a Presbyterian enters the jury box, carefully rolls up his umbrella, and calmly and critically sits down, let him go. He is cold as the grave; he knows right from wrong, although he seldom finds anything right. He believes in John Calvin and eternal punishment. Get rid of him with the fewest possible words before he contaminates the others; unless you and your clients are Presbyterians you probably are a bad lot, and even though you may be a Presbyterian, your client most likely is guilty.

If possible, the Baptists are more hopeless than the Presbyterians. They, too, are apt to think that the real home of all outsiders is Sheol, and you do not want them on the jury, and the sooner they leave the better.

The Methodists are worth considering; they are nearer the soil. Their religious emotions can be transmuted into love and charity. They are not half bad, even though they will not take a drink; they really do not need it so much as some of their competitors for the seat next to the throne. If chance sets you down between a Methodist and a Baptist, you will move toward the Methodist to keep warm.

Beware of the Lutherans, especially the Scandinavians; they are almost always sure to convict. Either a Lutheran or Scandinavian is unsafe, but if both-in-one, plead your client guilty and go down the docket. He learns about sinning and punishing from the preacher, and dares not doubt. A person who disobeys must be sent to Hell; he has God's word for that.

As to Unitarians, Universalists, Congregationalists, Jews and other agnostics, don't ask them too many questions; keep them anyhow; especially Jews and agnostics. It is best to inspect a Unitarian, or a Universalist, or a Congregationalist, with some care, for they may be prohibitionists; but never the Jews and the real agnostics! And, do not, please, accept a prohibitionist: he is too solemn and holy and dyspeptic. He knows your client would not have been indicted unless he were a drinking man, and anyone who drinks is guilty of something, probably much worse than he is charged with, although it is not set out in the indictment. Neither would he have employed *you* as his lawyer had he not been guilty.

I have never experimented much with Christian Scientists; they are too serious for me. Somehow, solemn people seem to think that pleasure is wicked. Only the gloomy and dyspeptic can be trusted to convict. Shakespeare knew: "Yond' Cassius has a lean and hungry look; he thinks too much; such men are danger-ous." You may defy all the rest of the rules if you can get a man who laughs. Few things in this world are of enough importance to warrant considering them seriously. So, by all means, choose a man who laughs. A juror who laughs hates to find anyone guilty.

Never take a wealthy man on a jury. He will convict, unless the defendant is accused of violating an anti-trust law, selling worthless stocks or bonds, or something of that kind. Next to the Board of Trade for him, the Penitentiary is the most important of public buildings. These imposing structures stand for Capitalism. Civilization could not possibly exist without them. Don't take a man because he is a "good" man; this means nothing. You should find out what he is good *for.* Neither should a man be accepted, because he is a bad sort. There are too many ways of being good or bad. If you are defending, you want imaginative individuals. You are not interested in the morals of the juror. If a man is instinctively kind and sympathetic, take him.

Then, too, there are the women. These are now in the jury box. A new broom sweeps clean. It leaves no speck on the floor or under the bed, or in the darkest corners of life. To these new jurors, the welfare of the state depends on the verdict. It will be so for many years to come. The chances are that it would not have made the slightest difference to the state if all cases had been decided the other way. It might, however, make a vast difference to the unfortunates facing cruel, narrow-minded jurors who pass judgment on their fellow men. To the defendants it might have meant the fate of life rather than death.

But, what is one life more or less in the general spawning? It may float away on the tide, or drop to the depths of oblivion, broken, crushed and dead. The great sea is full of embryo lives ready to take the places of those who have gone before. One more unfortunate lives and dies as the endless stream flows on, and little it matters to the wise judges who coldly pronounce long strings of words in droning cadence: the victims are removed, they come and go and the judges keep on chanting senseless phrases laden with doom upon the bowed heads of those before them. The judge is as unconcerned about the actual meaning of it all as the soughing wind rustling the leaves of a tree just outside the courthouse door.

Women still take their new privilege seriously. They are all puffed up with the importance of the part they feel they play, and are sure they represent a great step forward in the world. They believe that the sex is cooperating in a great cause. Like the rest of us, they do not know which way is forward and which is backward, or whether either one is any way at all. Luckily, as I feel, my services were almost over when women invaded the jury box.

A few years ago I became interested in a man charged with selling some brand of intoxicant in a denatured land that needed cheering. I do not know whether he sold it or not. I forgot to ask him. I viewed the case with mixed feelings of pity and contempt, for, as Omar philosophized, "I wonder often what the vintners buy one half so precious as the stuff they sell?" When I arrived on the scene, the courtroom looked ominous with women jurors. I managed to get rid of all but two, while the dismissed women lingered around in the big room waiting for the victory, wearing solemn faces and white ribbons. The jury disagreed. In the second trial there were four women who would not budge from their seats, or their verdict. Once more I went back to the case with distrust and apprehension. The number of women in the jury box had grown to six. All of them were unprejudiced. They said so. But everyone connected with the case was growing tired and skeptical, so we concluded to call it a draw. This was my last experience with women jurors. I formed a fixed opinion that they were absolutely dependable, but I did not want them.

§ 9.8 Selection Basis—Generally

Comments on this approach, if one can be presumptuous to comment on the old master, will appear later, for now let us consider a few amplifications to supplement the traditional approach.

The basis for choosing your "throw aways" from among the panel is basically a two step process: identification of the jurors and recognition of any similarities that exist with that identification and your case. The identification will seek out relationships that may exist between the prospective juror and the four "C's:" counsel, client, confederates and cause.

§ 9.9 Selection Basis—Identity With Client

The litigants, if individuals, are usually present in the courtroom and the standard procedure is to have them stand and inquire of the panel, "Do any of you know my client Mr. Brown? He lives on 2315 Elm and is a bank teller at the First National Bank. Or, are you acquainted with Mr. Smith, the defendant in this case?" If a litigant is a corporation or other business or institutional entity, then knowledge of the organization alone will not suffice. The usual inquiry will be "Are any of the jury panel members employed by or have any financial interest in the ABC Corporation?" Of course the identity of the organizational defendant will dictate the nature of more specific inquiry designed to establish potential affiliations. These might be business relationships, such as customer, supplier, agent, landlord, etc. or emotional relationships, such as contributor, fan, member. Two types of corporate defendants should be given special attention: utility companies and insurance companies. As to the former, they are frequently involved as named defendants. Everyone on the panel is familiar with them and many have experienced specific incidents which have created hostility ("They cut off my services."—"I was dunned for a bill") or friendliness ("The nicest young man fixed my phone"—"They came out on a holiday to connect my stove"). Such probable experiences must be probed. As to the latter, the extent of inquiry, if at all, will depend on the jurisdiction.

Insurance companies are seldom involved as named defendants but usually are behind the scenes directing the litigation and providing the source of recovery. What, if any, inquiries as to the jury's relationship to the insurance company will depend on the jurisdiction but in every case the subject matter must be approached in the spirit of the proverbial love-making porcupines—"very carefully." A misspoken word about "insurance" might well precipitate a mistrial. Check out your local West Digest, Trial Key Number before you hazard interrogation.

Asking if the panel identifies with the clients is the first step. If there is no affirmative response you are off to another line of inquiry. But what do we do when the hands shoot up? Additional questions suggest themselves and should probably be asked. "How long have you known Mr. Brown?" "What is the nature of your relationship?" and the ultimate, "Would this in any way prevent you from sitting on this jury and rendering a fair trial to both parties?" The "should probably be asked" is intentional. Recognition must be made of the fact that further probing may result in an unsolicited endorsement of an opposing litigant ("Yes, Mr. Brown and I serve on the same Church Board"—"I've been a customer of ABC for twenty years and I know they are a fine company") or an embarrassing disclosure about your own client ("Is that the Fred Smith who used to tend bar at the "Red

Dragon?") Of course these spontaneous embellishments can fall either way. Whether they hurt or help depends on the caprice of the gods.

§ 9.10 Selection Basis—Identity With Confederates

The title heading is an unconscionable concession to the "apt art of alliteration." What we're really talking about are witnesses. Too often they are overlooked as the identifying link with the jurors. The need to inquire into this possible relationship is in direct proportion to the importance of the witness. Does your case depend upon the testimony of one person? You must determine if the jury identifies with that person. Will there be a swearing match between experts? You must identify those experts and find out what relationship exists between them and the potential jurors.

Again you must recognize that, if a relationship is uncovered, there is a decided risk in probing that relationship.

"Do any of you know Dr. Wilbur Jones who treated Mrs. Smith?" An affirmative response.

"And what was the nature of that relationship?"

"He was our family doctor."

Now there's a pregnant response—"was" our family doctor? Did the professional relationship end because of some dissatisfaction, maybe even a malpractice claim? To dig further and have that bit of information injected into the case might very well prove disastrous. Gauge the tone and mood of the juror and if a negative comment is anticipated either let it alone or follow with the inquiry, "Will that previous relationship with Dr. Jones prevent you from giving both sides a fair trial?" If you receive a "yes" response to this, you'll have a challenge for cause.

§ 9.11 Selection Basis—Identity With Cause

This is the most significant item of them all—determining how the prospective juror identifies with the issue of the lawsuit. Which leads us to the favorite topic of those who write and speak about jury selection—how to recognize the "good" and "bad" jurors those which will identify and those which won't. Every advocate seems to have his own "tried and true" axioms. Various ethnic groups, occupations, religious preferences are neatly categorized and slipped into an appropriate slot.

Plaintiff's Jurors	*Defendant's Jurors*
Italians	Germans
Jews	Accountants
Old people	Women
Irish	Executives
Laborers	Young people
etc.	etc.

Such a scheme is stultifying and fails to recognize a number of factors. One, as to the ethnic choices there are few hyphenated Americans left. Most of us now are into the third or fourth generation and the ethnic characteristics of our forebears have all but disappeared through the "melting pot" syndrome.

Two, personality is a many faceted thing with shifting identities. We say "accountants are conservative" therefore in the representation of a plaintiff we will strike the accountant on the panel. But what of *this* accountant? Maybe he worked his way through college as a taxi driver and plans to quit accounting at 45 years to spend the balance of his years as a beachcomber. Is this accountant "conservative?" But even if each such occupational category were constant is it realistic to tag someone by occupation alone? This same accountant is also a man, a husband, a father, of Irish descent, Catholic, stamp collector, baseball fan, dog owner, Playboy subscriber, etc. Each of these activities, socio-economic factors and organizational affiliations might be identified as orienting him one way or the other. But we can't ascertain all these factors quantitatively much less qualitatively. Is he a devoted dog owner and a casual Catholic or vice versa—a sometime stamp collector and an avid accountant or just the opposite.

Three, we have no empirical studies to verify these truisms. How do we know what goes on in the jury room and how the different identities argued and what issues they supported or rejected? And if an Italian agreed on a "liberal" verdict of $20,000, how do we know a Swede wouldn't have given $30,000?

In the absence of other guides some of these old bromides might have to be considered but consider them with caution. Don't perpetuate the myth that "all accountants make good defendant jurors." Unless, of course, you believe that all blacks like watermelon, and all Scotsmen are tight, and all Italians are good lovers, etc.

Laying these generalizations aside there are pertinent questions to be asked of prospective jurors that will provide insight as to which of the litigants they might identify. Relationships, experiences and present activities will be your best guide in establishing these potential identifications. You represent a teenage, long haired motorcyclist. There is no such type on the panel. But what of parents of long haired teenagers—or present or past drivers of motorcycles—or those who had had accidents with a motorcyclist? There are relationships and experiences which obviously must be covered. Sometimes the identification with a litigant will be less direct and thus more difficult to recognize. This presents a test of the trial lawyers' knowledge of human nature.

If you will tolerate a personal reference, some years ago I witnessed an accident in which a neighbor driving an automobile struck a young boy (luckily with very little injury). When I returned home I reported to my wife that "Mrs. Jones just struck the Miller boy." Do you know what her knee jerk response was? "She must feel awful." *She* must feel awful? What about the boy? There was no identity with him, even though he was a familiar, likable lad and she was a mother of five. The immediate identification was with the woman driver and the sympathetic response was directed to her.

Perhaps that provides some insight into why child pedestrian cases are so difficult for a plaintiff to win.

The trick of voir dire is to know enough about life to develop a feeling for such identifications and to supplement this knowledge with well directed questions.

§ 9.12   Selection Basis—Identity With Cause—Illustration

Suppose you represent a black accused of raping a white girl. Several white women are on the panel. You will want to know how closely they relate to the victim. Let's analyze the three areas for representative questions.

Relationship — Do you know of any rape victims?
Experience — Have you ever been assaulted or threatened?
Activities — Do you carry any type of device to ward off would be attackers? Do you have a dog? What kind? Have you taken any instruction in self defense?

You might draw a blank on the first two but if your panel member carries a can of mace in her car, owns a Doberman Pinscher and has taken a course in Judo you know where her identity lies and that she must be removed.

Note that the interrogation along these lines deals with *facts* and not *feelings*. No need to ask, "Are you prejudiced toward blacks?" or "Do you think rape is a horrid crime?" The facts of her private life will speak much more clearly than the feelings expressed in public.

§ 9.13   Selection Basis—Identity With Counsel

Relationship between counsel and venireman could be a significant factor in choosing your jury. Perhaps it would be well to inject at this point that we have been assuming a forum in an urban setting. There is still a lot of litigation handled in small rural communities in which all the members of the legal drama are known by the prospective jurors. The superfluity of making such inquires in those circumstances is best illustrated by the rebuff that was suffered by the city lawyer who made a perfunctory inquiry into whether any of the panel members knew opposing counsel. "Son," said the judge, "everybody here knows everybody else—except you. Now proceed."

But in the urban setting the situation is different. Some inquiry should be made into the possible relationship between panel and paraclete. The question is "how?" Some lawyers find it embarrassing to simply say, "Do any of you know me?" This is particularly so when a client is on the panel. Clients expect to be recognized and a confession of ignorance on your part can be interpreted as the ultimate insult (being forgotten) or ultimate unfairness (an attempt to get a friend on the jury by feigning a lack of acquaintanceship). If you recognize someone on the panel, acknowledge that recognition. It might be after doing so, that you'll ask the judge to excuse the juror. It frequently is good judgment to do so. First, such a request from you, rather than the opposing counsel, creates an aura of fairness. Second, there is such a thing as friends on a jury "bending over backwards."

It is not unusual for a lawyer to take advantage of this line of interrogation by acquainting the jury, not only with the opposing counsel, but also the firm with which he is associated (the thought being that some jurors will relate big law firms with big business—and deep pockets). Thus it goes something like this. "Are any panel members acquainted with Mr. John Brown? (pause) Or have any of you ever done business or have any acquaintanceship with members of his firm Diddle, Dawdle, Doolittle and Stall?"

(Turning to opposing counsel) "John do you have a letterhead there?" "Thank you." "Let's see, that's Tom Diddle, Fred Dawdle, Robert Doolittle"—and on and on.

§ 9.14 Ingratiation—Generally

The second purpose of voir dire might best be described as an effort to establish support with the jury and create a relationship with them that will enhance your chances of persuasion. This constitutes that part of the voir dire sometimes characterized as "visiting with the jury." Of all the phases of the trial there is none which affords an opportunity for a lawyer to display his personality than at this time. There is little value in suggesting lines of patter or sure-fire quips. Best that we take a look at the jury panel and do a bit of psychological analysis to ascertain what approaches may be most effective.

§ 9.15 Ingratiation—Pretrial Conditioning

Most of the jurors will probably be serving on a jury for the first time. For many it will be their first experience with any type of legal proceeding. What is their general feeling? Fear, that's what it is. A gut wrenching apprehension of the unknown. They don't know exactly why they are there and what will be expected of them. So need number one of the juror is to be comforted and put at ease. Help them to relax and relieve that "uptight" feeling. In a phrase—"soften the sphincter." Be at ease yourself. Develop a spirit that reflects warmth, concern, humanity. Remember that you are in a court of law and you are an officer of the court—but also remember that you're a human being. The two identities need not create conflict. You can be both "careful and casual" (as the ad for men's sportswear says), and exude a feeling of both friendliness and formality (witness Henry Kissinger). The achievement of such demeanor demands attention to your relationships with the humans around you, the bailiff, the clerk, the client—everyone.

§ 9.16 Ingratiation—Pretrial Conditioning—Illustration

Every advocate should be aware of the pretrial conditioning that occurs before the panel walks into the courtroom. Most jurisdictions have prepared jurors' handbooks which are presented to the panel members at the time they are sworn in. Some supplement this written material with a film outlining the role of the jury. Knowing the content of such official propagandizing will be of inestimable value. The content of a typical juror's handbook follows:

HANDBOOK FOR TRIAL JURORS

YOUR COUNTRY CALLS

As a citizen, you are a partner and shareholder in the state and nation. You have long enjoyed the privileges and protection of your government. Now you are called into service. You are summoned to serve for a short time as a juror.

To serve as a juror is an honor. It is also a very interesting experience. As a juror you will gain first-hand knowledge of the workings of a most important branch of government. Service will bring you satisfaction and pride in your government and in yourself. You should not overlook this opportunity.

PURPOSE OF THIS BOOK

The purpose of this booklet is to explain to you in a general way the manner in which lawsuits are tried and the part which you, as a juror, will have in seeing that justice is done.

CIVIL JURY CASES

THE PARTIES AND PLEADINGS

A person starting a lawsuit is known as the plaintiff. A person against whom suit is brought is called a defendant. Suit is commenced by service of a summons. The plaintiff's claim and demand is stated in a petition. The defendant's answer is called an answer. If the defendant claims from the plaintiff, such claim is called a counterclaim. If a counterclaim is made, the plaintiff's answer is called a reply. These papers, called pleadings, have been exchanged between the parties sometime before the trial commences. If a party has more than one claim against the other, each claim may be stated as a cause of action.

SELECTION OF JURY

A group of citizens qualified to serve as jurors has been summoned. The entire group is called the jury panel. The first step in a trial is to select from this panel the number required to try the case—12. Names are drawn from the jurors present until the jury box is filled. Those called are required to answer truthfully all questions asked of them touching their qualifications to act as a juror in the case. After a short statement telling what the case is about and the parties who are involved, the lawyers or the judge will question the men or women in the box to see if they are qualified to act as fair and impartial jurors. There are certain legal grounds for which a juror may be challenged for cause and excused. In addition, each side will excuse a certain number of jurors without giving any reason. These are called peremptory challenges. The parties may suspect that a prospective juror has had some experience, or that there is some reason which, although not a legal ground of challenge for cause may yet be justification for excusing the juror. The lawyer or judge may ask you questions about your personal life and beliefs. You should answer these questions fairly, and if there is any reason why you feel that you should not serve as a juror, you should make it known. When all the challenges are used up, the jurors who have been called but not excused are sworn to try the case upon the merits.

Any person excused from jury service during the qualification process, or by having his name stricken by the lawyers for the parties, should not consider the challenge or retirement from the jury panel as any reflection on his integrity or intelligence. None was intended by the judge, the parties, or the lawyers.

OATH OF A JUROR IN CIVIL CASE

Each juror is required to take a solemn oath (or to affirm) that he will "well and truly try the matters in issue and a true verdict render according to the evidence and the law." When you take this oath you become a judge of all questions of fact, and are in duty bound to act fairly and impartially in considering them.

OPENING STATEMENTS

The plaintiff's lawyer may then make a short opening statement telling what his client, the plaintiff, claims, and will outline to you the evidence by which he expects to prove this claim. The defendant's lawyer, before he opens his side of the case, may make a similar statement as to what his client claims and the evidence he expects to produce. You should remember that these statements of the lawyers are not evidence, but only explanations of what each side claims, and that claims must be proved by evidence. The conflicting claims constitute the issues.

WITNESSES AND EVIDENCE

Anything which tends to prove or disprove a claim about the facts is called evidence. Evidence may be something in writing, or it may be an article such as a gun, a photo, or the like; in which case it is called an exhibit. Evidence may also be the statement of a person, in which case it is called testimony. If a witness is absent, his testimony may have been taken before trial and reduced to writing. Such testimony is taken under oath and both sides have been given a chance to be present. Such written testimony is called a deposition. It may be that a witness has already testified in court under oath and his testimony taken down in shorthand and then put into typewriting. Such testimony is called a transcript.

EXAMINATION OF WITNESSES

Unless his case can be proved by writings, the plaintiff will call witnesses to testify. The witnesses are sworn (or affirm) to tell the truth, the whole truth, and nothing but the truth. A lawyer who has called a witness proceeds with his direct examination. In so doing, the lawyer asks questions to bring out the facts he wishes to show. In any important matter, he is not allowed to "lead" the witness by asking questions in such form as to suggest the answer. The question asked must appear to have some bearing on the case, and the witnesses shown to know what he is talking about. If these and other rules are not followed, the other lawyer may properly object and if for any reason the judge thinks the question improper, he rules that the objection is sustained, which means that the question cannot be answered. If the question is proper, the objection is overruled, and the answer is given. When the direct examination is finished, the lawyer on the other side may cross examine, which means that he may ask questions. The cross-examining lawyer may ask "leading questions." When cross-examination is finished, the first lawyer may ask questions on redirect examination to clear up points developed on cross-examination. To keep out improper matter, witnesses are allowed only to answer the questions asked. Both sides may ask questions and find out all he knows that is proper. If the witness makes a statement which is not an answer to a question, it may be stricken out, that is, you must disregard it entirely.

HEARING AND SEEING WITNESS

Each juror should pay close attention to the witness who is testifying both to hear what the witness says and watch his manner and actions. If you cannot hear plainly, do not hesitate to interrupt and let the judge know that you cannot hear.

RESTING THE CASE

When the plaintiff has put in all his evidence, he indicates that he is through by "resting" his case. When the defendant is through, he also "rests."

DEFENSE AND REBUTTAL

The defendant calls his witnesses and offers his evidence when the plaintiff first rests. Then the plaintiff may offer evidence in rebuttal to explain or deny the defendant's evidence.

MOTIONS TO STRIKE; DIRECTED VERDICT

When a lawyer requests a court to take action, it is usually done by making a motion. Thus, he may make a motion to strike out certain testimony because it was not properly received. If the judge orders that testimony be stricken out, the jury should disregard the stricken testimony. At the close of the plaintiff's case, or at the close of the defendant's case, or at the end of all the evidence, one or both sides may ask the court for a directed verdict. If the undisputed facts show that either one of the parties is entitled to judgment as a matter of law, the judge directs the verdict, because there is nothing for the jury to decide. In such a case the judge alone is responsible and the jury must do as the judge directs. Often the judge refuses to grant a motion. That does not mean that the judge thinks the other side is entitled to a verdict. It only means that the jury ought to consider the matter.

JUROR'S CONDUCT DURING TRIAL

There are certain rules that a juror should follow throughout the trial in order that he may be fair to all sides. These are:—

Discussing the Case: During the trial jurors should not talk about the case with each other, or with other persons, or allow other people to talk about it in your presence. If anyone should insist upon talking about the case to you, tell him that you are on the jury and must not listen to him. If he insists, then learn his name if you can and report the matter to the judge at the first opportunity.

Radio and Newspaper Accounts: In order that the mind of each juror be kept open until all the evidence, argument, and the instructions of the court have been heard, jurors ought not to listen to radio accounts of the trial or read articles about it which may appear in newspapers during the trial. Such articles sometimes give one a biased or unbalanced idea of the case.

Talking with Parties or Lawyers: Do not talk with parties, witnesses, or lawyers during a trial. Someone may believe that something unfair is going on.

Promptness: It is most important that jurors should not be late in reporting for duty. One juror who is late wastes the time of all the other jurors, the judge, the lawyers, the witnesses, the parties, and the other court employees. A lawyer, witness, or juror may be fined for contempt of court for being tardy.

Delays During Trial

During the trial there may be delays for any one of many reasons. Something may have happened to delay someone. Possibly the judge is looking up the law on some point which has suddenly come up. The lawyers may be presenting to the judge a point of law which ought not to be argued in your presence. You may not know the reason for a delay and should not guess at it. Very often a delay actually saves time and more quickly brings the case to an end. Be patient.

Conference Out of Your Hearing

There are occasions during a trial when a judge may call the lawyers to the bench, or the lawyers may approach the bench, and there engage in conversation with the judge out of the hearing of the jury. At such times law matters or procedural matters are being discussed and this manner of doing it is to save the inconvenience of sending the jury from the court room. Inasmuch as a jury passes only on factual matters it is felt to be the best policy to discuss law matters and procedural matters out of their hearing in order to avoid any chance of confusion to the jury. This practice should give you no concern and you should not even attempt to draw any conclusions as to what is being said out of your hearing.

Arguments

After all the evidence has been given, each lawyer may make his argument to the jury, giving the reasons why he thinks his side should win. If the testimony of witnesses is contrary to each other, he will tell you why he thinks the witnesses on his side should be believed rather than those on the other side.

You should listen to these arguments carefully, always remembering that a lawyer is giving only his side of the case and that what he says is not evidence. Of course, a juror should not make up his mind on anything until he has heard all sides and the instructions of the judge.

INSTRUCTIONS

Toward the close of the case the judge will read you his instructions, which will state the law which applies to the case. You should listen to these instructions very carefully and try to understand and remember them. They are the law of the case.

CONDUCT AND DELIBERATIONS IN JURY ROOM

FOREMAN

Your first duty upon retiring at the close of the case is to select your Foreman. The Foreman acts as chairman. It is his duty to see that discussion is carried on in sensible and orderly fashion, to see that the issues submitted for your decision are fully and fairly discussed, that every juror has a chance to say what he thinks upon every question. Where ballots should be taken, he will see that it is done.

SECRECY

Discussion in the jury room should never be so loud that it can be heard outside. Until a verdict is announced, no outsider should know what goes on in the jury room.

EXHIBITS

If any papers or other things marked as "exhibits" are sent out for your examination, care should be taken not to injure or change them in any way. No marking should be put on them.

VIEWS OF OTHERS

Quite often differences of opinion arise between jurors. When that happens each juror should say what he thinks and why he thinks it. By reasoning the matter out, it generally is possible for jurors to agree. A juror should not hesitate to change his mind if he decides that his first opinion was not right, but one who has an opinion on a question should not change it unless his reason and judgment is changed. It is wrong for one juror to try to bully another into changing his mind. It is just as wrong for a juror to refuse to listen to the arguments and opinions of others—in other words, to be bullheaded and stubborn. When one has listened to all the opinions of others, and considered the reasons for their opinions, and has reasoned the matter out and formed his own judgment, he should, of course, stick to it unless he is persuaded to change his mind. No juror should ever vote against his conscience. He should vote according to his honest judgment.

LAW OF THE CASE

The judge will tell you what the law is for each case, so that you may apply the law to the facts as you find them to be. The kind and amount of proof required will be pointed out.

YOUR VERDICT

Your verdict will show how reasonable, fair, just, and sensible the jury is. Verdicts may indicate to other people who have disputes in the future, whether they can wisely and safely submit their disputes to a jury for settlement or whether it is better judgment to suffer wrongs in silence, or to pay claims which are unjust, because they are afraid of jury justice. In all verdicts you must be careful to be just.

CRIMINAL CASES

IN GENERAL

With some exceptions which will be pointed out, criminal and civil cases are tried under much the same rules and in much the same manner.

THE CHARGE

The charge or complaint is made in writing. If made by a grand jury, it is called an indictment. If made by the prosecuting attorney, it is called an information. If more than one offense is charged, they may be combined but they are separately stated and each charge is called a count. For instance, an information may charge that the defendant (count 1) robbed the prosecuting witness, and (count 2) that he assaulted and beat the prosecuting witness.

THE PLEA

Some time before the case is called, usually, the defendant is arraigned. That is, he is brought before the judge and the charge is read to him. For each offense he is asked "How do you plead?" and he pleads "guilty" or "not guilty."

THE PARTIES

The person charged is the defendant. The state is the prosecutor, and all crimes are prosecuted in the name of the State of Missouri, for when a crime is committed, it is the laws of the state that are broken and the offense is against the people of the state. The lawyer who represents the state is called the prosecuting attorney or circuit attorney.

DIFFERENCES FROM CIVIL CASES

The principal differences in the manner of trial between civil and criminal cases are these:

1. More proof is required to find one guilty of crime than is required to return a verdict for plaintiff in a civil case. Crime must be proved "beyond a reasonable doubt," while a party in a civil case to be successful need only prove his case "by the greater weight of the evidence."

2. In a civil case 9 or more jurors may return a verdict, whereas in a criminal case the verdict must be unanimous.

CONCLUSION

The importance of your position as a juror cannot be overstated. It might be that others could serve as well as you and with less loss and trouble but you have been regularly drawn according to law. We hope you will find the service interesting. We believe and expect that you will do your full duty as a citizen and juror.

(Approved by Order of Supreme Court of Missouri, December 17, 1959.)

§ 9.17   Ingratiation—Establishing Credentials—Generally

Whenever a group of strangers congregate there is a tendency to display their credentials in order to ascertain their place in the pecking order. We all do this, consciously or unconsciously. We like to get the feel of where we stand. Theologians and political scientists may condemn such statements as being expressive of an anti-egalitarian philosophy violative of more lofty concepts of the "brotherhood of man" and the equal creation of all persons. But psychologists know differently and lawyers, dealing with people as they are and not as they should be, must recognize that such a phenomenon does exist and must be dealt with. Each juror should be given an opportunity to display his credentials in order to elevate himself in the eyes of his fellow jurors and settle into an appropriate and comfortable niche. The challenge is to go about this in a considerate and understanding fashion. Will Rogers reportedly said, "We're all ignorant, it's just that we're ignorant about different things." Similarly all of us have marks of merit, it's just that our marks are made in different endeavors—and these areas of achievements can be uncovered by a sensitive and sympathetic advocate. Perhaps you recall the story of the woman who prided herself on her ability to always uncover some good quality about her acquaintances and comment upon their particular attractive characteristic. But one day her insight and imagination was stretched to the breaking point. She found herself at a party dancing with a stout, ungainly, unattractive partner. She strained to find a good characteristic upon which she could comment. At last her face lit up and with a sense of relief she said, "You know, you sure don't sweat much for a fat man."

What are the nice things we can uncover about jurors and, conversely, what are the bad things that they would just as soon not go into?

§ 9.18   Ingratiation—Establishing   Credentials—Illustration

Occupation of Juror

Each of us likes to think that the particular job with which we are involved is of some importance. If it isn't important it can at least be made to sound important. Personnel managers know this. There is no such animal as a "janitor" anymore. That job description is now classified as "maintenance engineer." Same with "housewife." The more appropriate title is "home manager." It's surprising how often in the course of a voir dire examination the lawyer has the opportunity of employing one type of job description or the other. Be conscious of the sensitivity of your panel members in this regard and opt for the "nice" way of saying things.

Sometimes the occupational obfuscation that comes from euphemistic titles can present a problem. What if a juror identifies himself as a "lead man" employed at General Motors? Sounds pretty important doesn't it? An inquiry into the nature of the work, however, will disclose that he is simply an assembly line worker. Don't unfrock him in front of his fellow jurors. If he had wanted to say "assembly line worker" he would have. Instead he chose to be known as "a lead man." His resident address, his clothes and his bearing will give you sufficient insight into his occupation for you to make your appraisal. Let his job description go unchallenged.

On the other hand some persons want to disclose the importance of their jobs. You should be able to sense this in the nature of their response. If with a self assured smile they claim that they are "foreman" at the local plant, then it would be advisable to let them crow a little. "Do you have any men under you, Mr. Smith?" "What are some of the responsibilities that such a job entails?" Now he can elaborate a bit about his importance—he has elevated himself in the pecking order, and you've made a friend.

What happens when a venireman acknowledges a rather modest occupation that creates no particular status in the eyes of his fellow jurors? That might be a good time to ask, "And how long have you worked for your employer?" The response of "Twenty-three years" establishes stability, trustworthiness and loyalty and your reaction with an approving smile and a "Fine" will confirm that appraisal to him and his fellow panel members.

History of Prior Litigation

Another delicate area that must be mentioned is that of prior litigation. It is usually considered to be a matter of some import to ascertain whether a juror, particularly in a personal injury action, has been involved in similar litigation as a plaintiff or defendant. The desire to uncover such information has merit but the manner in which the question is posed may prove embarrassing to the juror. "Have any of you ever been involved in a lawsuit?" A few hands hesitatingly go up. "Yes Mr. Jones, what was that all about?" Now you might have put poor Jones on a spot. Maybe it was a simple personal injury claim—but what if it wasn't? It might have been a hotly contested divorce suit or a claim on a delinquent account, or a bastardy proceeding. Perhaps this is the very kind of information which you seek, but in most cases you would be content to know if the venireman had been involved in litigation similar to that which is the subject matter of the instant suit. If such is the thrust of your inquiry, frame your question accordingly and avoid embarrassment for the juror.

Age

An acknowledgment of age can also be the source of concern with some jurors. If the juror is identified as Miss Jones employed as a telephone operator at Bell Telephone Company, prudence dictates that you not ask the length of employment. This response of "Twenty-three years" will trigger some quick computations in the minds of her fellow jurors that will immediately tag her as a middle aged spinster. You won't make any friends that way.

Occupation of Juror's Spouse

Good practice dictates that you uncover the occupation of the prospective juror's spouse. The manner of seeking such information is critical. An unthinking lawyer will confront the men on the panel with a straightforward, "Does your wife work?" Now this is potentially offensive on two grounds. First, it implies that if she is "just" a housewife she doesn't "work." Not too good public relations toward the housewives on the panel who probably regard themselves as the last of the true laborers. Second, some men are still uncomfortable about the fact that they are not the only bread winner in the family. Granted that the younger members of our society seem to be completely indifferent to such an implication, a man of middle age might still be victimized by an earlier concept of man's role as the sole provider. Ease into it in this fashion. "Nowadays we find that it is quite common for the wife to be employed outside the home so I would like to ask you Mr. Smith if your wife is currently employed?"

Summary

Well, the list could go on indefinitely reciting those areas of interrogation in which the lawyer can ingratiate or alienate a prospective juror. Be sensitive in your interrogation and elevate when you can. As John Russell noted, "As one lamp lights another nor grows less, so nobleness enkindleth nobleness." Your kindness to the jurors will light their kindness to your client. It's good morals—and good advocacy.

§ 9.19 Indoctrination—Generally

Most litigation transcends the particular problems of the litigants and most lawyers attempt to find and exploit the universalities that might be involved. Thus a product liability case develops the theme of "consumer safety," a charge of aggravated assault is translated to the issue of "crime in the streets," the defendant who had two beers before the accident is apt to be confronted with the "age old problem of the drunken driver." Most persons have predisposed feelings about such issues and the verdict which they render will be shaped as much by these prejudices as by the law or the evidence. Voir dire presents the advocate with the opportunity to seek out these pre-dispositions and indoctrinate the panel member to be a receptive fact finder. The methods for accomplishing these ends are numerous.

§ 9.20 Indoctrination—Techniques

Let us consider a few of those situations in which indoctrination becomes necessary and examine those techniques most frequently employed.

One, the panel may be acquainted with the particular circumstance and confronted with a distasteful challenge as to their state of mind. "I represent a Negro in this case. Are any of you panel members prejudiced against blacks?" Few persons consider themselves "prejudiced." That is a dirty word and it is unrealistic to expect a lay person in the strange environment of a court room to make such a confession. You might as well not make any inquiry at all as to ask a question such as that.

Two, the panel may be led into giving the "right" answer. This is the "some of my best friends are prostitutes" approach. It goes something like this. "Now my client was convicted of a crime approximately five years ago. You're not going to hold that against him are you? You will give him the fair trial that he deserves, won't you?" This type of patronizing pap is best left unsaid. Of course they will give him a trial he deserves. The trouble is that some might think he deserves to get kicked out of court because of his previous criminal record. This line of questioning—or is it lecturing?—will never develop such thoughts which might be lurking in the minds of the jurors.

Three, the lawyer might express a solicitous understanding of a point of view and then make a genuine attempt to ascertain if such view is accepted by any members of the panel. Perhaps a student of transactional analysis might express this as an "adult-adult relationship."

"I would be naive if I didn't recognize that many persons have strong feelings regarding the use of intoxicating beverages by persons who operate motor vehicles. Many of us may belong to religious denominations which prohibit the use of intoxicants and consider such behavior as being morally wrong. In this case the evidence will be that my client, Tom Brown, drank several beers before the collision occurred. The evidence will further indicate that he was not under the influence of liquor at the time of the occurrence. Now my problem is this—that some one may be so offended by Tom's behavior in drinking the beer that they might find it difficult to sit as a juror in this case and return a verdict based solely on the law and the evidence. (Addressing a juror personally) Mrs. Green, how do you feel about this?"

The style might vary but the pattern is clear:

1. Recognize the potentially dangerous attitude.

2. Speak solicitously of those who share this attitude.

3. Acknowledge that the problem exists.

4. Confront the jurors personally.

5. Seek an expression of opinion, not a monosyllabic affirmation.

6. Get a commitment.

It is true that the open ended invitation for an expression might draw a withering blast. Mrs. Green might state, "I think that anyone who drinks and drives ought to be thrown in jail." When that occurs you simply thank her for her frankness and ask that she be excused. Best have her speak her piece in the jury box than in the jury room. On the other hand she might reply, "Well I don't approve of drinking but if the evidence shows he wasn't affected, I won't hold that against him." That gives rise to a "thank you" and the final point—a commitment. "Mrs. Green if you are accepted on this jury, can I rely on you to lay aside this feeling you may have and return a verdict based on the law and the evidence?" When she says "yes" you will have minimized the threat as much as possible and have "indoctrinated" the juror as much as the law allows.

It appears that this last approach is the most effective, however, it is probably the least employed. Most lawyers think that a jury panel can be lectured or shamed into laying aside their prejudices. Such a belief is contrary to human nature. A five minute sermonette cannot obliterate a life time of conditioning. Some jurors might have pre-dispositions and principles that seem unfavorable to your client's cause but remember they have other principles as well. Are you afraid that a "law and order" juror will react unfavorably to your client's criminal record? Then ask him, "Mr. Thompson, When my client robbed a store five years ago he received the full measure of justice, a two year prison term. Are you willing to give him a full measure of justice in this case?"

You have not tried to talk him out of his law and order attitude. You have not been judgmental about his views. You have taken him as he was, appealed to his sense of fairness and either neutralized his potentially prejudicial point of view or turned it to your advantage.

§ 9.21   Indoctrination—Use of Jurors

The instrument for indoctrination need not be the advocate alone. Sometimes the prospective juror himself can become the vehicle by which the other jurors can be conditioned to accept your client's cause. Assume you represent a client in a personal injury action who has had a series of injuries and resultant claims. You recognize that such information cannot be left for revelation through cross-examination. You want the jury panel to be advised of this in order to minimize its possible ill effect. You solicit the help of the panel members themselves.

"Have any members of the panel ever been the victim of an injury inducing occurrence which necessitated the filing of a claim?" By that question, in that form, you have identified such persons as "victims" who found it "necessary" to file a "claim." Rare indeed will be the jury panel that won't include several such "victims." "Perhaps some of you were unfortunate to have suffered more than one such occurrence?" Again, a good likelihood that some member on the panel has had such a history. "If so, follow it up with, 'And how many such instances were there?'" Now if a panel member, one of their own group, has had multiple claims it will be difficult to condemn the plaintiff as a litigation minded claims artist. Don't be too defensive and apologetic. A sympathetic soul might appear on the panel to help enhance your client's stature with the others.

One more example. You represent a fourteen year old who has been injured while riding a motor bike. You are afraid that some panel members will condemn the parents of the boy as the real culprits for having provided the lad with such a sophisticated piece of machinery. Some might blunder ahead with a direct, "Will anyone hold it against the parents for providing my client with a motor bike?" How much more effective if you abandon such a defensive posture and take the approach that such behavior on the part of parents is quite normal. "How many of you have teen-age boys?" A few hands go up. "Well, if they are typical of today's teenager I'm sure they have requested that they have a motor bike of some kind. Have any of you had such a request?" The hands go up again. Addressing them individually. "Now Mr. Stein, were circumstances such that you purchased a motor bike for your son?" Even a "no" answer isn't too bad. The inference is that "circumstances" (inadequate financing? inadequate surroundings?) prevented the purchase. On the other hand if you receive a "yes," now you have the endorsement by a juror of the very act which the defendant was going to condemn.

On some rare occasions an opportunity will present itself by which the juror can supply some "extra legal" evidence in the case. An abstract explanation is difficult to frame but an example should make the point. An electric company is charged with negligent procedures in the installation of a utility pole. A panel member identifies himself as a safety supervisor of the telephone company.

"Mr. Klein does your job as safety supervisor involve the promulgation of safety rules for the installation of utility poles?"

"Yes."

"And are such rules found in printed form in some type of manual?"

"Yes."

"Do they encompass regulations as to the number of men in the crew?"

"Yes."

"And the type of warning devices to be used during installation?"

"Yes."

"And the proper type of equipment to be utilized."

"Yes."

"By reason of your experience in the safety features of erecting utility poles would you consider yourself somewhat of an expert in this field?"

"I guess you could say that."

"Thank you Mr. Klein."

No doubt Klein will be stricken by the opposition but do you see what you have accomplished? The remaining jurors know that the opposition are fearful of a safety expert and the panel member, before his demise, has indoctrinated his fellow jurors with the formality of safety rules (written in a manual) their importance (a supervisor of safety) and their scope (number of men, methodology, type of equipment). Sworn testimony from the stand will have no greater weight.

§ 9.22 Indoctrination—Final Consideration

Perhaps the foregoing comments have made it appear that voir dire is mechanistic in nature, a computer like operation involving the presentation of a series of questions the responses to which will automatically reveal the undesirables. Such is not the case. After all the information is gathered and all the rules are applied, the typical advocate will fall back on some sixth sense, some intuitive feeling of whether the prospective juror generates "good vibes" or "bad vibes." Remember these are the people to whom you will be selling your case. If you don't feel the proper rapport with those jurors, you will have one difficult time selling them regardless of the paper credentials they may possess. And you need not feel apologetic for such behavior. It is rather typical of lawyers.

CHAPTER 10

OPENING STATEMENT

"We have never forgotten the essence of what we do—Tell a story"
Don Hewitt, executive producer 60 Minutes

Analysis

---

§ 10.1 Dramatic Context

The trial of a lawsuit is frequently likened to a drama. If the comparison is legitimate, and most would agree that it is, then it behooves the trial lawyer to study the techniques of the dramatist and emulate his art.

303

One dramatic device that was frequently employed by the best of them all, Shakespeare, was the prologue—an introductory speech which set the stage and stimulated the interest of the audience. Perhaps that example which demonstrates the device at its best is found in Henry V. The author was dealing with an awesome task, recreating historical events which spanned a number of years, involved thousands of characters and matters of such magnitude as the Battle of Agincourt. Listen to the prologue as he stimulates the audience and challenges them to sharpen their imagination and supplement the characters and the scenery and overcome the limitations of the Globe Theatre.

Pardon gentles all the flat unraised spirit that hath dared to bring forth so great an object.

Can this cockpit hold the vasty fields of France?

May we cram within this wooden O the very casques that did affright the air at Agincourt?

Suppose within the girdle of these walls are now confined two mighty monarchies—

Piece out our imperfections with your minds and make imaginary puissance.

Into a thousand parts divide one man.

Think, when we speak of horses that you see them, printing their proud hooves in the receiving earth.

For 'tis your thoughts which now must deck our kings carry them here and there, leaping o'er times and turning the accomplishments of many years into an hour glass.

To aid you in the which admit me, chorus to this history.

Who, prologue like, your humble patience pray.

Gently to hear, kindly to judge our play.

The juror faces the same challenge as the play goer and the lawyer finds that the courtroom has the same inadequacies as the stage. You, as an advocate, will often be dealing with the re-creation of an event of great physical dimensions of extended periods of time and of profound human emotions. Well might you question whether the "cockpit" of a courtroom can accommodate the re-enactment of an airplane crash, or the "hour glass" of a truncated trial can convey a time dimension of a nine month hospital confinement or mere verbalization can approximate the inexpressible anguish of a quadraplegic. The opening statement may be a vehicle by which these inadequacies of the trial process may be confessed to the jury and the exhortation made that if a valid re-creation is to take place it can occur only through their own stimulated imagination coupled with a gentle hearing and a kindly judging.

§ 10.2 Purposes—Generally

The amount of empirical studies which have taken place in the advocacy area has been slim indeed, but some testing has occurred in this phase of the lawsuit. It has been discovered that jurors, interviewed after verdict, have confirmed that their ultimate decision corresponded with their tentative opinion after opening statements in over 80% of the cases. In other words, convince them with your opening statement and you have a four out of five chance of winning!

The explanation for such a phenomenon lies in a pithy epigram from the pen of Francis Bacon, "Man prefers to believe what he prefers to be true." An effective opening statement is designed to get the jury to prefer our side of the dispute. If that goal is accomplished, the instinctive screening of the evidence to follow will kick in. Thomas Gelovich in a book with the oxymoronic title, "How We Know What Isn't So" and the humbling sub-title "The Fallibility of Human Reason in Everyday Life" reminds us that "if we read an article or hear a news story that confirms our views, we readily accept its validity; if it goes against our beliefs, we question its source and scrutinize it for errors."

See how important the opening statement is? And do you see what your initial purpose will be? If you can start with the jury preferring your case, that preference will effect all the evidence that will follow.

§ 10.3 Purposes—Providing Overview

Aside from the establishment of a receptive mood, other purposes should be accomplished. The first and perhaps most important, is to present a synopsis of the trial that is to follow. The significance of this initial preview is established in a number of ways. First, there is an old bromide concerning the most effective methodology in a teaching situation: "Tell them what you're going to tell them, tell them, tell them what you told them." The first step is the opening statement; the second, the evidence; and the third, summation.

In the past, the typical opening statement was (but what creative advocate wants to be typical) prefaced with the explanation that the opening statement will be "a bird's eye view of what the case is about;" or that the opening statement "will serve as a road map to let you know where we're going and how we'll get there;" or that "the evidence will be introduced bit by bit and in such a state resemble the picture on a puzzle box—an indication of what those pieces will look like when they are all put together."

But the conventional wisdom of the past is always subject to review. As the art of advocacy progressed, the efficacy of such cliché beginnings began to be questioned. Are those golden moments of first impressions well spent in spewing such generalities? Does an advocate who wishes to establish himself as a dynamic storyteller advance his cause with such a trite beginning?

Consider the devices employed by those in other forms of communication, be it advertising, electioneering or storytelling. There is always a "grabber" up front. Louis L'Amour, our most successful western adventure storyteller, learned the importance of a boffo beginning the hard way. He recounts that it was only after his first two hundred offerings were rejected that he realized his error. "I was talking about the story for three pages before I ever started writing." His solution was to exchange the positions of Chapter One and Chapter Three and start his stories in the midst of the action. How can you profit by Louis L'Amour's experience? Provide an overview with the first words out of your mouth. If you feel compelled to introduce yourself to the jury, defer that to Chapter Three. Isn't that what the celebrity endorsers do on those television ads? You first hear about the merits of the product, and only then does that speaker introduce himself.

Your job is to identify the grabber that will provide an overview of your case. Is it breach of contract? Try "A promise made is a debt unpaid" (a bit of plagiary from a Robert Service poem). Is it a child pedestrian case with a claim of driver inattention? How about a modest corruption of an old adage, "Children should be seen and not hurt?" Maybe your opening shot will come from the evidence itself—a recitation from a police report ("Driver of vehicle number two left over two hundred feet of skid marks.") A discharge note from a medical record ("Patient was hospitalized for forty-one days, during which she had three operations.") or an admission in a deposition ("How fast were you traveling when you entered the intersection?" Answer: "I guess around thirty-five").

There are numerous advantages to a dramatic beginning:

1. It establishes you as a person worth listening to.

2. It initiates the persuasive process when the jury's attention is at its peak.

3. It creates a context in which subsequent information will have meaning.

To illustrate this last point, read the following factual statements and stop when you understand what is being described.

The procedure is actually quite simple. First, you arrange things into different groups. Of course, one pile may be sufficient depending on how much there is to do. It is important not to overdo things. That is, it is better to do too few things at once than too many. In the short run this may not seem important, but complications can easily arise. A mistake can be expensive as well. At first, the whole procedure will seem complicated. Soon, however, it will become just another facet of life.

You're probably still wondering. Think how more easily understood these descriptions would have been if prefaced by the statement, "I'm going to tell you how to wash clothes." Give the jury the benefit of such a thematic framework with the very first words out of your mouth.

The value of this introductory overview is immeasurably enhanced for the plaintiff in a civil case or the prosecution in a criminal case by reason of the fact that it will be the first such impact to which the jury will be exposed. The layman recognizes that these "first impressions are lasting impressions." The psychologist would talk in terms of the phenomenon of "primacy"— but the result is the same. If a strong image can be engrafted in the minds of the jury they are apt to more readily accept that evidence which supports their initial impression.

§ 10.4 Purposes—Establishing Theme

Every lawsuit has a theme which pervades the entire presentation. The establishment of this theme must be sounded in the overture—the opening statement.

The decision as to the theme has been made from the very start, through the selection of parties, choices of theories, etc., but the first opportunity that the advocate has to present the theme with all its interplay and nuances is during the opening statement. Let us assume a simple fact situation to illustrate the point.

Illustration

Plaintiff is injured when struck by a blade which disengages from a rotary lawn mower operated by A and owned by B. A is a college student who earns money during the summer cutting grass. He has operated many lawn mowers, is an engineering student and is familiar with their mechanics. He has worked for B on other occasions, was familiar with B's lawn mower. On a previous occasion he had noticed that the blade was wobbly and had notified B. B had owned the lawn mower for four years and had never had it repaired or overhauled. B acknowledges that A had told him that the blade was wobbly.

Assume your suit is against A alone. Your opening statement will attempt to exonerate B from any wrong doing and lay the blame at A's feet. The theme to be developed will be as follows:

A is trained and experienced with lawn mowers. He discovered that the mower was faulty but continued to use it knowing and appreciating the risks that were involved. B on the other hand, had reason to believe the lawn mower was in working order. It had functioned properly for four years without the need of repair. He was told by A that the blade was wobbly but he didn't think that this was a dangerous situation. He knew that A was an engineering student, well versed in the handling of lawn mowers and relied on him to make any necessary repairs or at least tell B that the mower was dangerous and needed repair.

If the suit was against B alone the theme would be substantially different and proceed as follows:

B had owned this lawn mower for four years and during the entire 48 months had not attended to its servicing or repair. He had been told specifically that the blade was wobbly but rather than have the blade replaced at minimal cost he elected to expose A and others to the dangers of a malfunctioning power lawn mower. A, a hard working and conscientious college student, having told B of the defect assumed that the simple repair had been made.

The facts are the same only the slant is changed.

308

§ 10.5 Purposes—Filling the Voids

In almost every case there are some loose ends which, if left unexplained, can provide some anxious moments during closing argument. The opening statement should provide the peripheral embellishments which fills the voids and smooths the story. Again an example is necessary to translate the general to the specific.

Illustration

Plaintiff has been treated by two doctors, one of which has indicated an uncertainty about his availability at trial. If he doesn't testify defendant is apt to argue, "Where is the missing doctor? If the doctor would have agreed as to plaintiff's claim of injury he would have been called to testify. Since he wasn't here, you can infer that his testimony would have been unfavorable to plaintiff." An explanation, made during opening statement would have squelched that argument before it was made. "The plaintiff was also treated by Dr. Smith and we hope his busy surgical schedule will permit him to come to court and testify. If the demands of his profession doesn't permit his appearance here, you will have the benefit of his observations and treatment as they are recorded in the official hospital record."

Let us consider a second situation where the lion must be defanged before being turned loose. The plaintiff's injuries are such that it is apparent that he must have the benefit of a specialist. The lawyer recommends to his client the names of several doctors who are known by the lawyer to be competent practitioners willing to become involved in medical legal matters. The client chooses a doctor so recommended. This relationship should be covered in opening statement with a simple explanation. "When Mr. Jones was advised that he should come under the care of a specialist he was uncertain which doctor to choose inasmuch as he was unfamiliar with any specialists in this area. We consulted about this matter and I recommended several competent men in the field and he chose Dr. Reinhart."

Absent such an explanation the jury might be acquainted with this situation during plaintiff's cross-examination by the inquiry, "Now your lawyer sent you to this Dr. Reinhart, didn't he?" Don't rely on your client to come up with the right answer. You anticipate that question—and answer it in opening statement.

§ 10.6   Techniques—Generally

The opening statement is basically a story and the techniques to be followed are those of the traditional story teller. How are most stories structured? First, we are established in time and place (Once upon a time in Never–Never land—). Next, we are introduced to a protagonist, a central character around which the action revolves (—there lived a Princess—). Then we are acquainted with the problem (—who had been bewitched). The plot that unfolds deals primarily with the struggles which precede the ultimate conclusion (—and they lived happily ever after).

The effective opening statement will have these same features—a setting of time and place, a dramatics personae, an identity of issues, a chronological flow—and a suggested "happy ending."

Of course variations of this general format may be pursued. The protagonist need not be a party litigant. Perhaps in a product failure case the story might revolve around the article involved and the chronology relating to its planning, design, manufacture, sale, use and, finally, its failure. There are a million ways to tell a good story and the theme and style might differ as much as Homer to O'Henry, or the brothers Grimm to the sisters Bronte. Whatever your style is, you'll have good dramatic material with which to work. What, after all, is more exciting than a lawsuit? If you can catch half the drama of the intrinsic romance that is to be found in a legal confrontation you will be able to spin a yarn that will at least hold the jury's attention if not persuade them to your cause. Consider the advantages that are yours:

> You have a select audience sworn to do their duty (and in this instance, it's to listen to you);
>
> You are unlimited as to time (unlike summation);
>
> You are free to employ whatever phraseology, theme, mood (and sometimes props) which you choose;
>
> You have a fact situation which involves human conflict, real people in trouble seeking help.
>
> What story teller could ask for more!

§ 10.7   Techniques—Attitude

Although a sense of confidence should pervade the opening statement there should be a sense of restraint also. Nothing can

310

be quite as embarrassing as to have your expectations of the evidence as expressed in the opening statement exceed the realities as they develop at trial. The picture you paint on opening statement is the one that must be fulfilled during trial. A lawyer is not a huckster using seed catalogue psychology to make a sale. If you state that the evidence will reveal that your client suffered "permanent injury," there had better be such medical testimony forthcoming. The higher you build the jury's expectations during opening statement the greater your evidence must be to meet those expectations. It is for this reason that some lawyers choose to understate their case on opening statement. Utilizing this technique, they argue, they are assured that they will not suffer any loss of credibility with the jury if the case doesn't measure up 100% to its potential. And if the evidence does transcend the introduction, then the jury will know you are an honorable advocate who doesn't overstate the case.

This situation is not unlike that which occurs in an audience's reaction to a play. The approval of the evening's entertainment depends not on the isolated merits of the dramatic effort but rather on the response as measured against the expectation. "I really didn't like it. I guess I expected too much" is a rather common analysis. The flip side goes like this, "I didn't expect much so I was pleasantly surprised." Is this psychology translatable to the lawsuit? Some lawyers think so and play down the opening statement to enhance the likelihood of a pleasant evidentiary surprise.

§ 10.8　Techniques—Pace and Structure

The pace and structure of a lawsuit are perhaps the two most essential dramatic devices in the presentation of a legal claim or defense. The lawsuit as a whole, as well as each unit of the lawsuit, must be so paced that an interest builds and climaxes at the most propitious time.

Every athletic coach is aware of the need to bring his team along so that it is "up" for the big game. There is always the nagging fear that Saturday's game will be played at Friday afternoon's scrimmage. And so it is with the advocate. The opening statement may be likened to a preparatory scrimmage. It serves a tremendously important function but it is not the big game. The real action will follow with the adduction of evidence and the climax will occur with the summation. A highly dramatic, enthusiastic opening statement may result in a peaking of the juror's

311

interest long before they are unleashed to do their job. Remember, the opening statement is an introductory stage in your courtship with the juror. It is meant to be interesting and titilating—but not seductive. Keep your courtin' under control and avoid the embarrassment of a premature climax.

§ 10.9 Techniques—Visual Aids

Since it is designated as an opening "statement" there is an inclination to confine this feature of the trial to the spoken word. There is no such proscription that fetters the lawyer so. The recitation of most factual situations which give rise to litigation is sufficiently complex that the juror's understanding will be enhanced by the use of visual aids. These aids should be utilized at that point in the trial when they will be most effective—and that will be at the time of first impression. Why should a lawyer in opening statement verbally describe:

A damaged vehicle when he has photographs in his briefcase;

The construction of a product when the blueprints are face down on the counsel table;

The chronology of a series of events when a blackboard and easel repose in the clerk's office?

The audio-visual aids are recognized as valid tools in opening statements whether previously authenticated as evidence to be properly submitted or merely non-evidentiary devices employed for illustrative purposes. There is a third identity of material potentially supplementary to the statement—the court file itself. In some instances it might be advantageous to refer to and read a portion of an opponent's pleading or a witness' deposition. This practice also has been approved by those courts confronted with its propriety.

§ 10.10 Potential Judicial Restraints

These suggestions regarding an effective presentation of an opening statement are made from the standpoint of persuasive advocacy. Be aware that some judges may balk at your attempts to present a persuasive opening. Unfortunately there is a paucity of court rules or appellate decisions which spell out the range of styles available to the advocate. Most of us, including judges, accept the propriety of any act on the basis of familiarity, "We've always done it that way" is a universally persuasive argument that we continue to do it that way, and it's especially persuasive to a tradition conditioned judge. Conversely, "I've never seen *that* before", raises suspicions and an inbred sense of resistance. Some judges hearing an opening statement with an "It was a dark and stormy night" beginning might very well intrude with the statement, "Just tell the jury what evidence you'll produce." Similarly, if you attempt to display an exhibit to explain your case, a judge might interject with the observation that, "Evidence is supposed to go in during the trial. Don't *show* them the evidence just *tell* them about the evidence."

What's an advocate to do?

1. Minimize the likelihood of the first intrusion by beginning your opening statement by turning to the judge and saying, "Your honor, the evidence that will be produced by the plaintiff (defendant) will be as follows." Then turn to the jury and tell your story of the dark and stormy night. The prefatory remarks to the judge assures him of your recognition of the rule that the opening statement is not evidence but only a statement of what evidence counsel will produce and lessens the chance of a sua sponte intrusion. It also serves as the first part of your bracketed presentation. When your story is over you can again turn to the judge and say, "That will be the plaintiff's (defendant's) case."

2. Advise the judge beforehand of your intention to use certain exhibits (in most cases they will have been already authenticated and marked) during your opening statement. He or she might be remnants of a troglodytic-era (yes, there are still some out there) and prohibit the use of exhibits in opening statement.

   If such is your luck, best to know before your presentation is interrupted.

3. Adopt the proper mind-set regarding your duty to your client and your relationship with the judge. The manner in which you conduct yourself in court should be measured by what is good advocacy—not what will please the judge. Judges who arbitrarily limit you in your quest to present information to the jury which is meaningful and memorable must be challenged. Who knows, they might be converted.

313

§ 10.11 Caveats to Consider—Generally

Lawyers are great at emulation. Our first instinct when confronted with a new problem is to seek the solace of precedent, find a form book and dutifully follow the wording and style of some unknown draftsmen. Well might we ask, "Upon what meat did these first formulators feed that they have grown so great?" But we don't. We follow the path first broken and over the years that path through continuing affirmation of use becomes a rut that directs our travel without the need for thought as to direction or destination. We become experts at mimicking mediocrity.

So it has been with certain phases of a trial, and particularly opening statements. Let's consider some of these well worn ruts, these ancient practices, which have as their only claim for accreditation that "trial lawyers have been doing it this way for years."

§ 10.12 Caveats to Consider—Disclaimer of Credibility

"At the outset let me explain that what I tell you during opening statement is not evidence and you are not to consider it as such." Can you imagine Dr. Suess prefacing "How the Grinch Stole Christmas" with the explanation that the characters and events are fictional and should not be confused with reality? Of course not. For he, as any good communicator, is anxious that the communicatee be caught up in the story, identify with the characters, respond to the crises, hiss the villain, cheer for the hero—indeed get lost in the story. Contemplate the devastating effect of the following disclaimers in the following situations: (Shakespearean prologue) "Remember playgoers, the story of these star crossed Italian families is simply a figment of my imagination and there is no historical basis for either character, Romeo or Juliet. Of course the death scene is merely a theatrical device and although they will appear to die, the same two characters will be right here tomorrow for the matinee performance." (Radio announcer) "Hi kiddies. In today's Lone Ranger adventure there will be the usual sounds of Silver and Scout galloping over the prairies. Don't be misled. Those aren't real horses. What you'll be hearing is our soundman Fred Finkle hitting some rubber cups on an office desk." Don't be guilty of a similar practice. If such a reminder must be made it will come from the judge in the form of an instruction to the jury.

§ 10.13 Caveats to Consider—Uncertainties of Evidence

"I think that the evidence will show that the defendant manufactured a defective widget. I hope to prove that the defective widget caused injury to my client and it is my expectation that the evidence may be such that you will find that the injuries were serious and permanent." Why is this lawyer so uncertain of his case? Doesn't he know that defendant manufactured the widget? If he hasn't ascertained this through pretrial discovery he shouldn't be in court. Won't his client unequivocally state that the widget failed? Doesn't he have a doctor's report which establishes that the injuries are indeed serious and permanent? If so— then say so—and in an affirmative unapologetic fashion. "The defendant manufactured a defective widget which failed and seriously injured Mrs. Jones." No "hopes" or "expectations" or "ifs" or "buts." That's what happened and that's what we'll prove.

§ 10.14   Limitations—Generally

Aside from those features of the opening statement that may be tactically unsound there are others that are legally improper. Opening statements should not be an argument—a tool of persuasion yes—but not an argument. It is objectionable, for instance, for your opponent to state that "the evidence will show that the defendant negligently drove at an excessive rate of speed" or "the poor plaintiff has suffered a most grievous injury that will severely affect her for the rest of her life." How best to recognize an objectionable argument? As you listen to your opponent's opening statement ask yourself, "Will a witness testify in such fashion?" Relating to the examples, who will testify that "the defendant was negligent and drove at an excessive rate of speed?" These are conclusions and as such inadmissible. The testimony will relate to "tearing down the road at seventy miles an hour" and this should be the verbiage employed in opening statement.

Or who will testify that "plaintiff suffered grievous injuries?" This too is conclusionary thus inadmissible as evidence and consequently improper in opening statement. The lawyer should avoid these argumentative, conclusionary statements, not only because they are objectionable but because they are usually less effective than a detailed recitation of the facts on which those conclusions or arguments are based.

§ 10.15   Limitations—Evidence

The content of the opening statement should be confined to the evidence that the speaker will adduce. Most courts will condone a brief introductory comment as to its role and scope, and some writers on the subject even endorse such an approach, but both from a legal and tactical point of view such introductory remarks should always be brief and frequently never given at all. A three or five minute sermonette on the obligations of jury duty and the joys of Anglo–American jurisprudence can best be left to the civics classroom. For those lawyers who persist in this preliminary pep talk, it is apparently justified as a ritualistic icebreaker necessary to get themselves warmed up. And that is how it usually appears to a jury—a perfunctory, plastic performance of no importance. You are there to tell them the story of your case so it's best to get on with it.

That story will consist of verbal and physical evidence and consequently, that should be the concern of your opening statement. Which leads to our next problem which arises from this legal limitation. How can we know what evidence will be deemed admissible by the court? How can we mention in opening statement the colored photographs of the murder victim when the court might exclude them as unduly inflammatory? How can we advise the jury that an unknown witness was heard to exclaim, "That driver must have been crazy running that red light!" when the trial judge might exclude that evidence on the basis that it did not possess all the ingredients of an excited utterance?

§ 10.16 Limitations—Evidence—Questionable

When there is a question as to the admissibility of evidence the lawyer on opening statement may elect one of a number of options.

First, the questionable evidence may be referred to with the genuine expectation that it will be received when offered. The consequences of such a choice are that counsel will be afforded utilization of a persuasive and pervasive ingredient in this all important initial recitation of the case; that once the subject matter is heard by the jury it will be a factor in their deliberation even if there is no subsequent formal presentation; that to avoid mentioning relevant evidence in the opening statement will be indicative of the counsel's own doubts about its propriety and jeopardize a ruling permitting its introduction when that issue is later raised.

Second, the questionable evidence may be ignored with the converse of the consequences stated above—a deprivation of its persuasive value and a concession as to its marginal credentials. On the other hand there will be no risk that you have overstated your case and that the promises you made as to the nature of your proof have gone unfulfilled. It is extremely discomforting to sit through your opponent's summation when it is laced with rhetorical queries concerning the whereabouts of the evidence which had been promised on opening statement but which had never materialized.

A third option is to state your problem with the trial judge before the trial commences and seek a ruling as to the propriety of the evidence. It is true that some judges are not too receptive to such Motions in Limine (or literally "at the threshold") and will respond with a pithy, "We'll cross that river when we get to it." But others will appreciate the opportunity of pondering an evidentiary problem in the serenity of their inner sanctum rather than shooting from the hip in the crucible of the courtroom.

Of course this third option may be invoked by either party as an offensive or defensive device. With present day pre-trial discovery procedures most counsel know the prospective evidence and can request a pre-judging to determine its propriety.

§ 10.17   Limitations—Making the Record

One word of caution. Sometimes procedures in chambers can be frightfully informal and decisions may be reached that are never recorded. If the court in chambers has sustained your opponent's position then you should follow one or two courses of action. If an unsuccessful attempt to exclude evidence, make your record in chambers duly noting your reasons and receiving the assurance of the court that this will preserve your complaint of error. This will obliterate the need of publicizing an objection before a jury which is foreordained for failure. If an unsuccessful attempt to adduce evidence, you might wish to withhold an objection to the court's ruling at that time in order to make a formal offer before the jury thus letting them know that you are able and willing to adduce further proof but that you are being frustrated by an objecting opponent. Of course an alert opponent will request that the ruling be made in chambers in order to prevent such public proffering of improper evidence. Regardless of the tactics employed (and finessing the possibility of the ethical improprieties of the latter), if a ruling on the scope and content of your opening statement has been made contrary to your client's interest, make sure that you have made your record.

§ 10.18   Legal Effects

Some mention should be made of the legal effects of this preliminary, informal introduction to the trial. The jury has been cautioned "that which the attorneys state is not evidence and must not be considered as such in your deliberations." How then can there be any legal effect to this extra-evidentiary monologue which precedes the "real thing"?

Well, first of all, an attorney acting as his client's agent may, within the scope of his authority, make binding admissions.

That is what can happen if you say too much. On the other hand, if the party with the burden of proof, doesn't say enough he may find himself scratched before the race begins. It doesn't occur too often but there are recorded cases in a goodly number of jurisdictions in which a motion to dismiss has been sustained at the conclusion of the plaintiff's opening statement. And why not? If it clearly appears that the admitted facts viewed in the light most favorable to the plaintiff or prosecutor are such that reasonable minds could not differ as to their legal effect—then there is nothing to litigate.

§ 10.19 Waiver

The giving of an opening statement is not compulsory. If good reason dictates that it be waived by either of the parties then, of course that choice may be made. The defendant in both civil and criminal cases has an additional choice. The opening statement may be given immediately following that of the opponent or reserved until the defendant's evidence is to begin.

The reason most frequently advanced for opting in favor of the former is that the initial advantage of "primacy" must be diminished as soon as possible.

The jury has received an adverse impression of the case and if left unchallenged it will be more deeply embossed upon the juror's mind and less easily erased. Further, an invitation to explain the defendant's case left unaccepted might be interpreted by the jury as a confession of weakness.

The reasons most frequently advanced for reserving opening statement may be categorized as follows:

1. The defense theory may be concealed and the defendant relieved of "tipping his hand;"

2. The perfectly passive posture of a non-response permits the defendant to utilize any theory which might surface during the opponent's case;

3. The thrust and force of your own case will be enhanced if it is preceded by a forceful opening statement immediately before the adduction of your evidence;

4. Concessions, if made in an opening statement, will relieve the opponent of certain technical elements of proof which might have been overlooked or neglected by an inept prosecutor or plaintiff's attorney.

Don't underestimate the importance of this last item. Every case and particularly every criminal case, entails the adduction of certain elements of technical proof upon which the very viability of the case will depend. The commission of the crime within the jurisdiction, the majority of the defendant, the identity of a street as "open and public," the authenticity of the ordinance by which a stop sign was erected—the list could go on and on. An opening statement is apt to concede some of these indisputable trifles. But these are tremendous trifles which are frequently overlooked even by experienced counsel. Foregoing the opening statement and the concessions which it will inevitably express, reserves the opportunity to complain of any inadequacies of the opponent's case.

§ 10.20   Overcoming Problems Encountered in Opening Presentation

Since opening statement is speech making time, the problems most often encountered are those common to every effort as oral communication.

Public speaking is a universally frightening experience. It ranks alongside snakes and heights as the terror trilogy. (Fear of death lags behind all three).

Under test conditions subjects have recorded heart rates as high as one hundred twenty beats a minute as they began their public address. (That's the bad news. The good news is that within a minute the rate had plummeted to near normal.)

There are other physical signs of nervousness along with the ubiquitous butterflies which inevitably manifest themselves. Knocking knees, sweaty palms, shallow breathing, tightened muscles, incontinence, quivering voice—almost anything that can afflict the parasympathetic nervous system can occur as you stand in front of the jury to address them at opening.

A few suggestions to overcome your fear.

§ 10.21 Overcoming Problems Encountered in Opening Presentation—Reduce Your Heartbeat

That racing heart is dictating but two alternatives—fight or flight—appropriate enough for the fear that was generated when our ancestors stared down a sabre toothed tiger. But neither works in opening statement. We don't want to seem too contentious at the get-go and there's no place to run to. You don't want the jury to hear the quivering voice or the resonance of knocking knees. You must find some way to buy some time until things more nearly return to normal. What to do?

Structure your beginning

Let your initial movements be slow and deliberate.

Do something with your hands.

Take a deep breath.

Look at the jurors.

Have your opening shot faultlessly memorized.

Putting all those things together, the scenario, scripted by a screen writer would read as follows:

Judge: "You may proceed counsel."

Lawyer (seated at table) nods to the judge as he arises and takes hold of a trial notebook that is on the counsel table in front of him. He strides purposefully to the lectern. Places the trial notebook in front of him and turns a page. He looks to the entire panel, takes a breath then turns to the judge. "Your honor, the evidence to be adduced by the plaintiff will be as follows (Turning to the jury)

"November thirtieth was a dark and stormy night ...."

§ 10.22 Overcoming Problems Encountered in Opening Presentation—Maximize Your Instincts

Don't attempt to suppress these natural defense mechanisms triggered by your nervous system. When the juices are flowing, as they must if you are to present an animated and interesting presentation, things happen. Recognize that they exist, give them time to abate and regard them (the sweaty palms, shallow breaths, etc.) as a help and not a hindrance—nature's way of getting you up for the big event. (Remember Joseph's response after his brothers sold him into slavery. "You meant it for evil but God meant it for good.")

§ 10.23　Overcoming Problems Encountered in Opening Presentation—Adopt a Communicative Mind-Set

The focus of your attention must be on talking *to* the jury not *at* them. Effective communication (the word comes from the root "common") is a shared experience. It is not a sole exercise which consists of sounds dribbling out of your mouth into the ether. Communication exists only when a receptor is there to receive and comprehend the sounds. That old conundrum, about the tree in the forest crashing to the ground when no one is there to hear it, is easily answered by the discerning advocate. No one to hear it— no noise. An absent jury, or a non-receptive jury, equates with silence. You must adopt a metaphysical concept wherein you are connecting with your audience. (The communicator who connects is described as "engaging"—a good word that confirms connection.) Think of reaching out and embracing the jury with your life forces (substitute "vibes" if you are a child of the sixties). Only then will the magic of transferred thought take place.

CHAPTER 11

DIRECT EXAMINATION—GENERALLY

"Just the facts ma'am"
Dragnet—Sgt. Joe Friday

Analysis

A. IN GENERAL

A. IN GENERAL

11.1 Basic Consideration

Direct examination is a dynamic exchange between lawyer and witness. Before embarking on the formal aspects of direct examination we must consider the other half of the dramatis personae. Witnesses are to a lawyer what customers are to a store owner. They provide the sustenance upon which you and your client must feed. No witnesses, no claim for recovery, no rebuttal for defense. Consequently, your ability to relate with the witnesses in your lawsuit, both those appearing for you and against you, will be critical to your success as an advocate.

The secret of a satisfying relationship is to recognize their needs and allay their fears. Are you nervous and concerned about the pending courtroom conflict? What about *them?* For most witnesses their knowledge of the role they are to play has been gleaned from viewing dramatic presentations of trials. The setting and script are indelibly imprinted in their consciousness.

The courtroom will be crowded with curious onlookers.

The judge will be stern but benign and enthroned atop a walnut walled dias.

The jury will be alertly suspicious, eagerly awaiting an opportunity to detect an inconsistency in the testimony and share their discovery with knowing nods to their neighbors in the box.

The lawyer on direct examination will unctuously coax the witness with helpful hints and treacle tones and for his efforts will be periodically punctuated with indignant accusations of "leading", "irrelevant" and "immaterial."

The cross examiner will be the embodiment of scowling evil, his questions either gushing with nefarious accusations or dripping with sneering sarcasm. He will attack the witness with the same relish that a predator torments his prey, boldly bellowing recriminations from the front, hissing insinuations from the rear, and suggesting duplicitous motives as he leans on the jury rail and smirks at the jury.

The cruel cross will culminate in a clamorous crescendo of accusations, the courtroom voyeurs gasping in shock, the judge banging his gavel and threatening to "clear the courtroom if any further outburst takes place."

The drama concludes with the perspiring, chalk faced vacant eyed victim being assisted from the stand by the solicitous direct examiner who exposed him to this hell and who now whispers to this weak-kneed witness "You done good."

Why shouldn't a prospective witness by wary of such a scenario, the reality of which has been reinforced through years of repetitive recreations on the silver screen and the telly tube. You overcome this tendency of non-involvement by invoking the Golden Rule, putting yourself in their place, anticipating their concerns and providing the assurances they seek.

Let's identify what these concerns will be. First, a court appearance intrudes upon their regular routine. A day at the office, a day on the road, a day at home will be replaced by a day in court. Wrenching readjustments will have to be made:

appointments rescheduled,

chores assigned,

substitutes located, etc.

First, find out what turmoil will result and attempt to resolve the readjustments that will result.

Second, there will be financial consequences due to the absence from job or home, anything from lost wages to baby sitting expenses. The only relief the judicial process affords is witness fees and mileage expense. Assurance must be given that other expenses will be borne by the client (a perfectly ethical offer.)

Third, logistical problems will arise in getting to and from the courthouse. "How will I get there?", "Where will I park?",

"Where do I go?", "When do you want me there?", "How long will I be?" are all legitimate questions that you should anticipate and answer.

Fourth, and perhaps the greatest concern will be the expectations of performance. Most relationships may be expressed in contractual terms. The lawyer-witness relationship is an exchange of mutual promises which creates a duty of performance. The witnesses promises are rather simple: to show up and tell the truth. The lawyer promises are more complex:

to orient the witness to the environment and the process;

to advise the witness of the specific areas of interrogation, their significance to the case and the anticipated nature of the cross examination; and

to assure the witness of his or her importance in the administration of justice.

Summing up, your initial task is to replace the witnesses distorted view of this prospective role and to do your best to convey the truth of the place where he will perform and the process in which he'll participate—and then keep your fingers crossed that the "truth will set him free."

§ 11.2 Limitations of Interrogation

The manner in which testimony is adduced in a court of law is unnatural and stilted. The lawyer asks a question which can be neither leading, suggestive, immaterial to the issues nor call for a narrative response. The witness answers and that answer must be responsive to the question, within the knowledge of the witness and neither narrative in form nor speculative in content. There are other proscriptions applicable but these will suffice. The point is that the lawyers can't simply call the witness to the stand and let him "spill his guts" as it were. Have you ever wondered why we have such artificial limitations? The Continental system has no such restraints. The witness takes the stand, recites his name and everything he wishes about the matter at hand. Of course there is a decided difference. The recitation is made to a pride of tribunes rather than a rabble of jurors. The jury of course is ill suited to hear the "truth, the whole truth, and nothing but the truth." They do not have the perspicacity necessary to sift the wheat from the chaff, the "rose from the poison ivy." Let the hint be made that the defendant is insured, suggest that the plaintiff is a widow, let them hear of a subsequent repair or an offer of settlement and the whole fact-finding process breaks down.

Stupored by a heady draft of "hearsay" or a sip from the vial of "irrelevance" they are sure to forget their sworn duty as fact-finders and return an irresponsible verdict. Now a judge is a different breed. He feeds on Caesar's meat and thus has grown so great that he'll not be deterred from the truth by such distractions. He is equipped with a "final filter" which enables him to hear all the evidence, be unmoved by that of an incendiary nature, minimize that of questioned probative value, ignore that which is irrelevant and fashion a verdict from that evidence which his legal training, mental acumen and innate sense of fairness dictates should alone be considered. Now if jurors had these same gifts there would be no need for exclusionary rules of evidence and absent these there would be no need for the verbal ping pong match called legal interrogation. But as long as the jury can't be trusted to "hear it all" there will be rules of evidence and as long as there are such rules the advocate must learn to develop his story through interrogation—the simple question, the pause to allow the interposing of an objection, then the direct response. It is not unlike being nibbled to death by ducks.

The problem is that the nibbling can become downright dull at times. The repetition of question and answer too often simulates the Chinese water torture as the soporific rhythm rolls relentlessly on and on.

Question	*Answer*
What is your name?	Sylvester Brown
Where do you live?	At home with my wife
What is your job?	Inspector of parts
Da da da da?	Da da da da da

Strange how often the interrogator and witness slide into this lock step cadence and turn what should be a lively recitation into a deadening dirge.

Some effort to control interrogation and presentation of evidence in the federal courts has been made through enactment of Federal Rule of Evidence 611(a) which provides:

(a) *Control by court.* The court shall exercise reasonable control over the mode and order of interrogating witnesses and presenting evidence so as to (1) make the interrogation and presentation effective for the ascertainment of the truth, (2) avoid needless consumption of time, and (3) protect witnesses from harassment or undue embarrassment.

But it is still up to the advocate to keep the jury awake.

B. METHODS OF VARYING INTERROGATION

§ 11.3 Generally

Rule number one then for proper interrogation is to dramatize the interrogation in whatever manner possible in order to fight the ennui that will otherwise smother the proceedings. Remember the trial of a lawsuit is an educational process and before a student can learn he must first be kept awake. Do you recall your best teachers? Weren't they the ones who brought drama into the classroom?

Perhaps you have read of the experiment conducted with medical educators and students who were exposed to a nonsensical lecture entitled "Mathematical Game Theory as Applied to Physician Education" delivered by a bogus educator "Dr. Fox" with a string of phony degrees and publications. The presentation was given for the purpose of determining whether the audience would be seduced by the impressive credentials and a humorous animated style into accepting a lecture composed of double talk, contradictions, and meaningless references to unrelated topics. Not one of the fifty-five listeners detected the hoax. In fact, most of them gave favorable critiques and some ranked the presentation as "brilliant."

A second experiment was conducted, as reported in The Chronicle of Higher Education to test whether student ratings of their instructors and student performance on tests are affected by "lecturer seduction" and by the content-coverage of a lecture.

They used the same Hollywood actor who had posed as "Dr. Fox" the year before. He delivered six 20–minute videotaped lectures on the biochemistry of memory. Three were delivered with enthusiasm, humor, expressiveness, friendliness, charisma, and personality. One lecture was high in content, the others medium and low in content. The content was lowered by removing substantive teaching points from the lecture and substituting experimental details without results, discussion of unrelated examples, short stories, discussion of what "was going to be covered," and circular discussions of unimportant or meaningless thoughts.

The other three lectures—with the same high, medium, and low content—were prepared so as to be "low in seduction."

Then each of the lectures was shown to a separate group of students enrolled in a general studies course at Southern Illinois. Some 207 undergraduate and graduate students participated, chiefly from the liberal arts and biological and physical sciences, but also from education, engineering, business, and home economics.

After the lecture, students were asked to evaluate the presentation using rating forms like those in general use, and they were given a multiple-choice test on the lecture topic.

The results, according to the authors, suggested that the "Doctor Fox effect" was "more complicated than was originally thought."

It turned out that, of the two factors studied, lecturer seduction was the more important factor in affecting student ratings and student test performance, but content-coverage also played an important role, and the two factors interacted in a complicated manner.

Students who viewed lectures higher in content tended to perform better on the test than students who viewed lectures lower in content. However, when students received lectures of identical content, those who had viewed a seductive presentation did better on the test than those who had viewed a lecture delivered so as to be low in seduction.

The "Doctor Fox effect" appears to be much more than an illusion. Whereas teaching style is a major factor in determining student ratings, it is also a powerful influence on student test performance.

All to confirm a truism expressed by Quintillian two thousand years ago. "Indifferent discourse well delivered is better received by a popular audience than a good discourse badly delivered. It is not so important what our thoughts are, as in what manner they are delivered, since those whom we address are moved only as they hear."

And so it is in the trial of a lawsuit that style will be a major factor in getting attention and conveying ideas.

Ed Wynn at one time was asked the difference between a comic and a comedian. "A comedian," he replied, "says funny things, a comic says things funny." A good advocate must blend these talents and say interesting things, interestingly.

§ 11.4   Postural

Some local court rules limit the ambulations of counsel by requiring that he position himself at the counsel table or a lectern. Some require that the interrogatory stand or, in some few jurisdictions, that he be seated. The suggestions that follow regarding postural changes are reserved for those enlightened jurisdictions that permit counsel a bit of mobility.

One way of dramatizing a series of questions is simply to alter your posture. You begin your interrogation while seated, developing the preliminary identification of the witness and a few perfunctory facts. Now you head into the meaty part. You rise from your seat and by that simple postural change the jury senses that something important is about to develop.

Recognize also that your position relative to the witness and the jury can be critical. Most witnesses tend to engage in a dialogue with their interrogator. If you stand too close to the witness his voice will be pitched to your accommodation and the jury might not be able to hear. As the witness' voice softens, back away, and give a silent challenge to increase his volume. And if local practice and courtroom design permits, when you feel the jury is "out of it," sidle over behind the jury box and let him pitch his responses to the persons that count.

§ 11.5   Verbal

Don't ask all your questions as if it were a private exchange between you and the witness. When an important issue is coming up, preface your question with "Will you tell the jury, Mr. Witness _____." That will prompt the witness to look toward the jury and "give it to 'em right between the eyes." Other prefatory phrases can be effective if used sparingly. An occasional "Let me ask you this" can be tolerated as a means of emphasizing a line of inquiry. Whatever means you employ, it's certain that sometime during a long questioning session you're going to have to grab the jurors by their lapels and say "Hey! listen."

That leads to the second rule. Structure your direct examination so that some of your offerings will be questions. That sounds obvious. Indeed won't the entire interrogation be questions? It needn't be and really shouldn't be. How do most interrogations proceed, first, an identity of the witness, second, a recitation of some perfunctory background detail, then third, into the controversial part of the lawsuit. Many lawyers handle all three in the same way. Item one: What is your name? Where do you live? Do you own an automobile? etc. Item two: What street were you traveling on? What direction were you traveling? Item three: How fast were you operating your automobile? When did you first see the other vehicle?

By the time you reach the guts of the case, the questioning form of direct examination has lost its impact. Save it for the real questions. Let the witness *state* his pedigree "State your name and address." "Tell the jury where you work". Guide him by leading questions (tolerated at this point) through the admitted portions of his testimony. "You were traveling north on Grand were you not? and driving a 1978 Belchfire?" Then ask him the *real* questions "Who had the green light? Why didn't you see the other vehicle sooner?".

Too often the whole presentation of direct examination seems "hokeyed up," artificial, sterile, rehearsed. Sure the lawyer is asking questions but he knows very well what the answers are. Who was driving? Where were you going? (As if he didn't know!) Let some of the questions be genuine inquiries put to the witness not in a perfunctory way but as if you are earnestly seeking information. "Well, why didn't you swerve to the right?" The response to that one will seem much more spontaneous and authentic and consequently carry much more persuasive power than if it were sandwiched among such routine askings as "What is your name?" and "Where do you live?"

§ 11.6 Dramatic Emphasis

Rule number three is to accentuate the positive, that is, give dramatic impact to those features of your case which you feel are important. Illustrations are tough to come by but let's try a few. On frequent occasions a police report or similar type document will be a key bit of evidence in a case. How do we enhance its importance before the jury? Well for one thing don't refer to it simply as a police report. It's really more than that. It's an *official* police report. When your witness first makes mention of it, ask if it is an "official" police report, he will acknowledge that it is and you will refer to it as such throughout the case. It's remarkable how self authenticating that phrase is!

Assume you are representing a plaintiff injured by a defective product advertised as a "Saf Tee Widget." In reality it's not safe at all and you have ample proof of its dangerous design. The offending instrument shouldn't be referred to by its generic name but by the boastful appellation chosen by the defendant. Each reference to the "Saf Tee Widget" will hammer home the irony of the name and make recovery that much easier.

One more. The employee of a private detective agency has shot your client. You claim that they were negligent in selecting their personnel. How should the defendant be referred to—as "Home Guard International Detective Agency" or as that "rent-a-cop outfit"? All of us are familiar with the claims of outstanding service, personnel and equipment advanced by the rent-a-car businesses. Will these same expectations of excellency be associated with their "sister" industry, the rent-a-cop companies? Hopefully so. At least it's worth a try.

Each case will present opportunities for such emphasis. Search them and dramatize—right up to the point of being hammy.

C. STRUCTURING THE INTERROGATION

§ 11.7 Introduction

Many of the suggestions made in Chapter 1 regarding the organization of your case will be applicable to the organization of your direct examination. The individual's testimony is a microcosm of your case in chief. There will be an introduction, a theme, and a climax. The difference is that the organization is more easily accomplished.

The chronological order will run something like this. First, an introductory session for the benefit of witness and jury. In any social situation there is a preliminary ritual in which the parties feel each other out until they are comfortable in each other's presence. This period of social preening, nuzzling and sniffing is part of the animal kingdom and man is no exception. So don't fight it. Ease him into the courtroom situation, let him become acclimated to the geography and to the judicial environment. If invocation of a court rule doesn't prevent it, have the witness present while someone else is testifying just so they can benefit from the "ease of familiarity." Fear is generated by the unknown and for most witnesses an appearance in court is one of those unknowns. Do you recall when you first gave blood? The medical attendants were most casual as you sat on the edge of the table, shirtless, not knowing whether the needle was round or square or whither it was going. How could *they* be so cavalier when such an awesome thing as draining blood from *your* body was imminent? Well, witnesses are apt to feel the same way. They need assurances before taking the stand and once they are there they should be led into their testimony with an easy smile from you and an opportunity for them to identify themselves and establish their credentials.

§ 11.8 Body

Now we are ready for the story. We know who the story teller is but we must know more. Under normal out-of-court storytelling it would probably develop this way:

1. A statement establishing the relationship between the story teller and his subject;

2. A conclusion (sometimes including a hint as to the reason for the conclusion); and

3. the explanatory details.

Let us see if our analysis is valid. You encounter a person who has witnessed an accident. His explanation might well be something like this. "I was standing on the corner of 10th and Main last night when I saw this poor ole lady get clobbered by some fellow who went through the red light." Or maybe "I was sitting inside when I heard this crash. I went outside and here was this crazy drunk who had smashed into a tree."

Even if the subject matter doesn't relate to a specific instance the same format is apt to be followed. "I've driven a Belchfire 8 for ten years and I know they're good cars. Why I've gone 30,000 miles without as much as a tune-up."

If there is some validity to this premise, then we can emulate that format in developing a natural sequence to our direct examination for it is the role of the trial lawyer to "hold a mirror, as it were, up to nature." It will be a three step story—*how* I know, *what* I know, *why* I know. This old chestnut is usually related to illustrate the dangers of improper cross-examination, but it also serves to illustrate this point. A laconic farmer was testifying in a mayhem case. "Yep", he said "I saw the fight and Jed bit off Luke's ear." "Did you see him bite it off?" queried the defense counsel. "Nope" said the witness. "Then why do you say he bit it off?" "I saw Jed spit it out" came the logical reply. That's the gist of any witness' testimony—the how, what and why.

Frequently the information sought from a witness will necessitate a more detailed organization. If you are attempting to recreate an automobile accident it is not enough to deal with the dynamics of the event (the speeds and movements of the vehicles) you must also recreate the static conditions (the physical lay out, the weather) in which the section occurs.

If we think in terms of images we can appreciate the difficulty that a juror has in imaging two cars colliding in a vacuum. They have to be somewhere (on a street, in a parking lot) at some time (daylight, dark, etc.) under some conditions (rain, sun, snow). The direct examiner must emulate the story teller. Even something as simple as "It was a dark and stormy night" can be of universal help in creating the proper setting in which the action will take place.

The general rule to follow in adducing information from a witness regarding a dynamic event is to proceed as follows:

Witness identification ("Introduce yourself to the jury");

nexus with event ("Did you see a car collision—")

describe the general physical location permanent (terrain, buildings, streets, etc.) and transitory (traffic, weather, etc.);

describe significant physical characteristics (traffic lights, stop signs, speed limits)

Now you're ready for the dynamics of the event.

§ 11.9 Conclusion

Will this order alone assure a successful direct examination? Hardly. As every vaudeville performer will attest you have to know how to "get off." Hector was asked if he was living a happy life. He replied that he didn't know, and couldn't know until he died. In the Greek scheme of things it was the way life ended that determined its previous value. So it is with your direct examination. It must be brought to a happy end, a ringing affirmation of that which went before, a well defined conclusion, a bang and not a whimper. The dramatist knows this. Show me a T.V. murder trial and I'll show you a climax to the defendant's testimony that goes like this:

> Counsel (approaching witness stand): "Fred, did you shoot your wife?"
>
> Fred (turning toward jury): "No sir, I did not!"
>
> Counsel (reeking with smugness): "I have no other questions, Your Honor."

And why shouldn't he be smug? He has put an exclamation point at the end of his witness's testimony. He has tersely summarized his case. He has ended on an affirmative note. The "death" has been superb. Hector can rest well.

§ 11.10 Other Considerations

Your job of structuring your questioning into a logical and chronological recitation consisting of introduction, body and conclusion will not ensure an effective direct examination. There are other factors, to consider and other techniques to employ in order to keep the jury engaged.

§ 11.11 Length

The first maxim: get in, score, and get out. Let's be perfectly honest. The average trial is a drag. Ask any onlooker at a typical trial how he would describe it and chances are he'll say "boring." The reason is the laborious pace, occasioned by a host of things: the "ten minute" recesses that always last a half hour; the conferences at the bench; the wait for the professional witness to arrive, etc. There are enough of these inherent problems without the trial lawyer aggravating the situation. Keep the jury awake by a hard hitting, well organized, brief, direct examination. Remember, it's the fang at the jugular that brings the crowd to its feet. Gumming the capillaries can be pretty dull. The jury will appreciate your efforts and the verdict is apt to reflect their appreciation.

How can we assure ourselves that our direct examination will fulfill this double standard of being well structured and to the point? First of all determine exactly what it is that you want from the witness. List the elements of proof that the witness will supply. Arrange them in logical order.

§ 11.12 Illustration

It is an automobile accident case. The witness has observed your client's car traveling at twenty miles per hour go through the intersection with the green light. He also observed the defendant's vehicle traveling in the curb lane at a speed of thirty miles an hour enter the intersection at an unabated rate of speed and strike the right side of the plaintiff's vehicle toward the rear. The witness can describe the location of the debris and the position of the vehicles as they came to rest.

These are the most important facts that this witness can supply: The condition of the traffic lights, the speeds, paths of travel, final positions—perhaps five elements in all. Now, of course, the witness *could* supply additional information of an uncontested nature (weather condition, time of day, color of vehicles, etc.) or other embellishing minutiae. But why dilute the testimony with such drivel? If five important responses are hidden amidst a clutch of twenty inconsequential replies, the witness is operating at a twenty percent efficiency. If every other question is important, you're up to fifty percent. Keep the percentage up and end with the best attention grabber.

There's one further benefit. Every trial lawyer should be concerned about the crowded dockets, the length of time to get to trial, the perennial gripe of the law's delays. There have been plenty of suggestions to remedy the problem from computerized dockets to more judges. The simplest remedy is seldom utilized— a firm resolve on the part of bench and bar alike to try cases quickly, to present testimony with dispatch, keep the proceedings lively, conclude the case and get on to the next.

§ 11.13 Clustering Relevant Information

There are a few modifications that should be made in the traditional chronological sequencing of testimony. The first is the need to group together facts which are relevant to each other. Let's take a simple example. You have a group of random sized jars in the dishwasher and a similar number of random sized lids in a kitchen drawer. How do you match them? Bring the jars and the lids together. Physical proximity will reveal the matching size and assure that you will get the right lid for the right jar. Let's go to the experts to affirm what we already know (the usual role of experts)

Psychologists have devised a test to measure the intellect of chimpanzees.

A chimp is put in a cage. A banana is placed outside the cage and beyond his reach. A pole long enough to reach the banana is placed in the cage but in the direction opposite to that in which the banana is positioned. Some of the chimps tested are intelligent enough to see the pole in isolation and recognize that it can be used to gain access to the coveted banana. Others fail to see the connection between the two, to recognize that the pole can be utilized as an extension of their reach. However, when the pole is positioned so that it is in the direct line on sight with the banana, the connection is plain to all the chimps. The pole is seized and maneuvered to bring the banana within the grasp. Our first maxim, expressed in the words of the psychologist, "Spatial proximity enhances the perception of relevance."

One more example. Consider a standard device employed by the murder mystery writer. As the story begins to unfold some trivial event is recorded—a passing comment, a casual observation, a seemingly unimportant activity—followed by multitudinous machinations which constitute the bulk of the drama. Now we are ready for the ending, a climax as predictable as a fast food burger. All the suspects are corralled in the library. Each is reminded of the particular motivation and opportunity which marks them as a likely criminal candidate. "But," our hero sleuth declares "the real murderer is the butler!", who, depending on the whimsy of the writer, either makes a tearful confession or reaches for a gun and is shot.

The denouement follows with a befuddled police chief inquiring, "How did you know it was the butler?" Our hero smugly replies, "Do you remember last week when (he then recounts the trifling event recorded supra) "That's what gave him away" The author or playwright has successfully obscured the relevance of the tell-tale event by isolating it from its meaningful counterpart. The intervention of other events dulled the memory and obscured the connection. If the description of the butler's muddy shoes had been recorded simultaneously with the fact that the body was found in a muddy field there would have been no mystery. The corollary to our maxim: "Temporal proximity enhances the perception of relevance". How do these observations apply to the organization of direct examination. You must arrange your evidence in clusters of related items.

§ 11.14 Clustering Relevant Information—Illustration

Your witness will testify that there was a traffic sign indicating a speed limit of forty miles an hour for northbound traffic on the trafficway. He will also testify that the plaintiff was traveling at fifty five miles per hour. Do we adduce evidence of the posted speed limit when we're creating the physical scene and then inquire about plaintiffs' speed fifteen minutes later when we're into the dynamics of the collision? Of course not. We bring the two together. Establish the witnesses observation of plaintiff's car, then:

Q. Were there any speed limit signs posted for northbound traffic near the scene of the collision?
A. Yes, just south of the intersection there was a sign that stated forty miles an hour.
Q. How fast was the plaintiff's car travelling?
A. Fifty five miles an hour.

The same principle applies regardless of the subject matter of the litigation. If there has been a series of letters that constitute the basis of a contractual claim, don't present the letters in a cluster. Introduce the letters with other evidence that is relevant to the legal issues of offer, acceptance or performance.

Don't isolate bits of information about which you want the jury to make a connection. If you insist on doing so, drop trial work and take up mystery writing.

§ 11.15 Emphasizing Legal Relevance

Every bit of evidence adduced at trial should be relevant to the legal issues that must be resolved by the jury. (At least that's the law of evidence.) If that is the case what should we do to demonstrate to the jury the connection between the numerous facts which we dump upon them and the multiple legal issues which they must decide? Clustering relevant information will help them relate one fact to another fact. Taking the process further, now we must connect those facts to the relevant issue.

§ 11.16 Clustering Legal Relevance—Illustration

Q. Mr. Montrey in his opening statement stated that you did not properly maintain your lawn mower. Let me ask you about that. Did you ever change the oil?
A. Yes, sir.

337

Q. How often?
A. As directed in the manual, after every ten hours of operation.
Q. Did you inspect the blades?
A. Yes, regularly, before every use.

———————

The question is, would the jury listen to such perfunctory information about lawn mower maintenance and retain it if it had been thrown in the questioning without red flagging is significance. The same technique can be used with experts.

Q. Dr. Hart, this jury will be asked to determine if Miss Niffs present complaints were caused by this accident. Are you prepared to express an opinion as to that?
A. Yes.

Or else

Q. Mr. Quirk this jury must decide whether or not this product was unreasonably dangerous when used in a reasonably anticipated manner. Does your background, education and experience relate to the study of widgets?
A. Yes.
Q. Have you studied this widget in order to evaluate its safety for the jury?
A. Yes.

———————

§ 11.17 Ending With a Bang

Previous mention has been made regarding the need for a boffo conclusion, the instruction bears repeating. We must end our interrogation with a bang and not a whimper. Illustrations of the latter abound.

1. (Returning to counsel table and whispering to co-counsel "Did I forget anything?)

2. "I think I'm finished, but may I review my notes your Honor?"

3. "Did you appear here voluntarily or under subpoena?"

Forget those scenarios. Do it this way. Identify and list the facts about which the witness will testify. Select the most significant item of evidence and put it last on the list. If it's a fraud case the most important testimony might be that the defendant represented himself to be a rocket scientist with a graduate degree from Massachusetts Institute of Technology. If the witnesses recollection of events were recited chronologically, this misrepresentation would appear somewhere in the middle of the testimony. If you want to enhance the likelihood that the jury will remember it, hold off to the end and provide as much drama as possible.

§ 11.18 Illustration

Q. Just a few more questions Mr. Nichols (that helps to reawaken them). Did Mr. Pearce ever make any representations to you regarding his profession and education?

A. He did.

Q. Turn to the jury and tell them what he said.

A. He told me he was a rocket scientist with a Ph.D. from M.I.T.

Q. Did you believe him?

A. I did.

Q. Did you rely on that information that he was a rocket scientist with a Ph.D. from M.I.T. when you signed the contract?

A. I did.

Q. Was he in fact a rocket scientist?

A. No.

D. TECHNIQUES OF INTERROGATION

§ 11.19 Generally

There are several suggestions of a general nature that will prove to be beneficial in developing information from your own witnesses. Both are communicative devices which seem particularly adaptible for courtroom use—and yet few advocates take advantage of them.

§ 11.20 Topic Sentences

A series of questions and answers covering a number of topics has a way of merging into an amorphous, unstructured mass. The lawyer most often proceeds from one facet of the case to another with no indication to the witness, the judge or the jury that such shifts are going to take place. No one would expect to ingest a novel in one gulp. The author conveniently creates bite size chapters for easier digestion. Any written offering has topic sentences, paragraphs, titles to aid in the understanding of the subject matter. Certainly if that technique is valid for written information which can be studied and re-studied at leisure then it seems reasonable that the same technique would be beneficial in presenting verbal information.

§ 11.21 Topic Sentences—Illustration

Instead of launching into the witness' identity try prefacing the series of questions with a brief, "Mr. Schmidt let me inquire into your background. Where do you live?" etc. When that topic has been exhausted shift emphasis with a second topic sentence. "Now let me inquire into your knowledge of this incident. Where were you on the evening of January 25th?" etc.

This style of interrogation is particularly effective in dealing with medical experts who have conducted a long and complicated examination and have reached certain conclusions concerning distinct areas of medical prognosis. Absent an orderly interrogation with identifying lead-in questions the jury will be lost.

§ 11.22 Graduality

There are certain areas of interrogation in which the impact of a given fact may be intensified by gradually unfolding the individual elements which constitute the basis for the ultimate conclusion.

Sometimes the recitation consists simply in a listing of the ingredients which lead to an obvious conclusion. Such would be the case in establishing drunkenness. The witness could be asked, "What was the condition of the driver?" to which he would respond, "He was drunk."

§ 11.23 Graduality—Illustrations

Applying the theory of gradualism the inquiry would be:

Q. Did you observe the witness' gait?
A. Yes, he was stumbling around.
Q. And did you observe his appearance?
A. Yes. His eyes were blood shot and his hands trembled.
Q. Did you have occasion to hear him speak?
A. Yes I did. His speech was garbled.
Q. And from these observations, did you reach a conclusion as to the driver's condition?
A. Yes, he obviously was intoxicated.

On other occasions the gradual unfolding of cumulative evidence will proceed from a position of lesser import to one of greater import concluding with the ultimate fact.

Assume a case where the lessee of premises is injured when a defective balcony collapses. The information sought to be elicited from the plaintiff is whether the lessor had warned of the condition. Again, the ultimate question could be put to the witness, "Did the defendant ever warn you of the condition of the railing?" But how much impact would a single negative response have?

Q. At the time the lease was signed did the defendant advise you that the balcony railing was rotten?
A. No, he didn't.
Q. After you occupied the premises did he ever write you about the rotten railing?
A. No.
Q. Or come by your home to advise you of the rotten railing?
A. No.
Q. Or even give you a telephone call?
A. No.
Q. Mr. Talbot during the entire six months of your tenancy did the defendant do *anything* to warn you of the dangerous condition of that railing?
A. Absolutely nothing.

If the jury doesn't get the picture after that, they never will.

§ 11.24 Repetitive Use of Key Phrases

There are some advocates who advise that each case that comes into the office be given a name which characterizes the theory of recovery or defense. Thus the case used by way of illustration in the preceding section would be entitled "The case of the concealed rotten railing."

The purpose of such an exercise is to identify the main issue of recovery or defense that will be hammered home to the jury.

It is surprising how often during interrogation, either on direct or cross examination the witness will employ a particularly effective phrase which epitomizes the guts of his testimony. When this occurs, pick it up and incorporate that same verbiage into related interrogation.

§ 11.25 Repetitive Use of Key Phrases—Illustrations

Assume you represent a motorist who has struck a child pedestrian. The interrogation of the facts of the occurrence commences with:

Q. Did you see the plaintiff before the accident occurred?

A. Yes, I saw her when she darted right in front of my car. (There's the magic phrase)

Q. How fast were you traveling when this girl *darted right in front of your car?*

A. Approximately twenty miles per hour.

Q. And where in the street were you traveling when this girl *darted right in front of your car?*

A. About two feet from the center line.

Repetition is a form of education and you can believe that the jury will be "educated" about that little girl darting in front of the car before the witness is through.

The principle applies regardless of the cause of action. There will always be operative words that bear repeating. If the case involves a breach of contract you as plaintiff's attorney want to keep that fact before the jury. When inquiring about the circumstances of its signing you could proceed in one of two ways. Note the differences in these series of questions.

First example

When was the contract signed?

Who was there?

Where was it signed?

How many copies were made?

Second example

When was the contract signed?

Who was there when the agreement was made?

Where did you and the defendant sign this contract in which he agreed to pay you ten thousand dollars for your machine?

How many copies of this contract were made?

The theme of the case is being constantly reinforced in the second example. How can you discipline yourself to do it the better way?

First, avoid the presumption that the jury knows as much about the case as you do and that they are continually attentive to the questions and answers that are playing out in front of them. The truth of the matter is that they are ignorant of the case and even though intent on learning about it, their attentiveness will not be constant and they will lapse in and out of comprehension. You've experienced the phenomenon yourself. Someone in the midst of relating a tale will say, "and he said" and the confused listener responds with "Now who is he?". Take your time, make your points emphatically and repeat the operative phrases.

Second, avoid pronouns. They are devices to speed up communication and they do so at a terrible cost to the communicator. They cannot stand by themselves, they are substitutes. "It," "they," "our," are meaningless substitutes absent context and reference to something else. Pronouns are colorless and can be confusing. As the ad man says "Don't be fooled by substitutes, demand the original."

E. PROBLEMS AND REMEDIES

§ 11.26 Generally

As one observes the typical direct examination, whether conducted by a veteran or neophyte, it becomes apparent what is the greatest impediment to an effective presentation. It does not concern rules of evidence. Most of the issues regarding admissibility of evidence are resolved with pre-trial motions. The difficulty lies not with *what* is presented but rather *how* it is presented. The objections that interrupt the attempt to tell a story do not involve matters of substance but matters of form.

First we'll identify the pesky objection you're apt to hear. Then the reasons why you have strayed from proper interrogation and the objection was evoked. And finally how to avoid the interruptions.

§ 11.27 Leading Questions

Why does the interrogator succumb so often to the temptation to lead his witness? It is an intuitive effort to control the exchange. And why should he want that control? Because he is unsure of the answer that might follow an open-ended question. And why is he unsure? (At last we get to the bottom line.) Two possible reasons: either he and his witness inadequately prepared or despite preparation, the interrogator still doubts the capacity of the witness to respond properly. Identifying the reasons identifies the remedy.

§ 11.28 Leading Questions—Witness Preparation

Properly prepare the witness for the job ahead. But don't take too narrow a view of that word "preparation." It encompasses something far greater than merely scripting a question and answer decision. Think back on how you prepared yourself for a performance in the school play, a musical recital or an athletic contest. It wasn't merely a matter of memorizing the lines, reading the notes or learning the plays. You had to be "psyched up" for the big event. You had to *want* to be on stage or on the field. That was what characterized the good director and the good coach: one who is a good motivator, who brings out the best in those in his charge.

The first step in preparing the witness directs itself to this problem of motivating the witness. Why should anyone want to appear in court as a witness on behalf of someone else? Maybe there is some self interest in that the witness knows the litigant and wants to help. But unfortunately that is not the typical case. Absent that connection, the witness will ask, "Why should I get involved?" There are a host of reasons why he should not be involved. A court appearance will be:

> inconvenient (schedules will have to be rearranged and plans postponed or abandoned);
>
> upsetting (any new experience is an inherent threat to one's peace of mind);
>
> expensive (there will be costs involved in losing work, travel, parking, etc.)

Your first step in preparing your witness is to overcome the natural resistance to get involved by removing or at least diminishing the witnesses concerns. This has been dealt with before (§ 9.1) but it bears repeating.

> 1. assure him that there will be no economic consequences to his appearance in court. In addition to his witness fees, you will compensate him for any lost wages and attendant expenses such as travel, parking, baby sitting fees, etc.

2. find out when it would be most convenient for them to appear in court (witnesses usually respond by saying, "It's never convenient" Best to ask, "When is it least inconvenient to appear in court")

3. acquaint them with as much peripheral information about their role as witness as you can, i.e., where to go, where to park, how long it will take, etc.

4. acquaint them with your expectations of them.

A witness must be made aware of why they are being called to court. This means that they should know the nature of the claim or defense or at least that issue of the claim or defense that is relevant to their first hand knowledge. If your witness has vital information regarding the time when the banana skin was dropped on the floor, tell him how important that information is; that Mrs. Roberts who slipped on that banana skin at 1:30 P.M. must have proof that the proprietor of the store know or should have known of its presence in time to have removed it (read the witness the instruction of law that spells out the elements of your claim); that the testimony from the witness that she saw the banana skin on the floor at 12:45 P.M. is essential to demonstrate defendant's actual or constructive knowledge of its presence; that absent such testimony Mrs. Roberts can't recover for her grievous injuries.

5. familiarize them with the outline of your questioning.

6. ask them if they have any questions about anything regarding their role as witness.

7. thank them profusely for their cooperation.

Proper preparation will minimize the likelihood of using leading questions but the threat remains. Best to remove the threat completely by utilizing a technique of interrogation which makes it impossible to lead the witness.

§ 11.29 Leading Questions—Use of Journalistic Language

Begin each question with those inquiries which typify the jargon of the journalist: who, why, where, when, how.

To illustrate the point let's take a conventional exchange between two lawyers who meet at an annual bar meeting.

Joe: Hi Jane. Good to see you. Did you just arrive?
Jane: Yes. Are you staying at the Hilton?

Joe: Sure. Did you bring the family?

Jane: Yeah. Will you be here during the entire week?

Joe: I think so. Have you tried any big one's lately?

How many of those questions do you think are leading? Of course the question put in that form is meaningless. How many do you think some trial judge would think are leading? The answer is every one.

In analyzing the problems associated with leading questions we begin with the realization that the definition of "leading" is up for grabs. Appellate decisions will be of no help. Forget Black's Law Dictionary and West's Descriptive Word Digest. The answer lies in the subjective uncertainty of the particular judge before whom you are appearing. At one pole are those who will not consider a question objectionable unless the answer is suggested in the question ("You were present at the signing of the contract, weren't you?) At the other pole are those who believe any question that calls for a "yes" or "no" answer is beyond the pale (Don't ask, "Are you married?" The proper form is "What is your marital status?")

Knowing that the offense of leading is so mushily interpreted, best that you conduct your interrogation in such a way that the possibility of interruption be eliminated, or at least minimized. How then would you question our lawyer friend (in a courtroom setting) on meeting him at a convention?

"When did you arrive"

"Where are you staying"

"Who has accompanied you?"

"How long are you planning to stay."

With these journalistic introductory words there can be no challenge that you are leading the witness. Your chief problem in direct examination will have been solved.

§ 11.30 Lack of Foundation

The give and take in a courtroom exchange does not simulate natural conversation. In our usual intercourse we jump to conclusions, skip the sequencing and perform other less athletic fashions of communication. When those same techniques translate to the courtroom you are apt to draw a number of objections, such as:

"Objection—assuming facts not in evidence,"

"Objection—speculation"

"Objection—lack of foundation"

"Objection—calls for a conclusion"

In reality they are all expressions of the same symptom—a failure to patiently and thoroughly develop facts in an orderly, chronological fashion.

§ 11.31 Lack of Foundation—Illustrations

Your witness is a police officer who has arrived at the scene of an accident. He has been called as your first witness to identify the final resting place of the automobile in which your client was riding. You claim that the defendant driver negligently drove off the road. He claims that there was a sudden blow-out wrenching the car out of control.

Q.   Officer, where was the car located.
A.   It's left side was ten feet eight inches from the northernmost edge of the asphalt roadway.
Q.   Were there tire tracks on the shoulder?
A.   Yes.
Q.   How far had the car been driven on the shoulder?
A.   Objection—assumes a fact not in evidence.

And indeed it does. The officer doesn't know how the car got there. The word "driven" suggests a deliberate act. You have not had any evidence *so far* that it had been driven. Your witness will so testify later in trial. It is merely your sequencing that is out of whack.

———————

You represent plaintiff in a product liability case including an injury to your client while operating a lawn tractor. You claim the injury was caused by a defective product. Defendant claims it was operator error. You want to eliminate any conclusion on the part of the jury that the malfunction was the result of poor maintenance.

Typical out of court questioning might lend you to ask the following:

Who saw to it that the lawn tractor was properly maintained?

Was it in good shape at the time it malfunctioned?

If this were on the game page of the Sunday Supplement we'd ask, "What's wrong with this picture?" (Turn to page 10 for the answers)

Page 10 would explain:

1. The first question *assumes* that some one saw to it that the tractor was maintained and further *concludes* that such maintenance was proper.

2. The second question seeks the witnesses *conclusion* as to the meaning of "good shape" and further *assumes* that the cause of the incident was the malfunctioning lawn tractor.

§ 11.32 Lack of Foundation—Patience

How do you avoid that problem? Take your time, assume nothing, start at the beginning.

Q. Did anyone see to it that the tractor was serviced?

Once you get an affirmation of that, start your journalistic list,

Who was it?

What did you do?

How often did you do it?

Now for another threshold foundational question.

Were you familiar with the condition of the lawn tractor when it turned over? (If evidence of the turn over is in evidence, alright. If not) the incident occurred?

Now after this foundation, you're ready for a conclusion.

Describe the condition of the lawn tractor at that time.

There's no guarantee that your opponent won't object on the grounds that the question calls for a conclusion. However, the jury has heard the basis of that conclusion and would no doubt themselves conclude that it was a legitimate question within the knowledge of the witness. Besides you have a good legal argument that you are entitled to a favorable ruling on the objection based on Federal Rules of Evidence 701.

The objection "lack of proper foundation" is beguilingly generic and could be based on anything from an absence of fundamental qualifications of a witness or legal pre-requisites for authenticating a document. Let's start with the foundational questions that are less legalistic and more easily understood.

§ 11.33 Lack of Foundation—Establish Witness Competence

Everyone is not qualified to be a witness. Those traditional perfunctory questions which so often initiate the questioning (State your name, Where do you live? What is your occupation?) do serve a purpose. The answers serve to establish the witnesses' qualification as someone with sufficient capacity to perceive, retain and recite the relevant facts which are to follow. If the responses, or the identity of the witness himself, indicates a lack of sufficient maturity or intellect to fulfill the basic qualifications of a witness, an objection raising the question of the witnesses' will be raised either by the opposing party or the judge sua sponte. The lawyer tendering the witness has not laid a proper capacity foundation.

More often the foundational element that is lacking is the witnesses' personal knowledge. What is wrong with the following testimonial excerpt?

Q. Where were you on April 20th at eight p.m.?
A. At the corner of Sullivan and Clay.
Q. Were you aware that an automobile collision had occurred?
A. Yes, I saw the cars collide and heard the crash.
Q. How fast was the green Ford traveling?

Hearing such testimony being adduced by your opponent, would you object? Of course. There is nothing before the court which establishes that the witness has personal knowledge of the automobile's speed. There might be an answer based on the sound of the crash, the ultimate resting place of the vehicles, etc. but nothing to indicate when the automobile was first seen nor how far it traveled while being observed.

An objection is made "Objection, lack of personal knowledge" It is sustained and your opponent regroups.

Q. Did you see the green Ford before the collision?
A. Yes.
Q. Where was it when you first saw it?
A. Approaching the intersection and about one hundred feet from the point of the collision.

Q. Did you continue to observe it as it proceeded into the intersection?
A. Yes.
Q. Now tell us (smirking) how fast was the green Ford traveling as it traveled this hundred foot distance?

Has the foundational test been met? Only if you're willing to concede that the witness has personal knowledge regarding the speed of moving automobiles. Perhaps that's a given in our automobile oriented culture but another lack of foundation objection could be legitimately raised. If sustained, the scenario would continue.

Q. Do you drive an automobile?
A. Yes.
Q. For how long have you driven a car?
A. Fifteen years.
Q. During that time have you had experience in observing and estimating the speed of moving vehicles?
A. I have.
Q. How fast was the green Ford traveling?

That should do it.

§ 11.34 Lack of Foundation—Satisfy Rule Requirements

Some foundational requirements are more legalistic and the grounds for establishing them are to be found in the Federal Rules of Evidence rather than in the rules of common sense (See Rule 803 establishing the requisition for exceptions to hearsay). But regardless of the source, when your opponent raises the objection, "lack of foundation" he is simply reminding you that you have gotten your chronology out of whack and have impatiently sought information from a witness or a document without proof that the witness or document is qualified to give such information.

§ 11.35 Lack of Foundation—Establish Basis for Conclusionary Evidence

When your opponent raises the objection of "conclusion" it is an indication either that:

you have violated the basic rule of seeking only that information of which your witness has personal knowledge, or

you have prematurely sought a bottom line ultimate fact without first adducing the basis of that testimony, or both.

An example of the first is the question that asks for the witness to state the mental processes of a third party.

Q. "Why didn't Mrs. Platte sign the contract?

"Objection, speculation and calls for a conclusion. The witness doesn't know what motivated Mrs. Platte."

"Sustained"

But what if the witness does know? Can this testimony though excluded when presented in the above form, be admitted? Sure. Prove that the motivational information was within the personal knowledge of the witness.

Q. Did Mrs. Platte explain to you why she didn't sign the contract?
A. Yes.
Q. What did she tell you? (Don't worry about a hearsay objection.)
A. She said that she didn't think that the other party had the resources to perform."

An example of the second is the question that seeks a response of a person's condition.

Q. "Was the driver drunk?"
      "Objection, leading and calls for a conclusion."
      "Sustained"
Q. Did you observe the driver when he left the car?
A. Yes?
Q. Describe his walk.
A. He stumbled and weaved?
Q. What was his appearance?
A. His clothes were dishevelled, his eyes blood shot.
Q. Did you hear him speak.
A. Yes, his speech was slurred and incomprehensible.

Now the jury has all the facts from which they can draw the conclusion of drunkenness. Whether the judge permits the witness to do so (some do as an exception to the general restriction of a lay opinion Federal Rule 702, some don't) really doesn't make a difference.

CHAPTER 12

USE OF DEPOSITIONS AND OTHER WRITTEN MATTER

"The spoken word perishes, the written word remains

Latin proverb

Analysis

A. USE OF DEPOSITIONS

A. USE OF DEPOSITIONS

§ 12.1 Introduction

Deposition testimony frequently comprises an important element of a litigant's proof. It usually takes two forms: admissions of a party opponent *or* testimony of an unavailable witness. The former usually consists of isolated statements scattered throughout the deposition, the latter, a complete recitation of the testimony. Each has its special problems as to admissibility, mechanics of admissions and judgment regarding use.

352

§ 12.2 Statement of Party–Opponent—Generally

The Federal Rules of Evidence promulgated for use in United States District Courts define an "Admission by Party–Opponent" in part as a statement which is "offered against a party and is his own statement, in either his individual or a representative capacity...." Such statements, as the Advisory Committee's Notes to Evidence Rule 801(d)(2) explain, are not considered hearsay. "No guarantee of trustworthiness is required in the case of an admission. The freedom which admissions have enjoyed from technical demands of searching for an assurance of trustworthiness in some against-interest circumstance, and from the restrictive influences of the opinion rule requiring first hand knowledge, when taken with the apparently prevalent satisfaction with the results, calls for generous treatment of this avenue to admissibility."

§ 12.3 Statement of Party–Opponent—Mechanics of Admission

This type of testimony is usually brief, punchy and of substantial probative value. The dramatic effect of its introduction should not be marred by the interruption of an objection. Consequently it is usually advisable to advise the court in chambers of that portion of the deposition sought to be read in order to afford the opposition and opportunity to object at that time. The presentation to the jury can then take place in this form:

> "Your honor at this time I wish to read to the jury certain portions of defendant's deposition taken on April 30, 1992 in the office of his attorney Mr. Sanders. At that time he was interrogated under oath and gave this testimony...."

§ 12.4 Statement of Party–Opponent—Judgment as to Use

Sometimes the admission of a party opponent constitutes the only source of proof of an essential element in your case. In such an instant there is no option available—the admission must be read as a part of your case. Most frequently you will have additional proof, either from your own client or a witness, to establish your prima facie case in which case you must decide whether the incriminating statement should be introduced as independent evidence in your case in chief or whether it should be reserved for impeachment purposes on cross examination. Let us again assume the intersection collision with the admission made in deposition as follows:

Q. "How fast were you traveling as you entered the intersection?"
A. "About thirty miles an hour."

The plaintiff's lawyer has established through other testimony a prima facie submission on another theory such as failure to keep a lookout. He elects to reserve the use of this deposition testimony for cross examination. The defendant testifies he was traveling twenty miles an hour as he entered the intersection. The cross examination proceeds as follows:

Q. "Do you recall when your testimony was taken under oath at your attorney's office?"
A. "Yes sir."
Q. "And do you recall being asked at what speed you were traveling as you entered the intersection and do you recall this response that you made on page 36 'About thirty miles an hour.' "
A. "Yes, I do—but I thought you meant the speed I was traveling as I *approached* the intersection. I applied my brakes before I entered the intersection and at that time I was traveling only twenty miles an hour."

Further cross examination will undoubtedly follow but if the witness sticks to his guns there may be no substantive evidence upon which the plaintiff can submit a theory of excessive speed. The deposition will have served its purpose as an impeaching tool but it may not suffice as a building block when utilized in this manner.

§ 12.5 Unavailable Witness—Generally

The applicable Rules of Civil Procedure will determine whether the deposition taken to perpetuate testimony may be received in evidence. Most state rules parallel those of the Federal Rules of Civil Procedure. Proof concerning that circumstance which justifies the reading of the deposition must be adduced at trial and the easiest manner to adduce such proof is through the deposition itself. Let us assume the witness is going to be absent at trial time. The interrogation would include this prefatory information:

Q. "Doctor, will you be available as a witness when this trial is set the week of December 6th?"
A. "No sir. I will be attending a seminar on 'The Economic Squeeze on the Rural Practitioner' being held in Acapulco that entire month."

If a physical disability is the qualifying condition the interrogation might proceed as follows:

Q. "What is your present physical condition?"
A. "I am suffering from recurrent attacks of extreme nervousness."
Q. "Are you under a doctor's care?"
A. "Yes, and he has prescribed complete bed rest for the next month."

§ 12.6 Unavailable Witness—Mechanics of Admission

The need for dramatization is never more sorely felt than when you are called upon to introduce deposition testimony in your lawsuit. Translating the printed word into an oral presentation presents problems enough. When the printed word is in the form of question and answer the problem is compounded. Add to this the necessity of conveying the personality of the deponent and you are confronted with a real challenge—how can we "flesh out" this written inquiry and present it to the jury in an interesting, persuasive fashion?

Let us start with what we *shouldn't* do. Don't just read the deposition. Can you think of anything more deadly than a one-man dialogue in which the communication is compartmentalized by the twin book-ends of "Question" and "Answer?"

Yet lawyers have been known to hold forth with such soporific soliloquies for hours at a time "reading into the record" the testimony of a deponent. The reference is apt. Such a performance is little more than "*reading* to the *record.*" Neither the manner nor the target of the pitch is appropriate. One should rather *dramatize* to the *jury.* You can't do that with unilateral utterings. You will have to secure the services of someone to play deponent, take the stand and respond to the questions propounded by the interrogator. This technique supplies two pluses: first, it will provide a natural vehicle for the adduction of the testimony; and second, it will clothe the obscure deponent with the traits of the stand-in reciter. Of course the jury will be advised that "with the aid of my associate, Mr. Jones, we will present the deposition of Tom Brown." The only personality to which they will be exposed will be that of Jones. Brown might be a rough-hewn, cantankerous and consequently an offensive witness but he will be known to the jury only by his written word so spoken by Jones—a Cyrano de Bergerac play in reverse. So choose your surrogate witness well. One who through his own appearance and demeanor and dramatic emphasis can "use all gently" and enhance the value of the deponent's testimony.

The manner of reading is only part of the problem. The jury must be acquainted with the nature of the deposition. So often it's assumed that jurors are acquainted with legal lingo. How do they know what you mean when you announce to the court that, "I am now going to read Tom Brown's deposition?" No doubt they'll recognize it as his statement—but it's more than that. Do they know it's been given under oath? that it is a bilateral proceeding? that the opposition had a chance to cross-examine? This they must know and they will if before pushing ahead with the interrogator-interrogatee exchange the jury is advised, "The deposition of Tom Brown will now be presented. His statement was taken on October 13th in the office of Mr. Black the defendant's attorney. Present were Mr. Black and myself. Mr. Brown was sworn and we proceeded as follows with the initial questioning by myself."

Usage varies regarding the scope and manner of reading the deposition. In some instances the offering party must read the entire direct examination and the opposing party then must offer all or none of the cross-examination with the offeror given the opportunity to read those portions excluded by his opponent. Sometimes each party is given the opportunity of reading whatever portion of the deposition is considered desirable, the plaintiff offering portions during his case in chief and the defendant offering his selected portions during its case in chief. Find out the practice followed by the trial judge and act accordingly.

§ 12.7 Unavailable Witness—Judgment as to Use

It is a rare witness who will present information to a jury that is one hundred per cent favorable to the party introducing his testimony. Even though he may be guided carefully through direct examination, the inevitable modifications and elaborations will take place on cross-examination and the initial advantageous effect might be completely compromised. With live witnesses at trial time the effect of the cross-examination is never known until it occurs. Not so with the witness whose testimony has been perpetuated through deposition. The testimony becomes a "packaged deal," the goodies developed on direct are there in black and white—and so are the zingers that pop up on cross-examination. The lawyer confronted with the choice of offering the deposition

356

must weigh the good with the bad and judge accordingly. The uncertainty of the cross has been removed and he is able to make his judgment with eyes wide open. Exhibits can be settled either informally between counsel or formally through the device of a pretrial conference. Whichever device is followed, it behooves the trial lawyer to get the preliminaries out of the way and be assured come trial time, that there will be no objection to the proffered evidence.

B. USE OF OTHER WRITTEN MATTER

§ 12.8 Introduction

For the evidence instructor the area of utilizing written matter as a source of evidence has been generally divided into the categories of business records, past recollection recorded and present recollection refreshed. For the advocate the problem is not segmented that neatly. It will be profitable for us to approach this matter from a different point of view.

Basically any written matter can be identified as either an evidentiary aid or evidence itself (but sometimes the identity is not too clear). Thus, the spontaneous diagram is usually simply an aid or adjunct to the verbal testimony which accompanies it. Sometimes it aids verbalization which isn't even testimony, as when it is used in opening statement or summation. In those cases when used as an aid it need not be formally marked as an exhibit nor offered into evidence. It serves merely as an adjunct to expression (such as a gesture) and has no evidentiary value standing alone.

Other written matter has intrinsic evidentiary worth. The prepared diagram, fully authenticated, is marked as an exhibit and entered into evidence. Once authenticated it has an identity and probative value all of its own.

The same recognition should be afforded written matter. The advocate should determine how a specific item is to be utilized at trial, as a simple adjunct to oral testimony or as independent evidence or as both.

§ 12.9 Illustration—Generally

Let us take the example of a police report. In most cases the information on the report will be utilized by the investigating officer who appears as a witness. For persuasion purposes it matters little how the information on the report reaches the jury, as a refresher of memory, past recollection recorded, or business record. The officer takes the stand with the report on his lap. Preliminaries are accomplished and the interrogation proceeds:

§ 12.10 Illustration—Refreshing Memory

> Q. Officer did you investigate an accident occurring on Main and Broadway this past May 15th?
>
> *Witness*: May I refer to my report?
>
> *Lawyer*: Certainly.
>
> A. Yes, I responded to a call at 8:15 A.M. etc.

The balance of the officer's testimony is a paraphrasing, or perhaps a quoting, from "my report" all of which was triggered by the confident assurance of the lawyer that he could "certainly" refer to the report.

Suppose, however, that after the interrogating lawyer had so gratuitously opined, the opposing lawyer had interjected.

"Pardon me your honor, May I voir dire the witness?"

> *Court*: Certainly.
>
> Q. How long ago was this accident, officer?
>
> A. Over three years ago.
>
> Q. And I assume you have investigated hundreds of accidents since then?
>
> A. Yes, many hundreds.
>
> Q. You don't have any personal recollection of this particular accident do you?
>
> A. No, I'm afraid not.
>
> *Lawyer*: Your honor, I object to the officer's use of any written material in this fashion.
>
> *Court*: Sustained.

The problem with which the counsel is now confronted is of his own making. His pretrial briefing of the witness should have acquainted him with the necessity of testifying from his own memory and that the police report could be used in this fashion only if the magic incantation was evoked that the report "refreshed his memory."

Now that the report has been eliminated as an aid to oral testimony (the witness has no independent recollection to refresh) the lawyer must attempt to establish the validity of the report as an independent source of evidence.

Two avenues lay open; to establish the report as a past recollection or as a business record.

§ 12.11 Illustration—Past Recollection Recorded

The interrogation continues.

> Q. Officer, are reports habitually made by the police investigator at the scene of the accident?
> A. Yes they are.
> Q. And was a report made on this occasion?
> A. Yes, sir.
> Q. Does the investigating officer have first hand knowledge of the facts recorded on the report?
> A. Yes, we do.

Lawyer 1: Your honor, I ask that police report, previously marked plaintiff's Exhibit 4 be introduced into evidence.

Lawyer 2: Your honor, may I see the report?

Court: Certainly.

Lawyer 2: Q. Officer, is this your signature on the report?
> A. No, that's the signature of Patrolman Fields, my investigating Partner.

Lawyer 2: Q. Did you ever prior to today actually read this report as signed by Patrolman Fields to verify its accuracy?
> A. No, I don't recall that I ever did. I just assume that it is correct if he signed it.

Lawyer 2: Your honor, I'll have to object to Exhibit 4.

Court: Sustained.

The usual requisites for admission of a past recollection recorded, as pronounced in McCormick on Evidence (2nd Ed.1972), are as follows:

1. The witness must have had firsthand knowledge of the event,

2. The written statement must be an original memorandum made at or near the time of the event and while the witness had a clear and accurate memory of it,

3. The witness must lack a present recollection of the event, and

4. The witness must vouch for the accuracy of the written memorandum.

Requisite number four not being met, the court correctly sustained the objection. One more possibility however is yet open—qualify the report as a business record.

§ 12.12 Illustration—Business Record

Q. Officer tell the jury how these reports are prepared?
A. We fill out the form right there at the scene.
Q. And then what is done with the report?
A. We turn it over to the clerk back at the district headquarters, who prepares a typewritten original which is signed by one of the investigating officers.

Lawyer 1: Your honor, I offer Exhibit 4 as a business record.
Lawyer 2: I object. There has been no showing how the record is kept, or who has been the custodian of this report. Furthermore there has been no showing that this is the original report prepared by the clerk, signed by the officer and maintained by the record custodian.
Court: Sustained.

Federal Rule of Evidence 803(6) and (7), relating to business records provides as follows:

(6) *Records of regularly conducted activity.* A memorandum, report, record, or data compilation, in any form, of acts, events, conditions, opinions, or diagnoses, made at or near the time by, or from information transmitted by, a person with knowledge, if kept in the course of a regularly conducted business activity, and if it was the regular practice of that business activity to make the memorandum, report, record, or data compilation, all as shown by the testimony of the custodian or other qualified witness, unless the source of information or the method or circumstances of preparation indicate lack of trustworthiness. The term "business" as used in this paragraph includes business, institution, association, profession, occupation, and calling of every kind, whether or not conducted for profit.

(7) *Absence of entry in records kept in accordance with the provisions of paragraph* (6). Evidence that a matter is not included in the memoranda reports, records, or data compilations, in any form, kept in accordance with the provisions of paragraph (6), to prove the nonoccurrence or nonexistence of the matter, if the matter was of a kind of which a memorandum, report, record, or data compilation was regularly made

and preserved, unless the sources of information or other circumstances indicate lack of trustworthiness.

Again, all of the requisites were not established and the plaintiff's lawyer had to withdraw his witness.

§ 12.13 Preventive Medicine

Problems regarding the use of written memoranda should be anticipated and the following "preventive medicine" applied.

1. If the memorandum is to be admitted as either a past recollection recorded or a business record, the tender of the exhibit should be made at pretrial conference in order to ascertain what objections, if any, your opponent has to the proffered exhibit so that the complained of deficiency, if valid, can be supplied.

2. If the memorandum is to be used as a means of refreshing memory, the witness should be advised of the propriety of such use and the reasons for that propriety. In addition it is best to have the memorandum prepared by the witness himself. Assume that the witness is testifying to the chronology of a series of events. Some lawyers will be tempted to prepare a typed list for the plaintiff's use. A certain question on cross examination will be "Where did you get that paper from which you were testifying?" "My lawyer gave it to me" is not the most desirous response in the world. Better if the witness could respond, "I prepared it so that I would be perfectly correct about the dates involved."

CHAPTER 13

DEMONSTRATIVE EVIDENCE

"Don't speak of love—show me!"
My Fair Lady—Alan Jay Lerner

Analysis

A. IN GENERAL

B. COURTROOM DEMONSTRATIONS

C. PHOTOGRAPHS

D. MOTION PICTURES AND VIDEOTAPES

E. MODELS

F. DIAGRAMS

G. STATISTICAL INFORMATION

A. IN GENERAL

§ 13.1 Introduction

During the past decade there has been a great deal of emphasis placed upon the use of demonstrative evidence in the trial of cases. Countless articles, speeches, seminars, and panel discussions have concerned themselves as tools for an effective presentation. The significance of demonstrative evidence cannot be overstated. The visual stimulus is always more impressive (at least more easily understood) than the aural stimulus. If we accept this as a truth, why is demonstrative evidence used so sparingly? And, perhaps a better question, why do we not utilize the advantages of the visual stimulus throughout the trial?

It was an Oriental who recognized that a picture was worth a thousand words—but it was a Greek who explained why. Aristotle made the observation that the thought process was a process of imagining—that we think in terms of images. It isn't too difficult to prove the statement. Thinking of a house, one's mind creates a picture of a house. What color is it? Perhaps the original image did not encompass such a detail; but with the thought of color, a color image is formed. What kind of fence does it have? Of what is the house constructed? Is there smoke coming from the chimney? Each query demands an answer—and the answer is given by a continuing elaboration of the image of a house.

The validity of Aristotle's observation may be proven in another way. The writer Tolstoy told that as a boy he sought to be initiated into an exclusive club. Before being granted membership he was asked to perform a series of tasks to prove his worthiness. Each succeeding task was more difficult and he passed them all—until the final challenge was assigned to him. He was asked to stand in a corner for five minutes and not think of a white bear. Of course it was impossible. The words "white bear" created an image of a white bear in his mind. He was "thinking" of a white bear. One cannot create an image without thinking, and conversely, one cannot think without creating an image.

If the jury is to think, to understand a presentation, they must be presented with information that will easily create images. The better the stimulus, the easier the thought process. It isn't difficult to imagine the scene of an accident when one is presented with a photograph of the scene. Nor is one apt to misconceive a broken leg when X-rays create the image of the misplaced bones. But these bits of conventional "demonstrative evidence" will constitute but a small portion of a trial. The jury will receive the bulk of their information from oral testimony; words that must stimulate their thought processes. What kind of images will they create? How can an oral presentation be utilized as demonstrative evidence?

The client has suffered an injury as a result of an automobile accident in which her head struck the windshield. During the course of her testimony she is asked to describe what happened to her at the time of impact. Her response, "My head came in contact with the windshield." A less effective image inducing phrase could not have been used. "Came in contact" is the barest of descriptions. It imparts no idea as to the intensity of the contact—and that is the point which is sought to be developed. The jury is left to supply, with their own imagination unaided by the witness, a most important element of the case. A witness is obligated to tell not only the truth but the "whole truth." In this instance the oath has been violated. The jury will create a picture in their mind's eye of the force of the impact. Most will picture a mild impact—the mild phrase "came in contact" suggests such. If the impact *wasn't* mild, then the witness has been guilty of perjury. Passive in its nature, perhaps, but still perjury, for through the witness' neglect the jurors have perceived false information.

A host of image producing words can be thought of to cover the range of intensity with which the impact might have occurred—"touched," "tapped," "bumped," "crashed," "slammed." Sometimes the less sophisticated words do the better job— "zinged," "thudded," "bammed." It is difficult to think of a more descriptive phrase than that employed by an unlettered lady who was thrown to the floor of a bus by a sudden stop—"I was jerked down."

The use of verbal demonstrative evidence should pervade the entire trial. Let us consider its application in describing an injury.

The 40 year old housewife has suffered a traumatic bursitis of her shoulder which prevents the elevation of her arms above the shoulder level. How is this disability to be described? "I can't lift my arms above my head." There is little there to drive an image into the minds of the jury. It might better be stated as follows:

Q. Tell us if this injury has interfered with your day-by-day routine.

A. "I find it impossible to raise my arms above the shoulder level. Two or three times a week I do the family washing. I used to hang out the clothes in our back yard. I cannot lift my arms up to the line anymore because of my injury. Just last Saturday I wanted to reach the sugar canister on the shelf over the stove. I couldn't lift my arms that high. I had to climb a step stool until I could reach out and get it."

A pretty fair picture of the disability can be visualized. The more detail ("sugar canister," "shelf over the stove," "last Saturday") the easier it is to paint the mental picture.

Consideration will now be given to the traditional sources of demonstrative evidence, the photographs, motion pictures, exhibits, but in labeling them so it is not to be understood that these alone "demonstrate" the case. Every effective piece of evidence, be it oral or real, is in fact demonstrative evidence, evidence which creates an image and stimulates the thought processes of the jury.

B. COURTROOM DEMONSTRATIONS

§ 13.2 Generally

It is incomprehensible that a potential buyer contemplating the purchase of a major appliance would be content with a verbal description of what the product will do when there is an opportunity to actually "see it work." So it is that the man of the household takes a "demonstration ride" before he commits himself to a new Belchfire Eight while mother must peer through the plastic dome to see how vigorously the dirty clothes are pummeled about before she purchases a new Wonder Washer.

Logic would dictate that the advocate demonstrate his capacity before he asks a jury to accept his product.

Why should a doctor describe a loss of motion, an inability to perform certain tasks or a pain while undergoing certain movements while the plaintiff sits in the courtroom?

Although logic might suggest a demonstration by the plaintiff in such a case, a knowledge of human nature injects a very real doubt as to the wisdom of such a course. There are some obvious differences. A machine can be controlled and made to perform to the limits of its capabilities. A person, particularly a plaintiff, has a will of his own and despite attempts at outside control, the ultimate performance will be volitional. A second difference is apparent. The salesman selling a product will benefit from a maximum performance demonstrating how much the machine will do. The plaintiff will benefit from a minimum performance demonstrating how little he can do.

The threat that a plaintiff's performance of his physical limitations will in truth be a "performance" has led most courts to rule that a voluntary demonstration by the plaintiff is inadmissible.

There are some exceptions to the general rule. If there are surrounding circumstances which give some assurance of a genuine demonstration the jury may be allowed to view the plaintiff's incapacities. Such assurances may arise from the age of the plaintiff or his mental condition. Who is so cynical as to think a four year old would feign an injury or that a victim of mental retardation would exaggerate a disability? Even under these circumstances a trial court might question the propriety of a courtroom demonstration of a disabled plaintiff.

§ 13.3   Mechanics of Admission

Hopefully the demonstration itself will be sufficiently dramatic that there need be no fanfare associated with its introduction. Assuming you want your plaintiff to display a scarred arm, the "lead in" might be a simple, 'Will you roll up your sleeve Mr. Jones so the jury might view your arm." There might be a question of preserving the visual evidence for the record but it seems a bit stilted to say, "Now you have exhibited a three inch reddish scar about one-half inch wide running from the tip of the elbow toward the shoulder on the outside of the arm." Aside from the awkwardness of the recitation it will probably draw an objection from your opponent that the scar "really appears to be only two inches long and it's not very red at all."

The same is true of a demonstration of disability. If a witness is asked to rotate his neck to show limitation of motion it is not advisable to verbalize the visualization of the demonstration. There is such a danger that the demonstration be considered an "act" that its presentation should be handled gingerly and in almost casual fashion.

Judgment as to use

There are a number of potential pitfalls inherent in the utilization of hortatory histrionics. The first is that they will be considered just that—histrionics, theatrics, play acting. Sometimes the "demonstration" will be an inherent part of the witness ambulating to the stand or attempting to articulate. If a deliberate demonstration is necessary weigh carefully the manner in which it might be interpreted by a cynical juror. Nothing devalues a claim any more than the feeling that the plaintiff is "putting on."

Secondly, the demonstration might transgress the bounds of propriety. This is a danger associated with photographs as well as demonstrations. How well is recalled a photograph taken of a man who had suffered the amputation of a leg. The shot was taken from the rear and although it was introduced to show the level of amputation the visual impression was that of shorts and slacks lying rumpled on the floor and a pair of bristly buttocks. Suffice to say the photo didn't have the same winsome appeal as that of a baby on a bearskin. How much better to have simply described the length and appearance of the stump! Such an approach would have benefited the plaintiff in two ways: one, there would be no question as to the tastefulness of the evidence; two, the verbal description would have probably been more effective. One problem of demonstrative visual evidence is that it is limiting in scope—nothing is left to the imagination. The advent of television precipitated the demise of the horror series. How could any theatre set match the visions unleashed by the radio sounds of a squeaky door, a howl of wind, a slapping shutter and a sepulchral voice inquiring "Do you believe in ghosts?" Not too many people have seen the stump of an amputated limb. It's likely that their imagination, triggered by some good descriptive words, would be "bigger than life."

C. PHOTOGRAPHS

§ 13.4 Generally

Legal writings regarding photographs were formerly concerned with their admissibility, use and abuse. The ubiquity of the Brownie and the popularity of the Polaroid has, for the most part, left those problems behind. The science itself is sufficiently refined that there should be no questions as to the availability of authentic photographic reproductions for most purposes. Some inherent limitations remain, but for the most part the limitations as valid evidence occur through deliberate distortions. Charles Scott in his Photographic Evidence work affords comprehensive coverage of the technical problems of photographic evidence. Consideration of the proper use and methods of introduction of photographs follow.

§ 13.5 Subject Matter

The Roman philosopher Terrence remarked, "Nothing that is human is alien to me." The same universality might be attributable to the camera. A modified application may be, "Few things admissible as evidence are alien to film." (Terrence, admittedly, had a better talent for pithy epigrams). If a witness can tell about something, it's highly likely that a photograph will show it—and with a damn sight more accuracy. Doesn't that mean, then, that the lawyer will seek the use of photographic evidence as frequently as possible? No, not so. Remember your role. You are an advocate, not a theologian; a partisan paraclete, not a eunuchoid umpire. The beliefs that you will attempt to make the jury adopt will cover a broad spectrum and, if categorized, will fall into one of three slots: those which are less than true, those that are true, those that are more than true. Photographic evidence will be reserved for the center slot. Indiscriminate use will either overshoot or undershoot the mark. Consequently the election to use photographic evidence will not depend on the subject matter but on your version of the facts. It's naive to say "A photograph is the best way to introduce evidence of automobile damage." Best for whom? If you represent a driver of a Volkswagen that was broadsided by a bus, then the axiom might apply, the picture being a "true" representation of the force of the impact as recited by your client. But the counsel for the carrier would keep such a photo in his briefcase claiming it to be a more-than-true distortion of the bus driver's testimony that he was travelling only ten miles an hour at the time of impact. And what if you represent a whiplash victim of a minor read end collision? The photo of an insignificant bumper scrape could hardly be considered the "best way" of explaining the accident. It would be a less-than-true representation of the sharp unexpected blow from the rear that snapped the sinews in your client's neck.

368

Of course there are some subjects of photographic evidence that will be recognized by the jury as being of particular value. Arguments can be advanced about the validity of a photograph of automobile damage in determining speed at time of impact but a photograph showing "line of sight" is almost conclusive as to the issue of visibility. Many an automobile case turns on the question of when a traffic hazard (be it an oncoming vehicle, a parked truck or a road surface defect) became visible to a motorist. A series of photographs taken at drivers' eye level, from his position on the roadway, at various points of distance from the hazard, will pretty well put that issue to rest. Hopefully, the truth of your client's recollection will jibe with the truth of the camera.

§ **13.6** Mechanics of Admission

The introduction of photographs into evidence is a twofold problem, identity and authentication of the exhibit and presentation to the jury. The first can usually be accomplished quite readily with the enactment of this simple ritual:

1. Have the court reporter mark the photograph as an exhibit.

2. Show the photograph to opposing counsel.

3. Ask the witness if the photograph, referring to it by exhibit number (in some jurisdictions "marked as Exhibit 1 for identification only") is a fair and accurate representation of the (here insert proper phrase "scene of the incident" "condition of the vehicle," etc.) as it existed on (insert appropriate date).

If there are a series of photographs of the same subject matter lump their presentation together and inquire if "exhibits 5 through 10 are fair and accurate representations—." As an elaboration of step two you might proffer the exhibit to the judge at this time or wait until the identity and authentication has been made and display them to his honor when requesting their introduction into evidence. At either time the judge may respond with an interested examination, a perfunctory perusal or a disdainful wave of the hand signifying "never mind." If the judge is apt to respond in this last fashion, it would seem advisable to eliminate the tender. If he wants to see them, let him ask, then respond with "Oh pardon me, your honor." Better to have it appear that you were guilty of an oversight in failing to offer the exhibits to the judge, than to have the judge undercut the value of your evidence by refusing to be bothered with a look.

There is only one hitch in the little trial vignette presented above. The assumption is made that the witness can respond in the affirmative regarding that query about the "fair and accurate representation." But what if he can't? What if the accident occurred with snow on the steps and the photograph of the offending stairway was taken in July? Or what if recent construction had altered the appearance of the intersection? The changes will not necessarily frustrate the use of your photograph. Acknowledge the change and qualify your presentation through an inquiry fashioned thus: "With the exception of the absence of snow from the steps, is this photograph, exhibit 4, a fair and accurate representation of the physical construction of the stairway as it existed on January 6, 1973?" Or perhaps, "It has been conceded that there has been a great deal of construction that has occurred in this area since the date of the accident, but as to the widths of the street, the terrain, the surfacing and the location of the stop signs is this photograph exhibit 2, a fair and accurate representation of those features as they existed on June 4, 1992?" In most instances the qualifications will suffice and the exhibit be accepted. If the changes would create confusion or surreptitiously introduce inadmissible evidence (i.e. subsequent repair) an opposite result can be anticipated.

In many cases the lay witness is adequate to authenticate the photographic exhibit but in some instances the professional photographer will have to be utilized. Not always "have to," sometimes the professional will be used for effect—simply to demonstrate the bigness of the case, the thoroughness of your preparation. The use of the pro in those instances is merely window dressing. But many times his role will be more vital and his testimony will be needed to either establish or buttress the authenticity of the physical evidence represented by the photograph.

Assume the use of a color photograph. Absent corroboration of the photographer as to the validity of the color print, the red scars on the purple bruises might be considered distortions by the judge and the exhibit rejected. A professional photographer who can explain the type of equipment used and the technique employed and further buttress the authenticity of his work by identifying the color bar on the photographs as that produced at trial (so a comparison, between the colors can be made), should have no trouble in authenticating the color photo.

And what of the series of photographs which seek to demonstrate the line of sight of a motorist approaching a curve or the crest of the hill? The problem demands something more than a series of random shots from a Rollex with the affirmation of an interested litigant that "I was one-hundred paces from what looked like the crest when I took this one." The professional photographer will have a profile map from the highway department to establish the location of the crest; determine the distances with his tape measure; shoot from a tripod the height of a six foot man seated in a '92 Corolla at a point from the center line where the driver in the center of the lane would be located. Now the court will admit the exhibits—and the jury should accept them as Gospel.

§ 13.7 Mechanics of Presentation

Once authenticated, the photograph, or photographs, will be offered into evidence and, if accepted, will be available to the jury. If the photograph is large enough it can be placed on an easel or pinned to a board and simply displayed in the jurors' view. If a conventional sized photograph, it may be passed to the jury, then if its importance warrants such practice or if it is to be referred to by subsequent witnesses, it may be put on display. The only techniques involved in the introduction of photographs is the timing of that event and the sequence of your offer. Most often counsel should be concerned with moving the trial along and conserving time. Thus, if ten photographs are to be introduced and there is no significance to the order in which they are to be viewed, it will help to start five at one end of the jury box and five at the other. The time consumed in the viewing of the exhibits will be halved. But it is false economy if the photos should be seen in sequence. The mechanics of introduction should be left to counsel and, in that case, he should insist that the exhibits pass through the hands of the jurors in the order presented.

Another false economy in time occurs when the interrogation continues as the jury views the exhibits. If a time conscious judge is apt to order you to "Proceed with interrogation" after the exhibits are offered into evidence and passed to the jury, it is wiser to complete your direct examination, then make your tender to the jury. In that event, your opponent's cross examination will be diluted by the jurors' split attention rather than your own examination.

371

D. MOTION PICTURES AND VIDEOTAPES

§ 13.8 Generally

Motion pictures or videotapes are of value only in that the movement depicted on the film is a fair representation of the movement observed. In the single photograph it is necessary to show that it is a true representation of the scene depicted. The law demands the same from the motion picture and in addition the assurance that the series of pictures are produced in such a time sequence that the illusion of motion is a true representation of the movement observed. Everyone is familiar with the distortions which can be effected with an ill-timed taking or projecting of motion film. Such a possibility necessitates proof that the film was taken and will be projected at such a rate that the movements depicted will be true and life-like.

As in the case of the single photograph there is the necessity of adequately identifying the plaintiff as the person portrayed in the motion pictures. Other technical proof must accompany the offer of the film into evidence to assure the court of its validity.

For instance, there should be proof of the continuity of the film. Again it is commonly known that certain distortions can be created by splicing the film and creating an artificial continuity. The party offering evidence of this nature undercuts the value of the film if it is edited in this fashion. In every instance it will affect the weight with which it will be regarded, in some instances it might even affect its admissibility. Even if there has been no splicing, as such, the editing may occur through the selective choice of the scenes chosen to be photographed. Ten or fifteen seconds of film depicting the plaintiff mowing the lawn followed by another abbreviated episode of climbing a ladder will certainly arouse suspicions as to the film's probative value. What happened during the other twenty minutes that he was mowing the lawn? Did he stop frequently to rest his back? Did he wince with pain as he bent to clean the blades? For a fair and convincing submission, the defendant should present an unedited event of sufficient length to establish the plaintiff's capacity for physical activity.

§ 13.9 Plaintiff's Use

The motion picture as a device for portraying plaintiff's injuries encounters the same objections as those raised against the courtroom demonstration. There is danger that the plaintiff will be caught up in the romance of "play acting" so that the filmed activity will not be a genuine portrayal of the condition which is sought to be shown. If the circumstances under which the motion pictures were taken provide some assurance of their validity, then they will be received in evidence, assuming other tests of admissibility are met.

Videotapes have been utilized to demonstrate the daily routine of a young child who suffered serious injuries resulting in substantial disability. Under such circumstance the court's decision to admit such evidence is supported by several factors:

1. The age of the child and the obvious seriousness of the injury dispel the fear of "play acting."

2. The magnitude of the injuries and the resulting extensive disability compel the use of some type of evidence other than oral testimony to convey the full impact of the injury.

3. The nature of the disability pervades every aspect of the victim's existence and hampers his ability to perform the simplest of tasks. In the interest of time alone it is desirable to utilize the motion picture as a succinct, realistic and believable representation of the injuries and thus avoid a lengthy oral description which would be limited by the communicative capacity of the witness and perhaps distorted by his subjective attitude.

The motion picture may also be used to portray certain medical experiments or clinical tests to which the plaintiff was subjected. The use of motion pictures in this regard can be most effective if the tests are such that the results cannot be feigned. If the plaintiff has suffered a nerve injury resulting in a loss of sensation, a motion picture showing a lack of response to pin prick would obviously be more persuasive than a doctor simply stating the fact.

§ 13.10 Defendant's Use

The motion picture is more often utilized as a tool for defendant. Nothing is more effective to disprove a plaintiff's claim of disability than a motion picture portraying the plaintiff doing the very things that he claimed he could not do.

In this instance there is no problem concerning the authenticity of plaintiff's actions. The only legal question of admissibility which might present itself to the defendant is the matter of identification. Most frequently surveillance motion pictures are taken under "cloak and dagger" type circumstances which don't always lend themselves to the best picture taking techniques. If possible, the film should show the features of the plaintiff with sufficient clarity for identification. If this is impossible the locale or activity should provide additional proof of identity. The pictures are more likely to be accepted as authentic portrayals of the plaintiff if the subject is photographed at his home or his place of employment. Film of a person which does not clearly reveal facial features that resemble the plaintiff in his body build, gait and other physical characteristics might well be rejected if taken in a public place with no buttressing proof of identity.

§ 13.11 Defendant's Use—Policy Considerations

Any consideration of the use of motion pictures by the defendant for the purpose of impeaching a plaintiff's claim of injury must include the recognition of "backlash" effect that may result from the use of evidence surreptitiously acquired. With pardons to Robert Frost, "Something there is that doesn't like a snoop." More ill will might be directed against a "Peeping Tom" lying in wait with a telephoto lens than a plaintiff who has overstated his injuries.

Before introducing motion pictures into evidence these factors must be weighed.

1. What were the circumstances under which the plaintiff was filmed? In this regard, consideration must be given first to the place of the taking. Did the camera invade the sanctity of the home or was it content with the backyard shot? Next, was any deceit practiced upon the plaintiff? Did the cameraman assume a false role to gain access to the plaintiff? Or worse yet, was a situation staged so as to lure the plaintiff into the performance of a physically demanding task? (It is not unknown for an ambitious sleuth to seek the help of a plaintiff to help change a flat tire. While the "good Samaritan" strains over a jack an accomplice is recording his physical capacity on film. Quaere: with whom will the jury identify and who will more offend their sense of fair play?)

2. How successfully do the films dispute the claim of injury? If the cameraman has recorded some disability but less than that claimed by the plaintiff, the pictures will cut both ways. They might restrict the claim to some extent

but they will indisputably verify some injury. For motion pictures to serve the best interests of the defendant they must fulfill a two fold purpose: establish the fact of plaintiff's physical capacity, and make the plaintiff out as a liar. The second function will not be served if they merely reveal a tendency to exaggerate the injury. This may be excused as a natural "rationalization." If such explanation will suffice, the films might best be kept in the can.

The defendant must be careful in the manner in which motion pictures are used in settlement discussions. Basically they are impeachment evidence and, as in the case of evidence of this nature, their chief value lies in surprise. The plaintiff who is forewarned of the existence of incriminating motion pictures is in position to mitigate their effect to such a point that they may be valueless. Knowing that the defendant has taken pictures of him mowing the lawn or climbing a ladder, the plaintiff explains on direct examination that on one or two occasions he has endeavored to do certain chores around the house and although he was able to do them without discomfort he had a terrible recurrence of pain that night.

Even if the defendant's counsel does not disclose the nature of the films but merely hints "We know that your client is lying about his injuries," the plaintiff's lawyer is alerted and the client admonished to carefully review his protestations of disability lest he overstate them.

The defendant's counsel must decide which course to follow. If he feels that a disclosure of the incriminating films will effect a reappraisal of plaintiff's demand and bring about a favorable settlement, then the disclosure should be made. Perhaps the films are so incriminating that the plaintiff will be revealed as a complete fraud to his unsuspecting attorney and the case will be dismissed. If either of those two events are not likely to occur, the possession of the films should remain unrevealed and their use reserved for trial.

E. MODELS

§ 13.12 Generally

Although not to be found in any hornbook, there is an expression of law that lies somewhere between codification and

"Confucius say"—"The more esoteric the evidence, the more resistance there will be to its introduction." The trial judges find a great deal of comfort in knowing that other courts on other occasions have done the same thing. Their choice of roads is the one more traveled by. Many shun the role of trail blazer and view an untrodden way not as a possible route to the sunlit uplands but rather as a sure path to the slough of appellate review. Knowing the likelihood of such hesitancy that might be encountered, the lawyer seeking to introduce an anatomical model, chart, or drawing should lay a foundation that will assure the court of the need for the exhibit and its common place use. Neither of these two elements should be taken for granted, nor need they be established by counsel's argument in the judge's chambers.

§ 13.13 Mechanics of Admission

It is the medical expert that should lay the foundation for the introduction of the exhibit. The interrogation may proceed in this fashion.

Q. Doctor, before you attempt to explain this injury to the jury, could you tell us whether or not in your study of medicine in medical school certain visual aids were used to help the students learn of the various structures of the human body?
A. Yes, we used such things as films, models, charts throughout our medical training.
Q. Have you brought with you an anatomical model of the spine such as those which are used in the medical schools?
A. Yes I have.
Q. Would the use of this anatomical model aid you in explaining Mrs. Jones' injury?
A. Yes and I'm sure it would aid the jury in understanding the medical problems involved in her case.

The model may then be marked as an exhibit and utilized by the medical expert in his oral testimony.

The use of any exhibit as a supplement to oral testimony presents a problem for appellate review. The natural inclination of the witness is to point to the exhibit and state, "This is the area in which we found the fracture." The demonstration is meaningful only to those present and is unintelligible to an appellate court reading the record. This problem has even greater implications if an exhibit has been used in connection with a deposition that is to be read to the jury. In that case the interrogating lawyer must be sure that the references to the exhibit and the identification of its parts be described orally so that the written record can easily be followed by the jury. The testimony might be preserved in the following manner:

Q. Doctor, will you refer to the model of the knee marked Exhibit A as you testify?

A. Alright.

Q. What did your initial examination reveal?

A. At the time of our initial examination he had a marked effusion, which is fluid on the knee joint. He also had laxity of the tibial collateral ligament, the main ligament that is on the inside of the knee.

Q. Now, you have made a reference to a ligament and I wonder if you could mark the name on a piece of tape, doctor, and attach it to that part of the model that you were referring to.

Q. Upon that tentative diagnosis what did you undertake to do, doctor?

A. On July 17th under general anesthetic an operative procedure was performed on the right knee of Mr. Brown.

Q. And could you demonstrate on the model where the incision was made and what you did?

A. An incision was made over the outer part of the model as I have indicated with this red mark.

Q. Then after making the incision what did you do?

A. There was blood found in the knee joint space.

Q. Is this an unusual condition?

A. This is an abnormal finding and indicates that an injury had occurred. A tear in the anterior portion of the tibial collateral ligament was noted; so this would mean the front part toward the kneecap of this ligament was torn. The anterior cruciate ligament was found intact.

Q. Now, where is that to be found on the model?

A. It runs in a semi-vertical position, beginning on the back of the thigh bone, runs between the notches, or these condyles of the lower end of the thigh bone and attaches to the upper end of the leg bone on the front portion.

Q. Will you mark that with a tape bearing its name?

A. Yes.

Q. According to my observation it appears to be the ligament that attaches the thigh bone to the shin bone, is that true?

A. This ligament is on the inside of the knee and is one of four major ligaments that attaches the thigh bone to the leg bone.

Q. Did you identify this as being a source of Mr. Brown's trouble?

A. I did.

377

Q. Now, you indicated you had found some effusion over the medial aspect of the knee. Where is that to be found on the model?

A. He had an effusion in the knee joint. The knee joint is the area that is in gray so that this was swollen larger than it should have been, with fluid in the knee joint.

Q. You have removed a portion of the model in order to reach the gray area and that seems to be right in what we would call the front of the knee?

A. The front of the knee and it's the entire front of the knee. This is what in layman's terms would be termed water on the knee.

Q. Now, upon receiving this history and upon this initial observation what course of treatment did you attempt to follow?

A. On the basis of physical examination it was my opinion that he had a tear of the tibial collateral ligament and a tear of the medial meniscus. He also had a tear of the anterior cruciate ligament.

Q. Now, you have referred to two additional parts of the knee and I wonder if you could identify those on the model, write their names on these strips of tape and append them to the appropriate parts.

A. Yes.

Q. It appears that the medial meniscus is a cartilage which lies to the side of the knee, is that right?

A. To the side.

Q. And in this instance was it that meniscus which was to the inside of the knee which was involved?

A. To the inside. This is correct.

F. DIAGRAMS

§ 13.14 Generally

The beginning of any story seeks to orient the listener to a geographical location—and so it is with most trials.

The prosecutor or plaintiff is anxious for the jury to comprehend the physical environs of the bank that was robbed, the room in which the murder was committed, the intersection where the accident occurred, etc. Verbal descriptions alone seldom suffice. Photographs frequently distort distances. The obvious solution is a diagram.

§ 13.15 Spontaneous

Depending upon the complexity of the information sought to be conveyed and the use to which it is to be put, it may be that a free hand drawing of a geographical area will be acceptable, that is, adequate to inform the jury and tolerated by the court. This need may arise at any time, from opening statement through closing argument. The first consideration is the medium to be employed. Don't let the facility in the particular court room dictate your choice. If the situation demands a visual aid of a particular type see to it that all the ingredients are available. Most modern court rooms have blackboards, chalk, easels and grease pencils, but the in-house accommodations stop there. It will be up to you to supply the paste board, the artist's pad, the colored chalk, etc.

The factors to be utilized in choosing an effective medium for the spontaneous diagram are:

1.   how easily can the illustration be made;

2.   how readily can it be utilized by the jury;

3.   how can it be incorporated into the record.

The last two factors practically eliminate the use of a black-board even though it probably ranks first for ease of illustration and convenience. But a blackboard is easily erased (most often by opposing lawyer who wants to use a diagram of his own) and seldom will the illustration survive either for later reference by the jury or for inclusion in the record for appeal. Note should be made that these inadequacies can be resolved by making a Polaroid shot of the blackboard but the logistics of such an effort leaves little for recommendation.

A more effective medium is the artist pad and grease pencil. The 3×5 sheet is easily seen, the grease pencil is a facile tool, the pad is readily displayed on a movable easel and, perhaps most significantly, each sheet may be marked as an exhibit, sent to the jury room during deliberations and included in the written record on appeal.

The most serious impediment to the use of the free hand diagram or illustration is its probative value. The opposition might very well raise the objection that "the drawing is not to scale and will mislead the jury." The usual counter is, "We are using the drawing for illustrative purposes only and it is meant to assist the jury to orient themselves to the location of the incident."

It's then up to the judge to decide whether the value outweighs the possible confusion and that decision is a discretionary call that will rarely be grounds for reversal.

§ 13.16 Prepared

The prepared diagram meets the objection of "misleading and confusing" for now we are dealing with a geographical location drawn to scale. The only possible error might arise from the use to which it is put. A properly scaled drawing of a highway has little authenticity if it is used with model vehicles not drawn to the same scale. Or a scaled drawing of the murder apartment has little authority if a lay witness sketches in, with no consideration for relative size, the location of certain landmarks. Once the scale is established all other referential use of the diagram should be similarly scaled.

The scaled drawing is more readily accepted for evidentiary use because of its authenticity—but that authenticity must be established. Labeling something as a scaled diagram doesn't make it so. There must be proof of accurate measurement, then accurate draftsmanship. This authentication is most readily accomplished at pretrial conference. Indeed, local court practice may dictate that such exhibits be identified and authenticated before trial. If the option lies with the attorney, the following considerations should be reviewed before electing to utilize pretrial procedures or formally authenticate the diagram before the jury. Pretrial admission is simpler, cheaper and faster. An examination of the proposed exhibit by your opponent will usually satisfy any doubts as to the accuracy of the diagram and an agreement will be reached as to its admissibility.

Authentication before a jury will necessitate the expense of calling the person who prepared the diagram and the time of adducing proof of the measurements taken, scale employed, etc. On the plus side, however, is the fact that such time and expense may enhance the value of the exhibit to the jury and demonstrate to them that here is an advocate who cares.

One parting caution to the opposing advocate. The use of diagrams, even when properly measured and accurately scaled can be misleading through the selection or omission of landmarks. A diagram which depicts an intersection showing only the curblines, traffic markings and stop signs will unduly emphasize those characteristics of the scene. Locating on the diagram the buildings, trees, parked cars, etc., will give a more realistic representation of the conditions confronting the drivers on the day of the accident. Making sure that the diagram is accurate as far as it goes, is not sufficient to protect your client. Make sure that it goes far enough.

G. STATISTICAL INFORMATION

§ 13.17 Life and Work Expectancies

A civil case seeking recovery for serious injuries will involve the presentation of certain statistical data. In the event that a permanent injury has been suffered, most jurisdictions will entertain evidence of the life expectancy of the plaintiff. In the event of wrongful death, the life expectancy of both the victim and his dependent survivor become relevant. The expected longevity of human life is not a fixed scientific fact to be likened to the speed of light or the rate of descent of falling bodies. Life expectancy tables are compiled by actuarial experts using scores of factors and hosts of figures to arrive at a conclusion as to the length of survival of a person of a particular age. Because life expectancy is an opinion and because that opinion will be based upon the factors considered (race, occupation, sex, geography, social status, etc.) there will be some variances among "the standard tables."

Thus if the life expectancy of several persons are in issue and proof of several tables are submitted, the jury will have presented to them a compilation of statistics that might not be readily retained. If these figures are of sufficient importance to be submitted to a jury they are of sufficient importance to cause them to be remembered. An exhibit in the form of a chart listing the appropriate statistics will provide the aid to the jury's memory.

The need for a visual presentation is in direct proportion to the number of such statistics which are introduced into evidence. If the plaintiff's injuries have rendered him incapable of further employment then the work expectancy of the plaintiff becomes relevant.

The projection of work expectancy will be determined by a number of factors; gender, type of work, retirement plans, etc. Again the testimony of an expert will be desirable, and in some cases necessary to present these figures to a jury and the verbal presentation will be greatly enhanced through the utilization of a visual aid.

§ 13.18 Present Value Tables

Of course the ultimate issue is the economic loss suffered through this impairment of work capacity and consequently additional figures must be introduced to establish the present value of the earnings to be lost in the future. The plaintiff cannot be content with proof that the plaintiff would have been expected to work another ten years at his present wage of eight thousand dollars and that he is therefore entitled to eighty thousand dollars for this loss. The problem is to determine what lump sum, awarded now and invested, would allow periodic withdrawals in the amount of monthly earnings for the ten years of expected work length. The amount representing this present value of periodic payments over a length of time will vary according to the interest rate which it will draw. Since the future interest rate is impossible to ascertain with certainty, the actuarial witness will usually give a range of figures based on several rates. This entails still additional figures which are likely to be forgotten without the aid of demonstrative proof.

Some jurisdictions demand that the plaintiff adduce such proof of present value in the event that a claim is made for future losses. Others make no such demand and the issue may be submitted without such computations being made. In such a circumstance the plaintiff is left with a tactical decision: should he adduce proof of present value thus reducing his claim but achieving an appearance of fairness, or should he leave such proof to the defendant thus creating the necessity of defendant dealing with the damage issue? Most opt for the former.

CHAPTER 14

EXPERT WITNESSES

"An expert is an ordinary person fifty miles from home with a briefcase"
Anonymous

Analysis

---

§ 14.1 Introduction

The testimony adduced in court is basically factual in nature. It is left to the jury to reach opinions and conclusions from those facts. On occasion an opinion is tolerated from a witness and (with the exception of the "collective facts rule") such occasions are confined to instances when the subject matter is beyond the ken of the jury and the witness possesses certain qualifications.

The qualification that the opinion testifier must possess is frequently stated as being that of an "expert." There is some question as to the advisability of employing that term for such a purpose. The word itself is ill-defined having some connotations which are incompatible with its use as a legal term. Webster says an expert is, "A person who is very skillful and highly trained and informed in some special field."

Two additional connotations blunt the meaning of the word. There is a suggestion of quackery about it. One finds himself unwittingly inserting a prefix to create a term more readily understood. "Self styled expert" and "so called expert" are phrases found with such ubiquity that the first two appendages are often read into the mother word automatically. The same deprecating connotation inspired the quipster's definition of an expert as being "anyone with a brief case who is more than fifty miles from home."

While this first connotation suggests a belittlement, the second does just the opposite. There is an element of comparison that is incorporated into the meaning of the word. Given a group of persons who have special knowledge in a particular subject, there is a resistance to label everyone as an expert. It is quite predictable that someone confronting the group would inquire, "Who are the experts?", in the sense of "Who are the wisest of the wise?" Ask a group of trial lawyers a question of law and quite likely they will defer to the judgment of the most learned among those present with the explanation, "Ask Bill, he's the expert." Used in this sense there is no absolute standard to determine a person's expertise but rather a "marking on the curve" which identifies the better or perhaps the best as the true expert.

§ 14.2 Role of Expert Witness

Federal Rule of Evidence 702 provides:

> If scientific, technical, or other specialized knowledge will assist the trier of fact to understand the evidence or to determine a fact in issue, a witness qualified as an expert by knowledge, skill, experience, training, or education, may testify thereto in the form of an opinion or otherwise.

Before considering the role that the expert is to play in the preparation and trial of a lawsuit, it is pertinent to be reacquainted with the role that the lawyer must play. The lawyer is an advocate. He is a partisan seeking a result that is beneficial to his client. He becomes his client's alter ego, gathering those facts and setting forth those arguments which the client himself would advance if he were able.

To support those arguments he must have evidence. Witnesses must be interviewed, measurements taken, opinions sought. The marshaling of this evidence is not simply a quest for the truth—it is rather an effort to uncover those facts and opinions which will buttress his client's position and support his claim or his defense. This is the genius of the advocacy system. The truth seeking is left to the finders of fact, the judge or the jury. That truth can best be determined by two partisan advocates presenting their respective cases as vigorously as possible.

Some elements of the case, of course, will be absolute in their nature. The factual content is self evident and indisputable. The street in question is 30 feet wide and that's that. Neither argument nor wit can add a foot or take an inch from it. But for every such irrefutable fact in a contested lawsuit there are a host of other facts the validity of which depend upon subjective evaluation. The width of the street can be measured by an objective standard. Begging Miss Stein's pardon, a yard is a yard is a yard. But what of the testimony of witness A who says that the plaintiff was traveling down that street at 40 miles per hour? There is no objective standard to apply. The truth of this fact depends upon a number of things: the propensity of the witness to tell the truth, the position from which he viewed the automobile, the period of time he witnessed the automobile, his experience in driving, etc.

What does an advocate do when the name of a potential witness to the accident is uncovered? A personal contact is made with an attempt to establish a friendly rapport. A sympathetic climate is sought to be developed for his client. Once the proper mood is established, the investigator does not simply invite the witness to tell all she knows with a reassuring, "All we want are the facts, ma'am." He will question her carefully, seek to develop the points favorable to his case, minimize those which are unfavorable and, in so doing, provide evidence that will advance his client's cause. If unsuccessful, other witnesses are sought who will provide the testimony necessary for a proper presentation or defense. Summing up, we might say that the role of the advocate in the preparation of his case will vary depending upon the nature of the evidence which he seeks to advance. If it is pure factual objective data (the width of a road, the view from a crossing, the time sequence of an electric light) he is a gatherer of statistics. But if the evidence is characterized by subjective appraisal depending for its value upon the credibility of the witness and the quality of his observance, then he is a full-blown advocate, picking and choosing the evidence he will use and seeking to develop that evidence to his best advantage.

What of the evidence from an expert? Into what category does it fall? Is it purely factual objective data? If so, the lawyer should take it as it comes, find the most competent expert to make the examination (just as we'd use a 12–inch ruler to measure the street) gather his statistics and lay the unvarnished results before the fact finder and hope that they aid his client. On the other hand, if expert testimony has the element of subjective appraisal, if it is an art as well as a science, if there are still areas of dispute among the experts (a question as to how many inches are in a foot) then the lawyer as an advocate is free, and perhaps compelled, to approach the expert witness as he would the lay witness, establish the rapport, create a sympathetic climate for his client and develop those points favorable to his client's case.

§ 14.3 Attributes—Generally

There are a number of factors which will substantially affect the attributes which you seek for your expert. The more important such factors are:

1. Professional Background

Certainly it can be of help if the nature of the expert's own background is known, particularly his own professional background. If a doctor has been a practicing physician over a number of years and is successful in his practice it usually will mean that he has developed a certain bedside manner, a warmth and concern for his patients that will carry over into his testimony if he is called upon to appear in court. On the other hand if his professional background has been in the area of research, if he has been a salaried practitioner on a hospital staff, it is more than likely that he has never had the opportunity to develop to the same extent a concern about his patients' welfare. His attitudes will have been directed along scientific lines rather than in dealing with humanity and undoubtedly his personality will reflect his background.

2. Previous Expert Opinions

Another thing of significance to ascertain is whether or not the particular expert has taken a professional stand in regard to a controversial area which might be involved in the case. Assume that the plaintiff is afflicted with a cancerous condition and the proof will attempt to relate a series of traumas to the inception of the malignant condition. This subject matter has been explored by many doctors and many medical articles have been written concerning it. If the doctor had previously expressed a skepticism of the likelihood that trauma is related to cancer and has published some monographs or medical articles in this field, then it would be difficult to expect him to render a decision which would be in contradiction to a previous point of view. He might fulfill all the other favorable characteristics, but if he has already taken a position in regard to this matter, it is a pretty good indication as to what his conclusions will be and there is no need to waste his time and that of the lawyer and client in seeking out an answer to medical causation which will be hostile to the point of view which must be adduced.

3. Point of View

The trial practitioner, having had the opportunity of hearing medical practitioners testify, realizes that doctors and other experts being human, frequently consider the problems of medical causation and the nature and extent of injuries from a predetermined point of view. They will, by nature, tend to be sympathetic or callous; or somewhere in between. They may accept complaints of injury as presumptively bona fide or reject them on the basis that all claimants are malingerers. If the attorney acknowledges that such personality characteristics exist, then he must consider them in seeking out the doctor who is to serve as his medical expert.

Regardless of how capable an expert might be within his particular field, if he is of the nature that he views a claimant with distrust, decries the effort to secure money through litigation, and suspects all plaintiffs as thieves then it would be foolish for a plaintiff's attorney to submit his client to such an expert.

§ 14.4   Attributes—Personality

With this preliminary information to guide him the lawyer should arrange a personal interview, hear the expert talk, note his mannerisms, grasp some understanding of his professional ken and, most importantly, determine his attitude toward the client's case. If he appears sympathetic to the cause, if he displays a winsome personality and if he articulates well, he very likely will be a good candidate as an expert witness.

Admittedly the guidelines for ascertaining the proper personality are rather vague. When in doubt fall back on the ole reliable, "Would you buy a used car from him?"

§ 14.5   Attributes—Professionalism

This qualification of the expert is more easily stated than described. It is an element quite apart from a pleasant personality. It is an aura of erudition that somehow emanates from some learned persons and not from others. It might be in the physical appearance: the greying temples, the mustache, the effusive eyebrows—any number of traits which contribute to the appellation of "distinguished." It might be in the bearing: the tilt of the head, the slump of the shoulders, the manner of dress, the style of speech, etc. Whatever contributes to it, you'll know if your expert witness has this mystique of professionalism or not. If he doesn't, his worth will be sorely diminished. If he does, his words will be heard and heavily weighed for he will "speak not as the others but as one with authority."

§ 14.6   Attributes—Translating Expertise

The ability to analogize a complicated problem into understandable language for a lay jury is a gift that too few experts possess. Without it, however, the expert despite his pleasing personality, attractive looks and broad knowledge in his field, will not be the best witness. It is difficult to conceive of any area of expertise that will not take some type of explaining in order to be fully understood by a lay jury of "average ignorance." He must be able to express his esoteric knowledge in simple terms. A few illustrations will suffice to indicate the importance of a picturesque ability to analogize in each of the foregoing fields.

§ 14.7   Attributes—Translating Expertise—Illustration

Assume that the case before the jury involves the rupture of an intervertebral lumbar disc. The doctor has been asked to describe the pathology of the lumbar disc. His "explanation" follows:

"The intervertebral disc is composed of cartilagineous plates enclosing it above and below, the nucleus pulposus and the annulus fibrosis. The nucleus pulposus is a semiliquid consistency attached to and contained within the annulus fibrosis. Microscopically the nucleus pulposus is composed of a loose network of fibrous strands. These run irregularly, but at the margins where the nucleus joins the cartilage plates these strands have a firm attachment. The elasticity in the turgescence varies with the age of the person involved and can be affected by the presence of certain diseases. With age the elasticity of the nucleus pulposus decreases and the disc frequently becomes degenerated and fibrosed.

"The function of the intervertebral disc is to act as a shock absorber in the intervertebral space. It also permits and limits the flexibility of the spine. If the limiting structure of the nucleus pulposus is impaired in strain or if the pressure within the annulus fibrosis is increased the whole structure may be prolapsed.

"Trauma may be an ideologic factor in the rupture of an intervertebral disc. If there is undue torsional strain the nucleus may be caused to herniate through the annulus fibrosis. Prolapse may also occur if there is a lifting strain and it is applied to the lumbar area. If the herniation of the nucleus pulposus occurs through the posterior portion of the annulus fibrosis it will encroach upon the spinal cord and the nerve roots. This in turn will cause pain and symptomology in the lower extremity."

Now undoubtedly a recitation such as this in a medical class would result in the student receiving an adequate grade because of his ability to articulate with the jargon of the proper medical terms. However to a lay jury the recitation will have little or no meaning. Following is a transcript of an actual case in which a doctor who could very well fulfill his role as a medical reciter in a medical class, also happened to possess the earthy quality of being able to translate this medical cant into understandable terms for the lay jury.

Q. Did you have occasion to see and treat the plaintiff, and, if so, tell the first time you saw her and what her complaints were to you and what, if anything, you did?

A. The plaintiff came to my office on April 30, 1993 at which time I obtained a history from the patient prior to the examination. The examination of the patient showed her to be about thirty-nine years old, white, female, normally developed, 5′ 8″ tall, weighing 150 pounds. The patient was wearing a plastic neck brace. Examination with particular reference to the head, neck, shoulders and upper extremities showed that there was marked limitation of motion in the neck in all directions. There was tenderness over the front part of her cervical spine in its midportion. There was tenderness over the insertion of a certain muscle group on the neck which is referred to as anterior scalenus muscle on the left. And there was tenderness along the vertebral border of the left shoulder blade. There was no limitation of motion in the shoulder joints. There was no significant difference in muscle measurements of the upper extremities of the two sides. I found that the biceps, triceps and brachioradialis reflexes were active bilaterally. These reflexes are obtained by hitting certain areas with a hammer and observing the responding reactive jerk. If there is a jerk, the vigor of the jerk is compared with the same jerk on the other side. These are muscle reflexes we talk about. I found them to be active, and they did respond, and symmetrical.

The clinical picture, as judged by the complaints of the patient and the pattern of distribution of sore spots, as elicited by pushing at certain key areas, I came to the conclusion that the picture was one of discogenic pain syndrome. This term means a pattern of pain which by experience we know most likely produced by deranged or damaged disc. In this particular case, in the neck. And in order to substantiate this clinical diagnosis, which is so far based primarily on subjective findings, I recommended that a special test be performed, which is called discogram. Discography was recommended.

Q.   Would a model of the spine or of the neck be helpful to you in explaining the anatomy and in explaining the situation in this patient?

A.   Yes.

Q.   Can you tell me what plaintiff's Exhibit 17 appears to be, and identify this for me?

A.   Exhibit 17 is a plastic model of a cervical spine. Attached to the cervical spine on the top is a portion of the skull, the occipital portion of the skull. As you can see, the cervical spine is composed of one, two, three, four, five, six, seven cervical vertebrae. Each one of these little white bodies are cervical vertebrae. The things sticking out to the side like little crossbars are the transverse processes, which in the back articulate with each other, uniting these bodies by these small joints. In the back we see the so-called laminae and spinous processes, which cover the spinal canal, and cover the spinal cord which runs inside of the spinal canal. The part we are

interested in here are the connections between the vertebral
bodies established by the discs. These slightly darker areas
here represent the cervical discs. The cervical discs can be
compared somewhat to a tiny small hockey puck. It consists
of a tough outer ring, the annulus fibrosis, and a softer center
portion, the nucleus pulposus. They have the function of
joints, connecting the vertebral bodies to each other. And
also the function of shock absorbers, giving a degree of resil-
iency to the spine. If we suspect that the internal structure is
damaged, either by degeneration or by trauma, we perform
what is called a discogram. The discogram is done by introducing a fine needle, actually two of them, a heavier and finer
needle, and a few drops of a substance, watery substance, is
then injected, which can be seen on the X-ray. Now, if the
center portion is surrounded by a normal, healthy annulus
fibrosis, then the dye will remain in the nucleus pulposus and
outline it. If, on the other hand, there are tears in the
annulus fibrosis, then the dye will go along those tears, and
we can see them when we take the picture. A disc may be
deranged internally and show tears on the discogram and not
hurt. In this case, it would indicate that the particular disc
has nothing to do with the patient's pain. On the other hand,
if the patient reports pain on injection, then the patient will
be able to tell whether or not the pain goes into similar areas
as his own pain, and whether or not the pain has the same
character as his own pain. Usually if this occurs the pain is
momentarily more severe. So the discogram gives us two
types of information: one, visually, and the other the pain
response of the patient. And in this manner we can determine whether or not a damaged disc is responsible for what
the patient complains of.

Q. After you performed the tests at Missouri Baptist Hospital,
    did the test reveal that there were internal ruptures?

A. A discogram was performed on May 4, 1993, under local
    anesthesia. The discs were examined. At the levels of C–5–6
    and C–4–5 the injection of the disc space caused the patient to
    experience pain radiating into the right shoulder and right
    arm. The patient recognized this pain as being identical with
    a type of spontaneous pain she does experience in these same
    areas. Review of the spot films showed that the dye had at
    both of these levels extended into the right joint and to the
    back, indicating the presence of posterial tears between the
    sixth and seventh cervical vertebrae. The pain initially went
    into the right shoulder and the right arm, down to the elbow.
    Upon additional injection the pain also went into the left arm.
    The pain at this level was also associated with pain at the
    base of the neck. Again, the patient recognized these pain

areas and the character of the pain to be identical with portions of her own spontaneous pain pattern. This is a rather tedious and somewhat painful process, but her pain responses were very accurate, and with regard to the distribution of dye, which corresponded to the site on which she experienced the pain, as well as to referred pain with regard to the area of the front portion of the spine touched by the needle tip. I mention this merely because it indicates that although we are dealing with pain responses we have here an immediate control as to whether or not such a subjective response has value, and the patient's responses were such that they could be checked by facts and, consequently, they must have been correct. In view of the fact that the patient was suffering from quite severe chronic discomfort and had not responded to extensive conservative measures, I recommended treatment consisting of disc removal and fusion of the cervical bodies, at C–6–7 and 5–6.

Q. And did you perform the operation, Doctor?

A. Yes.

Q. In an operation such as you have mentioned, will you tell us briefly how it is performed?

A. The operation consists essentially of completely removing what you have seen here of the discs. They are excised and removed, so that in place of the disc we have now an empty space. This empty space is then enlarged by making a drill hole in the center portion of the vertebral bodies, which removes a half cylindrical-shaped portion from the body above and below, so that if you will look at it now then you have a picture like you would be looking down into a cylindrical-shaped well. This hole goes all the way through the vertebral body to the point where it is touching the spinal canal. Before this is done a piece or two pieces, as many pieces as is needed, of bone, previously have been removed from the hip bone of the patient with a circular saw in such a manner that that piece of bone fits that cylindrical hole exactly like a peg fits a hole in a piece of furniture. And after the disc is removed and the hole is made, this piece of bone then is tapped into place so that it now unites the two adjacent vertebral bodies solidly in a mechanical sense. It doesn't become solid in a medical sense until the living bone cells have performed what we understand by a fusion, causing a knitting between the piece that we have within and the surrounding vertebral bodies. In this patient's case this principle was used at two levels, between the 5th and 6th and the 6th and 7th vertebral bodies.

§ **14.8** Attributes—Defense of Position

There is yet another quality that the good expert witness must possess. That is a willingness and a capacity to defend the opinion he is giving when, under cross-examination, he is subject to perhaps conflicting authorities or qualifying circumstances. It is one thing to lead an expert through direct examination and have him supply the necessary proof. It is quite another to have him withstand a searching cross-examination which is designed to have him qualify his opinions and perhaps even back away from them to such an extent that the initial testimony no longer has any probative value.

The expert cannot afford to be a passive, compromising personality willing to accept all conflicting points of view and tolerant of each of them. When the chips are down and the confrontation arises he must be willing to stand flatfooted on the opinion that he has given, basing it upon his own expertise, his own experience in the field. If his background is challenged, he must be willing to defend it and not be hesitant to unapologetically tell of his background and training.

Again then, the attributes that an expert must possess in order to fulfill his role are: (1) a predisposition, determined by personality and background, which will dispose him to an appraisal compatible with the advocate's interest; (2) a professional background which will be compatible with the point of view which is sought to be developed in the case; (3) a pleasant personality and an ability to articulate and express himself in terms understandable to a lay jury; and (4) a willingness and capacity to defend the opinion that he has given and perhaps even assume the role of an advocate if and when the situation develops.

§ **14.9** Dealing With the Expert

There is a downside to the selection of an expert who possesses these attributes. The self same characteristics will make it difficult, or at least awkward, for you to work with him. Consider a comparison of the two of you in respect to those attributes which so often, (we might say too often) reflects the case system that exists in our society. If typical of the lawyer-expert relationship, the figures tote up as follows:

Age—older than you;

Wealth—richer than you;

Education—more academic credentials than you;

Experience—(the most embarrassing of all) more time in court than you.

When you get together to confer, add another psychologically significant factor: it will be at his convenience and at his office. Add all these factors together and guess who is apt to be dominating the discussion? But if you're the advocate you must assume the lead role. It is you that has the primary responsibility for the welfare of your client. It is you who knows (or should know) both the content and the form in which the expert's testimony should be presented. Draw upon those realizations and take charge. Typically, taking charge means that it will be necessary for you to do the following. First, acquaint the expert with the rules which govern his testimony. Artificiality in which information is presented to a jury is at its height when it involves expert testimony. Who would ever say, in scientific or lay company, "My opinion, based on reasonable scientific certainty, is _____" Yet that is the verbiage that establishes the threshold of admissibility in most jurisdictions.

Nor would most experts recognize the difference between saying

"I'm twenty five percent certain that this head injury will develop into traumatic epilepsy" and

"I'm one hundred percent certain there's a one out of four chance that this injury will develop into traumatic epilepsy."

We have word games to play and they must play with our rules.

Another basic problem is the gap that lies between science and law. The expert trained as a scientist is functioning in a foreign field when he enters the legal arena. The certainty of the slide rule is abandoned for the rule of law. The immutable laws of physics is forgotten for the shifting concepts of reasonable care and foreseeable results.

These differences are not merely of a philosophical nature of interest only to the casuist. In some instances your experts' willingness to forget his scientific training and accept the language and pedantry of the law will determine his use in the courtroom. One such instance is the problem that arises in proving causation. The word has different meanings for the

394

scientist and the lawyer. Ask a doctor if cigarette smoking causes cancer and the answer will be "no." From a scientific point of view, if it did every smoker would contract cancer. The legal concept of causation is less demanding. The legal requisite of causation will be satisfied if an event precipitates, aggravates or accelerates a condition. Don't assault your medical expert with an inquiry about causation. Ask him if there is a connection between the event and the patient's condition. Once you have established the scientifically accepted "connection" you can semantically evolve into the legally accepted "causation."

§ 14.10 Purpose of Expert

In order for us to understand the purpose of the expert witness in general it might be more easily understood if we examined a particular kind of expert. The one most often found in litigation, the medical expert. His purpose as a witness will fall into three distinct categories:

1. A description of the injury;

2. The cause of the injury;

3. The consequences of the injury.

Assume a simple case where a client walking down a flight of steps stumbles and falls. He experiences immediate pain in his lower leg and observes the bone sticking through his skin. The leg is casted and knits, but at trial time there is tenderness at the site of the fracture and pain upon prolonged use or a change in the weather. How will the three elements be established? Must a medical witness be called? Can lay testimony suffice?

The injury can be easily described and just as easily understood by any juror: "a broken leg."

The cause of the injury is apparent: "I fell and broke my leg."

The consequences of the injury might not be quite so apparent, but still it would be hypertechnical fatuity to deny the probative value of the victim's testimony that "my leg still hurts from the accident."

But not all injuries are so easily described, so apparently traumatic, with such obvious results. If they are not, if the injury, its cause and its consequences are beyond the pale of the average juror's understanding, then a medical expert will have to testify in order to fill the void of ignorance and establish the quantum of proof necessary to establish a jury issue. It will take an expert witness, qualified in a particular area of expertise, testifying to things outside the realm of common knowledge and, consequently, permitted to give opinions which will form the basis of legal proof.

But expert testimony serves a function beyond merely getting the case to the jury. A lawyer rarely thinks in terms of adducing the barest amount of testimony necessary for his case. Getting beyond a motion to dismiss is hardly to be considered a victory. It merely establishes eligibility to compete for the real prize—a jury verdict. To achieve a favorable jury verdict the lawyer must adduce clear, convincing, moving testimony. He must think in terms of maximums—not minimums. He will not be content with the injury being described as a "broken leg." The jury must be acquainted with those elements of the injury which are beyond their normal ken—the attendant splitting of the periosteum, the ruptured vessels, the torn ligaments, the damaged nerves.

The disability will not be shrugged off with a simple "It hurts when I walk." There must be proof of the loss of motion in the joint, the area of hypesthesia, the extent of disuse atrophy. Nor will the extent of harm be confined to the site of the injury. The swelling in the foot will be associated with the impaired circulation, the pain in the low back will be related to the unnatural posture necessitated by a favoring of the injured limb.

This then is the function of the plaintiff's expert witness—

     1. to *establish sufficient proof* to create jury questions on the legal issues of proximate cause and extent of the consequences; and

     2. to *convince the jury* of the extent of the injuries and that these consequences were the result of the accident.

In serving these two functions he will in turn be serving two roles. First, as a witness having pertinent information regarding the injury, the treatment and the result. In this respect the doctor is no different than any other witness. Any layman could testify to the appearance of a plaintiff after an accident. This testimony is competent and very meaningful. Its competency is no way affected by the medical education or lack of it by the testifier. The doctor who views the plaintiff in the emergency room may be more technical and perhaps more accurate ("The victim was suffering from a large, flap type laceration extending from the right temporal region through the outer borders of the right brow, across the eyelid to the glabellar region. Another laceration extended from the outer canthal region of the left eye inferiorly and medially to within 2 centimeters of the left nostril, etc."). But the ambulance driver's testimony might be more vivid ("Her face was cut to ribbons"). Indeed, the value of this type of testimony is frequently in inverse proportion to the medical knowledge of the witness.

In addition, the description of what was done by way of treatment may be completely recited by a lay witness as well as a doctor. "He set my leg. I was given a series of shots. I had to take whirlpool baths and other kinds of physiotherapy. They operated on my leg and put in a pin." This is typical testimony from an injured plaintiff. In so testifying he is not usurping the function of the doctor nor is he assuming the role of an expert. The plaintiff is simply telling what he saw or experienced. When the doctor so testifies, he too is fulfilling this role as a witness.

The result of the injury might also fall within the same category of testimony. The doctor is merely a witness testifying to whatever any layman could recite when he states, "The plaintiff now has a one inch shortening in his leg.—He walks with a decided limp—The leg swells with prolonged use."

Of what significance is it that the medical practitioner is serving the role of a typical lay witness in many aspects of his testimony?

First, the lawyer might have a medical witness who does not qualify as a medical expert. What of the homeopath, the masseuse who treated the aching back, or the correspondence-course chiropractor? Even though such witnesses may not qualify as experts their testimony will be received if it stays within the bounds recited above.

Second, sometimes the lawyer encounters a qualified medical expert who is extremely uncooperative or perhaps even hostile to his cause. When contacted about the possibility of testifying he flatly says he won't come to court "and if you subpoena me I'll charge you $5,000.00 as an expert witness." Under those circumstances it's rather comforting to know that the law still has some claim on the doctor's knowledge. The plaintiff's lawyer may not be able to entice the doctor into giving an expert opinion (and no doubt he wouldn't want to) but he can make him respond to a subpoena and force him to tell the things he observed and the things that he did. If such is the case the threat of a $5,000.00 charge can be ignored. The doctor is entitled to no more than the minimal witness fee afforded to all witnesses who have personal knowledge of relevant facts and appear as witnesses in a case. Of course, it is seldom that such tactics will be employed by the trial lawyer. Calling a medical expert as a lay witness is a last resort which can usually be avoided.

The more significant role of the medical witness will be to establish the causal relationship between accident and injury and to prognosticate the effects of the injury. Both necessitate opinion evidence and in order to express such opinions the medical witness must satisfy the court that he possesses knowledge beyond that of the average person in an area of knowledge beyond that normally to be expected of an average person. Thus, for opinion evidence to be given the civil court must consider both the subject matter of the testimony and the person himself who seeks to testify.

§ 14.11 Mechanics of Interrogation—Generally

The expert witness should not be interrogated in the same fashion as a lay witness. A number of reasons dictate that the questioner take a different approach. The expert witness is usually a professional person; in most instances self employed. He will be busy, anxious to get about his business and consequently desirous that the interrogation be well organized, brief, and to the point. His scientific training demands the same, leaving no time for speculations, conjectures or guesses. He will appreciate questioning that is direct and well defined, that isn't diverted to the capillaries but goes straight to the jugular.

Aside from the expert's press of time and his scientific training, there is yet another reason which dictates the nature of expert evidence. The subject matter is relatively complicated and the jargon comparatively confusing. Despite all efforts at explanation and simplification there will be some aspects of the testimony that will not be comprehended. The attorney's presentation of his expert's testimony must therefore be direct, simple and well organized.

§ 14.12 Mechanics of Interrogation—Qualifications

Regardless of the legal requirements for qualifying a witness for opinion evidence, the attorney will want to do his best to enhance the credibility of the expert witness in the eyes of the jury. The witness should be advised of the necessity of establishing his special training so that he will be in position to advise the lawyer of special accomplishments and to review in his own mind the statistical details which will be inquired into.

The usual areas of inquiry for an expert witness are the following:

1. Basic Formal Education. Schools attended for undergraduate and graduate study, including the degrees received. A chronological recitation is usually more readily recalled by the witness and more easily understood by the jury.

2. Service Training.

3. Licensing Boards.

4. Specialized Training. This might include formal schooling or in-service training at additional institutions.

5. Professional Boards. Recognition within the expert's profession of competence with a specialty.

6. Teaching Positions.

7. Professional Writings.

8. Professional Memberships.

9. Awards Received.

§ 14.13 Mechanics of Interrogation—Qualifications—Illustration

The direct examination of an expert witness will follow a general pattern whether a witness for plaintiff or defendant. The following illustrates the general line of questioning:

Q. Will you state your name, please?
A. Frederick North.
Q. What is your business occupation?
A. I am a physician.
Q. Will you state your background and your qualifications, doctor?
A. I graduated from Washington University medical school in 1952. I then spent my time in training, essentially in general surgery, until April 1958 at which time I spent one year in a general rotating internship at Lutheran Hospital. From there I moved to Binghamton, New York, where I spent two years in residency training in neurology and psychiatry. This was followed by three years of training in neurological surgery at the Upstate New York Medical Center at Syracuse, New York. I finished training in 1964, and then spent one year in private practice in Syracuse, practice limited to neurological surgery. During this time I was parttime chief of the neurosurgical service at the V.A. Hospital in Syracuse, and

also instructor in neurosurgery at the medical school. In 1965 I entered the armed forces and spent two years at William Beaumont Army Hospital in El Paso, Texas, as chief of the neurosurgical service. I returned to St. Louis in 1967, the summer of 1967, where I associated in the practice of neurological surgery with Dr. Smith until 1970 at which time I went into practice on my own.

Q. Do you maintain an office here in St. Louis?

A. Yes, my office is at 500 Grand Avenue.

Q. Are you on the staffs of any hospitals?

A. I am on the staff at Missouri Baptist Hospital, at Firmon Desloge, St. Mary's, St. Mary's Infirmary, St. John's, Deaconess, Cardinal Glennon, Incarnate Word, Lutheran, and St. Joseph's Hospital in Kirkwood.

Q. Have you done teaching, doctor?

A. I have been on the faculty at the Syracuse University, and am a member of the faculty of St. Louis University now.

Q. Do you specialize in your practice?

A. My practice is limited to neurological surgery.

Q. And what does the practice of neurological surgery concern itself with?

A. Neurological surgery is a surgical sub-specialty which concerns itself with conditions affecting the brain, spinal cord, peripheral nerves, and the spine itself, which can be treated by surgical means.

Q. Are you a member of any medical societies, and, if so, will you state them for us, please?

A. Well, I belong to the St. Louis Medical Society, the Missouri Society, The A.M.A. I am a fellow of the International College of Surgeons. I belong to the Congress of Neurological Surgery. I belong to the Association for Research of Nervous and Mental Diseases; the Southern Medical Society; and I am a member of the Neurosurgical Society of West Germany.

Q. You mentioned you were a fellow. What is a fellow?

A. Well, the memberships in the International College like the American College, the degree of a fellow indicates that you are a full member as opposed to associate members or junior members. In other words, you have fulfilled all the requirements of a fellow. This involves a series of examinations by others in your specialty to determine if a candidate for the degree of fellow has sufficient experience and skill to qualify.

§ 14.14 Mechanics of Interrogation—Relation to Case

The next step is to establish the expert's relation to the case. In many instances he will be a "manufactured witness" who has been brought into the case at the instance of the lawyers for specific litigation purposes and paid by them for such services. If such is the case it is advisable to disclose such facts to the jury at the outset. They will hear about them at some time and if left to cross-examination the whole relationship might be depicted as unfair and sinister.

§ 14.15 Mechanics of Interrogation—Relation to Case— Illustration

The medical witness will continue as our vehicle of illustration.

If a treating physician, the plaintiff need only ask:

Q.   Did Mary Brown ever come under your professional care?

A.   Yes. I have seen Mrs. Brown over a period of years as a family physician. Most recently she came to me for treatment following an automobile accident on June 30, 1992.

If the doctor is an examining doctor for plaintiff or defendant, further information might be necessary:

Q.   Doctor at my request did you examine Mary Brown for the purpose of evaluating her claim?

A.   Yes, I did.

Q.   Have you on other occasions conducted such examinations for evaluation purposes?

A.   Yes. I serve as a consultant to the Veterans Bureau evaluating service disabilities. I am frequently asked by the referees at the Workmen's Compensation Commission to evaluate injuries. And frequently lawyers, such as yourself, seek my professional judgment in civil litigation.

Q.   Doctor, when you conduct these examinations and appear in court, what is the basis of your professional charges?

A.   My fee is based upon the time spent in my office and in any court appearance that might be necessary.

§ 14.16 Mechanics of Interrogation—Observations and Tests

A chronologically cohesive examination of the medical expert will inquire into the observations made and tests conducted.

History of Accident

Most doctors will initiate their office record with a history of the event which has precipitated the need for medical attention.

This history is usually requested by the attorney (at least by plaintiff's attorney), and just as usually objected to by the defendant. It is of a self serving nature but then again it is usually only cumulative of what the plaintiff has already testified.

Previous Medical History

The doctor will have taken a medical history which will be the logical background against which to consider the present complaints. The record will include those previous conditions or events considered to be of importance by the doctor. The recitation of the previous medical history itself is of little value to the injury. The important question will be:

> "Doctor, what if any role did this previous medical history play in your diagnosis, treatment or conclusions pertaining to the injuries suffered by the plaintiff?"

If there is no significant medical history the plaintiff should rule it out as soon as possible. The jury should not be left to speculate throughout the medical testimony about the possible effects of the usual childhood diseases, or the other injuries, or the previous sicknesses which plaintiff has suffered.

A firm response by the doctor to the effect that "the medical history of this patient was of no significance whatever," will wipe the slate clean and allow the jury to concentrate on the present injuries resulting from the accident.

The mere fact that the doctor has taken complete medical history does not compel the lawyer to adduce proof of such information. Although insignificant to the case at hand it might prove embarrassing to the plaintiff and detrimental to the case. Certainly nothing will be gained with a recitation that the plaintiff was treated for acne as a teenager or had an operation to correct hemorrhoids. Two simple inquiries should handle the matter, "Doctor, did you take a medical history?" followed with "Was there anything in this patient's history which in any way related to these injuries or their prognosis?"

Present Complaints

The treating or examining doctor usually precedes the examination with a request that the patient recite the problems that have occurred and are still recurring. The patient is free to disclose the problems in his own manner and frequently the doctor's notes will incorporate the phraseology of the patient.

Examination and Findings

Chronologically, the doctor will then conduct an examination and record his findings. During the course of this portion of the testimony the medical witness will undoubtedly use medical terms beyond the ken of the jury. The lawyer has the option of interrupting the testimony as the esoteric word is used or wait until the doctor's recitation is complete and then seek definitions for the words used. Most lawyers prefer the former approach in order to keep the jurors abreast of the testimony as it is given.

Many of the tests given might be more readily understood if they are demonstrated as well as described orally. It is one thing for a doctor to say, "The patient could flex his elbow one hundred degrees" and quite another for him to supplement the description with a simple movement of the arm.

Frequently the doctor will identify the clinical test through its medical term "The patient had a positive Babinski." If the test is sufficiently significant to mention, it is significant to describe. "The sole of the patient's foot was stroked by the end of a pencil, and the big toe bent up and the other toes fanned outward. Normally this stimulation causes the toes to flex or bend downward. When we get this abnormal response, as we did in this case, it is an indication of some disturbance in the brain or spinal cord. This test is a standard neurological test which we refer to as Babinski's reflex."

§ **14.17** Mechanics of Interrogation—Observations and Tests—Illustration

Q. Doctor, did you elicit a statement of complaints from the plaintiff?

A. Yes, she was seen in the emergency room at St. Mary's Hospital and X-ray films were made and Dr. Nash there in St. Louis saw her and hospitalized her and put her in traction and she remained in traction until she came back to Dallas on the 18th.

Q. All right.

A. Following the accident she had a great deal of pain in her neck and she said that her left eye felt as if it would pop out. She had pain between her shoulders and pain in the left arm. She had numbness and tingling of the left hand and she had more numbness and tingling in the right hand than she did in the left hand, at that time. She had nausea at the beginning, which had lasted for several days.

Q.   Now, those were her complaints to you on that first occasion, is that correct Doctor?

A.   Yes sir.

Q.   Did you conduct any examinations or tests at that time?

A.   Yes. I hospitalized her and gave her a thorough examination. My first finding was that she had definite limitation of neck motion. Actually there was 40 degrees limitation of bending the head to the side. Normally the head can be bent from the straight position, approximately 70 to 80 degrees to either side and this was limited by 30 degrees. That was the limitation to each side. Normally the chin can be rotated toward the shoulder from a 90 degree position to 180 degrees so that she had about 60 degrees of limitation in rotation, or turning the head, the chin towards the shoulder. Bending the head forward was limited by 20 degrees. Bending the head backward was limited and this caused pain, incidentally, a part of the limitation of motion, of the other motions, was due to the pain, also. I found tenderness over the joints of the neck on the right side and also on the left side I found tenderness and muscle spasm in the muscles just below the base of the skull on the left side.

Q.   You mentioned muscle spasm, doctor, what is it?

A.   Muscle spasm is a contraction of a muscle or a portion of a muscle, which is due to either an injury to the muscle itself or an injury to the nerve supply which causes the muscle to go into a spasm. It is a protective mechanism with which we are blessed and it's Nature's effort to protect injured joints by limiting the motion.

Q.   Sort of like a splint, Doctor?

A.   It is Nature's splint, yes. A muscle that is in contraction actually splints a joint.

Q.   Where did you find the muscle spasm?

A.   She had muscle spasm of the neck muscles, the lateral neck muscles, the muscles at the front of her neck and also in the muscles just above the shoulder blades.

Q.   Is this something you could see and feel, doctor?

A.   Oftentimes it can be seen. It can always be found with examining fingers.

Q.   Doctor, can the patient control muscle spasm voluntarily?

A.   Muscle spasm as such is not under the control of the patient.

Q.   Is this what is sometimes known as so-called objective sign of injury?

A.   Yes, it is an objective finding.

Q.   All right. Go on, Doctor.

A.   There was also tenderness and muscle spasm in the muscles just above the shoulder blades on both sides and also in the muscles between the shoulder blades and the thoracic portion of the spine, which is that portion of the spine to which the ribs are attached. I tested her reflexes and in the left arm the reflex at the front of the elbow, which is called the biceps, where the reflex was sluggish. The reflex at the wrist on the left side was also sluggish. At that time, the reflexes in the right arm were active and equal but I tested her sensation and there was no indication of any sensory change or any loss of feeling in either arm or shoulder. The arms were measured. The right arm, which was measured halfway between the elbow and shoulder was $10\frac{3}{4}$ inches. The right forearm was $9\frac{1}{2}$ inches. That is measured just below the elbow. And the left arm was 9 inches. The grip in the hands were the same being 35 pounds.

Q. Going back just for a moment, doctor, the measurement of the arms, is there anything significant about that or is that within the range of normalcy?

A. The measurement of the arms was within normal limits. There was a quarter of an inch difference between the left arm and the right arm, the right arm being a quarter of an inch larger than the left and in a right handed individual this is within the normal limits, in my opinion. The measurement of the forearms, however, showed that there was a half inch difference in the forearm on the right side as compared to the left side, indicating some atrophy or shrinking of the muscles of the left forearm.

Q. Doctor, going on for just a moment, did you make any test in connection with her eyes?

A. Yes, I tested the pupils for their reaction to light and distance and I also looked at the pupils to ascertain if there was any difference in the size of the two pupils and the left pupil was definitely dilated. It was larger than the right pupil. Also we checked her blood pressure and the blood pressure in the right arm was 100 over 74 and in the left arm it was 120 over 86. This indicated to me that there was, at that time, irritation of the sympathetic nerve supply in the neck, which supplies the blood vessels of the arms. When these fibers, the fibers are irritated, it causes what we call vasoconstriction, which simply means that the blood vessels constrict, or become smaller and therefore the blood pressure in it may be different in the two arms and it was in this instance, higher in the left arm than in the right arm, indicating to me irritation of the sympathetic nerve supply.

§ 14.18   Mechanics of Interrogation—Results

The results of the observations and tests should provide a distinct phase of the interrogation before proceeding to the conclusions that were drawn from those results. In that area of medical expertise the results are usually expressed in terms of diagnosis and course of treatment.

§ 14.19 Mechanics of Interrogation—Results—Illustration

Diagnosis

The listing of the findings has little meaning unless the medical expert reaches a conclusion as to their combined significance. One of the key questions will be, "Doctor what was your diagnosis of plaintiff's condition?"

Q. Doctor, taking into consideration the patient's history, her complaints and your findings, did you make a diagnosis of her condition?

A. Yes, sir. My diagnosis was that this patient had received a sprain injury to the ligaments and the capsules of the cervical spine. These are structures which hold the bones together in their normal relationship and as a result of this she had definite evidence of irritation of the cervical nerve roots or the nerves as they come off the spinal cord and leave the spinal canal. She had also evidence of irritation of the sympathetic nerve supply.

Course of Treatment

Labeling plaintiff's malady, as important as it is, still leaves some important questions unanswered. If the medical witness is the treating physician, he will be interrogated as to the course of treatment that was prescribed with an explanation as to what he was attempting to accomplish.

Q. Upon making this diagnosis what course of treatment did you undertake?

A. "I applied cold packs to the swollen ankle and advised Miss Brown to remain in bed, and after twenty four hours to begin periodic hot soaks to the ankle. The swelling and discoloration was caused by hemorrhaging within the tissue. My first concern was to stop this internal bleeding with the cold packs and then to absorb the blood and reduce the swelling with the application of heat."

The examining doctor, whether a witness for plaintiff or defendant, may be asked to describe the course of treatment that should be followed in the case. If the defendant's doctor makes a finding of existing disability or pain but thinks that the condition will subside with proper attention, it will aid the defense if testimony is forthcoming concerning the treatment available that will provide the necessary relief and improvement.

On the other hand, if the examining doctor for plaintiff entertains the opinion that little improvement can be expected, he should be queried about the need for treatment:

Q. Doctor, what course of treatment, in your opinion, should be prescribed for Miss Brown?

A. Well, she will have to continue on some type of medication to control the pain. If the pain and disability continues, as I think it will, some consideration will have to be given to the possibility of surgery. However, I'm afraid that this should be considered as a last resort, in that the chances of improvement, even with surgery, are very slim.

§ 14.20   Mechanics of Interrogation—Conclusions

The previous testimony has been in the nature of the "wind-up." That portion of the testimony dealing with prognosis is the "delivery." Now the medical expert is free to look into the future and express his opinion. The facts have been laid through the testimony concerning the history, the clinical tests, the findings. Now the expert is free to relate the consequences. These will fall into well defined categories:

1. Future pain and disability. Will the plaintiff continue to have trouble? Will he improve physically? And more importantly, will he be able to return to his work, resume his normal activities, be restored to society?

2. Permanency. Has maximum improvement already occurred? If there will be future improvement, will a residuum of pain and disability remain? What will be the effects of these permanent conditions?

3. Future medical treatment and expenses. Will additional medical attention be necessary? How much of an economic burden will this entail? What will be a reasonable charge for these expenses if it is reasonably certain the plaintiff will incur them?

4. Reduction of life expectancy. Have the injuries lessened the life expectancy of the plaintiff? Will he prove vulnerable

to other diseases or conditions which will reduce his length of life?

These are the matters which should climax the plaintiff's presentation.

The same is true of the defendant's doctor. The battle will no doubt be joined on these grounds and, if so, the defendant will want to emphasize the more optimistic prognosis of his medical expert by reserving the prognosis until the last.

§ 14.21 Mechanics of Interrogation—Conclusions—Illustration

Q. Do you have an opinion, based upon reasonable medical certainty as to whether or not the collision of February 3, 1992 was the competent producing cause of her present difficulties that you have told us about?

A. Yes I have an opinion.

Q. All right. What is your opinion?

A. My opinion, based on reasonable medical certainty, assuming all these facts to be true, as you have stated them, is that the collision which occurred in St. Louis on February 3, 1992 was the competent producing cause of the condition as I have outlined it, concerning this patient.

Q. Do you have an opinion based upon reasonable medical certainty as to whether or not Miss Brown will have future pain?

A. Yes I do.

Q. Will she have future pain?

A. It is my opinion, based on reasonable medical certainty that Miss Brown will have, from time to time, pain in the future.

Q. Do you have an opinion as to whether or not she will need future treatment?

A. Yes I have an opinion.

Q. What is that opinion?

A. It is my opinion, based on reasonable medical certainty, that Miss Brown will need further treatment, including further medication and treatment.

Q. Do you have an opinion, based upon reasonable medical certainty as to whether she has a permanent injury?

A. Yes sir, I do.

Q. What is that opinion?

A. It is my opinion, based on reasonable medical certainty that Miss Brown does have a permanent condition.

Q. Doctor, are you familiar with the type of work that she has done in the past as a member of the national staff of the Girl Scouts, U.S.A.?

A. I am familiar with the work that she has been doing, yes. Without actually being present when she was doing the work.

Q. What, if any, recommendation have you made with respect to future activity?

A. I have recommended to Miss Brown that she should, because of her physical condition, give up her work that she has been doing with the Girl Scout organization which necessitates a great deal of traveling, riding in taxicabs and airplanes and getting where she has to go to meet a schedule, the best way she can get there, it has been my recommendation that she will have to give up this type of work and I honestly don't know what she is going to be able to do. I have, last month, or maybe the month before, I advised her to try something— her brother has a drug store and I advised her to go to the drug store and maybe do what she could do at the drug store, even acting as a cashier, which is quite a comedown from her former job but I thought that perhaps trying to do something might give us a clue to what she would be able to do. I'm afraid that her condition is such that she is unable to do even this kind of work.

Note that in this particular testimony each question or answer which concerned the doctor's opinion included the shibboleth "based on reasonable medical certainty". No doubt there is the necessity, in most jurisdictions, for the expert to express his degree of certainty in some such fashion but there are other ways to do it.

"Doctor, I am going to ask you a series of questions seeking your opinion about the injury that Miss Brown suffered and their consequences. If you have an opinion on these matters I would ask that such opinion be based upon reasonable medical certainty. Doctor, do you have an opinion as to the cause of Miss Brown's condition?"

§ 14.22 Mechanics of Interrogation—Hypothetical Question

As an advocate your primary concern in adducing evidence from an expert should be the persuasiveness of that presentation. Too often we slip into traps of tradition and permit our trial behavior to be dictated by the "usual procedure." Such is the situation with the hypothetical question. It is employed again and again as a device to elicit the opinion of an expert, not because it is the most effective way to elicit such information but simply because it's always been done that way.

Some lawyers, recognizing that it is traditional, insist that it is a good tradition, an effective tool of persuasion that presents an opportunity to restate the evidence, highlighting those features which are favorable and thus make, in essence, a mini-summation. But in the hands of most lawyers the hypothetical question falls far short of such hopes and is regarded by the jury as a legalistic, artificial, confusing interruption to the normal presentation of evidence.

Consider the hypothetical question as it is usually presented (the illustration comes from a well known text on trial procedures).

Q. "Doctor I am going to ask you a rather long hypothetical question. It is necessarily a little long, and I wish you would pay close attention to it in order that you may carry all the facts in your mind."

There follows some seventy-seven lines of printed facts the gist of which is that a pregnant woman fell while alighting from a bus, miscarried thirty-six hours later and currently suffers from anemia and a prolapsed uterus.

The text next acknowledges argument on objection to the question, (which were overruled) and concludes with the doctor stating he has an opinion and in response to "What is that opinion" states that the fall did indeed cause the miscarriage and subsequent complaints.

Only lawyers could make such a production out of such a simple matter. The advocate, seeking to make a straightforward, lively, convincing presentation will avoid such pontifical proceedings like the plague. Before being victimized by the hypothetical question consider these points:

1. Some medical issues need no expert testimony in order to present the issue to the jury. It is bad enough to wade through all that recited factual minutiae in order to have a doctor opine that a fall caused a miscarriage. It is preposterous to hypothesize a healthy person falling down a flight of stairs and discovering a bone sticking through her panty hose and then ask the doctor what in his expert opinion caused the fracture.

2. If the expert himself has all the necessary information through first hand knowledge to form an opinion, then he need not "assume" such facts as hypothetical. Perhaps in a

product liability case an expert has witnessed a product failure. He simply tells what he saw and expresses his opinion.

3. The rules of evidence in federal courts (Rule 705) have all but eliminated the need for hypothetical questions.

If a hypothetical question must be used, follow these suggestions:

1. Keep it sufficiently abbreviated that you can state it without reading it. True, there are some courts which insist that written hypothetical questions be submitted as part of the pretrial procedure but such demands of the court for procedural tidiness should not dictate the manner in which counsel ultimately elects to adduce evidence. The preparation of a written hypothetical beforehand does serve two good purposes. It alerts your expert to the question with which he is to be confronted and it presents your opposition with an opportunity to make his objections beforehand and not interrupt your interrogation with an objection. It has become a trial ritual for any hypothetical question to be followed by an objection that something was included that should not have been and something excluded that should have been. By the time the argument subsides, witness and jury have forgotten the question.

2. In reciting the facts, dramatize the evidentiary information. If the facts involve a client who slipped with her left foot and slammed to the floor wrenching her back, use those color words "slammed" and "wrenched"—and you might act out the slipping at least if not the fall. After all we are dealing with one of the most important and dramatic aspects of the trial. Don't turn it into a dry, mechanistic, formal recitation which bewilders the jury. Make it an animated educational experience.

§ **14.23** Cross–Examination of Expert

See Chapter 15, §§ 15.38–15.55, *infra.*

CHAPTER 15

CROSS–EXAMINATION

"Go ahead, make my day"
Dirty Harry

Analysis

A. IN GENERAL

B. TECHNIQUES OF INTERROGATION

C. FORMS OF QUESTIONING

A. IN GENERAL

§ 15.1 Importance of Cross–Examination

There isn't a text written about trial tactics that doesn't introduce the topic of cross-examination as the "most spectacular phase of a trial," "the most publicized aspect of trial procedure" and conclude by stating that "the test of the trial lawyer is his ability to cross-examine effectively." No doubt there is merit in the position that cross-examination is important, that it can hold the key to success or failure and that it may be highly dramatic. But such statements can be made of any facet of a lawsuit. The unique aspect of cross-examination is that it is that phase of the trial which is most likely to lead to confrontation, anger and bellicosity. It is to a trial what the fist fight is to a hockey game. As entertainment it is tops. Look at the scripts of the television shows that seek to portray courtroom drama. They deal largely with cross-examination in its most savage form. So it is natural that lawyers tend to believe that the dramatic highlight of their case will be a hostile confrontation on cross-examination. But case after case is tried with no such confrontation, no heated exchanges, no on-the-stand breakdowns, no sudden confessions of error nor moans of mea culpa. Perhaps if Erle Stanley Gardner had had a flair for writing closing arguments we would have been spared the unrealistic portrayals of those devastating cross-examinations which terminated the trials and made summations superfluous. Despite the lack of authenticity of such portrayals the images linger on. To paraphrase an old saw, "The dramatic presentations are distorted but they rule us from the tube."

This attempt to put cross-examination in proper perspective is not an effort to merely express a personal pique. If one approaches cross-examination as the "high point of the trial, the true test of the trial lawyer" he is affording his opponent's cause much too much importance. He is adopting a defensive posture and in effect is stating that the merits of his own case will never be sufficient to persuade a jury and that victory can be achieved only if the opponent's efforts can be discredited. Think of it this way. If your direct examination is well organized, dramatic and persuasive, your case will be won. After all "The best defense is a good offense."

§ 15.2   Characteristics—Generally

A realistic analysis of the approach and technique of conducting this phase of the trial is initially burdened by the name itself—"cross-examination." The implication is that it must be an interrogation that must be "cross" or as Webster elaborates "Showing ill humor, annoyed." In an attempt to overcome these dramatic distortions and semantics, let us start off with a fresh concept and a new name.

§ 15.3 Characteristics—Unrehearsed

The most obvious aspect of this phase of the case is that it is unrehearsed. Everything else that we have done has been the product of deliberate thought generated in the comfort of our office. We have drafted and redrafted our pleadings, listed our questions to be asked on voir dire, outlined our opening statement, organized our direct examination and reviewed the questions with our witnesses. Now the pensorum shifts from the office couch to the counsel table. A whole new approach must be adopted, a different set of talents relied upon. You have not had the opportunity of preparing the witness, of rehearsing the order or manner of interrogation so, consequently, you are not certain how he will respond. Some planning can be made but for the most part you will be "winging it," "flying by the seat of your pants." The synapses must crackle and the thought processes flow with speed and spontaneity.

§ 15.4 Characteristics—Unendorsed

Your opponent has presented the person who now occupies the witness chair. He has not been called as part of your case. You have not, and cannot have, vouched for his credibility. He might be a charlatan or blackguard, confused or mistaken and you will be free to attack the validity of the evidence which he endorses.

§ 15.5 Characteristics—Secondary

In point of time this phase of questioning will occur after your opponent has had the initial opportunity to adduce that information which he desires. The first fruits have been harvested and you are left to pick over the "leavins." It is possible that the witness has stated all that he knows and that there is nothing left for seconds.

B. TECHNIQUES OF INTERROGATION

§ 15.6 Generally

What advantages, if any, does this three-fold identity afford?

First, it de-emphasizes the inevitability of hostility. Most factual lay witnesses consider themselves to be unbiased reporters of the truth. They do not envision themselves as "plaintiff's" witness or "defendant's" witness. They are in court to tell what they know. For the "cross" examiner to approach them otherwise, creates a hostility not necessarily there to begin with.

Second, it should enhance our ability to analyze and appreciate the handicaps under which we labor. Dare we ask an unrehearsed witness a question to which we do not know the answer? Can we hazard an opinion or explanation from a witness whose honesty or knowledge we cannot endorse? Need we interrogate further if the initial interrogation has been adequate and innocuous?

Third, it should permit us to break out of old patterns and recognize the possibilities inherent in this phase of the trial.

Let us proceed to structure some rules that will be applicable to unrehearsed, unendorsed, secondary interrogation.

§ 15.7   Unrehearsed Witness—Pretrial Preparation

Note that the witness who is being called by your opponent is not described as one whose identity is unknown or even as one whose knowledge is unknown. Modern day discovery procedures have all but eliminated the surprise witness as to the facts of an occurrence. (The surprise impeaching witness may still lurk in the weeds undiscovered through interrogatories, depositions or pretrial orders.) If even the most modest of pre-suit investigation or pretrial discovery tools have been utilized you have ascertained who your opponent will call and the substance of the testimony. Of course such has not always been the case. Old timers in the trial game claim that the real test of cross examining comes when you are suddenly confronted with an unknown witness giving unanticipated testimony—and that was what they had to live with in every case. Proper pretrial deposition will usually dictate that the opposition's witnesses be ascertained and documentary evidence produced. Note the qualification. In some unusual circumstances the prudent counsel may elect to forego such discovery.

There are a few additional caveats.

First, any discovery demand initiates trial preparation on the part of your opponent. Let us analogize trial preparation to a martial setting in which hostile countries have rights of pre-war discovery. Transylvania sends a set of interrogatories to Cathay

416

demanding to know the number and displacement of troops guarding the Kyber Pass. "So they are interested in the Kyber Pass, are they? Rush two divisions to the area and deploy them in bunkers", commands the defending general.

And so it frequently occurs in litigation. Defendant in a product failure case wants to know what experts have examined the product, what tests were performed, how many other cases of similar product failures are known. The lethargic plaintiff counsel is now forced to respond—usually by generating the evidence that has been requested. There is nothing like an enemy's request or a court order to stimulate activity on a file.

Second, the generation and preservation of all the essential evidence in a case puts your opponent in a devil-may-care posture of "meet my demands or we'll try it." Some pretrial procedures are so demanding (see § 5.5) that all the hard work of trial preparation is completed a week or two before trial. The legal issues are identified, instructions prepared, witnesses listed, exhibits numbered—the troops are mustered, cannons loaded and it's all over but the shooting. Many a lawyer (usually those representing plaintiff who is saddled with that onerous burden of "going forward") will discount a claim if it can be settled without the time, effort and expense of final trial preparation. An aggressive opponent has forced him into a posture of preparation and all the time, effort, etc., has been expended. Might as well fire the guns and see what happens.

The thinking advocate will recognize these possibilities before blindly inaugurating a thorough program of pretrial discovery.

§ 15.8 Unrehearsed Witness—Pretrial Preparation—Identity

The means of ascertaining the identity of your opponent's witnesses will be through your own informal investigation or through utilization of the tools of pretrial discovery.

As to the former, potential witnesses may most easily be ascertained through reference to public reports that may be filed directly or indirectly regarding the litigation producing incident. The number of reports generated by governmental agencies which will serve as independent evidence of several names of witnesses are legion: police reports, fire reports, autopsy records, Civilian Aeronautics Board Reports, Interstate Commerce Commission Reports, Consumer Safety Reports, Congressional Committee Hearings, etc. The next obvious source is investigation through neighborhood checks, newspaper advertisements, etc. The sources explored are limited only by the investigator's imagination and enthusiasm.

As to the former, you may employ interrogatories which directly seek the names and addresses of those persons known to have been present at the scene of the incident. Check your jurisdiction as to the proper language to employ. Some reject a request for "witnesses" because that assumes the party at the incident (objective) actually has knowledge (subjective) of the incident.

Many jurisdictions follow a pretrial hearing practice which dictates that the parties list the names of witnesses and exhibits before the trial begins (the sole exception being impeachment type evidence). There is no question but that the "surprise witness" should be a thing of the past.

§ **15.9** Unrehearsed Witness—Pretrial Preparation—Content

Once the identity is established, the content of the witnesses' testimony may be ascertainable, if desirable. Isn't the testimony of all the witnesses always desirable?

An affirmative response would come from a large number of modern day litigators who approach the fact gathering stage of a lawsuit as a vacuum cleaner operation. All of the potentially pertinent information is indiscriminately sucked up by depositions and other formal discovery processes and then the counsel sift out what is favorable to each side then begin their settlement negotiations. There are a number of reasons why such a process is desirable:

1. It gives the illusion of truth seeking.

2. It provides plenty of work for attorneys.

3. It gives the clients the impression of intense, spirited and conscientious representation.

But there are other reasons why such a process should not be followed and they are equally persuasive:

1. It is a time consuming and expensive procedure.

2. It produces information as likely to be detrimental as helpful.

3. It shifts the main role of the lawyer from that of trial advocate to that of pretrial investigator.

The first set of reasons is more persuasive to the defendant. He has less concern for time or money. In fact, if defendant's resources are sufficient the trial can be turned into a war of attrition, not a test of right or wrong but a contest of who can outlast the other. Witness anti-trust litigation as such an example.

The second set of reasons is more persuasive to the plaintiff. Most often the client is in need of funds and has no stomach for costs or delays. And the attorney is frequently working on a contingent fee contract and there is no meter running while the deposition process agonizingly grinds forward.

But aside from those differences of time and money, neither advocate, if worthy of the name, should seek to go about their partisan endeavors by willy-nilly witness interrogation by deposition. As mentioned before, the information you receive might hurt more than it helps. Furthermore it is preserved, to be available at trial even if the witness dies, is transferred to Perth, Australia, committed to an institution or otherwise "unavailable." And, one more demerit, you might legitimatize evidence that would not have been received at trial. Deposition taking will waive certain witness incapacities (such as that imposed by the Dead Man's Statutes) and certain lines of inquiry will waive privileged testimony. Consequently, good advice for either counsel is to learn the content of the witnesses—but only if you can do so selectively without harm to your own cause.

One way to execute this advice is through informal investigation, an art form that is slowly dying. We are witnessing another application of Gresham's Law, bad investigation is driving out good investigation.

Why should I make a call at a witness's home, in the evening and try to seduce him into giving me information when I can set up a deposition in my office, during office hours and force him under threat of contempt to answer my questions? If convenience were the only criterion the option would be for the deposition. But the advocate must measure matters in terms of success for the client. Go see the witness, establish rapport, find out what he knows, groom him for your side—that's your job.

§ 15.10 Unrehearsed Witness—Pretrial Preparation—Motivation

The motivations of a witness are not as easily determined. Certain objective facts which might suggest a reason for the witness testifying as he does can be uncovered by deposition (relationship to a party, continuing role as a testifying expert, etc.) but other factors less obvious and more subjective can only be suspicioned by intuition and only hinted at by way of proof.

If you have done your homework properly you will have been able to have discovered what the witness knows and what motivates him. Knowing this, the lack of rehearsal can be minimized and the risks of receiving an unanticipated answer practically eliminated. I say "practically" because we can never be assured that a witness will stick to a previous story but if such a change occurs you at least will have an opportunity to impeach.

§ 15.11 Unrehearsed Witness—Seeking the Unknown Answer

Will there ever be a situation where you will need to ask an unrehearsed witness a question which calls for an unknown answer? Perhaps the key word is "need." If you represent a plaintiff and are confronting an unrehearsed witness it means that you have already survived a motion to dismiss. Consequently there is no "need" for such unknown information to make a submissible case. If you represent a defendant you have undoubtedly structured a defense upon witnesses of your own and no "need" would arise to invoke a defense during plaintiff's case. No, the "need" is usually nothing more than a need to know, a curiosity on the part of the attorney that prompts him to satisfy this urge. If such is the only justification let the question calling for an unknown answer from an unrehearsed witness go unasked. Curiosity kills cases as well as cats.

But in our anxiety to axiomize, let us not be drawn into the temptation of adopting a course that dictates "*never* ask a question for which you do not know the answer." There are many instances when a clever cross-examiner can recognize a situation in which the answer to a properly asked question cannot possibly be harmful.

Assume that a doctor has prescribed a drug to a patient for which that patient has a history of allergy as recorded on the doctor's own records. What is the danger in asking the doctor,

420

"Before you prescribed the drug did you review your records?" Either a "yes" or "no" suffices to help your cause—even though you don't know (and don't care) what the answer will be.

§ 15.12   Unendorsed Witness—Generally

What are the credentials that are the hallmarks of a credible witness to the facts of the case? The proper recitation of any past event demands that the reciter possess the capacities of:

1. reception (internal);

2. reception (external);

3. perception;

4. preparatory set;

5. recall;

6. expression.

Take the person who claims that they have witnessed a flying saucer. Proceeding in the order as outlined above we would normally inquire:

1. How is your eyesight and hearing? (innate capacity to receive the stimuli).

2. Were you in a position to see and hear the flying saucer? (situational external capacity to receive the stimuli).

3. Was the image that you saw as a flashing two dimensional oval properly perceived as a spinning three dimensional disc? (experiential perception).

4. Were you alert and attentive? (situational internal capacity to receive stimuli).

5. With what was the event associated? What has transpired in the meantime? How long ago did you witness this phenomenon? Did you make notes or preserve a record of what you witnessed? (retention).

6. What is your educational background? How familiar are you with the language? (expression).

It is apparent that the potential for error exists in three distinct areas: the physical, the psychological and what is frequently a combination of the two.

§ 15.13 Unendorsed Witness—Physical Capacity

This is the phase of witnessing that intuitively is regarded as the primary source of error. Why did the umpire make a wrong call? "He's as blind as a bat!" comes the ready response. Why did the fellow slip on the banana peel? "He didn't look where he was walking" is the obvious explanation. Physical circumstances then should be the first order of business in questioning the capacity of an unendorsed witness and thus it is that when the witness says he saw a certain event we instinctively inquire, "How is your eyesight? Where were you positioned? Where were you looking?"

Once these facts have been established a second reason must be explored as an explanation of faulty observation. Why is it that a motorist with good eyesight, looking straight ahead, rear ends the car in front? Again the intuitive accusation, "Why don't you keep your mind on your driving?" There has been a mental lapse of some sort, a lack of perception. The brain received the necessary stimuli but it just didn't put it all together. The explanation? Other stimuli, other distractions, something which fouled the synapses. And so the inquiry goes "Was your radio on? Were you worried about anything? What were you thinking of?"

§ 15.14 Unendorsed Witness—Psychological Factors

Now for a more subtle explanation for faulty observation. The witness has good receptors, good position, good attentiveness—but a distortion occurs in what has happened and what he reports. Why? For years psychologists have been conducting experiments which illustrate this phenomenon. The most common is that in which a group of observers is suddenly confronted with an unexpected dramatic event, i.e., a stranger enters a classroom and is involved in an altercation with the teacher. Shortly thereafter the group is asked to describe what they observed. As you might imagine the accounts will vary in every respect from the identity of the stranger (height, clothes, features) to the nature of the altercation ("they wrestled" "a knife was used" "a gun was drawn"). The reasons for these differences can not be explained on the basis of physical disparity among the observers. Their visions and lines of sight may be the identical— but their testimony differs. The explanation why one saw a gun and the other a knife is not readily explained. At this stage we simply chalk it up to the vagaries of the human mind. There is one phenomenon that does have an explanation however. In such cases the "blame" for the altercation is almost always laid at the feet of the stranger. He is the one that is the aggressor, the villain that made the threatening gesture, who threw the first punch or brandished the knife. Regardless of how a film of the occurrence may confirm a different version, the witnesses will take the side of that party with whom they identify and in the given case it is the familiar teacher in the familiar classroom who is "seen" as a victim of the invading stranger. Here is one psychological factor that should not be overlooked as a possible explanation for a distorted observation. With whom does the witness identify? Against whom does he feel hostility? These subliminal subjective attitudes might well be determinative of the "facts" as they are honestly perceived.

§ 15.15   Unendorsed Witness—Psychological Factors—Illustration

Several years ago a young man was shot by a security guard in the lobby of a busy downtown building. Six witnesses observed the incident. They all agreed that the victim had been verbally abusive and had physically attacked the guard before he was shot. Only the victim disputed their version.

Cross-examination of the witnesses was not directed to the circumstances of the event but rather the identities of the persons involved. All agreed that the victim was tall, young, bearded, slovenly dressed and had all the physical attributes of a "hippie" (some said, "dirty hippie"). The guard had been employed at that post for a number of years. The witnesses were encouraged to relate their liking for the guard, his friendliness, how he had helped them in the past, how they called him by his first name. The stage was now set for the testimony by the psychologist who explained the phenomenon previously referred to and presented the jury the opportunity to reject the testimony of the witnesses and accept the testimony of the victim.

§ 15.16   Unendorsed Witness—Retention

Cross-examination which tests the retentive capacity of the witness occurs with such frequency that it merits special attention.

The usual attacks on the memory of the witness fall into three distinct categories.

The *first* is that the event recalled was routine and that there was nothing associated with the event to make it memorable.

The *second,* frequently associated with the first, is that there have been countless events of a similar nature that would blur one's memory of this particular event.

Thus, when an investigating officer of a vehicular mishap testifies to his recollection of the event he will typically be confronted with a series of questions such as these:

Q. Officer this was just a routine investigation of a routine accident was it not?
A. Yes.
Q. And you investigate many such events in the course of your daily duties.
A. Yes, on the average twenty to twenty-five a week.
Q. Now can you recall any of the accidents that you investigated, let's say on March 15 of last year?
A. No. I sure can't.

The inference is clear; how then do you recall the incident occurring on this other routine day?

The *third* line of inquiry is utilized if there has been a previous statement of the event related which differs with that version given at trial. It is expressed in the axiom that such a previous statement of an event, being more closely related to the event in point of time, has a greater degree of credibility. Frequently the variation exists between testimony given by deposition and that given at trial. The usual interrogation follows:

Q. You recall when your deposition was taken do you not?
A. Yes.
Q. That was last December just four months after the event?
A. I believe so.
Q. And I'm sure your memory of the event was clearer six months ago than it is today.
A. It probably was.

Other embellishments may be made but this represents the basic approach.

Another factor, quite distinct from those recited, which might affect a witness' capacity to retain is psychological in nature. All of us are familiar with the homicide defendant who testifies: "I remember seeing the gun in the drawer and I took hold of it—then

424

everything went black." The driver of an automobile involved in a fatal collision testifies, "I can recall leaving my home and heading for work but I have no memory of the events of the accident." Perhaps there is the physical explanation that a blow on the head had caused "retrograde amnesia"—a blocking out of the memory of events preceding a traumatic injury to the head. Or maybe the witness is just lying. But there is a good chance that the witness honestly can't recall the shocking, ugly event. Perhaps some kindly mechanism of the mind has blotted the occurrence from the memory or subliminated it so deeply within the super ego that it can not readily be resurrected. Persons of science have recognized the validity of such occurrence but, of more importance to us, so have persons of the law. On several occasions lawyers have recruited the aid of hypnosis and the so-called "truth serums" to probe the recesses of memory and draw to the level of consciousness past events. With the endorsement of properly qualified experts such testimony has been received in evidence.

§ 15.17 Unendorsed Witness—Falsifier—Generally

Another source of error that might affect the validity of the testimony of the unendorsed witness concerns neither physical limitations nor unconscious distortions. The time has come to speak of the "forked tongue," the deliberate liar who, for one reason or another, violates the oath and testifies to something other than "the truth, the whole truth and nothing but the truth." For the purpose of our problem (how to interrogate the unendorsed witness) it becomes necessary to determine those factors which might precipitate fraudulently false testimony. A cursory analysis suggests two basic explanations for fabrication, exaggeration or suppression on the witness stand:

1. *A lack of credibility.* Is the witness one of those frequently referred to "congenital liars" incapable of telling the truth? Does he have some chink in his moral armor that affects his respect for the oath?

2. *A background of bias.* Is the witness prejudiced in such a manner so as to reflect favor for one litigant or disfavor toward the other?

Assume these general categorizations are correct, we must become more specific and identify those particular events of a personal history which suggest a general lack of credibility and those particular relationships or experiences which suggest a prejudicial proclivity.

§ **15.18** Unendorsed Witness—Falsifier—Credibility

As to the first, the law recognizes the following to have sufficient probative value in establishing a general lack of credibility to warrant their admission into evidence:

1. *Conviction of a Crime.* The state jurisdictions are not uniform as to what limitations if any, should be imposed in receiving such evidence. Perhaps the best expression of the rule is incorporated in the Federal Rules of Evidence which state:

Rule 609.

IMPEACHMENT BY EVIDENCE OF
CONVICTION OF CRIME

(a) **General rule.** For the purpose of attacking the credibility of a witness, evidence that he has been convicted of a crime shall be admitted if elicited from him or established by public record during cross-examination but only if the crime (1) was punishable by death or imprisonment in excess of one year under the law under which he was convicted, and the court determines that the probative value of admitting this evidence outweighs its prejudicial effect to the defendant, or (2) involved dishonesty or false statement, regardless of the punishment.

(b) **Time limit.** Evidence of a conviction under this rule is not admissible if a period of more than ten years has elapsed since the date of the conviction or of the release of the witness from the confinement imposed for that conviction, whichever is the later date, unless the court determines, in the interests of justice, that the probative value of the conviction supported by specific facts and circumstances substantially outweighs its prejudicial effect. However, evidence of a conviction more than 10 years old as calculated herein, is not admissible unless the proponent gives to the adverse party sufficient advance written notice of intent to use such evidence to provide the adverse party with a fair opportunity to contest the use of such evidence.

· · ·

In some jurisdictions there is no restriction as to the time lapse between conviction. The theory being evidently, that anybody who has ever committed a transgression is likely to violate the oath. In such jurisdictions where the law itself does not impose a discreet limitation of the admissibility of prior convictions, the lawyer himself must do so. More will be said of this later.

2. *General Reputation for Veracity.* Again, reference is made to the Federal Rules of Evidence which provide the evidentiary limitations involved:

Rule 405.
METHODS OF PROVING CHARACTER

(a) **Reputation or opinion.** In all cases in which evidence of character or a trait of character of a person is admissible, proof may be made by testimony as to reputation or by testimony in the form of an opinion. On cross-examination, inquiry is allowable into relevant specific instances of conduct.

(b) **Specific instances of conduct.** In cases in which character or a trait of character of a person is an essential element of a charge, claim, or defense, proof may also be made of specific instances of his conduct.

Rule 608.
EVIDENCE OF CHARACTER AND
CONDUCT OF WITNESS

(a) **Opinion and reputation evidence of character.** The credibility of a witness may be attacked or supported by evidence in the form of opinion or reputation, but subject to these limitations: (1) the evidence may refer only to character for truthfulness or untruthfulness, and (2) evidence of truthful character is admissible only after the character of the witness for truthfulness has been attacked by opinion or reputation evidence or otherwise.

(b) **Specific instances of conduct.** Specific instances of the conduct of a witness, for the purpose of attacking or supporting his credibility, other than conviction of crime as provided in Rule 609, may not be proved by extrinsic evidence. They may, however, in the discretion of the court, if probative of truthfulness or untruthfulness, be inquired into on cross-examination of the witness (1) concerning his character for truthfulness or untruthfulness, or (2) concerning the character for truthfulness or untruthfulness of another witness as to

which character the witness being cross-examined has testified.

The giving of testimony, whether by an accused or by any
other witness, does not operate as a waiver of his privilege
against self-incrimination when examined with respect to
matters which relate only to credibility.

3. *Peripheral Personal History.* The law is rather liberal in
permitting the adduction of information about the witness which
might provide the jury with some insight as to whether the
witness is believable or not. How else can we justify such questions as "Are you employed? How long have you worked there?
Where do you live?", etc.

§ 15.19 Unendorsed Witness—Falsifier—Bias

Perhaps this is the type of information most frequently relied
upon to discredit the testimony of a witness. Establishing some
relationship between the party and the witness is the goal—with
the hope that some inference will follow that the witness will color
his or her testimony to favor the related party. The theory is
sound but in practice it often goes awry.

First, the lawyer must be discriminating in recognizing those
relationships that might give rise to an inference of bias. It will
do little good to inquire of a treating physician whether it isn't
true that he has been the family doctor of the plaintiff for a long
time. The answer might well be, "Yes, in fact I delivered Susan,
treated her for childhood diseases and I feel I know her medical
background as well as anyone can. That's why I can say that she
was a perfectly healthy girl until she suffered this permanent
injury".

Second, even if the relationship is suggestive of a bias on the
part of the witness, the advocate must be careful as to how that
relationship and its concomitant inference is developed. Long ago
some hack script writer of a courtroom drama authored the
following:

Lawyer: Mrs. Green you are the mother of the defendant
             who is accused of murder, aren't you?
Mrs. Green: Yes, I am.
Lawyer: And you would do anything to save your boy
             wouldn't you?
Mrs. Green: Yes, I would.
Lawyer: Even lie to this jury, wouldn't you?

Mrs. Green: Well, I . . . .
Lawyer (interrupting):   No further questions.

Oddly enough some lawyers have adopted this fatuous ploy in real, live cases. Such heavy handed grilling is bound to fail. The interrogation must be much more subtle if, indeed, needed at all. (A good direct examiner will bring out the relationship himself and leave nothing for the cross-examiner to develop.) If required, then the device frequently used is a terminal "throw away" question:

Lawyer: Incidentally, did you happen to know the plaintiff before this incident?
Witness: Yes, we were roommates in college.

The lawyer quits then and lets the jurors draw their own conclusions. One such conclusion might be that the witness colored his testimony. The other, and often the more important, that the opposing lawyer was unfairly concealing relevant information.

Oddly enough the inference drawn from biased witnesses is more often a subject matter of closing argument than cross-examination. The party fails to produce the spouse, relative or friend who has knowledge of the litigation producing event or its consequences. The opposing party argues, "Where was the plaintiff's wife? If anyone should know about the injuries claimed by the plaintiff—she's the one. You can infer that the reason she wasn't here was that she would have had to say something unfavorable to her husband's case."

To prevent such a tirade the lawyer is usually well advised to produce the witness, reveal the relationship and let it go at that.

§ 15.20   Unendorsed Witness—Falsifier—Summary

One general caveat. Regardless of the area of interrogation which you may choose, any attack upon the credibility or bias of a witness carries with it some inherent dangers. Most jurors will identify with the witness as another layman caught up in the judicial process and they will be sensitive to any abuse which their comrade may suffer. Remember the advice followed by revolutionists, "When you shoot the King, shoot to kill!" If you are questioning the truthfulness of a witness you had best have the evidence to make your attack successful. If you have dispatched a witness by proof of his dishonesty you will be hailed as a seeker of truth. If you have merely wounded a witness by insinuation of his dishonesty you will be cursed as a bullying pettifogger.

§ 15.21 Second Hand Witness

The third characteristic of this phase of the examination is that it is secondary to direct examination. The pessimist will regard this as a worrisome handicap claiming that the initial interrogation has the advantage of introducing the witness, creating the mood and organizing the testimony. The optimist will emphasize the other side of the coin—the advantage of having the last word. This is a factor that can be of tremendous importance and, depending upon the organization of your interrogation, a dramatic plus or a devastating minus.

A second advantage lies with the second interrogator—he might not have to interrogate at all. In some cases the initial series of questions propounded may have satisfactorily exhausted the relevant information to be contributed by the witness. In such a case there is no need for you to elaborate and a well disciplined "No questions your honor" will fulfill your duty to your client.

C. FORMS OF QUESTIONING

§ 15.22 Generally

The manner in which any question is framed is important in a lawsuit—but particularly so in cross examining. Here we are dealing with the unrehearsed, unendorsed witness and consequently we must maintain a tight rein. In addition we must be careful concerning the mood we convey. In reality we are conveying two moods. One to the witness and one to the jury.

As to the witness himself we wish to be sufficiently non-hostile that we don't generate harmful responses. But as to the jury we wish to convey an attitude toward the witness of suspicion, or distrust or even contempt.

A too friendly interrogation may be interpreted by the jury as an endorsement of the witness. A too hostile interrogation may be interpreted by the witness as unfair haranguing which justifies some retaliatory responses.

At any rate, cross examination presents some unique challenges in the form of questioning to be employed.

§ 15.23 Leading and Suggestive Form

The law recognizes the difference between the interrogator questioning his own witness and the interrogator confronting his opponent's witness. The latter has unbridled use of the leading and suggestive question—a tactical tool that is designed to offset the handicap of an unrehearsed and perhaps hostile witness. And a powerful tool it is. The wonder is that it is used so sparingly by many practitioners. It has two obvious advantages: *one*, it permits the advocate to choose his own words in describing the event with which the witness is confronted; *two*, it limits the response requested of the witness.

Suppose the witness has observed a child move into the street and get struck by an automobile. On direct examination the key question would be submitted in straight interrogatory form, such as, "What did you observe?" followed by a narration such as, "This little girl started to cross the street. She moved about ten feet away from the curb when a north bound car struck her." The cross-examiner, unfettered from the restraints of the direct examiner can inquire, "Now this little girl darted right in front of the oncoming car didn't she?" The "darted" and "right in front" are lawyers' terms taken from the lexicon of any experienced defense attorney. And the invited response is a monosyllabic "Yes." There are some advocates who maintain that all of cross-examination should be a recitation by the examiner and mere affirmation or denial by the witness. This tactic is available to those advocates who have a particularly forceful personality (by which the witness is intimidated into a monosyllabic response) or a particularly pleasing one (by which the witness is seduced into the proper response).

"You pays yer money and you takes yer choice." It is either a driving or a coaxing operation. Whatever tack you choose, through the device of the leading question you are pointing the witness in the direction of your choice and you are saying things your way.

§ 15.24 Interrogatory Form

Despite the countless questions that can be asked on cross-examination, whether leading or not, all of them should fall within one of three general categories. The first is the simple interrogative form. It is a non-leading, open ended invitation to answer a question. It can be utilized by the cross-examiner on two occasions only: when the answer is known; or when the answer is unknown but meaningless.

§ 15.25 Accusatory Form

This is the form of question most frequently associated with cross-examination inasmuch as it is much more effective as a theatrical device and consequently most often utilized by the nasty prosecutors that infest television land. It is characterized as aggressive and leading.

The classic accusatory interrogation is illustrated in the story of the man who killed his wife by stabbing her, shooting her, burning the body with gasoline then running over her with a power mower. The questioning proceeded:

> Lawyer: You stabbed your wife with the butcher knife, didn't you?
> Defendant: Yes, the devil made me do it.
> Lawyer: Then you shot her with a twelve gauge shotgun, didn't you?
> Defendant: Yes, the devil made me do it.
> Lawyer: And then you poured gasoline on her body and burned it, didn't you?
> Defendant: Yes, the devil made me do it—but the lawn mower was my idea.

§ 15.26 Anticipatory Form

The third form is leading in nature but much less aggressive. Instead of thinking the worse of the witness and accusing him of some impropriety, the examiner thinks the best and anticipates proper behavior. Of course the key to the effectiveness of this form of interrogation is in knowing that the anticipatory "good" behavior will draw a confession of "bad" behavior.

§ 15.27 Illustrations

Now let us take a simple fact that you wish to develop on cross-examination and see how each of the three forms of questioning would be utilized. Assume that you are aware that at the time a surgical operation was performed on your client the defendant "doctor" was not licensed to practice medicine.

That simple bit of information could be introduced in three ways:

Interrogatory: "At the time of the operation were you licensed to practice medicine?"

Accusatory: "You weren't even licensed to practice medicine at the time of this operation were you?"

Anticipatory: "And of course Doctor, you were licensed to practice medicine when you performed this surgery?"

Which form you employ will depend on your personality and that of the witness. If you have a hostile witness who has offended the jury with his bellicose manner you might think the accusatory form appropriate. If you are a young advocate confronting a Marcus Welby type you will probably opt for the anticipatory form. During a lengthy interrogation keep all three forms in mind and, as the interior decorators say, "mix and match as your taste dictates," and keep the interrogation lively and varied. Remember that as we "suit the action to the word and the word to the action" we must also "suit the form to the witness and the witness to the form."

D. STRUCTURING THE INTERROGATION

§ 15.28 Generally

The tight rein of cross-examination dictates a well structured series of questions designed to elicit specific responses. Cross-examination was never meant to be a free wheeling inquiry into every facet of the direct examination. Deposition is the proper vehicle for such fishing expeditions. Questioning which is open ended and uncontrolled can only lead to a repetition of the damning testimony given on direct. The cross-examiner must be conscious of several rules before embarking on his mission.

1. Analyze the testimony on direct and appraise how it has helped or hurt.

2. Analyze the witness and identify his or her vulnerability.

3. Identify the purpose of your examination.

4. Employ specific tactics to reach that purpose.

§ 15.29 Limiting Response

It has previously been mentioned that one of the advantages of the leading question was that it helped to limit the witnesses' response. Such control being recognized as a necessary restraint on an unrehearsed, unendorsed witness. The limitation must go beyond the response to a given question. If possible we must restrict the witness to a definitive source of information for the questions posed.

Tying down a hostile witness is not unlike trying to catch a colt. If a colt were loose in a corral the first thing one would do would be to close the corral gate and limit the area in which the colt is free to roam before the pursuit would begin. Similarly, before moving in on a hostile witness, it is necessary to close the gate and limit the area in which he can roam.

§ 15.30 Limiting Response—Illustration

Let us suppose that you are confronted with a medical witness who has testified, in contradiction to your own medical expert, that your client has no evidence of a back injury. You have a copy of the doctor's report and you note that there is no mention of a straight leg raising test, a basic, well recognized clinical test utilized in the diagnosis of back complaints. The lawyer might be inclined to attack the witness directly with no attempt to limit the basis for the doctor's response.

Q. "Isn't the straight leg raising test a basic, well recognized method of diagnosing injury?"
A. "Yes."
Q. "Why didn't you perform such a test on my client?"
A. "I'm sure I did."
Q. "It isn't in your report."
A. "Well, I frequently don't bother to record negative results for tests that are given."

The quarry that was thought to have been trapped has escaped. And no wonder. The colt was left with an open gate—and he took to pasture.

Compare the result when this rule is obeyed.

Q. "Doctor, after examining this person you made a report didn't you?"
A. "Yes."
Q. "And the purpose of that report was to provide a basis for your professional evaluation?"
A. "Yes."
Q. "And then I am sure that it incorporates a complete recitation of the patient's history?"

A.   "Yes."

Q.   "And his complaints?"

A.   "Yes."

Q.   "And, of course, all of the tests which you conducted to ascertain the nature and extent of his injuries?"

A.   "Yes."

Q.   "This examination was made six months ago doctor and I'm sure you have seen many patients since then."

A.   "Yes I have."

Q.   "So that your testimony today concerning that examination is derived solely from the report you prepared. Is that a fair statement?"

A.   "I think it is."

Q.   "Doctor will you refer to your report please and read to the jury what your findings were in regard to the straight leg raising test."

A.   "It doesn't seem to be in there."

Q.   "Well then, you didn't conduct such a test did you?"

A.   "I guess not."

The point is you closed the gate. You confined the doctor to his report as the source of his information then asked the question to which you already knew the answer.

§ 15.31   Flanking Approach

The direct confrontation with a hostile witness, particularly one who is well versed in courtroom combat, is fraught with danger. Your mood is translated to the witness and the tougher the inquiry, the tougher the response. Let us take a simple fact situation which will serve as a vehicle to demonstrate the possible dangers for a frontal attack and the alternative of a flanking maneuver.

The witness, a psychiatrist, has testified to the state of mind of the defendant. The opinion which he has rendered is based upon a review of the defendant's record of ten visits as an out-patient in a hospital over a three-week period. There has been no personal examination by the witness.

There would be a natural inclination to "dig right in" and pepper the witness with a series of questions the essence of which would be "How can you possibly render a professional opinion based on such scanty evidence?" Such a direct inquiry would trigger a lengthy response, the essence of which would be, "I am an expert in my field and, as such, I recognize the significance of certain observations which to the layman would seem unimportant but to me are very revealing. I, and other psychiatrists, frequently render opinions based on information such as this."

§ 15.32 Flanking Approach—Illustration

The peripheral approach is characterized by a series of questions designed to elicit obvious, brief responses the cumulative effect of which establish a thesis contrary to that upon which the witness relies. In this instance you might proceed as follows:

"A man of science bases his opinion upon his observations, isn't that true?

And, of course if his observations are inadequate or improperly interpreted the opinion will be correspondingly inadequate and improper. If the condition being observed is a static condition, such as the physical property of an object, I assume that a single observation may suffice upon which an opinion could be based?

That is, if I asked you your scientific conclusion as to the height of a mountain or the width of this room you could reach a correct answer with a single measurement.

Now if the condition is not static, but varies from time to time—like the state of the weather, or traffic flow—then a person would have to make multiple observations before reaching a valid conclusion concerning the true nature of such condition?

For instance, it has rained here for the last five days and a person whose observation of our weather would be confined to such a limited observation might conclude that it rained all the time. But a man of science would have to make observations or study records for a long period of time before being able to make an accurate, scientific conclusion as to the condition of our weather here.

Now, Dr. Jones, when we talk about an individual's moods and an individual's behavior are we talking about a static condition which remains constant or a variable condition which changes from time to time?

So it is not unusual then that a person may be happy and outgoing at one time and sullen and morose at another.

And if an observation would be confined to that limited period when the subject was depressed it would be unfair and certainly unscientific to conclude that the person was a sullen

436

and morose personality. Now doctor did you ever, even once, observe the defendant yourself?

And the hospital notes that you consulted, how many observations do they make reference to?

Over what period of time?

Thank you doctor."

Note that the bulk of the questioning concerned matters that the witness could not dispute. The jury knew the answers before they were given. The questions were general and nonthreatening to the witness and couched in such a way that an affirmation was merely perfunctory. Only the last two questions call for factual information—and you know what those responses will be. Hopefully you have led the jury down a line of sequential reasoning that has completely undermined the witness conclusion—and all with such innocuous responses as "yes," "no," "ten times" and "three weeks."

§ 15.33   Peripheral Amplification

On some occasions it might be necessary to develop from an opponent's witness certain concessions that will be beneficial to your case. Such an effort to evolve *peripheral amplification* must be differentiated from an attempt to gain a direct affirmance of evidence adduced in your case. Assume that your client has testified in a product failure case that the product had been used properly at all times. The defendant has produced the retailer who has not disputed this testimony concerning the use of the product. On cross-examination, seeking to buttress an undisputed issue, plaintiff's lawyer inquires, "There was no evidence of improper use, was there?" To which the retailer replies, "Come to think of it, when she returned the widget there were some dents on the side indicating to me that someone had tampered with it or misused it." Your attempt to bolster an undisputed fact has now created a contested issue. Well enough was not left alone. Remember, "Don't add cream to the custard if there's a chance it will curdle".

The tactic of peripheral amplification is quite different. You know where you are going and have restraints on the witness. Your only job is to create a friendly climate and proceed in a nonthreatening manner to unfold some facts which amplify (not merely confirm) evidence previously adduced.

§ 15.34 Peripheral Amplification—Illustration

Assume a case in which the driver of a vehicle has been killed in a grade-crossing accident. The investigating officer, a part time deputy sheriff, has made a report indicating the final position of the vehicle and the train, the physical surroundings of the crossing and the notation that the autopsy revealed .07 alcohol in the decedent's blood. The plaintiff has called the witness to the stand to testify as to the physical conditions and that the crossing gate was not functioning the evening of the accident.

Step one, establish rapport:

Q. Officer Calvin, you have served in your capacity as deputy sheriff for how long? (Note the "officer.")
A. Four years.
Q. And I'm sure that before assuming that position you received some formal instruction regarding the duties of a law enforcement officer? (He read a four page manual).
A. Yes, sir.

Step two, identify the subject matter:

Q. And you spend a substantial part of your time in following your profession as deputy sheriff. (In reality he works 40 hours a week at a Quick-Stop and rides patrol 3 nights a week and on Sunday).
A. Yes.
Q. Now the official report that you prepare when you investigate an accident is sent to the State Highway Department, is that not true?
A. Yes.
Q. And the information contained in that report is utilized to promote safety on the highways and help reduce traffic accidents?
A. Yes sir.
Q. So in that regard you note everything of interest that would reflect on the cause of an accident and include it in your official report?
A. Yes.
Q. And of course you did that in this case?
A. Yes.

Step three, adduce the favorable conclusions:

Q. Now I note that you ordered that a sample of the driver's blood be analyzed for alcoholic content.

A. Yes, I requested that the coroner do this.
Q. You, of course, have been instructed as to the relationship between fatal accidents and drunken driving?
A. Oh, yes.
Q. And you thought that it would be significant in determining the cause of this accident that the Highway Patrol have this information.
A. Yes, I did.
Q. And you note on your report the presence of a stop sign for northbound traffic approaching the railroad tracks?
A. Yes.
Q. And again, you realized that this was important in determining the cause of the accident.
A. Yes.
Q. Incidentally officer, I note that you found no skid marks of northbound cars near that stop sign, did you?
A. No.
Q. Nor any other physical evidence that the driver attempted to stop.
A. No, Sir.

The witness was given very little opportunity to contradict the "opposing" lawyer and very little reason to do so. He was endorsed as an important person doing an important job and simply acknowledged matters about which there could be little dispute. His peripheral amplification was of substantial benefit to the second interrogator.

One final caveat. It might be that other facets of the witness' testimony must be sharply contradicted. If so, be aware of the chronology of your interrogation. Get your concessions first—then attack.

§ 15.35 Degradation by Degrees

Generally the advocate will handle interrogation with dispatch in order to keep things moving and hold the jury's attention. There are a few exceptions to that general rule. If on cross-examination you discover that an opposing party has been guilty of some indiscretion, some act or omission that is of some significance in the case, then such failure should be developed with some degree of thoroughness avoiding mere repetition and argument.

Don't let the dramatic event consist simply of a single question and a single confession. Take a tip from the strip teasers. They don't stride on stage and discard their scivvies accompanied by a drum roll. They slink onstage, start unpeeling the long gloves and do their disrobing by degrees. So too the cross-examiner should do his degrading. He must structure a series of questions designed to elicit a series of responses each one more damning in its implication. The purpose is to take the jurors by the hand and lead them into a deeper and deeper conviction of the impropriety of the witnesses' action.

§ 15.36 Stopping Short of Climax

The trial lawyer must be a disciplined individual and the need for this particular trait is most sorely needed during the examination of a hostile witness. You have become righteously angered by the inconsistencies of his testimony, you have carefully structured your line of inquiry, you have elicited some damning concessions and now you are ready for the kill or to mix the metaphor (and run the risk of a damning Freudian analysis) you are ready for the climax.

And so it is that the neophyte rushes into the trap and hoping to emulate Perry Mason by reducing the witness to a blubbery shambles and consummate the case, the one last question is asked that undoes all the previous efforts.

Of all the dangers of cross-examination this one is the most destructive and the one that most often victimizes the inexperienced advocate. Remember, the consummation comes at closing argument. Cross-examination supplies the facts from which the arguments will be made at a later and more propitious time. When the urge arises to go all the way remember, "coitus interruptus isn't half bad."

§ 15.37 Stopping Short of Climax—Illustration

The witness on direct examination has testified that he saw the northbound defendant vehicle go through the red light. On cross-examination he has been led to state that he had been standing on the northwest corner of the intersection and was walking northwardly immediately before the accident occurred. The lawyer could conclude at this point and argue that the accident occurred behind the witness who was not in position to observe the condition of the light. The neophyte will hazard, "How then could you have observed the traffic signal when you were walking away from it?"

And the response, "Well, I heard the squeal of brakes, turned and saw the light just as the collision occurred."

440

The exculpatory conclusion will always be there for the glib witness. Don't test him in the hopes that there will be a confession of error. Stop short of the climax—and score on closing argument.

E. EXPERT WITNESSES

§ 15.38 Generally

The expert witness provides a special case for the cross-examiner. First, there are several features of the expert and his testimony that are of unique value to the direct examiner.

1. The expert will no doubt be an experienced testifier. Indeed sometimes his expertise as a testifier exceeds his expertise as a doctor, metallurgist, or actuary. He will know the forensic arts and will enjoy the give and take of verbal jousting.

2. His testimony will deal with the esoteric and his conclusions will seldom be refuted simply with an application of common sense. Consequently the interrogator will have to be sufficiently versed in the subject matter of the expert to detect errors in his observations or judgments.

On the other hand, there are several aspects of the expert and his testimony that inures to the benefit of the cross-examiner.

1. You will usually have advance information of his testimony. Most jurisdictions will permit pretrial discovery of the identity of a manufactured witness and the conclusions which he has reached.

2. The expert is a hired gun and as such is subject to a charge of bias.

3. The expert is usually a person of unique accomplishment and as such is usually endowed with a sense of favorable self-appraisal that borders on conceit. Frequently, overweening pride will draw him beyond his area of expertise and subject him to refutation and a subsequent loss of credibility.

Much has been written concerning the challenge of handling an expert on cross-examination but few, if any, such attempts match the scholarship and perspicacity of the observations of

Richard M. Markus of Cleveland, Ohio, an astute observer and successful practitioner of the art of advocacy. Mr. Markus is a past president of the Association of Trial Lawyers of America which has distributed these comments, which are set forth in §§ 15.39–15.50, as one of its excellent series of ATL Counseling Cassettes.

§ 15.39 Purpose of Cross–Examination—Generally

Every demolition expert knows that almost any structure can be destroyed if the explosive charge is set at a critical location. For a trial, the structure of an adversary's case often depends heavily upon expert conclusions, and explosive cross-examination directed toward that expert can often cause an opponent's attack or defense to crumble. Unlike other witnesses, this witness will testify on ultimate conclusions which may be controlling if accepted. Typically, the expert's testimony is given very substantial weight by the jury. At the same time, although jurors may often identify with ordinary witnesses, they do not easily associate themselves with expert witnesses, and they are therefore willing or even anxious to see him cross-examined effectively. For these reasons, and because the expert can also be the source of information helpful to the cross-examiner, he can be the most vulnerable witness in the trial. Indeed, you are entitled to a sigh of relief when your own expert survives cross-examination without having an opponent inflict any truly serious wounds.

Since the identity of the expert and the substance of his testimony can usually be learned well in advance of trial, the strategy for his cross-examination can be developed before he answers a single question on direct examination. At least five separate goals are available to the cross-examiner in planning that strategy:

1. To create an impression for the jury that the cross-examination was successful.

2. To establish the examiner's theses on subjects not covered expressly by the direct examination.

3. To induce the expert to modify conclusions expressed on direct examination.

4. To discredit his conclusions expressed on direct examination.

5. To discredit the expert personally.

Of course, more than one of these goals may be part of a well structured cross-examination, and the examining counsel may well wish to plan alternative approaches which depend upon the answers that the witness gives during the progress of the questioning.

§ 15.40 Purpose of Cross–Examination—Seeming Success

The appearance of success in cross-examination is essential for this type of witness. One might wonder whether the attorney can make a favorable impression on the jury without in fact making any major substantive headway. Experience suggests that he can. Even the most sophisticated trier of fact will gather a central impression of oral cross-examination; that impression does not necessarily correlate with conclusions which would be formed by a careful study of the written transcript. While a jury may be offended by vigorous cross-examination of some witnesses, they know that the expert is important, and they expect him to be treated with special attention. Thus, it would be most extraordinary to pass up or abbreviate cross-examination of this type of witness. At the outset, your opponent's expert can be fairly shown (a) to be less than impartial, (b) to have significant limitations on the fields of his expertise, and (c) to lack certain helpful factual data.

§ 15.41 Purpose of Cross–Examination—Seeming Success—Illustration

Q. Now doctor, am I correct that you examined Mr. Roberts at the request of the defense lawyer?
A. Yes.
Q. And you knew at that time there was a lawsuit which concerned his condition?
A. Yes.
Q. Following that examination, did you prepare a written report of your findings and conclusions?
A. Yes.
Q. And that report was sent to the defense lawyer?
A. Yes.
Q. You did not send a copy of that report to me, did you?
A. No.
Q. Or to Mr. Roberts?
A. No.
Q. Or to Dr. Wilson, his treating physician?
A. No.

Q. Of course, you charged for your services in making that examination and report, didn't you?

A. Yes.

Q. That bill was also sent to the defense lawyer, wasn't it?

A. Yes.

Q. And not to me, or Mr. Roberts, or his doctor, Dr. Wilson?

A. That is correct.

Q. Am I also correct that you expect to charge the defense lawyer for the time involved in your testimony here?

A. Yes.

Q. Doctor, you testified that you are a neurosurgeon?

A. Yes.

Q. Are you also a psychiatrist?

A. No.

Q. Are you an x-ray specialist, a radiologist?

A. No.

Q. Are you a specialist in orthopedic surgery?

A. We do some of the same kinds of work.

Q. Are you a specialist in that field?

A. No.

Q. There has been testimony in this case about brain waves or electroencephalograms. Are you a specialist in interpreting those tests?

A. I review many of them.

Q. But doctor, aren't there physicians who do that type of work almost exclusively?

A. Yes.

Q. Often they practice at hospitals, don't they?

A. Yes.

Q. And when your patients have brain wave tests done at such hospitals, you generally rely on those specialists for interpretation of such brain wave tests, don't you?

A. Yes.

A general impression that the cross-examiner is making further headway can often be created by causing the witness to agree continuously to questions posed in a leading form. Even if those questions cover material that is not critical to the case or are simply preliminary background, the examiner appears to be obtaining concessions from the witness who repeatedly answers "yes" ... "yes" ... "yes."

Q. Professor Armstrong, can we agree that safety is an important consideration in good design?

A.   Yes.

Q.   And the greater the danger involved, the greater a good design should include efforts for safety?

A.   I suppose so.

Q.   And certainly where the machine could cause its operator to lose his hand if it malfunctions, that would be a very serious danger, wouldn't it?

A.   Yes.

Q.   Is it good practice to test a machine design after the machine is constructed by operating the finished product?

A.   Yes.

Q.   And such tests should be conducted enough times to see how the machine will function over a period of time, shouldn't they?

A.   Yes.

Q.   Would good practice also require that important maintenance procedures be specified in the maintenance manual for the machine?

A.   Yes.

Q.   And wouldn't it be desirable to have those maintenance instructions as specific as possible for critical maintenance?

A.   Yes.

§ 15.42   Purpose of Cross–Examination—Establishing Collateral Support

Too often, counsel spends all his efforts and time in attacking the adverse expert, without using that witness to develop portions of the cross-examiner's own case. A trial may involve a very broad range of subjects, so your opponent will often fail to prepare his expert on subjects not directly covered by his own examination. As a result, your cross-examination may develop such subjects before the expert can consider the significance of his answers or any way to avoid giving apparently obvious answers favorable to your total position.

§ 15.43   Purpose of Cross–Examination—Establishing Collateral Support—Illustration

Q.   Mr. Alberts, in your attempt to reconstruct the circumstances of this accident as an accident reconstruction expert, did you consider the ultimate destination of the Ace Way truck?

A.   Only that it was west of the accident scene.

Q.   You are familiar with the roads and cities in that area, aren't you?

A.   Yes.
Q.   And as I recall, you told us on direct examination that you had worked as safety engineer for a commercial trucking company for eight years?
A.   That's right.
Q.   In that capacity, did you sometimes consider preferred routes for your company's trucks?
A.   Sometimes.
Q.   Did you confer with dispatchers from your company to learn routes that company drivers followed in making deliveries and pick-ups?
A.   Yes.
Q.   Now, Route 236, where this accident happened, is north of Foxville, where the Ace Way terminal is located, isn't it?
A.   Yes, it is.
Q.   But on the basis of your knowledge of this area and your experience with truck drivers' route selection, wouldn't it be fair to say that it was a possible route to reach Foxville from Orson City?
A.   I suppose it could be used.
Q.   Certainly. We can agree, can't we, that the Ace Way driver wasn't off on an errand of his own, simply because he was going west on Route 236 to reach his terminal at the time of the accident?
A.   Not from that fact alone.
Q.   And since he was killed in the accident, so that we can't ask him why he selected Route 236, don't you think in fairness we can conclude he was still on company business?

Defense Counsel: Objection.

Q.   Let me withdraw that question and put it another way. Would you agree, Mr. Alberts, that the place of the accident and the direction the Ace Way truck was traveling are consistent with one reasonable route for a truck driver going from Orson City to Foxville?
A.   Yes.

An artfully prepared line of questioning may cause a defense medical expert to agree that the nature of injuries is more consistent with your position as to the liability facts. Almost every case has a similar group of issues which are tangentially related to the opponent's expert testimony, and which can be explored to establish or strengthen other aspects of your own case.

If nothing else, your opponent's expert is an invaluable source of testimony that will repel some of the attacks made by your opponent on your witnesses. For example, when an opponent asks your witness about an alternative possibility as cause for the accident or the injury, he plants a seed of doubt in the minds of some jurors. That seed can be rooted out, where the possibility is clearly spurious, by asking his expert whether that cause is in fact highly improbable.

In the same way, dubious statements made by other witnesses called by your opponent can be highlighted as improbable through the opponent's expert witness, who is technically able to express "opinions" on a broad range of subjects within the field of his specialty.

Q. Doctor, did you see any evidence that my client's condition was caused by lead poisoning?
A. Did you say lead poisoning?
Q. Yes.
A. No, I saw no evidence of that.
Q. Can we rule that out?
A. Yes, I would have seen other signs if there had been any lead poisoning.
Q. Did the defense lawyer tell you that an earlier witness considered that a real possibility?
A. No, this is the first I heard of it.

The adverse expert will typically not know where you are leading or why you are going there until after he has helped you (or harmed the counsel who has retained him) on these collateral matters. The cross-examiner's demeanor in this type of questioning can be conciliatory or even friendly, displaying considerable objectivity for the witness and the jury. If the witness does not follow the examiner's lead, he may well appear to be unreasonable. And, in any event, the skillful examiner can usually discontinue the collateral course of inquiry before any adverse answers become too serious.

§ 15.44   Purpose of Cross–Examination—Modification of Opinion

Unless the expert is adamantly rigid, a good cross-examination can frequently seek to accomplish minor changes or even major reversals on the key opinions expressed on direct. Quite often, expert conclusions are based upon assumed facts contained in one or more hypothetical questions. Although those questions may be extremely lengthy, the witness will be able to remember only a few specific facts when asked to specify the data contained in the hypothetical question which were necessary for his answer. To emphasize that these limited facts are the necessary predicate for the conclusions expressed by the witness, it may be helpful in appropriate cases to list those assumed facts for the jury on a blackboard or chart, particularly when they are disputed facts. The witness is then routinely asked whether his answer would change if each of the facts individually was modified or contradicted.

§ 15.45 Purpose of Cross–Examination—Modification of Opinion—Illustration

Q. If the straight leg raising test had been positive, would that have been significant?
A. It would be relevant.
Q. And if muscle spasm were also present in the lumbar muscles, would that cause you to modify your opinion?
A. I didn't find any spasm.
Q. I understand, but if a competent orthopedist did find that spasm and a positive straight leg raising test, on the day after your examination, wouldn't that cause you to modify your conclusion that he had fully recovered when you saw him?
A. Well, if you assume that, I suppose so.

Ultimately, if the witness seems to show some reasonable objectivity, counsel may ask the witness his own hypothetical question employing his own version of those same disputed facts or supplementing those disputed facts with additional facts. A well propounded hypothetical question virtually demands a given answer, since it is an abbreviated final argument. Therefore, the witness is again given the unpleasant choice of agreeing with your conclusion on the basis of your facts, or of seeming unreasonable to the jury.

If a favorable answer is obtained, and if the modified or supplemental facts are reasonably well established, the same use of visual aids to display the assumed facts and the resulting conclusions can be helpful. Whenever facts are added or changed, the onus for their omission or inaccuracy should be placed squarely upon opposing counsel, by asking the witness whether he had been advised by your opponent that the additional fact exists or that the assumed fact was disputed. Since the jury will usually identify more with a witness than with any lawyer, and since this technique tends to place the blame for the inaccuracy of the first answer on the opposing lawyer rather than the witness, the jury can then more readily accept the new answer as reliable.

§ 15.46   Purpose   of   Cross–Examination—Discrediting Opinion

When the witness is unwilling to modify his conclusions to any significant extent, the cross-examiner's goal may now become an attempt to discredit the conclusions entirely. This is typically accomplished by showing that the witness has reached conclusions that are inconsistent (a) with each other, (b) with testimony of other experts, (c) with reported conclusions of other experts in recognized publications, (d) with reported statements by the same witness on other occasions, or (e) with the common experience and logical thinking of ordinary jurors.

If the witness fails to modify his conclusions, the cross-examiner may well seek to push the expert to the most extreme *adverse* position possible, so that by such polarization the witness can be made to sound unreliable. Thus, a defense physician who testifies on cross-examination that the plaintiff is "a malingerer" or "a liar" probably hurts his own image more than he hurts the plaintiff's case, at least if there is any reasonable justification for the plaintiff's medical story. When the witness has been pushed to the extremity of his somewhat obtuse position, any demonstrable inconsistencies can be developed fully by the cross-examiner. Thus, the defense physician who ultimately calls the plaintiff "a malingerer" has trouble explaining why his medical-legal report describes the plaintiff as "cooperative." Other statements made during direct or cross-examination prior to the statement of the extreme position may also be held in juxtaposition for the witness, so that his efforts to extricate himself from his own inconsistency make him seem bewildered. However, in many cases, the best effect is created by simply asking the witness whether he did in fact testify earlier as to a certain fact, which fact the jury can see is inconsistent with his present conclusion. In this way, the jurors note the conflict, and the expert has no concurrent opportunity to attempt explanation.

The extreme nature of his conclusions can also be highlighted by showing his disagreement with other experts. Perhaps the most interesting technique is the use of authoritative statements in apparently reliable publications, which in effect call upon the witness to denounce his previous statement or acknowledge his disagreement with well respected text or journal authors. Remember that those authors expressed their opinions to advance science, not to advance the cause of any litigant. Before asking the witness whether a certain writing is authoritative, or whether he agrees with it, it is wise to make some investigation of the availability of this source to the witness. Thus, when you attend the medical examination of the plaintiff, make a list of the medical texts on the doctor's own personal library shelf. If he practices at some hospital regularly, visit that hospital library and note the publications that are available in that library as reference sources for the medical staff. Perhaps the witness had an instructor at school who was the author of some relevant article or text, or perhaps some other academician at the same institute authored a worthwhile publication on the subject involved.

It is often helpful to pile those articles and textbooks on the counsel table at the beginning of the direct examination. This action creates the distinct impression to the jury that you are prepared and causes the witness to feel some trepidation which will restrain him from making too many extraordinary statements. Then, when the books or articles are the subject of inquiry, they should be first identified in the questioning with the author's name and the author's full qualifications shown in the article. If the witness denies that the source is authoritative, even after he is asked whether he knows that it is located in his own personal library or his own professional library, all is not lost. Of course, in some jurisdictions, it is possible to ask the witness about the publication even though he denies its authoritative status. [Note, Federal Rule of Evidence, 803(18)] But, even if further inquiry is blocked by the rule of your jurisdiction, some impact has occurred from the witness' refusal to acknowledge familiarity with the publication. That impact compounds as the witness refuses to identify or acknowledge a second and a third and a fourth and a fifth of these seemingly authoritative publications, by authors with seemingly impressive credentials. Ultimately, the trier of fact is impelled to conclude either that the witness is ignorant in his own professional field or that he is adamant, stubborn, and untruthful.

The best source of conflicting expert opinion is, of course, prior statements by the witness himself. Certainly, no trial preparation is adequate if a search has not been made for books or articles by the anticipated witness. Similarly, if he has given speeches in a place where they may have been transcribed, that transcript should be obtained and reviewed. In jurisdictions

which permit pretrial depositions of expert witnesses, those depositions should be retained in a file for that witness after the case is
closed. Reference can then be made to those former depositions
for use in cross-examination when the witness appears again. If
the witness has testified with some frequency previously, his
testimony has probably been transcribed as part of a record for
appeal which is available for inspection at the courthouse. For
counsel who have a substantial volume of litigation involving
expert witnesses, it may be wise to prepare an index of expert
testimony contained in appellate records filed at the courthouse.
This is a simple project for a law student, or even a secretary.
However it is obtained, nothing is quite as devastating to a witness
and his testimony as being confronted by a completely contrary
statement made by him in another circumstance or context.

§ 15.47 Purpose of Cross-Examination—Discrediting Opinion—Illustration

Q. All right. Now, you were asked by Mr. Fisher to express an
    opinion about whether this boy did or did not have epilepsy, is
    that correct?
A. That is correct.
Q. And I believe you said that in your opinion he does not?
A. That is correct.
Q. And you premised that, if I correctly wrote down the reasons
    in my notes, on three reasons; one, he had a normal electro-
    encephalogram; second, he had a normal neurological exami-
    nation, and the third was that he was not rendered uncon-
    scious; is that correct?
A. Yes.
Q. All right. Now, doctor, would you agree with this statement:
        "I don't think that unconsciousness could be used as an
        index at all in connection with epilepsy because we have
        penetrating wounds of the brain in which very frequent-
        ly consciousness is not lost at all. Yet, these are the
        most frequent developers of jacksonian epilepsy. I don't
        think that unconsciousness or duration of unconscious-
        ness has any prognostic significance in regard to the
        possibility of later epilepsy."
A. Absolutely not.
Q. Doctor, I am reading to you, if it will assist you, a special
    address you gave at the Cleveland Academy of trial lawyers
    on February 27, 1960. Now, would you like to read your own
    speech? Did I read it correctly?
A. No, you didn't.

451

Q. All right. Do you want to read it all over again to us?

A. "I don't think that unconsciousness could be used as an index at all in connection with epilepsy because we have penetrating wounds of the brain in which very frequently consciousness is not lost at all. Yet, these are the most frequent developers of the jacksonian epilepsy. I don't think that unconsciousness or duration of unconsciousness has any prognostic significance in regard to the possibility of later epilepsy."

Q. Thank you doctor.

Finally, the ultimate inconsistency is the conflict between the witness' conclusions and the jury's own common experience. When the witness can be pushed so far in the direction of his extreme position that the jury finds his conclusions offensive, he has lost all value to your opponent.

Q. Let me ask you this: If Mr. Hadley has a traumatic neurosis—assume that he does have, for a minute. If this case is concluded and he gets every single penny he asks for, will he get well the next day, the next week, or the next month? When is it going to happen?

A. I think he will feel very much better as soon as he gets a check in his pocket.

Q. How about headaches, dizziness? Those will disappear the same day he gets the check? Put it in his pocket and that's it?

A. He may have headaches from different causes.

Q. But this condition is going to go away on that day, you can count on that?

A. That is medical opinion, yes, sir.

Q. It won't even take a week, it will be just that day, that first day?

A. That's right.

Q. You were going to say, doctor, I think, if you were able to, what percentage of the population you would expect to get a traumatic neurosis after a traumatic incident.

A. My experience is that it's about 50 percent.

Q. So that we have in this court room 13 jurors and a Judge. That makes 14. If they are in accidents which would cause them to have some injury, and it was somebody else's fault, you would expect that seven of them would have traumatic neurosis, is that fair to say, on the average?

A. I would think that would be a little high. If they were successful people, no, they would not. There are many factors to contribute to this.

452

Q. But you wouldn't be surprised if a number of these 14 people would, would you?
A. No, I would not.

He becomes a "monster" who discredits his own testimony on all subjects because he takes a ludicrous position on some particular subject. He has demonstrated his own lack of objectivity and his own partiality. In that instance, most juries are ready, willing, and able to accept a final argument that characterizes the expert as an advocate who wishes that he could be the lawyer rather than a disinterested professional person evaluating relevant facts.

Of course, at least some procedures that could be used for causing the witness to modify his conclusions can also be used to discredit his conclusions. Therefore, emphasis can and should be made during this phase of cross-examination on the limited opportunity by the witness to observe necessary facts, or the limited twisted facts supplied to him by the counsel by whom he was called to testify.

§ 15.48   Purpose of Cross–Examination—Discrediting the Expert Personally

The last and probably most dangerous cross-examination goal is to discredit the witness himself. This type of *ad hominem* attack can lose all the ground that the cross-examiner may have gained in his previous efforts. Keeping in mind that juries are more willing to identify with any witness, even an expert witness, than with any lawyer, no attack should be launched against the witness personally unless the examiner has every reason to anticipate a high degree of success. Nothing is quite as catastrophic as a personal attack that falls flat.

If a personal attack is undertaken, the same criteria for credibility which apply to ordinary witnesses are applicable here as well. Ultimately, the success of this procedure will depend upon a showing that the witness displays bias. That bias may be an objective bias, in the sense that the witness has financial benefits from this testimony and similar testimony in other cases. It may likewise be a subjective bias, which merely represents his own attitudinal set, and which is capitalized upon by those who wish to use a man with that viewpoint. Both objective and subjective bias can be shown by causing the expert to acknowledge that he has testified on many occasions for the same side or for the same position. Show that he accumulates a substantial portion of his total income in this way *or* that his personal attitude has made him particularly attractive to parties taking a specific position in that type of litigation.

§ 15.49 Purpose of Cross–Examination—Discrediting the Expert Personally—Illustration

Q. How much did you charge Mr. Swanson for examining this man?

A. I charge $50 for an examination and report.

Q. What is your regular charge for appearing in Court?

A. $150.

Q. How many times have you appeared for defendants in the last six months for testimony?

A. I think I have appeared in Court three times.

Q. You received $150 or more on each occasion?

A. Yes, sir.

Q. And how many cases have you examined for defendants within the last six months?

A. I would say on the average of perhaps three times a week, three or four a week.

Q. In six months that is 4 times 25, that is 100 times $50, that is $5,000; is that right?

A. In the last six months?

Q. Yes.

A. If that is what it adds up to, yes, sir.

Q. And you say it's *Mr. Hadley* that has a compensation neurosis; is that right?

A. No, I did not say that.

Again, methods of demonstrating bias for an ordinary witness are still available for an expert witness, if he has some special relationship to one of the parties or their attorneys.

§ 15.50 Order of Interrogation

While the order of cross-examination may vary with different cases, or with different experts in the same case, the safest order would be the sequence we have used to review the subject during this discussion. After a few preliminaries to show limitations on the expert's impartiality or expertise, the cross-examiner begins by gaining agreement from the witness on relatively unimportant things, then seeks to establish agreement on somewhat more important collateral subjects, then seeks to cause him to modify conclusions previously stated on direct, then seeks to discredit conclusions made by the expert on direct, and finally makes any attack he chooses to venture against the witness personally. This climactic order obtains favorable testimony from the witness at a time when he is receptive to the examiner, and increases the intensity of attack as the jury is persumably more willing to accept that attack.

Of course, the effectiveness of any cross-examination will depend upon the perceptiveness of the examiner in interpreting the mood and reaction of the witness, so that he can anticipate whether the witness will follow his lead over previously uncharted territory. This necessarily means that a relatively tight rein must be held by the form of questioning so that the witness is not free to make lengthy explanations which are beyond the control of the examining counsel. At the same time, if the rein is so tight that the witness is virtually gagging on it, such extreme restraint may offend the jury's sense of righteousness and brand the examining lawyer as totally unobjective and unfair. Of course, the efficacy of any of the above suggestions will depend upon the personality of the examining counsel and their suitability for his skill and experience.

§ 15.51   Caveats—Generally

There are a number of techniques of cross-examination that arise with such frequency in the trial of a case that it is advisable to forewarn the expert of the likelihood of their occurring. Some are employed by both plaintiff and defendant counsel. For instance, "How much are you getting paid to testify in this case?" Perhaps a sum has already been agreed upon. If so, the unthinking expert might simply respond "One thousand dollars". Of course, an answer such as this is apt to be misinterpreted by the jury. The question itself is a loaded one meant to imply that the expert is getting paid to give the "right" opinion. The implication should not go unchallenged. The expert should be alerted to the unfair nature of the question at a conference in preparation for the trial so he can give a more meaningful response. "I am not getting paid to testify. My presence in court has necessitated my absence from my office and the cancelling of a number of professional obligations. Of course in my absence the expense of the office continues, the salaries of my staff, the cost of maintaining the laboratory equipment, the rent—all those costs which are generally regarded as 'overhead.' Consequently I will have to charge for my appearance in court and I believe a fair charge is one thousand dollars."

More frequently the amount to be paid to the expert is not prearranged but is determined by the amount of preparation and length of time involved in his court appearance. If such is the case, think how devastating it would be if, in response to the query, "How much are you getting paid to testify?", the expert would respond, "It depends on how things develop." Again he should state, "I am not being paid to testify. My charge for my appearance in court will depend on how long I will be kept from my other professional obligations." Sometimes this loaded question can backfire on the inquiry lawyer. Confronted with this question at the close of a laborious and meaningless cross examination some experts have been known to reply, "It depends on how many foolish questions you intend to ask."

Other techniques of cross examination are more subtle—and more effective, giving more reason to advise the expert of the probability of their occurring.

The following illustrations deal with the medical expert but the problems are translatable to any area of expertise.

§ 15.52 Caveats—Causation

Assume the case of a claim for a ruptured intervertebral disc. The doctor in direct examination has given his opinion that the accident in question caused the injury and subsequent disability.

The cross-examination begins:

Q. "Doctor there are many things which can cause ruptured intervertebral discs, isn't that so?"
A. "Yes."
Q. "Sometimes they're caused by serious accidents, sometimes by minor mishaps, and sometimes merely by reason of the aging process, isn't that so?"
A. "Yes."
Q. "And Doctor isn't it true that in this case the plaintiff might very well have sustained this injury by bending over and tying a shoe?"

The moment of truth has arrived. Is the doctor to again answer with a simple "yes" (manifesting the attitude that anything is possible) and allow the jury to imply that the lawyer's version of cause and effect was as valid as the doctor's? The lawyer should advise his expert that the opponent will try to advance the argument that what caused plaintiff's injury "is anybody's guess." So, forewarned, the doctor can reply,

> "It is true that people have been known to slip a disc while tying a shoe, but that certainly didn't happen in this case. The plaintiff was a young man in perfect health before the accident, working full time as a manual laborer. He was a passenger in an automobile that was involved in a violent collision and immediately thereafter he experienced pain in his back which I have diagnosed as a ruptured intervertebral disc. In this case we're not talking about a disc brought on by old age or a minor mishap. This injury was caused by the accident."

§ 15.53　Caveats—Results

Other common pitfalls might confront the plaintiff's medical expert. The doctor has testified on direct examination that the plaintiff has suffered an injury which will leave him incapacitated permanently so that he will never be able to return to the type of hard labor that he had engaged in before the accident. In cross-examination the defendant's attorney asks a series of questions such as this:

Q. "Doctor, did you provide the care and treatment for the plaintiff?"
A. "Yes."
Q. "You did provide him with good medical attention and care to the best of your ability, did you not?"
A. "I did."
Q. "You were pleased with the result and, in fact, your surgery in setting the leg was considered to be quite satisfactory, was it not?"
A. "Yes it was."
Q. "And you did achieve an excellent result, did you not, Doctor?"
A. "Yes, I did."

Now the defendant's lawyer may very well stop interrogation at that time and if the doctor has answered in the nice, simple, direct, pithy fashion as illustrated, the jury will probably conclude that inasmuch as there has been an excellent result that really the plaintiff's residual disability was not as bad as it was originally pictured. The doctor should be advised in the conference before trial of the implications of such interrogation. If not so advised, the doctor, particularly if he is pleased with his management of the injury, will hesitate to amplify his answer. On the other hand how much more meaningful would the response be, if, in reply to the last question the doctor would state,

> "Yes, I did get an excellent result and I was very pleased that we were able to prevent this initial injury from being more serious than it is. The extent of the injuries were such that it might very well have been that this plaintiff would have been bedridden for the rest of his life. With the surgery that was performed we were able to rehabilitate him to the point where he is able to get about as you have witnessed him in the courtroom, but the injuries are still of such significance that even with the best of results, in my opinion it is impossible for him to ever regain the full strength and use of that limb which would enable him to resume his duties as a ditch digger."

§ 15.54 Caveats—Conflicting Opinions

The doctor must be advised that his opinion will be questioned by the opposition and that he might very well be confronted by opposing opinions. The matter might arise in this fashion. Assume the doctor has testified on direct examination that in his opinion the trauma that was suffered by the plaintiff in an automobile accident resulted in the miscarriage of her child some six days later. Cross-examination follows:

Q. "Doctor, you've indicated that miscarriage occurred some six days after the accident?"
A. "That is true."
Q. "And that there were no tissue changes in the fetus?"
A. "That is right."
Q. "Are you familiar, doctor with the works of Hertig and Sheldon regarding their observations of trauma and abortion."
A. "Yes, I am."
Q. "Doctor, you are aware of the fact that these men are considered to be expert in their field and that their writings are authoritative in the area of obstetrics?"
A. "Yes, I am."
Q. "Doctor, are you not also aware that they state that if trauma does not result in an immediate abortion that there should be evidence of tissue change before the trauma can be considered the cause of the abortion?"

A. "Yes, I am aware of their point of view."

Here again if the defendant's attorney completes his interrogation at this point it would appear to the lay jury that the doctor has been confronted with experts who entertain a professional point of view that is directly contrary to his and that upon being confronted with them in cross-examination he had to acknowledge their expertise and abandon his own opinion that he had given on direct examination. The doctor must be advised of the necessity of explaining his opinion and the reason for his disagreement with other experts.

Q. "Doctor, are you not also aware that they state that if trauma does not result in an immediate abortion that there should be evidence of tissue change before the trauma can be considered the cause of the abortion?"

A. "There has been a great deal written in medical circles concerning the relationship that a blow has to a subsequent miscarriage. Although these two gentlemen seem to entertain a point of view that it must occur shortly thereafter, or else that there be evidence of tissue change in the fetus, there are a great deal of others, including myself, who believe that the miscarriage can result as long as six days after with no apparent injury to the fetus. In fact, I have had cases of my own in which the miscarriages have occurred as long as two weeks after the blow and, in my opinion, the blow was the precipitating cause of the miscarriage. Medical science still has many areas in which there are some disputes. A doctor has to rely upon his own training, his own experience, and particularly his experience with the particular client involved. Now I have treated Mrs. Jones for three other pregnancies and I have delivered three children for her. I am familiar with her own health, I am familiar with her own medical history and I was called into this case immediately after the accident occurred, I witnessed the bruises and the contusions about her abdomen. I took a complete history. I followed her closely in the hospital for the six days interim between the blow and the time the miscarriage occurred and in my judgment by reason of my personal information of this plaintiff and her medical history and my own experience handling hundreds of these cases, in my opinion in this case the blow definitely caused the miscarriage."

§ 15.55 Caveats—Previous Courtroom Experience

Many of the previous caveats are more applicable to the plaintiff's expert even though the defendant expert must also be willing to amplify his answers when an unfavorable inference might otherwise be implied and explain his opinions when confronted with conflicting experts. But in many cases the defendant's counsel need not be so careful in advising his experts of these potential pitfalls. In the case of medical testimony particularly, the defendant's expert might have a greater familiarity with the courtroom than the lawyer. The reason is apparent. The plaintiff's lawyer takes the treating doctor as he finds him. The defendant gets to choose his own, and the choice usually falls to a veteran examiner who has sharpened his responses and honed his wits in many previous courtroom confrontations with hostile attorneys. It is this very experience, however, which sometimes proves to be the "Achilles heel" for the veteran defendant doctor.

It is not unusual for the defendant's medical expert to effuse an easy air of familiarity as he enters the courtroom scene. When his name is called to take the stand he walks straight to the bailiff, raises his hand in a perfunctory manner, responds to the oath with a flat "I do," nods to the judge and takes the stand. The recitation of his qualifications (the schools attended, the medical societies, the hospital staffs) is apt to be stale and lifeless and sound as if he has recited them a thousand times—as indeed he has.

On direct examination he may be brusque and seemingly impatient with the deliberate questions of defendant's counsel, responding to half asked queries and volunteering information he anticipates will be asked for.

As cross-examination begins, he leans forward in the chair as if relishing the opportunity to match wits with the opposition. He refuses to answer "yes" or "no," elaborates on every response and states his opinion without equivocation or compromise.

Such is the syndrome of the testifying expert and if all the symptoms are present it is time for him to be turned out to pasture. If, however, he will still take counsel, he must be advised to refrain from a display of courtroom familiarity. The juror, acting for the first time as an officer of a court, is impressed with his awesome responsibilities as an administrator of justice. The prudent lawyer will be sensitive to this attitude of the jury, treat the court with deference, the witnesses with courtesy, and display an attitude of respect, perhaps even reverence for the judicial process of which he is a part. The same attitude should be expected of witnesses, be they neophytes or veterans.

The plaintiff lawyer will seek to exploit this vulnerability of the defendant's medical expert,—ask about his previous appearances in court, his frequent examinations for defendant's counsel, the percentage of his practice given over to such activities. The defense lawyer must advise him of the proper tack to take. No resentment should be shown at this implication of bias. The doctor should explain: "For over thirty years I have been privileged to aid the court and juries in determining the nature and extent of injuries claimed to have been suffered in accidents." When asked what proportion of his business is given over to such examinations he might reply, "I have been requested more and more during the past few years to appraise these cases, not only in matters of this nature but for the state in Workers' Compensation Proceedings and for the United States Government in rating Veterans' disability, until now I devote about two-thirds of my professional time to such activity."

"A soft answer turneth away wrath" and the veteran expert must be well versed in this adage. After all, the better the expert, the more damaging his testimony and the more likelihood that he will be attacked. One should be concerned that if his expert is dismissed with "no questions, thank you" that he hasn't done the job. If heated cross examination is to take place, however, let it be initiated by the plaintiff's lawyer. The expert, or any witness, always appears in the better light as a counter puncher. Witness the following exchange:

Q. "And Doctor you spend quite a bit of your time testifying in the cases where you have examined injured plaintiffs?"
A. "No, not really. Most of the cases in which I am asked to appraise an injury are settled on the basis of my medical report."

F. LIMITATIONS ON SCOPE OF EXAMINATION

§ 15.56 Generally

There is one legal limitation that is imposed in some jurisdictions which provides that the scope of the cross-examination should be limited to those matters covered in direct examination. An example of this is Federal Rule of Evidence 611(b) which provides:

461

Cross-examination should be limited to the subject matter of the direct examination and matters affecting the credibility of the witness. The court may, in the exercise of discretion permit inquiry into additional matters as if on direct examination.

The rationale for this limitation is difficult to defend. If a witness is called to tell the truth, the whole truth and nothing but the truth it seems incongruous to relate a portion of direct examination and then have further disclosure withheld because the endorsing party had not found it to his advantage to explore such other areas of inquiry. "But you have your remedy" argues the proponents of such a rule. "Call the witness as your own and ask any question you desire." That remedy is far from satisfactory. Why should an opposing party endorse the credibility of a witness with unknown or perhaps even faulty credentials? And why should a lawyer through a restricted line of inquiry on direct examination thrust such a burden on his opponent?

If there is any merit to such a rule the effects can be ameliorated by a third approach. Let the judge retain the witness as a witness of the court and permit both counsel to cross-examine as to the heretofore unexplored area of inquiry. This is provided for in the above quoted Federal Evidence Rule.

CHAPTER 16

OBJECTIONS

"You're charged with treason"

"I object!"

"On what grounds"

"I couldn't think of anything else to say"
Duck Soup—The Marx Brothers

Analysis

A. GENERALLY

463

A. GENERALLY

§ 16.1 Introduction

Let us initiate discussion with a recognition of the broad scope of objections. Traditionally we think of an objection to evidence made during the testimony of a witness, questioning the propriety of a given question. We must not confine ourselves to such a narrow view. An objection is the device by which we call to the attention of the trial judge any imminent, existing or executed impropriety. The individual accused of the impropriety will probably be our opposing counsel and the subject matter of the complaint will likely be a matter of law. But your complaint may be against the actions of a witness who is weeping on the stand; or a litigant in the courtroom who has shouted out "That's not true!"; or a juror who, in violation of the court's instruction, is taking notes; or a judge who has grimaced in disbelief as your client has testified to a key element in the case. Nor must the complaint occur during the reception of evidence. Objections will occur during voir dire, opening statement, summation and the charge. It is surprising how many neophyte lawyers sit through an offensive opening statement or closing argument and explain their failure to object with an incredulous, "I didn't know I could interrupt." No matter who the offender or when the offense occurs if redress is sought, there must be an objection made. The mechanics may differ depending on the instance, but the gist remains the same. Something is about to happen, is happening or has happened which is adverse to your client's interest, you want relief and if that relief is not afforded you are going to claim "foul" to the bosses upstairs.

B. MECHANICS

§ 16.2 Specificity

Keep in mind that if the basic function of the objection is to tell the judge "that can't be done and if you permit it, I'll have you overruled" then, to fulfill that function it is necessary to give a judge adequate warning of his impending error and make your objections specific in form.

Rule number one, make your objection and state the grounds. "I object" will not suffice. If the judge overrules you, it is not proper on appeal to bushwack him from a belated explanation to the appellate court that the proffered testimony was hearsay. The trial judge should be afforded the benefit of your legal sagacity at the time of your objection concerning the basis of your complaint and if the judge rules improperly you can't complain because it was your own silence which led him into his error.

Rule number two, is the converse. If you are to complain successfully on appeal about the court's ruling then specificity must characterize both the objection and the ruling.

There are a fistful of cliches employed by some judges which neatly sidestep a direct ruling.

> "Will you restate the question counselor?"

> "Sustained as to the form."

> "You are straying a bit but proceed."

How has the judge ruled? It is difficult to tell, if indeed he has ruled at all, and a complaint on appeal will probably be fruitless.

Suppose you have asked your witness:

> "How did the defendant appear to you?" and your opponent responds,

> "Objection, calls for a conclusion" and the judge contributes,

> "Restate the question."

The inexperienced advocate is now put into an embarrassing dilemma. He has received an order from the court, he is eager to please, he assumes that if any impropriety has occurred it has probably resulted from his own ineptness. But how can he state the question differently? "How did the defendant *look* to you?" No wonder in a goodly number of cases the question is abandoned and a relieved interrogator goes on to something else. Incidentally, it is not only the intimidated interrogator which is relieved, so is the judge. He has finessed the ruling and there is nothing now in the record by which he can be accused of error. You can expect a continuing use of this sidestep maneuver throughout the trial. The proper response for the advocate in such a situation is to state firmly but politely, "Your honor, may I have a ruling on that objection?"

That should evoke a "sustained" or "overruled" but if the judge continues the gambit with "I have ruled" then the advocate must reply, "Was the objection sustained or overruled?" With this illustration it is not meant to imply that only judges on occasion can be devious in their rulings. Counsel can be just as devious in their objections—and when that occurs it is the judge's turn to clarify the meaning of the counsel's position.

Q.   "Did the witness state to you how fast he thought the car was traveling?"
       Lawyer: "That's an improper question."
       Court: "Are you objecting?"
       Lawyer: "Yes, your honor. I object."
       Court: "What are your grounds?"
       Lawyer: "The question calls for a conclusion."
       Court: "Are those your only grounds?"
       Lawyer: "Yes."
       Court: "Overruled."

(The inquiry as to the "only grounds" was an invitation to give the right grounds, hearsay, but failing to receive the proper grounds the objection was properly overruled.)

The lesson to be learned is simply this: judges are entitled to be advised with specificity that an objection is being made and the grounds on which it is based—and lawyers are entitled to a specific ruling.

§ 16.3 Timeliness

If the question is offensive it should immediately trigger a response. A momentary pause and the damning response has entered the consciousness of the jury. A favorable ruling at that stage is of little help. Besides if the judge rules erroneously your lack of timeliness will probably eliminate any grounds for complaint on appeal. And it is no excuse to say, "Well, I knew the question was improper but I just couldn't think of the grounds." Make your general objection anyway. In the time it takes you to say "I object your honor" you might have thought of the proper incantation. If the gray matter lets you down maybe the judge will sustain you without a specific ground being stated.

§ 16.4 Courtesy

Some questions or statements of opposing counsel may be so outrageous that you can properly respond with righteous indignation. In such cases show it. But if you respond with bellicosity or disgust with each objection you will be guilty of emotion overkill. Most often the appropriate tone will be one of patience and courtesy perhaps even prefaced with "Pardon me, your honor, I must object to that question because I am afraid it calls for a hearsay response." It is pretty tough for a jury to be offended by that.

§ 16.5 Insistence

Courtesy, however, does not dictate that the objecting counsel be vacillating or perfunctory. You should convey to the jury that you have reluctantly interrupted the proceedings only because a matter of significance has prompted your action. A weak "I object" will be ignored by an aggressive witness and will serve no purpose. Rise from the counsel table and with a firm voice address the court. If the witness continues to talk, remain resolute and if the court doesn't instruct him to withhold his response, you tell him to do so. The jurors know the ground rules and they will not punish the lawyer for attempting to thwart a "cheap shot" by a witness ignoring a timely objection.

§ 16.6 Sequential Relief

Seek your relief in an orderly sequential fashion. Do not mimic the aggressive advocate who rises with each objection and asks for the whole bundle from admonition of counsel to mistrial. Assume the following:

Q. What did this witness tell you that he had heard the defendant say?
Lawyer. I object your honor, hearsay.
Court. Overruled.
A. He said that the defendant stated it was his fault but that he had plenty of insurance.

A response like that could trigger a request for several distinct types of relief:

1. That the response as to "plenty of insurance" be stricken;

2. That the jury be instructed to disregard the remark;

3. That counsel be admonished for soliciting such obviously improper evidence;

4. That a mistrial be granted.

If all these requests are lumped together, or if only the most substantial relief sought, you will have a much more difficult time on appeal to convict the court of an improper ruling. Afford the

court an opportunity to consider the relief sought in proper
sequential order, beginning with that relief most apt to be granted
and continuing through until your request is overruled.

You will then be in position to argue that the least of your
requested reliefs was not granted rather than argue that it was
prejudicial error not to grant the greatest relief that was sought.

§ 16.7 Physical

A second mechanical consideration aside from the verbal form
of the objection is the manner in which it is made.

Assume that an opposing litigant has started weeping on the
stand. You can hardly boom out from the counsel table "I object
your honor. The plaintiff is weeping on the stand and is obviously
seeking to gain the sympathy of the jury." A more discreet
maneuver would be to request permission to approach the bench
and out of the hearing of the jury, state, "May the record show
that the plaintiff is weeping on the stand. I must object your
honor to this display of emotion and its consequent effect on the
jury and ask for a mistrial."

Some judges disdain such sidebar conferences and adopt a
policy that objections will be made from counsel table. If such is
the case, then the manner of making the objection (being within
the hearing of the jury) becomes even more critical. It would be
advisable in such a case to state, "Your honor, in order to protect
my client I must point out that the plaintiff is weeping on the
stand. I am afraid that the jury will be unduly affected by such a
situation to the prejudice of my client and I must ask for a
mistrial."

If the court permits objections outside of the jury, use the
privilege sparingly. Nothing breaks the flow of testimony nor
frustrates the jury more than the interminable conferences at the
bench. And besides most of your objections you'll want to share
with the jury, so let go from the counsel table.

C. PURPOSES

§ 16.8 Generally

In the free wheeling system of American advocacy the objection has assumed a role far greater than that which it plays in the

English system. For our well behaved barrister brethren an objection is a finely honed instrument utilized for the sole purpose of excising from the fact finder's attention those bits of information which fall beyond the pale of proper evidence. Consequently the barristers employ its use with a great deal of restraint. If an objection is improperly made the ill founded request for relief is a reflection on the professional competence of the advocate who failed to recognize the impropriety of the evidence which he sought to admit. The overruling of the objection, on the other hand, is a professional put-down for the complaining advocate who obviously failed to recognize competent evidence sought to be introduced by his opponent. Good barristers should know the rules of evidence and it should be that knowledge and a highly developed sense of professional pride which determines what evidence should be proffered. Subtle refinements of evidentiary interpretations may be properly submitted to the trial judge for ruling but these will occur with great infrequency.

Not so on this side of the ocean. Objections have become an integral part of the art of advocacy and a typical trial is shot through with interruptions by counsel objecting to some attempted action on the part of his opponent. A good question might be raised as to the ethics of some of the uses to which these objections are put but let us reserve judgment as to that at this time and simply recognize the functions which the objection might serve.

§ 16.9   Legal Purposes—Excluding Information

The first and most common legal purpose of invoking an objection is to exclude information from the jury. This might take place at any time during the trial. The reasons might range from irrelevant to privileged but the request is the same—don't let the jury know! The secret is to know the exclusionary rules of evidence and to have a hair trigger mind that immediately responds when the offensive question soliciting excludable information is asked or when the offensive statement is made on voir dire, opening statement or closing argument.

§ 16.10   Legal Purposes—Modifying Interrogation

A secondary legal purpose of the objection is to modify the manner in which the questioning is taking place. The complaint is directed not to the content of the interrogation but to the manner.

Q. "You mean to say that although you saw this young child in the street you didn't even bother to blow your horn?"
Lawyer: "I object your honor, the question is argumentative."
Court: "Sustained."

As illustrated, the abuse is merely verbal. On occasion the offensive interrogation might include an approach to the witness stand or some other type of intimidating gesture which would provoke the objection that "counsel is badgering the witness." Perhaps the worst by-product of dramatized trials is the artistic need to include interrogator and witness in a single close up scene. The prosecutor in a literal nose to nose confrontation shouts, "And that is why you killed your wife isn't it?" The seasoned advocate watches such pyrotechnics and wonders how long such tactics would be tolerated in the average court room.

The sensitivity to the possibility of such abuse has often led to the enactment of court rules that compel the interrogator to address the witness while standing at a lectern or seated at counsel table.

§ 16.11 Legal Purposes—Preventing Prejudice

This is the third, "garbage can" category which includes those numberless occasions when the court's attention must be drawn to some circumstance which adversely affects your cause. Unlike the previous illustrations, the event complained of will not necessarily be a part of the record. The function of the lawyer, consequently, will be to describe for the record the event which gives rise to the complaint and then enunciate the objection. Most frequently this will be out of the hearing of the jury.

Assume that during a recess you have witnessed a juror talking to your opposing litigant. In judge's chambers you must state for the record what you observed—and don't be content with "I saw the juror talk to the defendant." Describe the time, the place, the length of the conversation, the content, if possible, the reactions of the individuals—and then ask for your relief. Frequently these "for the record" descriptions may be subject to modification from opposing counsel or the judge. Lawyer One states, "Let the record show that the witness when being sworn turned to the jury and winked" to which lawyer Two responds, "Your honor, the witness obviously had something in his eye and blinked in order to relieve the pain."

The real crunch comes when a record must be made by reason of some misconduct of the judge. "May the record show that the judge scowled and in a loud and threatening voice told the witness 'Speak up!' and in sarcastic tones added, 'If you want the jury to believe what you said they will have to hear you.'

To which the judge no doubt will add, "My voice was neither loud nor threatening nor my manner sarcastic."

Remember, again, that the purpose of the record is to preserve your grounds for complaint to an appellate court. To do this, the appellate judges must know what happened. This requirement that the objection be made a part of the trial record is set forth in Federal Rule of Evidence 103(a) as follows:

> Error may not be predicated upon a ruling which admits or excludes evidence unless a substantial right of the party is affected, and

> (1) *Objection.* In case the ruling is one admitting evidence a timely objection or motion to strike appears of record, stating the specific ground of objection, if the specific ground was not apparent from the context; or [(2) by offer of proof].

§ 16.12   Extra–Legal Purposes—Generally

Now we enter the area of penumbral propriety—the objection raised to tactical purposes only. The lawyer, given the right of interruption to make a legal complaint as to content or manner of interrogation, utilizes that right for some other purpose. To be sure the objection may be couched in the traditional matter and perhaps there is even a touch of legitimacy to it, but the reason for the objection is something other than the "legal" reasons cited above. Something "extra" is sought to be accomplished.

§ 16.13   Extra–Legal Purposes—Changing Momentum

All of us are familiar with the situation in a baseball game when the batting team manages to launch a series of hits. The tempo of the game increases, the enthusiasm of the successful hitters spreads to others on the team and the success of one feeds on the success of the other. It is then that the manager of the fielding team calls time out, deliberately walks to the mound, confers with the pitcher, the catcher and their infield cohorts, then slowly returns to the dug-out. Perhaps the discussion concerned itself with baseball strategy but most likely the conference was employed as a simple device to break the rhythm of the succeeding team and help settle down the other.

This same phenomenon occurs in trial. The interrogator uncovers an embarrassing line of inquiry, he asks a series of probing questions, the pace of interrogation increases, the witness becomes rattled and confused—then the opposing lawyer rises and, in as deliberate a fashion as the baseball manager moseying to the mound, states:

> "Pardon me your honor, may we approach the bench? (out of the hearing of the jury). I'm going to have to object to the manner in which counsel is interrogating this witness. He has continuously used argumentative questions and his tone and manner have been threatening. As a result of this method of interrogation the witness has obviously become confused and rattled."

> Court: "Your objection is overruled."

> Lawyer: "Your honor, may I note that it is about 10:30 a.m. and we have not had our mid-morning recess as yet. May we recess now?"

> Court: "No. We will complete the cross-examination of the witness."

Counsel has achieved a two minute relief for the witness. The rhythm of the interrogator has been broken and hopefully, the witness has "settled down" and can cope with the cross-examination a bit better.

Some judges, aware of the purpose of the objector might not be as solicitous and refuse a request for a side bar conference, summarily overrule the objection and instruct the interrogator to proceed. One judge when confronted with a frivolous objection and a request for a recess for the obvious purpose of "regrouping" a harassed witness, responded with this Ozarkian philosophy, "Mr. Lawyer, you never call off the hounds when they have just about treed the coon. Proceed." A comment like that in front of the jury can take the romance out of an extra-legal objection.

§ 16.14   Extra–Legal Purposes—Instructing the Witness

A more questionable practice utilized by some lawyers is the employment of a speaking objection to instruct the witness concerning the "proper" response to a question.

Q. "How many times was the plaintiff absent from work during this period of alleged disability?"

Lawyer: "I object your honor, this witness has no specific memory as to this and besides the work records would be the best evidence."

Court: "Overruled."

A.   "I really have no specific memory as to this."

This type of abusive use on an "objection" is employed even more frequently during deposition. The witness is asked a question concerning speed, distance, or length of time. The lawyer, fearing a harmful response interjects by stating, "I object, the question calls for speculation and unless the witness knows for certain he should not guess." The message has come through loud and clear and in too many instances the witness says, "Any answer I would give would be a guess."

How do you counter a tactic such as this in the courtroom? The only answer is an objection of your own. "I object to counsel instructing the witness as to the desired answer." Repeated abuse could prompt a request for admonition of counsel or even a mistrial. At any rate, make your record so that the trial judge or appellate court are given the opportunity to provide a remedy.

§ 16.15   Extra–Legal Purposes—Instructing the Jury

The speaking objection is also a tool to instruct the jury and usually takes the form of a comment on the evidence. Whether such a comment is within the bounds of good ethical practice and legitimate advocacy will depend on the situation. Consider your response when confronted with the following:

Q.   "Now after being advised by your lawyer about getting medical attention when did you see Dr. Young?"

In reality Dr. Young is the family doctor and had been consulted for treatment long before the client had sought legal advice from you. You have two choices:

"I object, there is no evidence that I advised my client to seek medical attention."

The objection to that objection is obvious. Semanticists might term that a negative pregnant. Your only complaint is that there is *no evidence* of such conduct. It is a bit like saying "It couldn't have been my fingerprints on the safe, I was wearing gloves."

The second choice instructs the jury as to the facts:

"I object, I never so advised my client. He went to his family doctor long before he sought legal advice."

Ideally, such pettifogging interrogation should be dealt with summarily by the judge with a harsh reprimand in front of the jury. But too often the advocate must protect his own flanks and frequently the best manner, and perhaps the only, is with a speaking objection instructing the jury.

D. CONSEQUENCES

§ 16.16 Legal Consequences

An objection should not be made in a cavalier fashion without substantial legal grounds for its validity. You may seek relief from the trial court, and be sustained in your position only to be told by an appellate court that the court ruled improperly. Sometimes a lawyer finds himself making a knee-jerk objection, having it sustained, then on sober second thought realizing that he might have introduced reversible error in the proceedings. If this second appraisal occurs quickly enough you can withdraw the objection immediately or after the offer of proof by your opponent. If that opportunity passes, approach the bench at the conclusion of the witness direct examination and withdraw the objection. Under these circumstances the response might be unduly highlighted but it might be better than risking a reversal.

§ 16.17 Extra–Legal Consequences

Every lawyer seems to be sensitive to the dangers of continually obstructing proceedings with objections. Many attempt to ameliorate that adverse effect by inquiring on voir dire whether the jury members understand that during the course of trial, it might be necessary to lodge objections and then seeking a promise that they won't hold that against him. Or perhaps during summation that stock statement will appear, "If I have done anything to offend you, such as making the numerous objections which I thought necessary to protect my client, hold it against me but don't penalize my client."

The efficacy of such tactics is questionable. Some may buy it, others not. The fact is that most jurors like all the cards on the table and want to share in every facet of the controversy before them. The lawyer who tries to obscure the facts by a profuse precipitation of those exclusive tete-a-tetes at the bench will be looked upon with disfavor. Legalistic obstructionism will never have the persuasive effect of ingenuous open-handedness and

before you employ the former you had better decide that the
evidence which you seek to exclude is of sufficient importance to
run the risk of alienating the jury.

CHAPTER 17

OFFERS OF PROOF

"If it ain't in the record, it didn't happen"
Billy Roy Wilson

Analysis

§ 17.1 Generally

When an attempt to adduce evidence is frustrated by an opponent's objection sustained by the court it is necessary to include within the record a recitation of the attempted proof in order to argue on appeal that its exclusion was of a prejudicial nature. Assume for instance, that your inquiry of a witness is, "What did the defendant tell you after the accident?" Your opponent objects, the judge sustains, and you proceed with another question. The record is silent as to the subject matter of the defendant's comment, consequently, you have no cause to complain as to the prejudicial effect of its exclusion. As far as a reviewing court is concerned the response might have ranged anywhere from "It was all my fault" to "It was all your fault." In order to preserve the record for review the adducing lawyer must make an offer of proof.

§ 17.2 Methods of Making—Narrative

Assume a fact situation in which a locomotive has struck an automobile at a grade crossing. The engineer immediately walks back to the scene of the impact and hears an onlooker state, "That crazy driver didn't even slow up. He went right past the signal into the side of the locomotive."

The interrogation of the engineer proceeds as follows:

476

Q. After the collision what did you do?

A. I stopped the train as soon as I could, hopped off the engine and hurried back to the crossing.

Q. Were there any persons there?

A. Yes.

Q. Did you talk to any of the persons there?

A. Yes one fellow said—

Lawyer. Object your honor, hearsay.

Court. Sustained.

Lawyer. May we approach the bench? (Out of hearing of the jury). Your honor it is our position that such a statement would fall within the res gestae or excited utterance exception.

Court. The evidence as it now stands does not so indicate. My ruling stands.

(Interrogation continues)

Q. How far did the engine stop beyond the crossing?

A. Approximately five hundred feet.

Q. How long did it take you to get down off the cab and return to the crossing?

A. No longer than two, maybe three minutes.

Q. Could you describe the demeanor of the person who talked to you at the scene?

A. He seemed pretty excited. He ran up to me and started blurting out what he had seen.

Q. And what did he say?

Lawyer. Same objection your honor.

Court. Sustained.

Lawyer. May we approach the bench? (Out of hearing of jury). Your honor, I wish to make an offer of proof. If the witness would be permitted to respond he would testify that the person stated: "That crazy driver didn't even slow up. He went right past the signal into the side of the locomotive."

Judge. The offer is received. My ruling remains. Proceed.

§ 17.3 Methods of Making—Interrogative

In some instances the evidence which is sought to be adduced covers an extensive line of questioning which cannot be succinctly recited by the lawyer or the exact nature of the witness' response may not be known. In such a case the usual procedure would be to have the jury retire and then make an offer of proof through the usual interrogation of the witness.

Q. State your name.

A.   Lee Travers.

Q.   What is your occupation?

A.   I am in charge of construction and maintenance for the Reading Railroad.

Q.   In response to my subpoena have you brought with you the records of your company concerning the installation of safety devices at the crossing of your tracks and Highway 32 near Prairieville?

Lawyer.   I object your honor to this line of inquiry. We have stipulated as to the safety devices that existed at the time of the accident and any change in conditions subsequent to the accident is irrelevant.

Court.   Sustained.

Lawyer.   May I make my offer of proof?

Court.   Yes. Ladies and gentlemen of the jury you may retire to the jury room for a short recess.

Court.   Proceed.

Q.   Were there any changes subsequent to the accident of October 11th?

A.   Yes there were.

Q.   What changes were there?

A.   We installed an electric flasher signal and a crossing gate.

Remember that the purpose of the offer of proof is to establish for a reviewing court that the evidence which was excluded from the fact finder was of sufficient importance that its exclusion was reversible error. For that reason it is mandatory that the proffered evidence be developed as fully and persuasively as if the jury was hearing it. In addition, the offer must meet the usual rules for the reception of evidence. If in the preceding illustration the subject matter of subsequent repair was excluded because of lack of relevance, the proof of that subject matter was properly adduced by a witness with personal knowledge of the changes made. If hearsay testimony had been offered to establish this fact then the offer of proof itself could have been subject to a valid objection and the record would still be devoid of the information on which an appeal would be based.

§ 17.4   Record of Offer and Ruling

Federal Rule of Evidence 103(b) provides that the court may add any other or further statement which shows the character of the evidence, the form in which it was offered, the objection made, and the ruling thereon.

CHAPTER 18

CLOSING ARGUMENT

*"And for the first time I've been seeing
the things I never noticed without you"*
Winterwood —Don McLean

Analysis

A. LEGAL SETTING

B. MECHANICS

C. ORGANIZATION

D. DEVELOPING THE ARGUMENT

E. CONTENT

A. LEGAL SETTING

§ 18.1 Generally

The closing argument is an exercise in persuasion. To that extent it should meet the test of any good persuasive effort. Those universal rules developed over the ages by debaters and rhetoricians merit the study of anyone seeking to become an effective advocate but we will not incorporate such universalities here. We shall limit ourselves to those unique circumstances which characterize the legal process and render the closing argument a singular form of persuasion.

§ 18.2 Unit of Persuasion

First, as to the identity of our object of persuasion. We are dealing with a multi-personality single unit. Not an individual nor even a group of individuals but a unique totality. This jury has (note how it takes the singular verb) heard the same evidence, been instructed on the same issues of law, and will render a collective verdict. The importance of this should be self-evident. The arguments that are to be advanced must, if at all possible, have group appeal. Except in rare cases (such as in the defense of a person accused of crime in which a hung jury might be advantageous), the advocate will be seeking to persuade the entire group or at least a substantial number of the group (as in those jurisdictions where two-thirds or three-fourths determine the verdict). An argument that will attract some and repel others serves no purpose. The jury should be addressed as a unit, appealed to as a group, brought together so that they can function as a team.

§ 18.3 Identity of Jurors

Second, we must consider the nature of the group background. They will be selected members of society with a sense of civic responsibility a cut above the random citizen.

Consider the elements of their identities:

1. Registered voters (most potential jurors are selected from the registered voter lists).

2. Willing to serve (most often an excuse can be invoked to evade jury service).

3. Conditioned by pre-service instruction (jury manuals or a film will have instructed them on the importance of their service).

4. Survivors of the selective process of voir dire.

5. Under oath to "well and truly try the issues."

These are not ordinary people unexpectedly confronted with a run-of-the-mill sales pitch. The trial lawyer doesn't face the sales resistance encountered by an encyclopedia salesman making a random house call and encountering a harassed mother with a cake in the oven and a two year old on the potty. These potential buyers have been selectively chosen, carefully groomed, placed in a jury box and committed under oath to listen to your presentation. No need for any foot in the door tactics, no explosive introductions nor gimmicky interrogations. You have them before you under the watchful eye of the court. They are anticipating the most romantic part of the trial. They are ready to listen.

§ 18.4 Group Dynamics

Third, let us recognize the importance of the manner in which the decision takes place. The jury is isolated. They are taken to the jury room by the bailiff, given the written instructions of the court (if such is the practice) and turned loose with the simple direction that they should summon the bailiff when they have reached a decision or have a question.

The proceedings are secret. No record is made of the comments nor the deliberative process. A number of years ago when several juries were "bugged" for the purpose of acquiring empirical data on how juries function, there was universal outrage at the encroachment on the sanctity of the jury room.

The deliberations take place with all the jurors present. Most jurisdictions give specific instructions that the jurors must defer their comments concerning the case until all the trial has been completed and then only when all the jurors are present.

This last feature is perhaps the most important. Everyone is in on the give and take. Individual jurors can't seek out others to sound out their sentiments and establish cliques. Consequently the juror must be circumspect about the argument that he or she articulates. Does the juror think plaintiff should win solely because the defendant is a big corporation? If such an argument is advanced it will likely draw criticism from those on the jury who have been a bit more sensitive about those instructions concerning the identity of the parties and the right to a fair trial regardless of corporate status.

Does the juror want to find the black defendant guilty simply because "We gotta teach these people how to act?" A statement like this will destroy his credibility as an impartial fact finder and lessen, if not obliterate, his persuasive powers with his fellow jurors.

This factor of peer evaluation among the jurors is a two edged sword. As already indicated it can be an elevating influence on the deliberative process by holding the risk of shame to those who might be inclined to violate their oath and consider matters other than the evidence and the applicable law. On the other hand, it might prompt the naturally reticent juror to remain silent for fear that some matter thought to be of importance would draw the condemnation of the group.

B. MECHANICS

§ 18.5   Order of Presentation

As one might expect, there is no universal procedure that dictates the order of the closing arguments. First, there may be a difference as to when the arguments take place in relationship to the court's instructions. In federal courts the arguments precede the instructions. The judge has the last word. In many state jurisdictions the opposite is true. The judge reads the instructions, then the arguments begin. The lawyers have the last word.

In all jurisdictions that party having the risk of non-persuasion has the opportunity of the last argument. In some jurisdictions that party will open as well as close. Thus if each side is afforded thirty minutes for summation, the plaintiff may open with fifteen minutes followed by thirty minutes from the defendant and concluding with a balance of fifteen minutes for the plaintiff. In such cases several limitations are imposed:

> The concluding portion may not exceed in length the opening portion;

> The content of the concluding portion must be confined to rebuttal argument; (thus new topics cannot be introduced at such stage and if the subject of damages or amount has not been argued before it cannot be introduced in this concluding rebuttal portion).

§ 18.6   Time

The summation will usually be limited to a given amount of time and this limitation may be imposed upon each side rather than each party. In other words, in a civil suit by P against defendants A, B and C, the plaintiff may be afforded thirty minutes and the defendant a total of thirty minutes, or ten minutes each. The arrangements for the time for arguments are usually made in judge's chambers and a time mutually agreed upon. If the court resists a litigant's request for a specific time to argue, then the court reporter should be summoned and a record made of the request and the reasons why the requested time is necessary.

The time requested will vary with the complexity of the case, but it is well to remember that jurors are conditioned to the thirty minute chunk into which most television offerings are segmented and it is difficult to stretch their attention span beyond the limits of their favorite sit-com.

C. ORGANIZATION

§ 18.7 Generally

The organization of the closing argument is critical. Your appeal will be either rational, emotional (or most likely a combination of both) and regardless of the selection or the mix, the argument must be structured to have an impact. The rational argument must unfold in logical order and the emotional argument must peak with a concluding appeal. Whether your target is the head or the heart, the key to hitting the bullseye is organization.

The form of organization will not always be the same but regardless of the form which is employed, you will arrange your summation so that you will create a mood, establish a base for your argument, develop that argument and conclude with an appeal. Let us analyze each of those elements and consider the variations that are possible.

§ 18.8 Creating the Mood

This appears to be that part of the summation most neglected by the advocate. The reason for the neglect is that too many consider this phase of the argument as simple salutation and the salutation employed is as perfunctory as a "How do you do? Haven't we had lovely weather?" For the lawyer there is a slight variation. "Good afternoon ladies and gentlemen of the jury. We have now reached that part of the case called the closing argument in which each of the lawyers have an opportunity to tell you what the case is about. First I want to thank you for your attentiveness. You have paid close attention to the witnesses and me and my client appreciate that...." How many times have you heard that opening shot? Is is profound? sincere? eloquent? effective? No, but, they argue, it has some advantages.

First, it is traditional. We lawyers are always impressed by what has gone before. We take the path most traveled and heaven knows, this one has been stamped smooth.

Second, it is comfortable. Most of our social introductions are nothing less than ritual. Confrontation with a stranger provides a bit of concern so we put the mind and emotions into neutral while we mouth an automatic "How do you do?" We buy a little time while we shake hands and exchange smiles and by then, hopefully the minor trauma of meeting a stranger has been overcome and we are ready to ease into communications of heavier import. Sometimes lawyers feel this same need to "buy time" in order to warm up and the acceptable way to do this is to recite an innocuous salutation followed by a ritualistic "thank you."

Third, it is flattering to the jury and consequently will make them more receptive to your presentation. It would appear that to the seasoned advocate none of the aforegoing reasons would suffice to justify such a trite beginning to the dramatic highlight of the trial. Certainly it is traditional in the sense that it has often been done in the past, but the best definition of tradition is "that which we have done before and we wish to do again." Why should anyone wish to make such an introduction again? The only valid explanation is that it is easier to passively accept what has been done before than to actively generate a new approach. We might realize that it isn't the best, but we are assured that it isn't the worst. Witness the franchised food chains. Their success is proof enough that most of us are content with predictable mediocrity.

And no doubt such a beginning provides comfort to those that feel the need to overcome the shock of a new confrontation. But why should you feel the discomfort of a confrontation and a new one at that? You have addressed the jury before, on voir dire, opening statement and certainly a few glances have been exchanged during trial. If your attitude has been right during trial, by now the jurors should at least be comfortable acquaintances if not old friends. Nor does the third reason, flattering them for their attentiveness, justify such an unimaginative beginning. Chances are your opponent will commence his summation in the same fashion so the generation of good will should be canceled out.

If we analyze this "thank you for listening" approach carefully we may conclude that it is in reality an offensive remark to these "officers of the court." All the participants in a trial are called together to perform the awesome task of dispensing justice. Everyone who is caught up in the procedure is there under compulsion—the judge and the coterie of courtroom attendants are elected or appointed public officials, the lawyers have contracted for the services, the witnesses and jurors are subpoenaed (too often we forget the Latin derivation, "under penalty") to appear and receive compensation for that appearance. Who are we to thank them? When they do their job well, it is because of their obligation to the state or to the concept of justice—not as a personal favor to the litigants. Perhaps it is time we abandon our traditional, comfortable flattering introduction to our summation.

Considering what not to do hardly solves our problem. How do we commence our closing argument? First of all don't think of an "introduction." If you do, you will fall right back into the ritualistic mouthings. Think in terms of the mood you wish to create in order that the jury will be ready to accept the body of your argument. It is surprising how often during a trial there will be certain incidents that have occurred or certain lines of inquiry developed which are foreign to the general theme of your presentation. Your initial task in opening argument is to neutralize these occurrences and create a proper climate for the jury's receptiveness.

§ 18.9 Creating the Mood—Illustrations

Perhaps an illustration or two will clarify the point. Sometimes during a case involving serious injury there will be certain moments of levity that will result in laughter by the jurors, attorneys or even the judge. A series of such events over a four or five day trial can threaten the intensity and sincerity of a plaintiff's presentation. Under such circumstances it might be wise to commence the closing argument in this fashion.

"During the four days in which we were presenting the facts of this occurrence and the consequent results of that occurrence on the life of Dan Trotter there have been a few times when certain events occurred which provoked a laugh—from all of us. There is certainly nothing improper about laughter in a court room. For the law deals with life, and laughter, thank goodness, is a substantial part of life. And perhaps in a case such as this laughter can be further justified for it has provided some periods of momentary relief from the catastrophe which most often has occupied our minds. But now the time for laughter has passed and we are confronted with another aspect of life which is the concern of the law, the suffering of Dan Trotter".

Just as often, the defendant will feel that the evidence has drifted away from the legal facets of the case and has overemphasized the issue of damages. Before launching into the body of the argument it might be well for his "creation of mood" to follow a form such as this.

"Anyone who undertakes the task of doing justice must be a whole person with the breadth of feeling that all sensitive people have. Such a person will have the capacity of sympathy. I am sure that each of you have at sometime during the course of this trial have felt sympathy for the plaintiff. But doing justice is not extending sympathy—it is more, much more, than that. And now that we have reached that stage in the trial that judgment must be rendered and a just decision reached there are other attributes of a whole person that must be called upon to see that a right result be reached—attributes of intellect, of analysis, of appraisal and most importantly the attribute of fairness."

You might note that in neither of the illustrations did the advocate fuss with the jury about the state of mind which they might have entertained during the trial. Take the jurors as they are. Acknowledge the moods that they might have developed— then generate the mood that will be most beneficial to your client.

§ 18.10   Establishing the Base—Generally

Military strategists usually agree that one of the most critical decisions that will affect the ultimate outcome of battle is the choice of ground on which the battle will take place. And so it is with the trial strategist—the ground, or issue, to be selected is of the utmost importance. Some difficulties do exist in the use of the military analogy. If one side chooses a site for battle the opposing side must accept that site or no battle ensues. Battles are not inevitable (only wars seem to be so) and the clash of arms signifies a bilateral approval of the battle ground. Not so with a trial. That battle will take place regardless. The plaintiff might choose one issue as his battle ground, the defendant might accept that challenge or choose another. And the jury might reject both of their offerings and decide that the real issue is something else. Despite these possibilities it is advisable that early in the summation, the advocate choose his battle ground and challenge the opponent to meet the issues that he presents.

The issue that is selected will of course depend on the evidence as it has developed. There is a lot of wisdom in that old saw that if the law is against you, argue the facts, if the facts are against you, argue the law and if both the law and facts are against you, scream for justice. The only modification could come with the recognition that such an approach is negative oriented. Most advocates would probably think in terms of what is "for" them rather than what is "against" them.

§ 18.11 Establishing the Base—Legal Issue

For the plaintiff who has made a submissible case it is not unusual to pick as the main issue and establish as the base of his argument the ingredients of the cause of action. Typically the lawyer will make reference to the verdict directing instruction, enumerate the essential elements which constitute the cause of action and thus form the framework upon which his argument will hang.

The defense may do the same, electing to emphasize the elements of the affirmative defense, thus finessing the legal arguments of the plaintiff and countering with a legal argument of his own.

§ 18.12 Establishing the Base—Factual Issue

Sometimes the base established will be a "key" fact upon which the advocate claims the whole case revolves, "You have heard much evidence over these past three days but I am sure that you have recognized the one issue that holds the answers to who should win this lawsuit—and that is, Was a warning placed on the packing case or was it not? If you find from analyzing the evidence that there was a warning, then in all fairness I must concede that the plaintiff is not entitled to recover. But if you find that there was no warning then your verdict must be for the plaintiff."

§ 18.13 Establishing the Base—Philosophical Issue

In choosing the battle ground the unfolding of the evidence might dictate that you avoid the law and the facts and choose a more philosophical base. When such is done you will hear plaintiff's lawyers say, "We are interested not only in whether Johnny Barton is compensated for his broken leg. The real issue here is whether we are going to approve of motorists who speed through school safety zones."

Or the plea of a defense lawyer, "Are you going to say to drunk drivers everywhere, 'Sure, drink all the booze you want, drive your car while you are drunk. If you get hurt there's always some jury that will take care of you.' That's the issue, ladies and gentlemen."

D. DEVELOPING THE ARGUMENT

§ 18.14 Generally

You have heard the adage, "The lawyer who represents him-self has a fool for a client," but have you analyzed the rationale of that maxim? The reason that you cannot serve as an adequate advocate for yourself is that you are deprived of the objective evaluation of an outsider. It is not that you can't articulate your position—it is that you cannot properly evaluate the position that should be articulated.

Now translate that to your role in dealing with a client other than yourself. What does he deserve of you? Someone who can be his "mouthpiece"? One who can articulate the argument that the client would make if he had the "gift of gab"?

Certainly, but that's only one service that you offer. The other is objectivity, the ability to recognize how the argument sought to be articulated will be received by others. The exercise of such objectivity creates a risk of client discontent. "Don't you believe me when I tell you that other driver was doing at least ninety? The answer of course is, "Whether I believe you or not doesn't count. It's what the jury will believe that determines your success or failure." If your goal is simply pleasing your client, then a polarized presentation portraying the issues in terms of black and white with your client the epitome of righteousness and your opponent evil incarnate will achieve that result. But the cost of such tactics, the loss of credibility and a consequent lessening of your change for a favorable verdict, is much too high a price to pay.

Producers who seek a prognostication for the success of a play don't simply rely on their own reactions. The classical question is, "How will it play in Peoria?" Similarly, the advocate shouldn't advance an argument simply because it is attractive to the client. It must have a more universal attraction. Your metaphor for such "down home" appeal is not "Peoria," it's the jury."

Without attempting to reduce an argument to some type of stylized recitation that would threaten its spontaneity and sinceri-ty, let us examine some techniques that seem to have had some measure of success in the past and which could be readily applied in a host of cases. Some you will recognize as having been employed in the previous illustrations.

§ 18.15   Universalizing Your Cause

Make the claim or defense bigger than the litigants. Transcend from a broken leg to speeding through school zones. Almost every case presents such an opportunity. The good advocate will find it.

§ 18.16   Stressing Importance of Decision

A necessary corollary to the universalism pitch. Tell the jury that their decision is a pronouncement to the community as to how that community regards drunken drivers, shoddy products, sharp dealing store owners, etc.

§ 18.17   Subliminal Suggestions

Few persons like to be hit over the heads with persuasive facts. Leave some at least to the jury to "discover" by themselves. Give a hint but hold off the complete revelation.

§ 18.18   Presenting a Key

Most of us have a Rosetta stone complex. We like to believe that at the heart of every complicated problem there is a simple truism that holds the secret to understanding. Tennyson put it much more prettily:

> "Little flower if I could but understand
>
> What you are root and all, all in all
>
> I should know what God and Man is."

Provide an understanding of that key.

§ 18.19   Appearing to Be Fair

It sounds a bit cynical to be expressed in that fashion but fairness alone in a trial setting is ineffectual unless that fairness is apparent to the jury. The application of this rule is to be found in the illustrative argument, "If what I say isn't so, I shouldn't win— but if it is so, I should win." It is difficult to argue with that approach.

§ 18.20   Holding the Offensive

Again a military analogy seems appropriate. We have all heard that "The best defense is a good offense." Well the best offense is a good offense too and, synthesizing the two, we reach the conclusion that good offenses are pretty important. Prior mention has been made that the establishment of the base of your argument is important and this is merely an extension of that concept. Establish *and hold* the base. You may achieve such a goal in a number of ways. The most effective of which is to advance arguments of such persuasive force that your opponent will be forced to respond thus, obligating himself to fight on your field. If deemed advisable confront your opponent with a direct challenge. "I have indicated my analysis of the damages in this case and I'll be waiting to hear how Mr. Stevens has analyzed the testimony." Two or three challenges like this and the opponent will have the major portion of his allotted argument time usurped by responses to issues chosen by you. That is what is meant by "holding the offense."

§ 18.21 Concluding Appeal

Each oral presentation of a persuasive nature should conclude with a specific request for action. The story is told of a football coach who gave a stirring half time speech in the visitors' locker room and concluded by exhorting his players to "go out that door and bring glory to ole Siwash!" The players unfamiliar with the surroundings ran through the door and fell into the swimming pool. The advocate on occasion is guilty of the same inadequate exhortation. The jury is duly aroused but they are sometimes led through the wrong door and into the swimming pool.

So rule number one is, be specific. For the defense lawyer this is a rather simple admonition. He will usually be requesting that the status remain quo. For the plaintiff it means not only a verdict be rendered but that guidance be afforded as to the amount. Few experiences are more frustrating than to have a juror approach the plaintiff's lawyer after verdict and anxiously inquire, "Did we give you what you expected?" Here is an obviously pro-plaintiff juror wishing to please but with an inadequate instruction as to what would be pleasing. Does that mean that in every case the plaintiff's lawyer should ask for a specific amount? Not necessarily so. There are some cases that just don't develop in the manner expected and by the end of the trial the plaintiff's lawyer might be happy to salvage any kind of verdict at all. Under those less than promising circumstances it might be ill advised to ask for a sizeable recovery. That just might be the final blow. Under those circumstances your specificity will be satisfied if you ask for "an amount that will fairly compensate my injured client."

Rule number two would be to rehearse the concluding two minutes. There is nothing magic in that particular time allocation but the point is clear. The very end of your closing argument must reach some kind of dramatic climax. To assure the success of that climax think out the note on which you will conclude, determine how long your epilogue will take to deliver, request the bailiff to warn you when that time approaches—then shift gears and have at it. Much of your earlier presentation will have been spontaneous, particularly that which has been rebuttal, but you will not want to trust a fickle muse to provide the inspiration for this last effort.

This is the one part of your courtroom presentation that you can practice in front of the mirror and preview before your spouse. Make your final forensic fling a polished, professional effort.

E. CONTENT

§ 18.22 Proscribed Areas—Generally

The general rule concerning the content of closing argument is that it should concern itself with the evidence that was adduced as trial and the legal issues that have been raised. Whether a given argument falls within the approved parameters will depend on the specifics of a particular case. There are however a number of rules of law which give added guidance to the legitimate grounds over which argument may roam.

§ 18.23 Proscribed Areas—Identification With Jurors

How tempting it is for an impassioned advocate to say, "How would you like to have a broken leg and go through life as a permanent cripple?" Or, on the other side of the coin, "How would you like to be sued for $100,000 just because your brakes failed?"

Putting the jurors in the role of litigant in such a blatant fashion is improper and obviously so. The thoughtful advocate will never be so crude. Of course it is good argumentation to have the juror identify with your client and every proper attempt to do so will be made. The refinements would result in a more obtuse approach. As in many facets of trial law it isn't the purpose that offends, it is the heavy handed mechanics of fulfilling that purpose. When the directness approximates the Golden Rule and there is a specific request to "do unto my litigant as you would want to be done to you," the courts blow the whistle.

§ 18.24 Proscribed Areas—Sympathetic Appeal

Again the general rule is clear—closing argument cannot incorporate a blatant appeal to the sympathetic inclinations of the jury. The *first* rule precludes empathy, the *second* it's first cousin, sympathy. But again the rule is limited to the heavy handed appeal for the "poor widow" or "helpless orphan." Any speech of persuasion will attempt to generate the "same feeling" (the literal meaning of sympathy) between the litigant and the jurors. It has become quite common for some lawyers to deal with the sympathy issue in the following manner.

"The court will tell you that in reaching your decision that you should not be influenced by sympathy for the plaintiff and I would certainly agree to that. Tom will receive all the sympathy that he needs from his family, his friends, his neighbors—those who knew him before he suffered these permanent injuries. This lawsuit was not brought in order to secure sympathy but rather to secure justice in the form of a substantial money award."

§ 18.25 Proscribed Areas—Prejudicial Appeal

And now the *third* in the series of proscriptions—no empathy, no sympathy, no prejudice. This will also be the subject matter of a cautionary instruction from the court wherein the jury will be advised that their verdict should not be the product of prejudice against the litigants and that regardless of the differing identities of the parties, each should be afforded the same regard under the law.

§ 18.26 Proscribed Areas—Extra–Legal

The rules of law tell us of certain matters that are improper subject matter for argument. Common sense and experience dictates other matters which should be avoided. Too many advocates consider the closing argument simply as an opportunity to review the evidence and relate the evidence to the law. Such a narrow view stultifies the noble art of argumentation. The collective memories of the jurors have probably retained the testimony of the witnesses much better than you. The advocate's memory of the testimony is garbled by his memory of what was said in deposition and in pretrial conference and is further colored by his hopes of what the witness would say. In all likelihood, the jurors remember best what the testimony actually was.

Argument is not the time to tell them the *what* of the case but rather the *why* of the case. Help them analyze the testimony, suggest a reason for the conflict in testimony, give them an insight into those facets of the case which the evidence could only hint about. This is what argument is all about.

§ 18.27   Response to Improper Argument

When your opponent transcends the bounds of proper argument you should be prepared to make a response that is appropriate to the transgression. Your arsenal consists of three weapons: a simple objection, a speaking objection, retaliatory argument. To illustrate your choices, consider the following:

"You recall that Officer Slade measured those skidmarks and told you that they were eighty-five feet long."

Option one — "I object your honor, he has misstated the evidence."

Option two — "I object your honor. Officer Slade testified that the length of the intermittent marks totalled only fifty feet over an eighty-five foot distance."

(In either case the court's response will be "The jury will recall the evidence. Proceed.")

Option three— remain silent and clarify the testimony during your argument.

The offensive argument in this instance is of a fairly inconsequential manner and apparently a good faith mistake on the part of your opponent. In this instance any of the three options might be an appropriate way to handle the situation.

Remember, of course, that option three might not be available if you are not in position to reply.

The real test comes at the conclusion of a hard fought trial when good faith on the part of your opponent can no longer be presumed and the potential ill effects of his improper argument are of a substantial nature.

> "Are you going to let a million dollar corporation get away with something like this?"

(Good practice would indicate that additional relief be sought beyond an objection. An argument as egregious as this would probably lead to a mistrial or admonition of counsel. We are confining our consideration in this instance, however, to "self help.")

A simple objection would hardly suffice. In fact it would simply highlight the foul blow that had been landed. A speaking objection might be more appropriate and sufficiently effective if in truth your client is not a "million dollar corporation." "I object your honor, Acme Industry is a small family owned operation with limited assets. The statement made by counsel is false and prejudicial." But what if you do represent a million dollar corporation? In that case consider option three as a retaliatory argument.

"Counsel mentioned that I represent a million dollar corporation and implied that you should somehow penalize us on the account. If he would have been fair in characterizing Acme Industry he would have told you that we employ hundreds of employees and contribute over half a million dollars in wages each month into this community. He would have told you that there are over ten thousand stock holders,—widows, retired folks, working people—who have their savings invested in this company. And yet these are the persons he wants to penalize."

The option which you choose will depend upon a number of factors, the chief of which will be the identity of the judge. If the judge runs a tight ship and is sensitive to the bounds of proper argument, he will respond favorably to your objection and perhaps even, sua sponte, chastise the offending advocate and instruct the jury appropriately. If the judge permits free wheeling argument then you had better be equipped to defend yourself accordingly. It is little comfort to ponder the possibilities that error might have been committed on closing argument. We are usually dealing in an area of the judge's discretion and the likelihood of relief on appeal is pretty thin. So, advocate, in such a case it will be up to you.

F. TECHNIQUES OF DELIVERY

§ 18.28 Generally

Nothing is more personal than a closing argument. This is the one facet of the trial in which your own traits and characteristics will be revealed. Consequently it is difficult to suggest techniques of delivery that will be compatible with your style and personality. Some general rules, however, seem sufficiently universal in their application to merit attention.

§ 18.29 Proximity to Jury

Psychologists tell us, as does experience, that there is such a thing as optimal distance in communication. What that distance is depends on the size of the group with whom you are communicating and the physical surroundings. If you are engaged in conversation with another individual you will assume positions about three feet apart. A farther distance impedes the connection, a closer distance encroaches on our "territorial imperative." A similar phenomenon occurs in addressing a jury. Position yourself twenty feet away and you cannot "reach" them. Stand right at the jury rail and you are intimidating them, creating a feeling of discomfort as you encroach on their area of personal domain. Be aware of the "right" distance, baby bear fashion, and you will find that for a jury of twelve it will be about eight feet, for a jury of six, a little closer.

§ 18.30 Use of Lectern

Any physical impediment between communicator and communicatee presents an obstacle to a free flow of expression. Professional counselors will arrange the furniture in their office so that they are not talking over a desk to their client. They prefer an unobstructed space so that the vibes can flow.

A lectern presents a physical obstacle that can result in the same restraint on communication.

Besides, continual use of a lectern presents a preacher-like aura to your presentation which is hardly the identity that an advocate would like to assume.

A lectern can be justified only if argument necessitates a reference to bulky notes and that is a need that is difficult to envision.

§ 18.31 Use of Notes

An ideal summation could be characterized as structured spontaneity. However it is quite a trick to develop your forensic ability to that degree which accommodates both features. Usually a choice must be made—shall I sacrifice some organization in order to enhance the spontaneity of my argument or shall I sacrifice some spontaneity in order to enhance the organization?

Whether you use notes will depend on the choice which you make. If you find that notes are necessary then use them judiciously. Confine them to topic sentences or simply stated points you wish to cover. And don't feel confined to a legal size pad. Paper pads come in all sizes and you might find you function best with a six by four pad or three by five cards. As a rule of thumb, the less apparent the notes, the better.

§ **18.32** Mobility

The suggestion as to the optimum distance one should assume in addressing a jury does not imply that the advocate will be glued to one spot during the entire presentation. He might wish to refer to an exhibit, utilize an artist's pad to illustrate a point or do a number of things which will animate his presentation. Mobility is a substantial ingredient to animation and most closing arguments will involve some movement, some gestures. There are exceptions to this rule (which prompts the use of the word "most.") When an argument deals with matters of great human emotion the cadence, movement and volume of an argument will adjust accordingly. Deep emotions evoke subtle responses. The most profound thoughts are dealt with in monosyllabic terms, softened tones, subdued rhythms, almost indiscernible movements. But for the bulk of the argument we are attempting to sustain interest with a lively interesting argument and this will necessitate the use of appropriate gestures, varied inflections and movement.

§ **18.33** Clarity of Expression

This entails two concepts: a lucid and cogent formulation of thoughts; and mechanically understandable delivery of those thoughts.

As to the *first*, remember the axiom that it is the role of the lawyer not to state ideas so that it is possible to understand them, but to state ideas so that it is impossible to misunderstand them.

As to the *second*, no finer advice can be found than that given by Hamlet to his players:

> Speak the speech, I pray you, as I pronounced it to you, trippingly on the tongue: but if you mouth it, as many of your players do, I had as lief the town-crier spoke my lines. Nor do not saw the air so with your hand, thus; but use all gently: for in the very torrent, tempest, and, as I may say, whirlwind of your passion, you must acquire and beget a temperance

that may give it smoothness. O, it offends me to the soul to hear a robustious periwig-pated fellow tear a passion to tatters, to very rags, to split the ears of the groundlings, who, for the most part, are capable of nothing but inexplicable dumbshows and noise.

Be not too tame neither, but let your own discretion be your tutor: suit the action to the word, the word to the action; with this special observance, that you o'erstep not the modesty of nature: for anything so overdone is from the purpose of playing, whose end, both at the first and now, was and is to hold, as 'twere, the mirror up to nature; to show virtue her own feature, scorn her own image, and the very age and body of the time his form and pressure. Now this overdone or come tardy off, though it make the unskilful laugh, cannot but make the judicious grieve: the censure of the which one must in your allowance o'erweigh a whole theatre of others. O, there be players that I have seen play, and heard others praise, and that highly, not to speak it profanely, that neither having the accent of Christians nor the gait of Christian, pagan, nor man, have so strutted and bellowed, that I have thought some of nature's journeymen had made men, and not made them well, they imitated humanity so abominably.

G. SPECIAL TOPICS

§ 18.34   Generally

There are certain topics associated with each side of an argument in a civil case which recur with regularity. Certain techniques of arguments associated with those topics have become standard themes through repetitive use. They are worthy of special attention.

§ 18.35   Plaintiff—Pain

The most difficult challenge that the plaintiff's lawyer will face in his closing argument is that of presenting an evaluation of the plaintiff's pain and suffering, past and future. Arriving at the value of material things is difficult enough. Dent a fender and take it to three repair shops for an estimate of repair and there will be three opinions given as to the damage to the automobile. Experts disagreeing about the evaluation of dented steel and scraped chrome! The jurors are not experts. Many will be serving in that capacity for the first time. And the commodity on which they are asked to hang a price tag is neither steel nor chrome but human pain and suffering. Their opinions are going to differ, and the range of evaluation is likely to be pronounced. Their own experiences with pain and illness will no doubt create a certain attitude with which the medical testimony will be received, but they will be looking to the attorneys in closing argument for help in fulfilling this most difficult obligation.

The expected differences of opinion in the evaluation of pain and suffering suggest that the plaintiff's attorney avoid a flatfooted, uncompromising appraisal. The evaluation comes as a suggestion with the realization that his concern for human life might be at variance with those of others. Indeed, the genius of the jury system is that it represents the judgment of six or twelve persons from different walks of life, having had different experiences. The verdict doesn't reflect merely the thought of one individual who might have a distorted sense of value. The lawyer might confess that he is not "the seventh son of a seventh son," nor does he possess powers of divination by which he is more capable of reaching a true evaluation of plaintiff's case. He might even confess an inability to fairly judge the injuries by reason of his intimate knowledge of the plaintiff and the problems he has had. But regardless of these preliminary protestations, the lawyer must proceed to advise the jury of the claim that is being made for this element of damages.

§ 18.36   Plaintiff—Pain—Illustrations

Several arguments are available, the essence of which may be stated as follows:

"There is one situation in which a person has an opportunity to evaluate pain in terms of dollars and cents. When the dentist advises that a tooth must be pulled or a cavity filled and questions whether Novocaine is desired, the intended victim must answer the question: Is it worth twenty dollars to avoid the pain? The response is obvious. When confronted with a choice like this we have no problem. The twenty dollars is little enough to pay in order to avoid the pain. But the pain with which the plaintiff is cursed is not the transitory pain that's experienced in the dentist's chair but the continuous nagging discomfort that haunts him at work and at his home, night and day."

A second approach is an attempt to evaluate the plaintiff's pain from the standpoint of "what would you take to change places with the plaintiff?" Any argument couched in these terms is more apt to be considered improper but the idea behind that approach may be advanced in some ways less likely to give offense.

"Suppose there appeared in the want ad section of our local paper an opportunity for a job opening such as this: the pay will be fifty dollars a day. There will be no responsibilities. You'll not have to report to work. No forms to fill and no calls to make. In fact, you will not have to do anything. The day will be free to spend in whatever way you choose. There's really only one feature to the job—you're going to have to endure pain, a continuing, unrelenting pain. And, once the job is taken, it will be a permanent commitment. No weekends off, no chance of retirement. The pay and the pain will continue until you die.

"Do you think the ad would be answered? Would anyone voluntarily accept a position such as that? Well, plaintiff has just such a future for him. The acceptance of the job was not his choice, but the job is his. The pain, the constant pain, will follow him to the end of his days. The job obligations are established, it is up to you to determine the fair wages that should be his."

§ 18.37 Plaintiff—Disability

A plaintiff's disability is usually expressed in terms of impairment of work capacity. Perhaps it is a testimony to our culture's emphasis on the utilitarian that we think that the most devastating effect of a disabling injury is that the victim, if a man, can no longer engage in his business, or mow the lawn, or paint the house. If a woman, the concern is that she can no longer engage in her business, wash or iron, or do the other household chores that "are never done."

True enough, the incapacity to perform these tasks is more readily translated into pecuniary terms; but other activities from which the plaintiff has been foreclosed by reason of his incapacity are of equal significance. "Man does not live by bread alone" nor does his life consist in performing the tasks necessary to buy that bread. In the twenty four hour day one third may be devoted to work and one third to sleep, but the golden hours are those of leisure. These are the hours spent as one wishes to spend them. The plaintiff's disability must be related also to the usurpation of these leisure hours and an evaluation sought for the deprivation of the right of doing what the plaintiff wants to do, even if it's doing nothing.

It's even reasonable to argue that this feature of the disability is to be evaluated more highly than the plaintiff's impaired earning capacity. After all, industry must pay time and one-half or even double time in order to lure workers from their leisure, and even then the average worker resists the encroachment upon the time to be spent with family and with friends. This aspect of disability must not be given a short shrift.

The plaintiff's lawyer will find it necessary to aid the jury in comprehending the disability of either a young or old plaintiff. In either instance the significance of a disabling injury is not as readily appreciated as it is in those cases involving a person old enough to have found his niche and yet young enough to have been deprived the fruits of it.

§ 18.38   Plaintiff—Disfigurement

Another element of damage quite distinct from pain and suffering or economic loss is that loss which results from a permanently disfiguring injury.

The poet wrote, "Vanity thy name is woman." The observation was valid as far as it goes. A more objective person might well say "Vanity thy name is people." Our features may not be comely—but they are ours. As one philosopher observed, "All our geese are swans." An injury that results in a cosmetic defect is of consequence regardless of whom the victim might be. The winsome face should not be marred and the homely countenance can little afford any further impairment.

To most, the face is regarded as the very center of our being, the reflection of our personality, the window of our soul. If that window is cracked or blurred the outlook on life will be distorted with its imperfections. Criminologists have discovered a high correlation of physical deformities among those who have broken the laws. If a defect is significant there is apt to be a pronounced withdrawal from society with resultant antisocial behavior. The statistics from the sociologist merely confirm a phenomenon which is well known—attitude and mood are closely related to appearance. If milady is blue, she purchases a new hat or submits to a change of coiffure. A feeling of attractiveness is essential to a person's sense of well being. The ingenue sings, "I feel pretty, I feel pretty, I feel pretty and witty and gay." The wit and gaiety are but natural sequelae to the prettiness that she feels.

Disfigurement may not be confined to the face alone. A loss of limb involves the same psychic effect as that experienced with the infliction of a facial scar. The loss might not offend the senses, the stump might be concealed behind a folded sleeve, but the victim is conscious of his loss. The integrity of the body has been violated and the frame with which he was born has been lessened and is no longer whole. Many medical articles have been written of the personality changes which frequently attend a loss of limb. This sense of loss must be comprehended by the plaintiff's lawyer and projected to the jury.

§ 18.39 Plaintiff—Injury to Infant

The lawyer who represents the young plaintiff who has suffered a disabling injury must call upon the jury to consider the effect of that disability. In all likelihood there will be little to go on. If the plaintiff is of school age there might be some indicia of future accomplishments. Perhaps he has demonstrated capacity as a scholar, a talent for music, or a craftman's skill. Aptitude tests, scholastic grades, and social acceptance among his fellow students will give some insight into his capabilities and establish a basis for arguing the effect of his disabling injuries. But if the plaintiff is of pre-school age there will be no such information. The injury has struck down a being in the process of becoming. The lawyer will have little facts from which he can argue his plaintiff's loss, but he will have some well-established traditions that will be of even greater value. There are few American traditions that are more deeply rooted than that which holds out the promise that "my child may one day be President." The Horatio Alger story has become a reality with predictable regularity. If one thing characterizes our culture it is the social instability of our citizens and the capacity of a child, humbly born, to reach the highest rung on the ladder of life. Every juror knows this and is proud of it. The disabled plaintiff may have appearances of an average child, from average parents, and with an average future. But who knows? He may be an Abraham Lincoln, a Hank Aaron, a Sandra Day O'Connor. The point is, the victim might have been, but now will never be. He has been taken out of the competition, scratched from the race, disqualified before the starting gun was ever fired.

The disability of a minor plaintiff should never be discounted. The child who suffers an injury before his potential is ever known invokes a peculiar sense of sympathy. Here is the epitome of the innocent victim. None can match the sweetness of children, for they are "freshest from the hand of God."

§ 18.40 Plaintiff—Injury to Elderly

A second type of case in which the jury may not appreciate its value is that which involves disability to an elderly plaintiff. Younger jurors might assume that old age is the time for disability, that elderly persons have no interest in the normal activities, that theirs is a rocking chair existence, and that an accident induced disability is of little consequence. If such might be their inclination, it behooves the plaintiff's lawyer to advance several arguments to refute such an attitude.

Everything derives its value from its ease of acquisition. A rare gem is a valuable one. The less of an article, the more valuable it is. This is not simply a rule of the market place. It is a rule of life. We value the special event, the family gathering at Christmas, and the annual picnic on the 4th of July because we know that they come but once a year. And we cherish the visits with our parents and the baby's birthday for we know that precious few are left. Ask the poor man and he will say that the last dollar is the most valuable. Ask the old man or the old woman and they'll confirm that the last few years, like the last few dollars, are those which are cherished the most. These are the years that should climax a happy life. A life filled with work and worry should hold some promise of rest and serenity in the latter days. Yet this is the time that the plaintiff now faces in pain and disability. The "sunset slope of life" has now been paved with thorns and thickets.

§ 18.41 Defendant

The approach to a closing argument from a defendant's standpoint is not so easily stated as that of the plaintiff. It is the plaintiff who, in most jurisdictions, opens and closes (a procedural plus to balance the burden of proof minus), and in so doing chooses, at least to some degree, the grounds on which the verbal battle is to be fought. The defendant's argument on damages is essentially rebuttal. Frequently he finds himself in the role of a counter puncher. His role in presenting the liability issue might be more aggressive but it is seldom that the defendant's counsel will seize the initiative. Such a situation might present itself if the essence of defense is a fraudulent claim based on nonexistent or highly exaggerated injuries. But, absent those grounds, the

503

defendant will usually be meeting the arguments on the injuries advanced by the plaintiff and hoping to divert most of the jury's attention to the issue of liability.

The mood of defendant's closing argument in regard to injuries and damages will have been established during the reception of evidence. It must be compatible with the theory of defense that permeated the trial.

Basically, there are three techniques of a damage defense. One ignores the issue. Defend on the issue of liability alone. Request no medical examination, engage in little or no cross-examination of the medical testimony offered by plaintiff and his medical experts. If such is the course that has been followed during trial, the theme must prevail to the end. The argument must explain the reasons for the stand-offish attitude. It may acknowledge the possibility of injury (without relieving the plaintiff of his risk of nonpersuasion) and deny responsibility.

"We have not endeavored to dispute the injuries which the plaintiff claims he suffered. Our reluctance to question his claims has not been prompted by indifference. They may be of some significance—but not as an issue in this case. We do not know if the injuries are serious or not but this we do know—the defendant is not responsible for those injuries."

A second technique meets the issue head on and disputes the existence or the causal relationship of the injuries. This defense may be based on a sterile medical question (Can a single blow cause cancer?), or on a highly emotional personal attack on the plaintiff (Is the plaintiff lying when he claims disability?). In either instance there can be no half hearted effort. The jury is given little ground for compromise. The tactic might be likened to Pickett's charge. Either the breastworks will be overrun or the corps will be demolished. The verdict might well be "double or nothing," depending on whether the jury is incensed by the attack on the credibility of plaintiff and his doctor, or whether they are convinced that the plaintiff has sought to peddle a fraudulent claim.

The third approach concedes the injury but questions the extent of the disability and the amount of the claim for damages. In case of "good" liability (or "bad" liability from the defendant's point of view) with legitimate injuries, the defendant has little choice but to assume the attitude that "we're sorry, but it's not all that bad." This defense must be based on facts and not just a closing argument of glib optimism. The plaintiff's medical proof must be questioned and the defense must encompass medical testimony of its own. The final argument must be structured on the foundation of a medical prognosis rather than be an inspirational message invoking a "stiff upper lip" and a "grin and bear it" philosophy for the plaintiff.

The most important tactical decision that the defense attorney must make is whether or not he will merely seek to minimize the plaintiff's demand for damages or present a definite evaluation of his own. Both courses entail some risks. If the plaintiff makes an argument outlining specific items of damages and requesting a verdict based on his computations, the jury might expect the same consideration from the defendant in aiding them in reaching a just verdict. The force of the argument might be dissipated by a lack of positive direction and an ill-defined request of the jury. On the other hand if the defendant suggests a specific sum he might run afoul of that strange reasoning process of some jurors that presumes a 100% discount of any mention of money by an attorney. A demand for $50,000 by a plaintiff's attorney is equated to mean $25,000 ("They always ask twice what they want"). And the corollary to the rule: an expression of value by a defendant's attorney of $5,000 is presumed to mean $10,000. Fearing the doubling process, the defendant's counsel might find it advisable to confess to the jury his understanding of this rather typical attitude and explain that the figure given is not one-half of a reasonable amount, but rather is a frank and full appraisal of plaintiff's injuries.

H. SUMMARY

§ 18.42   Summary

The various elements of a claim or defense must be presented to the jury in an integrated argument. Little else can be said. Each case will present its own problems. Each lawyer will have his own style. Each presentation will be before a jury having its own unique characteristics. There can be no pat formulae, no stemwinder phrases to fit any occasion, no standardized conclusions (Thus avoiding the embarrassment of the criminal lawyer who concluded his closing argument with his usual "Send this boy home to his mother" when defending the "boy" on a matricide charge).

A closing argument is meant to persuade. Therefore there are no "good" closing arguments nor are there "bad" closing arguments. They must be judged as "winning" arguments or "losing" arguments. If it is to be the former it will follow a logical pattern, the language will be direct and easily understood, the style forceful but not overbearing, the mood intimate and frank, the appeal sentimental but not maudlin, the overall effect—persuasion.

CHAPTER 19

EVALUATION OF CASE

Analysis

A. IN GENERAL

B. IDENTITY OF PLAINTIFF

C. MEDICAL EVALUATION

1. PLAINTIFF

2. DEFENDANT

A. IN GENERAL

§ 19.1 Introduction

Statistics indicate that approximately nine out of every ten lawsuits which are filed are disposed of before trial. With the increasing liberality of discovery rules and the graduating costs of litigation it is likely that the percentage of cases which actually go to trial will become even less than the present ten per cent. But regardless of our projections it is apparent that the complete advocate cannot confine himself to the development of trial skills. He must know how to handle the other ninety per cent of the cases in his office and, consequently, must know the skills of evaluation, negotiation and settlement. These latter skills of negotiation and settlement are treated in Chapter 20, *infra*.

In so stating the challenge there is no implication that trial and settlement skills are unrelated. No lawyer can be an effective negotiator until he has established his clout in the courtroom. Good settlements emanate from a two-fold reputation: willingness to litigate and competence in litigating. After all, every type of negotiation is based upon a form of threat—"Do what I want you to do—or else." The legal negotiator is saying "Accept my offer of settlement—or else" and the only "or else" there is, is "I'll see you in court."

§ 19.2 Initial Appraisal

An advocate is fundamentally a salesman. The product, for a plaintiff in a civil case of a defendant in a criminal matter, is the client with the potential buyer an opposing lawyer or the jury.

Regardless who it is to whom the sale will be made, the requisites of good salesmanship must be met. What are these requisites? Consultation need not be given to "how to sell" books nor reference made to "pep talks" from some high powered sales manager. Consider only those qualities that have always been and always will be associated with effective salesmanship; faith in the product, sincerity, knowledge of the product. Relating these attributes to the trial lawyer, it is found that the first two concern the development of personality characteristics while the third concerns the acquisition of knowledge.

What knowledge must the salesman possess? If he's selling a washing machine, he should know who makes it, how it's made, what it can do, cost of operation, how it compares with competitors' machines. These facts must be known to evaluate the product. Similarly, there will be many factors, primarily of a legal nature, which must be taken into consideration in evaluating a lawsuit.

Matters such as venue, judge, type of witnesses, quality of opponent, sources of proof, etc., will significantly affect your appraisal of the case. But the most significant factor will be the litigants themselves, the plaintiff and defendant in a civil case, the prosecuting witness and the defendant in a criminal case.

For illustration purposes let us consider the evaluation, negotiation and settlement of a civil, personal injury case. The facts which determine liability are so unique to each case that it will serve little purpose to concern ourselves with that phase of the lawsuit. Instead we shall confine ourselves to the universalities which recur in the appraisal of an injury.

B. IDENTITY OF PLAINTIFF

§ 19.3 Generally

Too frequently the lawyer approaches the problem of evaluating personal injury claims from the standpoint of the injury alone. "How much is a broken arm worth?" is the query made by the neophyte lawyer seeking the advice of a fellow practitioner. The experienced lawyer can give no response other than a host of additional queries. How did it happen? What kind of break? Was it his major arm or minor arm? Are there any present complaints? How old is your client? What's his business? etc. The point is obvious. The evaluation is not that of an arm being broken—it is rather an evaluation of a person that has suffered a broken arm. The personal injury lawyer does not deal in injuries, he deals with people who have suffered injuries. The medical profession has recognized the difference. The modern doctor says, "I don't treat illnesses, I treat patients." The emphasis has shifted to the individual. The approach is to the whole. The modern lawyer representing an injured plaintiff must adopt the same approach.

§ 19.4 Pre–Accident Identity

If this Gestalt system is utilized, the first task of the plaintiff's lawyer is to "know his client." The job is not a simple one. Man is a complicated animal with many kinds of identity. A pollster interrogated a number of persons with the simple query "Who are you?" The types of responses were almost as numerous as the persons polled. The sample included "John Jones," "An American," "A mother," "An engineer," "A Lutheran," "A boy." Who we are includes name, age, gender, occupation, nationality and a host of other things. The client may never be totally known but certain basic facts of identity can be ascertained.

Social Facts

Where does the client fit into society? Or, as the sociologist would say, "What is the social milieu from which he came?" This area of identity would include family status, occupation, education, social activities, economic condition, etc.

Physical Facts

Attention is shifted to the physical identity of the client; his age, weight, height, condition of health, etc. The lawyer is primarily concerned with ascertaining the pre-accident physical condition in order to determine the effects of the accident.

Legal History

A third area of importance is the legal background of the client. Has he had any previous claims, been involved in any litigation, been convicted of any crimes? From a medical standpoint such information will have little or no significance but as a jury appeal factor this data cannot be overlooked.

§ 19.5 Post Accident Impediments—Generally

Now that the client's pre-accident condition has been determined the lawyer must ascertain the post accident sequelae, the complaints which have given rise to the legal consultation.

There are a number of difficulties that will be encountered. It might appear that there can be no problem in getting an expectant claimant to recite how he received his injuries and the difficulties that have resulted. But such problems do exist. The plaintiff's lawyer must be cognizant of certain human attributes which work to the detriment of an injured person seeking to render a full disclosure of an accident and the injuries that resulted therefrom. "What can they be?", the cynic will require. "Don't tell me that someone who intends to sue for a bundle of money has any inhibitions about reciting his injuries. There will

510

be distortions all right—but they will be exaggerations of the injuries and elaboration of how the accident occurred." The lawyer who accepts this point of view puts his client at a distinct disadvantage. He must be aware of those characteristics of a sudden and traumatic event; those traits of human character which will obscure an injury and hamper an effective presentation of a claim.

§ 19.6   Post Accident Impediments—Shock

When a person is involved in an unexpected, exciting event he frequently finds himself behaving in an odd fashion. Perhaps it is more appropriate to say that he discovers he has behaved in a peculiar manner. In the excitement of an athletic contest the exuberant fan discovers that in the exhilaration of a scoring play he has jumped onto his seat, flung his scorecard toward the field and pounded his neighboring fan on the back. The excitement of the occasion has triggered some "automatic" responses which seem to be beyond the control of the deliberative process. The "will" has been short circuited, and things "just happen" without their having been consciously dictated.

The excitement of an accidental physical injury will similarly trigger such a response. The injured person does things, says things which are beyond his conscious control.

Muscles contract, nerves are numbed, respiration and circulation are thrown "into emergency." Actions are instinctive. The body, in its efforts toward self-preservation, summons its reserves, temporarily subdues the pain, activates the muscular system and thus endeavors to carry itself beyond the emergency period. Some instances of this phenomenon are quite dramatic: the horrified bystander who lifts an automobile while a trapped victim is removed; the football player who plays the last half with a broken ankle; the frenzied mother who rescues her child from the burning home only later to discover that the flesh has been seared off her feet.

The physiological explanation is of no concern. Why or how such things occur are for the lawyer unimportant. What is important is the realization that when a client is involved in an accident and suffers an injury it is very likely that he, the injured party, will be the least reliable source of information concerning the initial stages of his own injury.

511

There will be plenty of evidence favorable to the defendant that will be available. Legion are the police reports that record, "No complaint of injury," the defendants who testify, "He said that everything was alright," the onlookers at the scene who relate how the "drivers of the cars looked as if they were fine and gave no indication that they were hurt." Yet the complaints do arise, the injuries manifest themself, the lawsuit results. What is the explanation? That a scheming accident participant belatedly decides to pursue a false claim? That after a "sober second thought" he opts for litigation? In some instances, perhaps so; but in the majority of cases the shock of the event has masked the severity of its results. It is only after the adrenalin drains and the pre-accident calm is restored that the head begins to throb, the ankle to swell, the neck to stiffen and the claim is belatedly born.

§ 19.7 Post Accident Impediments—Unconsciousness

Aside from the effects of shock, the accident victim might also suffer the type of injury that will render him unconscious. Unconsciousness might assume many different forms, but regardless of its intensity it will impair the victim's memory of events and might account for speech or actions seemingly incompatible with the true nature of the injury suffered. The least difficulty arises in those instances in which the plaintiff is completely "knocked out." This condition will prevent the recitation of the events immediately after the accident, but it will also foreclose the victim from optimistically prognosticating, "Everything is alright, I'm not hurt." The difficulty arises when the state of unconsciousness is not complete, when the victim is only "dazed," temporarily "blacked out" or episodically "comes and goes." It is when the accident victim is in such a semi-comatose condition that he is apt to say and do things which might lead an onlooker to conclude that there has been no injury. Such a situation is not uncommon. The investigating officer interrogates about the accident, the admitting intern takes a history—but the plaintiff recalls neither conversation. How will such testimony be regarded? Is the forgetful plaintiff feigning an injury or was he genuinely "out on his feet?"

§ 19.8 Post Accident Impediments—Embarrassment

Other factors, aside from the physical, will serve to hinder a plaintiff's recitation of his injury. A middle aged woman slips and falls in a crowded department store. She is sprawled awkwardly on the floor. She struggles to regain her feet, she hurriedly pulls her dress into place, and leans against a counter. A concerned floor walker takes her arm and asks her how she feels. She smiles wanly, insists she's alright, takes a step—and collapses. Why didn't she remain on the floor until she could ascertain her condition? What was she thinking of as she painfully steadied herself against the counter? Was she concerned about the possibility of a broken limb? Perhaps, but most probably she was embarrassed by the scene, distressed by the attention and anxious to get on her way. Again, it is dangerous to generalize and dogmatically state the motivations that will dictate the actions of all injured parties. Of course there are some persons who relish the attention that comes with an injury suffered in public but certainly there are a goodly number who react as the middle-aged lady. When an injury is suffered, the last thing on their mind is litigation—the need for medical attention isn't even their first concern. Their prime feeling is that of embarrassment, they want to be up and about, seek the anonymity of the crowd and not be the target of gawking onlookers.

§ 19.9   Post Accident Impediments—Reluctance to Admit Disability

There is yet another attribute of human nature which inures to the benefit of the defendant. There is a hesitancy on the part of a substantial number of people who have suffered injury to appraise realistically their physical condition and admit that they are disabled. Whatever may be the reasons many persons resist the admission of their own physical or mental weakness—even though that weakness is the subject matter of litigation. This attribute is more often found with male litigants. Many will not acknowledge that they are crippled, that they'll never work again, or that they no longer can perform the physical feats they could in the past. The "Peter Pan" promise of perpetual youth is a dream devoutly to be wished. The fact that such obstinacy will jeopardize their chances of recovery and lessen the settlement or judgment seems to have little effect. Ponce de Leon scorned the quest for El Dorado and sought the Fountain of Youth instead.

This resistance to the admission of an infirmity is particularly strong when it relates to a matter of personal hygiene, or to the functioning of those parts of the body the mention of which is proscribed by excessive modesty.

Mrs. Jones has suffered a blow to the kidneys. Her deposition is taken and she is asked to relate her complaints. She unhesitatingly tells of the sharp pain in her side. She pauses, and mentions that she has on occasion "passed some blood," she stops, knits her brow then says, "That's about all." Her real complaint is the involuntary urination that so frequently occurs to her great embarrassment. She is not sufficiently sophisticated to express her malady in the sterile jargon of the medical man, (incontinent, nocturia) and she cannot bring herself to a confession that she "dribbles in her pants" or "wets the bed." Better that the complaint remain unspoken.

The forty-five year old man has suffered a crushing injury to his mid-section. He tells his lawyer of his complaints: the painful back, the nausea, the stiffened muscles, etc. His real concern however has been a total loss of libido. Since the accident he has had no sexual appetite and he has lost the power of erection. He has kept the secret to himself. He will tell neither his lawyer, his doctor nor his wife. The claim might well be settled as a back complaint. The true value of the injury might never be known. Recognizing these impediments in the recitation of injuries, the lawyer must first listen to the complaints as recited and then probe the client with additional questions.

Assume the female client has suffered a blow to the abdomen and has told of the muscular aches and pains, stiffness, etc. But has related no problems beyond that. The lawyer begins his interrogation. "Mrs. Jones, in many instances when a woman suffers the kind of accident that you have suffered it is not unusual to find that there are complaints relating to a disturbance of the menstrual cycle, perhaps a heavier or longer discharge, an abbreviated cycle or something of that nature. If such is the case with you, then of course that should be disclosed so that all the facets of your injury can be considered in appraising your claim and in trying to work out a settlement."

If there is a likelihood that a male client has suffered an injury that would affect his sexual capacity, the same type of explanation should be given. "It would not be unexpected with injuries such as you suffered, that you may also have had some complaints in reference to your sexual capacity. This could manifest itself in a number of ways. Maybe as a physical disability where a person loses the power of erection, or perhaps there has simply been a loss of appetite. In any case, if there has been such a situation as this, it is extremely important that we know of it so that you can be compensated for all your injuries."

The embarrassment of reciting matters of a highly personal manner might also prevent a full disclosure of the results of the disability as well as a disclosure of the disability itself. Persons suffering severe injuries to the spine frequently lose the use and function of the lower part of the body. Many aspects of the resulting disability are apparent: loss of the ability to walk, loss of sensation in the lower limbs, loss of control of the musculature resulting in spasms, etc. The secondary results of those injuries however give a deeper understanding of the enormity of the disability, and yet they may never be disclosed to the attorney who is content with the obvious. The necessity of manually removing the stool, the constant attention to decubiti (pressure sores), the threat of infection to the digestive tract; these are the elements of injury that cannot be overlooked.

The age in which we live is certainly not characterized by prudery and delicate feelings. We have come a long way from Victorian modesty, an age in which propriety dictated that the sides of a triangle be referred to as "arms" instead of "legs." But modesty still prevails as evidenced by the thousands of persons each year who fail to receive adequate medical attention for such conditions as cancer of the cervix, hemorrhoids, etc., by reason of the vestigial remains of Victorianism. So it is that the lawyer must counteract this hesitancy with questioning of his own.

The interrogation and probing by the lawyer serves two purposes: it breaches the subject and assures the client that there need be no embarrassment; and it provides the client with acceptable terminology. Many times the client must first hear the lawyer speak of "incontinence," "menstrual cycle," "loss of erection" before they feel adequate to express themselves in these sensitive areas.

Hopefully, all these impediments will be recognized and overcome and the plaintiff's counsel afforded an undistorted identity of his post accident client.

C. MEDICAL EVALUATION

1. PLAINTIFF

§ 19.10 Generally

If the claimant's attorney is to sell his commodity he must have information regarding the nature of the article. There is no adjuster nor defense lawyer worthy of the name who will buy a "pig-in-a-poke." Oral representations as to the nature and extent of the injury will be given little or no regard in the evaluation of a claim for settlement purposes. If the attorney is satisfied that there has been adequate medical attention given to the injured client, then he must ascertain whether or not there is adequate medical evaluation made of those injuries. Written information, whether from hospital records, clinical tests results or office notes made by a treating doctor, will be of little help unless this information is presented in a context which will afford a valid appraisal.

§ 19.11 Medical Report—Contents

To be of value the medical report should contain:

1. A full recitation of the plaintiff's medical history.
2. A brief recitation of the onset of the condition from which the complaints arise.
3. A description of the objective findings.
   4. A recitation of the clinical tests made and their results.
   5. A diagnosis.
   6. A prognosis.
   7. An opinion as to the need of further medical attention.
   8. The cost of medical services to date.
   9. An expression as to the future cost of medical attention.

It is seldom that this information can be secured merely from a hospital record or from the cryptic notes that so often constitute the sole written record of an office visit. Medical evaluation can best be served through a complete and comprehensive medical report prepared by the treating or an examining physician.

Even if one is fortunate enough to receive from a doctor a medical report which contains all of the elements suggested above, there are frequently matters of legal import which must supplement the report itself.

§ 19.12 Medical Report—Causal Relation

The first is the question of proximate cause. Some conditions are obviously traumatic and the report need not spell out or affirm that the condition of which the doctor is speaking was directly caused or directly contributed to be caused by the trauma. While such might be the case of a lacerated face or a fractured limb, it is certainly not true of a bleeding ulcer, tuberculosis, heart condition or disability from arthritis. A mere recitation that such was the condition from which the plaintiff was suffering would not of itself carry convincing evidence of responsibility of the defendant for such condition. Frequently this aspect of the medical information is the prime factor in evaluating a claim. Without an expression of the causal relationship of the trauma and the condition the report will be valueless.

The doctor submitting the report must be requested to express himself on the issue of causation; but, before the request is made, certain precautions should be taken. It will be necessary that the doctor seeking to give the opinion be thoroughly acquainted with the quantum of proof necessary to afford legal recovery for injuries sustained. Medicine belongs to a branch of science which requires certainties before conclusions are drawn. It is a medical homily that there are two words absent from a doctor's vocabulary, one is "always" and the other "never." The gist of the saying is clear—from a purely scientific point of view, doctors are hesitant to give unqualified opinions as to relationships existing between cause and effect. Thousands of tests were conducted and numerous papers written on the subject of the relationship between cigarette smoking and cancer. Despite a great body of proof relating thereto, there were, and are, still only a few doctors who will unequivocally state that "cigarette smoking causes cancer." Such a bold statement offends their sense of scientific probity. It is scientifically unsophisticated to reach such a conclusion without taking into consideration such factors as the frequency of exposure, the type of atmosphere, age, family history of respiratory disorders and countless other conditions. True enough, the doctor might be willing to state that smoking "may" cause cancer or "could" precipitate a malignancy, but such carefully couched opinions frequently fail to measure up to the degree of certainty demanded in the law to establish that the tortious act was the proximate cause of the injury.

The law is less sophisticated and more direct in seeking to establish causation. The lawyer must adduce evidence that, in the expert's opinion based on reasonable medical certainty, the smoking did cause the cancer. Knowing what the law demands, and unsympathetic to the sophistry of the more casuistic doctors, the lawyer might impatiently inquire of the doctor, "does it or doesn't it?" If a doctor is given a "yes" or "no" alternative to a question such as that, he will probably respond in the negative. Consequently, before asking the doctor for his commitment, it becomes necessary to acquaint him with the difference between medical causation and legal causation.

The indoctrination, as it were, might assume this form:

> The quantum of proof to establish legally that a negligent defendant must respond in damages for the disability of an injured victim is much less than the quantum of proof necessary to establish a medical axiom. Seeking justice in a courtroom is a far more tenuous affair than seeking a scientific truth in the sterility of a testing laboratory. The ultimate decision in the trial, if this is not settled, will be determined by 12 jurors, average lay citizens, who must reach a verdict based upon their understanding of the injuries suffered by the plaintiff. In that regard they must rely upon your expert opinion. They will not be asked to find that the plaintiff's injuries positively resulted from the occurrence. But neither will they be allowed to speculate as to the causation without some evidence. That evidence must come from you. We must present your opinion as to the relationship between the accident and the injury and this opinion must be based on a certain degree of certainty. All testimony whether it be from the lay witness or an expert must reach such a degree of certainty before it has probative value and is admitted as evidence. A witness to an accident who testifies that "I *think* the defendant went through the red light" or "I *believe* he may have gone through the red light" will not have such testimony received in court. The degree of certainty is not sufficient. He must testify "I saw the car go through the red light" before the testimony will have sufficient value to be received in evidence. In establishing medical causation your opinion must be based on "reasonable medical certainty."

The question will be put to you in this fashion, "Doctor, do you have an opinion based on reasonable medical certainty whether the condition from which your patient suffers was caused or contributed to by the incident I have hypothesized?" An affirmative response with the explanation "It did" will suffice to support a jury's finding of causation. We are now attempting to settle this matter and in order to do so we must confirm that the condition for which you have been treating your patient was the result of the accident. If it is more probable than not that the accident did cause or contribute to cause the injury then I would appreciate it if in your report you could express that the injuries were the result of the accident.

§ 19.13 Medical Report—Disability

Further refinements in the medical report might be necessary in order to translate cold medical data into more meaningful information to the claims adjuster or defense attorney. Frequently, for instance, a medical report will describe a loss of motion in a joint in terms of degrees of movement. Thus; "patient moves his neck through a range of 15° rotation to the right." Degrees of movement are not readily translatable to the percentage of disability. What is the normal extent of rotation? If it is 90° then plaintiff has retained about ⅙ of normal movement. How much more easily understood if expressed in such a fashion. Such an expression, although of more meaning, is still subject to further clarification. The important question is what does it mean by way of loss of function for the particular individual involved. Would that percentage of loss prevent a person from driving a car and maintaining a safe range of vision? Would it prevent a housewife from hanging up clothes, scrubbing floors, ironing or performing some other daily chore that she is called upon to perform? Relating the disability to a specific loss of function will always portray the injury in more meaningful terms and will serve to answer the real concern of the injured person. It is of little significance to learn that the plaintiff suffered 40% instability of the knee. Will it prevent him from standing at a lathe, playing golf, ascending stairs? A statistical rating for eyesight might convey some meaning, but the real question is will the blurred vision allow the inspector to retain his job, or the locomotive engineer to keep his position.

Translating the raw medical evaluation into meaningful disability for the particular client involved is primarily a job of the lawyer but the task can be considerably lightened by the doctor through his report. However, such an appraisal can be of little value unless the doctor is thoroughly acquainted with the type of daily routine that the plaintiff follows, his family status, economic needs, recreational interests, nature of personality, etc. Perhaps the need for incorporating these factors in a medical report can best be illustrated by assuming identical injury to two different persons, "A" and "B." Each has suffered a fracture into the right knee joint which has left a permanently unstable joint and 50% loss of motion in each movement of the knee. Each was hospitalized three weeks; but, in the ensuing six months post-hospital period, "A" was seen 3 times and "B" was seen on 15 occasions. The medical reports, considering only the injury, would be identical. The greater number of visits by "B" and the consequently larger bill might suggest a higher value to his claim. However, investigation of the injured parties reveal these differences.

"A"		"B"
30 years	AGE	50 years
6' 2"	HEIGHT	5' 10"
260	WEIGHT	135
laborer	OCCUPATION	accountant
high school graduate	EDUCATION	college graduate
stoical	EMOTIONAL	self indulgent
married, four children	SOCIAL STATUS	single
cartilage injury, left knee pre-accident	PHYSICAL CONDITION	no prior disability

Obviously medical reports to be used in evaluating these injuries should not be identical in these cases. No prognosis could be complete without considering that:

1. A's size will create recurring problems and heighten the likelihood of post traumatic difficulties, such as arthritis.

2. A's occupation will expose him to continuous shocks and abuse which will impede recovery and increase the likelihood of further disability.

3. A's stoical nature and need for employment was a factor in the relatively light medical attention he received after hospitalization.

4. That the previous weakness to A's other leg created a greater burden on his right knee for weight bearing, stability and mobility, and the overall disability will be significantly increased.

Failure to consider these factors on behalf of A will certainly unfavorably distort the medical picture. The lawyer representing him would be remiss in his obligations if he did not consult with the doctor prior to requesting the report to confirm the doctor's knowledge of this peripheral information and request that the report incorporate these factors.

The representation of B would not necessitate an elaboration of the factors complementing his injury. If anything they would tend to minimize the injury and consequently they would be better left unsaid. The genius of the advocacy system will prevail. It will be for the defense counsel or his examining physician to introduce the ameliorating effect of B's slight physique, his sedentary occupation and his preoccupation with his physical well being.

§ 19.14   Medical Report—Pre-existing Condition

Special consideration in securing an adequate medical evaluation and report must be given in those cases in which the claimant has suffered an injury super-imposed upon a pre-existing condition or injury. A substantial number of claims involve persons who have undergone arthritic changes in their spine and have suffered a subsequent trauma. The arthritic condition is "inflamed, aggravated, rendered painful" in the language of the plaintiff's petition. The medical report which confines itself to a recitation of the present condition will be of little or no assistance in evaluating the claim. The important questions which must be answered by the report are:

1. Was the previous condition painful or disabling and, if so, to what extent? If a previous injury, was there full recovery or were its effects still present?

2. Was the previous condition or injury static, progressive or regressive? In other words, absent the injury, what was claimant's prognosis as to function and survival?

3. Was the trauma a competent producing cause of the resulting disability? Did the trauma trigger the underlying condition? Was it the precipitating factor in

converting a functioning plaintiff with a compensated weakness into a non-functioning plaintiff with a deteriorating disability?

This area of evaluating an aggravation of a previously existing condition or injury is one of the most difficult problems confronted by representatives of injured claimants. All the medical information and opinion that can be accumulated should be utilized.

§ 19.15 Medical Report—Extraneous Matters

Although the attorney should solicit such considerations from the doctor in drafting his report, there is some restraint that should be exercised. The doctor should not become an advocate— that is the role of the lawyer. If his opinion, by way of report or testimony, is to have any persuasive effect it must not lose the characteristics of an unbiased, scientific opinion. Consequently, the medical report should not comment upon the patient's economic needs, size of family, inability to seek a less demanding job by reason of limited education. These are legitimate arguments to be advanced by the lawyer. They assume no greater weight when expressed by the doctor and they would tend to lessen the credibility of those opinions expressed within the areas of his specialized knowledge.

§ 19.16 Thumb–Rule Appraisal

The average person sitting on a jury will seldom be convinced by the plaintiff's complaints standing alone. There's a bit of Missourian in each of us that demands that we be shown. That is particularly true when it comes to appraising the validity of a plaintiff's complaints. Will Rogers was able to conclude that something was true simply because "I read it in the papers." Few persons are satisfied with such modest proof of truthfulness, and fewer still will be satisfied with the truth of a plaintiff's complaints simply because he said it.

There are a few simple questions that suggest themselves to the average person to determine whether a person's complaints of pain and disability are valid. The lawyer might be advised to employ these same tests to a person seeking representation in his claim for injuries.

First, have you seen a doctor? Most persons who suffer an injury of any consequence will seek professional medical attention.

Health and accident insurance, union benefits, pre-paid medical plans, all encourage a medical check up in the event of an injury. There is some resistance, however, to medical treatment, the long waits in the office, the expense, the thought that "it will go away." If the client has not sought medical attention, it does not necessarily foreclose the possibility of serious injury but it does substantially lessen the likelihood. It might be said that the potential plaintiff has one strike on him.

Second, have you lost any time from work? If there is a genuine disability it is reasonable to expect that the plaintiff's physical activity has been curtailed and that he has missed some work. Of course, the more physically demanding the work, the greater the expectation of lost time. Again there are some valid explanations for a negative response, "I just couldn't afford to." "The boss put me on light duty." "Some of the fellows covered for me." "I thought I might as well be hurting at work as hurting at home." Regardless of the explanation, however, if the plaintiff has neither seen a doctor nor absented himself from work, the count stands at two strikes.

Third, what are you doing for yourself by way of treatment? A person who suffers a continuing pain in the back may not see a doctor, may not miss work, but he will seek some kind of relief by way of a home remedy. He will be under a heat lamp, have his wife rub his back with alcohol, or apply a heating pad. If he complains of "splitting headaches" that have continued unabated and has not sought relief by taking aspirin, or the "twice as fast" competitor, then it is virtually impossible that the complaints of pain will be believed. With the acknowledgment of "no home remedy" the third strike is called and the batter is out. The lawyer must recognize that he will be consulted by persons claiming injury whose claims are not sufficiently severe or valid to warrant representation. A silk purse of a substantial recovery cannot be made from a sow's ear of a spurious claim. The recognition of this truth will save hours of fruitless labor.

§ 19.17 Medical Research

It is usually most desirable for the attorney to defer his medical research until he is in receipt of a medical report or a hospital record and has an expression from a competent medical person as to the area in which he will be dealing. Once this information is available some medical research will become necessary in order that the attorney will be able to comprehend:

1. The meaning of the medical phrases recited in the report.

2. The anatomy of the structures involved.

3. The physiology of the structures involved.

4. The mechanics of the trauma and the effects on the affected structures.

5. The nature of commonly used diagnostic techniques.

6. An evaluation of the disability.

These are basic areas of information which must be comprehended in every traumatic injury case. Other cases might introduce the need for further research. Such is the situation in those matters in which the nature of the injury is such that neither the cause nor the results are easily ascertainable. No special research would be needed when an automobile collision results in a broken arm. But what if the client experiences a flare-up of his diabetic condition or an exacerbation of a tubercular joint? Can the slight blow to the temple be responsible for the mental depression and aberrations subsequently suffered by your client? Did the blow to the abdomen cause the stomach ulcer? For the lawyer to evaluate his case he must broaden his medical research in order to comprehend:

1. The diagnostic procedures and techniques including the purpose and interpretation of:
    a. Clinical tests.
    b. X rays.
    c. Neurological examinations.
2. Differential diagnosis—the technique of interpreting signs, tests and symptoms which are present in more than one condition or disease. If there is an issue as to the identity of the claimant's complaints, it becomes just as important for the lawyer to know those conditions from which his client *doesn't* suffer as to know those from which he does.
3. The relationship between the client's pre-traumatic condition, the trauma and the consequent disability.

The young child has a family history of epilepsy, he suffers a depression fracture of the skull, six months later he experiences a seizure. The medical research will have to answer questions such as these:

1. Pre-traumatic condition—Is epilepsy inherited? If not inherited, do certain persons have a pre-disposition toward developing epilepsy?

2. Trauma—What brain damage, if any, results from a depressed skull fracture? Was there a period of unconsciousness? Any neurological signs of brain damage?

3. Etiology—Can epilepsy be induced by trauma to the head? How extensive must the damage be? Could the onset of the seizure post-date the trauma by as much as six months and still be related?

The initial research will be on the basis of improving the lawyer's understanding. Of course, it will not stop at this level. Having a lawyer understand the nature and extent of the injury is, of course, only the beginning. Translating this understanding to the adjuster, defense counsel or the jury is the ultimate goal of any medical research. But before any information can be conveyed, it must be comprehended—so the first step is for the lawyer to become acquainted with what the doctor has to say.

§ 19.18   Medical Research—Illustration

The focus of the medical research usually will fall within one particular area or another. For instance, if you represent a client who has suffered a traumatic injury which has resulted in the removal of his spleen, it will become obvious that the chief area of your research will be in regard to the anatomy and function of the spleen itself. It will be impossible to evaluate this claim for settlement or trial unless the lawyer has a full understanding of the function that the spleen serves; the manner in which these functions are performed; what, if any, organs undertake to perform these functions upon the loss of the spleen; effect of the loss of the spleen upon resistance to disease, life expectancy, etc.

Another kind of injury might necessitate little or no research as to the anatomy or function of the part involved, but focus most of its attention upon the etiology or the role, if any, played by the trauma in the resulting disability. Of such a nature are those situations in which claims are brought claiming that a disease not usually associated with trauma (cancer, tuberculosis, arthritis) has been induced by an accident.

Still another area of medical research emphasis might be in the area of diagnostic testing. A 38 year old woman suffers a whiplash injury to the neck. Shortly thereafter, she develops muscle stiffness and is hospitalized for a week, undergoing traction and muscle relaxants. She is released from the hospital and continues to have intermittent pains about the neck. After a nine month period, she has related pain into the shoulders, with occasional attacks of numbness in her right hand which do not follow an anatomical pattern. A myelogram is performed showing a slight occlusion in the cervical area between the sixth and seventh cervical vertebrae consistent with an arthritic bridging. Later a discogram is taken indicating an effusion of pantopaque beyond the disc. Prior medical history indicates that the woman had an occurrence of spontaneous wry neck, occurring some four years before the accident in question.

The medical picture that is presented is such that one doctor is of the opinion that the woman suffered a muscle strain of the neck, that her complaints of numbness are functional in nature and "all in her head" that by reason of her past history, she is susceptible to occasional periods of muscle strain of her neck for no apparent traumatic reason. Another doctor opines that she has suffered an aggravation of an arthritic condition of her cervical spine basing his opinion upon the myelogram. Yet another interprets the discogram and the complaints of numbness as symptoms of a traumatically induced ruptured intervertebral disc. The question, of course, now depends upon the diagnostic validity of the various tests that were performed. The emphasis of the medical research will be not only in an understanding of the cervical vertebrae, the intervertebral discs, and the muscle and nerve structure of the neck. Research must also include the causes of wry neck, the relationship of trauma to pains in the shoulder and numbness in the hands, the diagnostic validity of the myelogram and discogram. Without an understanding of these the lawyer will be unable to evaluate his client's case.

2. DEFENDANT

§ 19.19 Generally

The defendant's lawyer must have the same breadth of medical knowledge as his opponent. The difference between the two lies not in the extent of information needed but in the results which each seek to achieve and the sources of information available.

§ 19.20 Sources of Information—Petition of Complaint

The first formal information that the defendant's counsel will receive will be the allegations of injuries outlined in the petition or complaint. The information will be of little value. In many instances the original petition will make general allegations of injury to the "head, face and body" or else will follow a "shotgun" approach and allege that "all the bones, muscles, nerves, tissues, organs, tendons, vessels, discs, cartilages, skin and joints of the plaintiff's head, face, neck, back, shoulders, arms, legs and spine were severely fractured, wrenched, sprained, strained, twisted, torn, bruised, dislocated, lacerated, ruptured and abraded."

The pleading will be of some value to the defendant in establishing a range of value to the claim only if the injuries are alleged with particularity and the special damages are outlined in detail.

§ 19.21   Sources of Information—Claimant

A second source of information will come from the plaintiff himself. If an adjuster has called on the claimant before counsel was engaged, there is a possibility that the file will include: observations of the adjuster as to injury, complaints, disability; a statement from the claimant; or a report from the treating doctor. Standard claims practice dictates that a medical authorization be received from a person claiming injury.

The defendant will encounter resistance from both the claimant in signing the authorization, and the treating doctor, in filling out the form. As a general rule the ease with which these instruments are executed is in inverse proportion to their length.

The claimant should not be led into believing he is "signing his life away." There is no need for small print nor legalistic language. The blanks should be filled in by the defendant's representative at the time of execution so that all the claimant is asked to do is sign his name. The authorization should be given to an individual rather than a business organization easily recognized as an insurance company. If the form itself indicates that it is a request by an insurance company it might adversely affect the chances of it being completed by the doctor.

The report itself should be brief and request only the pertinent points. Better to have a short report in the file than to jeopardize the chances for any information by presenting the doctor with a burdensome request that he won't acknowledge.

The doctor should be afforded an opportunity to disclose those facts which would be of significance in establishing a liability defense or limiting recovery. Contradictory statements regarding the facts of the accident which appear in medical reports can be devastating to the plaintiff. The history as described by the patient should be solicited in the report. Encouragement should also be given toward a disclosure of any contributing factor which might be affecting plaintiff's complaints. Further the doctor should be requested to establish periods of disability. If he has done so on a report and has indicated that plaintiff's disability terminated four weeks after the accident, any testimony at trial regarding permanent injuries would be subject to question by reason of the prior appraisal.

Once suit is filed, the defendant may elicit further information from the claimant (now plaintiff) by way of deposition or interrogatory. The deposition provides the easier method of adducing most information. The lines of inquiry will seek to establish the following:

1. Physical status of plaintiff
   a. Age
   b. Height
   c. Weight
2. Social Status
   a. Marital status—number of children
   b. Residence
   c. Employment—nature of work, length of service, earnings
3. Injury
   a. Parts of body injured
   b. Types of treatment given
   c. Length of treatment
   d. Treating personnel and institutions
4. Present Complaints
   a. Nature and frequency of complaints
   b. Specific disabilities
      1. Physical
      2. Social
5. Pre-injury status of plaintiff
   a. Physical—weight and height
   b. Employment—nature of work, length of service, earnings
   c. Residence
   d. Previous injuries or claims
6. Financial losses
   a. Medical expenses
   b. Loss of earnings
   c. Incidental property loss

Inquiry into those areas calling for statistical information (bills, number of doctor visits, earnings, etc.) can best be secured through the submission of interrogatories in contrast with other areas of inquiry necessitating narrative replies which can best be secured through oral depositions.

§ 19.22 Sources of Information—Medical Reports

A third source of information will be the medical reports from the personnel and institutions treating the plaintiff. If possible, the defendant should secure the complete reports and records. Frequently the treating doctor's report might contain information or opinion that is detrimental to the plaintiff's case. The history given of the onset of the complaint might vary with that claimed by the plaintiff. The family history or past history of the plaintiff might indicate a hereditary defect or prior complaint which would cloud the issue of causal relationship between the instant episode and the subsequent disability. A prognosis might be more optimistic than the bleak future of pain and disability claimed by plaintiff's attorney.

To avoid the unfavorable aspects of a doctor's report, the plaintiff attorney might submit a medical abstract, a synopsis or merely excerpts from the report or record which is favorable to his client's case. Anything less than the complete report should be a "red flag" for defendant's attorney and he should advise his opponent that the report or record has little or no appraisal value unless it is complete.

With the complete report or record available an analysis will be made in order to ascertain the following:

1. The present condition of plaintiff.
2. Presence of a previous or subsequent event or condition of health which might affect:
   a. The causal relationship of the instant event.
   b. The subsequent complaints.
   c. The extent of disability.
3. The need for further examination and evaluation.

§ 19.23 Sources of Information—Surveillance

Another method of securing information is available to the defendant through independent investigation and surveillance. If there is some question as to the objectivity of the fellow employees, neighbors and friends who have confirmed the disability and complaints of the plaintiff, it will behoove the defendant to seek a

sampling of his own. It isn't too difficult to find a hostile neighbor, ("Her kids are always stomping on our grass") who thinks
that plaintiff is "putting on," or to uncover a less than friendly
fellow employee who feels that "Joe never did carry his load
around here even before he was hurt." Discovering the dissidents
is one thing; utilizing the information is quite another. The fact
that a neighbor or fellow worker is willing to confide information
to an investigator does not mean that he or she is willing to take
the stand and publicly degrade or excoriate one of their own.
Many are the insurance files that are fattened with opinion
statements from hostile witnesses, the information from which
will never be transposed to testimony at trial. But although
unlikely witnesses themselves, these dissidents may be the source
of information that will produce evidence available for trial.
"Why do you think Joe isn't hurt?" "He still bowls every week on
the company team and he's got one of the best averages in the
league." Here is factual information that can be readily established. No need for a fellow worker to be embarrassed by giving
unfavorable testimony; no uncertainties of a subjective appraisal.
The records of the bowling league show uninterrupted activity
with undiminished results—perhaps enough to knock the pins
from under the plaintiff's case.

"And Mrs. Neighbor, why do you think that the plaintiff is
'putting on'?" "Well, she complains and mopes around one minute and the next she's scrubbing her steps or hanging out wash.
If she can do those things, her back can't hurt her that bad."

Translating this information into objective evidence is easily
accomplished. Establish a surveillance of the plaintiff and record
by video tape the back yard activities which belie the claim of
disability. To assure admissibility, the date of the taping must be
established, the "takes" should be continuous (no cutting or editing) and the plaintiff easily identifiable.

Although the mechanics of taking surveillance video tapes is
relatively simple, the decision of whether they should be used at
trial is not. Section 13.11.

§ 19.24 Sources of Information—Medical Examination

The defendant is not confined to passive appraisal of information supplied by the plaintiff. In any adversary proceeding one
must expect that the information supplied by the opposition is
designed to support their contentions and advance their cause.
One cannot, and should not, expect a non-partisan, down to earth

presentation of unvarnished facts. Deposition time will find the plaintiff on his good behavior, reciting the facts of the accident with sureness and conviction and enumerating his injuries with sincerity and concern. The statements of lay witnesses which have been supplied have come from friends and neighbors whose fondness for the plaintiff has sharpened their anxiety to help and dulled their capacity to appraise objectively. The medical information emanates from the family doctor who is expected to present a sympathetic report—and the expectations are usually fulfilled. (How can the prognosis be anything but "guarded" when the client has been advised that he should continue to "drop in" for periodic check ups?)

If the injuries are serious and the risk of exposure substantial, the defendant will no doubt seek information of his own. The most obvious source of such information will be a medical examination by a doctor of the defendant's choosing.

The desirability of having such a medical examination will depend upon defendant counsel's answers to these questions:

1. On what basis is the claim to be defended? Will there be a claim of no liability or will the nature and extent of the injuries be in issue?

2. If there is a strong defendant's case on the issue of liability, is our position weakened by contesting the issue of damages? Will an examination by our doctor give undue emphasis to that feature of the case and lead the jury to believe that we do not have confidence in our defense?

3. If we are contesting the injury are there sufficient inherent weaknesses in plaintiff's case to provide an adequate defense? Must we adduce independent medical proof contrary to that of plaintiff either in regard to causal relation or extent of injury?

In most instances the defendant's counsel will resolve to use an examining doctor of his own. As suggested, there are some dangers involved. If defendant's doctor confirms the findings of the plaintiff's medical testimony then the defendant is foreclosed from questioning this issue in the case. Such is the case in some instances and, mirabile dictu, on some occasions the defendant's doctor finds injuries hitherto unknown! In most cases, however, the examination is made near trial time, the injuries have in some measure subsided, the examining doctor is a bit more optimistic as to the future and a medical issue is drawn for the jury regarding the extent of the injury or disability.

§ 19.25 Appraisal—Generally

What will the plaintiff claim by way of present pain and disability, if the case is tried? What evidence will he have to support his claim?

The counsel for defendant must realize that the biggest factor in determining the value of a claim for personal injury is the persistence of the complaint and the threat of future, possibly permanent, pain and disability. Regardless of how serious plaintiff's injury might have been, even if it brought the victim to death's door, if, at the time of trial the plaintiff is restored to his ante-tort condition and faces no threat of further recurrence, then his case has a limited value. The injuries that precipitate the deepest concern of the jurors are the persisting, unrelenting complaints which threaten to become chronic, a thorn in the side to be borne throughout life. Which injury would one rather suffer? A broken limb which knits in six weeks and leaves no complaint of pain or disability—or a blow to the head which causes periodic headaches which continue unabated for six months with no indication as to when they might relent? The answer is obvious. Who won't submit to the excruciating but transitory pain of a tooth extraction rather than face the interminable growing discomfort of an impacted molar?

And so it is that the defense lawyer must first determine whether there is to be a claim for future or permanent injury and, if so, the type of evidence available to support such a claim.

§ 19.26 Appraisal—Plaintiff

Obviously, first reference must be made to the plaintiff himself. What is recorded as "present complaints" in the medical reports? How has he responded in interrogatories or deposition? The lawyer for defendant must look beyond a mere recitation of a complaint. First, he must consider the "quality" of the complaint. If the plaintiff's deposition has been taken there has been an opportunity to view the plaintiff, witness his demeanor, gauge his sincerity, and appraise his jury appeal. There can be no formula for such an evaluation. The reasons, if any, why one plaintiff will warm the cockles of a jury's heart while another raises its hackles are obscure. Perhaps the poet best expressed the inscrutable process of personality appraisal when he wrote ...

"I do not like thee, Dr. Fell

The reason why I cannot tell

But this I know and know full well

I do not like thee, Dr. Fell."

The defendant lawyer at the time of plaintiff's deposition must "size him up" and appraise those factors which will determine his effectiveness as a witness: physical appearance, ability to articulate, intelligence, personality, etc.

If the plaintiff ranks high in jury appeal his subjective complaints must be weighed accordingly; if he does not, his complaints may be discounted.

§ 19.27   Appraisal—Lay Witness

Aside from the plaintiff there will be other sources of proof available to establish the existence of present complaints. Members of the family, friends, neighbors, co-workers, may be in position to testify what they have observed about the plaintiff indicative of a state of ill health or disability. Indeed, corroborating evidence such as this is practically mandatory if the plaintiff wishes to establish his claim. If a plaintiff's injury has foreclosed him from continuing in his bowling league, should not a member of the team confirm his unsuccessful efforts to resume this activity? Why let the plaintiff's word alone suffice when he had suffered attacks at work which have necessitated treatment and rest? The attending nurse or fellow workman should be relied upon in such instances.

Nor are such witnesses confined to testimony concerning their observations alone. They may also testify to verbal complaints made by the plaintiff of present complaints. Thus the testimony of a friend that "plaintiff complained of a headache and 'begged off' neighborhood bridge" would be received as evidence.

Defendant counsel faces the same problem in regard to this type of testimony—appraising the jury appeal, the credibility, of the person so testifying.

§ 19.28   Appraisal—Doctors

A third source of evidence seeking to establish the existence of present complaints will come from the medical practitioners who have treated or examined the plaintiff.

An evaluation of this evidence by defendant's counsel will be affected by the same factors apt to be considered by the jury in determining the weight to be given by such witnesses.

1. General considerations in establishing credibility.

    Whether a professional person or not, the demeanor of the witness on the stand, his physical appearance, personality, willingness to directly answer the questions, etc. will be considered by the jury in accepting or rejecting his testimony.

2. Areas of expertise.

    Is the medical witness a chiropractor, osteopath, medical doctor, homeopath? Does he have a specialty within his profession which encompasses those areas of plaintiff's complaints?

3. Standing within his profession.

    How long has he practiced, to what professional societies does he belong, is he associated with hospital staffs, has he written or taught in the field of his training, has he received any professional recognition by way of awards, etc. Has his license ever been suspended, has he been discharged from a hospital staff, has he been named in malpractice suits? Is he vulnerable by way of professional incompetence?

4. Medical-legal background.

    Is the medical practitioner identified as a "defendant's doctor" or "plaintiff's doctor?" Does he derive a substantial part of his income from handling one side only of medical-legal cases? Does he have a relationship with the plaintiff's lawyer? Was the plaintiff referred to the doctor by the attorney?

Of the various factors to be considered by defendant's counsel the medical-legal background of the treating or examining doctor is, perhaps, the most important.

A doctor chosen by plaintiff's attorney for the purpose of an examination and report will not have his opinion of present complaint held in the same regard as that of a family doctor who has treated the plaintiff from the onset of his injury. The testimony of such an examining doctor is vulnerable to the claim that he is a "manufactured witness" a "testifying doctor" and that by reason of his association with the plaintiff's lawyer he has abdicated his role as a disinterested expert witness and has assumed the role of advocate.

Numerous appearances in court as an examining and testifying doctor will expose a professional person to such an attack. That same experience, however, has sharpened his wits and tempered his judgment and acquainted him with the rough and tumble forensics of a court room. Whether this background, with its plus and minus features inures to the benefit of the plaintiff or the defendant will depend upon the case, the doctor and the counselors.

§ 19.29 Appraisal—Medical History

The second area of inquiry by the defendant's lawyer in seeking to evaluate the plaintiff's injury will be medical history. Has plaintiff suffered from a condition or injury ante-dating the event which has given rise to the instant claim? If so, what effect, if any, has such condition or injury have upon plaintiff's present condition?

A 40 year old man is involved in an automobile accident in which his knee forcibly strikes the dashboard. Swelling and discoloration of the knee persists and after six months the treating physician reports "an internal derangement of the knee resulting in lateral instability, impaired movement and continuous pain." Prior history reveals a tubercular infection of the spine some three years before the accident which condition responded to treatment and has been quiescent since.

The defendant's counsel must answer two questions: Is the present disability the result of a tubercular infection or the trauma suffered in the accident? If the former, did the tubercular infection coincidentally manifest itself at the time of the trauma or did the trauma activate a passive condition?

Many laymen, plaintiffs and jurors alike, are concerned only with the chronology of events in determining the causal relationship between an accident and a subsequent disability. Consequently, defendant's counsel must be prepared to meet every claim of disability following an accident and to be in adequate position to do this he must acquaint himself with the medical history and then, through medical research, ascertain the significance of the history in regard to the present condition. Thus, a positive serology might well be the no-liability answer to a claim for post traumatic psychosis. A swarm of spirochetes is just as damaging as the thrust of a head through a windshield.

The plaintiff might sustain an injury or fall victim to a disease subsequent to the tortious act of defendant. Obviously, such a situation clouds the medical picture and, on some occasions, to such an extent that plaintiff is unable to bear the onus of proving to the jury's satisfaction what role the initial injury played in the present disability.

CHAPTER 20

SETTLEMENT OF CASE

Analysis

A. SETTLEMENT FACTORS

A. SETTLEMENT FACTORS

§ 20.1 Generally

Why is it that so many lawsuits are settled? There are undoubtedly many reasons why such an overwhelming percentage of the cases are disposed of voluntarily rather than submitted to a judge or jury for disposition. The factors which tend to precipitate settlement fall within distinct categories.

§ 20.2 Psychological Factors

There are many aspects of a contested lawsuit which are distasteful to the individual litigants. The most basic is "fear of the unknown." The prospect of doing almost anything for the first time is disquieting to the average person. For most litigants it will be their first time in court. They are unfamiliar with the procedures, uncertain of what will be expected of them, and apprehensive of the notoriety that will be connected with the case. Their concept of court procedure has been distorted by the fictional portrayals on television or in the movies, or perhaps by their viewing of a newsreel clip of the peripheral action of an actual trial which, because of its unique sensationalism, has been deemed newsworthy by the communication media.

The scripts and the newsreels are so doggedly repetitive that, after viewing the same ritual time and time again, the real life litigant comes to believe that all trials must fall into the same pattern. The client will assume that the court room will be crowded by curious onlookers. The judge will be firm but kindly. The opposing attorney will undoubtedly be cynical and flinty-eyed, ready with slicing insinuation and caustic innuendo to humiliate his hapless victim in full view of the audibly shocked spectators (at which point the judge will bang his gavel and threaten "to have the court room cleared if there's another such outburst"). Sometime during the course of the trial a request will be made to conduct a dramatic experiment which will draw the opponent's objection ("I've never heard of this before") and the court's reluctant approval ("This is highly irregular counsel, but ..."). The trial will be punctuated by spirited objections ("He's trying to bamboozle the jury"), asides to the jury ("I told you he was lying"), and harsh admonitions from the judge ("There are strict penalties for perjury in this jurisdiction"). The trial will conclude when the weaker of the two adversaries finally breaks down and sobbingly admits that the whole thing was his fault.

With visions such as this fuzzing the mind, it is small wonder that a substantial number of cases are settled simply because the litigants don't want to go to trial.

Mention must be made again of a factor which heightens the likelihood of settlement: the fear of condemnation by reason of litigiousness. "All the world loves a lover" and conversely, very few like litigious persons. The average person who has a lawsuit pending is quite content to keep that information to himself. If queried about it, he is wont to reply apologetically, "yes, but I'm sure we'll settle it out of court." The reason for this hesitancy to become involved in litigation is difficult to explain. Undoubtedly it is related to the aversion that some persons have to being accused of "trying to get something for nothing." The fear of this accusation appears to be felt most keenly by the great mass of persons categorized as the "middle class." The lower economic group unashamedly acknowledge that they must seek redress by court procedure to effect their financial rehabilitation. The upper economic group explain that their litigiousness is a matter of principle. The middle class unable to adopt the altruistic excuse of the "upper class" and unwilling to admit to their economic needs as do the "lower class," are most apt to be found among those thousands of injured persons who settle for the "specials" and a few extra dollars "to cover the inconvenience."

§ 20.3   Mechanical Factors

Every lawsuit cannot be tried. The structure of our judicial process cannot tolerate the strain of wholesale litigation. We would be hard put to supply the jurors, the bailiffs and the clerks much less the court rooms and judges. The lawyers who engage in trial work could not profitably limit their practice to such a specialty if every case necessitated a full blown trial. The habitual witnesses; the policemen and the doctors, could not bear the imposition on their time.

Consequently a substantial number of cases must be terminated extra-judicially—and they are.

§ 20.4   Economic Factors

The proper disposition of a personal injury claim should be based on economic considerations. Some litigation may be focused upon the vindication of one of the litigants, or the resolution of some principle, as in a slander case or an alienation of affection matter. These same issues will be present in some degree in personal injury litigation. The drivers who collide in an intersection will probably wish to vindicate themselves and their driving ability. The defendant who feels that he has been falsely charged with a negligent act will no doubt resist the plaintiff's claim because of the principle involved. Indeed, many defendants lose faith with their own insurance company for settling a case when, in the judgment of the insured, the claim should have been denied. It makes little sense to them that the principle of who was right or wrong was sacrificed because the claim could be disposed of for "nuisance value."

But, despite the presence of principle or personal feelings serving to color the picture, the plaintiff in a personal injury case should consider the possible settlement of his claim from the standpoint of whether or not it is "good business."

Several economic factors suggest that it is good business to effect a settlement.

First, a settlement brings about an immediate disposition of the claim and payment to the plaintiff. Any litigation is time consuming. The time lapse for the trial itself and the disposition of the usual post-trial motions usually takes three months, depending of course on the jurisdiction. If there is an appeal, there might be another eighteen months or two years wait involved. There is economic value in the use of money during the period when payment could be delayed. For this reason it is not unusual for a successful plaintiff to discount a verdict to achieve an immediate payment. Such is the lure of "ready cash."

Second, litigation is expensive, and if the claim can be settled before the suit is tried, a greater percentage of the settlement will inure to the benefit of the plaintiff. The expenses involved in trying a suit fall within three classes: those incurred for witness fees, travel expenses, court costs; those incurred by the plaintiff himself in the attendance of court proceedings; and the increased legal fees which may be incurred, in the event that the contract of employment has a sliding scale for fee depending upon the stage of litigation at which the case is settled.

Third, there is some economic advantage to reducing the unpredictableness of a trial verdict to the certainty of a settlement. In other words, "A bird in the hand is worth two in the bush." The discount rate of fifty percent may be unrealistic in the particular case, but the logic behind the saying cannot be denied. The applicability of this truism to the area of litigation settlement is based upon the realization that in every lawsuit there is an element of risk. There is no such thing as a predictable verdict. The "open and shut" case is a shibboleth for the unsure lawyer feigning an air of confidence for the sake of client or jury.

If this premise is accepted, and there is a recognizable risk in the trial of the lawsuit, then this risk should be capable of being expressed in terms of gambler's odds and the claim discounted accordingly. Assume that plaintiff has a claim for property damage in the amount of one thousand dollars, arising out of an intersection collision at a traffic controlled intersection. Each driver claims he had the green light. There are no witnesses or other evidence direct or inferential to tip the balance in favor of either of the two parties. The odds of winning such a case are 50–50. Expressing it another way, the risk of losing is fifty percent. It would be economically sound to dismiss that risk by settling the case for one half of the damages suffered. The only alternative is "double or nothing."

Of course, establishing the odds is seldom as simple as in the foregoing illustration. Most frequently the damages are unliquidated and the possible results are not as readily ascertainable. But the truth remains. The reality of a settlement is frequently worth more than the hopes of a bigger verdict.

For many litigants there is no free choice when it comes to settlement or trial. They are simply not in position to resist the lure of a substantial settlement, even though it might be inadequate for the injuries suffered and the damages sustained. Or perhaps there is a specific need to be met. If such is the case, that particular need outweighs all the sophisticated formulae that could be utilized to arrive at a fair settlement figure. The evaluation that they place on their own claim at least is simple and direct, if not relevant. "The broken leg must be settled for ten thousand dollars—because that's how much we owe on the car."

B. NEGOTIATIONS

§ 20.5 Necessity

Before considering what *can* be done by the plaintiff's attorney in effecting a satisfactory settlement, it might be well to consider what, if anything, *must* be done. Is there an obligation on the part of plaintiff's attorney to negotiate in the hopes of a settlement, or may he fling down the gauntlet, gird his loins and "have at it" without exploring the possibilities of an amicable disposition of his client's claim?

The answer lies in the identity of the litigation. It is in truth the "client's claim." Sometimes it is easy for the plaintiff's attorney to lose sight of this fundamental fact. One experienced, flamboyant plaintiff's attorney, when asked the amount of his fee, responded, "I give the client half of everything I get." True, the attorney may "get" the recovery, but it is the plaintiff that he gets it for.

If it is conceded, as it must be, that the claim is that of the client, then the plaintiff's lawyer must suppress those inclinations which invariably arise with the handling of claims on a continuing basis against customary opposing counsel.

Assume that the plaintiff's lawyer has lost a hotly contested case against a rival adversary. Within a few weeks he finds that he again is pitted against his rival. The case involves good liability and severe injuries. He is anxious for revenge and this is the case that he can serve his opponent his "comeuppance." There is an understandable temptation to disdain settlement and utilize his client's case as a vehicle for retribution. But the client feels no animosity toward the opponent's representative. He is not engaged in a running gun battle with some attorney. He simply wants a just disposition of his claim, and it is that to which he is entitled.

The attorney is similarly tempted to regard the cases he is handling as an economic totality rather than individual cases to be individually considered. Perhaps he has three cases arising out of the same collision. The liability is questionable but the likelihood is that two of the three cases will be won. As far as the lawyer is concerned the winning of two cases at full value with the loss of one may have the same economic effect as settling all three at two-thirds of their value. For the lawyer, considering cases "in the long run," the odds even out. But for the client with only a single case, there is no "long run." A verdict is apt to be all or nothing and if he loses he derives no comfort in knowing that his companions have won.

Good practice and proper consideration for the client dictate that the attorney representing an injured party engage in settlement negotiations. Once those negotiations begin, the attorney is compelled by conscience and law to relay the results of his negotiation to the client. Consider the fate of the attorney who refuses a settlement offer without consultation with his client and then suffers a defendant's verdict at the hands of the jury. He has gambled with funds that were not his and consequently the loss should be his and not his client's. A complete disclosure of all settlement offers must be made to the client. The attorney may, of course, recommend action but the final decision is that of the client. That decision should not be foreclosed by a withholding of the offer by the attorney.

§ 20.6 Preparation of Plaintiff

Before any settlement negotiations commence, the plaintiff's attorney should create a proper climate for settlement with his client. Many injured persons have very definite ideas as to the value of their lawsuit at the time they consult an attorney. If they do, their views should be ascertained at the outset. Most frequently their evaluation is hopelessly optimistic. Oftentimes it is based upon a cloud nine appraisal by an uncle "who is a notary public" or a friend who knew someone who received as much in a similar suit. Sometimes an abbreviated news release can be the contaminant. "Jury gives woman $400,000 for broken leg" heralds the newspaper article. "My case is worth the same" says the middle aged housewife with a green stick fracture of her fibula, not knowing that the newsworthy recipient of the $400,000 was a promising ballerina with a one inch shortening due to a comminuted fracture of her femur.

If the client has evaluated his claim at a figure far in excess of the true settlement value of the case, the lawyer should attempt to rehabilitate his sense of reality. The obvious starting point is those cases within the jurisdiction which have dealt with similar type injuries. For a complete listing of awards, one may consult the appropriate Damages key number in West's General Digest. If the remittitur doctrine is utilized within the jurisdiction, a top figure for the particular injuries beyond which the courts have been loathe to approve a jury award can be determined.

The client must be acquainted with these previous decisions so that he may be aware of the optimum. If, within the jurisdiction, there is an established practice of appellate review and reduction of verdicts the client should not be misled into thinking that the jury award will necessarily be determinative of the recovery in his case. With bright-eyed anticipation the plaintiff asks, "How much will the jury give us?" The slack-jawed trial veteran counters, "How much will the court let us keep?"

Of course settlement figures will never approximate the maximum awards rendered by the jury and approved by the courts. A settlement is a compromise and the defendant can not be expected to voluntarily divest upon the plaintiff an amount which represents the defendant's maximum exposure. The client should be advised that the potential jury award will be discounted in arriving at a settlement figure. He must further be advised that the biggest factor in discounting the potential jury verdict are the questions of fault and injury.

Who will the jury determine to be responsible? How badly is the plaintiff injured?

Many clients are unable or at least unwilling to recognize that they might possibly lose their lawsuit. They are convinced that they are right and the other party wrong and they expect to have their lawyer share their view. As soon as mention is made that, "No case is a guaranteed winner," they interpret this as an indication of lack of faith on the part of the lawyer. Unwilling to be considered a Benedict Arnold, some attorneys refuse to acquaint the client with the cold facts of litigation. It's much more simple to agree with the client, acknowledge that he has a good case, admit that the injuries are serious and agree that his case has a substantial value. This attitude is sure to better lawyer-client relationship—at least until trial time. The lawyer who does not realistically analyze the case and share his analysis with his client revealing both the strengths and weaknesses of liability and injury does himself and his client a disservice. First, an unwillingness to recognize the potential flaws in the case will practically foreclose the possibility of settlement. If the plaintiff thinks his case is a sure winner, his injuries substantial, and his attorney agrees with him, why should he accept a settlement for anything less than "top dollar?" Nothing undercuts the possibility of settlement with greater certainty than a "cock-sure" attitude on the part of one of the litigants. Secondly, the jury verdict is almost sure to bring unsatisfactory results for the attorney.

If the jury does return a substantial verdict it is a vindication of the client's judgment, the "only thing they could have done." The efforts of plaintiff's attorney is dismissed as routine, an expected result in an "open and shut case." If the result is less than optimum, the lawyer becomes the whipping boy, the only flaw in an otherwise good case. Or perhaps the judge is corrupt or the jury tainted. Whatever excuse is used, the chagrined client is turned loose to malign the lawyer, the judge, the whole judicial process.

In order to prevent such a distasteful possibility the lawyer should confer with the client on the eve of settlement negotiations and share with him his concerns with the case. The client should not be allowed to interpret the lawyer's observations as an expression of a loss of confidence in the client or the case. He should be reminded that when he seeks medical advice he expects the doctor to confide in him and relate the true state of his health, the dangers of an operation, and the likelihood of an unsatisfactory result. It is only through this frank disclosure that the patient is able to appreciate the nature of his condition, make an intelligent appraisal and share with the doctor in reaching a decision as to what course of action should be followed. Similarly, a conscientious lawyer will advise the client of the true state of his claim, the dangers of trial, and the likelihood of an unsatisfactory result. Without these disclosures the client cannot make an intelligent decision as to what disposition should be made of the claim.

The client should realize that a doctor's concern for the successful outcome of an operation does not diminish his skill with the knife nor minimize his desire that the patient survive. Nor should he think that the lawyer's anxiety about the case will lessen his legal ability or suppress his desire to win.

§ 20.7   Preparation of Plaintiff—Illustration

Once the client is satisfied with the necessity of a pre-settlement analysis, he should be acquainted initially with the difficulty of evaluating a claim. The orientation might follow these lines.

"There is nothing that is quite as unpredictable as a jury. No matter how many cases a lawyer has tried he is still unable to predict with any degree of certainty how a particular jury will act in a particular case. One reason for this is that it is never known who will constitute the jury. Most often they are an average group of twelve citizens but sometimes there's a disproportionate number of those who might be of sympathetic bent or those who might be skeptical of personal injury claims. As a result, on occasion some jury verdicts are unpredictably generous while others are unrealistically low. The range of verdict in any case could vary from three to four hundred percent and it is because of this broad range of possibilities that makes it difficult to determine what is the true value of a case. On the basis of experience and knowledge of jury verdicts in similar cases we do have some idea as to what a jury might do. If this case of yours were to be tried before ten different juries we could expect to find that one of the juries might return a defendant's verdict and give you nothing. That would be an unusual jury, but the possibility exists. Then again one jury might return the amount we have sued for, $10,000. That too, would be an unusual verdict. The greatest number, say five or six would return verdicts in the 4 to $6,000 range and the remaining two or three would return verdicts above or below that. It's a lot easier to forecast what would happen if the same case were tried before ten different juries than trying to decide which of those ten will be your jury. It's the difference between an economist's ability to predict that the stock market will rise and his capacity to choose which stocks will follow the trend. There's always a chance that he might pick a stock which falls.

"Now before I engage in any negotiations with the defendant I would like to know how you feel about your claim. I don't want to engage in long negotiations and find that we have arrived at a figure which is wholly unacceptable to you. If you have any idea regarding settlement we should consider it because, after all, it's your claim and we want to satisfy you that the best disposition possible has been made."

At this time the client might indicate a figure that is unrealistic and completely beyond the hopes of settlement. If so, he should be advised.

"I have no quarrel with your thinking that your case is worth that much money Mr. Jones. I'm sure if I had suffered your injuries I would feel the same. I feel certain, however, that the defendant will never approach that figure and if that is the figure we stand on, we'll undoubtedly have to go to trial. Now that presents no difficulty. Our case is prepared and we are certainly ready to litigate. But if we want to explore the possibility of settlement we will have to consider a lesser amount."

Sometimes at this point the client will confess that he would consider less but that "you've always got to ask twice as much as you want." The client should be assured that the negotiation will be handled properly and that the appraisal of settlement which is sought from the client is not to be a negotiating figure but an amount which would be satisfactory if offered in settlement. Regardless of what that figure is the attorney will attempt to settle the case for as much as possible.

The assumption has been that the client will express some opinion as to the value of the claim. This is not always so. In some instances they will defer completely to the judgment of their attorney ("That's why I hired you"). The point is this: before settlement negotiations are begun the client should be consulted and his attitude ascertained in order that the proper stage is set for a successful settlement.

§ 20.8   Developing the Pitch

Every good salesman designs his "pitch" to the particular buyer that he hopes to sell. The automobile salesman speaks to the fashion conscious madam of the "elegant styling," of the "maintenance free" construction to her economy-minded husband, and of the "get up and go" to the free-wheeling teen-age son. The pitch designed for the claims representative will, of necessity, be different than that fashioned for the jury. The potential buyers are different. The claims man is engaged in a business. He has had years of experience in dealing with claimants and their lawyers. He has dealt with some fakes and a few frauds. He has seen "nice" people with serious injuries settle their claims for their out-of-pocket expenses because they didn't want to engage in the "distastefulness" of litigation. He has seen poor people make quick settlements because they couldn't afford to "wait out" their claim. He has fretted about paying too much on a questionable claim and has crowed upon closing out a case of "bad" liability and "good" injuries for less than three times the "specials." His enjoyment of dealing with the individual claimants has palled after too many evenings spent in searching out witnesses, taking claimant's statements and haggling over sore necks. Now he finds more enjoyment in matching wits with opposing attorneys, and nothing pleases him more than settling a case with a hot-shot damage suit lawyer for a sum substantially less than that authorized.

This is the adversary in a settlement negotiation. He is a pro, a company man, a hard bitten realist who knows his business, and he is determined to save his company every dime he can.

Considering only the potential buyer, it would appear that the settlement of a claim provides more ominous obstacles than a jury trial. But when the atmosphere of the settlement negotiation is compared with that of the trial, it is apparent why more cases are disposed of by settlement.

Those factors that are considered in the evaluation of a claim by settlement are not necessarily those which are presented to a jury. The jury may consider only that evidence which from a legal standpoint, admissible and, from a practical standpoint, available. Such restrictions do not confine the negotiators in a settlement session. One of the tasks of the plaintiff's lawyer is to sell the claims representative on the merits of his client as well as the merits of his case. Consequently information will be provided indicating that the plaintiff is married and the father of two children, has an honorable discharge from the military service and has never had a claim before. None of such evidence would be admissible at trial. The medical reports of injury and the corroborating statements from lay witnesses will be presented, or at least the information from such reports, and with little thought given to the practicalities of adducing such proof at trial. This seeming indifference to the rules of evidence and the difficulties of producing evidence does not always inure to the benefit of the plaintiff. Statistics will be afforded to show that the plaintiff was earning $600.00 a week and as a result of his injuries was off work three weeks and that hospital costs were $3,000.00—all such testimony being admissible as valid proof of the economic loss occasioned by the accident. The claims man has little interest in such figures. Did he actually lose any wages? How much did Blue Cross cover? What were the actual out-of-pocket expenses?

Whether a claim is sought to be settled by jury trial or voluntary compromise, the same goal is sought—a just disposition by which "every person gets his due." Although the goal is the same the rules of procedure are quite different. But like all good rules which govern human affairs, each system is based upon reason and experience. In the jury system the dispensers of justice are a group of average citizens. Their random selection, inexperience and average capacity assures a verdict that will be representative of the contemporary mores of the community. However, those same characteristics of the jury necessitate that the information upon which that verdict is based be screened, for fear that full disclosure of all the facts will generate more heat than light and that the prejudicial effect of some evidence will outweigh its probative value.

When the method of settlement is a voluntary compromise, there need be no such concern. Full disclosures can be made, the realities of the situation considered and a just disposition made—if the parties can be brought to agreement.

When a case of liability is not settled it is because one of the two parties involved in the negotiations has failed to understand fully the nature of the case. It is the role of the plaintiff's attorney to so present his information that such an understanding will take place.

§ 20.9 Extent of Disclosure

There is a judgment factor in settlement negotiations that should be considered at the outset of any discussion concerning the efforts at a mutually acceptable disposition of a personal injury claim. It is a problem that faces both plaintiff's and defendant's lawyer. To what extent shall the facts of the case be disclosed to the opposition?

There are three types of information the disclosure of which might be detrimental. Two concern the plaintiff, the third, the defendant.

> *One,* facts which are adverse to plaintiff's position. Should the plaintiff voluntarily disclose a previous injury to that part of the body which is now injured and the subject matter of the current claim?
>
> *Two,* facts beneficial to the plaintiff which, if disclosed, might be countered at trial time by the opposition. The plaintiff is in position to adduce proof that if he hadn't been injured he could have secured a job paying seven hundred dollars a week. Investigation by the defendant would reveal that the company went out of business two months after the plaintiff's job opportunity became available. Should the defendant be advised of the claim for lost wages during settlement negotiations?
>
> *Three,* impeachment material which, if disclosed before trial, could be rendered ineffective by plaintiff's explanation. The plaintiff has claimed in deposition that his injuries prevent him from doing manual labor. Surveillance video tapes taken by defendant reveal him chopping wood, painting and doing other household chores. Should the defendant tell plaintiff of his tapes in order to effect a cheaper settlement? Will the warning to the plaintiff tone down his claim at trial and foreclose defendant from using this damaging evidence?

There has been a determined effort from a number of quarters to minimize the sporting contest aspect from civil litigation. Liberalized discovery tools and pretrial conferences have tended toward full disclosures. But the nature of the beast cannot be completely altered. Our differences are still settled by the adversary system and as long as we have partisan representation we will have lawyers employing those tactics which are the stock and trade of any combatant: a full utilization of their strong points, a masking of their weak points, and the most efficacious weapon of them all—surprise.

C. METHODS OF PRESENTATION

§ 20.10 Generally

Lawyers are constantly reminded that theirs is "a profession, not a business." Unfortunately this plea for competence and high ethical standards has been interpreted by some to mean that lawyers should give no thought to the economic realities of their profession. Obviously a case with a potential settlement value of less than ten thousand dollars cannot be handled in the same fashion as one with a settlement value ten or twenty times that much. The client is concerned with the net amount of the settlement and the lawyer who diverts a substantial percentage of that settlement for photographs, plats, etc., when the potential of the case does not deserve it, is guilty of dissipating his time and his client's money. Neither can afford to swat flies with sledge hammers.

But the smaller case has the same need of effective presentation as the larger one. Some format should be adopted that will have the advantages of a persuasive disclosure without the attendant expense of time and money in its preparation.

§ 20.11 Settlement Precis

The use of a settlement precis seeks to meet that need. Its primary purpose will be to present the claim in as persuasive a fashion as possible. It divides itself into six main sections:

> Identity of the plaintiff
>
> Facts of the case
>
> Theory of liability
>
> Medical
>
> Expenses
>
> Analysis of evaluation

The preparation of such a precis will precipitate two secondary advantages: it will discipline the lawyer to analyze his liability, marshal his evidence and appraise the case; and it will provide a dress rehearsal for trial in the event efforts at settlement are fruitless.

§ 20.12 Settlement Precis—Illustration

Social history—Sharon Williams was born July 10th, 1985 the fourth of four children born to John and Virginia Williams. The family lives at 2305 Grand Vista, Columbus, Missouri. Mr. Williams is employed as a machinist at Eagle Air Craft Co. a position he has held for six years.

Sharon is a student in the second grade of Middleton Grade School. She is a member of Girl Scout Troop 378 and is a member of the YMCA girl's swimming team.

Medical History—Sharon had a normal prenatal history and a normal birth. She has been attended by Dr. Grant Fry, a pediatrician, from birth. She has suffered from the childhood diseases of chicken pox and measles. She has never suffered any disability to her lower limbs and has never sustained any injuries to her legs, back or spine. Dr. Fry's medical report is attached.

Facts of Accident—On April 5, 1992 Sharon was enroute from her home to school. The attached police report confirms that the day was clear and warm and the streets were dry. Sharon was by herself and crossing Grand Avenue at its intersection with Washington Street moving westwardly from the southeast to the southwest corner approximately six feet south of the south curb line and within the designated crosswalk. Grand Avenue is forty feet wide with two lanes of traffic moving in each direction. It is straight and level and surfaced with asphalt. There were no cars parked within sixty feet of the intersection. A sign located one hundred feet south of the intersection on Grand has the legend "Caution Children." Police report confirming the description of the scene of the accident is attached.

Sharon was struck by the north bound automobile of defendant at a point five feet from the center line. The attached photographs show the following:

Photo 1 skid marks ten feet long, blood on street.

Photo 2 damage to left head light.

Sharon states that when she left the southeast corner of the intersection the light was in her favor. She never looked at the light again. She walked at a normal pace until she was hit. She was looking forward and never saw or heard the defendant's automobile. The accident occurred at 8:35 A.M. The school is two blocks away and convenes at 8:45 A.M.

A statement taken from the defendant, a copy of which is attached, acknowledges that he didn't see the plaintiff until she was fifteen feet from him and that his automobile came to a stop twenty feet after impact.

Theories of Recovery

The plaintiff has three theories of recovery:

1. That defendant violated a red light

2. That defendant failed to keep a lookout

3. That defendant failed to exercise the highest degree of care to bring his automobile to a stop or slacken after plaintiff came into a position of immediate danger.

The proof of the first theory is supported by plaintiff's testimony that when she left the curb that the light was green for westbound traffic. By reason of the plaintiff's age the court may not permit her to testify. In that event, the defendant's failure to keep a lookout could be submitted as an alternate theory of recovery. Defendant has acknowledged that he didn't see plaintiff until he was fifteen feet away from her and she was already in his path. This would place Sharon at least twelve feet from the curb. The court will judicially notice that the pace of walk is approximately two or three miles an hour or 2.9 to 4.4 feet per second. Wofford v. St. Louis Public Service Co., Mo., 252 S.W.2d 529. Sharon was in the street and visible to defendant for almost three seconds before the accident. At defendant's acknowledged speed of twenty five miles per hour he was traveling at approximately thirty six feet per second or was approximately one hundred feet away when he should have seen Sharon. He was further alerted by the warning sign as he approached the intersection.

By reason of her age, it is questionable whether Sharon would be held responsible for her own actions. Malott v. Harvey, 199 Mo.App. 615, 204 S.W. 940; Quirk v. Metropolitan St. Ry. Co., 200 Mo.App. 585, 210 S.W. 103.

In the event Sharon could be held accountable for not maintaining a proper lookout a third theory of recovery is available: defendant's failure to stop or slacken after plaintiff came into a position of immediate danger. By defendant's admission he came to a stop twenty feet after the impact and he did not attempt evasive action until he was fifteen feet from Sharon, therefore his overall stopping distance was thirty five feet. A jury could find that by reason of Sharon's obliviousness that she was in immediate danger as she approached the path of the vehicle and when defendant's automobile was more than the thirty five feet that was available to bring his vehicle to a stop.

The skid marks indicate that no slackening took place until the defendant's vehicle was within ten feet of the impact. The damage to the automobile indicates it was the left front headlight which struck Sharon. Sharon was within two feet of safety beyond the path of the car when she was struck. Moving at 4.4 feet per second, in one half second she would have escaped injury. From this the jury could assume that a failure to slacken at an earlier time was the proximate cause of the injury.

Medical

The police report states that Sharon was "bleeding about the face and mouth" and complaining of "pain in the right hip." She was taken by police cruiser to Welfare Hospital where it was discovered that she had suffered the loss of a front upper left tooth which was permanent, a laceration of the lip necessitating six stitches and a bruise of the right hip. Portions of the hospital record are attached. She was examined by her pediatrician Dr. Fry who referred her to Dr. William Jones a dentist for examination. He confirms the loss of the permanent tooth and outlines the dental prostheses which will be needed throughout her growth stage and into adulthood. His report is attached. The stitches were removed after six days by Dr. Fry leaving a hair line scar one-fourth inch long near the upper lip.

Expenses

Emergency room Welfare Hospital	$350.00
Dr. Grant Fry	$500.00
Dr. William Jones	
Examination	$135.00
Anticipated treatment	$360.00

Analysis of Evaluation

Actual out of pocket expenses total $985.00 with anticipated costs for dental prosthetic devices throughout Sharon's growth period adding $1,360.00 for a total of $2,345.00. The loss of the tooth is permanent and will necessitate special prophylactic care to maintain the prosthetic devices which must be employed. The scar above the lip is discernible and will be permanent.

It is anticipated that a jury verdict could fall within the $25,000 to $28,000 range. If the case could be settled without further legal procedure I would recommend a settlement of $17,500.00.

§ 20.13 Settlement Brochure

If the case is of sufficient potential to warrant the necessary time and expense, a settlement brochure should be utilized in pretrial settlement negotiations. It will attempt to serve the same functions as outlined before in considering the use of the Settlement Precis. The same questions will also arise. Should the file be opened to the adverse party? Is there a genuine desire on defendant's part to negotiate? Will an advance disclosure of the theory of recovery alert the defendant to the need for developing a defense? Could the information contained in the medical reports be used in cross-examination of the doctor?

Realizing the potential harm of such disclosure, an effort is sometimes made to restrict the use of the information which is supplied for settlement purposes only. The effect of such a restriction might be questioned, both from a practical and psychological standpoint, but if the particular situation suggests that some safeguard should be attempted the following form might be used.

> "The exhibits, statements and reports incorporated in this brochure are submitted for settlement purposes only. They are not to be copied or reproduced in any fashion. In the event this case is tried none of the contents of this report, neither facts, representations nor opinions, are to be used for impeachment purposes."

There are a number of reasons why the brochure will enhance the likelihood of a satisfactory settlement. It presents the case in an orderly, dramatic and persuasive manner. The typical claim is presented by the plaintiff's lawyer to the claims representative as an oral argument, more emotional than logical, more conclusionary than factual. "We'll have testimony that your man was speeding." The witness is not identified nor the testimony outlined. "The medical testimony will prove permanent injuries." Who is the doctor that will say this and exactly what aspect of the injury will be permanent?

Too often the settlement negotiation descends to a shouting match with each party becoming more vehemently partisan as the exchange continues with a concomitant lessening of the chances of settlement.

The oral, face to face confrontation is not the most effective vehicle for settlement negotiations. Each side feigns an air of confidence in his case. It is feared that any conciliatory move will be interpreted as a confession of weakness. The plaintiff's lawyer claims that there is "good" liability, the defendant insists it's "questionable." The plaintiff submits that the injuries are "serious," the defendant counters with the thought that "fortunately he wasn't hurt badly." The plaintiff boasts of his "substantial case" while the claims man commiserates with his "little claim." Frequently, after this preliminary puff and banter, the parties will get down to a serious exchange of facts about the claim. But on occasion this pre-settlement sparring seals the fate of any pretrial disposition. With each succeeding round of biased appraisals the representatives of plaintiff and defendant become more convinced of the merit of his own position and the exaggerated validity of his opponents. Relations inexorably worsen until the negotiation conference concludes with, "I'll see you in court."

A settlement brochure eliminates this possibility. The plaintiff's case is presented in a written documentary form. It is based on facts—statements, reports, exhibits. There is no oratorical flourish nor emotional argument. The claims representative receives the information in "cold blood" and can appraise the case rationally with his reasoning powers unimpaired by the partisan jibes of his antagonist.

There are some additional benefits. A well ordered, carefully planned brochure carries with it an aura of importance. The bulk alone suggests value. Plaintiff files might not be sold by the pound but there seems to be some correlation between the bigness of the file and the bigness of the case. The preparation of a brochure demonstrates that the plaintiff has sufficient confidence in the magnitude of his case to warrant a detailed presentation. It immediately creates an impression of importance.

§ 20.14 Settlement Brochure—Illustration

Table of Contents

Table of Contents

Personal History of Plaintiff

Catherine Brown was born June 8, 1966 and at the time of the accident was twenty-six years of age. She was reared in Texas where she completed four years of high school at Lockhart, Texas and four years of college at Southwest Texas State College. On March 13, 1988 she was married to Fred Brown and his change of employment necessitated a move before her last semester of college could be completed.

On January 29, 1989 Catherine gave birth to her only child, Carl Robert.

Upon arrival in the Kansas City area Catherine enrolled in the Music Conservatory of the University of Missouri—Kansas City and graduated with a B.M.E. in music in 1990. She served as a substitute music teacher in the public schools of Kansas City in the spring of 1991 and in the fall of that year was hired as Music Director of the R–7 School District in Center City, Missouri at a salary of $26,800 for the school year.

Catherine's responsibility included the directorship of three bands and two choirs. In addition she served as sponsor for the Pep Club and Cheerleaders. Her outside activities included membership in the Mu Phi Epsilon Music Sorority and the Center City Music Club.

Medical History of Plaintiff—Summary

Prior to the date of the accident, June 16, 1992, Catherine Brown was in excellent health. She had never suffered any physical disability and her only hospitalization was for the birth of her son.

The accident was unusually violent. The loaded gravel truck struck the vehicle in which plaintiff was a passenger with such force that the automobile was carried seventy-six feet and seven inches beyond the point of impact. The side on which plaintiff was sitting was literally "run over." (See attached photo from police report).

The injuries, detailed in the hospital record and medical reports which follow, consisted primarily of the following:

disfiguring lacerations of face;

multiple fractures of the jaws;

fracture of clavicle with loss of bone;

multiple fractures of the pelvis;

fracture of radius and ulna right arm;

fracture of left forearm;

severe cerebral contusion.

Medical History and Physical Report by Initial Attending Physician

[Date]

BROWN, Catherine.

CHIEF COMPLAINT: Auto accident.

PRESENT ILLNESS: The patient is a 26 year old Gravida I, Para I, Aborta O, white female who was involved in an auto truck accident. The patient was brought immediately to the Emergency Room of General Hospital at which time the patient was admitted thru the Emergency Room by Dr. Smith. The patient was then seen by this doctor in the Intensive Care Unit at which time the patient presented with a blood pressure systolic between 80 and 90. The patient had a very rapid pulse of 120. The patient was cool and appeared to be in shock.

PHYSICAL EXAMINATION:

NEUROLOGICAL: The patient was confused as to time and place with episodes of incoherence. The pupils were dilated and extremely sluggish but were reactive. Fundoscopic examination revealed the discs to be sharp. There was no evidence of papilledema. Cranial nerves appeared to be intact. There was no evidence of motor or sensory loss of the extremities. The patient had obvious multiple fractures.

HEENT: Tympanic membranes were intact. There was no evidence of fluid or blood in the auditory canals. Posterior pharynx was clear. Oral cavity: The patient had palpable fractures of the mandible bilaterally.

NECK: Supple with no palpable masses or tenderness. No bruits. Thyroid was not palpable.

CHEST: Lungs were clear on auscultation and percussion. The patient had palpable fractures over the right chest.

ABDOMEN: No palpable masses or tenderness. Bowel sounds hypoactive. No CVA tenderness. Patient had a mild suprapubic tenderness.

EXTREMITIES: Symmetrical. The patient had marked deformity of the right forearm and wrist area with marked swelling. The patient also had deformity of the left forearm with some swelling. Pressure applied to the pelvic cage caused excrutiating pain. Peripheral pulses in all extremities were grade III and equal bilaterally.

SKIN: The patient had multiple large facial lacerations that covered the entire right face, forehead and parietal area. The patient also had a laceration of the right submandibular area, and left face at the outer canthus of the mouth. The patient had multiple abrasions over the upper extremities and a large laceration over the dorsum of the left hand with no evidence of tendon involvement.

IMPRESSION: Shock syndrome secondary to blood loss and multiple fractures; fracture of the right radius and ulna; right thoracic fractures; pelvic fractures; severe cerebral contusion; multiple lacerations.

DISPOSITION: Patient will be treated for shock syndrome with intravenous fluids, plasma expanders, antibiotics, and patient will then have splinting of the extremities and lacerations closed.

DIAGNOSIS: Compound fracture right and left body of the mandible. The patient sustained the injuries in an auto accident.

RECOMMENDATIONS: Closed reduction by the application of maxillary and mandibular arch bars.

Thank you for this consultation.

[*Signed*]

C.A. JONES, M.D.

———

Operative Record of Initial Attending Physician

[*Date*]

BROWN, Catherine.

PRE–OP DIAGNOSIS: Auto accident with shock syndrome, multiple facial lacerations, laceration of the left lower lip, laceration of left hand, open fracture of the clavicle, fracture of radius and pelvic fractures, cerebral concussion, moderate, severe.

SURGEON: C.A. Jones.

OPERATIVE PROCEDURE: The patient was placed in the supine position. Utilizing 1% Xylocaine diluted to ½% the patient had local infiltration and field blocks for closure of lacerations. The patient had multiple lacerations around the right eye, eyebrow and scalp. The patient also had a thru and thru laceration of the left lower lip and mouth. The patient had multiple small lacerations on the left arm and dorsum of the left hand. All the lacerations were infiltrated and thoroughly scrubbed with Betadine and Betadine solution. The patient then had excision of the margins of the lacerations. The patient had a moderate amount of skin loss on the right temporal area which required undermining of the scalp flap for primary closure. This was repaired with interrupted 4–0 chromic suture and 5–0 nylon suture. Thru and thru laceration of the left lower lip was repaired by first closing the subcutaneous tissue beneath the submucosa of the oral cavity with interrupted 3–0 chromic. The wound was thoroughly irrigated with Saline. The subcutaneous tissue and muscle tissue was then approximated with interrupted 4–0 chromic. The skin was closed with interrupted 5–0 nylon. The subcutaneous tissue in the lower lip and muscle tissue was then approximated with interrupted 4–0 chromic. The skin was closed with interrupted 5–0 nylon suture. The lacerations on the hand and arm were handled in a likewise manner. The patient also had an open comminuted fracture of the right clavicle with a portion of the bone sticking up thru the skin and remaining attached by a piece of periosteum.

The bone had apparently been ground into the dirt. It was therefore thought advisable and with consultation by Dr. Peterson that this portion of the clavicle should be excised and removed. The wound was opened and thoroughly irrigated with approximately two liters of saline solution. The wound was then closed with interrupted 3–0 chromic and interrupted 4–0 nylon suture. All the wounds were then bandaged with Garamycin and 4 × 4 dressings. The patient also had obvious fracture of the right forearm. The forearm was thus splinted due to severe edema at that time, it was felt that casting was not indicated. The arm was splinted with a posterior splint and Ace bandage.

The patient was then returned to surgical ICU for further follow-up. Post-operative condition was guarded.

[*Signed*]

C.A. JONES, M.D., Surgeon

Consultation Report By Doctor Johnson, Orthopedic Surgeon

[*Date*]

BROWN, Catherine.

This 26 year old lady was seen in consultation with Dr. Jones. The initial care had been provided when the patient came into the hospital by Dr. Jones for a compound fracture of the right clavicle and thoracic fractures. The patient also had fractures of the pubis which were also treated by Dr. Jones. I saw the patient at Dr. Jones' request for treatment of a fracture of the right distal radius, and this was treated with a closed reduction on 6/18/72, and immobilized in a long arm cast.

Review of x-rays of the right clavicle revealed satisfactory position of the fracture of the clavicle and also fractures of the right pubis were in satisfactory position. The patient was treated with bed rest for the fractures of the pubis. The patient responded quite nicely to this.

Because of persistent pain in the forearm, left, x-rays were taken several weeks following the accident and these revealed a cracked fracture of the distal ulna. Although it was in good position it was felt that immobilization in a short arm cast was indicated and this was applied. At the time of discharge the patient was instructed to return to my office to be followed as an outpatient as treatment for fractures of the right radius and ulna and the left ulna.

[*Signed*]

A.B. JOHNSON, M.D.,
Consultant

—

Operative Record of Doctor Smith, Oral Surgeon

[*Date*]

BROWN, Catherine.

OPERATION: Closed reduction and application of maxillary and mandibular arch bar with manual reduction.

PRE–OP DIAGNOSIS: Compound fracture of the right and left body of the mandible.

SURGEON: A.B. Smith.

OPERATIVE PROCEDURE: The patient was brought to the operating room in satisfactory physical condition. General anesthesia was induced. The patient was intubated through the right nares and draped in the usual manner for an intra-oral procedure. Mouth and throat were thoroughly cleansed. Deep throat pack was placed.

Following this a maxillary arch bar was ligated to the remaining maxillary teeth. After this had been accomplished manual reduction of the fracture sites was accomplished, circumferential wires were placed around the teeth on either side of the fracture site. After this had been accomplished a mandibular arch bar was ligated to the mandibular teeth thus holding the fracture sites in good alignment. Deep throat pack was removed. Elastics will be placed this evening or in the morning.

Dr. Johnson then continued with his part of the procedure, reduction of the right arm.

[*Signed*]

A.B. SMITH, D.D.S.

—

X–Ray Interpretation

[*Date*]

BROWN, Catherine.

RIGHT FOREARM EXAM including the ELBOW AND WRIST REGION with multiple views with a metal splint in place reveals recent fracture of the distal one-third of the shaft of the radius approximately 2 inches from the wrist joint. There is minimal comminution. The fragments are not widely displaced or separated. There is very slight anterior angulation.

There is also a fracture of the ulna slightly more than one cm. from the distal end with minimal displacement of these fragments.

There is no dislocation.

RIGHT SHOULDER REEXAM with AP VIEW shows the lateral fracture fragments of the clavicle to be displaced completely inferiorly in relation to the medial fragment. The major fragments are separated approximately one-half cm. The fracture fragments of the right 2nd rib are separated almost one-half cm. There is little callus formation in the fracture region but the fragments are not stabilized by bony union.

There are also fractures of the right 5th and 6th ribs posteriorly in good position.

LEFT FOREARM EXAM reveals a fracture in the ulna about 7 cm. above the wrist joint. The fragments are in close apposition with less than ½ cm. displacement and no significant degree of angulation.

PELVIS EXAM with films made at the bedside reveals recent fractures of the superior and inferior pelvic rami and the symphysis pubis on the right side. The fragments show only minimal displacement. There is no dislocation. There is also irregularity in the right side of the sacrum due to fracture in this region with minimal impaction of the fragments.

The sacroiliac joints are not disrupted.

RIGHT FOREARM AND ELBOW reading included with reading of the films of night before of examination of the Rt Arm.

EXAMINATION OF THE SKULL AND MANDIBLE WITH MULTIPLE VIEWS reveals recent fracture of the body of the mandible on the left side. The anterior fragment is displaced medially one cm. No other definite fracture of the mandible is seen at this time. There is no apparent fracture of the skull or depression. The sella turcica is regular.

RIGHT CLAVICLE AND CHEST EXAM reveal the markedly comminuted fracture near the mid portion of the right clavicle. The major fragments are separated almost one-half inch. There is complete inferior displacement of the lateral major fragment. There is no definite rib fracture or lung injury.

RIGHT FOREARM EXAM WITH AP AND LATERAL VIEWS with films made at the bedside shows fracture of the radius 2 inches from the distal end with minimal comminution, and approximately 10 degrees anterior angulation of the fragments. The fragments are not widely displaced. There is also a fracture of the ulna approximately one cm. from the distal end with minimal comminution and slight impaction of these fragments. There is no dislocation.

[*Signed*]

_____

Radiologist

Discharge Summary

[*Date*]

BROWN, Catherine.

PRESENT ILLNESS: The patient is a 26 year old white female who was involved in an auto truck accident. The patient was apparently struck broadside by the truck and carried out thru a field. The patient was brought to the Emergency Room for treatment. The patient was admitted thru the Emergency Room by Dr. Smith, who initiated treatment. The patient was then seen in ICU with a blood pressure of 60 to 90 systolic. The patient was confused as to time and place. Neurological examination revealed both pupils to be extremely dilated and sluggish. Discs were sharp. The patient was able to move all extremities. The patient also had multiple facial lacerations and fractures of the extremities.

PERTINENT PHYSICAL FINDINGS: Revealed multiple facial lacerations involving the right face and right temple area. There was no palpable skull fracture. The patient had bilateral fractures of the mandible, fractures of both forearms and pelvic fracture.

562

The patient was also seen in consultation by Dr. Peterson, Dr. Johnson and Dr. Smith. Patient initially had closure of the facial lacerations, repair of lacerations of the lower lip and left hand. The patient had an open fracture of the right clavicle which was debrided. A small portion of bone was removed. The wound was thoroughly irrigated and closed. The patient had splinting of both forearms. The patient was treated vigorously for shock with intravenous fluids, vasopressors and blood. The patient was also started on massive doses of antibiotics. The patient became more responsive 36 hours after admission at which time the patient then had maxillary fractures and fractures of the radius and ulna bilateral corrected. The patient was then treated with bed rest for four weeks due to large pelvic fracture. The patient's hospital course following the first four days of admission was unremarkable except for slow progression of activity. The patient was ambulated on the 3rd week post-admission. At the time of discharge the patient was ambulatory without assistance, however, the patient had a wide base gait due to instability of the pelvis. The patient's forearms were in plaster splints. The patient's maxillae were still wired. The patient was on a full liquid diet. The facial lacerations had healed well with minimal amount of scar defect. The patient was given a one week return office appointment for followup examination. The patient was discharged from the hospital on Keflex 250 mgms q.i.d.

FINAL DIAGNOSIS:　(1) Shock syndrome, secondary to multiple fractures and blood loss.
(2) Fracture of right radius and ulna.
(3) Fractures of left ulna.
(4) Fracture of right clavicle and right second rib, anteriorly.
(5) Multiple pelvic fractures.
(6) Severe cerebral contusion.
(7) Multiple facial and extremity lacerations.

[*Signed*]

_____

C.A. JONES, M.D.

_____

Medical Report of Doctor Lee, Orthopedic Surgeon

[*Date*]

Re: Catherine Brown

History

The above captioned 27 year old teacher stated that 1 year ago she was injured in an accident on Highway 97 near Hollowell, Kansas. She described riding as a front seat passenger in a car making a left hand turn when it was struck on the right by a trailer-truck that carried their car into a ditch and then a field. She was pinned in her seat by the crushed automobile and was rendered unconscious.

Injuries were sustained to the head, face, jaw, right shoulder, both upper limbs, chest and pelvis. Vigorous bleeding occurred from her face, mouth and compound fracture of her right shoulder.

She was taken by ambulance to the Oswego Hospital and then transferred immediately to the General Hospital in Joplin.

One month of hospital care followed under Dr. Jones, a general surgeon, Drs. Peterson and Johnson, orthopedic surgeons, and Dr. Smith, oral surgeon. On admission she was in shock from blood loss and was given immediate transfusions. Under local anesthesia face and scalp and left hand cuts were repaired, the wound over the right collarbone was cleaned and closed. She was unconscious for 2 or 3 days. Two days after the accident she had an open reduction and wiring of her jaw fractures, closed reduction of the fractures of her right forearm with application of a cast. Three weeks after the accident a cast was applied to her left forearm. Bed rest was the treatment for her pelvic fractures, right collarbone fracture and rib fractures. She started walking 3 weeks after the accident.

The right arm cast was worn 6 weeks and the left arm cast worn 6 weeks. Her teeth were wired for 7 weeks.

Three to four visits were made to Dr. Jones after release from the hospital, the last visit being February 1993. Three visits were made to Dr. Johnson, the last visit October 1992. Three visits were made to Dr. Smith, the last visit September 1992. One visit was made to an orthodontist and one visit was made to Dr. Holt a plastic surgeon.

At the time of the accident this woman was a music teacher and taught all instruments, was a housewife on a farm with one child.

564

Two months after the accident in August 1992 she started working
1 hour a day five days a week for summer class. Three months
after the accident she started full time teaching and has been
working regularly since.

Past history

No previous serious accident, injury, illness or operation reported.

Present complaints

Complaints at this time, 1 year after the accident, are said to
concern the head, face, mouth, right shoulder, left hand, right
forearm, right finger, right upper back and pelvis.

This woman states that following the accident she was unconscious 2 to 3 days, was dazed and had altered consciousness for
several weeks. When released from the hospital she had no
memory of the accident itself nor does she today. Prominent
symptoms at that time were poor concentration, sleepiness, headaches, poor memory. She had poor comprehension and was irrita-
ble, wanted to be left alone. She was easily upset and fatigued
easily. Nausea was also present.

For the past year and up to the present time complaints concern
nervousness, irritability, fatigue, memory changes, headaches,
coordination difficulties and poor concentration. Nervousness,
irritability and anger persist and recur intermittently. Excessive
fatigue is noted. She says that her memory is poor and she must
work at it. She writes down notes which she did not do before,
makes mistakes at mathematics, is forgetful of multiplication
tables. Headaches only occur occasionally. Coordination of the
hands has been notably poor and is quite evident to her as she is a
musician. Her playing is not as good as it was before the accident
and is obviously so. Concentration is less and conversations often
have to be repeated.

The scars about the right scalp are still sensitive. Scars about the
left corner of the mouth both inside and outside are sensitive,
irregular and cosmetically undesirable. There is residual enlarge-
ment of the left side of her jaw. Pain occurs on eating and biting.
Pain and popping are noted about the left jaw joint. When she
opens her mouth widely there is left sided pain. Teeth are now
crooked and painful.

Complaints of the right shoulder concern tenderness and sensitivity about the right collarbone. Weather changes are aggravating.

There is weakness, soreness and deformity about the right shoulder blade.

The dorsal scar over her left hand is still sensitive to touch or pressure but does not apparently interfere with function. There are no complaints of the left forearm.

The right forearm is said to be stiff and weak about the fracture site.

The MP joint of the right 5th finger is painful on use, is notably weak and this is especially present playing the piano. The more she plays the more fatigue and the worse her technique becomes.

Right groin aching is described as being present since the pelvis fractures, especially noted with prolonged sitting or standing. Weather changes are aggravating. The tail bone hurts all of the time.

Physical examination

This is a pleasant and cooperative 27 year old woman who obviously has some difficulty with specific memory manifested by hesitation in recall and need to corroborate historical facts with her husband.

External examination of the head reveals scarring of the right scalp about the temple, right forehead and outer eye, right angle of the jaw, below the left corner of the mouth and including a ridge inside of the mouth. The left jaw is enlarged and protruding. Tooth alignment is irregular and she has notable restriction of full opening of the mouth.

Eye reaction and cranial nerves are apparently intact. The Romberg test is normal and gross coordination is adequate.

Reflexes, sensation and motor power of both upper extremities are intact.

Inspection of the left hand reveals a 1½″ scar on the dorsum over the 2nd metacarpal. Except for the skin scar no apparent difficulty is evident. Examination of the left forearm shows no evidence of disability.

Inspection of the right forearm shows no particular abnormality, no specific tenderness, but there are a few degrees restriction of full pronation.

In the right hand there is local tenderness to pressure and pain on terminal ranges of movement of the MP joint of the 5th finger.

Inspection reveals a 1″ scar over the middle third of the right clavicle, dorsal angulation and deformity at this site. Healing of the right collarbone fracture has apparently occurred with normal consolidation. Measurements reveal ¼ to ⅜″ shortening of the right collarbone due to overriding at the fracture site.

From the posterior aspect the right shoulder girdle is slightly lower than the left and the right scapula inferior angle protrudes more than the left. Scapulohumeral rhythm is normal bilaterally.

Examination of the spine shows normal alignment, normal movement, and no apparent difficulties except over the coccyx where palpation and pressure are said to produce pain.

Sciatic sensitivity and buttock atrophy are absent bilaterally.

Reflexes, sensation and motor power of both lower extremities are intact. Leg signs are negative.

The Patrick test is negative. Both compression and distraction of the pelvis are negative.

Radiographic examination

Views of the right shoulder girdle show that this woman had sustained a fracture in the middle third of the right clavicle. Full healing has taken place with some over-riding of the bone fragments, dorsal protrusion and angulation.

Anteroposterior and lateral views of the left forearm show a healed fracture of the ulna shaft junction middle and distal thirds in normal alignment.

X-rays of the right forearm, wrist and hand show a healed fracture of the right radius shaft junction middle and distal thirds in good alignment. Some irregularity of the distal ulna may be the result of a previous fracture but study of previous films would have to confirm this. The irregularity involves the distal ulna at the radio-ulnar joint. Position is satisfactory.

The lumbar and lumbosacral spine were viewed in multiple planes including obliques and anteroposterior and angled views of the pelvis were taken. There is no evidence of any specific abnormality in the lumbar spine, sacrum or coccyx evident at this time. As to the pelvis it is evident that this woman sustained bilateral fractures of the pubic bones. On the right there is a fracture of the superior ramus of the pubis and inferior ramus of the pubis with good position. On the left there is a fracture of the inferior ramus of the pubis and another fracture extending through the body of the pubic bone leaving some residual irregularity at the pubic symphysis. All fractures are fully healed. General conformity of the pelvic ring is satisfactory.

Summary

One year ago this 27 year old music teacher sustained multiple severe injuries while riding in the front seat of an automobile struck by a trailer-truck. Injuries were sustained to the head, face, jaw, right shoulder, both upper limbs, chest, pelvis. Extensive bleeding from the face and mouth as well as multiple lacerations and compound fracture of the right shoulder resulted in shock for which she needed transfusions. One month of hospital care was under a general surgeon, two orthopedic surgeons and an oral surgeon. Multiple lacerations about the scalp, face and left hand were repaired as well as the compound fracture of the right collarbone. Open reduction and wiring of multiple jaw fractures was carried out. Closed reduction of fractures of both forearms followed by cast immobilization was carried out. She remained unconscious for 2 or 3 days, had altered consciousness for several weeks, wore her casts 6 weeks and the teeth wires for 7 weeks.

This woman was unable to work at all for 2 months after the accident, then started 1 hour a day. Although she is now working full time as a teacher there are multiple problems secondary to brain injury and hand coordination that seriously interfere with not only her work and music playing but daily living.

Comment

Multiple scars about this woman's face and head are certainly cosmetically undesirable both as a woman and as a school teacher. A plastic surgeon obviously can better evaluate surgical needs for these multiple scars.

From the history as well as from the physical examination it is evident that this woman sustained severe multiple fractures of her jaw with secondary damage to tooth alignment, bite and chewing capabilities. It is obvious that she has been left with permanent residual jaw deformities and permanent dysfunction of the lower jaw and teeth with residual symptoms as well as disability. These can best be described by an oral surgeon and an orthodontist.

Severe head injury with unconsciousness for several days and altered consciousness for several weeks has been followed by residual post-concussion symptoms of nervousness, irritability, anger, fatigue, memory changes, forgetfulness, headaches, concentration difficulties, poor fine coordination, etc. Although there may be some improvement in the future, the elapse of 1 year and the notable persistence of these symptoms indicate permanency.

Although the fracture of the right collarbone began seriously as a compound fracture, excellent healing has occurred although with some residual angulation and shortening. From a functional standpoint this should cause no permanent problem of any consequence.

The left forearm ulna fracture has healed well with no apparent residual disability.

The right forearm fractures have also healed well and the only apparent residual difficulty noted at this time is some restricted pronation. This may be permanent.

Injury has occurred to the 5th MP joint of this woman's right hand and although in most people such ligament and joint injury would not be a problem it is with her. This is because she is a musician and needs strength, flexibility, stretchability as well as coordination. All of these are interfered with because of residual difficulties in the right hand.

I find no apparent basis for the complaint of continuing tailbone pain and can only speculate as to its origin and persistence.

Muscular abnormalities of the right shoulder blade are apparently due to nerve injury in addition to soft tissue injury. This is apparently permanent.

Four fractures of the anterior pelvis were sustained by this woman, two on each side of the pubic symphysis. Good healing has taken place with fairly good alignment. Some minor symptoms may occur with the basis of residual irregularity at the pubic symphysis.

Multiple serious permanent injury as related above has been sustained by this woman in the accident of 16 June 1972.

[*Signed*]

_____

Joseph Lee, M.D.

_____

Medical Report of Doctor Holt, Plastic Surgeon
JAMES P. HOLT, M.D.
PLASTIC AND RECONSTRUCTIVE SURGERY
MAXILLO–FACIAL SURGERY

[Date]

Mr. James W. Jeans, Attorney

U.M.K.C. Law Building

5100 Rockhill Road

Kansas City, Missouri 64110

Dear Mr. Jeans:

The following is a medical report on Catherine Brown, a 26–year-old music director, who was seen in my office on December 9, 1992, for evaluation of scars resulting from injuries in an automobile accident on June 16, 1992.

The patient states that she was hospitalized for over a month in Joplin, Missouri, with fractures of the pelvis, jaw, right forearm, left forearm, right clavicle and ribs.

She has multiple atrophic scars running from the eyebrow and temple to above the ear (4–5 inches in total length), a scar at a right angle to the mandible and lower part of the ear (3–4 inches) which is also atrophic, a transverse atrophic scar of the lower lip (2 inches) with a ridge inside the labial mucosa, a scar of the dorsum of the right hand (3 inches), two scars of the radial aspect of the wrist (1 inch) and a scar of the right lower neck (1½ inches).

There is sensitivity around the right temple and clavicle and over the right wrist due to the injuries and scarring. She has some limitation of supination at the wrist and difficulty in abduction of the right fifth finger. These limitations interfere with playing the piano which is her professional activity.

My recommendation in this case would be a revision of the scars mentioned above which would require hospitalization and general anesthesia. The surgical fee for the procedures over the entire areas could be estimated at $3,000–3,500 not to include the cost of hospitalization, anesthesia, surgical suite, laboratory fees, etc. After the initial revision, it is possible that a dermabrasion procedure might further minimize the scarring after a period of 4–6 months.

In any event, regardless of the improvement that could be obtained from the surgery, the patient would still undoubtedly have permanent, visible scarring and some cosmetic disfigurement in the areas enumerated.

[*Signed*]

James P. Holt, M.D.

Medical Expenses

The cost of the medical services necessitated by the injuries incurred in the accident are itemized as follows:

General Hospital	$ 8,557.98
Dr. Smith	1,200.00
Dr. Chess	360.00
Dr. Johnson	620.00
Dr. Jones	1,450.00
Hamm Funeral Home	500.00
Dr. Murphy	200.00
Dr. James Holt	200.00
Total	$13,087.98

In addition Dr. Holt, the plastic surgeon estimates $3,000–$3,500 for surgical fees for remedial surgery plus a like amount for hospitalization, anesthesiologist, etc. It appears fair to state that total medical will approximate five thousand dollars.

Effects of Injuries

The effects of the injuries upon Catherine Brown and her family have been pronounced. She has lost weight, has been moody and depressed and has been unable to resume her activities in music. Although rehired in 1993 at $27,000 (as evidenced by the employment contract) because of her physical and emotional effects of her injury she was unable to satisfactorily perform her duties and was not rehired. In addition her private music lessons (which accounted for approximately $300 per month) had to be discontinued.

571

Fred Brown at the time of the accident, was working towards a master's degree in Counselor Education at U.M.K.C. His wife's need for constant attention and encouragement has delayed the completion of his education and has worked a real hardship on the family. Even though Catherine is no longer employed in the Bronaugh area, they continue to live there because they secure their present housing by Fred doing farm chores for the owner. He must commute over 100 miles to Kansas City for his schooling and work forty to sixty hours on the farm for house rent and living money.

Evaluation of Claims

The injuries speak for themselves and anyone so victimized would be entitled to a substantial sum for the resulting pain and disability. For Catherine Brown the effects were particularly disabling. The loss of strength, flexibility and dexterity of her right hand has seriously impaired her capacity as a musician and thus has affected her earning potential. The effects of the disfiguring facial scars on this twenty-six year old woman have been aggravated by the fact that her employment brings her before the public as well as numerous students. Although future plastic surgery may ameliorate some of the disfigurement of the skin, others will remain. The contour of the jaw and teeth have been permanently altered. The loss of bone in the clavicle has resulted in a permanent postural change.

We evaluate the damages for Catherine Brown as follows:

Medical expenses to date	$13,087.98
Medical expenses projected	11,500.00
Loss of earnings school year '93	27,200.00
Loss of earnings private lessons to date at $300 per month	4,500.00
	$55,787.98

Future loss of wages depends on the hirability of a physically impaired candidate suffering from permanent head injuries manifested by "nervousness, irritability, anger, fatigue, memory changes, forgetfulness, headaches, concentration difficulties." The impairment of Catherine's earning capacity is a fact—only the amount is uncertain. A strong argument could be advanced that a fair estimate could be figured at $1,000 a year or a total of $38,000 'til her work expectancy of sixty five.

If permanent disability and future pain and suffering were to be evaluated on the basis of $10,000 for each year of expectancy, one could argue an additional $430,000 for the biblical life span. A total of these sums is $523,787.98.

This computation is advanced as an example of jury argument that could be legitimately advanced with, in my opinion, a good chance of acceptance. I appreciate that for settlement purposes the sum of $523,787.98 is not a valid figure—but it does represent the degree to which each of the parties is exposed as individual or joint tort-feasor. Add to this the loss of consortium claim of the husband and the injury to the son and that exposure, again in my judgment, exceeds $100,000.

The plaintiff is assured of recovery against someone. The nature of the accident, the extensiveness of the injury and the "jury appeal" of the plaintiff lead one to conclude that a jury would be generous in evaluating the case. Our settlement demand for all claims is $475,000.

D.   SELLING THE CLIENT

§ **20.15**   Generally

The settlement of a personal injury claim from the standpoint of plaintiff's attorney is a three-fold process: appraisal of the claim by the attorney, selling that appraisal to the opposition, acceptance of the settlement by the client. Too little attention has been directed to the third phase yet this is, perhaps, the most important.

What is the goal of the lawyer in representing an injured client? Perhaps the question is poorly worded. It's difficult to find a single goal. An instinctive response from the economically oriented practitioner might be "To get all the money we can." The more philosophical barrister might say "To see that justice is done." Neither answer goes far enough. Certainly a just settlement is desired (whatever that is) and the quality of preparation and skill in handling the case will be reflected in the amount that is secured. But, as mentioned before, there is no objective mark against which we can measure the adequacy of a settlement. If no objective standard prevails, then a subjective test must be employed. Should the subjective standard be that of the community at large (justice) or the greed of the lawyer (all we can get)? or is it more reasonable to seek a settlement that meets the subjective standards of the client himself? If this is the case, then the goal of the lawyer is to satisfy the client.

The groundwork for accomplishing that goal has been laid with the pre-negotiation conference. Section 20.6. Now the initial stages of negotiation have begun. Assume that the initial demand has been for $7,500 and the initial offer has been $3,000. The area within which the case will be settled, if a settlement is reached, has been defined. The client has previously indicated that he had no definite ideas on the value of his claim but had hoped to settle for $5,000. At this stage it might be desirable to have a second conference at which time the state of negotiations should be revealed and an explanation given along these lines.

"Before we commit ourselves to a lesser figure it is important that I have your approval for a final settlement. We are the ones offering something for sale so consequently we must mark the sale price. I believe that the defendant will increase his offer of $3,000. If the defendant indicates a willingness to offer $4,500 then I believe that serious consideration should be given to his offer. Less than that, I would advise that we reject the offer. The odds would favor us if we went to trial. If he offered $6,000 I would recommend that the offer be accepted because then the odds would favor them. It's difficult to make any recommendations if there is an offer between $4,500 and $6,000. The acceptability of the offer then depends on your own sense of values. Can you afford to run the risk of the trial? Do you prefer to take the bird in the hand or chase for two in the bush?"

The client will then be fully advised that the case is in his hands and that, guided by his attorney's recommendations, there is an area in which his own discretion must rule. A settlement which meets his own appraisal of value will accomplish the goal that the lawyer has sought—his client's satisfaction.

Some attorneys might not wish to have the client have such an intimate role in the settlement of a claim. They would prefer to handle all of the negotiations, reach a settlement that they know is adequate and then sell the client.

Several techniques may be utilized if such a modus operandi is considered desirable.

First, get the client to think in terms of a net recovery. If the lawyer has a contingent fee calling for one-third of any amount secured by settlement and there have been litigation expenses of two hundred and fifty dollars which must be paid, it might be misleading to tell the client that the case can be settled for three thousand dollars when in reality the net proceeds will be less than two. If not misleading it might cloud his appreciation of the settlement by directing his attention to the amount of the fee and necessary expenses.

Second, the client must be conditioned for a settlement that the lawyer knows is adequate and which, for the welfare of the client, must be accepted. A substantial number of clients will think that "the insurance company will always come up with more." If there has been an offer of ten thousand dollars they are sure that the company will offer fifteen thousand dollars, and if there has been an offer of fifteen thousand dollars they'll surely add another thousand dollars. Just where this spiral stops is uncertain, but the feeling is deep-seated that regardless of the offer communicated, the lawyer can always get a little more.

There may be some validity to this concept in the initial stage of negotiation. Seldom is the opening shot offer or demand an uncompromising figure from which neither party will budge. But the preliminary "feeling out" has already taken place and the settlement negotiations have reached the "serious" stage and the defendant is approaching the limits of his authority. Does the plaintiff's attorney push for the final figure and then present it to his client for his approval? What will happen if the client is presented with a "take it or leave it" proposition of X amount? Chances are he'll counter with X plus one thousand dollars and register pronounced dissatisfaction if the lawyer is unable to secure the added amount.

In anticipation of this, some lawyers think it desirable to suspend negotiations and advise the plaintiff of the defendant's last offer. The client indicates that if an additional thousand dollars can be secured it will be satisfactory.

The lawyer now knows what it will take to satisfy the client and he has not as yet completed the negotiation ritual. There is still an opportunity to secure the magic extra amount and in so doing achieve an adequate settlement but, more importantly, a satisfied client. Of course, ideally, the final settlement will be made for an amount which will not only meet the client's expectations but be "beyond the dreams of avarice."

A lawyer's reputation is built upon the expressions which come from the mouths of his clients. Their appraisal will be based upon their relationship with the lawyer and the results which are achieved. Both goals must be reached: an intimate relationship based on mutual trust and full disclosure, and an adequate settlement satisfactory to the client. If proper settlement psychology is employed, one goal need not be sacrificed in order to secure the other.

INDEX

INDEX

INDEX

INDEX

INDEX

INDEX

INDEX

†